Alasdair – with love

10/8/97

HARLEQUIN
IN
WHITEHALL

Portrait of Humbert Wolfe by Sir William Rothenstein RA, 1931 (photograph by John Douglas)

HARLEQUIN IN WHITEHALL

A LIFE OF HUMBERT WOLFE

POET & CIVIL SERVANT

1885 - 1940

by

Philip Bagguley

Nyala Publishing, London

Published by
NYALA PUBLISHING
4 Christian Fields, London SW16
Tel/Fax. 0181 764 6292

ISBN 0 9529376 0 3

Typeset, printed & bound in Great Britain by
The Ipswich Book Company Ltd., Suffolk

For Ann, who believed in him,

and Audrey, who believed in me.

Preface

Ronald Knox, who was an acquaintance of Humbert Wolfe's at Oxford, described in the Preface to his *Enthusiasm* how the writing of it had been his real life's work, how he had lived with it for thirty or more years, adding to it, patching it, rewriting it, in the time that could be spared from other occupations; how it had 'haunted his day-dreams like a guilty romance'. Without daring to claim, in the pursuit of my own goal, anything like Knox's unswerving dedication, let alone as accomplished a piece of writing to show for it, I can truthfully say that I know what Knox meant and how he felt.

By a curious chance I first encountered Wolfe's poetry at about the same time that I read *Enthusiasm.* It was as an undergraduate in the early 1950s that I came upon a quotation from *The Uncelestial City* in one of the novels of Elizabeth Goudge. Ever since, Humbert Wolfe has been my obsession, my solace and my escape. Throughout the years he has preoccupied my waking thoughts and not a few of my dreams. I have been alternately fascinated, tantalised, delighted or infuriated as my quarry eluded me or let me get close enough to imagine that I had him at last within my grasp.

The task has not been made easier by the fact that the sources are limited and, in many instances, partial - that is, both partisan and incomplete. J. Enoch Powell, reviewing Asa Briggs' *Victorian Things*, pointed out that history is not the same as the material of history; indeed, that history is only possible when a great deal of the material is unavailable, by reason of death or destruction. 'Only then can the mind begin to operate creatively upon the residue.'

Unfortunately, this creative challenge has one big drawback: each little piece which the historian works on is by definition something removed from its context, and context cannot be restored because that would be the totality which, also by definition, 'is continuously withdrawn from our knowledge and comprehension by the effluxion of time and the nature of life itself.'[1]

It is sometimes said that biography is largely an exploration of motive and is concerned chiefly with accounting for why the subject acted as he did. While this may be true in some cases, it is rarely the whole story and often it must be impossible to do more than speculate, with the constant risk of falling into half-baked psychology.

For the biographer, as for the historian, facts are a dissolving view. If, as Powell said, we are not necessarily the wiser about the Victorian Age for having accumulated the record of sufficient things with sufficient accuracy, then the biographer of Humbert Wolfe can take comfort: at least there is space in which to try to create a convincing interpretation of such facts as there are. Wolfe himself, in his book on George Moore, wrote: '(For) I conceive it to be the critic's task to make a mood in which his author can be safely and quietly approached.' (Would that all critics thought so too.) My task, then, is two-fold: to try to bring Wolfe to life for the reader and to attempt to convey the unique and abiding interest which his life and work hold for me.

His was on several counts a tragic life: its promise was somehow never quite fulfilled, it was cut short by a death which might be called untimely, and it was the life of a tragic hero in the Aristotelian sense of a gifted, good but not flawless man whose life was lived on a large and public stage. But the image of Harlequin which his poetry so often evoked is surely the aptest metaphor for the figure he cut upon the stage which was his lifetime and his world.

He was so widely admired and apparently successful a writer - practically a household name in the last fifteen years of his life - that the decline in interest in him since the War is all the more surprising. I want therefore to argue for a fairer verdict on his poetry than he received either in his lifetime or after his death.

Why a life of Humbert Wolfe? By any reckoning, he was a man of parts. Indeed, as the title suggests and as he himself liked to hint, he was many men and played numerous parts: civil servant, poet, critic, essayist, dramatist, translator, broadcaster, patron of rising writers, eccentric, romantic - the list is almost endless.

His background alone was sufficiently colourful, not to say exotic, to make him a figure of interest. Born in Milan of a German father and an Italian mother, both of them Jewish; brought up in Bradford; winner of an Oxford scholarship who graduated with a First in Greats, he combined the life of a singularly prolific man of letters with that of a busy Civil Servant - perhaps the last in a long tradition rich in such figures. For many years he not only occupied an important post in Whitehall but also represented his country at the International Labour Office in Geneva and subsequently became Deputy Secretary of the Ministry of Labour. He had been created C.B.E. in 1918, and C.B. in 1925. He never lived to receive the knighthood which was confidently predicted for him: overwork and the strain of equipping the country's labour force for war killed him in 1940.

Finally, the range and number of people upon whose lives he impinged was sufficient to warrant more attention than he has received since his death. He is listed, of course, in the reference books and occasionally (but more often than not unfavourably) mentioned in histories of twentieth century writing. A few of his poems appear in anthologies or are read in BBC poetry programmes; most frequently he is paid the ultimate tribute of unacknowledged quotation, usually of 'You cannot hope to bribe or twist, thank God, the British journalist'. Yet no Life has ever been written or indeed attempted and, apart from a handful of articles in the early 1940s and a project (later abandoned) for a symposium to be edited by Pamela Frankau, nothing substantial has been printed about him since 1944. A serious study of his life and works is long overdue, as is his restoration to the place in English letters which is properly his.

As in any venture of paternity, that which has for so long been so much part of oneself must eventually go out into the world and take its chances in the marketplace and the reviewers' columns, in the hope that, as Knox put it, 'there is some truth here worth the telling; or, if not that, tinder at least to catch the sparks of another man's fire.'

P. H. B.
Nottingham
5 January 1997

Contents

List of illustrations		xiii
Genealogy of Humbert Wolfe		xv
Acknowledgements		xvii
Prologue	New Year's Eve 1939	1
1.	'Boy in the dusk' 1885 - 1894	5
2.	'The call of the perilous margins' 1894 - 1903	31
3.	'Lit like a great house with candles' 1903 - 1907	47
4.	Not for world-shakers 1908 - 1911	77
5.	'The astonishments of war' 1912 - 1919	111
6.	'The secret architecture of the dream' 1920 - 1923	149
7.	'Some engagement with a star' 1924 - 1927	191
8.	'The echo of departing wings' 1927 - 1930	255
9.	'But how shall we find peace?' 1931 -1936	307
10.	'A distant lonely song' 1936 - 1940	353
Epilogue	'The high song is over'	379
Appendices	Ministry of Munitions Organisational Charts	381
	Administration, Ministry of Labour, 1916 - 1939	
	Works by Humbert Wolfe	
	Writings on Humbert Wolfe	
Notes and References		395
Index		427

Illustrations

Frontispiece Portrait of Humbert Wolfe by Sir William Rothenstein, R.A., 1931

1. The Hollow by Albert Rutherston (in *Cursory Rhymes*, 1927)
2. No.4 Mount Royd in 1986
3. The Wolff family c.1890
4. The Lord Mayor's Children's Party c.1890
5. Consola and Berto c.1900
6. Humbert and Jessie on their wedding day, 29 March 1910
7. Jessie's family, with Ann as a baby, c.1914
8. No.6 Whitehall Gardens in 1912, garden view
9. No.6 Whitehall Gardens in 1912, dining room
10. Montagu House, Whitehall in 1936, exterior
11. Montagu House, Whitehall in 1936, interior
12. British Empire Delegation, ILO Conference, June 1926
13. Cartoon of Humbert at Geneva by BON, Heraldo de Madrid, 1925
14. Sketch of Humbert at ILO Geneva, by Oscar Lazar, 1927
15. Humbert and Jessie at Trouville in 1932
16. Photograph of Pamela Frankau, c.1940
17. Jessie and her portrait of Humbert asleep, in their Mount Street flat, 1935
18. Low cartoon, Evening Standard, 1931

Acknowledgements

Frontispiece and plates 4, 5, 6, 7, 15 and 17, by kind permission of Ann Wolfe; 1, by kind permission of the Rutherston family; 3, by kind permission of Elizabeth and Sarah Clifton; 8, 9, 10 and 11, courtesy of the Greater London Record Office; 12 and 14, courtesy of the ILO Archives, Geneva; 13, courtesy of Hemeroteca Municipal de Madrid; 16, by kind permission of Timothy d'Arch Smith; 18, courtesy of Evening Standard/Solo Syndications Ltd.

GENEALOGY OF HUMBERT WOLFE

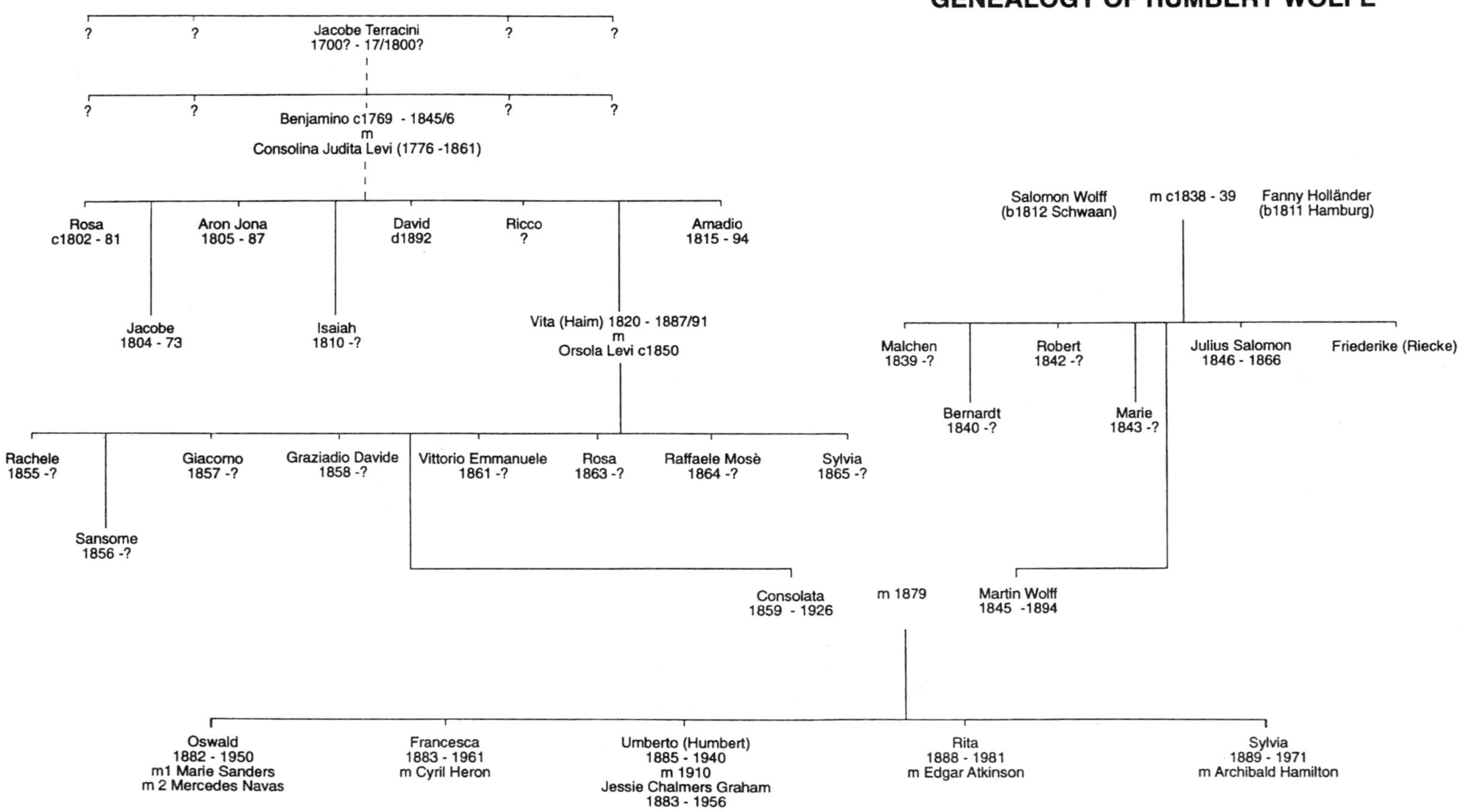

Acknowledgements

Every effort has been made to trace the owners of copyright material, and I hope that no copyright has been infringed. If any rights have been infringed I apologize and ask pardon, and promise to make the appropriate correction in any reprint of this book.

My grateful thanks are due first and foremost to Ann Wolfe for her unfailing support and help, and for giving me access to and permission to quote from the writings and the private papers of Humbert and Jessie Wolfe. I must also thank the other members of the Wolfe family, Elizabeth and Sarah Clifton, Mrs. Cecily Heron, Marie Padgett, Ruth Atkinson, and Mercedes Vizcarrondo for their interest and help; Dr. Rodney Lowe, on whose *Adjusting to Democracy* I have drawn extensively for Ministry of Labour history; the BBC Written Archives; Lucy Dynevor, for permission to reproduce a letter from Sir William Rothenstein; Professor Colin St John Wilson for allowing me to quote from the papers of the late P. J. St John Wilson; and the Controller of HM Stationery Office for permission to quote from papers at the Public Record Office.

For much patient and kindly help in connection with their printed and MS collections I am grateful to the librarians and staff of The Athenaeum Club, the Bath Reference Library, The Berg Collection, New York Public Library, the Bodleian Library, the Bradford Central Library, Bradford Grammar School, Edinburgh University Library, Haddington Library, the ILO in Geneva and London, the Walpole Library at The King's School, Canterbury, the University of Loughborough Pilkington Library, the University of Nottingham Hallward Library, the National Monuments Record, Wadham College Library, and the Royal Society of Literature.

I am deeply indebted to countless friends, colleagues and correspondents who have supplied information, read or listened to pages of manuscript and in various ways encouraged me to persevere, and especially to Margaret Cunningham, Eileen Budge, W. R. Chalmers, Timothy d'Arch Smith, Dr. Roger Davidson, Mr. Cyril Dennis, the late Sir Harold Emmerson, Professor Christine Fell, Sarah Fryer, Mrs Jessie Goodwin, Sir Alec and Lady Guinness, Professor B. Hamilton, Alan Longbottom, Mrs. Diana Marr-Johnson, Diana Raymond, Margaretta Scott, Dr. Lore Terracini, Francesca Vanke, Mrs. Gillian Warr, Elizabeth Watson-MacPherson, Sir John Walley, Mr. Alan Watts, the late P. J. St.J. Wilson, and Professor C. Wrigley.

I particularly want to thank Jane Franklin, but for whom I might never have read Humbert Wolfe; David Blay (Manager of the Resources Centre in the School of Education, University of Nottingham) and June Lemon, my former secretary, for untold help with charts, genealogies and indexing; John Spence, for his help with word-processing; and finally my old friends and colleagues, Gerald Hinchliffe, who encouraged my first efforts, and William Harpin, who over several years gave unstintingly of his time, his vast knowledge, and his boundless wisdom: if this book has a midwife, it is he.

Prologue

New Year's Eve 1939

Britain's first Christmas of the war is over and, as the year draws to its close, what Winston Churchill was to call 'the sinister trance' of the twilight war continues. On the Western front the opposing armies face one another across an undisputed 'No-man's land' in the uneasy, brooding calm of the hardening winter. At home, however, Britain is still warming itself with the news of the recent naval victory of the River Plate. The press has been full of the heroic part played in this action by the cruiser HMS Exeter which has inspired a poem printed in one of the national newspapers not many days since.[1]

In the theatres of London's blacked-out West End on this last night of the year the curtains are coming down on the evening's performance. The show at The Whitehall Theatre is a topical version of Cinderella, called *Who's Taking Liberty?*, a satirical pantomime by Miss Pamela Frankau.[2] Margaretta Scott appears as Prince Charming/Great Britain, Dorothy Hyson plays Cinderella/Liberty and Michael Wilding is The Demon King. Mischa Spoliansky's music is conducted by Muir Matheson. In the final scene, the producer, Leslie French, who also plays The Stage Hand, leads the cast and audience in the nightly singing of 'The Lily of Laguna'.

In the fourth row of the stalls, where he has sat almost every night since the pantomime opened on December 6th, sits the author of the 'HMS Exeter' poem, Humbert Wolfe, C.B., C.B.E., Deputy Secretary of the Ministry of Labour. He readily admits that he can no more sing or even detect a true note now than he could as a child when he joined in the same chorus at the end of *Aladdin* at The Theatre Royal, Bradford. But he still sings his heart out with the best of them in homage to 'my lily and my rose', putting aside for a few brief hours the cares of a wartime ministry and the sombre prospects ahead. Less than a week later, on January 5th 1940, he was dead, killed by a combination of overwork, high blood pressure and advanced arterio-sclerosis. It was his fifty-fifth birthday.

Pantomime had enthralled and fascinated Humbert Wolfe ever since that memorable childhood visit to see *Aladdin* at the theatre advertised as 'The Home of Pantomime'. For millions of children in Britain, their baptism as theatre-goers could be said to take place at the Christmas pantomime, that peculiarly British compound of music hall and fairy tale in which the perennial conflict of good and evil unfolds in all its familiar yet infinitely variable patterns. Miraculously it survives the assaults of fashion and the ravages of time, the easy boredoms of peace and the privations of war, constantly adapting to whatever has proved popular, from grand opera to vaudeville, yet managing somehow to remain itself, a national festival of irrational frolic, vulgar comedy and shallow sentiment whose roots lie beneath the Maypole.

That is one view of pantomime, and one which is perhaps closest to the spirit of Wolfe's reconstruction of his first childhood encounter with it. The half-dozen pages in *Now A Stranger* which describe the visit to *Aladdin* are full of a dizzy happiness, an ecstatic wonder and unbelievable delight which he would never forget.

> So from glory to glory, scene after scene, the pantomime touched all the gamut of song, humour and consummate thrill. The interval passed between a breath and a breath, and so moved was the boy that he left his bar of chocolate unfinished. . . . The transformation scene followed. Gauze curtain after gauze curtain drew heavenwards leaving behind bed upon bed of blossoms, tossed in armfuls from the first Garden of all. And now, when the grown-ups were beginning to shuffle their feet, there was the crack of a lath, and lighter than a whisper, and swifter than a dream, Harlequin was on the stage
>
> with a shout
> blowing life's starry candle out:[3]
>
> to be followed by Columbine:
>
> softly keeping time but he
> keeps, it seems, eternity.[4]
>
> Then Old Joey, the clown, and Pantaloon and the poker, and the illimitable strings of sausages and the tailor's shop with the two dummies marked "This style 38/6d." and the policeman rammed with the poker, beaten with the sausages, and danced round in a ring, by Harlequin, Columbine, Joey and Pantaloon. Suddenly they all took hands and ran to the front of the stage. The orchestra swung into "The Lily of Laguna - she is my lily and my

> rose." The curtain fell where lilies do not fade and roses never crumple their petals in any storm. The boy was accused of being sleepy. He had drunk the drowsy syrups of the other world, and had learned something not to be found in copy-books, nor in the multiplication tables, nor to be imparted by Miss Smith. He had sipped honey-dew. It might curdle with time or evaporate upon the air. But even if he were to suffer the slow, stale extinctions of life he had seen the palace of Xanadu and had heard the sound of the dulcimer.[5]

This first encounter with Harlequin was to be more significant than the young Umberto Wolff could have foreseen at the time, for the figure and the theme recur throughout his writings and his life. Humbert's Harlequin derives both from English and French pantomime, and from the Italian 'Commedia dell'Arte'. What liberties Humbert took with the character and the story may matter little; the significant elements are the mystery and enigma represented by Harlequin's invisibility, as well as by his mask, his parti-coloured dress, his agility, his sudden appearances and disappearances, his love-dance with Columbine, and finally the mysterious identification with death (as, for instance, in *Humoresque*). It is not excessively fanciful to see in Humbert's life, if not in his consciousness, the characteristics of Harlequin.[6]

Chapter One

1885-1894

'Boy in the dusk'
(*Humoresque*, 1926)

I

Genoa - Milan - Bradford

There can be little doubt that, had the choice been his, Humbert Wolfe could hardly have picked a more colourful setting for his own remarkable personality than his particular family and racial background or the circumstances of his birth and upbringing. His ancestry was Jewish - German on his father's side, Italian on his mother's. His father, Martin, came from a commercial background. He was the son of Salomon Wolff, who was born in 1812 in the town of Schwaan, some twelve miles south of Rostock, in the state of Mecklenburg-Schwerin. Salomon Wolff is described in the records as 'Kaufmann', but what branch of business he was in can only be conjectured. In or about 1838 he married a Jewish girl from Hamburg, Fanny Holländer (born in 1811), who bore him seven children. When Martin, their fifth child, was born in 1845 or 1846, they were living in Lübtheen, another small town in Mecklenburg-Schwerin, about thirty-five miles south-west of Schwerin and forty miles south-east of Hamburg.[1]

Humbert's mother, born in 1859, was Consola Terracini, of Genoa. Terracini is not now, nor was it then, a common name in Genoa. Today there are only four or five in the Genoa telephone directory, most probably all related. If so, it is equally probable that their family or families moved there from Asti where there were several Terracini households in the seventeenth century. Without a doubt the surname is, with Terracino, a variant of Terracina, a Jewish surname derived from the place-name Terracina, a coastal town in the province of Lazio, about sixty-five miles south of Rome, and for long the home of an ancient Jewish community which finally broke up in the sixteenth or seventeenth century. If those who borrowed the name originated from Spain, as has been surmised, it seems unlikely that they were refugees from the expulsions of 1492, for the medieval historian Michele Luzzati found evidence that some members of the Terracina family travelled in Tuscany before the fifteenth century.[2]

How any of them came to be either in Asti or subsequently in Genoa is not altogether clear. The industrial development of northern Italy in the nineteenth century and the freedom which Jews had enjoyed under the rule of the House of Savoy since 1848 offer a tempting explanation; the frequency with which Terracini children were named Umberto or Margherita suggests a firm devotion to the royal family. But the surname is to be found in the Asti records in 1614, while in the census ordered by Napoleon in 1808 one Beniamino Terracina declares that he is changing the surname of his descendants to Terracini. A more likely explanation for their presence is to be found in the Age of Enlightenment and the tolerance of the Hapsburg rulers in Lombardy and Tuscany.[3]

Whatever the explanation, in the second half of the eighteenth century there were in Asti at least three Terracini heads of families. One of these, Giaccobe, was Humbert's ancestor. Of his several children, a son, Beniamino (c1769 - 1845/1846) became a butcher who probably dealt with Jewish ritual slaughter. Beniamino had at least eight children of whom one, Vita (Haim) Terracini, born in Asti in 1820, married into another Jewish family in the area about 1850. His bride, Orsola, born in 1837, was the daughter of Raffaele Mosè Levi, of Chieri, a town between Asti and Turin. When the couple moved to Genoa in 1861 she had already borne him five children: a daughter, Rachele, in 1855, three sons in succession, Sansome in 1856, Giacomo in 1857 and Graziadio in 1858, and a second daughter, Consola(ta) - Humbert's mother - in 1859.[4]

By 1871 the Terracini family was living in a third floor apartment at No. 19, Via San Lorenzo, a street near the cathedral in the centre of Genoa, and Vita is described in the census of that year as a trader ('negoziante'), which may have meant among other things a dealer in ready-made clothes. By now his family had increased too: Vittorio Emmanuele was born in 1861, Rosa in 1863, Raffaele Mosè in 1864 and Sylvia on 14 July 1865, the only one of the children to have her date of birth recorded by the census. Other members of the household were a niece, Judita Cavalieri, originally from Ferrara, who joined the family in Asti, probably on the death of her father, and Maria Fascio, a domestic servant who had also been with them in Asti.

Already in 1870 the Terracini business was sufficiently established (under the name of Clava e Terracini) to be a signatory of the protest made by the 'negozianti in tessuti' of Genoa to the Chamber of Commerce against a new tax that the Commune wanted to impose. The records suggest a steady expansion from a shop selling ready-made clothes to a factory producing material and selling wholesale, and by the mid-eighteen nineties the premises included a second address near the first.

Why and when Martin Wolff came to be in Genoa is largely a matter of guesswork. His marriage certificate shows him to be a German national, born in 'Lüftheen' (a misspelling of Lübtheen) but resident in Bradford. It seems likely that he was already working for the firm of Simon, Israel & Co. of Hamburg, Manchester and New York, of which he subsequently became a partner. It is thought that the firm had business connections in Northern Italy and that Martin was sent there in the course of his employment.

On 23rd February 1879, at 9.30 in the morning, the thirty-three year-old Martin and the nineteen-year old Consola were married. Their first child, Oswald, was born on December 8th 1882, followed by a daughter, Fanny, in 1883. At what point the young couple moved to Milan is unclear but it was there that their third child, Umberto, was born in their residence in the Via Fattebenefratelli on 5 January 1885. Soon after Umberto's birth the family moved to the Yorkshire wool town of Bradford, where on 1 September 1885 Martin became a partner in the firm of Simon, Israel and Company, of Manchester, Hamburg and Bradford.[5]

The city and the neighbouring countryside which the newcomers found are eloquently described in *The Uncelestial City*, a work which Humbert wrote in 1930. The title, as it happens, was not intended to refer to Bradford but in the poem the city is easily recognised in the transparent disguise of Blackford, as are Manningham Lane and Lister's Mill:

> Do you know Blackford? Nature keeps the tally
> of those who found a smooth embosomed valley,
> waiting for dawn among her hills, and splendid
> with the shadow of her trees when day was ended,
> who found this valley, and, being business-men,
> swore that these things should not ocur again.
> They therefore added up a maze of brick
> by some unspeakable arithmetic,
> quietly boasting, as they clinched the sum,
> God makes the country, but we make the slum.
> Then where the dawn had slipped her hounds, and hunted
> her prey - the saffron mists - steam-engines shunted
> trucks full of coal with creaks and groans and jams,
> whole-heartedly supported by the trams
> with screaming brakes that skidded up and down
> the hills that make a nightmare of the town.
> . . . .
> The maze of streets, plunging down Walton Hill,
> swirl in an eddy about Stoneman's Mill,
> whose chimney tops the skyline with a dark,
> though self-contented, exclamation mark. . .

The story of Bradford's rise as a commercial and industrial centre in the nineteenth century has been told often enough and well enough to need no rehearsing here. What does require examination is the extent and nature of its influence on Humbert Wolfe and his family. It will become clear in the course of this account that for reasons of nationality, race and religion the Wolffs saw themselves as different from the native Bradfordians. Only one instance has been found when Humbert called himself a Yorkshireman and he was in fact criticised on occasion for appearing to speak slightingly of Bradford. Yet Humbert's prose and poetry captured and reflected in a singular way the distinctive individuality of this West Riding town, set in its moorland valleys, prosperous, self-confident, cosmopolitan and progressive yet still in some respects a provincial backwater. The late-twentieth century fashion is to glorify industry as heritage, but in the Bradford which the Wolffs found, industry, and particular spinning, was the life-blood of the population and showed in the appearance of the town. Civic and industrial architecture recalling Venice and Florence went cheek-by-jowl with long, dark rows of back-to-back freestone houses and steep, cobbled streets, and everywhere the all-pervading, all-prevailing smoke and grime that evoked the satanic mills of Blake's *Jerusalem* and inspired Caryl Battersby, Humbert's English Master at the Grammar School, to describe it as

> the town
> where all that is not black is brown.[6]

Socially, Bradford was equally monochrome, thanks to the predominance of a single industry, which made Bradford people, whether master or man, basically equal, sharing a broadly common outlook, proud, enterprising, fiercely democratic and contemptuous of airs and graces. Few areas were free of industrial development and both workers' and owners' houses could still be found in the same neighbourhood.

For all that, the moors were never far, practically within walking distance, certainly no more than a tram-ride away. Humbert thought it likely that 'hilliness' was in him from his earliest conscious days. He undoubtedly acquired in childhood the love of walking which directly or indirectly nourished so much of his later life and art. Indeed, the moors seem to have profoundly affected everyone who ever wrote of a Bradford childhood.

Foreign merchants, particularly Germans, had begun taking up residence in the town since the eighteen thirties. Germany was then the woollen industry's main buyer and the German firms were increasingly adopting the practice of setting up their own employees as their agents abroad. The warehouse of Simon, Israel and Co. was at No. 44 Vicar Lane, part of an area known as 'Little Germany', which still bears witness to the industry, determination and capacity for assimilation of the German businessmen. By 1902 between a half and two-thirds of the worsted merchants in Bradford were of German origin. Many if not most of them were Jewish. They predominated in the influential foreign element in this cosmopolitan city, particularly (though not exclusively) in the wool trade which, unlike the cotton industry, was enjoying a large development in this latter part of the nineteenth century. The consumption of raw wool in Britain more than doubled between 1870 and 1890 and the German businesses in Bradford were heavily involved in exports.[7]

By the time the Wolffs arrived, these German-Jewish residents formed a distinctive community whose economic, artistic and philanthropic contribution the town readily accepted. They helped to found the Chamber of Commerce, supported the building of St. George's Hall and the creation of the Bradford Festival Choral Society, founded hospitals and inaugurated benevolent funds, and generally enriched the cultural as well as the commercial life of Bradford, with which the names of Frederick Delius and William Rothenstein, of Charles Semon, Jacob Moser and Jacob Behrens will be forever linked as surely as those of J. B. Priestley and Titus Salt, of William Forster and Samuel Cunliffe Lister. [8]

Into this community, 'civilised, sophisticated and wealthy, wearing (its) foreignness and religion lightly',[9] as David James wrote, came the Wolffs with their young family, taking up residence in Manningham, which had become, with Heaton, one of the fashionable suburbs of Bradford where the development of enclaves of middle and upper-class housing attracted the business and professional families of the town, including of course a large number of the German-Jewish merchants. The immediate predecessor of the Wolffs in their Manningham house was, according to the census of 1885, George Simon himself, the senior partner in the firm.[10]

It seems safe to assume that the Wolffs rapidly merged with their surroundings and were indistinguishable from the other residents of Bradford. Had anti-Jewish prejudice been strong in the town, their ethnic and religious background might have constituted an obstacle to their acceptance. But, clearly, by the eighteen eighties the contribution of the Jewish community to the prosperity of the town ensured that the newcomers would be accepted in commercial circles, and J. B. Priestley, who grew up in Bradford in the 1890s, could recall no prejudice against Jews.[11]

It might, of course, be argued that Gentiles could not be expected to have a strongly developed sensitivity to anti-Jewish feeling, while the paranoia of some Jews removed the need for actual persecution. Questionable therefore though Humbert's claim may have been that from his childhood he suffered for being Jewish - as it will later be questioned - he may nevertheless have been correct in suggesting that the efforts which the German-Jews of Bradford made, not just to be integrated but to assimilate with the natives, testified to their fear of *not* being fully accepted, and induced in them a quasi-schizophrenic mentality which he clinically dissected in *Now A Stranger*:

> It is the common belief that there is no anti-Semitism in the British Isles . . . Now to be one of a beleaguered garrison in a world of declared enemies may be a gallant adventure. A

> sense of desperate comradeship against overwhelming odds might well fire the blood and exalt the head . . . But when the taint of Jewry means only exclusion from garden-parties, refusal of certain cherished intimacies and occasional light-hearted sneers, it is difficult to maintain an attitude of racial pride. Particularly, when with their habitual adaptation to environment, the Jews admired and eagerly accepted all the habits of the English . . . In spite of all this, or perhaps because of all this, they remained outside. Was it surprising that, instead of standing on their Jewry as upon a point of honour, some, if not many, were ashamed of it?[12]

The German-Jews of Bradford did indeed send their children to the same public and grammar schools as the native citizens, took their Sunday walk in Lister Park, the womenfolk in their bustles, the men in their bowler hats and tightly buttoned coats, and they appear not to have made any great parade of their religion. The synagogue (only erected in 1875) was, according to Humbert, an unprepossessing building in the middle of 'a row of blank grey tenement houses' in Bowland Street, approached through Lumm Lane, an unsavoury thoroughfare. The congregation was sparse, the finances precarious, the rabbi poorly paid - 'less than a clerk in a warehouse . . . His position . . . that of a chaplain in the XVIIIth century. He was definitely treated as being on a lower social grade than that of his richer parishioners. He and his wife formed no part of the regular social circle.'[13]

Although, therefore, no direct evidence survives to show how it felt to Martin Wolff to be a German and a Jew in Bradford, a reasonable guess can be made. By all accounts, both he and his wife were far from being fervent or even practising members of the congregation. From *Now A Stranger* we learn that the children attended the Synagogue and the Sunday School in a blind alley off Lumm Lane, but Consola herself took no interest in religion, limiting her practice to the almost compulsory attendance at the Synagogue on the Jewish New Year's Day and Yom Kippur (the Day of Atonement).[14]

II

No. 4 Mount Royd

The main difficulty with Humbert's early childhood lies in the nature of the evidence. When and where he was born, where the family lived, when and where he went to school, these and a few other bare facts can be ascertained from public records. But for the rest - the detail of everyday life in the Wolff household, the people and events which appear to have marked and shaped his personality - for all this we have (to put it bluntly) only his word, chiefly in *Now A Stranger* and *The Upward Anguish*, with a few tantalising scraps in *Portraits By Inference* and *A Winter Miscellany*. No family documents relating to the period have been found save for a few photographs and some unpublished recollections of his wife and his sisters.

That is not to say that his account is necessarily inaccurate, let alone untrustworthy. The meagre evidence supplied by his contemporaries mostly corroborates his version, although not in every detail nor in some important aspects, and *Now A Stranger* makes his early memories seem considerably sharper than those of his contemporaries. It is true that in the vivid, baroque vision of the child, glorified by the adult, there is always the risk of elaboration or embellishment - Humbert's reputation as a raconteur of stories taller with every telling is well attested - yet, where his recollection can be checked against other sources, his memory of people and places, of atmosphere and appearances was on the whole remarkably reliable. It diminishes nothing to allow that occasionally he probably conflated several events into one, either because that was how he remembered them or because effectively they constituted a single whole, and while the evidence that he sometimes manipulated the record is by no means inconclusive, there appear to be no grounds for dismissing his account of his childhood as totally unreliable. Nevertheless the possibility has to be recognised that what looks like a first sketch of the emerging personality may in fact have been an adult composition made with all the infallibility of hindsight. If that were indeed the case, it would confirm the other evidence that Humbert's several personae were largely his own creations.

One view of biography not only justifies but indeed requires an element of fiction in the imaginative recreation of the subject's life: the biographer must be something of a novelist if he or she is to succeed in bringing the subject to life. If that is so, it is even more true of autobiography, since the adult in rebuilding his past unavoidably selects from memories which, consciously or not, are themselves both selective and exclusive. The logical possibility always remains, of course, that in spite of himself the autobiographer may paint an accurate picture, selective memory and judicious artifice notwithstanding.

In Humbert's case, ambiguity was a deliberate choice. It is clear from a number of poems that he was determined not to reveal himself completely. One of the clearest instances of this was in a poem entitled 'Boy in the Dusk', from *Humoresque* (1926). It is difficult not to see in it the picture of himself which he wants or is willing to let the world see, while disclaiming any identification with it:

'Boy in the Dusk'

I will make a small statue
of a boy today,
that will half look at you
and half away.

I will have him standing
in darkness, but
he will be pretending
that he is not.

. . . .

And many will wonder,
and some will ask,
what I mean by my slender
"Boy in the Dusk."

. . . .

But I will not name him,
and every man
must find and acclaim him
as he can.

Since from childish and small things
the Boy in the Dusk
may flash into all things
the heart can ask.

Or he may be only
a small bronze statue
of a boy, who is lonely,
and looks half at you.

At the very beginning of this journey into his past, however, Humbert was only too well aware of the distance between himself and the 'inaccessible child' of whom he was in search. It was not simply that he had grown up, grown out of childhood, grown away from his origins, but rather that the child's experience of life was largely incommunicable not only to the adult but even to other children.

> If, therefore, I contemplate what this person - Humbert Wolfe - who writes this page, was or may have been when as Berto Wolff, he lived at 4, Mount Royd, Bradford, I am all

> but helpless. I am as strange in his small company as I would be if I tried to remember the inner life of Wyatt or Surrey.[15]

The decision, therefore, to write of his childhood self in the third person, as he was also to write of his Oxford days in his second autobiographical work, *The Upward Anguish*, was more than a fanciful gesture or a facile literary device to conceal a commonplace: it was his way of expressing his consciousness of the unbridgeable gap between then and now, which perhaps also painfully reminded him of lost innocence - like the souls of the dead 'reaching out with longing for the further shore.'[16] In the pages which follow, 'Berto', the name by which he was known in his family, will be used for his childhood persona, and for all references to him until 1918, 'Humbert' for the years thereafter.

The Wolffs lived for the first nine or ten years of young Berto's life at No. 4, Mount Royd, a cul-de-sac off Manningham Lane formed by a curving carriage drive which ran in front of four pairs of huge Victorian three-storeyed semi-detached houses and sloped down towards the canal and the railway. The Royd, as it was called, faced out over a canyon called The Hollow, an area of trees and lawns and shrubs, a semi-wilderness, a kind of private jungle whose gardens and thickets were the playground of the children of The Royd. Here is how Humbert remembered it nearly fifty years later:

> It is no serious strain on memory to recover the disposition of Mount Royd, and the great hole which separated it from Parkfield Road - a hole which could only be explained on the assumption that at one time or another it had been a quarry. The Royd curved in a sharply descending semi-circle away from Manningham Lane. It was protected from intrusion on its upper end by a high stone wall, against which one or two trees doubtfully ranged themselves. There were eight houses, each two forming a single, tall, gaunt and singularly ugly villa. They had an unpleasant stripped look, as though a row of starved middle-aged men had been disturbed in the act of bathing, displaying their pitiful ribs and their dim abashed eyes. Each house was approached by a row of some twelve stone steps which were cut between unkempt mounds of grass. In front was the long stone balustrade that fenced off The Hollow with its two lawns - the upper comparatively level and for some reason not to be used for cricket, the lower, twenty feet below, sloping through the long grass to a huge wall that shored up the garden of a house, towering above the sunk Hollow like a Roman villa above a Roman lane.[17]

A nostalgic poem in *Cursory Rhymes* (1927), recaptures some at least of the flavour of Humbert's childhood games of make-believe.

'The Hollow'

No one plays in the Hollow. Here
are no explorers. The traders in fur
trade no more dreams. Sir Bedivere
has broken the brand Excalibur.

No Mowgli, crouching in a thicket,
watches Shere Khan, nor wonders if
he wouldn't rather bat first wicket,
like J. T. Brown with Tunnicliffe.

Long John Silver has found the Island,
where all men leave their treasure behind.
There are no children now in my land;
no one plays there - except the wind.[18]

Their neighbours - six of whom Humbert remembered quite clearly half a century later - were mostly German and Jewish: Bronners, Lassens, Shalders, but also Mumfords and Meads.[19]

In addition to Martin, Consola and the children (Oswald, Fanny, Berto and later Rita, born in 1888, and Sylvia, born in the following year), the Wolff household included a nurse, Clara Hippe, Sarah, the cook, and a maid or two. Clara contrasted sharply with the family for 'her essence is to be German and not to be Jewish in a world where everything was Yorkshire and Israelite'. She was a neat, erect, slight and ugly woman with 'the deportment of a minute Pomeranian grenadier'. There was no love lost between Consola and the nurse, who jealously guarded the nursery against the young mother. Several times Clara threatened to leave or was threatened with dismissal and finally left the household when Berto was nine. He had by then grown out of her life but in the earlier years she occupied a significant place in his. She taught him strange German songs (which he probably wrongly quoted):

Wer will unter die soldaten
Der must haben ein gewehr

and another mysterious ditty:

Wo bist du denn gewesen
mein ziehender bock

With her hard voice and her briskly unsentimental ministrations to his cuts and bruises, she stood in the young Berto's eyes for orderliness and reliability - 'her hand . . . was not comfortable; it was firm and decisive . . . she was essentially the Greek chorus - known not by her words but by her inaccessibility.'[20]

On 28 January 1891 Martin Wolff was naturalised a British subject, together with the six year-old Umberto. The family nevertheless retained the German spelling of their name, and it was not until 1918 that Berto Wolff became Humbert Wolfe.[21] The boy was only nine years old when his father died, and consequently in the pages of *Now A Stranger* Martin emerges as a shadowy figure, not exactly unreal but more as a largely unseen presence influencing the on-stage performers than as the father one would expect to find. Humbert nevertheless remembered him as the unquestioned master of the house who occupied what can only be described as a solar position in Consola's life. 'He shouted for her as soon as he reached home each day and she, hearing his voice, would drop whatever she was doing and rush down the stairs to him.' [22] Humbert never heard them quarrel - and he seems to have had long ears. Although he was tone-deaf, Martin was given to singing in his deep bass voice what he took to be 'Down among the dead men', especially on days when business at the warehouse had gone well. In a family portrait his mild, bearded face is slightly at odds with his Napoleonic stance as he gazes out from the back of the group. Consola sits very erect, a slim, slightly built woman with a rather severe expression which, Humbert later surmised, probably intimidated the photographer (*see* photograph:5).

In the last chapter of *Now A Stranger*, Humbert described his difficulty in recreating the person of his mother. He was sure that her love for him as a child, though ardent, was without any sentimentality, and he dismissed any suggestion of an exquisite bond of sympathy between them. 'She was in no sense the boy's idol; it is doubtful whether she was even the centre of his life.' Nevertheless, she played such a predominant part in his upbringing that it is no exaggeration to say that she was, after himself, and perhaps even before himself, the central figure in his young life. She dominated, in every sense. Indeed, it will become apparent that she dominated his later life, too, and certainly the early years of his marriage. And from her, it is clear, he inherited many of his traits, including some of his less endearing ones.

What the photographs do not convey is the red-gold hair, the unexpectedly English complexion and the nose 'like a soft falcon', which made her such a striking figure and, according to the family tradition, one of the undoubted beauties of Bradford. Her daughter-in law, Humbert's wife, bore witness that the slimness, the red hair, the somewhat imperious manner and the assumption that no one could fail to see that she was right, remained with her all her life.[23]

What *Now A Stranger* inexplicably omits to say is that, at least from the time of Martin's death, if not from the birth of her eldest son, Oswald, she was stone deaf and taught herself to lip-read, a skill which she exercised to great effect, not to say advantage, in three languages.[24]

Within the Wolff household, three languages were commonly used: English - of a sort - , German - also of a sort, as far as Humbert's recollection goes - and Italian, this last particularly after the arrival of Consola's two sisters, Sylvia and Rosetta, who came to stay 'as inmates' (Humbert's word is carefully chosen) after the death of their father in Genoa, when Berto was five or six. Sylvia was 'a tall Venetian blonde' and Humbert recalled that the slight strain between Consola and Sylvia was due to their rivalry in looks.[25]

The household was largely Consola's empire over which she exercised an almost total sway, at least in the day-to-day activities - too much so, it seems, for the English lady of the house whom Martin wished her to be:

> Not for nothing did she wear her red hair like an oriflamme and shake it in the very heart of any struggle that presented itself. The terms, for example, upon which she lived with her maids behind the green baize door, that led from the hall to the kitchen, were mixed defiance and familiarity. Martin had explained to her without effect that English mistresses do not stand, arms akimbo, at the door of the pantry and exchange hot words with the cook, not so much as a display of temper as an exercise of the spiritual muscles before settling down for the day. In vain also was she warned that she must not make incursions to teach unwilling or slow workers how things should be done, and were done, in Italy.[26]

These assertions of authority were not always wholly successful. Descending at six in the morning to teach a housemaid how to polish boots, she had the misfortune to use grate polish instead of boot polish on Martin's new boots and had to make a present of them to the warehouse porter. On another occasion, instructing a visiting seamstress in the art of cutting trousers, she made for Oswald a pair of 'bags' which fully justified their name.[27]

Like most mothers, Consola resented criticism of her children, no doubt because it reflected badly upon herself, if not upon her husband, and anything approaching interference was sharply rebuffed. When her sister, Sylvia, not unreasonably suggested that Berto should be punished for breaking her mirror (the result of trying to force a drawer in which she was thought to keep a hoard of chocolates), Consola was not prepared to condemn him without proof and reminded Sylvia of her position as a guest in the house.[28]

The Wolffs would have been described as a comfortably-off middle class Jewish family. They had servants but not a carriage of their own.

They made excursions to the countryside around Bradford, to Bolton Abbey and to Rombald's Moor, 'the favourite excursion of all good citizens of Manningham', and took holidays at the sea-side in northern England and Scotland. They also formed part of the regular social circle in which each family possessed a group of what were known in the abstract as 'The Friends', groups which naturally varied from family to family but which were a definite corporate entity, with their own regular rules of entertainment, of exchange of visits and of companionship. Consola had her At Home day or went visiting, shopped in the centre of town and exchanged courtesies or confidences with her various friends and acquaintances.[29]

Among 'The Friends' were a couple, referred to throughout *Now A Stranger* as 'Mr. and Mrs. M.', 'a resolute and childless couple who were everybody's intimate and nobody's friend', with whom Consola maintained relations of armed neutrality. Humbert later described their friendship in terms of a Customs barrier: 'acquaintance for them was only justified by its inquisitions.' How Martin and the rest of the family got on with them is not known, but vis-à-vis Consola and Berto their standing resembled that of Jack Sprat and his wife: Mr. M.'s cordial dislike of the boy was matched by Consola's equally solid and unswerving dislike of his wife (who liked to be known as 'Tante Laura'). These feelings were never disclosed or admitted and Consola was more than a match for Mrs. M.'s hypocritical concern for Berto's well-being.[30]

It is apparent that within the restricted limits and slightly hot-house atmosphere of the Bradford Jewish circle susceptibilities were easily affronted, and slights might be nursed but were rarely forgiven and never forgotten. The Hegsteins were wealthy, childless and members of the 'County' set. Their cook and their cellar were said to be the best in Bradford. Mr. Hegstein was a prospective associate of Martin Wolff in some business dealings involving Brazil, and Consola had invited them to dinner. Whether or not social position outweighed business advantage, as Consola suspected, their request to be excused on the grounds of a prior engagement offended her deeply. She bided her time.

One Christmas when Berto was about six, Martin and Consola, together with Oswald, Fanny and Berto, were invited to the Mayor's Fancy Dress Party for children. Such invitations were not easily come by, for Martin, 'though a respected figure in commerce, had no municipal standing'. The chances, therefore, of either parent conversing with the Mayor, still less of taking a glass of wine with him, were remote: such privileges were reserved for the likes of Mrs. Hegstein.

Consola's choice of Garibaldi as the theme for her children's costumes owed nothing to political affiliation, for she had none: the idea came from the illustrations in a book. She made the uniform - peaked shako, belt and sword - for Oswald, and, drawing on a play called *Under Two Flags*, dressed Fanny as a *vivandière*, with a cocked velvet hat, short striped skirt and a little barrel (empty, alas!) strapped to her side. Berto was got up as a Neapolitan fisher-boy, in a velvet jacket, bright shirt and pants, and stockings 'most villainously cross-gartered . . . and, glory of glories, a little net slung over his shoulder'. (The photograph taken for the occasion authenticates Humbert's description.)

The night of the party arrived and they all trundled off in a four-wheeler to St. George's Hall. As Consola had feared, they were courteously but vaguely greeted by the Mayor, and went off to find their friends in this immense throng. Berto, who couldn't dance, was taken off by one of his father's staff to the buffet where he promptly acquired a large quantity of cakes and lost his companion, whose place was taken by no less a person than the Mayor. Berto, in his usual fashion, chattered away to the Mayor as he would to anyone willing to listen to him. Eventually the Mayor asked him what his net was for. 'For catching things,' said Berto and, suiting the action to the word, cast it - to his surprise and hers - over the head of Mrs. Hegstein who was waiting to exchange politnesses with the Mayor. In the struggle that followed she tried to box Berto's ears, her hair came down in disarray and the Mayor subsided into helpless laughter. Honours were even.[31]

III

'The Boy'

It is no doubt a commonplace to observe that in all childhoods certain names of people and places become charged with a special potency of image and association which may properly be called seminal. Quite how or why this should be so is a mystery. Memory, Humbert observed in *Now A Stranger*, is both exclusive and selective; the mind, like the body's digestive system, rejects unnecessary bulk, retaining only what is necesary to life and growth, which is why 'it is always a single fact or incident that gathers the significance perhaps of a whole period of time'. That more often than not this takes place at an unconscious level matters less than the capacity of these associations to trigger in later life powerful emotions, as words, colours, shapes and the like are invested with a unique and personal richness: 'Names . . . (which) have a significance for the adult mind as definite as a perfume and as clear as light.' [32]

Such seeds need a sympathetic environment in which to flourish. It is therefore legitimate to look for clues to the personality in the kinds of experience which created the deepest and most lasting impressions, and in the stimuli to which this child most readily responded. How Humbert's poetry, and indeed his adult life, reflected such seminal experiences will be matter for later chapters. For the present, our concern is with the origin of these images and associations in his early memories, and the evidence which they supply of his particular sensitivities.

Inevitably, many of these triggers are associated with Bradford itself: Manningham Lane, Parkfield Road, the synagogue, the Theatre Royal. Others, in proportion to their physical distance - Bolton Abbey, Rombald's Moor, Hellifield, Carnforth, Arnside - relate to escape from Bradford, to freedom and emancipation - a familiar theme in Romantic literature and therefore of significance for Humbert's own poetic beginnings. The journeys which they signified were not so much through space or time as from one dimension to another. 'The ruined (Bolton) Abbey, the angry Wharfe, and (in spring) the tidal bluebells, had no affinity that could be ascertained with shops, steam-trams, and much smoke'.[33] Along with the tales of Andrew Lang and Hans Andersen, and the legends of Greece and Rome, they were proof that another world existed.

A family holiday spent at Arnside, on the Westmorland (now the Cumbrian) coast near Morecambe, when Berto was seven, was one of the most powerful of these experiences. In addition to the heightened sensations accompanying the journey, with all its contradictions of the normal, Arnside always conjured up in Humbert's mind memories of 'a huge and dazzling curtain of purple clematis that covered and glorified one whole wall' of the inn on the front. 'Clematis - and Arnside and something changed in the movement of the mind.'[34] It also evoked apples, turkeys and donkeys - and, associated at least in part with all three, fear.

What Wolfe, across forty years, remembered most vividly and understood most clearly was his fear, even cowardice, as a child. He may not have wept more than most other boys of his age, but he remained acutely conscious not simply of the tears occasioned by the disapproval of adults, by physical pain, or by the frustration of his own desires, but even more of the sharp awareness of his own pusillanimity. He enjoyed the thrill of risk but lacked the stomach for a fight, save when anger made him forget to be afraid. In a passage reminiscent of Augustine's analysis of his youthful crimes in *The Confessions*, he described how he and his elder brother Oswald, by now eleven or twelve years old, together with some local children, raided an orchard in Arnside. With stones and a handy cricket ball the thieves dislodged the fruit which hung temptingly out of their reach in this forbidden Eden. (The recollection of the first bite, and the sweet, sharp and frightening taste, invited the inevitable parallel with that other initiation into the knowledge of good and evil.) But a flock of angry turkeys like a battle fleet in full sail put him to flight: terrified, he tripped and fell weeping with his squashed apple in his hand.[35]

Later in the same holiday he and a friend set out for the great adventure of a donkey-ride to Sandside, about a mile from Arnside along the shore road. They paid their twopence each in eager anticipation of a brisk canter, free from any interference or advice from elder siblings, and a triumphant return. The donkeys, however, true to their nature, were recalcitrant and defied all coaxing, tugging, yelling and even beating. The boys were in despair. Eventually the loutish youth in charge of the beasts lashed a pin to his stick and goaded the animals to the point of drawing blood. Young Berto's reactions were first sickness and then blinding rage, accompanied by the recognition that he lacked the courage to interfere. The donkey-herd, sensing this, shouted 'Don't you try none of your tricks, you little Jew-b...r or I'll stick it into you, too' and re-applied the goad. Berto, white and weeping, turned and ran back to Arnside. [36]

Similar anti-Jewish insults were shouted at them in the course of an outing to Rombald's Moor, in June of his seventh year. This was a long-awaited event in his life. [37] At one point they encountered a farmer holding a young thrush which he had killed for the crime of waking him with its singing. Characteristically, Berto reacted by urging his brother Oswald to 'lick him'. The farmer threatened to make Berto eat the bird but shrank back when confronted by an angry Consola: 'Always a red-headed Amazon, at such moments she was all Cleopatra'. When Berto, in his turn, had been sharply rebuked, for Consola was even-handed in her justice, the party set off again 'pursued by the cry, gradually dying on the air: "Oo killed Christ?"'

When finally they reached the edge of the Moor, the view of the valley of the Wharfe, four hundred feet below, was his breath-taking reward.

> Twenty minutes were allowed for restoration of faculties and for contemplation. The blood stole back into the boy's tired limbs, which was odd because most of it seemed to have left his heart and eddied to his brain. For once he had put aside all fancy, all fiction, all self-satisfaction. With undiluted vision he gazed upon the unconditioned valley. If he had known how, or had that lovely language at his command, he would have cried to his eyes, as George Moore did from the monastery terrace in Palestine, "I beseech you to remember." But, even if he had had the words, the plea would have been unnecessary. "Beauty born of murmuring sound" had passed not into his face, but into the texture of his life. The long trail across the heather, the tiring limbs, the sinking heart and this crowning mercy of loveliness seen not in a glass darkly, but, as it is permitted to a child, face to face, the deep scooped valley, the white Eastern house, the cold bare rocks, the long silken skein of the river, and the soaring bird - all these had passed into his possession - and neither Time, nor Mr. M., nor fate could ever rob him of this Real Estate.[38]

They clambered down to the 'White Wells' and thence descended into Ilkley for tea - not at the fashionable but expensive Hydro, for Consola meant the whole excursion to cost no more than ten shillings, but in a small tea shop where chocolate buns called 'Othellos' completed their happiness. The end of a perfect day, alas, was marred by further anti-Jewish insult. Consola having disputed the amount of the bill, the enraged proprietress reduced it by sixpence but complained loudly of having 'been doon aht of sixpence by a pack of Jews.'

The self-portrait given in *Now A Stranger* includes a description of his physical appearance at the age of six or seven, a picture which is supported by (and perhaps owes some debt to) the evidence of contemporary photographs. He was a plump child with a shock of dark, almost black hair, one unruly tuft standing on permanent sentry-duty above the rest. In his round face, the complexion of pale honey, two velvety brown eyes, 'like two half-pennies in a half-crown, a little too large and too deep for the face, as in a faulty drawing, are accentuated by the nose which already asserts its Eastern origin'.

> There is a picture of the Jew-boy at six years old, with the eyes of a startled girl. He is looking anxiously over the photographer's shoulder into distance, and there is a half-smile on a mouth that he must have borrowed from Robin Goodfellow, so like a mocking butterfly it seems. The eyes and the mouth are plainly at war - or is it only that his life's dichotomy is already displaying itself? 'What is my fault, nay, you shall answer mirror?' whisper the eyes. 'The supreme fault of all,' the lips answer, 'the fault of being born a Jew.' Suffer the little Jewish children to come unto Him, and His followers will promptly stone them! The eyes are not wholly convinced - nor are the lips. Perhaps that was the secret of the boy's character.[39]

Admittedly, our knowledge of these experiences is derived almost entirely from Humbert's adult recollection of them, and so the possibility must always remain that in re-creating his childhood he was, in point of fact if not of intention, reading into events a significance which was either a piece of wishful thinking or an 'ex post facto' conclusion. This would account for some at least of the discrepancies which exist between his recollections and those of his sisters and contemporaries.

It has been argued that the references to anti-Jewish insults and the claim that he suffered as a child for being Jewish owed less to fact than to the almost obsessively Jewish stance which he adopted in the last ten years of his life. This was certainly the view of J. B. Priestley who, after Humbert's death, wrote somewhere that as a schoolboy he had not suffered at all because he was Jewish, but that, when the Nazi pogroms began, Humbert had persuaded himself that anti-Jewish prejudice had always existed and that he had always been one of its victims.[40]

Be that as it may, the self-portrait quoted above prompts the same reaction that a similar self-portrait in Edith Sitwell's autobiography aroused in her biographer: '(It) has a romantic theatricality about it which diminishes the truth it may contain. It is a little embarrassing.'[41]

Besides foreignness and Jewishness, other factors contributed to making Berto a sensitive and precocious child. Some of 'The Friends' thought that Consola spoiled him. Berto, who for much of his childhood was incapable of distinguishing friends from enemies, was blithely unaware that they did not all approve of him. Unfavourable comparisons were made between Berto and his elder siblings: 'Oswald, so bright, with a man's head on his young shoulders; Fanny, so sweet, so gay'. The Friends pitied his mother - 'die arme Consola - Sie schwärmt für ihm; will nichts hören.' - who could not, would not see that he was conceited, untruthful and, for all that, stupid. They gloomily predicted that to a boy such as that no good could come.[42]

Admittedly, she did not isolate him from his peers. He played with other children, got into minor mischief and as often as not talked or bluffed his way out of trouble.[43] He suffered his share of scraped knees and nettle stings and at various times had croup, an inflammation behind the ear which may have been at the origin of his later mastoiditis, and perhaps even rheumatic fever. Whether or not he was particularly prone to illness, he did at the age of five or six suffer from a weak stomach, which for a time was thought to be a weak heart, and his indifferent health coupled with his mother's belief that he was too soft for a boy led her to treat him with a tenderness denied to her older children.[44]

When Oswald and Fanny were already attending school, and the two younger sisters, Rita and Sylvia, were in the nursery, Consola, instead of sending Berto to school, kept him at home and he had his lessons there - as far as can be ascertained, the basics of reading, writing and arithmetic. The regime was far from arduous. Lessons might be interrupted to allow him to accompany Consola on her shopping trips. He would read in her room while she rested in the afternoon, or sit with her while she awaited the return of Martin from the warehouse. It was this constant proximity to her which made him so well-informed about her life as the wife of a Bradford businessman, with her At Home day, her visiting, and the courtesies or confidences she exchanged with friends and acquaintance.[45]

It is impossible to say with certainty when exactly Humbert's love-affair with words began. His earliest memory of words used for any other than domestic purposes was of a nursery rhyme:

> A Turin, à Turin,
> A Cabal et biscottin

which his mother sang as she rocked him on her knee, and of the German ditties sung by Clara, his German nurse, of which mention has already been made. The first real book which he remembered was the story, read to him by Clara, of Jack and Floss, a young pair in whose fairly humdrum experiences he could recognise his own. So intensely did he share their pleasures and their terrors, that the single word 'sea' was enough to conjure up for him the whole of their summer holiday and was the inspiration for a poem called 'Seaside' which he wrote thirty years later.[46]

From this point onwards it was inevitable that he would not be content until he could read for himself. Unfortunately, this entailed lessons and effort, both of which he disliked. Such, in fact, were his difficulties with letters and numbers and handwriting that he passed for almost imbecile. Oswald and Fanny attended a private academy called either Miss Grove's or Miss Groven's. Berto was never a pupil there but the glimpse which he caught through an open door of desks and a pupil in a corner being mocked by the others induced in him such a terror that he would become ill whenever it was suggested that it was time he went to school.[47]

Matters were not improved when his sisters Rita and Sylvia, respectively three and four years younger than himself, were shown to be his superiors both in drawing maps and in handwriting. 'It was a curious fact that while words themselves were a delight and a constant surprise, the constituent letters the boy regarded with a personal hostility.' For the rest of his life his handwriting would always be difficult to read.

The little spare bedroom was converted into a schoolroom which he had only to enter for both his cheerfulness and any knowledge he had already acquired to vanish. The ink-stained tapestry cloth on the table reminded him of the illustration of the boy being held up by the hair and drowned in the ink-stand, in *Shock-headed Peter*, a book whose catalogue of senseless cruelty always symbolised for him the hatred of age for youth.[48] Fortunately his memory was good and he relied on learning by heart to make good the deficiencies of his handwriting.

At about the age of seven he began receiving private tuition from the head of the preparatory department of Bradford Grammar School, where Oswald was now a pupil. The tutor, referred to in *Now A Stranger* as 'Mr. X., known to the Grammar School boys as "Finny Crabs"', was in fact a Mr. Newton, whom the schoolboys nick-named 'Binnydabs'.[49] Humbert remembered him as 'a man with a large red face, a bushy black beard and a bushy black mind' and a belief, fortunately never tested upon young Berto, that knowledge was chiefly acquired through the seat of the trousers. It was perhaps as well that the fee he received (five shillings an hour) prevented him from beating the boy, for Berto had the baffling and irritating habit of withdrawing into some inner world to which Mr. X. had no access. On such occasions, we are told, Berto's eyes would veil over like a lizard's - a trait he displayed in adult life - and he would utter alarming and unexpected stupidities or offer some impudence but in such a mild manner that it was impossible to be sure that offence was intended. It did not seem to occur to Berto that he was in any danger from Mr. X.'s fury and the latter could only conclude that the boy was in some way lacking.[50]

We are not told what subjects he studied under this tutor, nor how many or how frequent were the lessons. Nevertheless, he made sufficient progress to be admitted to the preparatory department of Bradford Grammar School a year early, in April 1892. Oswald was already well established there in the Upper Fourth, which he portrayed to Berto as 'like nothing so much as a scene out of 'Old Heidelberg' minus the beer mugs. There the boys sat about at their ease, with desks and schoolbooks merely as a stage décor, and they fleeted the time carelessly as they did in the golden world.' Not so in the First Preparatory. Humbert recalled the shock of exchanging the cosy, sheltered but varied life of home for the bleak, strange and above all cold world of the old school buildings at the bottom of Manningham Lane. For most children, used to the manageable scale of the primary school, the sheer size of the secondary school is alarming. How much more intimidating, then, must have been the huge and 'barn-like ugliness ... of the school hall ... filled with the uproar of 450 boys, waiting for the headmaster to lead the procession of the staff to the prayers which he, in his capacity as a Doctor of Divinity, read daily to the assembled school with the air of a judge summing up against them.'[51]

It was in the bowels of this building that the Preparatory School was housed. The four years which Berto was to spend there would be crucial in the development of his distinctive self-awareness.

Humbert claimed that in his first class at the preparatory school he was ridiculed by the other children for whom anyone from Manningham or Heaton - and there were very few in the class - represented the hated Jewish employers: to them this plump, soft, round-eyed boy was a gift. They did not physically ill-treat him but made fun of his white socks, his sailor-collar, polite speech and of course the fact that he was a Jew. And although Berto did not set out to antagonize them further, he unconsciously did so by his behaviour. He boasted of his connection with and liking for 'Finny Crabs' (whom no-one liked), he claimed to know all the Latin irregular verbs by heart, and most of all, he talked - and talked, and talked; in class and out of class, about all sorts of things that were wholly uninteresting to his classmates - Arnside, books, the neighbours in Mount Royd, his older brother's prowess in the Upper School - without realising the hostility which he aroused. He was unstoppable and inaccessible to their jeers. They finally concluded that he was a half-wit and, as he constituted no particular danger to anyone but himself, they gradually left him alone or tolerated him with amused contempt.

Humbert later analysed this period as one of significant change in himself, in the course of which the discovery that he was unpopular was made not only bearable but almost welcome. The vehicle of this discovery was one Murgatroyd, a boy from a higher class in the preparatory school but living in Manningham and therefore an occasional companion on the way home from school. Murgatroyd was associated in Humbert's memory with two unpleasant events. On only the second time that he escorted the boy home, Murgatroyd attempted to explain to him the mysteries of sex. Berto had no idea what he was talking about. Words were to him winged visitors with strange and lovely migrant ways: Murgatroyd's obscenities were strange, ugly and meaningless. It was only many years later when he heard them again that he realised how simple or how protected he had been.

The second incident was much more devastating. It occurred towards the end of his first term when the attitude of the other boys was actually changing. He was walking home with Murgatroyd and as they parted at the entrance to Mount Royd, the other said that he couldn't understand why, since Berto wasn't such a bad kid, he was the most unpopular boy in the Preparatory. Berto simply could not understand it and was so shattered that he was ill for three days. He would give no explanation, and enquiries at school produced none, which simply increased Consola's anxiety and distress: 'the child that had gone to school three days ago had not come back.'

How he eventually got over the hurt, and the part played in his recovery by his English teacher, a Mr Rendell, is told in a long passage which begins with a fascinating and superbly ironic description of this master. In it Humbert also gently mocks a number of literary, social, religious and other targets of his wit, here less savage towards them than in other places. His keenest cuts appear to be reserved for Mr. Rendell himself, who 'understood boys as a stamp-collector understands postage-stamps...They were specimens ...collected...with a dispassionate and unloving eagerness.' His favourite, which might be classed as 'Exhibit A', was the manly, smiling, curly-headed type, unostentatiously pious and 'with enough brains to know that he was a fool and not enough to be a coward.' Unhappily, such specimens were rare in Bradford, whose 'lads, unlike those in Shropshire, did not tend to be creatures of romance or suitable heroes for books by Talbot Baines Reed. They had the habit of shouldering through time and fate like a herd of small, determined cattle with their heads down. In consequence, only once or twice in his long search did Mr. Rendell come upon this rare blossom.'

'Exhibit B, much less cherished, was the boy likely to qualify for Oxford or Cambridge. Here the collector's interest was faintly tinged with the commercial.' It appears that Berto was briefly weighed in this balance and found wanting, chiefly, it seems, because his capacity for memorising verse was not matched by any ability to understand it. Through Mr. Rendell Berto made the acquaintance of the poems of Longfellow and Tennyson, learned 'The Village Blacksmith' in record time and no less easily acquired 'The Charge of the Light Brigade' and the monkey-poem in 'The First Jungle Book'. Mr. Rendell sent for him, a signal honour, to enquire whether he liked poetry and which of the two poems he liked better, the Tennyson or the Kipling. When Berto finally confessed to preferring (although he could not say why) 'The Monkeys', with its 'jealous moon', Mr. Rendell sighed and said 'O, you Wolves, with your bright faces, if only you had bright brains,' and sent him back to the gymnasium.

By contrast, Exhibit C, 'the characters', abounded. Mr. Rendell 'professed no affection for this class. He had the vivisector's joy in their investigation - that abstract passion for knowledge in which the satisfaction of some obscure streak of cruelty culminates in something not unlike a spiritual orgasm. There was, for example, Bloggs, with the quiet inexpressive face of a tattered stocking. Bloggs hardly ever washed, and never all of himself at the one time. . . He would have been an unscrupulous liar if he had been able to think quickly enough. As it was - and this was his peculiar appeal to the collector - he constantly told the truth by accident.' Such a specimen was irresistible to Mr. Rendell, who 'watched over Bloggs and collected his sayings with a vigour which might perhaps have been directed to his improvement.' His patient 'investigation of a dumb and crippled soul' was finally rewarded, for Bloggs was caught stealing from the tuckshop, in full sight of five or six boys and the salesman, and, but for Mr. Rendell's intervention, might have been expelled. As it was, he escaped even a caning on the promise of a heart-to-heart talk with Mr. Rendell, who thereby 'added a unique speciment to his *hortus siccus*'.[52]

Humbert concluded that, having failed to gain entry to Category B, he was himself selected as a likely candidate for Category C after the *affaire* Murgatroyd. In the course of a dispute in the changing room, one boy had spat at his adversary. This was considered a womanly reaction, not to be tolerated amongst males. There followed a mass attack upon the offender, in which Berto heartily joined, thinking thereby to win popularity. When the rest withdrew, the weeping victim found himself face-to-face with Berto and, furious at being attacked by the prize muff of the form, rushed to attack him, whereupon Berto incontinently spat at him. This act surprisingly passed unnoticed and the entry of the School Sergeant put an end to the hostilities.

But Berto was immediately deeply ashamed and so upset that he dropped his dumb-bell on his foot. The Sergeant sent him off to sit by the vaulting horse for a rest. There Mr. Rendell happened to find him some minutes later, in tears. Mr. Rendell catechised him at length in an attempt to discover the cause of his distress. Eventually it all came out. He was weeping firstly because he had spat, secondly because that showed not only that he was unpopular but that he deserved to be, and thirdly because the Sergeant, instead of punishing him for dropping his dumb-bell, had been friendly. 'Would it make you feel better if I hit you ?' asked Mr. Rendell. 'No,' said Berto, 'because the other boys wouldn't believe you meant it.' 'Do you want to be a hero ?' 'I don't want to be a hero,' was the tearful reply, 'I want to be like them.' 'Listen, young man,' said Mr. Rendell, 'your job in life is to be different. It's not easy and the different ones aren't liked.' 'Never?' asked Berto. 'Never,' said the master, 'or very seldom.' 'But you're different,' objected the boy. 'And you like me ?' asked Mr. Rendell. Berto didn't answer. 'Good for you, infant,' said Mr. Rendell and sent him back to his gymnastics. At the end of the hour the spitting episode was forgotten and Berto was unexpectedly happy. He rushed home. All was well. He was different. He could be happy again.

> But the boy was wrong. Nothing could ever be the same again, and Consola had reason for her tears. He had tasted of the tree of knowledge of good and evil, and the gate had shut behind him. He didn't know, and if he had known, he wouldn't greatly have cared. He was singled out - in the Rendell class of the different. He proceeded to make himself excessively disagreeable and was finally clouted by C.... And still he didn't care. He wasn't even grateful to Mr. Rendell. He merely acknowledged his intelligence in discovering his qualities. . . The boy went to sleep smiling that night. The bruises in his heart had gone and there was no trace left. But, alas ! it was not so:
>
> With one pain, as one woman, when you love her and leave her,
> You carry her wound in your heart till you die.[53]

The capacity for accepting things as they were and a temperament of india-rubber enabled him to adapt to the environment and bounce not only back but higher and higher. The magnanimity which characterised his adult life may have had its source in his youthful inability to hate even those who hurt him; he rarely bore malice. Even the M's, whom he admitted to disliking, were described with an understanding kindness which made them almost endearing.[54]

Humbert described himself as being at this time ungainly in his movements and at best an inferior performer at sports. Surprisingly he was very fond of the sports field, less for the games which took place there than for the Field itself which held for him the magical attraction of a great garden or park in the middle of a city. Its appeal was less in the winter when his incompetence at rugby condemned him to be a frozen if excitable spectator. He much preferred the season and the game of cricket for which the duffers had a pitch set aside for them.[55]

He also wrote that by the time he was nine he had not only reached the top class in the Preparatory School, he had also settled comfortably into his surroundings and was beginning to lose his 'difference'. He rarely wept now, his lessons caused him no difficulty, save for arithmetic and drawing, and 'he had found, in fact, that he could learn almost anything by heart except courage and the capacity for popularity.'[56]

This perception of himself was only partially borne out by the recollection of his contemporaries. One of these, Geoffrey Burton, who entered the school in that same year but in the class below Berto, said that he attracted attention to himself by his dress, appearance and speech. His smallish, well-rounded figure, with big, gentle brown eyes in the middle of a large, dark face, surmounted by a shock of short, thick, dark hair, was habitually dressed in a navy blue sailor blouse, with the traditional wide collar and tie, and short trousers. He was usually to be found holding forth at the centre of a group of fellow-pupils, who mostly regarded him with good-natured curiosity and tolerance, and a good deal of secret admiration.

He was, by all accounts but his own, alert and attentive, wholesomely inquisitive and imaginative, just the sort of boy to reward a master's interest by producing good, original work, yet equally bright at amusing his fellows with his quips. He rapidly acquired both a reputation which soon spread beyond the school walls, and the nick-name 'Bugs' (pronounced with a broad Yorkshire vowel, more like 'Boogs'), thought to be a corruption of 'Humbugs', the nearest familiar sound to which his fellows could convert 'Umberto', and the name of a hard striped peppermint boiled sweet very popular in the area.[57]

By now Berto had also begun to enjoy the beautifully ordered words of the Prayer Book, no longer shuddering at the daily pronouncement of the Saviour's name.[58] At what point he stopped attending the synagogue and the Sunday school is not recorded but, although he was too deeply marked by his Jewish background ever to be completely free of it, it is clear that by now his religious allegiance, never very strong, was considerably eroded by the failure of Bradfordian Judaism to appeal to his needs. There was little in the architecture, the decoration or the ceremonial in Bowland Street to inspire or excite the young worshipper. Such events in the Jewish calendar as stirred his emotions - the flowers which transformed the Rabbi's house on the Feast of Tabernacles, or the desolating strains of the Shofa-horn blown once a year at Yom-Kippur - he enjoyed as pretty spectacles or well-performed tricks.

The Rabbi's failure to inspire either affection or respect, Consola's indifference to her religion, the irreverent behaviour of some of the congregation and Berto's own feeling that children were excluded from this private club for men, contributed to make him ashamed of his Jewishness and envious of 'the proud and overt way in which Christians paid their calls upon their God' of a Sunday morning, and when, on his way to Sunday School, he had to run the gauntlet of mindless anti-Jewish jibes, what he hated most was 'not his persecutors but the object of their persecution'.[59]

Mention has already been made of his brothers and sisters. From this account of his childhood it is clear that he admired Oswald, barely two years older than himself, although frequently referred to as three or four years older. Like most elder brothers, Oswald seemed herculean and omniscient to his infant brother, but since no further mention was made of him after Berto has reached the top of the preparatory school, it may be assumed that Oswald took on more normal proportions and importance in his younger brother's eyes. Nevertheless, they remained on excellent terms for the rest of his life, despite the different directions which their lives took and the fact that Humbert was determined never to enter the

Bradford 'trade'.[60] There is evidence, too, from Oswald's family that he had a high regard for Humbert and delighted in his younger brother's professional and literary success.

There is less indication in Humbert's writings of any deep feelings for his sisters at this time. The two younger ones he portrayed as simply appendages to the skirts of their mother or their nurse. One would expect to find at least a hint of his feelings towards his elder sister, Fanny, whether of admiration or dislike, but she too was simply a name in the cast-list of his dramatic world. Family recollections and some unpublished records show that they were in fact a close-knit family, with an almost mystic affection for Consola who had no interest outside her children. She disapproved of their absorption in books which they infinitely preferred to the enforced walks in the cold Park during the winter months. In their large and comfortable nursery a coal fire blazed behind the high green fender, on either side of which were long white cupboards in which they would hide, reading with the door left open just enough to allow them to see the print. When Consola invited other children to come to tea, the young Wolffs would hand them a book each and retire behind the chairs, hoping not to be disturbed. If their elders insisted that they play with their guests, the only game they could think of was to lie on top of the table and pretend to swim.

His sisters remembered him at this age as a bewildering mixture of fun, lack of worldly wisdom and a desperate seriousness about things which, at least to the two younger girls, seemed not at all to matter. His absent-mindedness was forever getting him into trouble: one day, to his mother's consternation, he arrived home from school in the middle of the morning. Was he ill? Had he done something wrong? No, he had simply mistaken the break bell for the lunch-time one. His sister Rita recalled a fragment of the doggerel verse which he began to write very early in his life and which he would recite at inopportune moments to set them off in fits of giggling. Every Sunday the children were sent to pay their respects to Mrs. Mahler, whom they all felt to be an almighty bore. As they approached the house Berto suddenly broke out with:-

> When I see you Mrs. Mahler
> Like a stuffed pig in your parlour
> Looking bored and very fat
> I am then constrained to wonder
> How Herr Mahler made the blunder.

The Mahlers, of course, were never made privy to the joke, and Consola was not amused to hear it, for she had a deep respect for Mr. Mahler, her co-executor, in whose financial wisdom she had a considerable, if misplaced, faith.

Humbert's sisters kept in quite close touch with him right up to his death, and relations were never less than cordial. Humbert himself maintained a warm affection for them all and often went to considerable pains to help them.[61]

By the autumn of 1894, his father had for two years been ill with angina. Despite Consola's steadfast belief in his recovery his condition steadily worsened. The long illness appears hardly to have affected Berto whose relationship with his father, though cordial, was, as we have seen, fairly distant. Before the onset of Martin's illness Berto had sometimes on Sundays been allowed into the little ebony and ivory boudoir where Martin opened the post which the firm's messenger brought to the house. Humbert recalled the pleasure which he got from the scent and taste of the pipe which his father now smoked instead of the cigars of earlier years, the rustle of paper as the envelopes with their exciting foreign stamps were opened, and his father's calm, even when he tore a cheque in two while trying to detach a Brazilian specimen. But now, although Berto was aware in a casual way that his father no longer went to the warehouse every day and the house no longer echoed to the rumbling notes of 'Down among the dead men', that Oswald sometimes had to go to comfort his father in the night, that The Friends inquired more frequently and more pressingly after the invalid's health, school crowded more and more into his life to the exclusion of all else. Already in the child could be discerned that faculty for forgetting everything but that which was immediately in front of him which was, on his own admission, to become habitual.[62]

In October 1894 the Nurse who had shared with Consola the care of the invalid was dismissed, either because Martin had seemed better or (as Humbert later thought more probable) because from the Nurse's point of view Consola had grown worse. Two days after the Nurse's dismissal, Consola had taken Martin in an open cab to Saltaire Park to enjoy the October sunshine. At the gates of the Park she helped him out and they walked a short way to a seat. When after a few minutes she became aware that Martin was not answering her, with the cabman's help she got her husband into the cab and drove the long road back - an hour's drive according to Humbert - with Martin dead at her side.[63]

Martin Wolff was forty-eight years of age, Consola was thirty-five, Berto nearly ten. His childhood was over.

Chapter Two

1894-1903

'The call of the perilous margins'

('The Well', *London Sonnets*)

Bradford Grammar School - 1894-1903

Entry No. 22489 of the Bradford Grammar School Register reads:

> Wolff, Umberto: admitted, April 1892; Senior, September 1896; left, July 1903.

The School Year Books and the Honours List for 1884 - 1911 reveal the following bare facts:

1896-1897	Umberto Wolff: Classical Third
1899-1900	Umberto Wolff: Classical Fifth. Oxford & Cambridge Lower Certificate (Distinctions in English and History)
1900-1901	Oxford and Cambridge Higher Certificate (Latin, French, Elementary Mathematics,English,History)
1902	Oxford and Cambridge Higher Certificate
1903	Oxford and Cambridge Higher Certificate (Latin, Greek, Scripture, English [Distinction], History [Distinction][1]
1903	Open Scholarship in Classics to Wadham College, Oxford; Lister Scholarship of £20 per annum for three years; Honourable Mentions for the Forster History Prize; the Classical Prize and the English Prize.

At that time the school was organised into a seven stage Preparatory School, and a Senior School which pupils were expected to enter 'as soon as possible after completing their twelfth year'. The prospectus for the period makes it clear that it was not necessary to pass through every form of the Preparatory School - in special cases pupils could move through two classes in one year - and it was thanks to one such 'double promotion' that at the age of nine Berto found himself in the top class of the preparatory department when his father died in 1894.[2]

The imposing perpendicular gothic and twentieth century brick of the present Bradford Grammar School stand at a great remove, both in space and in style, from the dreary, shabby ugliness of the original buildings at the bottom of Manningham Lane, which have since been demolished to make way for a ring road.[3] The headmaster, the Reverend Dr. William Hulton Keeling, was a formidable man with a ferocious stare and a harsh voice, whose 'huge square face like that of a tin statue of Thor that had been left to rust in some abandoned garden' had given rise to the soubriquet of 'Old Rusty', by which he was known to generations of boys.[4] He was appointed in 1871 to improve the school in the aftermath of the reforming legislation relating to endowed schools. During his long headship the school became renowned for the number of boys it put through Oxford and Cambridge, as a result (it seems likely) of the combination of skilful methods of tuition, single-minded concentration on able pupils earmarked for scholarships, and the scholarly staff which the school was able to attract.

The school in those days employed a system not unlike that of the old-style French *lycée*, that is to say that the Classical teachers were also responsible for English, just as in France they would have been for French, as well as for Latin and Greek. It was not until the nineteen-twenties that a teacher was appointed for the express purpose of teaching English. The masters to whom Humbert acknowledged the greatest debt were Caryl Battersby, the Fourth Form Classical and English master, author of a book of poems, *Song of the Golden Bough* (Constable), and J. E. Barton, his Fifth Form teacher, winner of the Newdigate Prize for English Verse, who later became headmaster of Bristol Grammar School after eighteen years at Bradford.

Among young Berto's contemporaries were Henry Clay, who preceded him to Oxford by one year, as a Scholar of University College, and later, after a spell in the Ministry of Labour, became Professor of Economics at Manchester University; the artists Edward Maufe and Albert Rutherston (William Rothenstein's younger brother and three years older than Berto); Oliver Onions (the novelist); and W. E. Barber, who became the first literary editor of *The Morning Post* thanks to its editor, Sir Fabian Ware, who had been his French master at Bradford.

Form lists and Speech Day reports in *The Bradfordian* record Berto's results in various subjects - not always as brilliant as one might have expected, partly because he was much younger than his classmates - and tell us something of his contribution to the life of the school. Only occasionally did he reach first or second place but he usually managed to be in the top half of the class in Classical and Modern Languages, History and English. Mathematics, Science and Art were his weakest subjects. When he reached the Fifth Form, however, he blossomed, taking first places in Greek, German and English, second in History, Geography and Latin. He was awarded the Special Prize for Modern Languages at the end of that year, a presage of the easy if not always quite accurate fluency in French and German which he was later to display in his Civil Service work as well as in his writing.

Physical prowess and muscular coordination were not his strong points. Such triumphs as he won on the sports field were in the nature of kingship in the realm of the halt if not of the blind: first place in the Under 13 Scratch 100 yards (time: 15 seconds) and a year later first in the 220 yards scratch consolation race.

He performed as Puck in an extract from *A Midsummer Night's Dream* at Speech Day in 1898, when he was thirteen, and the following year as the first niece in a performance of Act 3 of *The Critics*.

Among his 'extra-curricular' activities should be mentioned the hoaxes that he played from time to time. One which Geoffrey Burton remembered clearly, although Humbert unaccountably never recorded it, took place during afternooon school in the Classical Vth, just after J. E. Barton had come as form master. Berto electrified the rest of the class, most of whom were not privy to the transformation, by appearing in a theatrical wig of bright auburn hair. He also moved from his usual desk in the back row to one in the front and exerted himself to attract the greatest possible attention, at the same time maintaining his composure undiminished, and in every sense not turning a hair throughout the performance.

Barton, the master to whom Berto owed so much and whom he later praised so highly, was at a disadvantage, as he had not by then had time to size up and know all the various boys. He was obviously mystified by the air of suppressed excitement, but could not put his finger on the cause or take any disciplinary action. So he tactfully refrained from taking any notice and remained unaware of the explanation. Some years afterwards Burton, who by then had become Barton's brother-in-law, had the pleasure of enlightening him on this baffling but still-remembered incident.

Another mild joke in which Berto liked to take a lead involved the now defunct *Bradford* (later *Yorkshire*) *Observer*. Under pseudonyms or otherwise he and his friends started and maintained lengthy correspondence on topics of the day in pompous and platitudinous letters full of current clichés, and hoaxed quite a few of the paper's innocent readers into joining in their sham disputation.[5]

To judge from the pages of *The Bradfordian*, his entry into the Sixth Form marked the beginning of his fullest contribution to the life of the school. He was regularly to be heard in the Debating Society where his maiden speech in November 1900 (supporting the extension of the franchise to women) was thought to be 'admirable alike for vigour of treatment and freedom of delivery'. In a later debate, opposing belief in psychic phenomena he 'related with delicate and veiled satire a ghost story'. He was elected to the Committee of the Society at the end of the year and was increasingly heard as a main or a supporting speaker. In November 1901 he proposed the motion 'that this House would lynch all anarchist murderers'. In April 1902 he enjoyed his greatest oratorical triumph when proposing 'that the death of Cecil Rhodes is a disaster to the British Empire': the Secretary to the Debating Society, one K. Mossman, described the speech as 'a rhetorical masterpiece . . . (whose) easy, flowing oratory . . . equalled, if not surpassed the most eloquent oration the House had ever heard.'

He was also to be seen and heard on the stage, playing Sganarelle in *Le Médecin Malgré Lui* (1901) and a young aesthete in *Third Person Singular*, written for the Debating Society players by Barton, who by now was Senior Classics and Senior English master. Berto was highly praised by the magazine for his dress and speech. And, in place of the usual Greek play on Speech Day at the end of July 1902, he was called upon to recite William Watson's *Ode on the Coronation of King Edward VII.*

School magazines did not at this time set out to display a great deal of what it has become fashionable to call 'creative writing', and *The Bradfordian* was no exception, although during Berto's later school years it contained rather more original poetry and prose (as distinct from reports on matches and debates) than when he first joined the school. From the absence of editorial pleas for contributions it may be concluded that the magazine received at least as much literary copy as it had space for. From its pages some idea of his early poetry can be gained, but what little we know of the genesis of his vocation as a poet, how he wrote his poetry, or what poetry meant to him as a schoolboy, comes to us through brief mentions in *Now A Stranger* and *The Upward Anguish* and snatches of autobiography in the Preface to *Early Poems* and *A Winter Miscellany*, which whet but do not satisfy the appetite.

In *Now A Stranger* he recalled how, at the age of seven, on a fine June morning he composed his first poem. The occasion was an outing to Rombald's Moor - 'a favourite excursion of all good citizens of Manningham' - and represented the long-delayed satisfaction of one of Berto's most cherished ambitions. The trip involved a tram-ride to Saltaire and then a ten-mile walk across the moor to Ilkley. Berto's health had thus far been thought too frail for such strenuous exertion although, as it turned out, the constant ailments to which he was prone were due to a weak stomach rather than the suspected weak heart.

Brilliantly the day dawned and long before the household was stirring Berto sat for an hour at his window, drinking in the bright morning whose intense colours he found almost frightening.

> But what frightened him still more was the behaviour of the words used to represent them. "Blue, blue, blue," he murmured under his breath till the word lost all sense and began to belly out like the balloon that they blew up for the Gala at Peel Park. It swelled and swelled till it almost seemed as though it were minded to take off for a huge ascent with the boy suspended by a frail hawser. He pulled himself back

with a jerk, but he suspected, without admitting the thought, that there might be more peril in the dictionary than on the road to the Moor. He composed his first poem, which however he did not commit to paper. As far as can be recalled, it ran as follows:

> It was blue, blue, blue,
> And I hardly knew
> What to do.[6]

Whatever allowances may need to be made for over-imaginative hindsight in this account of his discovery of the poetic daemon, it is clear that from an early age Humbert was conscious of the peculiar magic of words and of their power, of which a significant aspect was their propensity to take possession of him rather than he of them. It is, however, equally clear that we are unlikely ever to know for certain which was his first written poem, for there appear to be three, if not four, contenders for the title.

In *Now A Stranger* he described reading his first poem to his mother at about the age of sixteen:

> Berto appeared in the drawing-room at Oak Mount, extremely flushed and tousled, with staring eyes and more ink than usual on his hands. He was carrying a sheet of foolscap. "Listen," he said, and proceeded to read his first poem as follows:
>
> Vintagers over the hill
> that turns up a cheek to the height,
> I can hear your gladness still
> as I pass away from your sight.
>
> Consola gasped. "It's a poem; yes, poetry. You made it up, Berto?" He admitted it. Consola did two things, one openly, one surreptitiously. The surreptitious act was to look in the Encyclopedia to discover the date at which Tennyson wrote his first poem. The overt act was to murmur with immense satisfaction: "Now let that Will (Rothenstein) criticize that."[7]

A typescript version of the poem in the Grammar School Library continues:

> And I see the luscious grape,
> How it stains your feet and hands,
> And the sun around your shape
> Like the glow of summer sands.

And you sing a mellow song
With such longing ling'ring notes
It seems the humming bees prolong
The music as it floats.

You know not care, and yet you sing,
How softly, sweetly, sadly!
Of one - a shepherd - suffering
So would I suffer gladly

If I could find such soothing end
As sung in country story
And every singer my true friend,
Comfort my prize, not glory.

The identification of this as his first poem presents several problems. The first is that, despite its simple, deceptively artless form, and the change of metre in the third stanza, suggesting that the author could not sustain the original metre, the technical skill and the imagery deployed make it unlikely that the lines had no predecessors but leapt new from the author's pen, like Athene springing fully armed from the head of Jupiter.

Furthermore, three years before the publication of *Now A Stranger*, in the Preface to *Early Poems*, the 1930 re-issue of the 1920 *London Sonnets*, he had identified another poem, even more technically mature than 'The Vintagers', as his first composition:

> I have a dim memory of a boy aged sixteen writing eagerly in an attic bedroom in Oak Mount at Bradford a poem called "The Well." Little did he know of love or loss or separation when he wrote:
>
> Lifted again is the voice of your singing.
> Golden again are the perilous margins.
> Sweet are your eyes, and young and immortal
> Our hearts are set to the day and the hills
>
> Moreover, it was not I, but some other, who stumbled down the stair and read the poem to Consola - that most beautiful red-haired lady, who was his mother. Nor did I see her surreptitiously look up "Tennyson" in a handbook to discover the age at which he committed his first poem.[8]

In the full text of 'The Well' which appeared in *Early Poems*, an old man speaks to his dead love as he sits by the well where they had played and dreamt and loved in their youth. From the sad reflection that if they, the dreamers, were real then, all must now be over since she is dead, he moves on to another, brighter possibility:

> But if we two are dreams of a dreamer,
> All is not over and here together
> Age falls from me, and from you the mantle
> Death seemed to cast, and here by the well side
> Lifted again is the voice of your singing,
> Golden again are the perilous margins . . .

Little though he may have known of love or loss or separation who wrote these lines, the mastery displayed in handling a difficult metre, and the confidence with which he breaks step when he feels the need - the pace is more that of the fells than the parade ground - no less than the sophisticated reflection upon the nature of reality, testify to something more than 'newly-learnèd art.' No matter, therefore, which poem he was prepared to own as his first-born, it is virtually certain that he had at least made some previous attempts and those not entirely unsuccessful.

But a third account of these poetic beginnings was given by a journalist, W. T. Cranfield, in *The Yorkshire Observer* in 1927. Reviewing the success of Humbert's increasingly prolific output, he wrote:

> Appropriately enough, the passing of the old Bradford steam trams provided the subject for his first poem. Written when he was sixteen, its appearance in the "Bradfordian" was of great encouragement to the boy of that time.[9]

Later articles in Yorkshire newspapers repeated the story right up to the time of his death. Thus, on the occasion of Humbert's visit to open a new Labour Exchange in Bradford in 1933, one Yorkshire newspaper quoted him as saying that his first poem was written at the age of sixteen "to mark the passing of the old steam trams" and *The Yorkshire Observer*, in the obituary notice which it devoted to Humbert on 6 January 1940, said:

> His first published effort was a crib of Milton's "Lycidas" offering farewell to the steam trams which at that time were abdicating before their electric successors.

'Dirge for the Steam-Tram - "Multis Ille Bonis Flebilis Occidit" -', which appeared over the pseudonym 'Bion' in *The Bradfordian*, was a clever and amusing pastiche of eighteenth century elegiac verse, in a splendid jumble of oats and neat-herds, gods, muses and SH_2. The following extract conveys something of the flavour:

Now, now, no longer shall some agèd sire
Rush forth to greet thee, and embrace the mire.
No more shall matrons, peering through the damp,
Threat thy conductor with infuriate gamp.
. . . .
Thou wast too fair to die. Besides 'tis taught
That matter cannot fade away to naught.
So weep not, Bradford, dry those eyes now red,
For the steam tram, your sorrow, is not dead;
Today he wanders through the jocund meads,
Where heroes thin attend their nitid steeds. . .

Now A Stranger quotes six lines from the middle of the poem but without any suggestion that they were his first or even his first published verses.

The final complication was added by an interview which Humbert gave to the the 'Special Correspondent' of the *London Mercury* in 1936, in which he was quoted as saying:

> My first poem was written at the age of fifteen, and was published in the Oxford Magazine. It was actually set for the Scholarship Examination the next year, and although I myself did not have to translate it, several of my contemporaries were compelled, despite their indignation, to translate a schoolfellow's work!

But the article did not identify the poem.[10]

Two years later, in *The Upward Anguish* (1938), Humbert enlarged upon this story. While still a schoolboy, he had written a poem apparently more remarkable for its brilliant fate than for its content. It was entitled, he said, 'To A Poet Scorned', and began:

My songs unheard I come to earth
Darkness I ask long sleep,
Why should I pray for second birth
Who would but wake to weep?

The verses had had the good fortune to please the editors of *The Oxford Magazine* who duly published it. When Berto went up for his entrance examination, by a coincidence so extraordinary as to appear preternatural, the poem set for translation into Latin verse in the Christ Church group of entrance examinations was none other than his *Oxford Magazine* piece. Berto, as a candidate in the Trinity-Wadham group, did not sit the paper, or what he would have made of that coincidence beggars the imagination, but he later confessed to having had 'the satisfaction of knowing that three or four people in my form were translating my bad English verse into worse Latin. I shall never again know such a thrill.'[11]

The date on the typescript copy of the poem preserved in the archives of Bradford Grammar School - 21 May 1903 - places it several months after the scholarship examination in which it was reportedly set. Moreover (although this is a less important detail), what Humbert twice referred to as the opening lines are clearly the second stanza of the poem.

The Oxford Magazine did indeed publish, in an Eights Week Number, the following poem:

'Epitaph of a Poet Scorned'

Carve not my name upon the stone,
Why give a name to dust?
But leave me quiet here alone;
Weep short, if weep you must.

My songs unheard I come to earth;
Darkness I ask, long sleep;
Why should I wish for second birth
Who would but wake to weep?

Bring poppies, poppies to my grave,
That I may sleep more sound,
And o'er my head the laurel wave
Wherewith I was not crowned.
'W'[12]

With the exception of 'wish' rather than 'pray' in line 3 of the second stanza, the text is identical with that of the 1903 poem in the School archives, and we may safely assume that 'W' was none other than Berto Wolff.

The perfection of this story is marred only by one detail: the year of publication, which was 1904 - the end of his first year as an undergraduate. Unfortunately, none of the Christ Church group of colleges has preserved the entrance examination papers for the period and so the story cannot be fully verified. There is no reason to suppose that Humbert invented the whole of the Scholarship Examination story but it does seem probable that if the poem was set as an examination piece it was in a later year than 1903.

It must be said that to conceal such a tale would have required, if not superhuman modesty, at least a greater degree of reserve than Humbert possessed, and we have his own admission that he talked ceaselessly about it at the time.[13] It must have seemed too good a story for a minor chronological discrepancy to be allowed to spoil it. Certainly none of the other participants or observers seems to have wanted to challenge what eventually became the received version.

According to the 1940 obituary notice in *The Yorkshire Observer*, however, the poem thus glorified by the examiners was *A Farewell to the School*, a poem with 'a more gravely romantic ring' which had won the approval of his English master, Mr. Barton, who encouraged him to send it for publication. The only poem bearing such a title which it has been possible to trace was called 'Farewell Remarks' and was printed in *The Bradfordian* in July 1903. Its length makes it an unlikely candidate for the translation paper and its ring is neither romantic nor grave, although it does have an engaging mock-gravity - almost a foretaste of Noel Coward - which perhaps concealed anxiety behind its typically British understatement, but Humbert never claimed it as a first poem:

. . . .
Old friends, good-bye. We go and leave behind
A life not ill;
Perhaps the world, though slandered, will prove kind:
Let's hope it will.

The most probable explanation is that Humbert wrote two versions of the story of his 'first poem'. In one, the poem was 'Vintagers'; in the other, it was 'The Well.' 'Vintagers' has all the marks of a less mature composition than 'The Well' and is the more convincing candidate. But the question of his first published poem gave rise to some confusion. In an article about Bradford Grammar School, written by Humbert for *The Yorkshire Observer* of 20 April 1939, he said quite plainly that 'Farewell to the Steam Trams', written when he was in the Fifth Form, was his first published poem and it is without a doubt the first poem bearing the pseudonym 'Bion' with which he signed his poems in *The Bradfordian*. He also made it clear that it was Barton, the Fifth Form master and a poet himself, who thought that a romantic poem which Berto had written was good enough to send to *The Oxford Magazine*. It was this one which Berto's fellows encountered in the examination rooms some months after its publication in the magazine, but although it was his first poem to reach beyond the Bradford readership, it was not stricly speaking his first 'public' poem.

The replacement of the old school door by a new, self-closing glass door inspired him to write 'To The School Door - Eheu! Fugaces!', in the school magazine in April 1903. The only prose contribution to *The Bradfordian* which can be identified as his was an imitation of Hardy in May 1903, entitled 'The Night Train'.

As to the amount he wrote and the manner of its writing, we have his own later testimony that by the time he was in his last year at school he was writing regularly, but for some unexplained reason he could only write at night time in his bedroom 'looking over to the single light of Scotland Farm on the left and to the line of lights past Peel Park'. He had, it seems, a prescribed allowance of one poem a week, presumably a self-imposed ration, conceivably in the interests of his Oxford aspirations, and he habitually spoke the words aloud as he composed.

What little more we know about his early writings is derived chiefly from his account of a week's holiday which he spent with his schoolmate, Geoffrey Burton, in the Lake District, a reward from their parents for winning scholarships to Oxford.[14]

At this stage in his life, if he believed that art expresses and interprets experience, he clearly did not believe that the experience had to be his own. One would expect to find him holding just the opposite view, namely that once the autobiographical novel has been written, the test of the true novelist is his ability to enter imaginatively into someone else's experience, whereas the poet has necessarily to be expressing his own. An incident during this holiday shows that he thought nothing of the kind.

Geoffrey and he had set out from Grange Over Sands to walk to Windermere and back. After several hours walking, the onset of hunger sparked off a discussion of the effect of bodily sensations on their perceptions and reasoning powers, whence they proceeded to consider the role of sex and love in their young lives. It appears that they were both fairly ignorant of these mysteries

> but their ignorance of the particular did not prevent Geoffrey or him from having clear views on the general.

They (or at least Berto) took the view that sex was a nuisance which interfered with everything, especially work. And far from being, as Geoffrey thought, an essential ingredient of poetry,

> love was a mere convention, as arbitrary, say, as a *ballade à double refrain*. Poetry could get on very well without sex or love. No doubt these things had a dramatic value and were indispensable to a novelist. But the poet was happily spared their odious insistence. . . He had, it is true, written a love-poem or two, as, for instance, the one which Geoffrey remembered he had composed after they had seen Barrie's fine play 'Quality Street' together. But that, as was proper, was somebody else's emotion recollected and recorded in tranquillity.[15]

It is not surprising that his youthful poetry was modelled on other writers, major and minor. Artists usually begin by imitating acknowledged masters and, flattery apart, there is no better means to understanding the methods and outlook of good artists or the nature and potential of the medium than to try to recreate the experience of the masters. Moreover, until the young artist has a comment of his own to make on life, the 'sincerity' of his work is bound to contain something of the second-hand: it need not be any less genuine for that. Wisdom lies in following the advice of Lecoq de Boisbaudran to his art students: 'Steal, if you must, from the rich, not the poor.'[16]

That this view was held and encouraged by Berto's teachers is borne out by the most casual inspection of *The Bradfordian* of this period: the poetic contributions were almost entirely imitative and consciously so. No entry bears the proper name of its author; the convention seems to have been to write anonymously or under a pseudonym. It is legitimate to infer that unattributed pieces were the work of members of staff if not of the editor himself. Thus, in April 1902, the first poem in a series entitled *The Poets at the Grammar School*, a sonnet on the subject of impending corporal punishement, was an unmistakeable imitation of Milton, from its title - 'When the Assault was intended on the sinner' - to its opening lines

> Sergeant, or Drill-Instructor, whoso'er
> Is destined my unhappy back to beat

Berto was perhaps less slavish in his imitation but both the fact and the intent are visible. Indeed, his choice of pen-name is revealing, for Bion was himself a Greek imitator of Theocritus and best known for his *Lament for Adonis*, while his own death was lamented in a beautiful dirge by a friend or pupil.

The most insistent model for his early poems, and notably in the 'Dirge for the Steam-Tram', was Tennyson - Lycidas is only a thematic echo - and it is interesting to note that Consola looked to Tennyson for comparison with his earliest poem and not, for example, to Pope or Keats. The Grand Old Man of English poetry had died in 1892 and featured strongly in school anthologies of the time. It is hardly surprising that Berto's early efforts betray the influence of such an all-pervasive model.

The adolescent Wolff judged the quality of his verse by its ability to please his mentors. His 'best' poems were those of which his English teacher, Barton, approved and which

> dealt with abstract subjects, or, in the Browning vein, with familiar matters of today.. . . He had written some nature-poems, one a blank verse ode to the dying beech, which began:
>
> > O dying beech against the light-blue sky.
> > O brown and blue in mingling wonderful.
>
> . . . He had also begun an Epic dealing with certain aspects of Asgard that had escaped Matthew Arnold's attention. Geoffrey (Burton) had surely not forgotten the first two lines:
>
> > Thus spake he cheerly, and through all the Halls
> > echoed the sounding voices of the gods

> . . . . And, finally, there was his tribute to a dead school-fellow, which had dealt with the subject of death conclusively, beginning
>
> Though surfeited with many carcases,
> Death, be not proud.
>
> Barton, it was true, had pointed out that John Donne had begun a sonnet with the first four words of the second line. As, however, he had never read Donne, this seemed to him rather to his credit than otherwise.[17]

The preoccupation with religious questions, which was to haunt a great deal, if not most, of Humbert's later poetry, appears to have surfaced quite early in his life and by the time he reached the sixth form he had become much concerned about religion.

> The faint shamefaced Judaism of Bradford and the distracted administrations of Dr. Strauss - the German-born Rabbi - had been of little use to one who asked serious questions of his God, if, as he concluded, there was a God. He had written a sharp poem or two to the address of Atheists, with whom he had little patience.[18]

He seems to have made a clear distinction between ethnic and religious Judaism, and, although he professed not to be ashamed of being Jewish, he said that for years, 'despite the persistent revelations of his profile, he hugged the belief that nobody could suspect his Jewish origins and took good care not to rub them in.' He was becoming increasingly attracted to Christianity and discussed with a school friend the desirability of being confirmed in the Christian faith. Unitarianism he found unsatisfactory, as much on aesthetic as on theological grounds, and he began, somewhat furtively, to attend evening service at St. Jude's, where his appetite for beauty of language and surroundings could be gratified. In addition to the comfort of being 'numbered among those to whom these spiritual elegances belonged,' he noted with engaging candour the advantage to his career if he were to pass over. 'But something - probably no more than a mixture of shyness and apathy - had held him back.'

At about this time (his Sixth Form years) the family went on a six-week holiday to Inveraray on Loch Fyne. As there was not room for him in the little house which Consola had rented, Berto was lodged with a Miss Macnab, a Salvationist spinster with whom he readily discussed the state of his soul.[19]

It is possible that an undated early love poem 'To My Friend - Lost' relates to an event which occurred during this holiday.[20], for by this time he had also met the girl who was later to become his wife. Two years older than Berto, Jessie Chalmers Graham was the eldest of the three children of Joseph Chalmers Graham, the first rector of the Knox Institute in Haddington, East Lothian. The precise date of the meeting is not known: no reference to it can be found in Humbert's autobiographical works nor can it be clearly inferred from any of his poems, but the family belief, supported by Jessie's own unpublished account, is that they first met as children one August during a seaside holiday at Ganovan Bay, on the west coast of Scotland near Oban, when Berto was about eight and Jessie ten. Her account does not say how old they were but simply speaks of 'my first sight of Berto, a far away figure of a boy, on the shore at Ganovan Bay, reaching out his hand for the spade that a little girl silently hands him.' The two families continued to meet on holiday and a warm relationship developed between Jessie and Berto, although their parents never became close friends.[21]

If, as *Now A Stranger* suggests, the consciousness of being different was both the cause of and a comfort in his early loneliness, by the time he reached his last years at school it had become a banner, or a distinction to be worn with panache. Lionised, according to Mortimer Wheeler[22] (who aspired to take his place in Barton's charmed circle), he was nevertheless endowed with a singular capacity for being hurt. In addition, his burning desire to succeed was matched only by an almost morbid fear of failure, not least because at this stage in his life failure to achieve his ambition would mean imprisonment in the warehouse. He had at all costs to escape from that. As he wrote in *The Upward Anguish*,

> He lived in acute terror of having to enter the Bradford "trade". The long untidy rooms of his father's warehouse in Vicar Lane had haunted him all his life with a dim, dull smell of mohair and sacking and with a vista of shabby clerks, pen behind ear, turning over bales or swivelling the great handle of the letter copy-book. He knew that he would be a failure in business, just as he had always been bottom of the class in arithmetic. . . He remembered with acute distaste Mr. Elsenhans, purple at the ears, shouting his head off at a clerk. "I vill teach you," he yelled, "that bizness is not being a shentleman at the Grammar School. We knock the nonsense out of toffs here." Emphatically he did not want to have the nonsense knocked out of him by Mr. Elsenhans.[23]

Oxford represented not only escape from trade but also promotion from the role of spectator to that of competitor:

> Always before, as he had written in the school magazine, he had
> Lolled within the grand-stand or ate pies
> in shilling seats,
> now we essay the race and hear the cries

the crowd repeats. (*Farewell Remarks*)

Most of all, Oxford embodied his perception that, as he was to write in *The Uncelestial City*,

> there was waiting somewhere sunwards
> a rendezvous with loveliness.[24]

Enjoying the respect of his classmates and the adulation of his juniors, anxious to be accepted as one of the rest while demonstrably seeking to be quite different from them, yearning for approval and fearful of exclusion, he betrayed an innocence amounting to naïveté about others and about himself, if his adult recollections are to be taken at their word. He resembled a chameleon in taking on the protective colouring of the prevailing environment, concealing as best he could, and even from himself, the insecurity of the alien immigrant which haunted him all his life:

> All his childhood and youth he had had a vision of an enclosed garden where some absolute compensation waited. Outside the world would beat and roar, but, safe within walls, the refugee would hear nothing but perhaps a light wind through the trees. [25]

Chapter Three

1903-1907

'Lit like a great house with candles.'
('Oxford', *The Unknown Goddess*, 1925)

I

The Scholar

Besides escape from the warehouse, 'Oxford stood for Classics and English.' So wrote Humbert in 1938. But what English meant at Oxford in 1903 was something rather different from English at Bradford Grammar School. English to Berto meant literature, including modern or contemporary writing: to the university of Oxford in the early nineteen hundreds it stood essentially for philology. There was a Rawlinson Chair of Anglo-Saxon but any other English literature was firmly excluded from the curriculum.

A Chair of Poetry, it is true, had been created in the seventeenth century - Matthew Arnold occupied it from 1857 to 1867 - but not for the purpose of teaching a course leading to a degree. In 1880 the Merton Professorship of English Language and Literature was established, but such was the controversy over who was to occupy that chair and what was to be taught from it that in 1887 the post was still unfilled. Cambridge had had no difficulty in admitting literature to the curriculum and although, under Professor Skeat's patriarchate, literature was firmly bound in with linguistic studies, it was nevertheless there. At Oxford, however, those opposed to the inclusion of literature argued that it was too nebulous a subject, with no reliable standards by which it could be examined or even be defined. There were fears that undergraduates might be attracted to it because it looked easy, or that it might be just another name for *belles lettres* and "chatter about Shelley". The university would be well advised to play for safety and appoint another philologist.

Against this it was argued, and most fiercely of all by J. C. Collins, one of the candidates for the Merton Chair, that philology contributed nothing to the cultivation of taste or to the education of the emotions and, far from enlarging the mind, it too often induced a narrowness and opacity of vision which could be corrected only by the study of literature in relation to the classical masterpieces which had influenced its development. Considering the esteem in which the classical literatures of

Greece and Rome were held at Oxford, this view might have been expected to command more respect. English literature, after all, was an important element in the general paper of the scholarship examination, and for some decades had been a set subject in the Civil Service examinations which were the next step after graduation in the career of large numbers of Oxford men. Collins, as a University Extension lecturer, had prepared many such candidates in his time. But against the traditionalists all this availed nothing; the chair went to A. S. Napier, a philologist who was said to lecture on no author later than Chaucer. It was not until 1904, at the end of Berto's first year, that a separate chair of English Literature was created, with Walter Raleigh as its first occupant.[1]

It was therefore no accident that at Bradford Grammar School English was taught by the Classics masters and, much as they encouraged Berto's poetic ambitions, there could have been no question of his aiming at anything but a Classical scholarship.

Humbert's account of his scholarship examination in *The Upward Anguish* conveys the clear impression that it was more in the nature of a dummy run than a serious challenge: at seventeen he was younger than most of his fellow contestants and was not expected to do brilliantly on this first attempt. Geoffrey Burton, however, who was his classmate, recalled nearly sixty years later that although Berto was the youngest member of the Classical VIth, 'his scholarship prospects were rated pretty high.'[2]

Nevertheless it may have been for prudential reasons that he was entered not for the Christ Church group of colleges but for the less prestigious Trinity-Wadham group where the competition might be presumed to be less fierce. He had been told: "Your chance is freshness and a sort of inspired cheek" - doubtless the *chutzpah* for which his race was famous - although he later professed to know better: 'His Latin and Greek were, admittedly, moderate, but let the heroes from Eton and Harrow beat him at English if they could.'[3]

The examination took place in late November or early December, 1902, and occupied four days in all, two for the written papers and two for the *viva voce.* As no records have survived against which Humbert's description of the examination can be checked, the same difficulty arises as was observed earlier in the matter of his poem in the Latin Verse examination. The main events are beyond dispute; it is in the details and the manner of their occurrence that one is tempted to see the work of a creative memory. Even so, the reconstruction is, to say the least, plausible.

Of the eighty or so candidates, only the top thirty in the written papers were selected for the Viva which continued through the third and fourth days. Berto was among them. *The Upward Anguish* contains two accounts of the Viva which together constitute in their ingenuousness an example of breath-taking sleight-of-hand in which the reader is led to become a ready if unwitting accomplice. Berto's Viva, conducted in the old Wadham Senior Common Room, was, he wrote, straightforward and unimpressive, but his description of it subtly dramatises his own nervousness, manifested in his clumsy, stumbling entry into the room - bruising his ankle in the process - , his half-audible replies to the simple questions put to him, and finally, when his spirits returned, his disgraceful exhibition of self-conceit in showing off his knowledge of *Henry Esmond*. His examiners included the president of Trinity, Dr. Pelham, and a Wadham tutor whom he was to know and love later as "Juffy" Wells. At the end, Dr. Pelham asked him why he had chosen Wadham. Unaware of the identity of his questioner, Berto replied: "I was told that it was a better College than Trinity." The ensuing laughter puzzled him.

> His description of the Viva when he returned to Bradford as compared with what in fact happened is not without interest,

he wrote in *The Upward Anguish*, and a second, embellished account of the Viva immediately follows the first.

> On subsequent reflection it seemed to him that so decisive an occasion in his life must have been more amply attended by incident. He convinced himself that, in his extreme perturbation of spirit, he had failed to notice a number of striking events. They began to suggest themselves with ever-increasing emphasis of detail. Ten rather colourless minutes became an Odyssey, a semi-comic saga.

After listening to the recital of this "improved" version, his great friend and future brother-in-law, Archie Hamilton, was suitably deflating: "And they only gave you a scholarship. I can't understand why they didn't appoint you Warden of Wadham straight off and save themselves the trouble of doing it later."

The results were expected in about a week. A week passed and no telegram came. Worse still, his friend Geoffrey Burton had already heard that he was elected a Hastings Exhibitioner of Queen's College, the award had been duly announced to the assembled school and the customary half-holiday to mark it. Consola professed to take no interest in the result but had not left the house for two days in case the telegram came. When eventually it did arrive, while Berto was at the theatre whither he had been dispatched to distract his anxiety, the effect was itself theatrical, as if to set off the quality of his success by clearing the stage of his fellow competitors. He had been awarded a Scholarship at Wadham: the School was given a whole day's holiday.

II

First Year

From the first time that he set eyes on Oxford on his scholarship visit it was and would forever remain an enchanted land. He made a vow to be true to Oxford and what it stood for, although quite what this meant and what the mysterious near-betrayal was to which he alluded in *The Upward Anguish* is not made clear.

At the start of his first term at Wadham in October 1903 Berto had rooms on the first floor of No. 10 staircase in the back quad. At dinner the five Scholars in the First Year sat together at the Scholars' table at the top left-hand corner of Hall:

> Here was Keith, broad-jowled as the young Augustus, but breathing with the heaviness of one cursed from youth with asthma; chubbily red, Allen, like an apple put in the front of the basket to conceal less showy specimens behind; Measham, with the loose action of a wolf-hound puppy; Evelyn-White, pale as papyrus. . . while a First Year Scholar with enormous gravity in his face of a rather too fat Ministrant in an Early Italian, an appearance further ruined by hair most unsuitably parted in the middle and a ridiculously high double collar. . . was reciting the Grace.[4]

Berto's resemblance to faces seen in Italian pictures was recorded by his contemporaries. Measham later said that his sharpest memory was of Berto's profile, his head characteristically thrown back, and his prominent nose and swept-back hair suggesting something avian in the outline, rather like a toucan, while a younger contemporary at Wadham, S. B. Ward, noted the thick black hair, heavy-lidded eyes, aquiline features narrowing rapidly from cheekbones to a firm chin, and a Mediterranean brown complexion.[5]

The degree course upon which he was now embarked was and still is most commonly known as 'Greats', a four year course of which the first five terms were devoted mainly to the study of Latin and Greek, which were examined at Classical Honour Moderations, while the remaining seven terms were spent studying philosophy and history and culminated in the examination called 'Literae Humaniores'. Besides the Dean, H. P. Richards, who would 'occasionally overlook your prose', his main Classics tutor was Mr. Jones of St. Barnabas, whose chief claim to fame, said Humbert, was that he had won several prizes for suggesting the names for new brands of biscuits to Messrs. Huntley and Palmer. For some inexplicable reason he and Berto conceived an instant dislike for one another and Berto counted him the first of his Oxford disappointments and 'the least Oxford thing which he had hitherto encountered in Oxford.' For Logic he went to J. A. J. Drewitt, of whom more will be heard later.

Fragments of reminiscence from his contemporaries testify to the zest with which Berto entered into Oxford life, joining societies, making acquaintances within and outside his college, going down early to the river to be 'tubbed' for his college boat, turning out once or twice for the college Rugger team and showing much more energy than skill. He was the star turn at the Freshers' Concert in College, with an imitation of Henry Irving in 'The Bells', and humorous sketches in broad Yorkshire. He was soon speaking at meetings of the college literary society and by the end of the first year *The Bradfordian*'s Oxford correspondent was reporting that 'Wolff alone makes more noise than all the rest of us put together. He has complete charge of Wadham; but after all Wadham is only Wadham.'

What his fellow scholars remembered best was his vivacity, his bubbling gaiety and effervescence, and above all the ceaseless talk, the continual up-to-the-minute commentary, delivered in what S. B. Ward remembered as a delicate, rather nasal voice. Another said that everything inspired his tongue; he passed from comments on the news to doggerel verse about his companions, or to short and not too lucid discourse on the last lecture. *The Upward Anguish* reproduces a number of fair imitations of the 'gaseous conversation' at which he seems to have excelled.[6]

Like all Junior Common Rooms, Wadham's had a Complaint Book in which members of the college voiced their grievances or their suggestions in comments frequently more witty than useful. Stephen Ward, the Secretary of the J.C.R., found in it one day a contribution in Berto's illegible handwriting which ended, punning Ward's name, 'quis custodiet ipsos custodes?' Ward riposted with an answer beginning 'Triste lupus stabulis', and recalled many years later Berto's kindly delight on finding the ball back in his own court.

One trait which the others found both lovable and childlike was his delight in talking about himself. And if what he told his audience provoked a laugh, as for example that he was nick-named 'Bugs', so much the better. They realised that there was a good deal of the actor in his make-up. He throve on laughter and applause, even if the comedy was unintentional, and took an innocent delight in his own cleverness. Humbert must at some point have realised this himself, for he quoted Keith as saying musingly to him one day: 'I like it when your eyes pop out of your head with surprise at what your mouth is saying.'

Geoffrey Burton remembered vividly the cheerful week-end they spent at the end of their first term at the Gloucester home of J. E. Barton, their former classical master, by now Headmaster of the Crypt School, later Headmaster of Bristol Grammar School, a critic and writer of some repute. The two went on from there to join a party of friends from Queen's College who were staying at a place called Farchynys under

Cader Idris on the southern shore of the Mawdach estuary in North Wales. Berto was by then in the highest of spirits. On a shooting expedition he managed to bring down the only 'bag' of the day, the first and probably the only pheasant he ever shot. They cycled to Harlech where he similarly distinguished himself in the primitive golf they played in foursomes on the links at the foot of Harlech Castle, and was generally the life and soul of the party.

Yet this self-disclosure was all on the surface. Friends though they all were, and constantly in each other's company, they were in no sense intimates and would have thought any attempt to 'open their hearts' to one another as embarrassing as the expression itself. On the publication, therefore, of *The Upward Anguish* thirty years later, they read with great surprise of the agonies of disappointment, jealousy, frustrated ambition and wounded pride which tormented him as a freshman and of which they had no inkling.

A poem from *Requiem*[7] supplied the title of this second volume of autobiographical sketches - for *The Upward Anguish* is clearly that, even though Humbert maintained the device he had adopted in *Now A Stranger* of referring to himself in the third person. The only difference was that The Boy had become The Scholar. The titles of both books aptly summed up their theme and were if anything more apposite here than in their original context. The poem in *Requiem* containing the line

> This is more than the upward anguish of the spire

contrasted the vocation of the teacher with that of the builder. But, beginning with his scholarship examination and ending with his last term, *The Upward Anguish* unmistakably and deliberately recorded the raw, ambitious grammar school boy's attempts to scale the social and intellectual heights of Oxford. It has to be said that this 'curious narrative of mingled pain and triumph', as Robert Lynd called it[8], was autobiography of the Borrovian type in which incidents were manipulated and rearranged so as to emphasize the growth and development of the hero's personality. It is nevertheless possible, with the help of contemporaneous records and contemporaries' recollections, to distil the substance of fact contained within the brilliant conversations and Homeric contests which Humbert epically, if not too accurately, recorded.

Berto began his Oxford career under two handicaps in addition to his Jewishness: he was a grammar school boy at an undistinguished college. Wadham had been his headmaster's college and Berto had been painfully surprised to learn during the scholarship examination that, despite counting among its recent alumni such men as F. E. Smith and John Simon, it was not highly regarded in the University. Even the Head Master, Mr. Keeling, recognised that Trinity was a better college but Wadham, he said, was "a very good College for you . . . plenty of work, no nonsense, good tutors and decent young men with not too much money to spend."[9]

The challenge he now faced was new and different from any he had hitherto encountered. It was no longer simply a matter of proving himself as good as if not better than his peers from Bradford and the Grammar School; he now had to pit himself against Public Schools and illustrious Colleges. All that he knew of Public Schools was through hearsay and the pages of *Stalky and Co.* and *Tom Brown's Schooldays*. It was a legendary country, the acme of civilisation, a cross between Mount Olympus and the Land of Cockaigne, and Public School Boys were untarnished idols. But the strong public school bias amounting almost to class distinction which others besides Humbert detected in undergraduate Oxford at that time constituted a barrier which could prove insurmountable.

In Humbert's account of the train journey to Oxford for the Scholarship Examination, a Bradford businessman (real or imagined) spelled out the risks for him: "You're Boogs Wolff, aren't you? . . . You're clever enoof, they say. It's being a Bradford Jew and thinking yourself a nob. Nay, ah'm not meaning to offend you. Just warn you to go slow-like." But since going slow was not in his nature, in the same way that he was forever grazing his knees and banging his head, so, with his peculiar capacity for being hurt, the emotional bruises which his haste earned him, if less visible than the physical scars, were no less painfully acquired.

For all his high hopes, then, Berto's feeling at the end of the first few weeks at Wadham was chiefly one of disappointment. His efforts to surmount the handicaps of school and college were not at first very happy. He cultivated assiduously the society of Public School men in the mistaken belief that they were all paragons, and to the other Wadham freshmen he boasted innocently but infuriatingly of his acquaintance with such grand foundations as New College and Magdalen. Most of his fellow undergraduates at Wadham he found dull if not brutish; he no more shared their interests than they did his. Whether or not the invasion of his rooms by the second-year hearties bent on ragging him actually took place, it would not have been surprising if they had decided that he needed to be taken down a peg. The same conclusion was reached on other occasions; this one was important chiefly because it marked the beginning of his friendship with Alan Davidson Keith, to whom *The Upward Anguish* was dedicated.[10]

Keith was the younger brother of the incredible A. B. Keith who, according to Humbert, 'got so many hundreds of marks above the highest ever in the Civil Service Examinations that they altered the curriculum and the marking system.' 'Drum', as the younger one was called, had won a Scholarship in Sanskrit at the age of seventeen the previous year but came up with Berto and the other three scholars of his year. He was believed to have a fellowship waiting for him and 'had achieved instant and deserved popularity with the whole College.' Through him Berto got to know and was accepted by a number of other first year undergraduates, chiefly his neighbours in the back quad where dwelt the less socially ambitious members of the College: Gilliat, the exhibitioner from Manchester Grammar School, Yates, known as 'Sloppy' because, wrote Humbert, 'he looked as though he had been hastily run together by a speculative builder', Bissett, the South African Rhodes Scholar, Measham and Marrs.

Although he still valued the acquaintance and approval of the Public School men, he gradually came to realise that he had to live and make his way in a more sober world, even at Oxford; a world in which 'he was not necessarily a swan among geese.' As Gilliat explained to him one day in a friendly but painful piece of advice, going up to Oxford, for the Public School men, was like moving up a form at school: they all knew one another and everyone knew them and their school. The Wolffs and the Gilliats with their grammar school background had to mind their step, had to establish themselves slowly. Thanks to Gilliat and Keith, he also came to realise that Oxford did not like people to rub in their cleverness; that he had to learn to keep himself back and never reveal what he was feeling, or appear in any way out of the ordinary. He may indeed have learned to conceal his feelings; there is little to indicate that he ever seriously strove to appear ordinary.

The Upward Anguish makes it clear that he frequently met friends and acquaintances with similar interests who read papers to one another and argued about poetry, philosophy and art, but it must be presumed that this literary activity was not on a scale or of a kind to attract public attention. Apart from 'Epitaph on a poet scorned', he received only one mention in any literary connection in the columns of *The Oxford Magazine*, and then not until his fourth year, when he gave a paper to the Wadham literary society on R. L. Stevenson. But in his first two terms he made regular contributions to College and Union debates, speaking with some modest degree of success on such varied motions as nationalization of the railways; Russia's Far East policy; reforms in the War Office; Labour representation; and Householder's Suffrage for women, on which he spoke third in support of the motion. This debate earned him several lines of comment in *The Oxford Magazine*, the last of which observed that he 'assumed the air of a lecturer, but his matter was good.'[11]

But not good enough, it would seem, for little or nothing more was heard of him in the debating chamber for the remainder of that year and the next.The explanation for his unusual silence may have been that he needed to work for Honour Moderations in which, as will be seen, he eventually did less well than he had hoped. Alternatively, it may have been that, as he maintained in *The Upward Anguish*, his attempts at oratory were taken as a sign of the 'cleverness' which Oxford men abhorred. He found increasing difficulty in being called to speak and, when he had spoken, suffered the humiliation of hearing a less eloquent speaker not only poke fun at the matter and the manner of his speech and the pretensions of its author but also receive the applause which Berto had anticipated for himself.[12]

Further trials and disappointments were in store for him. Overlooked in the Union, excluded from the company of the great, and only moderately successful in the examination room, he felt doomed to perpetual frustration. The account of the fluctuations in Berto's social life described in Chapter V of *The Upward Anguish* could have been modelled on a classical drama: a catastrophe precipitating a 'peripeteia'. The chapter begins with him outwardly satisfied with the companionship of the 'estimable dullards' of his own year, and asking nothing better than the acquaintance of three charming sisters visiting Oxford for Eights Week. It ends with him taking part in brilliant Meredithian conversations, in the company of his hero Keith; of Morrison and Fox, the intellectual and social dandies of the second year; of Flecker, the poet; and of his artist friend Albert Rutherston.

The catastrophe which brought about this reversal was the omission of Berto from a party given by one of his year to the sisters and their family, Berto's joke at the expense of the visitors and their host had caused him to forfeit any chance of meeting them. He was not the only one whose hopes were thwarted, but it was hardly possible for everyone to be asked to meet them. He concealed his disappointment as best he could, refusing to be dismayed when the small Oxford world of his boyish hopes crashed about his ears, though there are good grounds for thinking that he still felt the bruises three years later. But to attain the fiery citadel, and sip his nectar among the demi-gods was more than a single afternoon's scramble.

That he did eventually sit at ease among the demi-gods was chiefly due, it seems, to three unexpected and apparently unconnected but convergent events. The first was an invitation to lunch which he received half-way through Eights Week from a Second Year Scholar, J. H. Morrison[13], who lodged magnificently in the High with an Earl's son and a Canadian alleged to be a millionaire. The second was to be taken to lunch at Professor Raleigh's by his friend and fellow-Bradfordian, the painter Will Rothenstein; and finally, the visit of Will's brother Albert.

Walter Raleigh had arrived to take up the Chair of Poetry in Oxford the previous year. Berto's excitement at meeting him was understandably great: according to Barton, his teacher at Bradford, Raleigh and Matthew Arnold were the major critics of the last fifty years. Even greater, however, was his excitement at meeting the other guest, Gabriel Woods, not because he resembled the traditional picture of Shelley with his dark deep hair and broad bright brow, but because he was a brother of Maurice Woods, the former President of the Union, the moving spirit and organiser of Conservatism in the university, and arguably the most dazzling young man in Oxford. 'Now at least, even if by proxy, (Berto) was in touch with the great.'

A subsequent meeting with Gabriel Woods which brought about his first encounter with Flecker convinced him that 'a period seemed to be opening for him in which he was to be selected to meet persons of distinction.' And, finally, Albert Rutherston's visit unlocked the door to the only other person - and the most inaccessible - whose acquaintance Berto sought, the Beau Brummell of Wadham, Victor Fox, in whose rooms in the front quad the final party of Albert's visit was held. Among the guests were Frank Harris and 'that great poet "Bozzy" Douglas - as Albert was privileged to call him.'

Berto's disillusionment with so much that he had found in Oxford and especially in his contemporaries - 'He had wanted brains and blood and the large horizons to which they were the key' - was about to give way to an almost paradisial contentment and a new world in which he foresaw the realization of all his dreams, '- room to stretch wings he believed he possessed, men who held the Union by a brilliant speech and were watched by politicians in London . . . but above all, eager incessant minds like that of Maurice Woods, son of the Master of the Temple, who moved through Oxford like a white devouring flame.'[14]

Comparison of Humbert's narrative in *The Upward Anguish* with the recollections of his Wadham contemporaries suggests that he telescoped the Eights Weeks of 1904 and 1905 into one, omitting the intervening year. The missing year was the important second year in which, having found their feet and sized each other up as freshmen, they formed closer and more exclusive friendships with those they found congenial. Changes of rooms in College helped to break up associations based on mere contiguity. Measham remained in his attic on No. 9 staircase, but he had a new opposite number, the exhibitioner Marrs, and Berto moved from No. 10 to the room under Marrs, a grouping that foreshadowed closer association two years later.

Berto's unquestionable dissatisfaction with his second class in Honour Moderations, the examination in Latin and Greek in Year 2, may have inclined him all the more to drop the year from his account. His friendship with Keith and Morrison was growing closer but photographs of the 1905 Wadham Torpid and Eights showed that he had not yet risen above the pedestrian loyalties of the normal undergraduate, and the break in his life between first and third year, though in retrospect it looked to him complete and tragical, was not a sudden earth-rending cleft but a slow wearing away.

III

Third Year

That the scenes from military, literary, philosophical and political life at Oxford which the remaining chapters of *The Upward Anguish* purport to describe are all seen 'sub specie Umbertatis", so to speak, is in no way surprising. He was, after all, writing an account of his undergraduate life. Nor was he in any way unique either in seeking the company and the approval of the swells or in displaying a self-conceit, a desire to show off and a tendency to coin hurtful witticisms at the expense of others. Evelyn Waugh and John Betjeman were notable examples of the same pursuit of self-advancement. What is unusual in Humbert's case is that virtually all our knowledge of these unattractive traits comes from his own revelations. He went out of his way to spare himself no embarrassing detail; every unflattering brush-stroke was his own deliberate work.

Meanwhile, there remained the business of getting as good a degree as he could. As he embarked upon his Greats course, Berto's disappointment at the outcome of Honour Moderations was tinged with relief that Latin and Greek at last made way for philosophy. Twenty years after Humbert's death, Sir Geoffrey Burton's recollection was that Berto was never considered a good classical scholar, in the ordinary academic sense; there were few such at Bradford in their day, if ever; but he clearly remembered how sorely disappointed Berto was by his Class II in Moderations. Other contemporaries shrewdly recognised that, though exceptionally gifted and undoubtedly clever, he was too interested in his own mental workings to be a great scholar. It was when he had no longer to worry about syntax and accurate renderings that he came into his own.[15]

His philosophy tutor was J. A. J. Drewitt, whom he was to admire and love. He placed Drewitt in the same category as his English master, Barton.

> He taught metaphysics but with some distaste gave instruction in the infantilism of formal logic . . . He was a small stooping figure with a face so white that it would have put many a corpse to shame. He wore steel-rimmed spectacles with treble lenses like those of the smaller dog in the Grimms' fairy-tale. His manner was so acutely nervous that he instantly put the most timid pupil at his ease. Nobody in the world could be as frightened as Drewitt looked. But behind that manner was hidden one of the greatest philosophic minds of the last fifty years. Either his own self-depreciation or the fatal lethargy of Oxford made him a dumb mysterious Hegel. Only once did he condescend into print on metaphysics in the matter of the difference between dreams and waking. The Scholar still has the paper off-printed from "Mind". It is a fragment that might, *mutatis mutandis*, have graced Plato's page. Instead of which, Drewitt devoted years of his life to measuring the stresses in Homer as a contribution to the thesis that Homer was not written by Homer but by a number of men of the same name.[16]

Drewitt's tuition, though it led to many abiding intellectual pleasures, was hardly a straight road to what used to be called a safe 'First', and Berto almost certainly took precautions. One of these was his visit to Heidelberg at the end of his third year; he prevailed upon Consola to let him go for the last half of the Semester to hear Kuno Fischer who was said to be the greatest living authority on Kant.

The Upward Anguish mentions one other philosophy tutor, a Mr. Schiller of Corpus Christi College, a vociferous proponent of the doctrines of the Pragmatists and reputedly the author of a number of bad puns. Berto appears to have made some joke at his expense: he was certainly credited with the authorship of a joke about 'experimentum in corpore vili' which R. A. Knox also made in a debate in the Union.[17]

In *The Upward Anguish* Humbert professed that, after his failure to impress the Union in his first year, 'much time elapsed before he spoke at the Union again, and never, try as he would, could he establish himself there.' Be that as it may, in the autumn of 1905 he was once more to be heard speaking from the floor of the Union, this time on the diplomatic isolation of Germany, in what was reported as ' . . . a sound speech. A little more confidence would improve his style, for what he said was worth hearing.' The 16th November 1905 found him opening the debate on the Anglo-Japanese alliance and Russia, but this seemingly meteoric rise to fame may well have been more apparent than real, since only the day before the house had packed to hear Lord Roberts address an audience of more than eleven hundred. Nevertheless Mr. Wolff of Wadham was thought to have 'a pleasant manner and a good delivery. His arguments were sound, and though he needs practice and was a little too colloquial, he made a good impression on the House.'

No more was heard of him until the end of that season when in June 1906 he spoke against the Disestablishment of the Anglican Church in Wales.[18] For the first time *The Oxford Magazine*'s report seems to capture something of the flavour that was to be Humbert's:

> Mr. U. Wolff (Wadham) upholds Establishment at any price. The Nonconformists were the noisiest section of the Welsh people, but not necessarily the best. The Anglican Church might not be truly national but to disestablish it without establishing something else would be no remedy. This was rather subtle, and made us wonder what Mr. Wolff was doing in this particular galley, but it was not a bad speech.

In his fourth year he spoke in at least three Union debates. The first two earned him only faint and cautious praise, and some deflating comments: on the claims of Social Reform as against those of Imperial Policy 'he succeeded in interesting the House and from his speech, though it was hardly a success from a debating point of view, we gained a good deal of useful general information', while his speech opposing Women's Suffrage 'bristled with paradox, which did not have the benefit of contrast, for there was no 'case' behind it. Within such limits it was good and well appreciated.'

On 15 May he had what must have been his greatest triumph. Opposing Mr. Asquith's budget, 'Mr. U. Wolff (Wadham) was in the best form we have ever seen him 'on paper', awkward moments were smoothed over with success, and he handled the subject with a humorous touch throughout. The differentiation in the income tax and the provision for Old Age Pensions came under a brisk fire of criticism, then he debouched on the broadening of the basis of taxation, and ended somewhere about there.' Already, it seems, he managed to give the impression, which was still deceiving audiences thirty years later, that with him speech came before thought, as he would rise and blither gently for full minutes, his eyes glassy, before being coherent and - usually - amusing.[19]

The debating topics on which he chose to speak and his seeming inactivity in the literary field (to judge by the slight public impression any literary activity of his appears to have made), suggest a shifting of his interest from poetry to politics which is borne out by what he later wrote in *The Upward Anguish*. If the choice of a career at first appeared to be between metaphysics and verse, politics soon became another alternative. In somewhat oblique fashion he suggested in *The Upward Anguish* that it was not so much a case of his abandoning poetry as of poetry abandoning him; and that what he called 'his dazed struggles (as a schoolboy) to find words for the long thoughts of youth' were replaced and rewarded by 'thoughts longer still and actions to cap them . . . a path at whose far end Disraeli beckoned.' This change of direction was almost certainly gradual rather than abrupt but what sealed it definitively appears to have been his election in 1906 to a political club in Oxford called 'The Canning'.

In his tireless search for social and political success he had cultivated the JCR Debating Society, eventually being elected Secretary and College representative on the Union Committee. Thanks to his friendship with Morrison and Gabriel Woods, his contacts with the greater world of Oxford increased, but it was through his election to the Canning Club that he became at last a political figure, if only a minor one. Viscount Wolmer, the grandson of a Prime Minister, was the Secretary of the Club and it was to his 'genius for quiet intrigue' that Humbert attributed his own allegedly improper admission to the Club, but without explaining where the impropriety lay. The later account simply says that after an inter-Collegiate Society meeting at which Berto had read a paper on Imperialism, apparently a bravura performance which went down well with his uncritical hearers, Wolmer invited him 'to come on the Canning.'[20]

The Canning Club, founded in 1861, owed its origins to Disraeli, although he was never a member and never attended a meeting or a dinner. Maurice Woods, originally a Liberal, became a Tory and joined the Canning in 1903. Under his influence it became a centre for rejuvenated and progressive Conservatism.[21]

Both the fortunes and the morale of the Tory Party were at a low ebb in 1906. Far from emerging stronger from the quarrelsome disarray in which Balfour had thought to leave the Liberals by his resignation in December 1905, the Unionists had suffered a crushing defeat in the General Election of January 1906, Campbell-Bannerman and the Liberals winning 377 seats against the Tories' 157. The conflict between Free Traders and Protectionists is usually seen as the reason for their collapse, but the rise of the Labour Party (which gained 53 seats) and the fury of the Nonconformists at parts of the 1902 Education Act also played a part.

Oxford may have been insulated from these vulgar events, but the connections of gilded youth with the 'great and the good' would have informed their debates. The idealistic, visionary or simply impatient young may not have brought about the dumping of the Tory Old Guard but they certainly saw the possibilities both for revitalising the Party and for advancing their own careers. Into this new Oxford Movement headed by Wolmer and G. M. Young, a Fellow of All Souls, Berto was swept up along with a number of his contemporaries on a tide of Tory revival. Admittedly, the appeal of politics to many of his generation of Oxford men, particularly those like him from less than wealthy backgrounds, lay in all probability as much in the opportunities it offered for material and social success as in the possibilities it held out of satisfying a passionate personal commitment whether to preserving the status quo or to changing the face of society.

On the roll of members of the Canning Club Berto was No. 493. No. 492 was R. A. Knox, of Balliol, who became Vice-Secretary for 1906-07, and Secretary in 1908. The first chapter in *Portraits By Inference*, published in 1934, four years before *The Upward Anguish*, describes a meeting of the Club in 1906 and lists those present as Julian Grenfell, Patrick Shaw-Taylor and R. A. Knox, all of Balliol, together with Viscount Wolmer, of University College, and himself. Humbert admitted in *The Upward Anguish* that the earlier account was 'wholly unverifiable' and 'was not so much history as poetry - even if it was bad poetry.' He also apologized for omitting the name of Lord Eustace Percy. The original rules laid down that refreshment should consist of beer and sandwiches (for which coffee and mulled claret were substituted in later years), members (even non-smokers) would smoke churchwarden pipes, and meetings would open with the President's address followed by votes of thanks and The Paper, which was intended to have 'a bearing on politics.' At every meeting there would be the toast 'Church and Queen' (or 'King') and other toasts at the discretion of the President. In Humbert's account the 'historic loving-cup' became 'a dangerous brew of hot spiced beer with toast floating on its brown surface. . . the tankard passed from slightly scorched hand to hand to the accompaniment of the password

'Church and State', churchwarden pipes . . duly lit (and broken).' Then the business of the evening began - in this case, the reading of a paper by Knox, in whose rooms they had gathered, on the definitive canon of the Sherlock Holmes stories, a subject whose political significance is not easily discerned.

Other more overtly political activities of the Canning Club included occasional joint meetings with its sister Conservative Club, the Palmerston, and with the Chatham. G. M. Young was also responsible for getting Berto invited to a great luncheon in honour of the Colonial ministers given by another All Souls man, L. S. Amery. Eventually came the supreme vindication when, as President of the Wadham JCR, Berto entertained to dinner the two guests of the Club, Wolmer and Gladstone, both grandsons of Prime Ministers.[22]

By the beginning of their last year, the group of friends had moved out of college. Berto shared rooms in Holywell, below New College, with Cheatle, a Commoner of their year; Marrs and Measham were at 55 High Street, while Gilliat and Keith were lodged in Long Wall near the bottom of Magdalen deer-park. Although they all remained friends and met frequently, Berto saw rather more of Marrs and Measham, probably because their rooms were, or could be, on the way to most places to which undergraduates resorted. He wrote in *The Upward Anguish* that when he was with Gilliat and Keith he felt increasingly that he was a constant third to their pair, despite Keith's efforts to remove that impression, and that finally this drove him further and further into work, politics and other friendships.

Thanks in no small part to the refusal of the others in his Wadham group to be impressed by his titled and fashionable connections in the Canning, Berto, without losing in any degree his gift for startling and amusing talk, had acquired an urbanity, a readiness to listen and defer to others, and an evident desire to please rather than impress, which made him always welcome in their rooms. Nothing could prevent him from decorating his looking-glass and mantelpiece with notices of esoteric societies' meetings, and little notes signed by demi-gods. One of his friends, who had booked seats for "Peter Pan" by wire, noticed that in the confirmatory telegram from the theatre the final 's' in "Duke of York's" was illegible, so he stuck the telegram on his looking-glass. When Berto came in, he saw it, and the point, and was delighted.

IV

Poetry at Oxford

Berto's desertion of verse for politics has already been mentioned. In *The Upward Anguish* he confessed to having written in 1906, at an interval of six months, only two poems, the second of which was his annual poem for his mother on the anniversary of Martin Wolff's death, October 27th.[23] On this occasion he unaccountably read the poem, a sonnet, to Marrs who was very impressed by the lines:

> Chrysanthemum, gold trumpet of the dead,
> That sang him home, when no flower else dared sing.

Alas, the appetite thus whetted by this most promising couplet is doomed to remain unsatisfied, for no trace of the remainder of the poem is to be found, a loss all the more regrettable in that the surviving collections of his juvenilia contain no sonnets at all.

When, early in the autumn of 1906, Measham and Marrs conceived the idea of a Greats Week pantomime, as a protective device against university politics, Marrs remembered Berto's sonnet and enlisted him to help with some of the songs. They chose the form of a pantomime because Measham and Marrs, whose homes were respectively in Newcastle-on-Tyne and Gateshead, used to go together each Christmas vacation to Newcastle's two pantomimes, and Marrs boasted his ability to conduct any conversation in the traditional rhymed couplets. They hit upon the idea of a philosophical pantomime, with the title *The Old Man of Königsberg, or Kant and Re-Kant*, in which the eponymous hero stood for their tutor, Drewitt. Years later Humbert readily acknowledged that he had composed only the preface and a few lyrics; all the rest was the work of Marrs and Measham, although Measham seems to have persisted in the belief that Berto claimed to have written a song of which Measham was the real author.[24]

The finished work was read aloud to a select audience, which included Albert Rutherston, at 55 High Street, and publication was decided on. Albert even promised to use his influence in the theatrical world to have it produced in the West End, but nothing came of it. The text was duly printed and they hawked it outside the Schools during Greats Week. It received kindly reviews in *Isis* and *The Wadham Gazette* and just about recovered its costs.

If Kant/Drewitt was the hero of the play, the villain was beyond doubt a Pragmatist - almost certainly F.C.S. Schiller of Corpus. Berto's Preface, in the form of an 'Epistle Dedicatory to William Shakespear' from 'Bernard Pshaw', contained such barbs as 'What comic (is there) in Falstaff and his men in Lincoln green, when we know that the whole world is but a creation in Corpus green?', and the final mock-anguished cry: 'Oh, William, William, why had you not the courage to be always a pragmatist?'[25]

The ghost of the 'Old Man' rose to confront Berto at his Viva. He may also have paid the penalty for the joke about 'experimentum in corpore vili', since The Pragmatist was one of his examiners, but although he admitted, in *Portraits By Inference*, to having used the joke more than once, nowhere did he actually claim it as his creation, an unlikely extreme of self-denial had he really been its author.[26]

He had already developed the habit of quoting scraps of poetry when he had nothing particular to talk about: the last verse of the ballad of Clerk Saunders, fragments of Swinburne, lines from Henry Vaughan and from the 'Shrouding of the Duchess of Malfi', and so on. But none of his Wadham friends seem to have suspected, or not until his last year, that he was, even in embryo, a poet, as distinct from the author of the sort of verses all had occasionally written for their School Magazines.

'Poetry was not in the ascendant at Oxford in 1904', Humbert wrote in *Portraits By Inference*. 'The English School, it is true, greatly flourished under Sir Walter Raleigh, and there were some among the undergraduate population foolhardy enough to read John Masefield. But there was a tendency to do this in secret.'[27] He said that it was Gabriel Woods who introduced him to a poet at Trinity called John Flecker (later known as James Elroy Flecker). To judge by Humbert's account of it later, their first meeting was hardly propitious, chiefly because Berto found Flecker to be as stupid a philosopher as he was an inspired poet. At their second meeting, Flecker asked Berto to recite one of his poems. The one he chose contained the lines:

> They chose an island for her dwelling-place -
> the goddess with the sorrow in her eyes;
> where the slow waters of the ocean pace
> to seek a distant dawn, that island lies.

Flecker was very taken with the line

> the goddess with the sorrow in her eyes

and, though disparaging of Berto's thought and technical accomplishment, recognised that Berto had an 'ear' and exhorted him to 'continue to use it. You may overhear something. And. . . read the French, particularly Verlaine.'[28]

It is clear from *The Upward Anguish* that he attempted to write poetry - not just doggerel or purely comic verse - throughout his time at Oxford, and not merely in his first two years there. Part of his early disappointment at the philistinism of his fellow undergraduates arose from the amiable boredom they showed when he tried to read his poems to any of them, although both Ward and Mrs. Wells, the Dean's wife, gave him a kinder hearing. But the scraps of verse cited in the *The Upward Anguish* are mostly taken from works published in his later life. *The Oxford Magazine* for those years contains only one verifiable sample of his verse, the 'Epitaph On A Poet Scorned' to which reference has already been made.

In later life Humbert confessed that the politicians who eventually came into his life at Oxford 'constituted not a new interest but a flood that swept him away in a state of superhuman satisfaction.' It is significant that he interpreted the change not so much in terms of his forsaking poetry as of poetry forsaking him, almost as if to punish him for his infidelity. 'Nor, if we have judged and presented him with any accuracy, shall we wonder that the Scholar began not merely to forget Flecker but to be himself forgotten by poetry.'[29]

Although, therefore, there are grounds for believing that his Muse was less powerful or that he heard her voice less clearly, enough evidence remains to show that he never stopped writing verse while at Oxford. Even in 1907, his final year, when the attractions of the Canning Club combined with the pressures of impending final examinations would have been enough to distract him from verse, it is unlikely that his only exercise in verse was to write a couple of songs for *The Old Man of Königsberg*. All that can be said with certainty is that no poems can clearly be identified with that year.

The main evidence for what he wrote as an undergraduate is to be found in three typescript collection of poems, the only ones to have survived and possibly the only collections ever made. Two of them, *Verses* and *Poems*, are in the possesion of his niece, Ruth Atkinson. *Poems*, a collection of thirty poems bound in soft leather and inscribed 'December 24 1904 To my Mother: these small promises of future things', was clearly a Christmas or New Year present to his Mother and, although none of the poems are dated, all are *ex hypothesi* pre-1905. '*Verses*' contains fifty-three poems. Two poems, bearing the title '27th October - in Oxford', can reasonably be identified as poems he wrote for his mother on the anniversary of his father's death. A few others are dedicated to his mother and sometimes dated.

The third set, entitled *47 Poems 1904-1906* (although only forty-six can be counted and three of them are dated 1908), is to be found in the Humbert Wolfe Archive in The Clarkson Library, Bradford Grammar School. The contents of the three collections overlap, some poems occurring in two and occasionally in all three of them, but only those in the Bradford Grammar School archives are (for the most part) dated and they follow no chronological order. The survival of these three sets probably owes more to family piety than to the inherent merit of the poems - so far as one can tell he never in later life quoted or even referred publicly to any of them except for 'Vintagers', 'Epitaph of a poet scorned' and a verse from 'Their Island Altar' quoted in *The Upward Anguish*. Nevertheless they are worth looking at a little more closely for what they reveal of the young Berto and what they presage of the later Humbert.

After his death, his widow recalled her pride in receiving at the age of fifteen the first of the poems Berto sent her from Oxford:

Violet, small flower
    Hanging head aglow,
In thy golden hour,
    In a glade didst grow.

Sweet the throstle thought thee,
    Singing on his bough,
Little wood-things sought thee,
    But they mourn thee now.[30]

Some of the typescript poems could plausibly be identified with their courtship, as for example 'The Humble Lover', dated 'Oxford and Bradford Dec. 16th 1903'. Others were clearly anniversary poems. For most of the poems, however, in the absence of anything to show who or what inspired them, or for whom they were intended, firmer identification remains impossible.

The themes of these youthful poems are the customary adolescent concerns: love, aspiration, death, religion (or mysticism). In the poems dealing with love we find the traditional interpretations:

1. Love brings both joy and sadness. Out of sadness emerges a spiritual awareness of the loved one which strengthens and lifts the relationship to a plane beyond the physical. A typical example may be found in these two stanzas from 'Tears' (no later than 1904):

I had withstood the perfume of your youth,
    The sacred essences,
But your lone tears taught me the path to truth
    With mouthless messages.
They lay in secret places in my soul,
    I found them unawares,
Until a light from heaven on them stole,
    And turned them into prayers.

2. Love, though transient, aspires to permanence. In 'The Magic Summer', perhaps the best of the early love poems, the lovers share the delusion that, detached from circumstance, their love can achieve permanence in some idealized, timeless state:

'The Magic Summer'

We made a magic summer of our own,
    Shut off the winds and bade the birds to sing,
A little lonely garden in our lives
    Too fresh for autumn and too ripe for spring.
. . . .

A painless island which no afterwards
  Could come to trouble and no past make sore.

. . . .

So did we think and then the morning sun
  Reached out his golden arms, and caught us fast.
It was too late: the little god had won:
  And we had lost our future in the past.

The last stanza perfectly conveys the confused feelings aroused by adolescent love: regret that the magic garden cannot be preserved inviolate in memory struggles in vain against the strength of the morning sun - Eros up to his tricks again!

3. Love as loss or bereavement. Several poems express the adolescent's despair and dissatisfaction with love. Two poems in particular, 'Her Heart' and 'Her Smiles', voice his underlying discontent as fulfilment eludes him:

'Her Heart'

I hid my heart in silence long
  And never meant to show
My love, but ah! you did me wrong
  By looking at me so.

For from your eyes there fell the thought
  From which I first learnt pride.
Before I held my heart as naught,
  I only wished and sighed.

But then apparelled in the dreams
  I thought were in your eyes,
To me poor fool so fair it seems
  At last I grew unwise.

In hope I showed it to the light,
  You thought it poor and bare,
For that which raised it in my sight
  For you was wanting there.
  (probably November 1904)

'Her Smiles'

You seek upon my face the smile
  Your scorn killed long ago.
You watched it dying all this while
  And could but would not know.

. . . .

You wished it, so I gave you mirth
    And hid my pains and fears,
But all my laughter had its birth
    Deep in a world of tears.

. . . .

(1 November 1904)

Periodically, however, in spite of all that his experience has taught him, he is tempted to believe in the possibility of hope and confidence:

'Love II'

I have said good-bye to loving
    Since the time love hurt me so,
And I found a way of proving
    Love to be an idle show.

Now I know his gift is sorrow,
    And I know his touch is pain.
Hateful love! and yet tomorrow
    I shall be in love again.

(11 November 1904)

This insecurity in love is of a piece with his general insecurity which may have been racial in origin but also betrays the fear of failing to meet the high expectations which people have of bright adolescents. It probably accounts for his industry and desire for perfection. His use of traditional images and language (almost *ad nauseam*) and his obvious polishing and repolishing of language and metre stem from a concern to preclude criticism. As yet, he falls short of 'originality' and the perceptions that startle. His 'Imitation of Heine' of 20 September 1904 shows that the German poet to whom the later Humbert was to be so frequently compared had already begun to exert upon him the special fascination which was to endure throughout his life:

It is the old ancient story
    About a man and a maid,
He went from her with the glory
    For which the maiden had prayed.[31]

A longer poem, 'L'Amour Amie' (dated December 1904), beginning

A maid and youth there were who long had been
 Simply companions, - if you like it, friends,
But she one night the lighted wings had seen
 Of some gold god: for her the friendship ends,

echoes not only 'The Magic Summer' but also Robert Bridges' 'Triolet' (1890):

When first we met we did not guess
That love would prove so hard a master.

A second theme, explicit in some poems, implicit in others, is Berto's aspiration to fulfilment. It is not an uncommon image to envisage life as a journey. At this stage, although like any noble Greek he aspires to excellence, a fair degree of self-doubt vitiates his optimism. 'The Star' is a good example of both his hopes and his fears:

The heights to which I struggle they lie far,
 And, far beyond, a light
Which is the presence of the perfect star
 I shall not see till night

In some poems, there is the Wordsworthian concept of travelling from some pre-natal spiritual existence, in close affinity with God through a valley of tears ('Shades of the prison-house begin to close upon the growing boy.'). Certainly, he reveals the adolescent characteristic of aspiring to peace, to freedom from conflict, yet experiencing the pain of struggle. A good example is to be found in 'The failures of the past', dated August 12, 1904, of which the closing stanza -

O better to be satisfied
 With what was sought not won!
Yet God has pity on the pride
 Of high things left undone

- might almost sum up his life.

The chief poem, and the most moving, in this category is entitled: 'We are all born . . .' It stresses the struggle for peace, the desire to have the mysteries solved and the conflicts resolved. The opening lines -

We are all born with dreams set in our hearts,
And an unspoken message in our eyes
And therefore we go seeking through the world
To find interpreters . . .

- perfectly represent both his schooldays and his Oxford days. He was for ever looking for interpreters of his dreams, and the peace that would ensue:

> We are all searching for this quiet place;
> Our dreams all lean towards it. Ah! the peace!
> To bloom in such a garden! every bud
> Willingly opens to the soothing rain,
> A noiseless perfect progress until night.

- a vision which is recalled in the extract from *The Upward Anguish* (p. 17) quoted earlier at the end of Chapter 2.

There follows a lovely image:

> Thus do we come unfinished on the world
> Half poets waiting for the gleam and saints
> Yet unacquainted with the noise of wings . . .

He aspired to the affinities which would elucidate his life and bring him peace:

> - first through another's heart
> We understand the meaning of our own.

The last stanza of 'The Violets Again', with its echoes of Wordsworth's pantheism, takes the theme further:

> And in the path the sun had burned
> I knew the ceaseless will
> Working for ever, and I turned
> And saw a higher hill.

This takes us to a third group of poems, those dealing with religion or mysticism. There are reflections of Wordsworth's 'visionary gleams' in several poems, notably in 'The Flower of God', whose first two verses echo the beginnings of the 'Immortality Ode':

> Sometimes there comes upon me unaware
> A dying thought half lost among my dreams,
> . . . .
> As though a bell struck once within my brain,
> As though a bird had sung a single note
> Charged with sweet things once heard and not again, . .

The poem goes on to suggest that not only in man but in the whole of creation - 'and all the bitter silence of dumb things' - there is a yearning for the fulfilment which will come only with mystical knowledge -

> . . . when the heart from stain is free
> By sorrow purged or in the midst of prayer
> The knowledge of the thing we cannot see
> Comes far and faintly there.

Berto is wrestling here with a theme which will progressively and obsessively pervade the poetry of his mature years, the notion which is expressed in the Pauline image of 'all creation groaning in travail' (Romans 8).

Even at this age Berto understands clearly that the knowledge in question is not that of reason or of logic: to that extent he can appeal to the Gospel as much as to Wordsworth:

> Wisdom put off which makes you blind
> And be a child again.
>
> Come like a tired child at night
> Stretch out a humble hand,
> And be content to see the light
> You cannot understand.
> (from 'Lines written in a Bible')

Death was naturally an event to be marked and commemorated in his poetry. He had written a poem on the death of a schoolfellow; he had lived in the shadow of his mother's mourning since the age of nine and every year wrote a poem for her on the anniversary of Martin Wolff's death. In 'The Coming of Death', the idea that death is a kind of birth faintly echoes Wordworth, but equally reproduces a traditional element of Christian piety. The poem appears to draw on his own experience -

> There is one knocking at my heart
> With steady fingers - Death.
> . . . .

- but despite simplicity and apparent sincerity, the poem fails to be totally convincing.

'Their Island Altar', which he recited for Flecker, is dated 20 September 1904, and, like 'The Magic Summer' and 'The Torn Veil' (which will be referred to later), has a curious obliqueness about it which leaves the reader slightly mystified:

> They built an altar unto memory;
> She in the future must their goddess be.

They built it up together solemnly
In a high place which both could after see.

They chose an island for her dwelling-place -
the goddess with the sorrow in her eyes;
where the slow waters of the ocean pace
to seek a distant dawn, that island lies.

They were as quiet as a ray of sun,
The seabirds came and watched them without fear.
But when the whole of what they planned was done
Each went a diff'rent way and shed no tear.

When they were gone, at first no creature came
To trouble and no wind to break the spell,
But afterwards a single feather came
Against it, and behold the altar fell.

In this acknowledgement of the transience and insubstantiality of love and the memory of love - so fragile that the lightest of touches destroys it - we recognize a familiar strain. What is remarkable is the adolesecent's sudden insight that intensity of feeling is no guarantee of a permanent memorial, a discovery which chimes with attitudes revealed in other poems in this collection.

From the poems quoted above, it is clear that Berto deployed a traditional poetic language, rich with associations from his own literary experiences. Emotions, albeit conventional, are evoked and contrasts contrived after the pattern, though not the structure, of the traditional sonnet, by means of a vocabulary which recurs within poems and across the whole collection: golden, blazes, flames, fire, sun; silence, darkness, shadows, blindness, faded, death, pain, suffering, sorrow, weep, poppies, pray(er); joy, dream, glory, praise, light, laugh(ter); roses, violets (a life-long favourite of his), perfume, bees (they seem to hum everywhere), summer.

Images which have, or indeed already had, become poetic clichés -

love pierced through my heart like a sword
(Prayer Asked Of A Poet)

inevitably appear banal, as do such attempted conceits as this (from Dear Unkind Mistress):

a poor lost heart, a lady's tennis ball
from me to her how lightly was it hurled
'Tis now thrown back again and that is all.

Against this it must be admitted that other images, culled also almost entirely from his literary stock, have an impressive ring to them, whether he is writing of graves and wreaths, gardens and sunshine, sleep and awakening, or sounding an authentically poetic note with such lines as

> To make caresses to a single soul (A Disbeliever in God)

or

> Come through the dust of the road to my door,
> My garden is cool . . . (The Lover Alone)

Besides the influence of Wordsworth, echoes of Keats, Tennyson and Swinburne are detectable and also perhaps Robert Bridges, whose *Shorter Poems* (Books I - V) were published in 1896 and became a best seller in a cheap printing in 1897.[32] But, despite the echoes of earlier poetic styles, both Classical and Romantic, there is in the best of his youthful efforts (e.g. 'The Vintagers') a pleasing, uncluttered simplicity which he was to transmute into artful artlessness in later works such as *Kensington Gardens*.

Occasionally the tribute he pays to Lovelace and Suckling in the neat antitheses of quatrains such as: 'To my friend - lost' -

> What wonder that my cheeks are hot
> And that my eyes are wet
> You taught me all things, but forgot
> To teach me to forget

- heralds the epigrams of *The Uncelestial City*, while the echo of Ronsard's 'Bénissant vostre nom de louange immortelle' in the concluding stanza of 'The Humble Lover'-

> And therefore since I cannot make your fame
> By song, I prithee, come make mine.
> If the world knows that you have shared my name
> It will become divine.

- presages a later passionate affair with *Sonnets pour Hélène*.[33]

As with the work of any apprentice, much of this early verse partakes of the stock exercise on the stock theme; the young poet can be seen experimenting with ideas and verse forms, imitating the acknowledged masters, and inevitably protesting the sentiments appropriate to the attitude being struck. Like most beginners in his tradition, the young poet often falls back on archaisms and 'poetic' usages - apostrophising, past tense stressing (amazéd, closéd) and similar prosodic devices - in order to sustain the metre or the rhyme.

Certainly none of the audacities that were later to be almost synonymous with the name of Humbert Wolfe - unusual punctuation, rhyme stretched to almost unbearable loadbearing lengths, like the ethereal traceries of high gothic architecture - are to be found in these early poems. Piety aside, their significance lies chiefly in the very fact of their existence and in what they reveal of the emergent themes which would pervade his later writings. They testify to the fact that he kept up his habit of writing verse throughout his undergraduate years and that he served a diligent apprenticeship. Of Oxford itself or of his undergraduate life they reveal virtually nothing.

V

Exit From Arcady - The Indian Summer

Schools, as the honours examinations were called, came and went. Berto's adventures in the Viva have already been mentioned. He emerged, as everyone (including himself) had confidently expected, with a First. With it came the prospect of departure from the enchanted garden, and unavoidable contact with the big, cold world outside. At least five or six of them - Keith, Gilliat, Marrs, Measham and Berto - proposed to take the Indian Civil Service Examination 'and trust that the Government either at home or abroad would have them in their keeping.'[34]

Berto, with his eye on a political future, consulted Maurice Woods, Gabriel Woods' elder brother and by now an important and influential figure in the political world. Woods promised to occupy himself on Berto's behalf and suggested an Indian appointment as a stop-gap. But when no more was heard of this Berto raised the matter with Wolmer, who recommended that Berto try for an Indian appointment by way of the I.C.S. exam, adding: 'if you want a nomination for the F.O. [Foreign Office] I might be able to help you.' 'The Scholar was grateful,' wrote Humbert in *The Upward Anguish*, 'but he didn't want a nomination for the F.O. He wanted a safe seat, £600 a year, and an option on a place in the Cabinet.'

The I.C.S. exams were in fact the entrance examination for the Home Civil Service too. They took place several weeks after the end of the Oxford term and the group of friends arranged to spend the intervening time in Oxford, following a course of lectures specially designed to enable candidates to persuade the Civil Service Commissioners that they knew something of subjects of which they were profoundly ignorant. The crammer's they attended for this purpose was an establishment called Sturt's, one of a number which prepared young gentlemen for the examination. The subjects which Berto, Marrs and Measham chose were Psychology, Political Economy, Political Science, and General Modern History (800 to 1100 AD). Meanwhile, they were enjoying a sort of Indian Summer of undergraduate life. They were all back in College, the weather was kind, and deck-chairs under the lime-tree were favourite seats of learning.

The Civil Service examinations took place in London, in Burlington Place, and the three companions shared lodgings in a dingy street in Notting Hill. Eventually, their last papers done, the time came for them to part. As far as can be ascertained, they never saw one another again.

The Oxford Magazine for 21 October 1907 offered its congratulations to U. Wolff on his First in Lit. Hum. and on his performance in the ICS examination. Also to R. J. Measham on his high place in the same examination.

The magazine also reported annually on the results of the Civil Service Competition, with the rank order placings of the different candidates and their academic record. In the issue for 7 November we read:

> No. 43* U. Wolff (Wadham) 2 Cl Mod, 1 Lit Hum.; 4 years residence; Special Tuition outside the University: H. Sturt 6 weeks.
>
> NB * = appointment of candidate depends on final allocation of places.

His marks varied widely, some fair to high, other quite low.

His friend Gilliatt (2 Cl Mod, 2 Lit Hum) came 34th, with entry to the Indian Civil Service. Measham (1 Cl Mod, 2 Lit Hum) was placed 19th, with entry to the Home Civil Service. Geoffrey Burton, with a 2nd in both Cl Mod and Greats, made only 63rd and was, like Berto, asterisked but re-sat the examination in 1908, moved up to 31st place and was rewarded with appointment to the Indian Service. Of Marrs and Keith no trace at all can be found.

Such records and recollections as it has been possible to piece together convey the distinct impression that the experience of knowing Berto for those three years was, for Berto's Wadham friends, as much a part of their education as were their academic studies. It was not that they were ever intimate or discussed any subject very seriously, for such was not the custom. Others of their friends may well have been just as kindly and sympathetic, other companions of their work and play just as gay and gallant. They had met equally keen and piercing minds, equally industrious and ambitious competitors. What they perceived as unique and distinctive in Berto, and which endeared him even to those whom he annoyed, was not a typical English quality, nor is there an English word for it. What they saw was *panache*.

It is equally pertinent, at this turning point in Berto's life, to ask the question: 'What did Oxford mean to him? and how did it influence his personal and poetical development?'

Henceforth for him Oxford would always stand for something like Augustine's 'pulchritudo tam nova et tam antiqua' - timeless beauty and eternal youth, and this not least because the university's population was predominantly young and annually or triennially renewed. This may have contributed to his enduring affection, even preference, for the company of the young, and his constant concern to encourage them.

As a graduate of Oxford he was also a citizen of a state within a state, with rights and privileges there, and doubtless responsibilities too. Being a graduate of Oxford was rather like being a citizen of Athens or of Rome. Henceforward it would always have a power over him and a claim on him, tugging at his heart strings as well as giving him the right to call it home. Furthermore, it gave him equality (of a sort) with other Oxford alumni, a circle of acquaintance whose influence in the world of politics as well as of the arts was enormous.

Alongside his exuberant gaiety went a deep and unremitting hurt, the pain of slights that could not be assuaged and the knowledge that this could happen even to him and could happen again. He mostly managed to push it from the forefront of his mind: his life contains innumerable instances of his ability to forget slights and disappointments and to bounce back with seemingly irrepressible cheerfulness. Nevertheless, it is reasonable to assume that in this experience was to be found, at least in part, the source of the abiding themes of his poetry: that few things have permanence, love does not endure, fidelity is an illusion and beauty perishable; themes which pervade his poetry like a stream which moulds and shapes the landscape by which it is fed.

But what Oxford meant to him is perhaps most typically expressed in a poem he wrote nearly twenty years later:

> Some day I'll go back to Oxford -
> I shall take the 4.50 train from Paddington
> (Or its sweet ghost if it has ceased to run),
>
> . . . .
>
> I shall step out silently, and take a cab,
> that slides along the cobbles like a wounded crab.
> I'll say to the cabman, 'Wadham,' and then sit
> perfectly still, but my body will be lit
> like a great house with candles.[35]

Chapter Four

1908-1911

Not for world-shakers

Then there's the Civil Service. Any takers?
  It's honest work, though not perhaps a part
for turbulent world-savers and world-shakers,
  or those with fire underneath the heart.

(*The Uncelestial City*, 1930)

I

1908

The ambition of a career in politics which Berto briefly nursed in 1907-1908 was unlikely to be speedily realised. The promise of patronage and influence held out at Oxford showed no sign of materialising, and the second line of attack - the Civil Service Examination - was, on the face of it, neither a rapid nor a direct means of access to political life. The Civil Service might give him inside knowledge and experience of the world of politics, as well as contacts with politicians, but unless he entered as one destined for high office this was likely to be a slow process. His Civil Service Examination results were not spectacular enough to mark him out as a high flier. Indeed, the asterisk beside his name in the pass list made it clear that he would be placed, if at all, only after all the abler candidates had been appointed.

Another well-trodden route to political office was the legal profession, particularly advocacy. Then, as now, the Bar had a certain glamour, an element of the theatrical, and many a star of the Law Courts and the Palace of Westminster had cut his teeth in the debating chamber of the Oxford Union. Was not F. E. Smith, who became successively Attorney General, Lord Chancellor, Secretary of State for India and lst Earl of Birkenhead, a Wadham man and from a modest background in the North of England? Furthermore, the law was a career of which Consola approved. Jessie Wolfe later wrote that, according to Berto, Consola wanted him to go to the Bar, and had even planned to go to live with him in London, taking her daughters with her.[1]

Berto, however, either because he was still counting on his influential Oxford friends to smooth his path for him, or simply because he was waiting for the Civil Service Commissioners to decide where to place him, delayed a considerable time before setting foot on the legal ladder. His admission to the Inner Temple came on 2 May 1908, when he was described as "Umberto Wolff of Wadham College Oxford and the Board of Trade, Whitehall, civil servant, the second son of Martin Wolff dec., late of 4, Mount Royal (*sic*), Bradford, merchant."

His was, in fact, the commonest Oxford route to legal qualification at that time, and the one preferred by the profession: a first degree, preferably Greats, followed by the degree of Bachelor in Civil Law and then either by articles in a legal firm or by admission to one of the four Inns of Court, with a pupillage to follow in due course. The principal, if not the essential, features of the training offered by the Inns of Court were the obligatory 'dinners' - six per term over a three year period - and an examination at the end. The members of each Inn called themselves 'The Honourable Society of the Inner Temple' (or Middle Temple/ Gray's Inn/ Lincoln's Inn) and eating together was central to the initiation of new members into their corporate identity. Formal tuition was not a requirement and students were left to prepare for the examination by their own devices. It was therefore possible, and for such as Berto probably necessary, to earn a living in some other employment and study for the Bar in one's spare time.

Berto was still 'eating dinners' at the Inner Temple two years later but the records indicate that he was never called to the Bar. There is nothing to suggest that he ever sat, let alone failed, any of the examinations. He may finally have rebelled against his mother, or simply lost interest in the law; according to his wife, it was no secret by this time that he intended to be a writer as well as a Civil Servant. Furthermore, his energies were fully occupied with the succession of major and significant changes in his life between 1908 and 1910. These were, in order of occurrence, his entry into the Civil Service, his formal admission to the Church of England, and his engagement and marriage to Jessie Graham.

By the time he was admitted to the Inner Temple he had finally been certificated by the Commissioners (on 7 April, 1908) for appointment in the Home Civil Service (class 1) to an upper division clerkship in the Harbour Department of the Board of Trade at a salary of £150 per annum. To achieve this he had had to produce for the Commissioners his own birth certificate and his father's certificate of naturalisation. He was still known as Umberto Wolff and there is no evidence that he or anyone else thought that he should anglicize his name. On 2 April of that year his father's certificate of naturalisation was returned by the Commissioners to Messrs. Mahler, Sichel & Co., the executors of his father's will in Bradford. It was the practice at that time to retain the certificate of birth in the Commission's files.[2]

It may be supposed that he had been waiting for this assurance that his livelihood and his career, however modest, were now secure, before taking the next major step in his life, for on 18 May of the same year he wrote to

Mr. Graham in Edinburgh to ask for the hand of his daughter, Jessie, in marriage.

The acquaintance established between the two families on that first holiday near Oban had developed over the years. They took holidays in the same places, both in Oban and other parts of Scotland,[3] Jessie had stayed with the Wolffs in Bradford and, according to a belief handed down in the family, Consola at one time considered her a possible wife for her first-born, Oswald, who was a few months older than Jessie. This legend is hard to reconcile with what is known of Consola's later reactions to both her sons' marriage intentions, but whatever its basis in reality, it soon became clear that Jessie had a closer affinity with Berto, despite being his senior by eighteen months.

Jessie later claimed that she was fifteen when the undergraduate Berto wrote for her the poem beginning 'Violet, small flower', but she may have confused dates and poems. Another, less charitable, explanation is that in this reminiscence she had to lower her age since she had already made herself younger than she really was. A passage in *A Winter Miscellany* (1930) records a visit to

> Auld Reekie, whither I went to Jessie's party one Christmastime from Oxford.
> Do you remember - can you e'er forget? -
> How in the coiled perplexities of youth,
> In our wild climate, in our scowling town,
> We gloomed and shivered, sorrowed, sobbed and feared? . . .
> No! one could not forget. It was already dark when the train drew into that huge station crouching under Arthur's Seat. The East Wind, as always, blew down Princes Street as though Eurus himself stood by the corner of Lothian Road with apple cheeks and pursed blowing mouth. But the tram and youth took us easily through the utmost gale. There was a little snow on the ground, for the four-wheeled cab that came to fetch us for the ball slithered aimlessly down Hartington Gardens. . . All that - and to dance and to leave the dance for the return train at midnight with a waltz in my head and no winter at all in my heart.[4]

The difference in religion was undoubtedly an obstacle to marriage in the eyes of the Graham parents. Jessie never knew whether or not Consola had any religious grounds, in addition to her other reasons, for objecting to the marriage. Consola's three daughters all married non-Jews without opposition from their mother on that score, but Mr. Graham was unlikely to have been encouraged by Consola's lack of Jewish fervour, however reassuring the signs of Berto's interest in Christianity may have been.

From what Jessie recalled nearly forty years later it is clear that her father would not countenance their marriage until Berto became a Christian.[5]

In May 1908 Berto was able to make his formal request for permission to marry Jessie because this obstacle had been removed. In a letter dated Monday 18 May he wrote:

> I think Jessie will have told you that I have been accepted a member of the Church of England. On Wednesday night last by 'the mystical washing away of sins' I became a Christian. There is still for me the completing ceremony of Confirmation, & though I hardly feel ready for that yet, I owe it as a duty both to those who admitted me into the Church, and those for whose sake (as well as for my own) I entered it. Though I am not as yet ready for it, I have no doubt that I shall proceed so far before the day of the further consecration, the consecration which it now lies with you to permit or forbid according as you consider me worthy or not of the great trust & honour I now solicit from you.
>
> I am writing, dear Mr. Graham, now that the obstacles are cleared away to ask you, if when the time & the hour comes, I may be allowed the greatest joy & honour I can possibly attain - the joy of making Jessie my wife.
>
> I need not tell you that I have loved her, & will always love her, and ask you to consider the years that have passed as an earnest of what I feel, & a small promise of what I hope. It shall be the first business of my life to surround my dearest with all that love can give her. I cannot claim to great position, or great wealth (you know my position) but whatever that may be it shall be devoted unreservedly to the happiness of your daughter.
>
> If you and Mrs. Graham can trust me with this the greatest trust of all I hope that my life & Jessie's happiness (if I can secure it) will be in some small measure a return for what you are doing now.
>
> I will come (if I may) on June 5 or 6 to claim (if you grant) the lady who is the whole meaning of my life.[6]

Five years earlier, Berto had arrived for his first term at Oxford in something of a religious fog, and far from clear in his own mind about what the faith might be to which he was committed. He had ceased to be in any religious sense a Jew, but had not yet taken the plunge into

Christianity. Not that he was not tempted to do so, nor was he unaware of the religious as well as the mundane arguments for joining the Church of England, but he was loth to risk upsetting Consola and 'there was something stubborn in his blood, which remembered Zion.' He had been led to understand by the Warden of Wadham, the Rev. Mr. Wright-Henderson, that he would be excused attendance at Chapel, and was therefore surprised to learn that, as a Scholar of the College, he would have to read the lessons for one or two weeks of each term. He duly complied, but with a sense of committing a social as well as a religious impropriety, and he resisted without difficulty the attempts of the more pious in the College to enlist him in St. Andrew's Guild, an evangelical Christian student society.[7]

To judge by a passage in *The Upward Anguish*, his dealings with his tutor, Drewitt, were responsible for some kind of conversion *à rebours*. Drewitt held that no metaphysician could be an agnostic: to say that one did not know was an admission of defeat, and the thinker's first job was to know what it was that he could not know, and then proceed from that point. Doubt of the kind that afflicted Matthew Arnold and Arthur Hugh Clough 'was a sort of chicken-pox that one acquired in the nursery of the mind. One did not doubt; one formed a conclusion.'

Tennyson's lines:

> There lives more faith in honest doubt,
> Believe me, than in half the creeds.

seemed to Berto 'the reflexions of a Second-rate Sensitive Mind', the Victorian malady to which nevertheless his own painful self-examination bore a strange resemblance. 'It was difficult to go into one's bedroom and not address oneself to one's Maker.' Was he simply being cowardly and hypocritical in continuing to commit his cares into the keeping of a Protector who in metaphysical truth did not exist? Honesty seemed to require him to face up to the logical consequences of his thought.

> The conclusion of the struggle was inevitable. One night he went into his bedroom, undressed rapidly, hesitated and then jumped hastily into bed. The Scout, when he came to wake him next morning, found the light burning. "You didn't turn off the light last night," he grumbled. "Oh yes I did," he answered. Yes. Completely. And, true to his nature, he just restrained himself from quoting,
> "put out the light and then put out the light."[8]

But this was written thirty years after the event and perhaps for another purpose. If he did experience a loss of faith, it appears to have been fairly short-lived, to be replaced by a whole-hearted conversion to Christianity by the time he became engaged to his future wife. Whatever may be said about the fulsome tone of Berto's letter to Mr. Graham, there is no reason to doubt the sincerity of his conversion. Jessie herself later recalled 'how deeply he was moved by the beautiful Jacobean English of the prayer-book, and how he kept on repeating to me phrases from the Order of Baptism and the Order of Confirmation - "the mystical washing away of sin", "This Thy child".'[9]

It is also clear from Berto's letter to his future father-in-law that he had courted Jessie for a long time: there is a distinct echo of Jacob's long wait for Rachel. For most if not all of the time that the two young people had known one another, the Grahams had lived in Edinburgh, where Mr. Graham had his own school. Joseph Chalmers Graham was the son of a schoolmaster and grandson of a clockmaker. After schooling at the Royal High School, Edinburgh, he had read Classics at Edinburgh University and had married Euphemia Alexander, the daughter of an Edinburgh builder. From Jessie's description, the Alexanders appear to have been fairly well-to-do. They lived in a large house called 'The Grange', 'with its horses and carriages, its vinery, the flower garden with fruit on the red walls, the croquet lawn where the two pet lambs nibbled the ivy off the walls as high as their mouths could reach.'[10]

In 1879 Mr. Graham was appointed rector (that is, headmaster) of the newly created Knox Memorial Institute in Haddington, East Lothian, about twenty miles east of Edinburgh. The Institute was built both to replace the old and famous grammar school - which counted among its more noteworthy alumni the reformer John Knox and the poet William Dunbar - and to meet the requirements of the 1872 Education Act. The main speaker at the official opening in February 1880 was Arthur J. Balfour, Conservative Member of Parliament for Hertford and the heir to a sizeable estate at Whittinghame, near Haddington. The future Prime Minister, then thirty-two years of age, had barely begun to make his mark in politics but both his father and grandfather had represented Haddington in Parliament and the family ranked high among the local gentry.[11]

The present rector (1991) has written:

> Certainly Graham took charge at a most difficult time, following the dismissal (after almost thirty years of trying) of the infamous Rev. Dr. Whyte who reduced the grammar school roll to absurdly low levels - either to avoid paying doctors (ushers) any more or because of an incurable sadism. Under the 1872 Act the school became an 'omnibus school' - with rigid streaming - for all ages including primary. Under Graham . . . The

> Knox Memorial Institute was one of the original band of candidates of twenty-four presenting candidates for the first diet of Scottish Highers.[12]

'Craigneil', the Grahams' house in Haddington, had been built for Euphemia by her father as her first married home, which suggests that they married about the time of her husband's appointment to the rectorship in 1879. In June 1883 their first child, Jessie, was born. She was to spend the first ten years of her life in Haddington.

Mr. Graham's severe manner and fierce appearance (enhanced by a fiery red beard) augmented his authority as Rector of the Knox Institute. He was, it seems, as stern a disciplinarian at home as he was at school. His grand-daughter recalled:

> My mother spoke of him as a severe parent - for instance, she asked for a painting-box, for a birthday. He gave her one, but it was second-hand. "It's all broken", she said, and got a whipping for not being grateful. Another time she innocently repeated some swear-words which she had heard. Same result. Perhaps that was par for the course for Victorian parents, especially in Scotland. Later on he encouraged her to read, offered a prize for reading the whole of Scott, read the poetry of Goethe and Schiller to her, went on cycle rides with her. . . He knew she had brains, and asked her if she'd like to be a doctor, but paid no attention when an art-master suggested she should go farther with painting.[13]

But in 1893 Mr. Graham resigned the rectorship and the family returned to Edinburgh where he opened his own school in Spylaw Road.

> As to why he left the Knox, Jessie said he was persuaded by his wife, Euphemia, my grandmother. She was an Edinburgh woman, was terribly bored with Haddington, and longed to return to Edinburgh. And no doubt he felt it was a challenge to start his own school. Jessie said it was ill-timed - shortly after he resigned, another school in Haddington closed and the Knox would have got their pupils.
>
> He was a man who loved books. When he retired, after his school was sold, he continued teaching and tutoring, and started to learn Hebrew. He loved long walks. I have a silver tray which was presented to him when he left the Knox Institute.[14]

Jessie's father wanted her to study medicine but she could not face the dissecting rooms and so abandoned all hope of higher education, leaving school at the age of fifteen or sixteen. She studied cooking and dress-making for two years at the Atholl Crescent domestic science school in Edinburgh. There was plainly a strong artistic bent in her which she expressed in dress-making, in creating delightful domestic interiors, and (much later in life) in painting. While still in her teens she also taught in Sunday school. In one lesson on Nebuchadnezzar her pupils queried his eating grass. She told them that there were vegetarians who did not eat meat. When at the examination her class was asked what they knew about Nebuchadnezzar, they chorussed with one voice: "He was a vegetarian!"

She took a succession of posts as a governess, one with the family of Lord Howard of Glossop, whose son she was to teach during his school holidays. She set him the task of writing his own account of Cowper's poem, 'John Gilpin'. Her pupil clearly did not believe in wasting words: "John Gilpin had a horse and rode it to and fro'." Her pupil was killed in the First World War and Jessie's daughter Ann remembers coming across a monument to him while walking in the woods near Loch Shiel.

At about the age of nineteen or twenty, Jessie spent nearly a year at the Royal Eye Hospital in south London as a probationer nurse. To her family and social circle this choice was something of an embarrassment: they did not esteem nursing as a career and Jessie had to overcome the strong disapproval of her own family in order to try even as short a training period as this, and one of her aunts asked her not to go to see her in the uniform Jessie was so proud of. Jessie later said that in order to enter this small hospital she had to pretend to be older than she was, which would make her less than twenty-one.

Until then she had been slow and dreamy; her gruelling experience as a hospital nurse cured her of that. At the end-of-year examination, in which she came top, one of her examiners publicly complimented her on her answer to the question: "What symptoms would you regard as requiring you to call the doctor?" Jessie had listed 'Pain' as the first symptom, and the examiner said she was the only one who had mentioned pain, which showed some consideration for her patients. Her daughter recalled that she always remained very knowledgeable about eyes.

Next she became nursery-governess to the family of a British Consul in Egypt for about a year. Although she liked the children, she did not enjoy the job very much: the Consul and his wife seem to have been rather disagreeable. But Egypt enthralled her. She found its foreignness, its difference, its mystery entrancing. She later described in vivid detail an Arab wedding which she saw, the bride hidden in a tent on a camel, the outriders firing off guns in celebration. All her life she retained a love of travel and longed especially to see the East. During her last illness she was talking of India and longing to see Kashmir.

In the intervals of nursing and Egypt there was ordinary life in Edinburgh with her family and friends, dances (with eightsome reels), tennis, skating on Duddingston Loch in the winter and swimming in the summer. There were concerts at the Usher Hall. Jessie enjoyed music; she played the piano and had a sweet singing voice. Her closest friend was the lovely but foolish Kirstie (whom she called Chrys), who boasted of being engaged to six different young men at once, and whose story ended sadly: almost disowned by her family after becoming pregnant in a love affair with her music master, she was quietly married and isolated from her former friends, ending up in South Africa, unhappy, poor and with a large family.

From these snippets of her own and her family's recollections Jessie emerges as a strong personality, energetic, resilient and enterprising, with a degree of self-reliance and will-power unusual in a young woman of that period.

By all accounts Mr. Graham and Berto got on well. During a holiday with the Grahams in Oban, Berto and Jessie went sailing but were unable to get back before nightfall because of a storm. When they eventually returned the next day, Mr. Graham, who was on the quay to meet them, simply said, 'Oh, you're back', and quoted some lines from Campbell's poem 'Lord Ullin's Daughter'. Berto was much struck by his calm attitude which contrasted so sharply with the excitable nature of his own family, particularly Consola.[15]

In May 1908 Berto was fully occupied with penetrating the mysteries of the Civil Service and settling down to a way of life which was quite different both from Bradford and from Oxford. Years later Humbert said that his first experience of London was not too happy. His irrepressible ebullience was sometimes mistaken for pushfulness. Manners in those days were very much more conventional and oddities tended to be censured. He soon learned to keep his place, and became an acute and anonymous civil servant. Harry Balfour, one of the three Civil Service friends with whom he shared a house in St. George's Square, Pimlico (the other two were George Chrystal and Philip Lloyd-Green), remembered him as modest and agreeable - a curious contrast with the censures Berto received from others. Balfour was another who was struck both by the fine bone structure of his face which gave him a strong resemblance to the profile of Savonarola, and by the unusual circumstance that poetry kept composing itself in his head apparently without any effort on his part.[16]

In addition to his family there remained one other link with Bradford which was not only to enlarge and benefit Berto's social life but also to contribute to his and Jessie's difficulties with Consola when they were first married. That link was his friendship with the Rothenstein brothers, Will and Albert - the latter had not yet anglicized his name to Rutherston. Through them he became one of the group loosely associated with the New English Art Club, of which Albert was the youngest member. A chapter in *Portraits By Inference* describes Humbert's memory of the Club as it was in 1908.

Among the new friends Berto made in this group was Michel Salaman, the son of an ostrich feather merchant and a descendant of the musician who had been Haydn's impresario in London. Michel, his beautiful wife Chattie, and several of his brothers and sisters, had studied art at the Slade; he was there at the same time as Augustus John and his sister Gwen in the mid-eighteen-nineties but, while maintaining a strong interest in art and artists, increasingly devoted himself to the chase and became Master of the Exmoor Hunt. Whether Berto met the Salamans before his occupancy of Albert's spare attic at No. 18 Fitzroy Street in 1908 is not known, but evidently he soon became a recipient of the 'extraordinary sympathy and generosity' which Michel lavished on most of the friends of Augustus John.[17]

It was also about this time that Berto met Rupert Brooke and, as he later wrote in *The Upward Anguish*, 'was passed over by that poet as being a dull Civil Servant.' In the same passage he recalled how his friend Morrison, who had left Oxford to study philosophy at Cambridge, had described Brooke to him as 'as beautiful and lonely as a cloud, and thought to be a better poet even than Flecker.' Flecker too had fled Oxford in order to study Turkish at Cambridge, after passing the examination for the Eastern Student Interpretership. Humbert more than once paid tribute to him, in prose and in verse, and it is clear from both *Portraits By Inference* and *The Upward Anguish* that Flecker somehow represented the voice of conscience when Berto had been tempted to forsake poetry for politics and the Bar.

II

1908-1910

Mr. Graham clearly saw no reason to withhold his consent to the marriage, for on 20 May 1908, only two days after making his formal request, Berto was writing from 99 St George's Square, SW, to thank his future father-in-law:

> . . . I can only say to you and Mrs. Graham that it will be the first and highest ambition of my life to prove to you that you have not been mistaken in your trust. And I hope that the great happiness to which your consent opens a door may help to bring joy into your lives as it most certainly must into ours.

Berto and Jessie's engagement was to be a fairly long one but not unusually so for those days, and between May 1908 and March 1910 their chief concerns were finding somewhere to live and having enough to live on. Their anxiety was understandable since Berto would have no money other than his salary - then £150 per annum - until he received his share of the legacy left by his father.

The increase in Civil Service salaries voted by Parliament in 1908 meant a rise of £50 per annum for Berto, who was visiting Jessie in Edinburgh when the news came. £200 a year was only a beginning, but it seemed to them a good beginning and they 'celebrated the occasion by dining at the Caledonian Hotel and going to a music-hall afterwards.'[18]

Jessie was sure that they could manage on £200 a year. Consola was equally sure that they could not. She was in any case unenthusiastic about the marriage, as she had been about Oswald's. She had displayed one of her transcendental rages on receiving news that Oswald had become engaged to the beautiful daughter of one of the wealthiest families in Hamburg.[19] And Jessie was by no means either beautiful or wealthy. In truth, Consola thought no one a really suitable spouse for one of 'My Sons', to whom, said Jessie, 'she always referred with the air of a queen speaking of the young royal princes.' And in her first wrath that Berto was going to get married at all, she had not discouraged and may even have started a good deal of gossip about Jessie's extreme poverty and general unsuitability, gossip which she subsequently had to scotch in order to escape the mortifying commiserations of The Friends.

Jessie remembered vividly

> coming back one day from a game of tennis with Berto's sister, Sylvia, and meeting Consola with the red that meant anger and indignation flaming in her cheeks, and Fanny (Berto's oldest sister) saying to me as we met:-
> "We've been seeing 'most expensive'" (this was the nick-name of one of the Wolff's best-hated friends - she acquired it because her most frequent remark was said to be 'Most expensive, my dear!')
> "When you see her, Jakins darling," Fanny went on, "be sure to tell her you've a dowry of £10,000, and you're going to inherit three times as much."[20]

But although she could not prevent the marriage taking place, Consola did her best to discourage any haste to solemnize it. Jessie's visits to Bradford during her engagement alerted her sharply to the problems which Consola's notions of money and poverty were to cause them. Consola cast figures endlessly in her little book, making what she called a 'Boodja' (her pronunciation of 'budget') to demonstrate that they could not possibly manage on so little, let alone 'entratain'. She would remind Jessie that 'such things as soap for washing clothes and the floor, lavatory paper, Sanitas, polish, Brook's soap, knife powder, and matches cost money, and then she would add up her sum and say:-

> There will be nothing, not one penny for your hairpins, or the papier poudre to rub on your nose, not one penny for the doctor. . . This is terrible, I cannot make the end to meet.[21]

They spent that summer and the following year making plans and especially trying to think of some way of persuading Consola that on £200 a year they could perfectly well set out on their married life and in two rooms instead of what she called a 'propple' house.

Convincing Consola would not be easy. She had never been poor and even as a widow she could still afford two good maids in her house in Oak Mount. But setting her present circumstances against those of her early married life in Milan, and later at Mount Royd, she considered herself poor in comparison with her friends, and

> our proposal of two rooms on £200 a year suggested to her mind nothing but unspeakable squalor. Her weekly visits to the narrow back-streets of Bradford, where she used to exhort the poor to save their pennies, gave her a mental picture of what our life would be on £200 a year, which she contrasted painfully with her memories of the flat in Milan where she had begun her married life.

Consola was fond of describing her Milan home in loving detail:

> First you come in the hall, with rich, coloured rugs and curtains, and a jewelled lantern hanging down. Then you come in the dining room furnish' in ebony and red velvet. Then you come in the salon with golden furniture and brocade, and then you come in my boudoir, with the hanging in pale blue, and a pale blue rug.

She told Jessie that there had been a butler, too, who did not care to obey the seventeen year old Consola,

> but my husband spoke to that men, and after that he did always what I tell him at once.

> She did not believe that people could live like gentle-folk in two rooms, although I tried to point out that we could achieve a better standard of living in two rooms, on a working class income, than if we attempted to run a house in the only way she recognised as suitable for us.[22]

But Jessie refused to be daunted. She believed in Berto utterly: there was nothing he could not do and all Consola's gloomy prophecies counted for nothing as the two of them walked the moors in the summer of 1908, cheerfully digested the lobster salad (2/6d each) at the Welsh House (as Consola called the Wells House Hydro) at Ilkley, and threw hoop-las at China dogs and clocks at the Shipley Glen Fair in the Easter of 1909. Berto was by now most anxious that they should try to marry on his £200 a year as soon as possible.

The insights into the life of the Wolff family and especially into the personality of Consola which these first visits to Bradford gave Jessie were richly revealing but also deeply disturbing. She was to discover that

> Consola's sweetly-harsh voice, which had cooed at me when I was a child:-
>
> > 'Are you a very spoil' little girl? Who spoil you most, your father, or your mother?'
>
> could change so quickly into bitter, passionate scolding, whose intensity had to be experienced to be understood. She was often a termagant, but her potent charm, which Berto inherited, attracted every-one she met, and, usually, retained their affection. Her slim, erect figure, with its crown of bright red hair, which never had much gray in it, marched with determined footsteps up and down her house, and quickly climbed the steep road from Oak Mount to Manningham Lane, and darted in and out of the shops there. She mounted the tram for town as though it were a chariot, from which to storm the fortifications of the market, the trimming shop, Maufe's, and Wilson's. Her tempo was always *Allegro con brio*. On returning home from shopping, she would sit in the drawing room, waiting to be summoned to lunch. She walked across the hall to the dining-room with the air of a queen, and sat at the head of the table to serve out the food placed before her. One would not have been much surprised if a troupe of stewards and chefs had marched in, bearing dishes aloft for her inspection, as in *Chu Chin Chow*, singing:-
>
> > 'Here be lampreys, fried in whale's fat
> > And Caviar from Tartar.'
>
> Deafness, in her case, seemed to me a self-imposed barrier, a portcullis which she lowered with her eye-lids when she wanted to exclude the world from the citadel

> of her mind. She had only to open her eyes, and look at the faces of those about her to lip-read their words, in French, German, Italian, or English, but when she closed her eyes, with a "we are not amused" expression, conversation with her was, for a time, at an end.[23]

Apart from its usefulness as the instrument of her own purposes, Consola's deafness, by barring her in many ways from the present, also imprisoned her in the past. In any other town than Bradford, and before she became deaf, she might have acquired a more English outlook. But she and her husband were settled in the midst of a foreign colony, where German and Italian were spoken as much as, if not more than, English. She had a German nurse and a Viennese governess for her children. Her outlook, like her accent, remained irredeemably continental, indeed, pre-1900 Italian. Jessie wrote that her own 'first impression of Bradford was of visiting a foreign town, in which the English part, the shops and the market, appeared like the foreign concessions in the Treaty Ports of China.'

Christmas 1908 found Berto ill in his lodgings at 17 Hallam Street, W1.[24] Jessie had come to London to visit him and was staying with Consola, who sent her down to Eccleston Square for the doctor at 6.30 in the morning. The maid said she could not give the message for at least two hours, and by the time the doctor reached Hallam Street it was lunchtime and Albert Rutherston had brought in another doctor. Berto's doctor was understandably annoyed at what he saw as a breach of etiquette and went upstairs to reproach his patient. This was the occasion for another of Consola's towering rages. She rushed after the intruder to drive him away, returning in triumph to the table, 'her eyes alight with indignation, the rosy flags of anger in her cheeks rivalling the redness of her hair.'[25] What the illness was remains a matter for conjecture but it does not seem to have been serious enough to warrant a detailed record and we must assume that Berto recovered fairly quickly.

But money and house-hunting were not their sole preoccupations during this time, as is clear from those of Berto's letters which have survived. He wrote verses to Jessie for her birthday and in reply to her own shy excursions into poetry. A letter to her, dated 6 June 1909, shows that he was also submitting poems to *The Westminster Gazette* which, in company with a number of other weeklies, organized regular verse competitions. In this instance, the competition was for a sonnet about the suburbs.

He wrote to her from Cambridge where he had been attending a dinner. Morrison, his Wadham friend who had fled to Cambridge, was there and Berto had clearly enjoyed the other company he had met.

> We talked oh how we talked! All the shades of Oxford returned, looked wistfully a little, & then settled into

armchairs. The bells of Cambridge rang like my own bells in the other place. It was very exquisite.

He went on to say:-

The W. G. [Westminster Gazette] had such a kind little thing about me last Saturday. When I wrote to ask for my prize I said 'I admit it's not a sonnet, but surely it's suburban.' The Editor put in a little note at the end of the page 'No it isn't - it is poetry!' Wasn't it nice of him?

The letter also mentioned a poem entitled 'The Great Adventure' which he was submitting that day for a competition in *The Westminster Gazette*. He quoted the last verse which he particularly liked:

Still for the adventurers remains the goal:
for these the glory. And for us may be
an easy death what time the enfranchised soul
embrace and founder in the endless sea.

He failed to win the prize, as a letter for her birthday the following week makes clear (13 June 1909).

I really feel that my poem was better than the prizewinner's, and I pretend that they thought that I had won enough prizes lately. I'm sending you along with this letter the poem they didn't print. Perhaps it may appear somewhere else at a [later?] time.[26]

On 22 June he wrote to say:-

I didn't know I was going to marry a poetess . . . Well I was going to say that you should quite seriously try to write a poem and see what comes of it.

Her attempt at poetry (about her dreaming of Berto) has not survived but Berto tried to reassure her in a letter dated 29 June:

I can't imagine why you should be ashamed of your poem. It is very tender and touched with the grip of passion. I send you a sonnet in answer:

'Your Dream'

I came to you (you sing it) in your sleep
and love, as though he were not satisfied

with the old days, must turn again and reap
with burning kisses that our lips had tried
at his first coming. Did he find again
the fresh green trees, the unconditioned sky,
the world before the coming of the rain,
that like a shadow waited and went by,
soft, like a god, and like a god, aflame?
Did he still find that murmur at your lips?
still see you standing, as the morning stands,
with fingers stretched, that touched and fled and came
to mine again, warm to the tender lips,
once lilies and now roses. O your hands!

It is interesting and instructive to see what had happened to this poem by the time it appeared, reworked, as 'At Noontide Seeking', the first of Three Sonnets of Love, in *London Sonnets* (1920).

Can love being love and therefore magical,
When summer and the roses lie between,
Find back to spring? Or shall he know at all
The places where his golden feet have been
At noontide seeking. Shall he know again
The tune of dawn, the unconditioned sky,
The world before the coming of the rain,
That like a shadow waited and went by,
Soft like a God and like a God aflame?
Ah will he find that murmur at your lips,
Still see you standing, as the morning stands,
With fingers stretched that touched and fled and came
To mine again, warm to the tender tips
Once lilies and now roses - Oh your hands? [27]

Berto, meanwhile, had been doing some house-hunting by himself, sending Jessie descriptions of the flats he had found, and the districts they were in, and sometimes drawing a rough plan of the rooms he had seen. They wanted somewhere not too far away from Whitehall and costing no more than £40 a year to rent. He found several which might meet their needs - one in Chelsea, another in St. George's Square, Pimlico, rooms in the Temple, and finally the offer of two rooms, with the use of kitchen and bathroom, in Albert Rutherston's flat at 18 Fitzroy Street, Bloomsbury - and was eager for Jessie to see them and make her choice.

Jessie divided this last Christmas before the wedding (1909-10) between her own home and Berto's.

I had eaten hot roast turkey and plum pudding in Edinburgh, and had arrived in Bradford in time to eat

> cold turkey and fried plum pudding. The visit promised to be more exciting than I had imagined. Besides the fittings of the dresses being made for me by Rosetta (Terracini), there was a party, and Consola had announced her intention of taking me to London with her, when Berto returned to his work at the Board of Trade, so that we might all go house-hunting together during the week-end.[28]

Jessie had encountered the German Jews of Bradford *en masse* only once before, at a Schillerverein party to which Sylvia Terracini had taken her. Now, meeting the full Wolff entourage at Oak Mount, at something between a betrothal and a pre-wedding gathering, crystallised her first impressions of Bradford as a foreign town. Perhaps because the party represented chiefly the older generation, this collection of burghers, wealthy and solid men, and their wives in stiff, rich silks, and neat, severe hair-dressing, reminded Jessie of paintings by Franz Hals or Rembrandt. There were the Emil Mosers and the Jakob Mosers, the Mahlers, the Rothensteins, the Falkensteins, the Edelsteins, the Liebreichs, the Von Hallés, the Pinners and the Unners. There were only a few of the younger generation to support Berto and his fiancée, amongst whom were Albert Rothenstein, Juliet Pinner, a violinist and Berto's three sisters.

The first two of 'The Friends' (as Nannie Atkins later taught her to think of the Bradford circle) to arrive happened to be the Mahlers, known as 'Tante' and 'Onkel'.[29] Tante had already antagonized Jessie in the letter she wrote on hearing of the engagement, 'in which all the good wishes expressed seem to mean the opposite.' Jessie's later reference to 'their stuffy self-righteousness and grudging meanness' may well have been inspired by what she and her daughter, Ann, endured at their hands.

Jessie was well aware that Berto was not really approved of in Bradford. He had told her that they were suspicious of learning and that even his having entered the Civil Service did not seem to have appeased them. They thought him conceited and said so. Worse, on occasion they said so to Jessie. She had been taken one evening to meet an old governess who wished to inspect Berto's new fiancée. Over the black bread, the leberwurst, honey-cakes and coffee, she spoke enthusiastically of Berto's father, who had died before Jessie met the Wolff family.

> 'I have been told that Berto is like his father,' said Jessie.
>
> 'You haf misinformed been,' was the reply, 'his father was a good man. Berto is too conceited.'

On another occasion, while escorting Jessie to hear Sylvia Terracini lecture on Dante, Onkel had taken the opportunity

> to say what a pity it was that Berto was so selfish and conceited, and that it was only to be hoped that the heavy responsibilities he was shouldering on a too small income would have a steadying effect.[30]

But on the evening of the party, for all that they might deplore Berto's conceit, his originality in resolutely turning his back on business in order to be a Civil Servant, even a writer, and his determination to marry, on £200 a year, a girl who was not a Jewess and had no fortune, Jessie felt that they were regarding them with friendly eyes.

> I had been touched by the table of presents I had found waiting for me when I arrived - not the solid silver wedding-presents, which came later - but little personal things, to be of use in a small appartment, where there was to be no servant. There was a simple arrangement for making coffee for breakfast, from Mrs. Jakob Moser, a neat affair for boiling eggs, a tea-cosy with egg-cosies to match, a chafing-dish. Everyone showed an almost paternal interest in our house-hunting expedition. It all gave me a happy feeling of being admitted into the circle, and welcomed. Their warm and kindly interest in our plan to go and live in a very simple way, as they all said, delighted me.

Now that this so improvident marriage was going to take place, and Consola had decided to give it her blessing to the extent of helping the couple to find a house, it was as if the whole party was determined to reflect Consola's apparent enthusiasm. Berto's sister Sylvia sang 'The merry pipes of Pan', from *The Arcadians*, his other sister, Rita, declaimed with passion Kipling's poem from *Pook o' Pook's Hill*:- 'What is a woman that you forsake her?', and Juliet Pinner sang an aria from *La Bohême* with piano accompaniment and violin obbligato. Even the charade which Albert had arranged made house-hunting its central theme. He made Berto and Jessie pretend to go to Paris to find a house. The violinist played the part of a naughty little boy whom Albert had to slap. But Albert forgot to put his other hand against the cheek that was to be slapped, and nearly knocked the unfortunate violinist's head off. As Albert dealt out one resounding slap after another, Mr. Emil Moser clapped his hands with delight, shouting:- "How clever he hits him! How clever he hits him!"

On the train journey to London the next day, while Berto went to have lunch in the dining-car, Consola and Jessie ate their packed lunch of chicken and rolls in the compartment, and Consola explained once again the peculiarities of his digestion, giving Jessie detailed instructions on how to make the savoury rice and macaroni dishes he liked, and a recipe for a cheap tomato soup. These topics exhausted, she set about another 'boodja' to demonstrate the impossibility of 'making the end to meet.'

Jessie had received copious advice on house-keeping from her own mother. Berto's contribution had been a copy of George Gissing's *New Grub Street*, while his older sister, Fanny, was emphatic that now that 'Bugs' was getting to know such swells they must entertain a lot in order to 'get in' with them. Jessie ruefully reflected that Consola's 'boodja' did not include entertaining (except people to tea), although it did include birthday and Christmas presents of blouses (to be made by Jessie) for Consola and the girls. But, above all, Consola could not or would not see the importance of being get-at-able in London, especially if one was just beginning, and one's means and time, and those of one's first acquaintances, were limited.

Consola and Jessie had booked rooms at The Strand Palace Hotel, then the latest thing in hotels, with running water in every bed-room. They arrived there on the Saturday night, and set off on the Sunday morning to view some of the flats before going to Albert Rutherston's for lunch and to see the rooms he had to let. The day began inauspiciously. Consola was irritated by various delays and the morning was spent in fruitless searches: flats were either too expensive or could not be viewed without appointment. Consola's main concern was that there should be adequate accommodation for her future grandchild's pram, which she made the theme of the expedition. Eventually they took refuge in Westminster Abbey to rest their weary feet. Consola refused to look at anything else until after lunch, and retreated into deafness. Despite the service which was in progress at the time, voices were raised to an unseemly level and they hastily fled the disapproving looks of the other worshippers to take a bus to Albert's for lunch.

Albert's rooms were ruled out as being totally unsuitable for a grandchild of Consola's, as was a house in Edwardes Square, Kensington, which took them all afternoon to find and, though cheap, was due for demolition, a discovery which brought Consola to hysterical mirth. It turned out to be the missed chance of a life-time, for the house still stands today.

The next morning, although Jessie did not know it, their fate was sealed. Consola had seen an advertisemnent in *The Times* of flats in Prince of Wales Road, Battersea, from £55 a year. Berto had joined them for breakfast in order to go with them to see another flat before going on to his office. For the first time Jessie saw him in his London dress - top-hat and morning coat, 'looking very dashing and rakish.' He pointed out to Consola that south of the river was difficult of access; he would rather stay on or near the Chelsea side. Consola merely replied:- "We shall go, and we shall look, and we shall see what we shall see."

They went to several places in Pimlico and Chelsea: two unviewable, the rest too expensive. Berto left them to go to work, while Jessie went on with Consola to look at Battersea: York Mansions, Primrose Mansions,

Prince of Wales Mansions, and eventually Overstrand Mansions, where they found No. 16, a ground-floor flat, with a little garden. Jessie thought it much too large with six rooms, bathroom and kitchen, and too expensive at £60 a year, and said so. Against Consola's obsession with the thought of the baby they were to have one day, all this availed nothing.

> 'Here is the nursery,' she would say, 'here is where you will keep the pram, here is the dining-room, and this is the leaving-room - here is your baid-room, and a spare baid-room - so useful.' (Alas, how too useful!)'

They met Berto for lunch, but apparently without pressing the claims of Battersea too strongly, if at all. After he had returned to his office, they returned to the search in Chelsea, enquiring wherever they saw a 'To Let' sign displayed, but everything cost as much as or more than their whole income. Jessie hoped that they could delay a decision until they could please themselves, but Consola was adamant.

> 'I will make Berto come with us tomorrow morning to see that little parterre. I think it will be lovely. I can see you put the baby in his pram in that garden, and in the park opposite - oh, it is ideal!'

Berto's objections were dismissed as simply silly. 'It is quite near Victoria in that train', she said, 'and when you have made your way up in the world, you can choose your side of the river.' To Jessie Berto said that they might as well go and live as far out as Esher, as at Battersea. It was tantalisingly near, yet because of the bad means of communication at that time, quite far away. But he could not make Consola understand this. For her, the matter was settled and once more she had her way.

Berto was about to change his lodgings again, this time to 47 Ebury Street, where Edward Lascelles[31] occupied the ground floor suite. There was just time for Consola and Jessie to do Berto's packing and then they were on their way back to Bradford where Jessie was made sharply aware that further tussles were in store, as Consola dictated her plans for the use and decoration of the rooms in their 'doll's-house', promising to 'make a row' if when she came to visit them they had not carried out her wishes.[32]

III

1910

The wedding took place in the afternoon of 29 March 1910 at a church in Morningside, Edinburgh. Years later Jessie recalled looking out of her bedroom window in Hartington Gardens on the morning of her wedding day and craning her head to catch a glimpse of the Forth Bridge to the west and Edinburgh Castle to the east.[33] The wedding day was warm and sunny, as fine as a sudden foretaste of summer. Consola, who was staying at the Grahams' house, came with her daughters, Sylvia and Rita, and the black and tan terrier which had been a present from Berto, to help Jessie prepare for the ceremony.

As Jessie's mother arranged the wreath of orange-blossom she had worn at her own wedding over the bride's hair, and her veil over that, Consola warned Jessie to take care of her veil.

> 'Don't let it tear', said Consola. 'It is said to mean you will soon be a widow if the veil gets torn on the wedding-day. My veil was torn, and I was a widow after only fourteeen years.'

The story echoes one of Berto's earlier poems, entitled 'The Torn Veil':[34]

> She gave me a piece of the veil she had torn,
> It was white and salt with the sea.
> She had worn it, she whispered, at early morn
> And therefore she gave it to me.
>
> Had shielded her mouth from the kiss of the sun
> When he raised his lips from the sea,
> And guarded her cheeks when the rain had begun,
> And therefore she gave it to me.
>
> Had been on her eyes when she stood on the hill
> To look for one over the sea
> And had he not come would be wearing it still,
> And therefore she gave it to me.

Berto almost certainly knew of the association of the torn veil with Consola's widowhood, but how directly the poem refers to her tragedy is not immediately apparent. The poem exemplifies the obliqueness which characterised a number of his youthful poems and which here contrives to suggest an ominous if cryptic theme.

The wedding service was conducted by Mr. Mathew, the minister of the Free Church at Haddington, who had baptised all the Graham children and who now lived in their former house, 'Craigniel', purchased by the church for the manse. Jessie's later reminiscence of the occasion conveys both the centrality of her father in her early life and the ambivalence of her feelings about religion. She regarded Mr. Mathew with awe, but even he acquired his omnipotence because, besides being the voice of God, he was her father's Minister.

> He seemed, with his large fair beard (now turning grey), so like the men in the pictures in the big Bible, men who appeared on such easy terms with God. He inspired me more with fear than with the love of God, especially as I tended to confuse him with the old doctor who, by a nasty trick as it seemed to me, had removed one of my teeth, without any warning whatever. When I used to hear about God, walking in the garden in the cool of the day, I thought of Mr. Mathew walking with my father on the lawn at Craigniel.

Edward Lascelles, who worked with Berto in the Board of Trade and had rooms in the same house in Ebury Street, was to have been their best man but at the last moment he could not be there and Harry Balfour, another friend and colleague of Berto's, took his place, making a witty speech but not reading the sheaf of telegrams which he held 'so as not to delay the departure of the bride and groom to the North Pole' - Berto and Jessie had managed to keep secret the place of their honeymoon.[35]

At the station, Jessie's friend Chrys, whom she had not been allowed to invite to the wedding, appeared with a gift of roses. But even as they set off for their secret destination, the hand, and the mind, of Consola contrived to accompany them, for they found, tied to the door of their first-class compartment, a very worn, small red shoe, the recurrent bambino theme of their house-hunting of the previous Christmas.

They abandoned their first-class dignity at Carlisle and continued their journey to London as ordinary third-class travellers in a train filled with an Easter holiday crowd. Arriving at Euston at four in the morning they packed themselves and their luggage into a growler and set out for the Paddington Station Hotel, with Berto taking up the position that was to become so familiar - leaning half-way out of the window, telling the driver he was going in the wrong direction.

They spent the next day visiting London and in particular checking progress in the decoration of their flat at Overstrand Mansions which Jessie said looked more like Penelope's sitting room, in the Maugham play of that name. Mr. 'A', the builder in charge of the alterations, 'an unprepossessing individual with a wink', who seemed to have come with the flat, could not guarantee to complete the refurbishing before their return from their honeymoon, so they decided that on their return from Devon they would stay at Berto's rooms in Ebury Street until Mr. A. and his gang were out of the Battersea flat.

That evening they went to The Playhouse Theatre where they saw part of a Pinero play from the pit - Marie Lohr looking lovely in a very tiresome part; they did not see the play out but went for a walk along the Embankment, saw Polaire dancing at the Palace and 'ended the day with a 5/- supper in the hushed luxury of the Savoy. . .'.

They left Paddington the next day in another roaring holiday crowd and eventually reached their destination, Rock House, near Thirlestone, which Berto had visited once before with a reading party from Oxford, conducted by his tutor and friend, 'Juffy' Wells (later Warden of Wadham'), to whom he wrote:

> Here 'we fleet the time carelessly as they did in the golden world.'[36]

They fleeted it now on 35/- a head, and, between the inclusive meals, walked along the beach and the cliffs from Bolt Tail to Salcombe where from the headland above Bolt Head they could look down on the estuary and out to the wide waters of the Channel. They remembered that 'The Broken Heart' in Masefield's *Captain Margaret* had set sail from here and they compared it with the sailing of the 'Hispaniola' in *Treasure Island.* They built rosy hopes for the future to which Berto's present work on the Pilotage Commission would open the door: who could say, perhaps one day a colonial governorship?

They discussed books:

> the vastness and majesty of Hardy, the wind of energy that seemed to sweep through Meredith. We would agree about Dickens and Tennyson, both of whom we admired greatly, and disagree about Wells, whom Berto admired more than I did, though we both, cool and critical, watching the sea beyond Salcombe, decided that Wells was careless about style.

And as they talked, her anxiety about managing gradually left her:

> The bustle of preparing for the wedding, the conflicting advice from all sides had died away. Everything looked so much simpler, now that we could talk about everything without anyone interfering.[37]

Berto's poem, 'Thirlestone', was published ten years later.

Berto had taken two weeks leave, and when they returned to Ebury Street from their brief honeymoon, they spent most of the remaining precious few days in furniture shops in the Tottenham Court Road, using the money given as a wedding present by Berto's elder brother, Oswald, to complete the furnishing of the flat. They had bought most of their furniture 'in the dark cavern of Blaikie's in Edinburgh' (where Jessie also found the malacca cane, price 2/-, which Berto carried for the rest of his life) but they still had to find floor coverings, curtains and easy chairs, while keeping within their spending limit of £100. By buying what the salesman diffidently called 'second quality' chairs, and 'riminants' (Consola's version of remnants) of felt to use as carpet, they managed to keep the cost to £108.

Despite the inconvenience caused by the beery Mr. A. the builder, who had ignored their wishes in the matter of colours and where the bookshelves were to be put, they managed to take possession of their new home fairly quickly, and set about making it habitable. Until the furniture arrived they lived a kind of camping life, with picnic meals eaten off the top of a packing case, but they gradually made the flat not only habitable but comfortable and a home they were proud of. They hung their prints of Whitehall and St. James in the dining room, and some of Max's caricatures in the library.

Throughout their married life the library was to be the principal room in their house, moving with them to successive addresses and accumulating books and shelves on the way. It began here in Battersea, as they unpacked their books and sat on the floor, reading to themselves or to each other, before deciding which shelf to put them on. Berto would sit on the top step of the ladder, 'reading good-bye' as he called it, to something which could be relegated to the highest shelf.

> We loved to wander down the Battersea Park Road in the evenings when the flares were lit, from the fish and chip shop near the station, past the fruit and vegetable stalls . . . down to the busiest corner of the Latchmere Road, where the butchers stood outside on the pavement, chanting their staccato cry of 'Buy! Buy! Buy!'[38]

Their first visitor was Edward Lascelles, who came to tea on the first Sunday after their flat was in order. His fiancée, Leila Kennett-Barrington, had given them a little Wedgwood vase as a wedding present, but Jessie was not destined to meet her until a disastrous day ten months later.

They had decided that they should hold some 'At Home' days, and cards had been sent out announcing that Mr. and Mrs. Umberto Wolff would be At Home at 16 Overstrand Mansions on the 1st and 2nd of June. Towards the end of April Jessie's mother came to spend a fortnight with them, helping to make curtains and chair covers and generally get the flat as comfortable as possible. At the end of the second week Consola's sister, Rosetta, arrived on her way back from Belgium. She too suffered from deafness. Edward VII had just died (6 May, 1910) and on the morning of Rosetta's arrival his body was to be taken to lie in state at

Westminster. Berto, Jessie and Mrs. Graham were going to the Board of Trade to see the funeral cortège pass down Whitehall and thought that Rosetta might like to go with them. She was only half-pleased. Glad though she was to see them and the flat, she was very much concerned to use a bus-ticket which was included in her fare to and from Bradford, for a station bus from Victoria to 'San Pan Crass', and 'the passing of the King's funeral procession was a tiresome interruption of this delightful plan.'

At the Board of Trade they met Berto's chief, Garnham Roper, and his wife and little boys. From his magnificent office, which seemed far removed in every respect from Berto's modest room in Whitehall Gardens, they had a good view of the procession but were somewhat distracted by Rosetta's vehement and unceasing monologue on the subject of her bus-ticket. Their last sight of her was in Whitehall, brandishing her ear-trumpet in protest against entering the taxi which Berto had called, and calling him a 'spindriff' for not allowing her to go back to Victoria (crowd notwithstanding) to make use of her bus-ticket, which was now going to be wasted.

Jessie's mother duly returned to Edinburgh and shortly after that Berto's sister Rita arrived to stay with them on her way back from Liège. Jessie always thought Rita more like Berto than any of the rest of his family: physically a kind of pocket edition of him and in character possessing his gentler traits. Jessie had been upset at not being included in an invitation to a dance in Bradford which Rita had contrived to get for Berto during their engagement. She now hoped that the visit might restore confidence between them, and was encouraged by Rita's friendliness on her arriving at the Battersea flat.

Unfortunately Rita could not stay for the Days At Home but Jessie's younger sister Annie arrived a day or two before 1 June and together they made ready to receive Berto's friends. Cards had been sent to friends everywhere but they expected visits chiefly from the two or three dozen people in or near London whom Berto had invited.

1 June was a perfect summer day and Berto went off as usual to Whitehall, hoping to get back before everyone had gone. Jessie, for her part, simply hoped that the visitors would not all come on the first day. The invitation was for tea-time and the little dining-room was all set out, the pretty silver baskets they had been given as presents were filled with cakes and sandwiches and little rolls, and the beautiful silver tulip from Berto's philosophy tutor Drewitt was full of flowers. (On the card which accompanied the present, Drewitt had written "And so he married the Princess.")

Four o'clock passed, and half-past, and five, and no one came. Finally the bell rang and a visitor was announced. It was the wife of a man Berto had known slightly at Oxford; the couple now lived in the top floor flat above Berto and Jessie. The lady did not stay long, and she was the only person who turned up.

When Berto came home he was bitterly disappointed that none of his friends had come. The trio from St. George's Square with whom Berto had lived for a time (Harry Balfour their best man, George Chrystal and Philip Lloyd-Green) kept their promise to come for coffee after dinner, and the evening ended on a slightly more cheerful note. Lloyd-Green, later Lord Linten, invited them to come on a picnic one evening in his car.

Berto was relieved that his sister Rita had not been there to witness their humiliation and report on it to Consola. He promptly sat down to write to his mother, telling her of the throng of friends they had received. But Jessie later wrote that 'these ghostly visitors who only existed on paper were yet to do us an injury.'

Jessie prepared more cautiously for the second day and this time the bell did ring earlier and a few friends called, including Berto's old school-friend and future brother-in-law Archie Hamilton who was then Resident Medical Officer at the Women's Hospital in Chelsea. They spent a happy evening together and so the ordeal ended.

But not for Berto. He bitterly resented the humiliating discovery that people he had thought of as friends, and friends who had been pleased to know him, did not consider it worth their while to come and see his wife. And then to cap it all, a note arrived for Jessie from Will Rothenstein, who at that time lived in Hampstead, asking them to excuse him and his wife for not coming to call as the distance from Hampstead to Battersea was so great, but asking Berto and Jessie to go and sup with them instead. Unfortunately on the date he suggested they were already committed to dining with Sir Alfred Bateman, the chairman of the Pilotage Commission on which Berto worked.

Berto in any case was furious with the Rothensteins and wanted to pen a reply on the lines of the famous reply of Robert Burns to a similar rebuff, in which Burns pointed out that the distance from Lavender Hill to Mayfair was as great as that from Mayfair to Lavender Hill (which happened to be no more than a mile from Prince of Wales Drive). Jessie managed to dissuade him but, even so, the reasonable answer which she produced to Will's note evidently gave offence and was reported to Bradford, resulting in much trouble a few months later.

Berto blamed the fiasco on their being on the wrong side of the river, but they were determined not to let it spoil their lives. The people who had stayed away were of so little importance, compared with their importance to one another.

IV

1910 - 1911

Their life acquired a routine, comfortable and pleasant to follow. On April 1, 1911, Berto's salarty had risen to £220 per annum and their budget provided for a good breakfast and an evening meal. Berto would lunch out, at Lyons with Aylmer Digby, Secretary of the Pilotage Commission, or with Harry Balfour at Eustace Miles (a vegetarian restaurant) or the Saville, paying turn about. Occasionally he went to the National Liberal Club as the guest of another Civil Servant, an Irishman whose invitation, said Berto, was given in the words:- "Come and let me drive a shteak into your middle."

Berto had begun to write in the evenings and, as the days grew longer and warmer and the French windows stood open on their garden and the trees of the park, he would sit at a table by the light of a green-shaded lamp, writing his first novel, *Utopia*, which was never published, and sometimes poems, which were published ten years later in *London Sonnets*, in which the fried fish shop, the bun shop, and other familiar sights of their everyday lives had their place.

In the last lines of The Fried Fish Shop -

> But wanting won't mend 'oles up in your socks
> Nor cure that 'ungry feeling when you stands
> Clappin' your stummick with your empty 'ands
> And thinking gently of a wooden box,
> Where they will lay you at the parish charge
> Straight if you're small and doubled if you're large -

'there is', he wrote in the Preface to the 1930 re-issue, 'something that was pleading for the uses of satire long before I had begun to believe in that mode as one of the redemptions of the world.'

On evenings when Berto did not want to write, they would go for a walk, or to gallery-seats at some theatre; occasionally they had visitors after dinner. On Sundays some of Berto's men-friends might come to tea, or he and Jessie would go for a walk over Box Hill, or Ranmoor Common, or in Epping Forest.

Later in June the Pilotage Commission had to meet its French counterpart in Paris and Berto was appointed Secretary for the occasion. The dramatized and probably embellished account of this first visit to Paris which Humbert gave in 1934 in *Portraits By Inference* differs in a number of points from Jessie's account, but principally in omitting the fact that she went with him. At first it seemed that she must stay behind, much to their disappointment since the secretary of another Commission which went to Paris about that time had managed to take his new young wife with him.[39] To keep Jessie company during Berto's absence, Jessie's sister Annie, who had been staying with them, agreed to prolong her visit.

Berto had bought tickets for a fancy-dress Ball, the Red Devil in the Botanic Gardens, and had asked Victor Fox and Harry Balfour to go with them. He reassured Jessie that he would be back from Paris in time to take her to the Ball and so it turned out. He returned by the night boat, having to take a report to Sir Hubert Llewellyn Smith, the senior Civil Servant at the Board of Trade, who was away in the country.

He also brought back the news that he had to go back to Paris and could take Jessie with him. He had discovered a small unused room in the suite occupied by the Commission which they could have at no cost to the Commission or themselves. He speedily completed his civil service tasks and, after a little dinner party, they all set off for the Ball. Berto, in a dove-coloured suit and flowered waistcoat, with his trousers strapped under his boots and an enormous light beaver hat on his head, looked like someone out of *Pride and Prejudice*. Jessie went in a black evening-dress, with a red ribbon round her hair and her throat, and said she was an Apache.

As if in a vast Midsummer Night's Dream they danced until dawn. They saw Albert Rutherston for the first time since the pre-wedding party in Bradford. Somerset Maugham was there too. They did not meet him, although Jessie and Victor danced after him for a long time in an unsuccessful effort to catch up with him, and his scarlet pierrette partner, whom Victor Fox wanted to wrest from him.

Next morning Annie went back to Scotland. Jessie met Berto at Charing Cross early in the afternoon and by evening they were in Paris on their second honeymoon. It was Jessie's first trip to Paris and to be making it with Berto was pure enchantment. The Hotel Vouillemont, where the Commission was meeting, in the rue Boissy d'Anglas near the Place de la Concorde, was itself a new and delightful experience, with its rooms all looking on to an open central courtyard, with the café complet, rolls and honey which they had in bed, and most of all the mysteriously controlled front door which opened noiselessly to their ring, like the door to Aladdin's cave.

While Berto worked in the Commission, Jessie found her way to the shops in the Rue de Rivoli to buy presents for her sister and for Consola. She did not buy a hat, although everyone, including Berto, seemed to think she should, and the women in Paris all seemed to wear hats, very large hats, all day and most of the night. She braved the fiacres in the Place de la Concorde, where Alsace and Lorraine still wore their mourning crêpe, in order to walk across the river and browse among the bookstalls on the Left Bank. She sat in the Luxembourg Gardens, waiting for Berto to join her, and together they visited Napoleon's tomb. Thanks to the hospitality of Sir Alfred Bateman and the other members of the Commission they were able to save their money for extras, like the seats for Rostand's *Chanteclair* at the Porte Saint-Martin, which left them a little sad, and *La Dame de Chez Maxim*, which seemed to them to have the same deathless appeal in Paris as *Charlie's Aunt* had in England.

The Commission went back to London, leaving Berto to get the report typed, and then the week-end was theirs to do as they pleased. They decided to sample something of Parisian night-life. Berto had a list of things and places to visit: the Moulin Rouge, the can-can at the Bal

Tabarin, which they found silly, then the Rat Mort, a little restaurant on an upper floor. much as they might have found in Soho. They saw a man from the Treasury there, whom Berto knew slightly but who plainly did not want to be recognised. Maxim's was last on their list and to avoid having to eat another meal they simply pretended to be looking for someone - as, apparently, were a number of large-hatted ladies, and others who had found someone and were sitting at tables with gentlemen and bottles of champagne.

They left the hot, airless place. It was nearly dawn and they hired a fiacre to take them through the Bois and back to the Vouillemont. The next day was their last and as they were to sail on the night-boat they spent the day at Versailles, returning to Paris by tram. At Berto's suggestion, to keep her from falling asleep, Jessie smoked a cigarette, to the accompaniment of shocked comments at her abandoned behaviour from some Americans. The sea was like glass on the return journey and they sat on the deck, wrapped in rugs, in the clear starry night, talking of Paris and feeling very happy.[40]

Other delightful things happened: Berto's friend Michel Salaman and his wife gave them a wedding present of Wedgwood china and invited them to go and stay with them in Somerset in August. Life seemed so perfect that they felt they ought to invite Consola to stay. Her birthday was approaching and she was sure to want to see the flat. The fateful telegram was sent.

As Jessie described it, Consola's visit was like a developing thunder storm, beginning with distant rumblings which a practised observer might have recognised, and steadily growing, though not in a noticeably direct progression, until it burst with a fury which took them by surprise, and was only calmed by an equally heart-stopping intervention - rather as one fire may sometimes be extinguished only by another.

Berto's elder sister, Fanny, had become engaged to Cyril Heron who was working in London at the time of Consola's visit and who came to lunch either by invitation or by summons, to be catechized by Consola about his and Fanny's financial future. Consola compiled 'boodjas' for them, as she had done for Berto and Jessie, and by the time he left she was clearly simmering with anger.

It soon became apparent that she felt slighted and saw Jessie as the cause: Jessie's sister had not taken up her invitation to stay with her in Bradford; Jessie's mother, not Consola, had been invited to come and arrange the flat; the Rothenstein parents had been offended that Jessie had refused to go and meet them. Jessie and Berto knew that these were all distortions which could be easily explained, or pure inventions which it suited Consola to believe. But when Berto protested at her calling Jessie a fool her pent-up fury could not be contained. She banged the table, making the coffee-cups jump in their saucers, and screamed at him:

> May I not say what I please, do what I please in my own house? Is this not my own house, when I pay the rent?

When Jessie asked what she meant she could only repeat:-

> It is my house, I tell you, and I shall say in it what I please.

The money for the rent had been lent against Berto's interest in the Wolff trust, and was to be repaid out of his part of the estate, when it was divided, in a few months' time. It followed that it was his money, and his house.

Jessie was so distressed that she left Berto and Consola to their shouting and immediately set about packing her bags to go back to her father and get him to speak to Consola. But the voices followed her and, as her mind went endlessly over the arguments and accusations, she heard Berto shouting to his mother:- 'I tell you, Jessie is going to have a child!'

This was not how Jessie had planned to tell her the news. It was to be her real birthday present, not just the chocolates they had brought back from Paris, which Consola had found so offensive. Jessie determined not to let Consola spoil their marriage or herself be the cause of a break between Berto and his mother. Consola came with Berto to make her peace. Jessie felt sorry for her: how awful to be deaf, and suspicious, and jealous. Berto explained that he had had to tell his mother the news: it was the only way of stopping her tirade. And Consola's rages were legendary, both in their strength and their fugacity. Jessie said that she supposed that she might be regarded as one of the family now, although it felt like baptism by thunderbolt.

They had several times been invited to visit the Salamans at Porlock but put off accepting because of the expense and Jessie's pregnancy. They were in any case committed to a holiday with Jessie's family in the West Highlands later and, in spite of the row, to visit Consola in Bradford. But they had heard so much from Albert Rutherston about the Salamans' magnificent home at Doverhay Place that the discovery of a cheap excursion fare to Minehead for a few shillings seemed too good to miss. As they left for Paddington, Berto said:

> The hotel at 16 Overstrand Mansions is now closed for the season.

Despite a hide-and-seek journey to avoid arriving ahead of the the Salamans who were travelling down from London at the same time, they still managed to be on the platform at Minehead to meet their hosts, Michel - 'little, round, red-haired, with his rather charming, lisping voice' - and his lovely wife, Chattie, and their three children. Jessie said that the house at Porlock was the most beautifully furnished and decorated that either of them had ever seen, and the Salamans the most perfect hosts, whose delight was to entertain their friends, rich or poor, and to do so perfectly by giving them the freedom to entertain themselves and treat the house as their own.

'Wonderful meals appeared whenever a company of diners was ready to consume them. They even offered us the use of the horses in their stables, and I nervously listened while Berto was being tempted to ride something, and accompany Michel on a visit to the kennels.' Knowing something of Berto's past misadventures with horses in Manningham Park, Jessie was relieved to hear him decline, but on another day he did accept the offer of a horse and trap in which to drive to the Meet on Exmoor. The horse (which had been ridden regularly to hounds and only recently had to suffer the indignity of the trap) was docile enough, until they met the hounds. At the sight of them it flew into the middle of the pack, and out again, dashed madly around and finally crashed the trap in a ditch, upending both Berto and Jessie, whereupon it calmed down and sedately conveyed them back up the hill to Doverhay.

They went to the horse-show at Dunster Castle and to the Ball at Minehead, their return journey through the warm night enhanced by the presence of a hare which was caught in the light of the headlamps and ran steadily before them all the way back to Porlock, as it did, Jessie was told, on two succeeeding journeys to and from Minehead. Finally, as if they had not accumulated sufficient incident to stock Berto's store of tall tales, on the last night of their stay the chimney caught fire. Fearing for the thatched roof, the men set off to get out the fire-hose. By the time it was unrolled, and everyone and everything except the thatch had been more or less soaked, the sparks which caused the alarm had ceased to fly from the chimney, but the whole experience was thought to have been 'a good thing, because at least it showed the hose was in working order,' and they all went to bed, damp but satisfied.[41]

As Berto and Jessie made their way to Bradford the next day they discussed what it must be like to be rich like the Salamans, so rich that they did not need to bother about it, and yet managed not to make other people feel poor. The easy friendliness of their hosts contrasted sharply with the convention-bound families of Bradford and made Jessie all the more anxious to meet Berto's other friends, such as the members of the Friday Club, who might not be as wealthy but had the same attitude to life.

At Bradford it seemed as though Berto had been right, when he said that rows in his family came and passed and were completely forgotten. Nothing happened to ruffle the peace of their visit and at the end of it they went on to a peaceful fortnight's holiday at Clynder, on Gare Loch, where the Graham parents had taken a cottage.

Back in London - it was now well into September - they decided to buy a dog and find a servant to live in for the winter. On the recommendation of the Salamans they went to the Battersea Dogs Home and for 5/- bought a wire-haired fox-terrier called Dusty - 'too pretty to be very good' in Jessie's down-to-earth judgement. The servant was less easy to find but eventually they found one who resembled the Wolff family's nurse if only in name - Clara - and in her violent temper. After two o'clock, according to Jessie, she was all that a maid should be with her neat bright-coloured appearance, but before that, 'in carpet slippers tied on with string, an apron made out of a potato sack, her head tied up in an old duster, and her false teeth carefully laid aside till she was dressed, she looked terrible.' But she was clever at housework and Jessie taught her enough cooking to ensure that Berto got an evening meal if Jessie were unable to prepare one.

The weather continued fine and they still went out to walk in the woods and over the hills around Leatherhead and Box Hill at the week-ends. Old Mr. Coxhead, who had proposed Berto for confirmation, invited them to dinner to meet his niece who was engaged to Frank Sidgwick.[42] He also introduced them to the Ishmaelite Club, a literary and debating society, which held its meetings in the houses of its members. Papers were read and debated, and there was a cold supper, supposed to consist only of food that did not need forks and knives to eat it with, although there was an occasion, in a mansion in Bryanston Square, where turkey, trifle and champagne were served by powdered footmen, 'and,' said Jessie, 'so far as I could see, none of the members of the society objected.'

The Clive Bells invited them to dinner but in the event Berto had to go alone and Jessie never met them. Nearly every week Berto would say: 'Lascelles is going to bring his young woman this Sunday', and often they would alter their plans for the week-end, and go for their walks on Saturday afternoon so as to be sure to be in on Sunday, in case the couple came to tea. But though he came frequently, he always came alone, and each time, when he had gone, Berto explained to Jessie what a mistake it had been to take the flat in Battersea, and particularly when they learned that the Edwardes Square house had had a reprieve.

It was not only being south of the river that he found irksome, or the tiresome trains, or the smelly tram full of the unwashed - it was Whitehall and the Board of Trade and the people there he found difficult to put up with. There was one man in particular who had come up 'through the ranks', so to speak, and had reached a position of authority over the young men down from the Universities who had entered the Civil Service by examination. He saw to it that those who had enjoyed this advantage were not allowed to enjoy anything else easily while under his domination. And of all the young men he had to deal with, Berto was the greatest shock to him.

It was largely in order to give a good impression to this ogre and to the Board of Trade generally that Berto had chosen his lodgings carefully, forsaking Albert's studio and the purlieus of Soho for more decorous and sober addresses. Had Battersea been lodgings instead of a flat they would have left it then, but they were nailed in with their 'riminants' and their bookshelves, and had to make the best of it. And despite his feelings about the wrong side of the river, Berto was proud of his house. He would say to Jessie that his dim little room in 7 Whitehall Gardens looking on to Horse Guards Avenue, and the two foot square of carpet under the knee-hole of his desk, were not worthy of 16 Overstrand.

Towards the end of January 1911 his elder brother Oswald arrived from Hamburg for the wedding of Fanny Wolff to Cyril Heron. The terms of Martin Wolff's will left the bulk of his not inconsiderable estate (over £22,000 in 1894) in trust, to be shared equally among his children when the youngest reached her majority, which happened to be in December 1910. They could, however, 'apply for their share for their advancement as the trustees shall see fit', and some allowance was made for the possible need to provide for grandchildren. Whether the legacy for which Berto required his birth certificate in 1909 was part or all of his share of the inheritance, the terms of the marriage settlement which he agreed with Mr. Graham make it plain that he had not yet received it.[43]

> The time for the dividing up of trust-money had come at Christmas . . Oswald explained that it was thought better that the money should remain in a trust, and only the income be paid out to each of the family. "It will be better for Bugs to have the income only - he'd soon waste the capital." I was surprised. Berto had said he meant to invest the money, and settle it on me and the child. But he said nothing of the kind to Oswald.[44]

Berto seemed to have let himself be persuaded that the income from the trust would be larger than it would be if the money were divided, and told Jessie 'that he would have the right to obtain some capital, if he urgently required it at any time.'

They continued to prepare for the arrival of what he called The Wolverine, expected at the end of February or early March. Jessie made clothes and trimmed a cot, and turned the unused fourth bed-room into a nursery. But her feeling of being on probation with all her new acquaintance, and what seemed to her the contemptuous and critical attitude of her in-laws, was heightened by the absence of any intimate women friends at this period. The unexpected visit of an old friend of her mother's brought something of the warm, friendly atmosphere of Edinburgh for which she had been more homesick than she realised. In the succeeding days, until Jessie's mother arrived, shortly before the baby's birth, this lady called to see her often and cheered her up considerably.

Her mother thought the nurse should be in the house but the doctor said there was no need for at least a fortnight. On the evening of the fourth of March Jessie had gone for her usual evening stroll with Berto after dinner, along Prince of Wales Road, across Chelsea Bridge, along the embankment and back by Albert Bridge. She felt untired and untirable but went to bed about eleven.

Early the next morning she felt slight pain and Berto was sent to telephone for the doctor and the nurse. The doctor took his time and the nurse who eventually arrived was not the one Jessie had engaged but a young nurse without experience. Long before the doctor came the baby was born - a big boy, with dark hair and long eye-lashes, looking like Jessie when she was a baby, but with Berto's dimple in his chin.

But the baby made no sound, even when the nurse slapped him. When the doctor finally came, at nine, the nurse told him that it had been a breech-birth and that the baby had never breathed. The doctor said there was nothing he could have done even if he had got there sooner but Jessie was not to be comforted. Berto said to her: 'Don't be too unhappy, he'll come again when he thinks we can look after him better.'

He wired the sad news to Consola, and Fanny, informed by her, came with one of her sisters to enquire. On the door-step they met Edward Lascelles and with him, at last, his fiancée, Miss Leila Kennett-Barrington. At least, said Berto, now his sisters would never know that it was the first time he had brought her.

The death of their first-born is referred to twice in *London Sonnets*: first in the third section of 'Sometimes when I think of love':-

> Sometimes when I think of love
> I hear a heavy voice repeat
> "There's a good doctor up the street."
> . . . .
> . . . Has love in the darkness heard
> Of the little lost shadow, the small lost third?[45]

and later, in the third of 'Three Epitaphs', a poem entitled 'The Little Sleeper':

> This little sleeper, who was overtaken
> By death, as one child overtakes another,
> Dreams by his side all night and will not waken
> Till the dawn comes in heaven with his mother.[46]

1. The Hollow by Albert Rutherston (in *Cursory Rhymes*, 1927). The figures in the foreground are recognisably Rutherston (on the left) and Humbert (with hat). The stylised background of Mount Royd houses and mill chimneys shows a degree of artistic licence

2. No.4 Mount Royd (the right-hand one of the two semi-detached villas) in 1986. The houses have changed little in the last hundred years (*photograph by the author*)

3. (Above) The Wolff family c.1890: L to R, standing, Oswald and Martin Wolff; seated, Consola, Sylvia, Rita, Fanny and Umberto

4. (Right) The Lord Mayor's Children's Party c.1890: Berto as a Neapolitan fisher-boy, Fanny a "vivandière", and Oswald as Garibaldi (*see p.17*)

5. Consola and Berto c.1900

6. Humbert and Jessie on their wedding day, 29 March 1910

Chapter Five

1912-1919

'The astonishments of war'
(Labour Supply and Regulation)

I

(i)

Labour Exchanges

The records of the Board of Trade indicate that Berto was originally appointed to the staff of the Harbour Department in 1908. It is equally clear from *Portraits By Inference* that in 1911 he was still working in the Harbour Department, under Assistant Secretary the Hon. Thomas Henry William Pelham, son of the 3rd Earl of Chichester. Apart from the brief and unusual excitement of Berto's special appointment to the Secretaryship of the Anglo-French Pilotage Committee, requiring his two visits to Paris (already mentioned in Chapter 4), his main work at No. 7 Whitehall Gardens was the much less exciting task of collating information, providing statistics, and generally contributing to the drafting of the Port of London Bill.

The traditional role of the Board of Trade was essentially to furnish the Government with statistical information and advice on matters of trade and commerce. The 'strong and flourishing tradition of administrative initiative, of inventiveness, drive, innovation,' described by Caldwell,[1] may have been evident in the senior officials but it was unlikely to be strongly encouraged in relative juniors such as Berto. And it was against this irksome frustration of his imaginative and enterprising instincts that Berto chafed. His mounting dissatisfaction with his position in the Harbour Department may well have been a powerful factor in persuading him to accept the offer of an exciting if somewhat risky opening in William Beveridge's newly formed Labour Exchanges Department.

The history of the legislation which created the Trade Boards, the Labour Exchanges, and Unemployment Insurance is already massively documented; but the resultant expansion of the Board of Trade, and its monopoly, until the First World War, of the 'formulation, initiation and execution of labour policy' had a direct bearing on Berto's Civil Service career and therefore on the whole of his life, both professional and personal.[2]

Whatever the biographies and autobiographies of Winston Churchill, Lloyd George, the Webbs, Lord Beveridge and others may suggest to the contrary, the inception of social security in Britain at the beginning of the twentieth century was clearly not the emanation of a single brain. The government ministers, particularly Lloyd George and Churchill, were responsible, necessarily, for implementing if not for initiating the legislative measures, but the pressure for legislation came from a rising tide of concern over the condition of the working classes. R. Davidson has eloquently described the intellectual ferment in the Oxford of the 1880s, and the emergence therefrom of a generation of immensely able public servants deeply committed to public action in the face of 'sensational exposés of urban squalor.' Toynbee Hall, the concrete expresssion of the Oxford University Settlement Movement, was to become a hot-house of leading administrators, among whom were Hubert Llewellyn Smith, first Commissioner for Labour in the Board of Trade and subsequently Permanent Secretary of the Board, and William Beveridge, the first Director of Labour Exchanges, while 'another prolific field of apprenticeship for future office, the Oxford University Extension Movement, was making spectacular headway.'[3]

The ability and initiative of the official personnel recruited to the Labour Department of the Board of Trade were to have important consequences not only for their own Ministry but for the future social administration of the country. Thanks to a clause in the 1859 Superannuation Act, Llewellyn Smith and a number of his staff were appointed at an age exceeding that at which public service ordinarily began; in consequence, 'he had at his disposal. . . specialists with reputations as economists and statisticians who were recognizedly influential in labour circles before their appointment.'[4] Furthermore their branch of the Board of Trade enjoyed a number of features which made for administrative vitality: separated, like the Patent Office, from the Board proper they were spared its tendency to excessive formalization while enjoying access to its statistical resources and expertise, with the added opportunity for helping to formulate policy.[5]

The legislative success of Ministers (and often therefore their subsequent elevation to posts with substantially greater emoluments) owed much to the enterprise and efficiency of the permanent officials. For, paradoxically, the Minister at the head of this large, influential and continually expanding department was paid less than half the salary of any of the Secretaries of State. This, as Lord Beveridge later pointed out, led to relatively brief ministerial tenancies and so to the proportionately greater influence of the officials, particularly the Permanent Secretary. 'In my first six years at the Board,' wrote Beveridge, 'we had four different Presidents. . . It was natural that at times we should regard ourselves as the Board, and our Ministers as perhaps pleasant but certainly transient and occasionally embarrassing phantoms.'[6]

In the same month of 1908 that Berto was appointed to his clerkship in the Board of Trade, Winston Churchill became its President in the new Asquith government. He had already become increasingly interested in radical social reform while Under-Secretary of State for the Colonies. In particular he envisaged a system whereby those seeking work could find it, and employers seeking labourers could find them. Surplus of labour in one area might coincide with scarcity in another: Labour Exchanges would help to remedy this lack of balance.[7]

Churchill worked on his plan for Labour Exchanges during the summer of 1908. Through Sidney Webb, who thought the plan 'a quite admirable statement', Churchill made contact with William Beveridge, then a young journalist and lecturer much concerned with questions of social reform. Beveridge was brought into the Board of Trade to set up a new department in order 'to establish and manage National Labour Exchanges, with Unemployment Insurance in prospect.' Once the Labour Exchanges Bill became law in 1909, Beveridge became officially Director of Labour Exchanges at a salary of £700 per annum, rising to £900. C. F. Rey, then private secretary to Hubert Llewellyn Smith, the Permanent Secretary of the Board, became General Manager at £600 rising to £800. Basil Blackwood, son of the Marquess of Dufferin and Ava, became Assistant General Manager.[8]

For the other Head Office staff, Beveridge was allowed to select from the Board of Trade in general three upper division Civil Servants of exceptional ability. Berto was judged to be one such. The offer of an opening in Beveridge's 'uncertain adventure' was exciting. It was risky, of course, but the combination of an improved salary and the chance of escape from an atmosphere which he felt to be oppressive and stifling must have been powerfully persuasive. The two who went with him were Stephen Tallents and Thomas Phillips.

> Each of these, in coming to us, [wrote Lord Beveridge] gave up his place in the Board of Trade hierarchy, with the prospect of regular promotion there, in order to get an immediate rise of pay and to chance his arm with our new venture. They were a strong trio, each with a special gift added to general ability. Tallents was best of the three in judgement, Wolff in speed, Phillips in accuracy and mastery of detail.[9]

The Central Office was established at Caxton House, Westminster, but premises had to be found for the exchanges, and Beveridge and Rey spent a lot of time and energy 'combating the desire of H.M. Office of Works to place our exchanges in those parts of industrial towns which had the least savoury reputation.' On 1 February 1910, sixty-one exchanges opened their doors. A further eighty-seven were up and running by the end of the year. By the time unemployment insurance became a reality at the end of 1912 there were 414 exchanges and 1,000 local offices of the fund.

Although Lord Beveridge's account suggests that Berto joined the new department at its inception, it is clear that Berto was first appointed to it as Chief of Section on 24 August, 1912, at a salary of £500 rising to £600. Humbert's explanation, in *Labour Supply And Regulation* (1923), of the origins of the Labour Exchanges department accounts for the apparent discrepancy. It began, he said,

> as a branch of the main Labour Department (of the Board of Trade) to administer the Labour Exchanges Act of 1908. When the Insurance Act of 1911 was passed, Part II provided a system of unemployment insurance for a limited number of trades. The essential underlying feature of unemployment insurance was that benefit would only be payable to insured persons if they were willing and unable to find suitable employment. The only test of such willingness and inability was provided by the Labour Exchange, and accordingly the administration of Part II of the new Act was added to the duties of the Labour Exchanges Department, which thereupon became a separate Department of the Board of Trade.

Consola seems to have viewed this move unfavourably and expressed her disapproval in a telegram couched in her own highly individual form of English; it ended: 'GOD WILL BE DONE.' The reluctant acceptance of the inevitable suggested if not clearly expressed by this pious sentiment contrasted strongly with Consola's habitual reaction to decisions which diverged from hers.

As Lord Beveridge made clear in *Power and Influence*, the nature of this new department was such that existing criteria and procedures, both for appointing staff and for operating the exchanges, were almost entirely unapplicable. As a national, uniform system for administering insurance they unavoidably came directly under the Board of Trade, but their work required a greater degree of flexibility and humanity than, for example, Post Offices, and local officers had to be able to adjust the scheme to meet local conditions. There can be no doubt that the excitement and enthusiasm which this new departure engendered in its staff derived in great measure from the challenge of sheer novelty: there were no precedents at all, and consequently an unusual degree of direct responsibility was placed on the civil servants taking part in it, compared for example with compulsory health insurance, which was launched at the same time. Such a challenge would undoubtedly appeal to Berto and it seems probable that he acquired here both the skill and the taste for doing things his own way which he was to deploy to such good effect later.[10]

Doubtless the higher salary scale to which he was promoted on 10 April 1913 reflected his increased responsibilities within this enlarged Labour Exchanges and Unemployment Insurance Branch.

He may, nevertheless, have been hard pressed to decide which was more exciting at this time, his career or his domestic life, for on 14 August 1913, Jessie gave birth to their second child, Ann. She was to transform their lives in ways they could never have foreseen. Ann was a fine, healthy child, who gave both of them immense delight and comfort. Some of Humbert's best verse was inspired by and written for her. One cloud only marred the otherwise clear skies: she was born with a cleft palate and a hare lip. At two weeks old she had undergone the first of the long series of operations which punctuated her early life. Plastic surgery was then at a very experimental stage, and this first operation, although effecting a partial cure, caused the later operations to be more difficult and more numerous. But in 1913 neither Jessie nor Berto could have any inkling of the effect this affliction was to have, both on Ann's future and on their own.

Of the period between the death of their first-born and the birth of Ann very little record has survived. Although the Preface to the re-issue of *London Sonnets* in 1930 implied that most of the poems in it were written while they were living in Battersea, there is no means of knowing precisely how long they stayed there. By the beginning of 1914 they had moved from Battersea to No. 8 Neville Street, off the Fulham Road, as is evident from the description of domestic bliss given in the Preface to *A Winter Miscellany* and Chapter VII of *Portraits By Inference.*[11] *London Sonnets*, published in 1920, supplies some indirect light, while Jessie's recollections, written after her husband's death, and Ann's memories of her childhood, give a few pictures, like still photographs, of some of the typical and habitual aspects of their life (see earlier Chapter 4) - for example, their habit of meeting at midday on Saturdays when Berto finished work, to go off to the country; Jessie would wait for him by the lions in Trafalgar Square, or meet him at the entrance to the Board of Trade. Friends they had made in London would sometimes accompany them on these outings, Naomi Royde-Smith, for example, and Rose Macaulay. On one of these picnics Jessie revealed a superstitious side of her nature - perhaps the Scot in her - for upon observing that the party numbered thirteen, she insisted on sitting apart from the rest as a precaution against bad luck. Both she and Berto adored the theatre and the opera, and even before their marriage they had been devotees of the cinema. During their Battersea days they became balletomanes, too. They saw Nijinsky's historic performance in *Le Spectre de la Rose*, Jessie ever after insisting that he really did *hover* at the apogee of his famous leap.

During this period Berto wrote his first - perhaps his only - novel which was never published and seems to have been lost. Ann said that it was based on the life of Jessie's friend Chrys, whose tragic story has already been touched upon (see Chapter 4 above). He also became for a short time the theatre critic of a newspaper (alas, unidentified). If, as frequently happened, he found the play particularly dull, he would enliven his review with pen-pictures of people in the audience. When a reader wrote in to admire Mr Wolff's psychic powers - two of the people he claimed to have seen had been dead for some time - this budding journalistic career was abruptly terminated.

(ii)

War

The Labour Exchanges were to prove their usefulness as the prospect of war increased. As part of the War Book planning they had been used to collect returns from firms on the numbers and types of persons in their employ. In order to help the prompt dispatch of the Expeditionary Force, saddlers, blacksmiths and men in some other selected trades in Midlands and Western towns were marked down, to be sent converging on Aldershot on receipt of the starting telegrams. The Admiralty in similar fashion wanted shipyard workers to be sent to dockyards to complete the building of ships and to repair war damage.

Berto, as the headquarters officer in charge of the Expeditionary Force scheme, was to start the clock on a message from the War Office. In *Portraits By Inference* he described how on 3 August 1914, he was recalled to London from Frinton - under - Sea where he was on holiday with Jessie and their little daughter Ann. He said that the hired car in which he travelled 'had cost £5 10s., paid out of cash lying at the Paymaster-General's Office out of the total of £20 upon which Great Britain started upon the war.' He went on to describe the mood of excitement which swept the country on a tidal wave of enthusiasm for war in the first days of August 1914. It is, therefore, all the more astonishing that he kept silent about his own part in events, which he could justifiably have retailed under the title: 'How I nearly started World War I a day early.'

About mid-day on 3 August he had telephoned his opposite number at the War Office for instructions and had been told to 'carry on.' He interpreted this as confirmation that the telegrams for action should be sent out: the War was on. He rushed excitedly to tell Beveridge, who said that if that was indeed what the message meant he should proceed. But on his way to lunch Beveridge bethought himself that 'carry on' could have other meanings and so telephoned Berto from his club and told him to find out exactly what the War Office meant by the phrase. As he had suspected, it meant in this instance "stand by": Berto had all but started the War, as far as it concerned their department, a day too soon.[12]

The Labour Exchanges Department was to play an even more important role in the subsequent conduct of the War. Numerous published studies of the people and the events of the period testify to this, as does Humbert's own account, *Labour Supply and Regulation*, to which Cameron Hazlehurst paid tribute in his Preface to the *History of the Ministry of Munitions* (HMSO): ". . . earlier studies - especially those by A. L. Bowley, G. D. H. Cole, and Humbert Wolfe - in the series on the 'Economic and Social History of the World War'. . . have not been superseded."

Humbert's book began unequivocally: 'The labour problem for a State compelled to throw the whole of its resources into the conduct of a war is, in the phrase that gained currency during the late war, the problem of man-power. . . which, if the war is prolonged, is ultimately the problem of making one man or woman do the work of one and a quarter or even of one and a half.'

He then identified four simultaneous needs: a sufficient supply of fighting men; sufficient men and women at home to equip, clothe and feed the fighting services; a sufficient labour force to provide the necessities of the civilian population; and finally a sufficient labour force to maintain the export trades of the country at the highest possible level in order to offset the strain on the country's financial resources and its international credit. Meeting these needs was made more difficult because war makes greater demands on the total production of the country than peace time, and the difficulties were further exacerbated by interruption, through blockade and siege, of the normal sources of supply of raw materials, manufactured goods and, above all, food.

If one disregarded the actual facts of each nation's situation, he went on, the ideal method of solving the problem 'would be first to decide the proportion to be allocated respectively as between the combatant forces and the civilian workers,' and then to impose upon the latter measures of central state direction and control draconian in their rigour. 'That is the ideal attainable in the absolute form only in the words of Aristotle when the material to be handled is not man but ἢ θηρίον ἢ θεός' (that is, either below or above the nature of man). It also implied 'a central State machine fully equipped with experience, exact knowledge and power.'[13]

No such central machine existed in the United Kingdom at the outbreak of the War; there were, on the contrary, no less than three Departments charged with labour policy - the Local Government Board, the Home Office, and the Board of Trade - which had little control over or relation with the recruiting Departments of the War Office and the Admiralty.

> The first problem before the United Kingdom in August 1914 after the Navy had been mobilized and the Expeditionary Force had been dispatched, was to raise armies.

Labour Supply and Regulation went on to articulate with devastating clarity the problems raised by exclusive concentration on this objective. When Britain entered the War, such was the initial and universal enthusiasm to enlist that 'the difficulty was not to find 100,000 but to choose the most suitable.'[14] The problems which this generous but unthinking and uncontrolled rush to the colours was to create had never been remotely imagined by those in control of affairs.

The industries vital to arming, equipping and keeping the armed forces supplied, especially (though not only) with munitions, had lost substantial numbers of men to the forces - over 20% in some industries - and although reinforcements were drawn in from other trades which early in the War appeared thereby to suffer heavy unemployment, these could not, in the nature of things, immediately stem the haemorrhage or its effects:

> However the gaps were filled, wounds so suddenly inflicted on the body of an industry would be long in healing. Industries, like human beings, are apt to hobble after amputation.[15]

Some trades in the early days had been glad to see enlistment as a means of reducing unemployment, while

> the business community, not to be left behind, had determined to see the War through on the basis of 'business as usual', which, if it meant anything at all, meant that, in order to prevent unemployment, work which in many cases would be of no national advantage, and in some positively a disadvantage, should, even if at the employers' loss, be carried on. In the light of subsequent events it may seem strange that the most deep-rooted fear at this stage should not have been of a possible shortage of manpower, but a dangerous surplus.[16]

He recognised, looking back, that even the most far-sighted of men could hardly have envisaged the situation differently. 'No one could predict the size of the armies to be enrolled, nor the duration of the War.' The successful prosecution of the War in the field depended, therefore, on a satisfactory solution to the dual problem of man-power at home: in short, ensuring on the one hand an adequate supply of civilian labour, and on the other the maximum and most effective use of it.

The rest of the book not only rehearsed the problems and the solutions which were, with varying degrees of success, applied to them; it also encompassed, in a singularly self-effacing way, the whole of his professional life during the War. Although he was neither the only nor the most important person in either the Labour Exchanges Department or the Ministry of Munitions, he was nevertheless centrally involved in all the events, issues, discussions and policies which he described, and the importance of his contribution must not be undervalued. In a peculiar and unique way, he *was* Labour Supply and Regulation. It is staggering to realize that at the outbreak of war he was twenty-nine years of age, and not yet thirty-five when he was chosen as one of the 'men of judicial temper and adequate training' judged worthy to undertake the 'Economic and Social History of the World War.'[17]

It is fortunate that in his Introduction to the book he provided for his readers a coherent summary of those complex and far from coherent or consistent events and circumstances. The digest which follows is heavily indebted to his account.

The indiscriminate system of voluntary recruiting practised in the first enthusiasm of the war created irreparable gaps in the skilled producing power of the country. Devices such as badging in order to ring-fence the labour required for civilian purposes succeeded in stemming the blind rush to the Colours by the end of 1915, and once the War Office had been persuaded that it was both possible and desirable to spread the manufacture of munitions all over the country instead of concentrating it in a limited number of centres, the existing Employment Exchange machine made it possible to find the men required, if they existed, and to place them where they were neeeded, if they were willing to go. The next problem was how to increase if possible the net supply. This was tackled by bringing in workmen from abroad and from the Dominions, by the release of men from the Colours, by the massive introduction of female labour, and by other methods such as the use of prisoners of war for agricultural work.

These methods, which dealt with the question of supply of labour, left undiminished the serious deficit both in numbers of workers and above all in quality, for no substitute existed for the skill, the experience or the physical strength of the most skilled workers who had joined the Forces. The next question therefore was one of Labour Regulation, i.e. the intensive use of the available labour, so as to remedy the deficiency in numbers by requiring more of each individual. The Munitions of War Act (1915) set out to do this, by laying down the broad lines upon which labour, rationed between fighters and workers, distributed and augmented, was to be used to the fullest extent. It made work continuous, by prohibiting strikes and lock-outs, and by providing for a system of compulsory arbitration; it broke down restrictions on output, by persuading the Trades Unions to accept dilution - that is, the introduction of semi-skilled and unskilled men and women upon skilled men's work; it required the longest hours compatible with health (and no longer), by controlling workmen's hours and efficiency, and imposing legal penalties for indiscipline while improving working conditions, in factories (termed 'Controlled Establishments') where profits were limited.

It enrolled various mobile corps, such as the War Munitions Volunteers, in which workmen placed themselves at the disposal of the Government to be moved where their work was at the moment most required, and it kept them there by various means, chief of which was the leaving certificate which was given only with the consent of the employer. Finally, it attempted to control, where it could not solve, the wages problems which were in fact a condition precedent to the handling of all the others.[18]

But, as Humbert was at pains to stress, the problems did not in their historical reality present themselves even in chronological, let alone in logical, order. 'In fact, the greatest difficulty of all during the War was that each problem tended to provoke a new one, which had to be faced side by side with the other as yet unsolved.'[19]

The realisation of the need to supply and regulate the labour necessary to prosecute the war became apparent, if not for the first time, at least in a more acute form, when the shortage of munitions began to be felt. As Humbert put it, in characteristic style,

> War, if it has no other good qualities, is an accomplished teacher. . Certainly not later than October 1914 it became obvious that the supply of munitions would have to be multiplied out of all knowledge. It was not till the spring of 1915 that the shell shortage was to rivet public attention, but long before that, the dificulties arising from a general deficiency of munitions were causing grave anxiety.[20]

Labour Supply and Regulation required the controlled and sober language of the Civil Servant. In *Portraits By Inference* (1934), however, beneath the sharper satirical tone of his description of the situation in the first months of 1915 one can sense the bitter anger he still felt. He drew a clear parallel between the destruction of reasonable criticism by the military leadership and the murderous machine gun fire of the battle fronts:

> I had travelled a very long way from summer and Frinton when in the February of 1915 I first entered the room in which both Arthur Balfour and Lloyd George were seated. The glow and splendour had mysteriously begun to be lost in the mud of Flanders. The first blind belief in Kitchener had yielded to growing uneasiness. What of rifles, shells and guns? insistent voices began to ask, and voices not always ready to be silenced by the suggestion prevalent in some military and other quarters that to seek to remedy the Army's deficiencies was to help the enemy. Rank after rank of impertinents were

> mowed down by the powers of self-satisfied evasion. But at last the valiant resistance to the processes of thought which is the contribution of so many eminent soldiers to the process of war broke down before immense national uneasiness.
>
> The slow, historic wrath of England began to direct itself against apparent neglect and inefficiency. The Press, in all other particulars neither permitted nor anxious to deal with facts, seized upon this one. A confused murmur of ignorant rage began to clamour at the doors of authority. The armies were in danger, it seemed, but, what was perhaps more productive of action, the Government was also in danger. They acted. A committee, or rather several conflicting committees, covering the same ground, were appointed.
>
> At some later date in my life, when it will be possible for me to do so, and if it still seems worth while to correct some of the more outrageous misstatements on the munitions position at the beginning of 1915, I may deal at length with these committees and their ultimate absorption in the Ministry of Munitions. Like the ghost of Hamlet's father, "I could a tale unfold."[21]

Sadly, he never did; worse still, he was to see it all happening again in the last year of his life, as if the country, like the Bourbons, had learned nothing and forgotten nothing.

Employers and recruiting officers alike had to be dissuaded, the former from allowing, the latter from encouraging, skilled workers to enlist; the War Office had to be persuaded to spread munitions contracts more widely; trades unions had to be induced to suspend restrictive practices, as employers had to accept a limitation on profiteering. All of these proved difficult, the last two almost impossible, and the succession of committees to which Humbert alluded was evidence of the seemingly impossible magnitude of the task.

> The problem of getting the munitions was being simultaneously and vigorously attacked by the Treasury Committee, the War Office Committee, the War Office, the Board of Trade, Mr. Booth's rapidly improvised central organisation, and by the Engineering Employers' Federation. So many and such active agents were bound not only to throw up new ideas and methods continuously, but almost to throw them at one another. And in fact the period between Mr. Booth's original

> appointment in March and the creation of the Ministry of Munitions in June produced almost as many conflicts of jurisdiction as ideas. But the conflicts tended to disappear in the Ministry of Munitions; the ideas changed the whole military situation.[22]

The revelation of the deplorable shortage of munitions, and the admission that the War Office had failed to foresee and provide, led to a Parliamentary Bill establishing Government control over all armament factories and workers, and the setting up of a special Committee for mobilising industry on 12 April, with Balfour and Lloyd George as its two principal members. The Munitions of War Committee, as it was named, met under the chairmanship of the Chancellor of the Exchequer from 12 April to 13 May. Llewellyn Smith was co-opted to it and Beveridge became a fringe member and attended all its meetings, but was too high in rank to be its secretary and Berto was given the job.

In her diary for 15 May 1915, Lloyd George's personal secretary, Frances Stevenson, reported the struggles with the Munitions Committee which occupied most of Lloyd George's attention, and some of the problems Berto had to contend with. Despite the suspicion of partiality in her account, at least towards Lloyd George, it bears witness to Berto's close involvement at the centre of the munitions issue. But she does seem to contradict Humbert's account in *Labour Supply and Regulation*, particularly concerning the alleged opposition of Booth and Girouard to Lloyd George's attempts to widen the distribution of contracts for the manufacture of munitions.[23]

Balfour's niece, Blanche Dugdale, wrote in her biography of her uncle:

> The work of the Committee was, however, much hampered by the refusal of the War Office to give it proper cooperation. Before that difficulty could be overcome the Government had been changed and the chief importance of the Committee remains as marking the recognition that the supply of munitions must be considered a task in itself, not to be left for the other great War Departments to carry out according to their own ideas and capacities.[24]

By the middle of May 1915, the 'shell shortage' had become the 'shell scandal' and a major factor in precipitating the end of Asquith's purely Liberal government and its replacement by a Coalition. 'On the 26th May,' Humbert reported, 'the Prime Minister (Mr. Asquith) announced the creation of a Department, to be called the Ministry of Munitions, to carry on the work thus initiated, and on that day Mr. Lloyd George installed himself at No. 6 Whitehall Gardens as the first Minister of Munitions.'[25]

II

Ministry of Munitions 1915-1918

The first office of the new Ministry was next door to the Board of Trade, in the house of William Lockett Agnew, the art dealer and publisher, where Gladstone is reported to have lived at some time, although his name does not figure among the listed occupiers between 1825 and 1915.[26] In the chapter of *Portraits By Inference* entitled 'Ghosts at No. 6 Whitehall Gardens', Humbert's pen-picture of the tranquil grace of this late-Georgian house served to sharpen the contrast with the deadly purposes it now must serve:

> Grey, elegant and untroubled, the house stands outwardly as though it were still the home and resort of fashion. The windows have their old air of easy proportion, and the entrance hall has a cool rectilinear impertinence that all but scans you through a quizzing-glass.

When Lloyd George moved in on 26 May 1915, the new Ministry did not strictly speaking yet exist, or if it did, it was, as he was fond of repeating later, in his own person alone. The Parliamentary Bill creating it was introduced only on 3 June by the new Home Secretary, John Simon, and received the Royal Assent only on 9 June.

The *History of tbe Ministry of Munitions* charts in an Appendix the organisational structure at 6 Whitehall Gardens on 1 June 1915. Lloyd George is described as Chairman of the Munitions of War Committee, and Minister of Munitions (Designate). His Parliamentary Secretary (Designate) was Dr. Christopher Addison, M.P., and Sir Hubert Llewellyn Smith, K.C.B., was appointed General Secretary. William Beveridge was Assistant General Secretary, and under him were Berto, named here as 'Mr. H. Wolfe, Secretary to the Munitions of War Committee', and Mr. P. G. L. Webb, in charge of Establishment. The main text of the History notes that 'the chief posts (in the Secretariat and the Contract and Finance Departments) were held by permanent civil servants lent by other Government Departments - Sir Hubert Llewellyn Smith, Mr. Beveridge, Mr. Rey, Mr. Wolfe (sic), Mr. Hanson, and Mr. Dannreuther.'[27] *See* Appendix AI

Both the *History of the Ministry of Munitions* and Lord Beveridge's recollections bear out Humbert's more lively account in *Portraits by Inference* of the day the new Minister 'moved in'. With Lord Curzon at his side, Berto observed from the window of his office the mêlée in Whitehall Gardens:

> The excellent messenger at the front door, used to the rural quiet of the house, was overwhelmed by men bringing furniture, postmen bringing sacks of letters, inventors bringing anything from bales of cloth to some of the smaller parts of heavy siege artillery, members of the public with grievances and others soon to acquire them, Government officials looking for their rooms, their chiefs and their work, and, last, Members of the Government hurrying or strolling up the stone stairs, according as to whether they were new to the Cabinet or not.[28]

Beveridge covered the garden of No. 6 with a vast marquee to house the typists and the registry and thereafter ordered a new temporary building every Friday and expected it to be up by the following Monday - these were 'the bungalows' referred to in the *History* of the Ministry, and which a later author called 'unsightly huts'.

As Secretary of the Munitions of War Committee, Berto was in close and frequent contact with most of the important political figures in England at the time, and from what he wrote of them in *Portraits By Inference* it is possible to make a reasonable guess at his feelings about them. Balfour he clearly admired almost to the point of veneration; Lord Curzon, Edwin Montagu, Sir Percy Girouard, Lord Moulton, are all portrayed in warm tones - perhaps, indeed almost certainly, because they treated him with consideration and courtesy. Kitchener appears only once and then in a generally unflattering light. But the most intriguing question, because the most shrouded in mystery, is that of Berto's relations with Lloyd George. If he ever recorded what he really felt about Lloyd George it has remained a well-kept secret. In the rare private documents of Humbert's to be found in this country there is no mention of Lloyd George, and although the few references in his published works to The Man Who Won the War display to advantage Humbert's gift for the brilliant image and the telling phrase, as well as his fair-minded readiness to acknowledge England's debt to Lloyd George, they also leave the reader with a sense of incompleteness, as if Humbert were holding something back.

Thus, in *Portraits By Inference*, he described the Chairman of the Munitions Committee (early 1915):

> with his frame of a thickset little Welsh Rugby half-back and his general air of one waiting on tiptoe for the ball to be hurled out of the scrum.

A little later in the same chapter, he described Balfour and Lloyd George walking out into Whitehall together 'like a pylon with its dynamo.' In the chapter dealing with the Ministry of Munitions he conjured up the picture of 'the boisterous loud-voiced Hammer of the Hun, the human Miölner tossed from the strong right hand of the Welsh Thor.' Elsewhere he wrote of Lloyd George's speaking in a voice 'like buttered toast.' All very colourful, perceptive, and not unadmiring - but revealing nothing of how they got on together.[29]

Others have recorded what was said to be Humbert's view of him. According to Richard Church, Humbert thought that Lloyd George was

> a hundred per cent wicked. The Welsh Wizard had a mind and imagination that functioned from minute to minute, moving with an inspired power of extemporization as each necessity arose, either practical towards events or psychological towards men. But after that moment all was forgotten, promises and commitments obliterated from his memory, his conscience left treacherously virgin.[30]

If Humbert really did thus shrewdly pin-point Lloyd George's moral amnesia, it tells us nothing direct about their relationship.

Although there appears to be no evidence to support the belief that he was Lloyd George's wartime private secretary, it is clear that in the early days of the Ministry Berto worked closely with Lloyd George. Lord Beveridge, writing about the Munitions of War Bill of July 1915, said: 'Wolff - (who) from being secretary to the Munitions of War Committee, proceeded for a while to the personal entourage of Lloyd George, had not lasted long in the Minister's favour.' This, in Beveridge's view, was a stroke of good fortune for his Department which was busy in the last weeks of June with the huge task of dealing with amendments to the Bill. Beveridge recognised the value of Berto's experience of drafting legislation,

> and his quickness of mind can never have been tested more highly. We had masses of amendments in the paper every morning, with notes and answers on all of them to be circulated to Ministers by midday or before. The spectacle of Wolff keeping three shorthand typists in continuous action simultaneously while he dictated as fast as he could speak (except when he ran to consult me on a knotty point) is one that I do not forget.[31]

Concerning this Munitions Code, as the Munitions of War Act (1915) was commonly known when it reached the Statute Book, Humbert wrote:

> Acts of Parliament, it is generally recognized, are distinguishable from Acts of God in being unable to change hearts, and the Munitions Act was only peculiar in this respect because men's hearts at the time of its passing were unusually malleable.[32]

Perhaps we shall never know the reason for Berto's sudden eclipse after such a brief spell in the sunshine of Lloyd George's favour, or his true feelings about the latter. Some sense of Lloyd George's attitude to Berto may be inferred from the only reference I have found in Lloyd George's writings. In *War Memoirs* he briefly mentions, with acidulous suavity, Berto's arrival in the Ministry of Munitions:

> And through the portals of the Board of Trade there wafted into this Ministry of solid and material industrialism a breeze from the foothills of Parnassus in the person of Mr. Umberto Wolff.[33]

This reference to 'solid and material industrialism' echoes Lloyd George's frequently repeated assertion that the Ministry was 'from first to last a business-man organisation.' Lord Beveridge always maintained that this was at most only partially true. That part of the Ministry concerned with Munitions Supply - and it was undoubtedly the larger part - did import men with business and industrial experience to deal with the placing of contracts, the establishment and managing of new factories, and so on. But it was not true of the department of Munitions Labour, which had some businessmen but had begun 'in the main with civil servants; we were reinforced largely by a stream of academics and intellectuals; even the civil servants we borrowed from other departments had often an academic flavour.'[34]

Some businessmen were already assisting the War Office Armament Output Committee, notably George Booth, a director of Booth's Steamships and the Bank of England, and Sir Percy Girouard, a Canadian engineer officer who had retired just before the War to run Armstrong's huge establishment at Elswick. Booth has traditionally been identified as the original 'man of push and go', although according to Lloyd George's *War Memoirs* he was more of a tactful conciliator than a driver. Girouard soon fell foul of Lloyd George and by the end of July he had to go. Bentley Gilbert, commenting on the factors which commended the transfer of Lloyd George from the Exchequer to Munitions, stated quite bluntly that by the end of May 1915 Britain was fighting the war on credit, owing to Lloyd George's contempt for administrative niceties. 'He disliked Civil Servants and they disliked him.' In this instance, therefore, Frances Stevenson's confident assertion that everyone was keen to see him taking up Munitions of War was truer than she knew, but for quite different reasons from those she fondly imagined.[35]

Lloyd George's mistrust and dislike of civil servants was notorious and well documented. He was fond of underlining the distinction between experts and administrators. On 23 July 1915, the day that he forced the expert Girouard to resign, he told the House of Commons: 'Good administrators may lack technical expertise, but experts are rarely good administrators.' It might be argued that, as one who could legitimately claim to be neither, he was uniquely placed to judge. It is certain that he would never consent to be other than in charge, and it is probable that he feared the consequences of civil servants telling him what he could and should do. Nor would he give them the chance of claiming the credit which he thought was rightfully his, and this undoubtedly would account for his attempts to diminish their undeniable contribution, at the same time as it distracted attention from the criticisms which could properly be levelled at the businessmen.[36]

It is clear from *Portraits By Inference* that Humbert's admiration for the businessmen lay a long way second to the Minister's. Characteristically, he revealed this obliquely, by highlighting the qualities which he *did* admire, and the people who possessed them. For example, Lord Moulton, who

> unlike many other reputations, had a specific genius, and not that generalized lack of applied knowledge which is described as the gift of organization. I had many interviews with captains of industry, from which I returned with the uneasy suspicion that if that was all they had to impart, then either (which was probable) they didn't trust me or (what was possible) they had succeeded in business because their only competitors were businessmen like themselves.[37]

And later in the same chapter, he wrote:

> Meanwhile, I sat in my office - a large room with one chair which I relinquished to callers interviewing supermen on the Minister's behalf. By all accounts England was thick with them. Hardly a man, who trooped up the stairs, but was a born organizer or one, as Cyril Asquith said, able to cope with the national crisis owing to his long experience of crises in his private affairs.[38]

Humbert's biting comment was at least partially endorsed by a paragraph in the *History of the Ministry of Munitions* which stated fairly bluntly that Lloyd George's practical policy of giving the businessmen a free hand led to poor record-keeping and to the failure of these 'captains of industry' to subordinate departmental interests to those of the Ministry as a whole.

Lloyd George had ensured that as Minister he had total freedom to produce anything that he considered to be munitions of war, and whether they were requested by the military or not. Not surprisingly, the new Ministry immediately began to expand at a fantastic rate, as its increasing responsibilities required more and more staff and premises. In addition to Nos. 5 and 6, Whitehall Gardens, the Ministry also occupied premises in Storey's Gate and King Charles Street (where Explosives and Trench Warfare Supply Departments respectively were housed), while the Munitions Supply Department began in congested quarters in the War Office, with an overflow into the Hotel Cecil. On 15 June 1915, Munitions Supply moved into the unfinished buildings of the Department of Agriculture and Fisheries, now renamed Armaments Buildings, in Whitehall Place, and were joined by Sir Eric Geddes and all the business and production side. Before the end of the year they had begun to invade the Hotel Metropole in Northumberland Avenue, whither the Minister himself removed in March 1916, making it the Headquarters building, and leaving the Secretariat and Munitions Labour in sole possesion of No. 6 Whitehall Gardens.[39]

By 1 July 1915, the Ministry's Secretariat and Labour Division under W. H. Beveridge (who had the rank of Assistant Secretary) was already divided into five branches, three of which were entirely concerned with labour questions. Berto was in charge of the section dealing with Legislation, Controlled Establishments, Munitions Tribunals, General Labour Questions, Leaving Certificates, and Works Rules. [*See* Appendix AII] And since it was the Board of Trade, particularly the Labour Exchanges Department, which

> had hitherto been concerned with the supply of labour and the negotiations with Trade Unions, the information and organisation already developed for dealing with these questions was thus placed at the disposal of the new department.[40]

Humbert made it clearer still:

> Indeed, it would be true to say that if the Exchanges had not existed before the War, the War would have invented them. . . In fact the truth is that just as the War after one year produced the Ministry of Munitions, and after two produced the Ministry of National Service, so it would after a decent interval have produced the Exchanges.[41]

His description of the Ministry deserves to be quoted:

> the Ministry of Munitions, that mixture of the Sanhedrin and a Bank Holiday crowd at Liverpool Street Station. . . (at) No. 6 Whitehall Gardens. "There was. . . such a Department during the war - huge, industrious, all important, greatly directed by great men under the impulse of the greatest of all. At one time its staff outnumbered the population of Wakefield; twenty hotels contrived in vain, with immense overcrowding, to house its enrolled multitudes; it was the largest property-owner in the world; it built factories in a day and forgot them in a night; it acquired a county for the site of a new building, and lost the county and the title-deeds next morning; it did all the work that fell to its share as well as all the work that fell to everybody else's share; it was actuated by advanced Socialist and by advanced anti-Socialist principles; it socialized huge sections of industry for purely capitalist reasons, and refused to interfere with others on purely Marxian grounds; it spent more in a day than the nation could repay in a century; and it was the Man Who Won the War, or the Man Who Mislaid it somewhere in a poison-gas factory."[42]

By 1 July 1916, the Labour responsibilities within the Ministry had been separated from the Secretariat and reorganized into three sections under three Assistant Secretaries: Labour Regulation, under W. H. Beveridge (in which Berto may be presumed to figure, although the chart does not name him); Labour Supply, under C. F. Rey; and Controlled Establishments, under Owen Smith. The plan to perpetuate the Munitions of War Committee as an advisory and coordinating body was scrapped as being too unwieldy, and after only one meeting, on 23 July, it ceased to exist.*See* Appendix AIII[43]

The two chapters in *Portraits* which deal with the War are at one and the same time vastly entertaining and deeply moving. They glitter with starshell bursts which starkly but often all too briefly illuminate a face or an event. The pages sparkle with images which capture the essential in the same way as a caricature does: the pylon and generator image of Balfour and Lloyd George already mentioned; Sir Percy Girouard's voice 'whose colour might be described as cracked walnut'; Lord Moulton (in charge of Explosives Supply) whose

> services anticipated the creation of the Ministry. It was at a meeting of the committee plunged in gloom because of information as to the possible failure of supply vital to the Armies that I first saw the great lawyer and the greater man of science. He flapped heavily into the room, looking and moving like nothing on earth so

> much as Tenniel's picture of the Mock Turtle. This picture was accentuated by a shortness of neck and a habit of folding up what there was in a manner not common in humans. His voice, when he began to speak, had something of the richness of a good soup, but no man ever spoke with more sense or directness.... The dark and enigmatic eyes of Edwin Montagu, shrine of all the useless wisdom of his race, its tragic doubt, its secular sensitiveness, and its prevision of doom.

H. W. Garrod, Fellow of Merton, who joined them in 1915, is there, along with two Under-Secretaries, Neil Primrose (the son of Lord Rosebery), 'of all Junior Ministers. . . the most conscientious and hardest-working', and F. G. Kellaway; General Sir Auckland Geddes, Minister of National Service; Sir Max Aitken, 'a formidable Member of Parliament', whose practice of calling everyone by his Christian name upon very slight acquaintance prompted Berto to ask with his customary and disarming air of innocent enquiry: 'Doesn't he know any surnames, or is he only asked to use them when people know him well enough?'

A place of special affection is reserved for Sir Thomas Munro, County Clerk of Lanarkshire, who 'all the years of the War was dying on his feet, but that didn't prevent his putting in about ten hours a day at the office', and who had the engaging habit of keeping his taxi waiting, sometimes for hours. A colleague said to him, 'If ever you commit a murder I shall tell the police to go round London looking for a house outside which there is a taxi showing £8 5s on the meter. Within will be discovered the murderer.'

Among the portraits of the great and the good (and the not-so-good) of these times, one stands out above the others: A. J. Balfour whom Berto saw in the course of his duties about three times a week, occasionally lunching at his house in Carlton Gardens and, by way of respite from the events of the moment, discussing metaphysics, or Balfour's Burne-Jones paintings (which Berto had the courage not to like):

> The figure that made my heart beat faster as I entered the room at the Treasury was slender and stooping. It gave the impression of languid grace which would throw a pinch of snuff in the eyes of life, treating it as the plebeian it plainly was. It was attired in an ordinary office suit, but in some way suggested negligent ruffles. It . . . listened courteously. . . It was cool, carrying its own atmosphere in a vacuum that its aloofness created, and in a time of heat, hate and hysteria it was infinitely reassuring. It was in fact Arthur Balfour.

This was, of course, the same Balfour who had addressed the assembly at the official opening of the Knox Academy in Haddington in 1880, and the Conservative politician whom Berto and his friends in the New Oxford Movement had later done their best to oust, in a campaign whose main plank was 'B. M. G.' - Balfour Must Go.[44]

These and many more spring to life from these two chapters of compelling prose in which Humbert displayed his warmth, his generosity, and his mordant wit. Unshakeable in his patriotism and his belief in the rightness of the Allied cause, he was at the same time sharply critical of the inefficiency, the venality, the paltriness of motive and the sheer stupidity which so often endangered its success. But in the end he is all too oblique, leaving one with a wish for more on the whole topic of the War. It raises the wider question of his motives for writing the book, a question to be dealt with more fully in Chapter 8.

The death of Kitchener early in June 1916 led to Lloyd George's move to the War Office in July and the appointment of Edwin Montagu as Minister of Munitions, Dr. Addison remaining as his Under-Secretary. On 28 September Berto was promoted Principal Officer at £700 p.a. The Coalition Government fell early in December and with Asquith's departure Edwin Montagu went too, his place being taken by Dr. Addison who stayed as Minister of Munitions until the following July. One of the first things Lloyd George did, as incoming Prime Minister, was to create a separate Ministry of Labour, one of the three principal concessions which he made in order to secure the support of the Labour Party for his premiership.

The precise date of Berto's appointment to this new Ministry (which was to be his professional home for the rest of his life) has proved impossible to establish. No record of it has survived in the archives of the Civil Service, and although the 1918 issue of Whitaker's *Almanac* listed Berto as a Principal Officer in the new Ministry at the beginning of 1918, the *History of the Ministry of Munitions*, Public Record Office files, Humbert's own *Labour Supply and Regulation*, and Whitaker too, make it clear that throughout 1917 and 1918 he retained his responsibility as Controller of the Labour Regulation Department in the Ministry of Munitions, with the rank of Assistant Secretary (Acting). By 1 July 1917, the Labour Department of the Ministry of Munitions had become a two-section division, with Berto, now Assistant General Secretary, in charge of Labour Regulation, and Sir Stephenson Kent, KCB, Director-General in charge of Labour Supply.[45]

Care must be taken in interpreting the titles given to the functions exercised by officials in wartime Ministries. The Civil Service continued to adhere to a hierarchy of grades, with promotion through them as circumstances dictated, and quite often, as in the armed services, with temporary rather than permanent effect, as was the case with Berto's Assistant Secretaryship. Within the Ministries, however, and particularly in one such as Munitions with its huge and constantly expanding responsibilities, officials were named as Secretary to a Committee or a Department, Controller etc., titles which reflected a function, rather than a rank in the Service. In any case, it remains unlikely that Berto could have acquired simultaneous membership of two such separate and at times rival Ministries as Munitions and Labour. It may be that he was notionally transferred to Labour in 1917-18 but seconded to Munitions for the duration of the War; without a doubt he was *de facto* identified with Munitions until the end of November 1918. *See* Appendix AIV

On 1 January 1918, Berto's massive war effort was rewarded: he was was gazetted Commander in the Order of the British Empire under the name of Humbert Wolfe. Objections were raised in some quarters, including the House of Commons, to the honouring of men with German names. One Civil Servant who had the job of sorting out Humbert's office papers after his death recalls seeing a long paper written in characteristic green ink by Churchill, Humbert's Minister in 1918, which attempted to rebut the accusation that Humbert was a German, on the grounds that his father was born before Germany was united, and in what was then part of Schleswig-Holstein.[46] There is in fact no doubt that Mecklenburg-Schwerin *was* German in 1845, but as Martin Wolff, with his sons, was naturalized a British citizen in 1891, the argument was in any case otiose. But, as will be seen, anti-German feeling remained rife, and even the royal house of Saxe-Coburg-Gotha had prudently affirmed its Englishness by renaming itself the House of Windsor.

As the war dragged on and the department grew ever larger, central control became increasingly difficult. In August 1918 there were over 70 departments at the Ministry.[47] Already in a House of Commons debate on 25 April 1918, Winston Churchill argued that an enlarged Secretariat, with the best available permanent civil servants as its nucleus, was the only way to conduct the business of a Public Department satisfactorily. Accordingly the whole Department was reorganised under a Munitions Council which was designed to re-establish Civil Service control over departmental procedure while retaining unimpaired the Business Man's executive freedom. The chart depicting the new streamlined departmental organisation at 1 July 1918, shows Winston Churchill as Minister. In fact, he was not offered the post until the middle of the month, and announced the new structure of the Ministry only on 18 August. He took this opportunity to bring back into his own entourage his former Admiralty Secretary, James Masterton Smith, whom he appointed to be in charge of the Secretariat of the reorganized Ministry. Masterton Smith was later knighted and became Permanent Secretary of the Ministry of Labour and thus Humbert's chief. *See* Appendix AV

Under the overall direction of the Munitions Council the various parts of the Ministry were re-assembled into eight Groups. Group L, which was responsible for Labour matters, comprised four Departments, Labour Regulation under Humbert as Controller, two Labour Supply Departments (one for the civil, one for the military side), and a Labour

Adviser's Department under Sir Thomas Munro, CBE. Humbert remained in the post of Controller until 16 November 1918.[48] Among the other staff of the Ministry named in Whitaker's *Almanac* were two Section Directors, E. C. P. Lascelles, last heard of in the first year of Berto's married life, and whose name later appeared intermittently in public records as it seems to have done in Berto's life, and Mrs. Blanco-White, a lady more widely known for her association with H. G. Wells.

In the concluding chapter of *Labour Supply and Regulation*, Humbert was at pains to pay tribute to the contribution made by the new Ministry of Labour:

> [It] remained, as far as the War would permit, neutral in labour matters. . . and able in consequence to give cool, general advice to all the executive Departments struggling with the day-to-day incidents of Labour Supply and Regulation.[49]

He was equally generous about the new Ministry's role in preparing for the Peace. There is ample evidence, however, that from its establishment until well beyond the end of the war, the Ministry was, in the words of H. B. Butler, but a 'still, small voice.' Politically, it counted for little and, initially at least, it was administratively weak. Perhaps for those reasons it appeared to spend a good deal of time and energy in battles with other departments, notably with the Department of National Service, created simultaneously with the Ministry of Labour, and soon to become a ministry in its own right; with the Ministry of Reconstruction, set up in August 1917; and with Munitions.

In his capacity as Controller of Labour Regulation, Humbert soon found himself at variance with officials in these Ministries, notably in 1917 over the issue of establishing Works Committees to deal with cases of bad time-keeping, for one of the effects of the new Munitions Bill would be to make the Minister of Munitions responsible for undertaking all prosecutions under the Act, which at that time amounted to some 500 a week, the majority for bad time-keeping. Among those ranged against Humbert on this occasion were his former schoolmate, Henry Clay from the Ministry of Labour, H. B. Butler, Principal Assistant Secretary at the Ministry of Labour, and Arthur Greenwood for the Ministry of Reconstruction. On the basis of the Whitley Report, the Ministry of Munitions had produced a memorandum on the procedure to be adopted.

The conflict appeared to be between centralisation and decentralisation. Clay, writing to Butler, had doubts as to 'whether the Ministry of Munitions - or to be more definite Mr. Wolfe - was really convinced of the necessity of works committees, or was merely deferring to an unimportant demand by the Commission on Industrial Unrest.' Butler agreed: 'The danger is that the Ministry of Munitions may appear to be cooperating in decentralising administration without actually doing so.' The consequent weakening of trade union control, with employers provided with the means of evading it, would result in labour viewing Shop/Works Committees as an 'Employers' Dodge.' Greenwood advised Butler to 'deal very firmly with the situation. In my opinion, the (Ministry of Munitions) memorandum is. . . worse than a sham. The Whitley Report did not contemplate a Works Committee which would bolster up a system of industrial Prussianism in which, to quote from the memorandum, workpeople are to have "hopes and fears" only, and the management "wishes and intentions".' The matter was eventually settled more or less to the satisfaction of all parties, but the Cabinet's general lack of enthusiasm for the Whitley proposals can hardly have boosted the new Ministry's self-confidence.[50]

No account of Humbert's wartime career would be complete without mention of two particular qualities of which historians of the Ministry of Labour between the wars have made special mention, but which he first demonstrated to any remarkable degree at the Ministry of Munitions. One was his skill as a mediator, the other was his tenacious courage in standing up for what he knew to be right.

On the rare occasions when he referred to his activities as a conciliator, he described them in self-depreciating tones, as in this passage in *Portraits By Inference*:

> No less damaging to my prospect of transfer was the wholly unfounded allegation of my popularity as a negotiator. But the authority here was Sir Thomas Munro, who not merely never spoke ill of any one, but invented with every detail of veracity the most fantastic virtues in the least deserving. He had in mind, I imagine, 6 a.m. on Hackney Marshes when I addressed a crowd of strikers from an upturned tub. It appeared, later, that my speech had merely made the whole shift, who had been returning to work, twenty minutes late, but this, after all, Sir Thomas was entitled to urge, did not distinguish me from other able strike-settlers.

At the end of the war, large numbers of soldiers protested strongly against the scientific scheme of demobilization by industrial categories, for which the Ministry of Labour was mainly responsible. Volunteers with long service were angry when they saw other, more recent conscripts released as 'key men' while they had to wait months before returning to civilian life. Armed mutinies broke out in Calais and Folkestone early in 1919, and on 8 February 1919, a defiant mob of several thousand soldiers appeared on Horse Guards Parade. Harry Balfour, Humbert's colleague and best man at his wedding, wrote some forty years later:

> Humbert was always a good man in an emergency. In the difficult days at the war's end when slightly mutinous battalions used to march to the War Office with vague hopes of a happier time, Humbert was often induced by the responsible officials to address and soothe the seething soldiers, who even on occasion shouted on arrival "bring out your German Jew". Humbert was always courageous and enjoyed a complicated situation.[51]

Although Cameron Hazlehurst's account of the origins of the *History of the Ministry of Munitions* makes no mention of Humbert's disagreements with the official record, files in the Public Record Office from as early as 1917 show Humbert challenging, firmly and sometimes vehemently, what he considered to be inaccuracies in the *History*. The Editorial Committee, under G. I. H. Lloyd, Director of the Historical Records Branch of the Ministry of Munitions, who had taken over the general editorship from Professor W. G. Adams in June 1917, could hardly avoid submitting the draft *History* to Humbert's scrutiny. The lengthy battle between them - it went on well into 1919 - can be followed in Lloyd's correspondence with Humbert and with the chief members of the Editorial Advisory Committee, A. J. Jenkinson, a retired Fellow of Brasenose College, Oxford, Captain F. M. Cornford and Mrs. H. W. V. Temperley.

Humbert protested against a history which showed a bias "so strong as to make the document simply a criticism of the Government labour policy throughout the war and not an impartial presentation of facts." He was emphatic that the Ministry could not permit so serious an attack on its policy to be placed on permanent record "especially as the criticism seems to me wholly unfounded." He praised the volume as a piece of history but criticized it as 'partizan', and referred to 'pseudos en te psyche' (in Greek characters in the text: it means 'the lie in the soul'). A PS added 'It does seem a little hard that neither Beveridge nor I figure anywhere at all!'

He later acknowledged that 'partisanship' was 'ill-chosen' and explained that by it he had meant that the writer's view was that of sympathy with labour. (He compared his criticism to that directed against Macaulay's history - honesty of purpose and high ability but judgement discoloured by Whiggism.) As to the Greek phrase, he thought that it had 'long since lost its offensive quality. It is always open for a person who holds one principle to condemn the person who holds another on the ground that his spiritual attitude is false.., 'but he added that if either of his objections had given offence he withdrew them. And when his criticisms resulted in amendments and compromise Humbert was prepared to be conciliatory: 'I think that both you and Mr. Cornford have been very patient with my observations. I am afraid they were a little definite in form but I thought it as well to get the matters I was dealing with into a high light.'

He had also argued that some of the authors had only a partial record - a great volume of vocal labour criticism, a certain amount of official records, 'but a great absence of the real inner meaning of events' (because the enormous part played by Ministerial Conferences and Cabinet decisions was not officially if at all recorded, and could only be supplied by someone who was present). At the beginning of January 1918 Lloyd wrote suggesting that as an alternative to an expanded revision of a section now in its second proof stage, Humbert should write a retrospect of the whole period, i.e. a memorandum of up to, say, 10 - 15,000 words, 'Not in substitution for the present effort, but for inclusion in a later section - perhaps a summary of the Ministry's work.' Humbert's reply recognized that it was only just that he as critic should provide the document in question but said he had not the time and could not produce anything as good as the official record, and would not undertake to do it in under three to six months.

The PRO files suggest that by the end of September 1918 Lloyd and his colleagues regretted that Humbert should need to see the revised proofs at all. One letter to Lloyd from another colleague quoted "a delightful misprint" which Humbert would have relished: 'The Bill (i.e. The Military Service Acts 1916) had originated in ideas which had been germinating in the wind of Mr. Lloyd George for some time.'

Lloyd more than once wrote as if Humbert had agreed to write his own version of events. Humbert's replies show clearly that he gave no such undertaking. If he was already committed to writing *Labour Supply and Regulation*, that effectively ruled out another book which would entail the additional labour of condensing a large amount of complex material. Alternatively, Lloyd's suggestion may have given him the idea for *Labour Supply and Regulation*, although that seems unlikely, simply because the Carnegie series was designed well in advance and he would have been earmarked for it quite early on. But since the History was only completed in 1923, the year of publication of *Labour Supply and Regulation*, the possibility cannot be entirely ruled out.[52]

III

'To have lived through a great war as a civilian,' Humbert wrote in *Portraits By Inference*, 'is a vivid and abominable experience.' Like millions of other young men in the world in 1914, he said, 'I was borne forward on an impulse as though I was a part of some great clear wind that with one bright puff had murdered the sleep in the soul of man.' He had shared the delirium of the roaring, cheering mob that swept down Whitehall on the evening of the 4th of August. But the glow and the splendour mysteriously began to be lost.

It was not simply that friends, colleagues, acquaintances went away, some never to return; not just the anxiety and eventual grief for loved ones, nor the horror of an increasing daily toll of lives sacrificed as much to the incompetence and sloth of their own military leaders as to the superior strength of the enemy. To judge from *Portraits By Inference* and his poetry from this period onwards, he sensed that civilisation was being gradually destroyed. Indeed, the combatants, even the casualties, might be envied in that

> they have action; they are in the presence of undeniable fact. They do not hear rumours, repeat terrified and terrifying gossip, or live like cottagers on a lonely moor before the printing press split the dark. This is the civilian state. The first casualty of every war is truth, and with the death of truth the Middle Age returns. The General and the Cabinet Minister, each in his place, lie persistently, unremittingly and conscientiously. The small man, with his sure instinct for corruption, at first suspects, and then is infected by, the general miasma. Till by the gradual progress of the malady the seven deadly vices become the seven deadlier virtues.[53]

Mindless anti-German feeling, anti-Semitism, accusations of 'column-dodging' and prodigal distributions of the white feather were among the typical expressions of the disease. H. W. Garrod, a Fellow of Merton, who, having been rejected for active service (five times, according to Humbert), had left Oxford in order to serve in some more useful capacity in the Ministry of Munitions, was offered a white feather with the words,

> 'Don't you know that young men like you are dying in France for civilization?' Flattered though he was at being fallaciously described as young, he instantly replied as he pinned on the white feather, 'And, madam, don't you know that I am the civilization for which they are dying.'[54]

As a non-combatant of military age (though only just) and bearing a German-Jewish name, Berto was doubly qualified for such attentions. He had twice tried to enlist but was turned down on the grounds of a weak heart. This did not, however, spare him from attacks such as that launched upon him by Norman Douglas, the celebrated author of *South Wind*. The latter described in *Alone* how in 1916, having given up his job as Assistant Editor of *The English Review*, he had tried to find war work, hoping for a position in which he could put to good use his knowledge of languages and his experience in the Foreign Service, perhaps even his German background - he was one quarter German and had been brought up in Austria. To his extreme chagrin, no one seemed to want him and he went to live in Italy, an exile which lasted until 1941. According to Richard Aldington, Douglas attributed 'his resolution to go abroad at that uninviting period to the opposition of bureaucrats to employing him and to an unspecified 'God-sent little accident, the result of sheer boredom'.' Douglas's 'little accident' had in fact led to a charge of sexual assault upon minors, for which he was on bail awaiting trial, after having recently been acquitted on a similar charge.

In his version of his frustrating encounters with senior civil servants Douglas made a savage attack on what he considered to be the disproportionate number of young Jews in safe bureaucratic jobs.

> Was there some secret society which protected them? Or were they all so preposterously clever that the Old Country would straightway evaporate into thin air unless they sat in some comfortable office, while our own youngsters were being blown to pieces out yonder?[55]

Another biographer of Douglas, Mark Holloway, accepts that it is doubtful whether Douglas endured quite all the humiliations which he described in this scene, but two of the people (designated simply by the letters R and W) on whom he vented these anti-Jewish feelings certainly existed. One was Humbert's old school-friend, Albert Rutherston. The identification of the second - "A plump, though not ill-looking, young Hebrew was Mr. W." - with Humbert himself may be inferred from Humbert's dedication of 'The Locri Faun' (1925) to Norman Douglas "from his unknown admirer Mr. W.", an identification publicly confirmed only in 1934 in *Portraits By Inference*:

> 'But it seemed that in spite of his plumpness, his comparative absence of ugliness and above all his Hebraic ancestry 'Mr. W.' could not "place" Mr. Douglas. The writer permitted himself to wonder why this Jewkin was not dispatched to the front.'[56]

In the same passage Humbert, pressed for an explanation as to why he did not get Douglas a job, replied (with what Aldington described as 'an irony of restraint'): 'It had been indicated to me that at that particular moment in England he would not be a success.' What Douglas omitted in his account was supplied by Richard Aldington:

> To those who asked him Humbert Wolfe would explain that the reason he could not get Norman Douglas a job was that Wolfe had received a very disagreeable commission from his superiors, namely, to tell Norman

> that he had the alternative of getting out of England at once or of facing arrest on a certain charge.[57]

Berto's wife and daughter were also exposed to the effects of this warped patriotism. Ann Wolfe remembered being taken by her mother during the War to stay in a boarding house on the South Coast in order to recover from a bout of bronchitis. But the combination of bad war news, post-cards from Consola in her strange handwriting, and their foreign-sounding name, got them thrown out of the house despite Ann's condition.[58]

These experiences found echo in the poems which he continued to write amid the crippling demands of the Ministry of Munitions. They were eventually published in *London Pseudo-Sonnets* (1920) and *Shylock Reasons With Mr. Chesterton* (1921). The Preface to their re-issue in a single volume by Basil Blackwell in 1930 makes it possible to date at least some of them more precisely. Parts of the collection, it is clear, were written before the War, while he was at Oxford, or even earlier, if the Preface is an accurate record, which may not in every respect be the case (*see*, for example, 'The Well', referred to in Chapter 2 above).

'Sometimes when I think of love', in spite of its rhythmic echoes of Swinburne, poignantly evokes his and Jessie's courtship and youthful passion, their grief at the death of their 'little lost shadow, the small lost third' (also commemorated in 'The Little Sleeper'), and finally the tenderness almost too painful for words which the simple domesticities conjure up for him, the unforgiven (because Jewish) reprobate who owes his life to her:

> I am thinking then of your lighted face
> And your hands and the way your fingers lace
> As you sit quietly reading a book.
> Perhaps I move and you suddenly look
> Across the room, and the soul in your eyes
> Is bright as it looks with the old surprise,
> Changing for ever, for ever the same,
> And you break my heart as you speak my name.
> You must not wonder, you will not reprove
> If sometimes I dare not think of love.

The ten London pseudo-sonnets which gave the book its title constitute a series of observations of London life before the War. It seems likely that the idea, if not the poems themselves, originated in the 1909 competition in the *Westminster Gazette*, referred to in Chapter 4 above. They deal for the most part with working class London - 'The Old Clothes Dealer', 'Coves At Hampton Court', 'the flower-seller outside the Ritz', 'The Bun Shop', 'The Fried Fish Shop' (probably the one by the station at Battersea), 'The Streets Behind the Tottenham Court Road', 'a public-house' ('The Yorkshire Grey'), 'Wardour Street', 'The Suburbs'. The critical but not unsympathetic comment they make on the social conditions of the period announces the unmistakable tones of Humbert's later satires (*see* 'The Fried Fish Shop', mentioned in Chapter 4:

> And thinking gently of a wooden box,
> Where they will lay you at the parish charge
> Straight if you're small and doubled if you're large.).

In several of these sonnets Humbert has caught the authentic accent and rhythms of their subject's speech, and made it sound natural to the sonnet form; for example, 'The Old Clothes Dealer':

> It's not my fault, now is it? I'm a Jew.
> I'd a been born a Christian quick enough
> If only so I could have sold my stuff
> Double the price and not be called a screw.
> . . . .
> I often think when the Shemah begins
> "O God o' Jacob! Ain't we paid our sins?"

Similarly, in 'One Man Returns':

> He wanted me to tear me ands to bits,
> Along o' the box-makers, stead of which,
> I took and bought a basket, struck a pitch
> To sell me flowers by the Hotel Ritz.

Or the dismissed waitress talking of the marble tables in 'The Bun Shop':

> . . . . I believe
> If you rubbed hard on each one with your sleeve
> You'd find cut on them some gel's epitaph.
> They look like tombstones, don't they? in a row
> Quietly waiting in a mason's yard.

In others his own pity and anger speak out in tones which anticipate *The Uncelestial City*, as for example in 'The Streets Behind the Tottenham Court Road':

> The quiet folk who live in Kensington
> Mothers of pleasant girls and worthy wives
> Living at ease their comfortable lives
> Don't think what roots their homes are built upon,
> Don't think, or wouldn't listen if you shewed
> That beyond cure by love or change by hate

Like hooded lepers at each corner wait
The streets behind the Tottenham Court Road.
Row upon row the phantom houses stain
The sweetness of the air, and not a day
Dies, but some woman's child turns down that way
Along those streets and is not seen again.
And only God can in his mercy say
Which is more cruel, Kensington or they.

or 'The Suburbs':

Because they are so many and the same,
The little houses row on weary row;
Because they are so loveless and so lame
It were a bitter thing to tell them so.

And finally, the elegiac 'The Last London Sonnet':

All roads in London lead the one last way.
Like little streams that find a flowing river
They find the one great road that runs for ever
Yet has no London name . . .

Even without the confirmation of the 1930 Preface, the seeds of all that he attempted after 1920 can be seen in this first collection, in terms both of the range of poetic forms he was prepared to essay and of the themes he treated. Pierrot, Pierrette and Harlequin appear for the first time in these pages ('Pierrot', 'The Dancers', 'Columbine'). 'Judas', with its transfer of guilt - 'Not I betrayed thee, but . . . He who made thee . . . With such immortal longings' - and 'God gave us bodies' - 'Let them write in heaven"Love we forgive, but God is not forgiven."' - are the first attempts at formulating questions which will recur in most of his subsequent writings. Similarly, the debate about the triumph of love and beauty over time and death, one he never quite resolved, it seems, - these and other questions presage cognate themes in *Humoresque* (1926), *Requiem* (1927), and *The Uncelestial City* (1930).

Some of the *London Sonnets* poems were plainly written during or at the end of the war, for example, 'Victor Fox' - another version, conscious or not, of 'They shall grow not old' - while 'Battersea' registers his numbed awareness of the gulf between the survivors and the now eternally young:

I have always known where London river ends
(Or seems to end) that I shall find my friends,
Who are my friends no longer, being dead.

. . . .
Dear
In the moon, young and unchanging, they
Will cry me welcome in the boyish way
They had before they went to France, but I,
A boy no more, will greet them silently.[59]

The epitaphs also clearly belong to this period: 'Flecker' -

You have made the golden journey. Samarkand
Is all about you, Flecker, and where you lie
How youth and her beauty perish in the sand
They are singing in the caravanserai- ;

and 'Edith Cavell'-

Who died for love, we use to nourish hate:
Who was all tenderness, our hearts to harden;
And who of mercy had the high estate
By us escheated of her right to pardon.

With them belong, at least in chronology, the patriotic sonnets, 'England', 'The Moon In Flanders', and 'The Soldier Speaks'. The ten-line stanzas of the *ballade* 'Flowers At Hampton Court', which at first sight appear to do little more than marry 'Where have all the flowers gone?' with Rupert Brooke's 'some corner of a foreign field', nevertheless bring one up short with lines such as '. . . joyous bands of lilies, and the lean/ daffodils danced before or ran between.'

A number of the wartime poems sound alternate notes of gloomy warning and defiant, sometimes desperate optimism in what seemed a hopeless world. 'Victory' holds little comfort:

Let it be written down, while still the wound
Festers . . .
. . . . .Death we have not found
The worst, ...
. . . . But there's an ape
Out of the slime into the spirit creeping.

Conversely, 'The Gods Of The Copy-Book Headings', an explicit reply to a bitter, pessimistic poem of the same title which Kipling wrote in 1919, takes a more confident line: 'The devils come because the half-gods go/ but in the end the gods, the gods return.'[60] Another, 'The Woodcutters of Hütteldorf', prompted by Sir William Beveridge's account of the destruction of the Wienerwald to supply the Viennese with wood - 'it so completely sums up the misery of the people and the breakdown of civilisation', wrote Beveridge in *Peace in Austria* - inspired Humbert to appeal to an older song (which unaccountably had become a French nursery rhyme), 'Nous n'irons plus au bois, les lauriers sont coupés', and to end with the exhortation:

> Go back to the woods; replant the laurel trees.
> Still love than war hath greater victories,
> And while the devils beat the warlike drum
> Into their kingdom of peace the children come.

'Wheels 1919' is easy to date: it also identifies both by its title and its references a poetic trend from which Humbert firmly dissociated himself. Allusions to Aldous Huxley - 'Palm to palm in quiet sweat' - and acid apostrophising of 'the higher fornication' - 'You who at the higher level/Know love as he truly is' - suggest more than mere indifference to Imagists and Georgians.

There is very little if anything in Humbert's first published poems, and nothing at all in the documents in his family's possession, to suggest that he could be identified with either the Imagist or the Georgian poets. He came to know some of them but was never recruited by them, nor did he seek to be. Despite the attractions of associating with burgeoning movements in poetry, with the accruing advantages of a higher profile in the literary world, Humbert did not join, nor, in the case of the Georgian group, was he ever invited, as far as can be ascertained. Indeed, throughout the thirty years of his productive life as a poet, he showed remarkable consistency in his steadfast dedication simply to poetry, rather than to schools and movements. When the occasion called for it - as, for example in *Dialogues and Monologues* (1928) - he could analyse a movement or a trend, and identify its strengths and weaknesses, but to the last he remained his own man.

Imagism and more especially 'Georgian' poetry were creatures of the decade 1910 - 1920 (the last of the Georgian anthologies was published in 1922). The energy for identifiable 'movements' and 'schools' had exhausted itself by then; thereafter uniquely individual voices were seen as representing more truly the spirit of the times. The more accomplished 'movement' poets (Lawrence, Graves, Blunden, Eliot, etc.) resigned their membership (if indeed they thought of themselves as card-carriers at all); the old guard (Masefield, Drinkwater, Noyes, W. H. Davies) carried on as before, leaving the occasional oddity (for example, the Sitwells) as a reminder of 'manifesto' poetry.

It is the 'new' poet who is most inclined to look round for allegiances with the like-minded - the maturely established would expect followers to appear rather than seek models to emulate. Humbert paid a price for independence, as George Sampson noted: 'Humbert Wolfe stands apart from any movement of his time and has been harshly judged by contemporary 'sectarians' for his detachment.'

Thus, with the Georgians he favoured conventional metrics and aimed at intelligibility, while not disdaining a degree of romanticism. But with 'realism', homely rural English themes, and all that came under Orwell's disparaging heading of the 'beer and cricket' school of English poetry he would have no truck. Similarly, the Georgians' policy of reassuring rather than disturbing their English upper middle class readers was as abhorrent to him as the Imagists' categorical recipes for writing poetry. This poet-civil servant may superficially resemble Sir John Squire's typical Georgian poet at work:

> He would preside at committees, confer with officials, do all the routine work of a busy man of affairs. Then . . . he would take the train home to his suburb by the Crystal Palace, read an old or a new book, and lapse easily into the composition of quiet poetry,[60]

but the last phrase gives the game away: for all his apparent facility, Humbert was not interested in 'quiet poetry', while his satirical writing would have pained the sensitivities of such as Sir Edward Marsh.

These two books of poems, his first commercially published collections, mark a significant advance in his poetry. It would be wrong to dismiss his earlier verse - the contributions to *The Bradfordian* and the typescript collections analysed in Chapter 4 above - as mere exercises in versification and the simulation of poetical sentiments. Of course they *were* apprentice efforts, but some of them, at least, expressed personal experience, insights, a point of view, which there is no reason to suppose were purely factitious. Nevertheless, their chief limitation lay in the fact that many, though not all of them, although written for a particular person, appeared to address a wide and unspecified audience on universal issues in a moralistic, devotional or generally uplifing tone, but with little convincing effect - rather like a very young curate imitating Bossuet or Newman.

In this respect, *London Sonnets* breaks new ground. Not only is the poetic voice more confident (despite the technical weaknesses occasionally revealed); it also sets out, quite deliberately, to convey what may be called in the broadest sense a message, to raise issues - including moral issues - or to ask questions. Not that his purpose is narrowly didactic, even in his satirical verse. Rather does he appear to be struggling to embody in his poems the dictum of Aristotle so dear to Arnold (a moralist if ever there was one): 'the superiority of poetry over history consists in its possessing a higher truth and a higher seriousness.' Moral philosophers hold that for moral statements to be valid they must be universalisable. There is a sense in which the poet is tested by the same rule: does he evoke in the reader the response of recognition: "Yes, that's true, that's how it is!"? Even when Humbert is reflecting on his personal experience (of love, for example), he seems to be appealing to a shared experience in his readers: "Isn't it like this for you? for us all?" 'Message' then becomes the equivalent of 'universal truth', with something of the resonance of Pope's 'What oft was thought but ne'er so well expressed.' In Humbert's case, it was particularly fitting that *London Sonnets* and *Labour Supply and Regulation* should appear in parallel; poetry and history marching as it were side by side.

These two first books of poetry did not bring him fame; reviewers were muted in their enthusiasm. One wrote: 'A faintly religious note quavers through these verses', the first of many such observations which continued right up to his obituaries. It is true that fundamental religious themes increasingly haunted his poetry, like ghosts that could not rest. But was his preoccupation ever more than an aesthetically motivated attitude? There was certainly an abiding interest in the central Christian beliefs - death and resurrection, sin and forgiveness - as well as a romantic intoxication with the imagery, sounds, sense and colours of Christianity (tinged with what looks like a residue of paganism), but little evidence of ordinary, still less of extraordinary, piety. It is to be supposed that in the strongly Presbyterian atmosphere of the Graham household, Jessie would have been a regular churchgoer: her recollections after Humbert's death suggest it, without explicitly saying so. But their daughter, Ann, said that Humbert and Jessie rarely attended church and for her to be taken there as a child was a rare and memorable event.

It must be admitted that here and there poems are marred by elaborate conceits, occasional clichés, some sacrifices to the dictates of rhyme, and clumsiness resulting from abandoning the natural order of prose. Nevertheless, there are flashes of inspiration, that sureness of touch in the ordering of words which combine to say something new in a way that has the conviction of inevitability, the sudden (and often unexpected) felicitous image erupting into an otherwise unremarkable if technically adroit piece. Thus, on Icarus, the First Airman:

> Death with the powdered stars will walk and pass
> Like a man's breath upon a looking-glass,
> For a suspended heart-beat making dim
> Heaven brighter afterwards because of him.

Similarly, in 'Dancers': 'to a little wind the darkened trees / bend gravely and resume their silences.'; in 'Balder's Song': 'And maybe where the dog-rose remedies / with her wild flush the hedge, and spring begins.'; and 'The Skies':

> So large they are and cool the skies;
> God's frozen breath in dreams, or worse:
> Beautiful unsupported lies
> That simulate a universe.

or the poppies in 'France':

> The line these hold no force can break,
> Nor their platoons advancing shake,
> Whose wide offensive wave on wave
> Doth make a garden of a grave.

The last lines of 'The Reply', a sonnet dedicated to the thesis that the end of love, like the loss of beauty, is no cause for sorrow since both are necessarily transient - a favourite theme with Humbert - perfectly convey the cool, marmoreal indifference of a dead past:

> Cold, though they burn, untroubled, though they hurt you,
> And white, like gods, when through the sculptured portal
> The starshine enter and the moon's cold graces.

Although the exact date of this poem is unknown, the Ministry of Munitions paper on which it was first drafted (now in the archives of Bradford Grammar School) is clear evidence that war was not his only theme between 1914 and 1919.

In the poems inspired by family life the poignancy of 'Sometimes when I think of love' and 'The Little Sleeper.' is offset by the simplicity and tenderness which characterized much of his best later writing. Thus, for example, the Envoi:

> Past Buckhurst Hill the motor-bus
> Takes and shakes the three of us.
> When first we went, there were but two
> In Epping Forest, I and you.
>
> . . . .
>
> No one guessed and no one heard
> How, beyond the singing bird,
> Someone sang in solitude
> In the wood within the wood.
>
> . . . .
>
> Conquering the solitude
> A child is laughing in the wood.
> Past Buckhurst Hill the motor-bus
> Takes us back the three of us.

The rest of his family - brother, sisters and more distant relatives - appear to have inspired none of his published verse. Only Consola is ever mentioned, and even her name is not found in these first collections. The absence of much reference to Consola in Jessie's unpublished papers for this period might suggest that her influence waned after 1911. In fact, she still did her best to impose her will for a long time afterwards. When they lived in Neville Street (1914) she took it on herself to go through their accounts and point out their mistakes, an intrusion which predictably resulted in another titanic row. A later visit when they lived in Church Street, Kensington, was remarkable for being peaceful. On this occasion she took Ann to 'the pictures' - not to the cinema as Ann had assumed but to the National Gallery, much to Ann's disappointment. Humbert and Jessie had developed an early addiction to films, long before the talkies, and even before 1910.

Ann remembered visiting the Sidgwicks with her parents in a large house outside London. It seems likely that this was Frank Sidgwick, the founder of the publishing firm of Sidgwick and Jackson, who had married the niece of Humbert's friend Mr Coxhead (*see* Ch. 4 above). He published Rupert Brooke's first book of verse. If he and Humbert were friends, it seems strange that he never published anything of Humbert's. A brother, Arthur Sidgwick, is mentioned in *Portraits By Inference.* He died of wounds in September 1917, when Ann was only four years old, so it seems unlikely that they visited him.

When they lived in Neville Street, and perhaps before that in Battersea, they got to know Prebendary Webb-Peploe, a highly-esteemed Evangelical churchman and writer. A Prebendary of St. Paul's Cathedral since 1893, he was vicar of St. Paul's, Onslow Square, from 1876 until his resignation in 1916. It is possible that this was the St. Paul's where, according to Jessie, Humbert was baptised and confirmed, which would account for their acquaintance with the cleric. When they lost their third child (born in Neville Street, 1916/17, but surviving only a few hours), he told her she must thank God for the loss: his 'consolation' seemed to Jessie unbearably harsh. Unaccountably, there is nothing in Humbert's poetry which can be clearly identified with this their second tragic loss.

During the War they left Neville Street in order to avoid air raids and went to Hampstead, first to an unidentified house, known to Ann as 'The Dirty House', then to one called The Turret (after its single turret) in Frognal. Ann recalled watching air-raids and seeing an anti-aircraft gun on the Heath. She was five when they left in 1918; they could have bought the house for £500 but Humbert thought it too inconveniently placed for his work.

At the end of 1918, leaving Humbert to his duties in London, Jessie and Ann went to Torquay for the sake of Ann's bronchitis but returned to London before Christmas, only to succumb to the virulent influenza which ravaged the population in 1919; it was commonly said that the 'flu claimed more casualties than fell on the battlefields of the War. Ann had two clear memories of that winter: one was of waking up on Christmas morning in a furnished flat in St. George's Square, Pimlico; the other, of observing from the window an unending procession of hearses to the nearby church. They also took rooms for a short time in an hotel opposite the Natural History Museum, before moving to 25 Queen's Gate, in South Kensington.

Chapter Six

1920-1923

'The secret architecture of the dream'
('Labor Omnia Vincit III', *Out of Great Tribulation*, 1939)

I

Montagu House

In October 1919 Humbert's provisional promotion to Assistant Secretary (dating from 16 November 1918) was made permanent, on a salary scale of £1000 rising by £50 increments to £1200.[1] Another promotion recorded about the same time was the elevation to the substantive rank of Senior Clerk in the Employment Policy Branch (salary £400, rising by £20 increments to £500), of Mr. C. E. M. Joad, who later achieved notoriety as the incorrectly styled 'Professor Joad', of Brains Trust fame in World War II. His name will recur in the account of the chequered history of the Trade Boards.

The London headquarters of the new Ministry into which Humbert moved in 1919 was Montagu House, 'the last aristocratic town house in Whitehall to be commandeered by government.' [2] It was a quite splendid dwelling, in the Renaissance style of a château on the Loire, built between 1859 and 1862 on the former gardens of Whitehall Palace, by the architect William Burn, to be the London residence of the Duke of Buccleuch. Pre-War photographs of both exterior and interior bear out Richard Church's description of the splendours which met his eyes on his first visit to the 'state's new embassy to the working class'[3]

> every ceiling treble lacquered and insulated with sea-shells, all the doors rosewood . . . The entrance hall was wide, paved with coloured marble . . . The staircase rose to a landing . . . then parted in right and left curves up to the salon floors.[4]

At the same time it was hopelessly inadequate to house a staff of three and a half thousand in 1919, even with the erection of bungalows in the gardens and partitions in the larger rooms. This 'rude dissipation of the glories of Montagu House' is described in Harold Butler's *Confident Morning*:

> The magnificent reception-rooms with their marble chimney-pieces and their lofty painted ceilings were carved up into more or less spacious cells by hideous dun-coloured partitions, which effectively degraded their beauty, and bred an uncomfortable feeling of sacrilege in the minds of their occupants. The servants' bedrooms, attained by dusty, dimly lit staircases, were more readily adapted to official use, while the beautiful garden along the Embankment was soon obliterated by a fungoid growth of unsightly huts. One could almost hear the old house groaning under its mutilation. The whole effect was inexpressibly forlorn.[5]

The tale of the new Ministry's fortunes and misfortunes - now epic, now melodrama - in the inter-war years is not the primary concern of the present work, and in any case has been told, interpreted and re-interpreted sufficiently often to need no repetition here. Nevertherless, a minimum of explanation is needed in order to provide both context and intelligibility for Humbert's professional activities, and indirectly for his social and literary life too, over the next twenty years (*see* Appendix B).

The concluding chapter of *Labour Supply and Regulation* subtly conveys Humbert's awareness of the irony inherent in the architectural symmetry with which the first peace-time concerns of the Ministry of Labour neatly balanced the war-time objectives of the Labour Department of the Ministry of Munitions. It was not simply that his first task at the end of hostilities should be to dismantle the system he had spent the best part of five years helping to build up; but, even more, that the problems which the Ministry of Labour had to solve were almost exactly those of 1914 in reverse.

> For there were two questions. How were the Forces and the munitions workers to be demobilized so as to supply industry turning from war to peace with the necessary labour with least possible dislocation to production and hardship to the workmen, and what was the answer to such questions as the future of compulsory arbitration, the maintenance of a reasonable wages level during the transition period and the restoration of pre-War Trade Union restrictions in accordance with the provisions of section 4 (4) of the Munitions of War Act, 1915?[6]

The system of release from the colours by industrial categories was the answer found for the first question, and the anger and disaffection which this process fomented among the troops has already been mentioned (*see* Chapter 5). As for the second set of questions, the Ministry's energies from its very creation had been chiefly directed towards solving the problems of low wages and of the relations between employer and employed.

> The answers which it propounded were contained in a great extension of the trade-board system, in the establishment of joint industrial councils in a number of organized industries and in the creation of the International Labour Organization.[7]

Humbert made no claim to be the architect of any of these schemes, although, for the next ten years at least, he was to be centrally involved with all three of these, especially the Trade Boards and the International Labour Organization. The Trade Boards had existed for as long as Labour Exchanges; they 'established wage-fixing machinery in certain "sweated" industries for the purpose of determining statutory minimum wages.'[8] In 1918, thanks chiefly to the efforts of Harold Butler, Principal Assistant Secretary of the Ministry, the Trade Board Amendment Act enabled the Ministry to take the initiative in setting up Trade Boards and thus extend their influence. Butler's appointment to the I.L.O. in 1919 as Deputy Director was a great loss to the Ministry; had he stayed, the subsequent history of Trade Boards, until 1924 if not later, might have been very different.

The other major achievement in which Butler played a central role was the creation of the International Labour Organization, set up under the Treaty of Versailles for the express purpose of securing the permanent peace of the world by the establishment of social justice through an improvement of the conditions of labour. The Ministry of Labour was made responsible for all government business concerned with the Organisation, and, within the Ministry, International Labour came within the purview of the General Department, of which Humbert was made head in 1920, with the rank of Principal Assistant Secretary.[9]

From 1919 to 1924 the Civil Service underwent a drastic reorganisation. If economies had to be made, the Ministry looked a suitable candidate for abolition, and anxieties about the permanence of the Ministry were to haunt its staff for the remainder of the decade, as Humbert's letters to his wife reveal. Even when it did achieve permanent status in 1923 its troubles were not over. The Ministry's rapid growth to become one of the largest departments of state was finally proof against the recommendation of the 1922 Geddes Committee that the Ministry be dismantled, and when the suggestion arose once more in 1927 it was shown to be both politically and administratively impractical.[10] But, initially at least, the Ministry was regarded as little more than a second-rate department. The low salary of its Minister (£2000) and the low status of his department discouraged ambitious politicians. The real strength of the Ministry lay in its highly talented senior civil servants, but their potential was hampered by the lack of firm political leadership.

Among these senior officials Humbert stood out in every way. His striking personality was matched by an even more striking appearance and manner. Richard Church (whose transfer to Montagu House from the 'Dickensian oddity' of the Government Laboratory in Custom House Humbert had, against all the Civil Service rules, contrived), recalled that at his first interview with Humbert in the autumn of 1920, he heard the voice before he saw the man.

> Half an hour must have passed, before the inner door opened, and paused halfway with a figure still hidden behind it except for one hand on the further knob. I heard a high-pitched, chanting Oxford accent, saying: "Do come back, do, and explain just as briefly what you feel ought to be done!"

The visitor thus disposed of, Humbert then turned to Church.

> 'Do come in. So sorry', the piercing Oxford voice explained, 'People *insist* on telling me how to run the country, as though I were Prime Minister instead of a wretched anonymous Civil Servant slaving as much against his will as I can see you do'.[11]

Humbert's high-toned voice and clear articulation were often mistaken for affectation. They were in fact acquired quite early in his life and were the means whereby he and his siblings communicated with their deaf mother and aunt. Pamela Frankau remembered his voice as 'velvety, with an odd metallic note behind the velvet,' and his habitual greeting not 'How are you?' but 'How does it march?' There seems to be no evidence for the 'curious saucy lisp' which J. B. Priestley professed to remember. G. B. Stern, on the other hand, recalled Humbert's readings of his poems in 'a really beautiful voice.'

His room in Montagu House was as dramatic as its occupant. Formerly the Duke's library, it was huge, with a great bay window, a deep carpet, long curtains, and walls lined with elaborately decorated bookshelves, mostly empty save for those behind his enormous double desk, where gaily coloured dustjackets far outnumbered the drab official publications.

The voice, the flow of speech which 'poured from him as from a hydrant', the resemblance to Disraeli conjured up by 'the handsome Jewish features, the dandified costume, . . . the lock of hair which he tossed back with a hand which I noticed to be surprisingly powerful, with spatulate fingers, . . . the powerful mouth, the protruding nose and the strange eyes with deep-brown irises surrounded by a thin ring of grey, all held me spellbound.' Church noted also the 'lupine teeth' which could flash with a charming smile or were bared in a snarl of disgust when the needs of an importunate Minister intruded upon his time.[12]

Church's narrative is especially valuable in that it shows Humbert as more than simply a brilliant, gifted, charming personality. *The Voyage Home* succeeded in conveying also the formidable intellect which ruthlessly scrutinized and analyzed the person or the problem before him, the indomitable will, the astonishingly mature political sense, and the genius for handling irreconcilable groups and individuals.

By now Humbert had adopted a style of dress markedly different from the top hat and morning coat which Jessie had admired on her house-hunting visit ten years earlier. Whether Civil Service dress had become generally more casual as a consequence of the War, or whether his status as a senior Civil Servant emboldened him to adopt a more raffish style, it is hard to say. Photographs of groups at I.L.O. Conferences between 1923 and 1930 suggest that if morning dress was no longer always *de rigueur*, formality had not been entirely abandoned. In another letter to Jessie in the summer of 1920 he mentioned that after lunching with Geddes (of the famous 'axe') he was preparing to dine with Horne (recently Minister of Labour, now President of the Board of Trade) - '2 Cabinet Ministers in one day! and I haven't got my dress clothes.' But his independence in the matter of dress is borne out by the written testimony of contemporary eye-witnesses.

> He was an impressive figure . . . The fact is, he was different. Amongst all those frock-coated men with their winged collars and moustaches, typical of the Clemenceau-Lloyd George era, he was a non-conformist. He was clean-shaven, wore a light suit, and sported a bow-tie. Also his hair was thick and rather long. The long hair gave rise to an amusing incident. One afternoon his daughter, Ann, went to tea with a school-friend. At half-past six her father came to escort her home. The friend's small brother was sent to answer the door, and promptly reported back that there was a "funny chap with long hair" on the step. "Oh, that will be my father," said Ann.[13]

Richard Church recalled in a characteristic episode Humbert's picturesque appearance and eccentric, even exotic, taste. Civil Servants, even senior ones, worked on Saturdays in those days, at least until midday. Church went into work wearing a tweed coat and flannel bags in preparation for a walk over the Downs on his way home:

> As I entered the flowery iron gates of Montagu House I felt a tap on my shoulder. Turning my eyes, I saw an agate knob, at the end of an ebony stick. Turning

> further, I saw Humbert Wolfe dressed up to the nines: a huge bow tie, a heliotrope hat and overcoat to match. A whimsical, half-pained smile played about the muscular mouth, and the goat-like eyes glittered.
>
> 'My dear Richard,' said the high-toned voice, with exquisite affectation, 'why *will* you come to the office in fancy dress?'

Church went on to record that his slightly hurt reaction brought an immediate change in Humbert's mood, and an apology.[14]

In 1920 Humbert was thirty-five years old, a seasoned Civil Servant with an established reputation, his worth and service recognised by the award of CBE, and by his promotion to Assistant Secretary. It must have seemed to the world, and even to him, that he had 'arrived.'

And yet . . . one may wonder whether his world and his future looked quite as rosy to him. The Civil Service could have seemed a bathetic descent after the high promise of Oxford; the Board of Trade a prosaic round of fairly lowly tasks. The move to Labour Exchanges had held out the prospect of adventure, but the War set a strait-jacket on everyone. The value and importance of his contribution were beyond question, but once the war ended, his move to the Ministry of Labour was as much sideways as forwards.

His affectations of eccentricity were both a protest and an insurance against the stifling constraints of the Civil Service. His sometime colleague in the Ministry of Munitions, H. W. Garrod, wrote in 1927 that the chief disabilities with which Humbert had to contend were those of race, profession and environment: his racial origins created prejudice, his profession was 'commonly accounted humdrum . . . and more able men have been killed by environment than by drink or wars or women.'[15] Yet the Ministry of Labour was far from being the stuffiest ministry. Church described a number of officials who, like Humbert, cultivated an 'other life' outside as writers, painters, musicians, and indulged their penchant for less formal dress. And Humbert was responsible for attracting - even conjuring - a number of writers, artists and musicians into the Ministry. He found a home for Flint, the Imagist poet, in the Department of Intelligence and Statistics, where Church himself eventually fetched up under a head of department better known as C. K. Munro, the dramatist. Sadly, it turned out that, as far as poetry was concerned, Flint had shot his bolt.

No doubt playing the patron appealed to Humbert's vanity, but there was more to it than that. It was part of, and of a piece with, his belief that talent and originality could only benefit the Ministry and should be encouraged. He was anxious too to improve relations between the Ministry and the public in the aftermath of the War, particularly in the Labour Exchanges where the unemployed, predominantly ex-servicemen, were either patronized or treated with military harshness. Church believed that Humbert's efforts in this respect contributed substantially to preserving the peace during the General Strike of 1926. He was an early champion of what has come to be called 'equality of opportunity" within the service, and did his best to ensure that women with first class credentials and high ability were given the chance to deploy them. A high co-efficient of pulchritude was no impediment, as was observed in the case of Beryl Power, the sister of Eileen Power, the economic historian, of Amber Blanco-White, already mentioned, and of Miss Barfield, a solicitor and sister of the philosopher, Owen Barfield.[16]

Humbert's attitude to rank and seniority could be described as generally latitudinarian except towards those above him, whom he habitually accorded the degree of deference which he thought they deserved. He loved provoking senior officials who came urgently requiring information to enable the Minister to answer a Question in the House. Humbert was quite capable of keeping them waiting while he discussed with a relative junior the more important matter of the poetry of Sassoon or Edward Thomas.

Richard Church was not alone in thinking that Humbert's contempt for the stuffier aspects of bureaucracy, added to his outside interests and reputation, made him suspect among his more orthodox colleagues. And just as these manifestations of versatility and picturesque idiosyncracy damaged his professional career, so have they, in the fifty years since his death, done him some disservice in the sense that they served to distract attention from the genuine qualities which he displayed as a civil servant and as a poet. It is all the more necessary, therefore, to highlight the courage he showed in challenging Treasury orthodoxy and in urging his political masters to act out of of principle rather than mere expediency or laziness.

But much of that came later. In 1920 Humbert was experiencing a measure of professional success, but perhaps, too, some disenchantment. His appointment to the British delegation to the I.L.O. in 1921 was to offer the possibility, and at times what looked like the promise, of real success and advancement. His letters to Jessie show that for most of the time that he represented Britain at the I.L.O., and even after that, he entertained hopes of a senior post at the League of Nations (Secretary-General or one of his Deputies) or alternatively the Director's post at the I.L.O.

Meanwhile, as the decade advanced, his reputation as a poet gradually increased, slowly at first, but the succession of books after 1920 and the increasing volume of his contributions to reviews and literary magazines were steadily bringing him before the public eye. His circle of acquaintance widened too, through his writing and through the Civil Service. The names of literary and other luminaries whom he met in restaurants and his clubs (the R.A.C. and others) crop up regularly in his letters to Jessie.

This period (from 1920 onwards) is the best documented of his life. His name is frequently found in the recollections and papers of political, Civil Service and society notables. In addition, his letters to his wife and correspondence with other contemporaries make it possible to put flesh on bones and to restore something of the reality of his life.

One collection in particular is uniquely informative: a group of over five hundred letters from Humbert to Jessie, the majority written between 1920 and 1937. They were preserved by Jessie and after her death by their daughter Ann, who finally disposed of them to the Berg Collection in the New York Public Library in the nineteen sixties. They constitute a curious archive, for two reasons. Firstly because, in addition to the autograph signed letters, a handful of autograph signed notes, and a few telegrams and postcards, there is a typescript edition of most, though not all, of the letters, made by Jessie during the second world war. Humbert's biographer has reason to be grateful to Jessie for her patient transcription; deciphering Humbert's handwriting rapidly becomes a major labour of interpretation. Nevertheless her edition is precisely and undoubtedly that - an edited version - with omissions which she judged to be appropriate or necessary, and therefore leaves a permanent suspicion that it may be less than reliable in some details. I do not believe, however, that such surgery as she performed seriously altered the story which the letters tell.

The second curious feature lies in the peculiar uniqueness of the letters, for they are all from Humbert, none from Jessie. He wrote (almost daily) whenever either he or Jessie was away from London. The varying frequency and duration of their absences from one another account for variations in the number of letters from year to year, without one's needing to assume further editorial activity on Jessie's part. But none of her letters to him seem to have survived; Humbert once wrote from Geneva that when he received a reply from her he destroyed her preceding letter. Reading this one-sided 'correspondence', therefore, is rather like listening to one half of a telephone conversation: one can guess at most of the missing utterances but some mysteries remain unsolved.

From Humbert's frequent defensive protestations in these letters, one may infer that Jessie 'got on to' him quite often, took umbrage at what he had done or said, or had left unsaid or undone, and sometimes simply grew worried and upset, and needed reassurance. Knowing what one does of the subsequent unfolding of events, one has to admire her forbearance and selflessness. Nor is there any need to invoke neurosis or paranoia to account for her anxiety. At the same time it has to be said that, besides affording invaluable insights into the personalities of Humbert and his wife and the detail of their family life, the letters provide a fascinating commentary upon contemporary political events, as well as supplying vital information about Humbert's literary and social activity.

The first of the post-war letters are the nine which he wrote in July and August 1920, while he was waiting to join Jessie in Scotland for a holiday. They contain the salient features of all the subsequent correspondence: a seemingly perennial discussion about where they should live; money matters; current preoccupations and crises at the Ministry; what he was writing; and whom he met, lunched or dined with. Occasionally the letters show how national and international affairs impinge upon their personal lives. Towards the end of July he was suggesting to Jessie that they wait until the following spring to look for an inexpensive flat 'because everybody is saying that the boom is burst, and that we're on the edge of a slump', which would be to their advantage as purchasers. A week later, he reported that he had lunched in the office with Masterton-Smith, the Permanent Secretary, to discuss measures for the relief of distress during the forthcoming winter:

> There is a serious panic on about the winter. It really looks as though we were going to have bad times. I've written a long memorandum, suggesting
> (1) higher unemployment benefit
> (2) organized short-time
> (3) labour camps
> It's going to the Cabinet tomorrow.

And two days later he was reassuring her that despite 'a Poland panic' - the Bolshevik army had advanced to within a hundred miles of Warsaw - he expected to be joining her for their holiday as planned.

Although the Ministry worked him hard, and late, he found time to write reviews, articles and poems for various publications, and was thinking of writing a play, but feared 'that I'm writing too much. I'm going to keep the play for Scotland.' He mentioned having submitted a novel (unnamed) for publication; we must assume that he met with no success. Among the poems he wrote and quoted to her were 'The Japanese Mask' (which later appeared in his 1928 collection, *This Blind Rose*), and 'Mr. Kipps to his Maker', which began:

> You should have thought before you fashioned me
> of the huge weight of immortality
> for little men like me.

and may have been re-fashioned to become part of the 'Kipps' poem in the same book.

He told Jessie where and with whom he had dined: at his club, the R. A. C., with Morrison, his Oxford friend; at the Wyndham, with Sir Stephenson Kent, his old chief from Munitions and the Demobilisation Unit, who 'for all his wealth . . . secretly envies those of us who have to work. I don't really think that life can be fun when you can always have champagne even though it's 35/- a bottle. Though the champagne we had only cost 15/-!' One curious acquaintance whom he visited was John Fothergill, later to open a famous inn at Thame. Humbert found him 'really a little unbalanced. He does eat so queerly. But he is a very gentle poor lost old thing.'[17]

In one letter he explained that if his letters sounded far away. it was because 'I feel far away . . . Besides, I wanted to give "deltails" as mother always says and you know that I'm not good at that.' And in the next letter,

> This time I feel that to have you away is to be cut in two. Do you know I'm like Ann - I have the blind up at night, because the room feels so odd and lonely! I woke up the other night with a jump thinking that I heard Ann speak. . . But when I look back on the time since you came back I am so grateful. It isn't only my body you look after! it's my mind. The poems that I've written while you're away feel somehow thin. There is something about having you there that definitely adds to the quality of my thoughts. I hope this doesn't sound far away. It's meant to sound very close indeed.

On 10 August he reported a visit from his brother, Oswald, the previous day, 'on his way to Brussels, rather *piano* I thought. I'm not so sure that his Belgian adventure is being as successful as he expected.' Oswald had married a beautiful and wealthy Hamburg girl, and was living in Germany when the War broke out. He was interned, lost his fortune, and subsequently his wife. The Brussels venture appears to have been part of his efforts to regain financial security on his return to England after the War.[18] Consola, meanwhile, seemed to have lost nothing of her ability to stir up trouble, playing the hurt mother-in-law. 'I had a cold p.c. from mother asking for your address. I sent a letter telling her to "come orf it" as the saying is.'

The domestic detail one expects in all such letters is revealing, particularly about how they spent their money and what they regarded as necessary expense.

> I went into Harrod's on my way to the office yesterday and they faithfully promised the shoes . . . for Tuesday. They are villainously expensive - £3.19. [about £100 in 1990s money.] That damned feller Rendall squeezed out my article [in *The Saturday Review*] this week. So bang goes £3. I've written a snorter to A. A. B.

He was looking forward to his time in the hills, and asked if Jessie was buying golf clubs.

> I want you to play. Especially if we can have meals at the Clubhouse. That will reduce the housekeeping.

It is difficult to see this as an economy, unless it implied a saving on servants, but it goes some way to explaining why they had difficulty in living off his salary and what he earned from his writing, a recurring anxiety for the rest of his life.

The letters also reveal quite clearly the close relationship he had with his daughter, Ann. That he frequently wrote to her as well as to her mother is plain from references to such letters, though the letters themselves do not form part of the archive. But he frequently sent her a message via Jessie, showed interest in her activities and pride in her achievements, and shared her childhood world with its dolls and pet animals.

His friendship with A. A. Baumann, who edited *The Saturday Review* from 1917 to 1921, was of central importance to his advancement in literary circles. In *Portraits By Inference*, he described his first meeting with this 'contemporary of Curzon at Balliol, and by many considered the more remarkable of the two'. Early in 1919 Humbert had been taken by Martin Hall (of Chapman & Hall?) to meet Baumann for lunch at the St. James's Club, where Baumann, having listened to Humbert's lengthy exposition of the labour situation, asked "Will you write that for me?" What Humbert wrote and when is not known, and, said Humbert, was 'of no moment or interest, except to me who had to wait for my thirties to see my first proof.' But his account captured the overwhelming and unique experience of opening the envelope, extracting 'with reverent fingers the coarse paper with the ill-printed lines, and to know that, as long as paper endures and print does not fade, your work is a part of time - is there at the first glimpse of all any sensation to match it?'[19]

Later that year, while recovering from the influenza epidemic, he received from A. A. B., as he always called him thereafter, the first parcel of review books, one of which was *Jones's Wedding and Other Poems*, by Arthur Sidgwick, the brother of Frank Sidgwick, the publisher. Humbert remembered Arthur Sidgwick as his slightly senior contemporary at Oxford, who had died of wounds in France in 1917.[20]

Thereafter, the letters to Jessie record numerous articles and poems for *The Saturday Review*, and regular visits to Baumann's house in Tunbridge Wells for lunch or for a week-end. Baumann, who was in his sixties when Humbert first made his acquaintance, was a barrister and director of public companies as well as being a journalist, and had been an M.P. in the 1880s. Humbert's letters increasingly reflect his feeling of having taken on the role of 'heir' to A. A. B., and by the end of the decade he even seemed to be counting on this position to solve his financial problems. This 'inheritance', however, does not appear ever to have materialised.

II

The War of the Trade Boards

The aim of the major managerial reorganisation of the Civil Service between 1919 and 1924 was to reduce waste, to increase efficiency, and to instil, in the place of purely departmental loyalties, a sense of belonging to a single public service. The logical consequence of this was Treasury control of the service, especially when the Permanent Secretary to the Treasury was confirmed as head of the Civil Service, with responsibility for approving all senior appointments in every ministry.

Leaving aside the debated question of whether the Treasury should have even attempted, let alone whether it contrived or failed, to impose uniformity, it is clear that declared Ministry of Labour and Government policy on a number of issues was thwarted by Ministers and Cabinet, and by senior Ministry and Treasury officials. It is also clear that among the rare and notable exceptions Humbert stood out as a brave and independently-minded official who was not afraid to challenge Treasury thinking (often on the grounds that it showed no evidence of thought), and that he played an important part in overcoming Treasury restrictions and in developing the peculiar character of the Ministry in the inter-war years.

He had a short way with shoddy argument. The Treasury, for example, held the unshakeable belief that an industrial relations staff caused rather than reduced industrial unrest. This, said Humbert, was doubtless 'on the self-evident analogy that fire-brigades create fires.'[21] But perhaps his major conflict on the home front between 1919 and 1924 was what might be called The War of the Trade Boards.

The dramatic increase in the number of Trade Boards at the end of the First World War had been a major triumph for the Ministry. But, as prices fell and unemployment rose, pressure from employers and public opinion persuaded the Minister and the Cabinet to arrest their policy of expansion.[22] The lack of properly trained investigating officers hampered the effectiveness of the Trade Boards. Humbert, as head of the section responsible for Trade Boards, argued strongly, and initially with some success, for more funds in order to train an adequate inspection force. But Treasury economic doctrine held that in a climate of recession, public expenditure should be reduced. Trade Boards, by encouraging higher wages, led to higher public expenditure. Trade Boards therefore should be curtailed, and one of the easiest ways of bringing this about was to restrict their operations by starving them of investigation and enforcement staff. In a minute to his Minister, T. J. Macnamara, in January 1921, Humbert exposed the unsoundness of this argument, adding tartly, "the

Treasury reasoning is as unusual as it is fallacious. It would, I think, have been better for the Treasury before entering into the field of industrial economics, to attempt to acquire some knowledge of the rudiments of that science.'[23]

Humbert's principled stand in all of this was all the more exemplary for being virtually unsupported by his Ministerial colleagues and superiors. Hilton, the head of the Statistics Division, was the only colleague of comparable status to take a firm anti-Treasury line. H. J. Wilson, the Assistant Permanent Secretary who succeeded Masterton-Smith as Permanent Secretary in August 1921, and Sir David Shackleton, now the Ministry's Chief Labour Advisor, ensured that Treasury policy was in the main enforced. Wilson's complaisance did his career no harm, for he eventually rose to be Permanent Secretary to the Treasury and thereby head of the Civil Service.[24]

In addition to his isolation in the battle of principle concerning the Trade Boards, Humbert found that he was also a lone voice in the particular incident of the dispute over the Grocery Trade Board, where independent members of the Board had fixed a rate of wages (as was their duty), but the Minister, instead of confirming their decision, sent the matter to the Cabinet for a solution. Early in March 1921 Humbert warned that they risked 'destroying not only the Grocery Board but the whole Trade Board system.' In June he bluntly advised Macnamara that 'in the circumstances I should choose the course which, in my view, is right in principle.' Macnamara, with the approval of the Cabinet, managed to avoid his statutory duty to confirm the rates, on the grounds that economic conditions were too volatile.[25]

From the evidence of his letters to Jessie, Humbert had a low opinion of Macnamara, whom he called 'that donkey' for daring to call a meeting on August Bank Holiday 1922. A later letter refers to 'rotten old Macnamara.' The Minister, whose leadership was judged by Lowe to be 'erratic', was described by Richard Church as

> an ex-schoolteacher . . . a tall, horse-faced man with a large mouthful of teeth, and the boomimg voice of a bully. He had little respect for his permanent staff, and was apt to disclaim them, and criticize them in public, where they had no means of answering back.[26]

Church cited a typical instance of Humbert's way of dealing with the Minister's pomposity. Macnamara had one day summoned all his senior officials in order to catechize them about a leak of some confidential information to the Press.

> Having seated them all round the wall, he tossed his head so that one could imagine the rattling of harness.

> "Now, gentlemen," he snorted, "I am going to ask you categorically, one by one, if you know anything about this gross breach of official confidence. I hope you realize that the position of the Government has been gravely imperilled?"
>
> ....

The schoolroom inquisition then proceeded, drawing progressively nearer to Humbert, who had arrived last and taken a chair near the door, where he lounged with affected languor and made great play of hiding a yawn brought on by his boredom. When the inquisitor reached him,

> before (the Minister) could utter the now dreary formula, Humbert, half recumbent, rolled his eloquent eyes to heaven, and drawled:
>
> "It's no use asking me, Minister. My private secretary *never* lets me see important papers!"[27]

Further attempts were made to constrain and if possible abolish the Trade Boards. A Committee, chaired by the Lord Chancellor, Lord Cave, was appointed to review the Trade Boards Act. Humbert gave evidence before it in 1922. The Cave Committee eventually recommended that the Boards be retained but strictly with their limited pre-war purpose of preventing 'sweating'. Although the recommendations never became law, administrative decisions by the Ministry ensured adherence to the 'spirit' of the Cave Report.

The Report of The Cave Committee on the Working and Effects of the Trade Board Acts, 1922, listed Humbert as a witness on the first, second, third, and twenty seventh [last] days of the enquiry. It also emerges from the Report that Beryl Power was then a Trade Board Inspector. Humbert's admiration for Miss Power's beauty and professional competence was well known, but no evidence has been found to support the widely held belief that his relationship with her was other than professional.

A long memorandum submitted by Humbert in the course of preparing evidence for the Cave Committee highlights the fundamental differences which divided the Ministry's officials. The review of the Trade Boards inevitably raised the issue of the need for a court of appeal. Sir David Shackleton argued that this should not be part of the Ministry's functions. Humbert's experience of the Grocery Board convinced him that the Ministry's role could not and should not be merely to register decisions of the Trade Boards; it necessarily had to assume some responsibility for wage-rates and therefore should be and should admit to being a court of appeal.[28]

His memorandum reads as a forceful, confident and logical statement of the case. He spelled out the issues, faced the awkward and inevitable consequences, and gave clear and firm advice. A strong note of political and philosophical principle runs through the paper, notably on parliamentary authority and Ministerial responsibility, for the fundamental debate was about State intervention and industrial devolution.

Humbert accepted the general view that 'Government must interfere with trade as little as possible,' but argued that if a Trade Board needed to be applied, it followed that 'the Minister should accept a real responsibility for seeing that the wages fixed are the right wages.'

He recommended that the Department itself should obtain the necessary information to enable it to give informed advice to the Minister, which might mean appointing an outside Commissioner or hearing the case itself if it so wished - he quoted the precedent of the Piers and Harbours Act.

> The objection to this course is that it appears to involve bureaucratic interference with trade. The answer to this criticism is that it is always possible for enemies to describe the whole Trade Board system in this terminology and that any attempt to avoid this criticism by administrative confusion is foredoomed to failure. Any attempt to add semi-responsible bodies which have not the final decision is bound to lead to delay and to friction, and actually to accentuate the Ministerial nature of the ultimate decision. The simple truth is that the Trade Board policy involves an Act of Government: that Acts of Government can only be performed by and through Ministers, and that any attempt to evade that obligation is in effect an attempt to get away from the principle of the Trade Boards Acts. If it is frankly admitted that this political difficulty must be faced, (as in my view it must if the Acts are to be properly administered) then the cleanest, simplest and cheapest method is for the Minister to be able to get the really informed opinion he needs from his own officers.[29]

The reference to administrative confusion and delay was carefully chosen: Humbert knew from experience that Ministers, and Cabinet, as well as the Treasury, were past masters at prevarication. His gloomy warning proved only too well-founded, for although Wilson and Shackleton signified their agreement with his proposal, Humbert was defeated.

Occasionally the Ministry of Labour files strike an unintentionally droll note. One file is headed: '*Draught* Memorandum for the Cabinet

Proposals for continuing the establishment of Trade Boards', while the Summary of Evidence to the Committee of Enquiry into Trade Boards cites, among instances of visits by officers of the Department to Boards or Committees of Boards for oral discussion, 'Mr. Joad, Coffin Furniture Trade Board, to discuss questions of scope.'[30]

Whether Humbert personally engineered Joad's appointment, or simply ratified it, there was a poetic aptness in placing responsibility for this industry of ultimate repose in the hands of one so monumentally idle. Joad had come to the Ministry of Labour from the Labour Exchanges Department of the Board of Trade which he entered in 1914. The prodigious activity of his life in the 1930s and 1940s contrasts strangely with his legendary indolence as a civil servant. He ineptly tried to conceal his frequent absences from the office by keeping a coat hanging behind his door to suggest that he was somewhere about the building. His personal hygiene and habits were unpleasant and in addition he affected a superior, condescending manner. Church thought him a charlatan, while the typists spent their time avoiding his attentions. Invited by a clergyman to write for a pacifist journal, to which contributors gave their services free, he insisted on payment, claiming hardship on the pretext that he had lost his job for being a conscientious objector when in fact he was employed throughout the war. He eventually resigned from the Civil Service in 1930 to become head of the Department of Philosophy at Birkbeck College. He gained a reputation as a teacher, writer and broadcaster, but finally came to grief when he was caught travelling on the railway without a ticket.[31]

The Trade Boards issue resurfaced in 1924, first in the closing weeks of Baldwin's government and then under the first and short-lived Labour administration. But, as Humbert noted in November 1924, the months covered by the Labour Government did not produce any striking change of policy with regard to administration, although with regard to legislation the policy of their predecessors was reversed. Reviewing the history of the Boards, he remarked that the Labour Government (with Cave) went back to the spirit of 1909 and concentrated on wages rather than organisation as the test for setting up a Board - 'Nor was this the only instance of the conservative attitude of the Labour Government in this regard.'[32]

A marginal note to Humbert's Memorandum of 7 February 1924, on Distributive Trades provides a rare example of a Horace Wilson joke. Alongside a reference to the Hairdressing Trade, Wilson wrote: 'Is this a distributive trade: I hope not!'[33]

III

The International Labour Organization 1920 - 1921

It is generally agreed that Britain was the chief architect of the International Labour Organization, and certainly of the tripartite basis of its constitution, which made the partnership of governments', employers' and workers' representatives the essential feature of its annual conferences and of its Governing Body. The principal British contributors to the creation of the I.L.O. were George Barnes, a member of Lloyd George's War Cabinet and regarded by the Prime Minister as 'the authentic voice of Labour'; Sir Malcom Delevingne, a senior official in the Home Office; and two Ministry of Labour officials in the British delegation to the Peace Conference, Harold Butler and Edward Phelan.[34]

In August 1919, barely four months after the Peace Treaty, the first International Labour Conference was held in Washington. The first item on the agenda was the establishment of a maximum eight-hour day, 48-hour week, for people employed in any public or private industrial undertaking, known thenceforward as The Hours Convention. With only one dissentient vote the Convention was carried, but although Britain voted for it the Government failed to ratify it. At the first meeting of the new organization's Governing Body, Arthur Fontaine, the permanent head of the French Ministry of Labour, was confirmed as Chairman, a post he occupied for the next ten years. Albert Thomas, the wartime Minister of Munitions and a socialist député, was elected Director and when the Governing Body next met in January 1920, in Paris, Harold Butler was appointed to the post of Deputy Director.[35]

After a year of bouncing backwards and forwards between Paris, London, Washington and Genoa (where the second Conference, exclusively concerned with maritime questions, was held in 1920), the newly created International Labour Office finally made its home in Geneva, thanks to the firmness of Albert Thomas, who decided that the dignity and efficiency of the I.L.O. were too important to wait while the League of Nations made up its mind whether to choose Brussels or Geneva as its seat. The first headquarters of the I.L.O. were in a former boys' school in the Parc Ariana, on the Route de Pregny, about two miles above the town. For sessions of the International Labour Conference, the Casino /Kursaal was lent rent-free by the Geneva town council from 1921 until the new lakeside building was opened in 1926.[36]

Humbert was eminently qualified, by experience and seniority as well as by personal conviction, for his role as a representative of Britain at the I.L.O. In addition, he was known to a number of important people in the

League of Nations and the world of international labour, in both of which, particularly after the withdrawal of the United States, the two most important parties were Britain and France. But the explanation for his involvement with the work of the I.L.O. from the spring of 1921 is probably to be found in the simple, even banal, fact that his department at the Ministry was responsible for international labour affairs. Be that as it may, the time he spent at Geneva over the next dozen years was to be of crucial significance for every aspect of the rest of his life.

The first indication we have of this new turn in his career is in a letter, dated 12 May 1921, to Humbert at the Ministry of Labour from the Director of the I.L.O. in Geneva, Albert Thomas, regretting that he had been unable to chat with Humbert on 'our last day' (presumably Thomas had been to a meeting in London), welcoming any correspondence on subjects which concerned them both, and promising to call on Humbert when Thomas next came to London.

From Humbert's reply of 19 May it may be inferred that if the two had met they had not yet got to know one another at all well. Writing in fluent, slightly fulsome but not quite flawless French, Humbert expressed his appreciation of the warmth of Thomas's letter welcoming him to the I.L.O., and looked forward to making closer acquaintance soon either in London or Stockholm. The letter is interesting as a rare surviving example of Humbert's command of French. The general incapacity of most British representatives to express themselves in anything but English at international meetings, then as now, is well attested: Harold Butler, in *Confident Morning*, cited A. J. Balfour's admission that the only French he understood was Lloyd George's. It would be churlish, therefore, to be over-critical of Humbert's French at this time. The meaning is perfectly clear and the letter reveals a genuine 'feel' for the language, and for the register deemed to be appropriate in correspondence of this kind. Humbert's performances in French and German as well as in English at subsequent sessions of the I.L.O. became legendary.[37]

Chapter 13 of *Portraits By Inference* described Humbert's journey across Europe, from Berlin to Denmark and then on to Stockholm in the summer of that year. In this chapter, entitled 'Albert *Et* Arthur', Humbert was ostensibly concerned with portraying the complementary characters of Arthur Fontaine, Chairman of the Governing Body of the I.L.O., and his fellow countryman, the Director-General. Due allowance being made for changes in perspective and even of perception between the actual visit and the later account of it written in 1934, *Portraits By Inference* vividly conveys the stark contrast between the near starvation of Germany and the lavish entertainment the delegates enjoyed in Denmark and Stockholm. Jessie had been all set to accompany him but, only a matter of hours before they were due to leave, Humbert came home with the news that, after all, the Swedes had decided that delegates were not to be allowed to take their wives with them. Jessie took the set-back bravely but she was deeply disappointed. It is safe to assume that the crossing from

Warnemünde to Denmark in the course of this visit provided the setting for the poem 'Denmark', in *The Unknown Goddess* (1925).[38]

By the autumn of 1921, the Wolfes had moved from Queen's Gate to No. 72 High Street, Kensington; Humbert was writing to Jessie at that address in October. They occupied the two upper floors above a branch of Barclay's bank. It had previously been The Civet Cat public house, and two metal signs, in the shape of cats, still swing from the wall. It was a black and white, mock-Tudor building, which has since become a pizza parlour. Ann Wolfe had a clear memory of their four years there as one of the happiest periods of her early life:

> This was a different kind of move. The furniture came out of storage, remembered chairs, carpets and pictures reappeared. It felt like home in a way that other places hadn't. It was a light, airy flat, the top two storeys of a corner building, partly in High Street, partly in Church Street. Some windows looked across the High Street to Barkers, the corner ones along the High Street, so I could watch for Berto coming from the High Street Underground, when he came back from work, and other windows across Church Street to St. Mary Abbots, whose bells resounded often. I remember it as a happy period.[39]

There seems to have been no question of Jessie's accompanying him when he went to Geneva in October 1921, to attend the meeting of the Governing Body, followed by the Conference proper. On this first visit to Geneva he stayed at the Grand Hotel, Beau Rivage. The seven letters which he wrote to Jessie between 18 and 27 October repeatedly say how much he missed her - 'I thought with real pain of the pleasure it would have been to see Paris again together and Switzerland for the first time.' Geneva was so different from Stockholm - 'no banquetings and all damnation work. Never mind, my dear! Who knows, who knows - as Flecker says - if life won't burst open like a rose and all the decks put on their leaves again.'[40]

The official record of the 1921 Conference described Humbert as "Technical Adviser to the Government Delegation of Great Britain." The chief British Government representative was Sir Montague Barlow, M.P., Parliamentary Secretary at the Ministry of Labour. Barlow had had a successful career as a Director of Sotheby's, and enjoyed a reputation as a reformer in labour matters. He championed more comprehensive social security and stoutly defended the Ministry's role in the field of social service. For all that, Humbert had little regard for him, to judge from his derogatory references to 'that unspeakable horror Barlow. He is that most tiresome of combinations - a vain stupid man with a streak of cleverness in him.' His public speaking deserved the epitaph of the 18th century preacher: 'sleep at his bidding creeps from pew to pew', and he was hardly more stimulating as a travelling and table companion. In his first letter home, describing the Channel crossing, Humbert wrote, 'The sea - thank God - was as flat as Barlow's conversation.' And later there are various references to the 'inestimable pleasure of Barlow's company', and to 'dining with the really and truly Sir Montague Barlow.'

At the Conference the earliest issue to surface and the one which was debated the longest - it went on for years - was Hours of Work, on which Humbert had sharpened his teeth during the War, and which had already been debated at the Washington Conference of 1919. Thereafter, 'Hours' cropped up in Humbert's letters every time he went to Geneva, and from both I.L.O. and British records it is clear that it remained a problem issue at least until 1930, if not beyond. Another hotly debated issue was White Lead, which provided Humbert with one of his favourite diversions on the unreliability of statistics.

The 1921 letters, unlike those of later visits to Geneva, say little about the detail of the Conference, but convey quite plainly the tedium of the endless meetings: 'Life is infamously dull. Conferences, committees . . . the same dull people saying the same dull things at enormous length over and over and over again.' (27 October)

For Humbert the only compensation for the heat of the meeting rooms, the wearisome discussions, and the fog which for much of the time obscured Mont Blanc, was the discovery he made of the old town of Geneva where he went for a walk every evening after dinner. In one of the first letters of this visit he described 'Rue du Soleil Levant' (Street of the Rising Sun) which he had found the previous evening.

> It was a sheer tumbling little street that was so headlong that it would have fallen 100 feet into the lake below, if the railing at the end of it hadn't stopped it. Naturally I wrote a poem on it late last night. I won't send it to you, so that you may write one in competition!

He encouraged her to send off two poems, presumably her own, to *Country Life* and *Time and Tide.*

A few days later he described the old town in more detail:

> It is built sharp on the hill, and there are deep wynds like those on the Grassmarket only deeper - darker, and filled with strange ghosts of dead Genevese. You look up suddenly out of a well slap into the stars. And night - which was a night of astonishing moon - suddenly four swans slanted lamenting through the sky . . . I am writing a poem for each of the streets in the old town -

Rue du Soleil Levant - Rue des Barrières - Rue du Puits
St. Pierre and Rue de Toutes Ames. Here is the last:

Street of all souls, have in your moonless keeping
these English souls, who ask no more of you
than that smooth dark, where none awakes from sleeping
and no foot stirs the quiet all night through.

Street of many souls, these too admit
into your Order, where is none to call
Matin or Vesper and no lamp is lit,
and the long service has no end at all.[41]

One letter spoke of having found an amusing Swiss toy for Ann, a model Swiss chalet with animals and a peasant. Financial matters, always part of their correspondence, as was evident from 1920 onwards, took on a sinister aspect halfway through this absence when Jessie wrote in great alarm to tell him that he was overdrawn at the bank to the tune of £272 (at least £5000 in 1990s money) and that the bank was creating difficulties for her. He wrote to reassure her: the trouble was partly a misunderstanding (although the letters make clear that they had a permanent overdraft but of an acceptable size); steps had been taken to enable her to draw on their account, and in addition he had written to his friend and former colleague, Owen Smith, to ask for a loan. 'The thing is right and (touching wood) if Owen helps it can never happen in any case again.'

A few days later he wrote to announce that Owen had agreed and that once his cheque arrived the overdraft would be wiped out. It also meant that he would be able to help Jessie's brother, 'Gub', who was unwell at the time. The letters and Jessie's unpublished papers show that they were never without financial worries throughout the 1920s and 1930s. To judge from his letters Humbert generally took a matter-of-fact view of their debts; there is a strong suggestion of 'pay when you have to and no more than you must to keep them happy', but occasionally there is real desperation in his tone. Jessie, with good reason, as will be seen, tended to worry more than he did.

On his salary they should theoretically have had a comfortable life, but apart from the possibility that they were extravagant or just careless, the recurring cost of Ann's operations was a large additional expense. There may also have been some financial strain from the presence of Jessie's family as lodgers, first Gilbert, Jessie's brother, whose health had been badly affected by his wartime service as a naval doctor, and then, after Joseph Graham died in 1923, Jessie's mother and sister, to whom Humbert offered a home even though they had little liking for him. In addition, through no fault of his or Jessie's, Humbert's private income from his share in the family trust, and his hope of receiving the capital, had shrunk because a sizeable part of Martin Wolff's estate had been invested in German and Russian funds which collapsed disastrously as a result of the War and the Russian Revolution.

His hopes of returning home about 26 October, and so of restoring Jessie's spirits, were dashed as he was about to leave. Sir Montague Barlow had been recalled to London and the Minister had instructed Humbert to stay in Geneva until Barlow's return. The next day, 27th, Humbert wrote: 'That donk Barlow won't wire the day of his return. Meanwhile poor old Sir David [Shackleton, who was also with them in Geneva] clings pathetically to me. "Nay, laad", says he "tha moosn't leave me to all these foreign chaps."' On 27 October, however, he wrote that he expected to be back in London by Monday evening, 1 November, and enclosed the poem - here called Epping - which formed the Envoi to *Shylock Reasons With Mr. Chesterton* (1921).

IV

1922

Besides overseeing the ordinary business of his department, Humbert also had in 1922, as we have seen, to deal with the Trade Boards issue, the Cave Commission, and the challenge of the Committee on National Expenditure. This last, under the chairmanship of Sir Eric Geddes, was set up by the Government at the end of 1921 in response to an 'anti-waste' campaign promoted by businessmen and some sections of the Press, which focussed, somewhat late in the day, on the wartime extravagance for which, as temporary civil servants and government contractors, businessmen had been in part responsible. Fearing for its own survival, the Government charged the Committee with the task of finding ways of reducing gross expenditure in Departments of State. The economies which the Committee recommended in all branches of public spending were of such severity that they were known as 'the Geddes Axe'. But perhaps the most far-reaching effect of the Committee's Report was that it effectively set the tone for a decade or more in industrial relations by attempting to legitimize the extension to peacetime of wartime Government interventionism.[42]

In addition, even when he was not attending meetings in Geneva, Humbert had to deal with I.L.O. matters at home. For the decisions reached by the Governing Body and by the annual Conference had to be applied by individual States, which meant ratification, if they were to have anything more than a paper reality. And the private papers of Humbert and others support the evidence of the public records that sectional and national interests were just as powerful within the I.L.O. as they were within the League of Nations.

It is not surprising, therefore, that civil servants like Humbert, who were often among the more idealistic members of the I.L.O., faced with the task of defending their own governments' far from idealistic or unselfish policies, should have adopted a stoical realism with regard to the amount of progress they thought feasible, making every effort to achieve what they knew to be desirable but settling for what could actually be done, and hoping thereby eventually to bring about permanent and fundamental, if quiet, revolution. In this respect, the judgement made by Violet Markham, who came to know and admire Humbert during her brief period as Canada's representive at the I.L.O., was misleading though well-meant. In her autobiography, *Return Passage*, she wrote: 'Wit, charm, cynicism, and a keen sense of humour, all went to the making of a rare personality. *The idealism of the poet, the realism of the civil servant, were in separate compartments.*' [my italics] The likelihood is that in reality he was simply disguising his real feelings in order to preserve his sanity; poking fun at the antics of the I.L.O. delegations was probably the only way of saving the idealist from turning into a cynic.[43]

The I.L.O. from its creation had had as its aim the practical implementation of internationally agreed labour standards. But in practice the Conventions (as the agreements were called) constantly ran into difficulties, as each State argued that its own peculiar industrial conditions made the convention inoperable, or unduly exacting, or too inflexible. In addition, many States were unwilling to ratify Conventions, with the sacrifice which this would entail, so long as other States claimed exemption. And finally, as the 'Hours' Convention demonstrated, it was one thing to obtain general approval of a general principle, and quite another to secure agreement to its application to every industry. This probably explains why the 'Hours' issue cropped up, like King Charles's Head, in every Conference which Humbert attended: the 8-hour day, 48-hour week, had to be examined and voted upon in the context of every industry's circumstances. It was argued, of course, that a global Convention of the kind agreed at Washington was precisely the kind of unrealistic agreement which Britain could neither ratify nor implement. But there is ample evidence in the records to show that Humbert was quick to correct any attempt to misrepresent decisions of the Conference.[44]

He was twice in Geneva that year, for the Governing Body in the last week of July and for the Conference in the second half of October. As in 1921, he went as 'Adviser' to the Government Delegation, and to act as substitute for Sir Montague Barlow, on the Commission on Constitutional Reform. The decision of the Governing Body to hold its July meetings in the Kursaal at Interlaken enabled Humbert to take advantage of the programme of excursions which had been laid on and which provided him with the occasion and the setting for a number of later poems. His letters to Jessie said little about the meetings, save that at the end he thought they had been useful: 'We've done all the things that we meant to do.' He mentioned 'five lonely-looking ladies', wives of senior I.L.O. personnel, at the reception given by the Swiss:

> Madame Thomas, who is a little rude sharp-faced lower middle-class Frenchwoman, Madame Fontaine - old Fontaine's second wife a rather heavy type of Parisian, and Mrs. (Secker?) - wife of the Director of Intelligence in the office. She is aggressively even violently Yankee. Emphasizes her accent and hates the English. Finally Mrs. Butler had come. She is really a nice woman . . . very lame and just a little conscious of it . . . but she is pleasant and simple.

His letters and postcards give some idea of the profound effect this first real experience of the Swiss Alps had upon him. It remained forever a special place for him, inspiring and nourishing much of his poetry over the next two decades.

> Outside my window is the highest hill that isn't a mountain in the world. It's like the most enormous hedgehog with spikes right over the top - lovely soft green spikes - and looking over the hedgehog white, insolent, untouched is the Jungfrau. . . (Jungfrau means virgin, as you know, but isn't it German to call a thing like a dream gone frozen a young woman!)

One evening about 8 o'clock, at the end of the day's meetings, he walked the five miles to Zweilutschinen and back, accompanied by Barlow (who for once escaped scornful comment).

> We got there about 9.20. The Jungfrau was in front of us all the way and she changed from a deep true orange to golden-red. Then she grew dark. The great pine forests were hushed and green and the little Lutschinen (there are two - one from Mürren called the white, the second from Grindelwald called the black) rushed in a grey-blue torrent. We reached a little inn by a fork of the stream and there under a vine we had a supper of ham and eggs, Gruyère cheese, wild strawberries and Swiss wine. We walked back through the dark with the air far more alcoholic than any wine was ever distilled.

This walk and the meal were later described in the poem, 'Over The Fire', which begins: '"The Bear" at Zweilutschinen!' in *The Uncelestial City* (1930).

On another evening, the whole Governing Body went on a steamer trip on Lake Thun.

> We saw the whole Jungfrau range - Wetterhorn, Schreckhorn, Eiger, Monch, Jungfrau, the barrier at the end of the world (it seemed). On the way back they lit stars on the top of the mountains. We dined on board and got back about 10.

The excursion to the Jungfraujoch was spoiled by rain and then a blizzard of snow.

> We didn't see a thing till on the way home about 6 the sun came out on the Eiger, terrifyingly white, huge and beautiful. We saw an avalanche begin, rush, tremble, roar, and subside. But the height didn't agree with me. My wretched stomach sat up and took notice. The station at the top rocked under my feet as though it had been the deck of a steamer. I did however manage to get these Edelweiss, which I enclose.[45]

In 1922 Humbert planned, as he had in previous years, at least since the War, to take his annual holiday early in September, since Jessie had gone with Ann to Kilcreggan, in Dumbartonshire, to look after her mother who was convalescing after an illness. The score of letters which he sent to Jessie between the middle of August and the first days of September are rich with information about his activities and preoccupations, but perhaps their chief interest lies in what they reveal about the work in progress, whether this was poems fresh from his pen, ideas he had for books, or contacts with publishers and other literary figures. He wrote this daily report of his activities either from Montagu House or from the Royal Automobile Club, where he slept and frequently dined, calling at the Kensington flat only to empty the letter-box.

A number of the poems which were eventually to make up *Kensington Gardens* (1924) first appeared in the monthly *Chapbook* of the Poetry Bookshop on 24 August 1922, with a cover designed by Albert Rutherston. Published by Harold Monro, a frequent dining acquaintance of Humbert's, *The Chapbook* was a periodical which appeared from 1919 to 1925, the successor to earlier periodicals such as *The Poetry Review* and *Poetry and Drama*. Humbert's association with Monro and the Poetry Bookshop may have been responsible for the description of him as a 'fringe Georgian', since the Poetry Bookshop, founded in 1913, was responsible for the Georgian Poetry collections of Edward Marsh. Humbert briefly mentioned going with Monro after dinner on 19 August to the Poetry Bookshop 'where Richard Aldington and T. S. Eliot turned up.'

On 26 August Humbert wrote: 'Monro has asked me to dine on Sunday to meet a Director of Benn Bros a new and very rich firm of publishers who are going to make me an offer for *Kensington Gardens*.' (This may have been Victor Gollancz who had not yet left Benn to set up on his own.) After his dinner with 'Monro & the Benn creature' at the Holborn Restaurant, he wrote: 'The news is really good. . . He was most enthusiastic . . . he very much wanted to do them with special paper, and special printing and illustrated.' Albert Rutherston, who was 'doing' a large Shakespeare for them (probably the illustrations for *Cymbeline*, which Benn brought out in 1923), was suggested for the illustrations, and there was talk of a limited *de luxe* edition of signed copies, as well as a larger one. Royalties were discussed, and possible sales (with the expectation of as many as 10,000 copies sold), 'but I'm holding myself in in case it collapses, as so many other things have collapsed.' But the next day he was writing: 'If *Kensington Gardens* is a success I should get the same people to publish my other things. So who knows! we may still set up a motor-car next year and visit all the countries of our dreams' - two things they never did, together or apart.

He also reported dining at The Reform with Alec Waugh and 'hope to plant something on him.' He almost certainly meant Arthur Waugh, Managing Editor of Chapman and Hall, father of Alec and Evelyn, and himself the author of several books on literature. The next day he wrote:

> The old Waugh is rather a dear, but the young one [Alec] is a bit of a simp. He has written several novels e.g. "The Loom of Youth" about public-school life. He has got another coming out shortly.

At the beginning of September he was at the Holborn again,

> where I dined with Monro & Osbert and Sacha Sitwell. We talked almost exclusively of King Charles' Head - i.e. Squire & Shanks. How malicious, how cheap, how ridiculous. But we all rather wished we had their complaint.

Whatever it was that involved these two eminences remains a mystery. He expected publications that month to bring in £15 or £20. 'Next month there'll be the Spectator, the Sitwell Review, & "The Desk" poem. So there is a prospect of a steady income.'[46]

Another letter mentions dining 'at the Wyndham with Cuming. He was much reassured by *Kensington Gardens*. He thought that I had gone over to the Vers Libreists.'[47] Humbert sent a copy of *The Chapbook* to his former teacher, Caryl Battersby, who sent a most flattering reply from Scarborough, which ended: '. . . in short they are all little gems. A pity that Albert Rutherston's girls don't cut their finger-nails and cultivate better legs!' - doubtless a reference to the illustrations.

His poems frequently appeared in *The Westminster Gazette* which also gave him regular reviewing work; in the last week of August he received and reviewed Sacheverell Sitwell's *The 101 Harlequins*. Despite any similarities suggested by the title, there is no reason to suppose that Sitwell's book inspired or influenced Humbert's interest in the Harlequin theme. It seems more likely that there was a revival of interest in Harlequin in Britain at the time, principally through the ballet.[48]

At the same time, Humbert's 'Astronomy' appeared in *The Spectator*, (it was later included in *The Unknown Goddess*), and other pieces in *The Outlook*. On 23 August he wrote: 'The horrible news of the murder of Michael Collins greeted me on the tape at breakfast. What fools, what hopeless fools!' The next day he wrote a poem on the murder of this Irish patriot and sent it to *The Westminster Gazette*, which published it on 25 August. This poem too appeared later in *This Blind Rose* (1928), but dated 24 August 1922. With another of his letters to Jessie he enclosed a poem he wrote on 29 August, called 'The Garden-God' - 'It rather thrills me.' (The poem was later incorporated in *The Uncelestial City* as 'Two Suicides - A - Jones', p. 118.)

But nothing demonstrates so vividly the extraordinary speed with which he wrote as the fascinating account of the genesis of *Circular Saws* (1923). It seems to have begun with an exchange of letters between Humbert and his daughter during this fortnight of August 1922, and there is a strong inference that the idea for it came from something Ann had written. Ann's letters, sadly, are not extant, but two of Humbert's not only contain elements which later appeared in the book, but also bear out Ann's testimony to Humbert's powers as a story-teller. The letters also indicate that although Ann, who had just celebrated her tenth birthday, was treated as a child, she was not patronised or talked down to. Her world was taken seriously, and there was clearly a strong imaginative and emotional bond between her and her father which the letters and the book confirm.

The first mention occurred almost as a post-script to a letter to Jessie on 29 August: 'I'm very much obliged to Ann for "All's well, that ends well". It is a dignified and remarkable achievement.' The second, a letter to Ann, postmarked 30 August 1922, clearly refers to details of Ann and Jessie's stay in Scotland:

> My dear Ann,
>
> After your beautiful letter I am almost afraid to write! How is the new dolly? Has she bathed yet? Does she paddle? Is she as bad as Jane? I expect she has changed into a frog or toad with all the rain you have had, like the Princess in the Haroun-Al-Raschid story that I haven't made up yet. She did that because she

> couldn't afford an umbrella and her mummy had bought her a most un-becoming mackintosh. However when she changed back into a princess there was a drought. So all's well that ends well. Your loving, Daddy.

On Friday, 1 September, he wrote to Jessie:

> I've started a queer little book which I'm going to try to finish over the week-end called "Circular Saws". It is to have 30 little stories of about a page each on a proverb. So far I've written eleven, including (thanks to Ann) "All's well that ends well", "Extremes meet", "Faint-heart never won fair lady", "Let sleeping dogs lie". I'm just stuck in one about an unusually repulsive troll who specialises in psycho-analysis!' [This appeared as No. 11, "It's never too late to mend."] 'It won't be a book for children!
>
> (2 Sept. Sat) I'm going on with my "Circular Saws" over the week-end. I've finished 12. 20 to 30 will be sufficient for a book.'

In the end, forty-one stories appeared in the book, published by Chapman and Hall in 1923. The dust-jacket was designed by Evelyn Waugh, then nineteen or twenty years of age.[49]

He dined again, unexpectedly, with John Fothergill:

> . . . looking the funniest thing I have ever seen. He has slightly brown-tinted spectacles, a panama hat dating back to the early forties, buckled shoes, a cretonne tie, & a light yellow suit. There was almost a cheer in the dining-room when he came in.

Fothergill had been scouring the south of England as far as Glastonbury and Plymouth in search of an hotel to buy.

> He is going today to Thame to look at a hotel there. It is about 10 miles from Oxford in an agricultural district. I don't think he will ever take a hotel, but he enjoys going round. I tremble to think what the hotel proprietors imagine has arrived when John comes in.

Events proved Humbert wrong, and Fothergill's career as an eccentric inn-keeper at Thame has passed into legend.

Financial matters inevitably creep into the letters, but without any suggestion of crisis, and mostly in connection with fees for his writings and bills to be paid.

> At the moment we are only £16 overdrawn. . . With luck therefore we should reach the 23rd [presumably the date his salary was paid] with not more than £60 overdrawn and start the October month with a balance.

He dined, sumptuously, with Owen Smith and suggested repayment (of the 1921 loan), 'but he pooh-poohed it and just talked in his quiet amiable way about 2 thousand things.'

Several times he referred to purchases from Selfridge's, and Stricklands, and to the dispatch of food parcels (galantine, cake, Madeira, ham) to Jessie from Fortnum & Mason - small wonder that they experienced what the French delicately call *des fins de mois difficiles*. One might almost infer that there were no butchers or grocers in Scotland.

After a long and tiresome interview with the Home Office and a representative of the I.L.O. which lasted until 7.30, he rushed round to the Carlton Grill to dine with Barlow.

> Hilton Young, Secretary of the Treasury, was the only other person there. Young is a very charming person, who lost an arm in the war. He has written several quite good poems and apparently quite liked mine! I tried to get him to talk about back-pay, but nah-pooh! Both he and Barlow think that Horne [former Minister of Labour in 1919] is going to resign and accept the post of Lord Justice Clerk. I shan't be surprised, because Horne was always a man who liked the safe thing.

He also dined with Butler, the Deputy-Director of the I.L.O., at the Travellers' Club.

> I've half made up my mind to let myself be put up [i.e. for membership]. There's no entrance fee this year, and the subscription is only 7 gns. more than this place [the R.A.C.]. Butler would put me up or get someone else to do it.

At the same time he was involved in paradoxically contradictory discussions of finance at the Ministry:

> There are two Cabinet Committees at work, an Economy Cee under Worthington Evans trying to cut us down, and the usual Unemployment Cee with L. J.

> [unidentifiable] in the Chair trying to make us spend more. I spent most of the afternoon at the former y'day, defending an income of £6000 in the T.Bd Estimates, and the day before I protested in vain against a new grant of £10,000,000 to the Unemployed! What a world!

And interspersed through all this, graphic and at times scathing comments on the complicated lives his family seemed to lead. His sister, Fanny who, with her husband, Cyril Heron, was living in straitened circumstances in Putney, had kidney trouble and was to see a specialist. His brother, Oswald, was in London once again, as was Jessie's brother, Gilbert, who appeared to have obtained a temporary medical post.

> I had lunch with Oswald at the Carlton Grill. He's gone a good deal balder and fatter but looked smug and well. . . . He blew his chest all over the place, told me he was a bosom-friend of the King of Spain's and altogether one of the nuts of the earth.

A few days later,

> I lunched Fanny and Cyril at Simpson's. Fanny was unable to take food! but looked with interest at a fried sole. Cyril ate with great vigour.' At the end of that week, 'I lunched at the Argentine Club with Oswald. . . Fanny & Cyril were both there. Oswald had said nothing about them. I wish my family weren't so *mysterious* in their goings-on. (I expect you wish that one of them in particular wasn't!).

Having met a couple of Oswald's latest business associates whom he believed to be crooks, he wrote: 'Quelle galère & thank God you didn't let me go into the City in 1919. I should have been in gaol long ago!'

Occasionally people paid him court in the hope of obtaining work or a favour of some sort. On 2 September, in the last letter he wrote before Jessie's return and their departure for Frinton or Littlehampton, he wrote:

> I had lunch with my old friend Isidore Salmon (Major!) at the Trocadero. Again there was the magnificent scene of welcome & banzai. Again the bottle of champagne (refused) and the 5 ft cigar (accepted!). Of course he wanted something - 2 saxophone bands brought over from America to be licensed for admission into G.B.[50]

They spent their holiday at Rustington, near Littlehampton, where Jessie remained when Humbert had to return to his office at the beginning of October. On 4 October he wrote to her:

> everybody is spluttering and buzzing & in a quiet way it looks like August 1914 all over again. But it's all sham and we shall all settle down quite peacefully,

probably referring to the crisis with Turkey - the 'Chanak' affair.[51] He said also that the chief business of his short letter 'is to thank you exceedingly for almost the best time since Thirlestone' i.e. their honeymoon in 1910.

The I.L.O. Conference took place in Geneva from 18 October to 3 November. Humbert's letters home make it clear that the meetings were still held in the Kursaal, which was very uncomfortable: 'the rooms are steam-heated, & what with the smoke & the talk & the noise one emerges with a splitting headache.' (22 Oct)

From 1922 onwards he always put up at the Hotel des Bergues, on the Quai des Bergues, just as he always stopped overnight in Paris at the Vouillemont, where he and Jessie had stayed together during the Pilotage Commission meeting in 1910. At Les Bergues, he wrote,

> there's the whole of the British Empire Delegations. Nobody has brought womenfolk. . . The other deputations . . are practically the same as always. The French are Fontaine & Jouhaux, the Dutch Nolens & Oudegeest. . . The employers' group have at last come to their senses & sent a decent Scotsman called Lithgow, together with Sir Andrew Duncan & Irvine Geddes - Eric's much less repulsive brother.[52]

Sir Montague Barlow was detained in London and Humbert, as his substitute, had 'the true Parliamentary thrill of going to the Tribune and "on behalf of Great Britain" etc. etc.'

He took advantage of 'the interminable rain, the interminable speeches, and the interminable boredom' to describe the Conference Room at the Kursaal for Jessie's benefit:

> On the stage are arranged from side to side - Nutt (the translator), Pinot (Vice-President), Butler, Lord Burnham, Thomas, Jouhaux (Workers' Delegate). Behind them at a long semi-circular desk arranged exactly like the conventional Table of the Last Supper 12 Beavers, who all look extraordinarily suited to play the part of Judas.

> Beneath the stage there is a little desk like an auctioneer's pulpit. From there at this moment a Japanese worker is clucking and cooing in a most alarming manner. . . Ranged in front row upon row are the solid ranks of the Labour Parliament of the world. Great Britain is in the fourth row, and we sit Poulton [the Workers' delegate], myself, Sir David, & Lithgow (the Employers' delegate). As soon as the clucking has been allayed, I am to get up and make a speech on the 8 Hours' Day. I can only hope that while I am speaking the Venezuelan delegate - who is at the moment snoring loudly - will wake up. . . Best love. I've got to pop up now & astonish the world.

He bemoaned the absence of information about what was going on at home (despite telegrams asking for news, they appear to have had no reply), but without identifying precisely the crisis to which he was referring - possibly the Turkish crisis and the difficulties within the Coalition Government. Almost as soon as he reached Geneva he complained to Jessie that 'we know nothing of what is happening except that Winston [Churchill] has had an operation for appendicitis.' There were also serious anxieties about the future of the Ministry of Labour:

> 29 Oct. No news from London - only a confused babel of rumours. "Abolition of Ministry of Labour", "Transfer to Board of Trade - Home Office, Ministry of Health, & the Kensington Town Council!"

He was at pains to reassure Jessie on 30 Oct:

> 'You needn't of course worry about *me* individually. But I am far from clear as to what will happen to the Dept as a whole.'

He continued to hold the fort with Sir David Shackleton, and mentioned the large number of speeches he had made and the good job he had done for the Empire and Britain even though he knew that he would get no thanks or recognition.

A notable feature of The Official Bulletin and the daily Reports (which printed several of Humbert's interventions) was that the translations, whether into English or French, were always a summary, from which witticisms and barbs delivered in the original language were rigorously excluded. The reasons for this, as Harold Butler explained in *Confident Morning*, were both the self-evident one that witticisms rarely translate easily, even when the translator is capable of rendering them, and also that the summary removed the element of personal attack or animosity which could be accepted in the heat of the moment but might, if recorded, have damaged international relations.

A few of Humbert's shots have nevertheless been preserved. In the morning session of 27 October, on the proposal to have more than one reporter, he said:

> Although there may be more virtue in two heads than one, when those heads are in collision I do not think it helps.

In the afternoon of the same day, on the question of including experts on the Drafting Committee, he argued that drafting is an exact science:

> I know that there is a prevalent and, indeed, an amiable belief that the majority of men are born with a capacity to draft and to write verses; but I would venture to say that that amiable belief is a delusion and that in both cases training, knowledge and experience are required.

On 31 October, on the question of the number of privileged States who enjoyed or claimed membership of the Governing Body, he began a long speech by saying that he was not at the Washington Conference of 1919:

> I am not one of those who, like Mr. Mahaim (Belgium), are entitled to wear "W" on their coats as having been to Washington, and therefore it is not for me to explain what happened at Washington; but I think that it is possible, though perhaps not certain, that, in the first glorious outburst of enthusiasm, there was not that very careful regard for meticulous detail which might have secured a more permanent and more satisfactory arrangement for the States included.

Finally, at the last session, on the afternoon of 3 November, he made a short speech of thanks to Lord Burnham (the President of the Conference) on behalf of Canada, S. Africa, India and Great Britain: 'I will admit that I had prepared a speech, but I think that we can best show our appreciation of you at this late hour by not delivering it.'

One day he lunched with Shotwell, the General Editor of the *Ecomomic and Social History of the World War*, of which *Labour Supply and Regulation* was one volume. A further book by Humbert was under discussion, clearly a sequel to *Labour Supply* or on a cognate topic:

> The book is fixed. I told him that it wouldn't be more than 100-115 pages. He told me that I could make it as long as I liked. I said that glad as I was to get more pounds, the amount of stuff that could be written on the

> subject was limited. I said that I would have it done by next summer at latest. "Labour Supply & Regulation" probably won't be out till January. So that I should have to wait at least six months for a second.

For whatever reasons, the book was never published and perhaps was never written.

The ritual and generally farcical round of dinners as guests of other national delegations continued: 'these dinners are too silly. They only mean dining at different tables in the same hotel at the expense of other Governments than one's own!. . .' One day he wrote of the previous evening's dinner given by Lithgow on behalf of the Employers to the various foreign delegations: ' - same food, same drink, same truffles on the chicken, same speeches "inspired by sentiments of universal humanity" etc. etc.'

On 24 October: ' . . . I haven't written a thing except to complete the following new "Physical Energy." [for *Kensington Gardens*, 1924]:

> Children when you
>   sail your yachts:
> think of Cecil
>   Rhodes and Watts;
>
> those so great
>   than whom is greater
> now the smallest
>   navigator,
>
> & reflect that
>   being small
> has compensations
>   after all.

On 25 October he wrote once more of the endless waiting for news, but added, unusually, 'The only thing that makes the position possible is that the work is really extremely interesting.' He went on to describe a serious row which had blown up the previous day in connection with an uprising in the South African coal mines which led to the leaders being condemned to death for murder. The Conference had been asked to intervene to prevent the executions, which placed the British Empire delegation (and Humbert especially) in a difficult position. As the official representative, and without any preparation, he had to make a speech about the sovereign rights of Governments, which saved the day for the Empire, but not, alas, for the poor Africans who were executed.

A sharp pen-portrait followed:

> I am sitting at this moment between Shackleton & Poulton, with old Lithgow glowering in the background. He is the Scots employers - a large Glasgow ironmaster with a very red Gaelic head & an equally red gaelic temper. But he is a good soul & we are very harmonious.

The agenda of the penultimate day of the Conference was not untypical:

> the meeting of the Conference, followed by the last Meeting of the old Governing Body, the first Meeting of the new Governing Body, the Finance Committee & the Committee of Selection in addition to the Belgian dinner.

He regularly sent Jessie the minutes of the previous day's meetings, which were produced remarkably quickly by the typists.

The collapse of the Coalition Government aroused serious anxiety about the future of the Ministry of Labour. All that he knew in Geneva was that Churchill had had an operation for appendicitis. Eventually, on 15 November 1922, Churchill was defeated in the General Election and found himself, as he said, 'without an office, without a seat, without a party and without an appendix.' Humbert was among the first to commiserate with his former Minister, for whom, as has been noted, he had enormous admiration:

> Will you acquit me of impertinence if I write to say how profoundly I resent the Dundee result? Perhaps you will let me remind you how deep & how permanent is the affection which you inspire in all who have the honour to serve you. We all (I know) felt what happened as a blow personal to ourselves. It is of course the most transitory of reverses, but as it may cast a momentary shadow you may care to be assured that when you and Mrs. Churchill waited for the result & still more when you heard it you were not alone.[53]

V

1923

Sir Montague Barlow had been appointed Minister of Labour in October 1922, before the Election which his party won handsomely. His new Parliamentary Secretary, Major A. Boyd-Carpenter, M.P., was appointed as British Government Member of the Governing Body of the I.L.O., and Humbert Wolfe as Deputy Member. On their first joint visit to Geneva in January, Humbert wrote to Jessie that 'Boyd-Carpenter is a very pleasant change from Barlow.' In March Boyd-Carpenter, newly appointed Financial Secretary to the Treasury, was succeeded at the Ministry of Labour by the member for Rushcliffe, H. B. Betterton, C.B.E. Other British representatives at the I.L.O. were Sir Malcolm Delevingne, K.C.B., Assistant Under-Secretary of State at the Home Office, and Miss Margaret Bondfield, J.P. (Adviser), Chairman of the General Council of the T.U.C.

Violet R. Markham, C.H., who in 1923 represented the Government of Canada at the I.L.O., noted in her autobiography that Humbert was there as Sir Henry Betterton's chief official. She reported in some detail his party piece about statistics, drawn from the struggle over the White Lead Convention.

> The issue about white lead, stated simply, is that paint without white lead is very bad paint, while paint with white lead causes disease and death among the workers. The controversy was long and heated. "Statistics", sighed Humbert, "yes, statistics; how marvellous they are. I assure you incontrovertible evidence was produced by the manufacturers, buttressed by impeccable figures and supported by eminent medical authority, that the only really sound and nourishing diet for a baby was white lead."[54]

Humbert's 1923 letters are of particular interest both for the light they throw on his professional career, particularly at the I.L.O., and on his literary advancement, although the letters from his first visit at the end of January say very little. It is evident that when he left England Consola was staying with them, and he went out of his way to thank Jessie for steering Consola over the moments which threatened strain. He also made a point of telling Jessie that none of the representatives at Geneva had brought a wife, except for the representative of India, Sir Louis Kershaw of the India Office. The only remotely topical issue which he mentioned was the Ruhr which was vigorously discussed at the dinner table one evening.

At the beginning of April he was back in Geneva, this time with H. B. Betterton who had brought his wife with him, 'a grey-haired and very kindly lady.' Jessie was to experience their relaxed and supportive kindness in later years. The most surprising item of news was in his first letter of 4 April: 'The great enterprise of shifting M. Thomas has started.' Thomas was refusing to discuss the report on reduction of expenditure, and Humbert's committee retaliated by refusing to proceed with the discussion of the Budget. The letter ended: 'I'm so sorry you couldn't come. Perhaps (who knows) next time you'll come as Mrs. Director.' This was the first intimation that Humbert foresaw, even as a remote possibility, the prospect of a permanent post in Geneva. At the same time, it is clear that Jessie was disappointed at not accompanying him to Geneva.

By the next day the budget affair had become 'a spiritual dust-storm, mixed with a cyclone and a touch of east wind down Princes Street.' Thomas was accusing Great Britain of plotting the downfall of the office, the Dutch and French delegates burst into denunciations of Britain as the tyrant of Europe 'with side-references to "proud officials" who think that the workers exist for the purpose of being trodden on.' Betterton explained the grounds for the proposed reductions and Humbert made 'the speech of my life, so exciting that even Butler could hardly refrain from clapping when it was finished.' Thomas asked for an adjournment until the next day "in order to consider his position." 'In Great Britain,' wrote Humbert, 'that would mean "in order to consider his resignation". But here it only means "to consider how to get out of his resignation". . . Lithgow has instructions to press for my appointment! But it won't come. All the same it's exciting.'

Later letters continue the saga, which culminated in Thomas's resignation which he then conditionally withdrew. Although Humbert expected nothing dramatic in the short term, 'the developments for which we all 4 (including the pussy) hope are appreciably nearer!' He reassured Jessie once more: 'I am so sorry that you weren't here, but you wouldn't have enjoyed it. Meals have lasted half-an-hour. There has been no social life and the whole atmosphere is one of suspicion.' The absence of any further letters indicates that Thomas saw his way to carrying on as Director.

At the beginning of June Humbert and Jessie had a holiday in Littlehampton. Humbert left there to go to Geneva via London and Paris. On the way he collected an advance copy of *Labour Supply and Regulation*:

'It's an overwhelming-looking volume,' he wrote to Jessie, I feel ashamed to believe that I wrote it.' Once more he regrets that she can't accompany him and says how much he enjoyed Littlehampton. The main topic of discussion at Geneva was the new building, for which several different designs had been tendered. The committee began by examining the site by the lake 'as if we were a party of grave-diggers. We then went to inspect a perfectly bewildering display of plans, each one uglier than the next, but all equally meaningless.' The architects then waited upon him, each in order to press his own case and denigrate his colleagues. Finally, after discussing drains and cubic capacity, they discovered that the building would cost about twice the money available and the architect was sent to redraw his plans.

Jessie's father died in 1923 and July found her in Edinburgh, no doubt on family matters. Humbert wrote to tell her of the great heat in London and of the industrial inflammation which coincided with it. The Dockers'

Strike occasioned a long conference on 3 July: 'Lord! I was tired of Gosling and Bevin.' And on the 4th there was serious riot at Whitehaven.

> Things are being rather lively for us. . . That curious growth - Gavan Duffy - has asked for a debate upon it on the adjournment which may mean hours and hours. On the other hand yesterday after I wrote I went down to the House & we worked there till 11 at a statement on the cost of living figure to appear in to-morrow's papers. I don't really think that the Dock strike is serious. I think it is chiefly a hot weather rash. But the inflammation has been acute in spots! It is 6.15 & I am going down to the House at 6.30 where I shall dine (as I did last night) & then sit and stew in that horrible official gallery. It is really like war-days. We have had lunch in the Minister's room (sandwiches and beer) & are rushing about wildly and foolishly. But one smart thunder-storm would I think modify the whole position.

On 6 July he wrote to say that

> the Whitehaven debate fizzled out badly. Gavan Duffy was almost incapable of speech and Lane-Fox who answered for the Ministry of Mines satisfied the House. All the same I had to stay and swelter at the House until 11.45.[55]

And then a most revealing passage:

> I was too hot to go to bed when I got back to the Club. So I wrote a poem on Wormwood Scrubs prison - about the orchestra of London, fiddles of Piccadilly, the flute in the copper-beeches at Kew, & the brass round the fire in winter. But under it all
>
> ebbing, flowing, parting, meeting,
> as though it were my own heart beating
> a sullen distant drummer drubs
> 'Wormwood Scrubs! Wormwood Scrubs!'
>
> I was thinking of how you said that London rests on lunatic asylums and prisons, & I thought under all the the fiddles & flutes of life rolled this dull drum of death.[56]

Circular Saws had been published about five weeks earlier and was beginning to sell, thanks to favourable reviews in *The Observer* and *The Westminster Gazette* - he thought the style of the latter suggested that the reviewer was Philip Guedalla. Albert Rutherston had been slow to reply to his letters about *Kensington Gardens*, and Arthur Waugh, who had invited him to lunch at the Garrick, suggested that he give it to Chapman and Hall. Waugh was very pleased with the way things were going and asked to see 'The Undetective Stories' which Humbert had been writing.[57]

A few of the tales in *Circular Saws* had appeared in *The Weekly Westminster Gazette* and *The Chapbook*. These twentieth century fables after the manner of Aesop or La Fontaine display a great variation in tone and assumed audience. They cover a range of experiments in irony, wit, humour (both broad and high), sarcasm, and cynicism, which seem both to anticipate and to exemplify the detailed analysis which later constituted the first chapter of *Notes on English Verse Satire* (1929). A few of the pieces could be criticised: in some, the incursion of the author/publisher looks more than a little precious; in others ('Dis Aliter Visum', for example), there is excessive striving for effect, while to anyone unaware of the origins of the collection, fables such as 'All's Well That Ends Well' may sound a note of false naivety by appearing to be addressed to a notional precocious child, like modern fairy tales for smart young persons.

But alongside these there are some very skilfully sustained jokes. Perhaps the best of these is 'Quantity Is Better Than Quality', a cautionary tale worthy of Lewis Carroll about a certain constitutional monarchy in which the upper class were pledged to breathe only once a week, in an effort to discourage continuous breathing in the lower classes. The 'middling class', anxious to imitate their betters, took to practising reduced breathing. Of course they overdid it, with a consequent increase of business for the Guild of Sextons and Gravediggers. But as the middling class, though perishing in great numbers, would not admit to the social disgrace of being dead, the Sextons and Gravediggers became involved in a demarcation dispute with the 'The Society of Critics, Essayists, and Writers of Belles Lettres', who alone were entitled to bury the living (and by extension to resurrect the dead). The Press became involved, arbitrators were called in, and eventually the deadlock was resolved by the decision of the Head of State to begin continuous breathing. The middling class quickly resumed breathing, the Sextons and Gravediggers resumed their now diminished labours, and the critics, having found a living writer of genius, promptly set about his interment. And everyone breathed again.

Circular Saws also produced the first of his squibs against the Press - a delightful six-line tale called 'Let Sleeping Dogs Lie', one of several pieces which achieved an unerring aim in the perfection of their simplicity:

> Once upon a time there was a wizard
> who could find the truth in a news-

> paper.
> Fortunately he was discovered and hanged
> in time, and since then nobody has dared to
> tamper with the liberty of the Press.

In No. XXII, 'Men, Not Measures', Mr. Crayfish made his first appearance, as a government minister (The Senior Almoner) whom Humbert used to poke fun at the combined philistinism and stuffiness of politicians. The Prime Minister of Samaria and his Council are discussing the difficulties presented by the Poet's Birth (Prevention) Bill, whose object was 'to secure that in future poets should be made . . . and not born.' The Senior Almoner is quoted as having 'had a letter from a very respectable washerwoman in his constituency. She complained that there was a poet who wore soft collars. He did not wish to press the point, but popular feeling could not be neglected.' He then swims into the reported musings, first of the Prime Minister - 'There was Crayfish, the Senior Almoner. He sympathised.' - then, a few lines later, into those of the Minister of Commerce - 'Just ask old Crayfish - only chap in the room who's ever read anything except *The Morning News* - (. . .) - and *The Blue 'Un*. (. . .) Funny how (the Prime Minister) not being a man he gets real men like old Crayfish for instance. That's the one - no rhetoric for him. Look at his tense simple eyes. He thinks only of what's best and loyalty, and if sincerity can get the damned thing through he'll do it.' Initially, then, Crayfish was a mild figure of fun, but clearly different from the other ministers, and above all a man of principle. It is just possible to see here an adumbration of the character of Mr. Justice Crayfish of *The Uncelestial City* (1930).

Humbert's daughter thought that he may have intended to suggest Jewishness, in that many Jews in Britain had Germanic names ending in 'fisch'. Another possible source may have been Eliot's 'The Love Song of J. Alfred Prufrock', and especially the lobster image in

> I should have been a pair of ragged claws
> scuttling across the floors of silent seas.'

And again, perhaps, later:

> No! I am not Prince Hamlet, nor was meant to be;
> Am an attendant lord, one that will do
> To swell a progress, start a scene or two,
> Advise the prince; no doubt, an easy tool,
> Deferential, glad to be of use,
> Politic, cautious, and meticulous;
> Full of high sentence, but a bit obtuse;
> At times, indeed, almost ridiculous -
> Almost, at times, the Fool.

. . . .
We have lingered in the chambers of the sea
By sea-girls wreathed with seaweed red and brown
Till human voices wake us, and we drown.'

Humbert's identification with this and with Crayfish is plausible and chimes with his self-depreciation as well as with his frustrated professional and literary ambitions. The name, if not the identical character, resurfaced in *The Uncelestial City* (1930).

La Rue du Soleil Levant in No. XII has already been mentioned. There was also a verse lampoon on Geddes of the famous axe, who had declared war on waste within the Civil Service:

'Ici-Gît'

When at creation God was faced
With earth's illimitable waste,
We understand that what he said is:
"Let there be light," - and there was Geddes.

- given the circumstances of the time, a rather brave gesture, and a foretaste of what was to come in *Lampoons* (1925). There were a few anti-war pieces, a barely disguised mention of H. H. Asquith (No. 21, 'Quis Separabit?'), several religious fables, and two specifically Jewish ones, Nos. 26 and 35, the latter incidentally containing a superb pastiche of the hypocritical posturings observed at international gatherings such as the League of Nations and the I.L.O. To have written virtually all of this in a week-end was a veritable *tour de force*.

On 7 July he wrote to Jessie: '"Circular Saws" has made an appreciable difference in the way the literary people treat me. Constable's have . . . sent a message through Monro saying that they'd like to see some of my satires.' He listed those he sent them: 'Paul Arthur' probably an early version of *News of the Devil*, 'The Verdict' (possibly a poem later incorporated in *The Uncelestial City*), 'Kipps' (later published in *This Blind Rose*) and others which have proved impossible to identify with published work.

At his club he had bumped into Michel Salaman who told him that Chattie, his wife, had had an operation, but that as soon as she was about again they wanted Humbert and Jessie to go down for a week-end before the school holidays. Humbert had also dined with the Sitwell brothers who were about to go abroad for six months. Osbert had given him a copy of his latest book of verse.

There was also some discussion of a holiday house in Aberfoyle. Humbert made it clear that he was 'quite ready to have them all', that is, Jessie's mother and sister, as well as Jessie and Ann, which in the circumstances showed remarkable generosity on his part. Jessie's and Humbert's families did not get on well together. Both mothers thought the other family inferior or unworthy. Consola had wanted a 'successful', and preferably a wealthy, match for Humbert. The Grahams owned some property in Edinburgh but that did not provide much income, and after Joseph Graham's death, Jessie's mother came with her daughter Annie, and Jessie's brother, Gilbert Malise Graham ('Gub'), to live with them in Kensington High Street.

Ann Wolfe recalled that 'Gilbert also stayed with us for a time. He gave me lessons, showed me how to use my camera, took us to see Gilbert and Sullivan. I liked him a lot. I knew he was sometimes ill, as a result of the war (he had been a naval doctor), and had to go into Hospital.' Humbert got on well with Jessie's brother, as he had with her father, but Gilbert stayed with them only for a short time. From several of the letters of this period it is apparent that Humbert was busy on Gilbert's behalf, supporting his efforts to obtain a pension for his war service.

With all these guests the flat was now very crowded, the Grahams had money problems and Humbert did his best to help them, but they had always disliked him and the menage did not work. It was said that 'every woman who met Humbert half fell in love with him.' Annie and her mother were the exceptions. Consequently there was constant friction, and the Graham ladies proved to be unsympathetic lodgers. Eventually Humbert found them a place in Battersea.

Chapter Seven

1924-1927

'Some engagement with a star'
(*The Uncelestial City*, 1930)

I

1924

(i)

Kensington Gardens

Early in 1924 his new book of poems, *Kensington Gardens*, appeared. *The Times Literary Supplement* reviewer described it in the issue of 27 March as 'minor art'. The four-line verse Preface to these artfully simple poems proclaimed two things: one explicit - that Humbert's daughter, Ann, was the focus of the book; the other, implicit until the later Preface to *The Unknown Goddess*, that he had found a new place for a comma, namely at the beginning of a line:

> Into spring
> ,whispering
> "O," there ran
> my daughter Ann.

Although many other lines in the book also begin with a comma, the punctuation is in fact predominantly orthodox. Some critics thought, with H. W. Garrod, that 'Mr. Wolfe believed that there was something in the nature of poetry - or of *his* poetry - which compelled him to this whimsical punctuation.'[1] (Garrod was surely perverse to misquote Humbert as saying that 'he felt that "he could not change a comma without troubling of a star!"', when what he wrote was: 'Indeed I was almost assured that I could not change a comma without troubling of a star!', which is plainly not the same thing.) Humbert never really explained the significance of the displaced comma, but his daughter Ann told me that he wanted to suggest a slight, almost imperceptible catch of the breath before the next words, a subtlety which I confess is beyond my comprehension. But it is possible that, by accident or design, the unusual placing of the comma served to startle the reader into closer attention.

Such niceties apart, the whole work is what the Jacobeans might have called "an extended conceit", rather like Eliot's *Practical Cats*. It is divided, very unevenly, into two parts: 'Morning', consisting of ten sections and thirty-seven poems, and 'Night', with only one poem, plus a Tail-piece which is really a conclusion to 'Night'. But even that imbalance, like the eccentric punctuation, has no major significance. The poems, quite short for the most part, and written in a deceptively simple style, celebrate a spring day in the Gardens, and clearly draw upon his walks there with his daughter. These delicate and charming verses describe or comment upon first the flora and fauna of the Gardens, then its games, monuments, palace and lake, and finally the people to be seen there. What emerges most powerfully is the warmth of affection with which the book is suffused.

It is easy to see why so many of the poems found their way into anthologies - 'Tulip', for example:

> Clean as a lady
> ,cool as glass,
> fresh without fragrance
> the tulip was.
>
> The craftsman, who carved her
> of metal, prayed:
> "Live, oh thou lovely!"
> Half metal she stayed.

Similarly, 'The Lilac'

> Who thought of the lilac?
> "I," dew said,
> "I made up the lilac
> out of my head."
>
> "She made up the lilac!
> Pooh!" thrilled a linnet,
> and each dew-note had
> lilac in it.

Here and there the satirist escapes and takes charge:

> 'Thrushes'
>
> The City Financier
> walks in the gardens
> ,stiffly, because of
> his pride and his burdens.
>
> The daisies, looking

up, observe
only a self-
respecting curve.

The thrushes only
see a flat
table-land
of shiny hat.

He looks importantly
about him,
while all the spring
goes on without him.

And perhaps even more typically, in 'The Grey Squirrel':

Like a small grey
coffee-pot
sits the squirrel.
He is not

all he should be,
kills by dozens
trees, and eats
his red-brown cousins.

The keeper, on the
other hand
,who shot him, is
a Christian, and

loves his enemies,
which shows
the squirrel was not
one of those.

'Physical Energy' has already been quoted (*see* Chapter 6). Occasionally the assured light touch slips into the facile, as, for instance, in 'Peter Pan', 'Mr. Harris', and the ending of

'The Hawthorn Tree'

When I am old
and need a crutch,
and nothing I do
pleases me much,

I'll go and sit
where I can see
spring sunlight on
a hawthorn-tree.

And if that leaves me
cold, I'll have
hawthorn planted
on my grave.

It is perhaps of interest, however, to observe that his own grave was at his request marked only by a hawthorn tree.

A darker and more serious note sounds from time to time, in poems such as 'The Atheist Orator', who, mistaking Kensington Gardens for Hyde Park, climbs in one night and starts to preach with no audience save the trees.

. . . .

Those lovely trees
grew lovelier,
as he proved conclusively
no trees were.

Down poured the moon
on the great grace
of those green towers.
The small white face

shared the vast gift,
and, drenched with light,
his angry soul
shrilled in the night

(as the impartial
moonlight fell)
"Man needs no heaven,
and fears no Hell."

The effect that he achieved with this great economy of line marks the extent of his development since those earlier attempts at religious apologetics at Bradford Grammar School and Oxford.

(ii)

Geneva Hopes

In January, 1924, with the arrival of the first Labour government under Ramsay MacDonald, Tom Shaw became the new Minister of Labour, with Miss Margaret Bondfield, MP, as his Parliamentary Secretary. Within a week she accompanied the British delegation to the meeting of the Governing Body of the I.L.O. Humbert, writing to Jessie from Geneva on 28 January, said he was sure that although Harold Butler accompanied her ostensibly to act as interpreter (at Albert Thomas's request) the real reason for his presence was 'to rescue Thomas from the difficulties in which he had involved himself.'

Humbert did not elaborate on precisely what these difficulties were but among them would have been relations between the British government and the I.L.O. Government enthusiasm for the I.L.O. had begun to wane when Thomas was seen to have a firm policy of 'navigation as opposed to drift'; the Treasury begrudged the £30,000 annual grant to support the Organization; and critics in Parliament and industry accused the conferences of being no more than 'annual log-rolling competitions.'[2] This last charge squares ill with accounts of debates which Humbert sent his wife, as it does with the recollections of others, such as Violet Markham, who recognised that the solid achievements of the I.L.O., which was concerned with concrete industrial issues, enabled it to survive the débâcle of the League of Nations, despite the cynical window-dressing sometimes observed, when delegates agreed to conventions which they knew their Governments would never ratify.[3] But to Thomas the arrival of a Labour government must have looked like a golden opportunity to mend fences.

Humbert told Jessie that Margaret Bondfield was initially 'a bit frightened of me', and he was probably flattered that she relied on his experience and guidance in the early days, but he had a genuine regard and respect for her. A former senior official at the Ministry of Labour recalled that when she became the first woman to be a Cabinet Minister in the 1929 Labour government, 'Humbert was at his most charming, and we used to compare their relationship to that of Queen Victoria and Disraeli.'[4] She was, it seems, as kind and motherly as her photographs suggest. The story that she kept him from his lunch in order to draft a reply to a parliamentary question may have been true, but the end of the tale - that Humbert, asked by a colleague from another Ministry how she was getting on, replied, 'Oh, she's still *virago intacta*!" - is most unlikely. Beatrice Webb, no admirer of Humbert, was quite clear that he made the observation, 'which was as witty as it was true', about Susan Lawrence, Minister of Health in the same 1929 government.[5]

The occasion for another of Humbert's many witticisms which passed into Whitehall folklore is thought to have been provided by the head of the Ministry's Finance Department, F. W. Bowers, a deeply religious, if somewhat puritanical man. In this instance the 'bon mot' was one which it might have been kinder to restrain. The only eye-witness account I have seen does not name the victim, but simply says that a colleague who was a very religious man arrived late for a meeting and began making profuse apologies. 'Humbert checked him by saying: "That's all right. We'll say it was an immaculate misconception, shall we?"'[6] Less unfairly, though no less unkindly, he referred to the head of an accident-prone railway company as 'a man with an infinite capacity for breaking trains.'

At the end of March he was back in Geneva; writing to Jessie on the 30th he raised once more the hope of a permanent post there: 'It does seem wicked to be here alone in honeymoon week. . . Better luck next year!' Two days later he explained that 'Fontaine, the President of the Governing Body, is running for the Directorship', since he thought Thomas, despite the return to power in France of his arch-enemy, Poincaré, would be 'back in French politics very soon.' The financial crisis which both the League and the I.L.O. experienced at this time may well have had a bearing on the manoeuvring taking place at the highest level of both organizations. Humbert reported to Jesssie that Thomas had asked him if he was a candidate for the Directorship. Humbert replied that he would rather have Attolico's job at the League - that is, the post of Senior Vice Secretary-General .[7]

On 3 April he wrote:

> The air is still full of rumours and hints. I have had four deputations from the staff, who have been busily airing their grievances to me, as if I were head of the office! Jouhaux and Oudegeest - the two workers' leaders - have been most cordial to me. . . I am lunching tomorrow with Drummond and Attolico.

The Budget reduction was finally fixed at 400,000 francs, he told her on 4 April, 'for every single franc of which I am personally responsible. As usual the fight which I have put up has led to bitter recriminations. Late last night at his flat Thomas said "some day you will regret the way you have cut down the staff - when you want to use it yourself."'

From 1924 until, and even beyond, 1930, the hope of a permanent senior post at Geneva ran like a leit-motiv through his letters to Jessie. The focus oscillated between the Directorship of the I.L.O. and the post of Secretary-General, or Vice Secretary-General, of the League, according to every shift in the manoeuvres of the principal *dramatis personae* to achieve their ambitions. The chief difficulty seems to have been that of ensuring at least an appearance of fairness by not filling the two senior posts with men of the same nationality. The French were not alone in opposing the idea of an Englishman at the head of both organisations. Equally, Britain would resist attempts to appoint two Frenchmen, although eventually that was what happened. And Humbert was well aware that accepting a Vice Secretary-General's post, if it were offered, could easily ensure that he never rose above that level.

The Secretary-General of the League, Sir Eric Drummond (later 16th Earl of Perth), appeared more than ready to give up the League in exchange for some high office at home, a senior ambassadorial post or one in the Foreign Office, but would not commit himself until he got the post he wanted: nothing less would do. Attolico also wanted an embassy, and got one in 1926. Thomas more than once used the threat of resignation in order to get his own way at the I.L.O., but never seriously contemplated standing down and he died in office at the I.L.O. in 1932. Inconclusive discussions about the succession went on throughout the 1920s, sometimes with Humbert in the role of heir-apparent, but the king-makers seem to have taken good care to stop short of solid assurances, and it is difficult to ascertain whether they were cynically building up Humbert's hopes for their own mysterious purposes, or whether he was deluding himself that he stood a real chance of replacing either Drummond or Thomas.

Inspection of I.L.O. files in Geneva and London has thus far revealed no evidence to support his expectation, and his daughter has accepted that there may have been something of fantasy or self-deception in his hopes of such advancement. Nevertheless, it was the reason which he gave Jessie for decisions he made with regard to their accommodation at various times - that there was no point in taking this or that house or flat if they were going to be in Geneva soon. There is, however, no reason to doubt his tale of the ambitions and manoeuvres of Thomas, Drummond, Attolico and others, even on the unverifiable asssumption that he misinterpreted their bearing on his own future, always a possibility even for one of his shrewd and mature political sense.

His conversation with Drummond and Attolico on 4 April revealed that the latter's ambition of becoming an Ambassador was not yet realized. But his description of his job and his staff at the League convinced Humbert that it was 'infinitely better work than the I.L.O. Drummond is very friendly &, though he isn't a hero of intelligence, he's by no means a fool. He told me that he didn't expect to be here more than 2 years longer.'

On the evening of the first day's meeting of the Governing Body on Tuesday, 8 April, he wrote: 'The whole day has been devoted to a determined attempt by the employers to get Thomas to resign.' They felt the Director should be the representative of a nation not engaged in the Ruhr.

> . . . Everybody in the Governing Body - employers, workers and Govts are shewing themselves extremely friendly to me - & if the matter came to a vote now (which it won't) I have no doubt of the result.

But Thomas survived the attack and if Humbert made any further comment to Jessie on these events it has perished.

His next stay in Geneva was in June. From Paris his travelling companion was 'Monseigneur Nolens, who is the Catholic Mussolini of Holland,' and they arrived in Geneva just in time to say good-bye to Miss Bondfield who was returning to England. Thomas was at the station to do the same.

> It is common talk here that he means to resign after the Conference. . . . I have been formally nominated British delegate & have been appointed to the Executive Committee of the Conference, to the Committee on Workers' Spare Time & to the Committee on the Amendment of Conventions. So that I shall have my hands full.

On 18 June he reported that the Conference was moving on very slowly.

> The only incident is an excitement about Fascismo. An Italian Labour Delegate Mateotti was abducted last week by the Fascisti & has (probably) been murdered. In revenge there are plots here against Rusoni - a Fascist Delegate. He has been excluded from all work in the Committees & goes about under police protection. His chief claim to fame however is that he is the living image of the large gentleman in the films who knocks Charlie Chaplin about. I always expect to see his eyes glaze and his head rock slowly from side to side.

In her autobiography, Violet Markham described the boredom and sardonic amusement with which old Geneva hands like Humbert and H. B. Betterton greeted the noisy and violent exchanges which regularly disrupted I.L.O. meetings.[8]

On 19 June Humbert acted as conciliator in the Italian crisis.

> My real inclination was to adjure Rusoni to go back on the films & leave real life alone. But . . . I blarneyed de Michelis into the belief that the <u>other</u> two great powers - England & France - would feel lonely if Italy withdrew..

> . . I am now senior British Delegate - at any rate for the moment. . . Sokal the Pole has let it be known that he is a candidate for the Director's post. We have let it be known that we think he is balmy![9]

The next day Humbert told Jessie that Thomas at lunch

> went fully & completely into the whole business. He is not going at once. . . In these circumstances it is plain that there will be no change till the autumn, & we must make our plans with the clear understanding that for the next three months at any rate there can be no prospect of our coming here. I would only add that the whole British Delegation (of which I send you a photograph under a separate cover) are very anxious that I should succeed.

A letter dated 25 June assured Jessie that all was not lost. Justin Godart (Humbert mis-spells his name as Goddard), the new French Labour Minister, just arrived in Geneva, had been fêted by the French workers, with Thomas and Humbert the only other guests. Godart had spoken of Thomas as a hoped-for future colleague and eventual 'chief' i.e. Prime Minister. Thomas, thanking him, had looked at Humbert and said he would never leave Geneva until he could leave the sacred trust in safe hands. 'I was called on to speak and said that I cared for one thing only - & that was to modify & if it were possible end suffering. I was riotously applauded.'

However, he went on to advise her not to count on their going to Geneva; they must prepare for England. He favoured giving up the flat at the end of July and taking a house in the country, e.g. Worthing, for August and September, though what they would do after that if they did not go abroad would need serious thought. But almost immediately he was looking on the bright side again, describing Butler's house, which was just the sort of house that would suit them if they came to Geneva - 'not more than 6 or 7 bedrooms. A Press artist did 'a sort of Brighton Pier drawing of me [for the American Press] while I sat & wrote to Ann.' For the rest of that summer there was no more talk of leaving Kensington.

In order to escape the Flower Carnival and Ball held on 30 June, he took himself off to the Rochers de Naye, above Montreux. He had the hotel rouse him at 3.30 the next morning and climbed up to the snow-point.

> I reached it at 4 just before the sun & saw the loveliest sight of my life. Below me there was a sea of grey cloud & all round flying grey wisps of cloud. Suddenly the sea

> changed to rose, then to an incredible blaze of crimson, & the wisps of cloud that were blown at me hit me full in the face red as a rose. Then suddenly all round me the huge peaks blazed into colour from Mont Blanc at one point of the horizon to Jungfrau at another. . . I gathered on a high rock some Edelweiss for you . . . I do wish that you had been here with me, not only at the Naye but the whole time.

At the beginning of October he wrote to Jessie from the I.L.O. Conference in Prague. After describing the nightmare three-day journey (trains going through Germany provided no meals, to spite the Czechs and the French, he said), he gave his impressions of southern Germany - 'looking very prosperous, the Germans very offensive and anti-Semitic, the Czechs were very cordial to the British.' He painted lively and colourful pictures of the legendary Czech President, Masaryk; of the city of Prague with its Cathedral church of St. Stephen on the peak of a hill - 'a marvellous waterfall of Gothic' - and meals of strange dishes 'washed down with a Hungarian wine that tasted like a Sitwell poem. . .'

He found this Conference 'like all other International Labour affairs. One talks & talks & talks. It grows hotter & hotter, & towards afternoon there is a violent row between the French & the Germans. . .'

One letter gave an amusing but highly unlikely - and therefore probably true - account of an incident at an underground tea-shop 'vaulted and absurdly like the place where the plotters meet in the films', where he had gone with Sokal, the Pole.

> Sokal poured out the soul of Poland, to be suddenly interrupted by a gentleman wearing a furry hat, long top-boots, and an enormous silver knife stretching across his stomach. My experience of films told me that the proper thing for me to do was to draw out a revolver & shoot out the oil lamp. Only I hadn't a revolver. Neither had Sokal. The fur-hatted gentleman in fluent Russian informed Sokal that the Soviets were about to invade Poland, and that (as it seemed) he personally was going to begin the invasion by cutting Sokal's throat. At this point I intervened by observing in perfect English that if he didn't stop I should report him to Ramsay Macdonald. On hearing the English tongue he burst into tears, seized my hand & kissed it. And rushed out of the restaurant. The next thing, of course, should have been a close-up of Mr. R. Macdonald & me against a tree in the dawn. Instead of which I had to pay 24 kr for tea.

He was in the middle of one of his periodic attempts to give up smoking and reported that he had not smoked at all for 37 days, but doubted he could keep off much longer. He went on from Prague to Geneva for Committee meetings and almost immediately (7 October) recorded his astonishment at the forecast in the Paris Press of an immediate British General Election, although he had heard vague rumours in Prague.

> If the Labour Govt does go out I think that more than 1 Labour leader may be looking for a job in this part of the world! There have in fact been no developments. Fontaine told me definitely at Prague that T[homas]. was going at Christmas, but I think that was only in order to secure that F[ontaine]. should be re-elected Chairman of the G. Body. Thomas himself, who was at Prague, told me that he was going to S. America in Jan, & I gathered that he was going as Director of the I.L.O!

The rumours rapidly became fact, for on 9 October he wrote:

> Everybody here is buzzing with the news from England. And really I can't make head or tail of it. Why the Liberals turned the Labour people out & why the Labour people went on this particular issue [presumably he is referring to the Soviet loan and the prospect of an Anglo-Soviet Treaty] passes my comprehension.

But his own prospects at the I.L.O. preoccupy him more: on the 11th he told Jessie that Thomas had bought a farm in France for his retirement. 'In the meantime he is terribly torn between two alternatives - getting his money safe & getting back into politics.'

He went to inspect progress on the new I.L.O. building on 13 October:

> Markham [Office of Works] & I are to spend about 3 hrs today trying to persuade the architect - Epitaux - that what is wanted for the Council Room is a Council Room & not a cross between a public lavatory & a Persian favourite's boudoir! . . . Drummond now speaks of staying on for a second term! If he does my chances almost go because they would never stand an Englishman at the head of both offices! I think however that what he really wants is the Permanent Secretaryship of the F.O. - and I think he'll get it.

II

1925

(i)

In the wake of the overwhelming Conservative victory in the General Election of October 1924 came the appointment of Sir Arthur Steel-Maitland as Minister of Labour, with H. B. Betterton, M.P., once more Parliamentary Secretary. As before, Humbert would represent Britain at Geneva when Betterton was unable to do so. The Governing Body met at Geneva on 6 January. Humbert reported to Jessie that Oudegeest, the leader of the Workers' Group on the Governing Body 'was now definitely in the field [for the Directorship] and indicated that (failing himself, O), they might do worse than H[umbert].'

On 9 January he lunched with Drummond who 'definitely asked me whether I would take the Directorship [of the I.L.O.] , as a prelude to one of the Deputyships [of the League], which might fall in this year or next.' Humbert asked for guarantees, which Drummond naturally could not give, and Humbert pointed out that if Attolico stayed on after Drummond's departure and a new Secretary-General was appointed, 'Then I'm planted. He agreed - reluctantly.' A further meeting with him was no more fruitful.

At the beginning of March Humbert, replying to a letter from Albert Thomas, said that he had had a severe bout of influenza. He was very touched by Thomas's charming letter of 18 February, and hoped to be at the next meeting of the Governing Body but did not know if Betterton would be. Humbert went on to say that he was in great need of a change to Swiss air and hoped to take an extra week or two in the mountains.[10]

On 19 March he left for Geneva; finding himself with one and a half hours to kill in Paris between trains, he went to a cinema: 'There were two films,' he wrote to Jessie, 'both American, & both utterly unlike the sort the U.S.A. make for the English market. One, "Qu'en pensez-vous?" had that pleasant villain in it, whom we both like, & was quite frankly Parisian. Aren't the Americans extraordinary?'

He listed several hotels he was considering for the break which he had referred to in his letter to Thomas. He quickly made up his mind, for his next letter on Saturday 21 was written from the Grand-Hotel Bellevue, Monnetier-Mornex, a few miles southwest of Geneva. The hotel, situated near the top of the Little Salève, was quite small and virtually empty. All was very peaceful and the rest was doing him good. He had read in the

French press that Curzon was dead. 'Poor soul! he did have rotten luck. I expect that old villain Balfour will nip into his job.'[11]

He lazed there for just under a week, completely cut off from the outside world, with only three-day old French newspapers and no English papers at all. He did nothing more strenuous than a gentle stroll or a trip on the funicular to watch the skiing at Treize Arbres, and in the evening 'cockered up' some of the epitaphs which appeared later that year as *Lampoons*. Of the two he quoted for Jessie's benefit, the first is probably the best one in the collection, a perfect pastiche of Housman. He wrote:

> You know that he is always writing in "The [sic] Shropshire Lad" & "Last Poems" about young men of one and twenty being hanged (all his friends seem to have been murderers!) and that in "Last Poems" he has one beginning
>
> When lads have done with labour
> At Abden-under-Lee
> Then one would fetch his neighbour
> and both would send for me"
>
> well taking these two things together my epitaph runs
>
> "When lads have done with labour
> in Shropshire, one will cry,
> 'Let's go and kill a neighbour,'
> and t'other answers 'Aye!'
>
> So this one kills his cousins,
> and that one kills his dad;
> and, as they hang by dozens
> at Ludlow, lad by lad,
>
> all of them one-and-twenty,
> all of them murderers,
> the hangman mutters: 'Plenty
> even for Housman's verse.'"
>
> The Masefield one is [as if] written by Walter de la Mare to the tune of "Here lies a most beautiful lady" and runs:
>
> "Here lies a most difficult poet
> hard to read & scan was he.
> I think he was the most difficult poet
> that ever mangled poetry.
>
> But still they read him, still they praise him,

however rude, rude he be,
which makes me wonder, when I crumble
"Whoever will remember me?!"

In the published version, the first stanza was altered to:

Here lies a most vigorous poet,
hard of fist and thought was he.
I think he was the most vigorous poet
that ever assaulted poetry.

and the final line ran: "will anyone remember me?"

By 27 March he was back in Geneva for the Governing Body, from where he wrote to Jessie a wedding anniversary letter full of gratitude for all she had been to him during the fifteen years of their marriage. He acknowledged the sorrows they had had, more than she had deserved; his own failure to fulfil her dreams and expectations; and his selfishness and tiresomeness. But he passionately assured her that, despite the disappointments and the mistakes, he remained the boy she had loved all those years ago in Bradford.

The Governing Body argued for days about the Budget which Thomas had increased despite his solemn promises that he would reduce it. When Humbert showed up Thomas's attempted deception the latter first threatened to make the matter a vote of confidence but 'he won't do anything that might require him to resign.'

As soon as the meetings ended Humbert was to join Jessie in Folkestone for Easter. His last letter from Geneva on 1 April enclosed a plea from Consola for some financial assistance for Oswald who appeared to have fallen on hard times. Her letter is of unique interest, not least for the evidence of her idiosyncratic spelling and syntax. On 29 March from Park View Road, Bradford, she wrote:

> My dear boy
> I was so glad to hear from you it is allways a red letter day, whenn your handwriting greets me good morning, whenn I come down to my breakfast. I hope the change of air and of surrounding has cured your cold, I expect your usuall cough was troubling you. . . .
>
> Il mondo è fatto a scale, chi lo scende, e chi lo sale: say Dante and it is really your case, while I am glad and happy to say, you have after no end of worrie and strugel reached the top of the ladder Oswald has got to the bottom, and not only have I entirely the children to keep, but if I can, I must help him a little. I have sold

Maries pearl which however only brought £130 that is not much is it, however it is better than nothing, if you can manage to send him a £5 note, I am sure he will be gratefull, it will be little if you think how many £5 he has given you is it not! his add[ress] 225 apartado Madrid Spain. This month your name was mention, between all the up to date poem: my greatest wish has been realised with your success, has it not! so much love

Mother

(ii)

The Unknown Goddess

The 'up to date poem' may well have been *The Unknown Goddess*, a collection of sixty-one of Humbert's poems, published by Methuen in the spring of 1925. About half of the poems were new; the rest had variously been published in *The Spectator*, *The Weekly Westminster Gazette*, *The Outlook*, *The Queen*, *The Beacon*, *The Decachord*, and *Punch*. Two of the poems originally appeared in W. H. Davies' *Shorter Lyrics 1900 - 1922*, some had been included in anthologies and several had been broadcast from 2 LO, Aberdeen and Cardiff stations.

The Preface to the collection has already been mentioned in connection with *Kensington Gardens*. In his 1927 lecture on Humbert's poetry, H. W. Garrod's strictures on poets who insisted on writing Prefaces were aimed chiefly at Humbert's theories on punctuation and false rhyme. In point of fact, however, if Humbert advanced any theory at all, which is debatable, it was about *half-rhymes*: he was neither so brazen nor so foolish as to claim as a virtue, leave alone 'parade as a success in itself', what Garrod maintained was 'his defect of rhyming faculty,' exemplified (said Garrod) by the very first poem, 'Iliad', and by its very first couplet which he accused of rhyming 'false' with 'yours.' Garrod's argument, however, is weakened by his failure to note that the forty lines of 'Iliad' were not written in rhyming couplets, but in an *abab* pattern:

> False dreams, all false,
> mad heart were yours.
> The word, and nought else,
> in time endures.[12]

Humbert did not pretend to have invented the half-rhyme, nor did he claim for it any superiority over pure rhyme. He was too well-read to be unaware of Wilfrid Owen's use of what he called 'pararhyme', and of the half-rhyme to be found in earlier poets such as Vaughan and Hopkins in

English, and Jules Romains in French. Exact half-rhymes, however, which retain the consonant but change the vowel (as Owen did, for example, with 'sipped/supped'), inevitably impose some restrictions on the verse. For many words in English, particularly monosyllables, there are few if any possible half-rhymes. When they are combined with end-stopped lines in regular four-line stanzas, the exigencies of the rhyme tend to dictate the sense of the poem. It was perhaps for this reason that Humbert regularly refused to limit the sentence to the stanza, and at times chose outright the sentence and even the paragraph as the unit of verse, as in the one hundred and eighty-six lines of 'The Locri Faun.'

The Preface and the Table of Contents give no hint as to the choice governing the order of the poems, nor do the poems display any self-evident division into distinct groups by subject, chronology or form. The collection nevertheless displays a wide range and variety of verse-forms. Besides the quatrain, his favourite choice here, but with every variety of rhyme scheme, there are rhyming couplets, six- and eight-line stanzas with a variety of ingenious rhyme schemes - a-b-a-c-b-c in 'La Belle Au Bois Dormant', a different arrangement in each of the four stanzas of 'Betelgeuse', and totally unrhymed stanzas in 'The Son of Man'. He also uses the sonnet, and a twelve-line stanza form in 'Jupiter', consisting of two iambic pentameter couplets followed by four couplets in various arrangements of one-, three-, and five-feet lines. There are poems which mix rhyme and free verse, and others that are entirely free and unrhymed.

Occasionally the verse resonates with strange echoes - of Kipling's striding rhythms, for example, in a most un-Kiplingesque poem, 'Denmark', or of Verlaine's 'Les sanglots longs/ des violons' in 'Rhyme/in your clear chime/ we hear/ ringing, far-off and clear,/ in beauty's fairy granges/ at evensong the changes,/ and swells/ of her lost elfin-bells'.

Predictably, London gardens were essential features of Humbert's 'Dream City':

> On a dream-hill we'll build our city,
> and we'll build gates that have two keys -
> love to let in the vanquished, and pity
> to close the locks that shelter these.

It would be a transformed London, with

> A silent Square could but a lonely
> thrush on the lilacs bear to cease
> his song, and no sound else - save only
> the traffic of the heart at peace.
>
> And we will have a river painted
> with the dawn's wistful stratagems

7. Jessie's family, with Ann as a baby, c.1914. L to R, Joseph Chalmers Graham, Jessie, Mrs Graham with Ann on her knee, 'Gub' Graham, Annie Graham

8. (Left) No.6 Whitehall Gardens in 1912, garden view

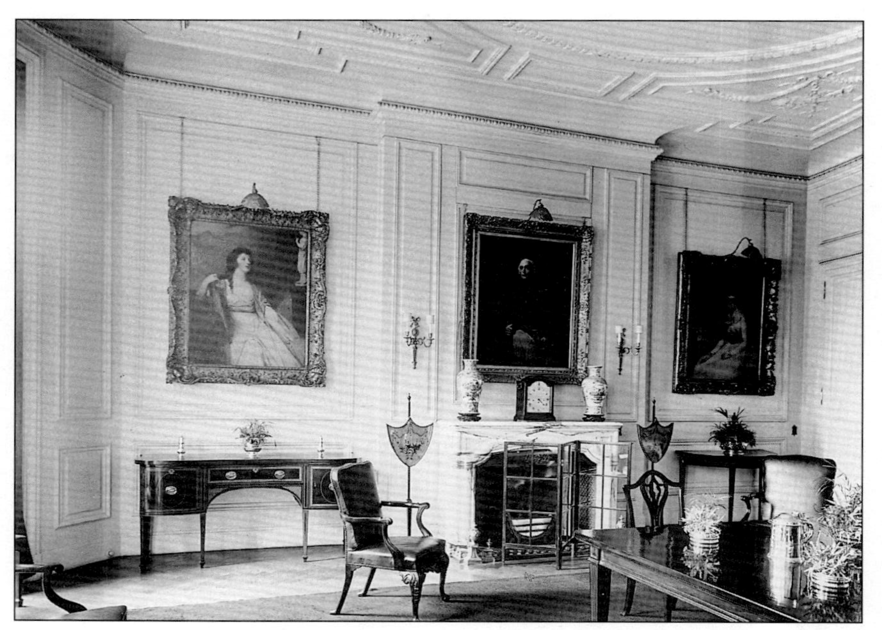

9. (Above) Dining room

10. (Above) Montagu House, Whitehall, in 1936, exterior view

11. (Right) A room of the kind that Humbert occupied

12. British Empire Delegation, ILO Conference, June 1926. Front row, left, is Margaret Bondfield; Humbert is in the centre

confident manipulation of the decasyllabic line, adjusting the old elegiac metre of Gray to express a new lyric passion:

> Look! we have loved all day, without asking or thinking,
>   and like Joshua, love has held back the sun,
> now when for all the Western world it is sinking:
>   for the long day of our beauty can never be done.
>
> Never, because the moments and hours it is made of
>   have ceased to be time, and have become a part
> of the one impulse of life that death is afraid of,
>   the unsubstantial fictions of the heart. . . [20]

The other two are 'The Incommunicable Surd':

> If with the greenness in our thought the trees
>   are vivid, if no other sweets than ours
> muffle the rose, yet something in all these,
>   not born of us, astonishingly flowers.
>
> Nor in our ears alone are musical
>   the birds: the dulcet mountain-lawns that swoon
> have their own peace, and the seas rounding all
>   hold bright cabal to cheat us with the moon. . .

and 'Death The Goth':

> In the Catalonian meadow
> electric lamps on trees
> coldly, between the tables,
> glitter like oranges.
> . . . .
> But your hat with the heron's feathers,
> is a helmet for death to see
> on the small proud head thrown backwards
> of the Wingéd Victory.
> . . . .
> Let the trees creep upon us,
> the bittern beat its gong,
> they will but find us sitting
> in the senate-house of song,
> pale upon marble benches,
> in neither fear nor wrath
> with love, - the quiet Romans
> despising death the Goth.

Pierrette adds her own triumphant voice:

> I am not afraid. For the truth is this
> that every woman for her one lover
> once in her life is Beatrice,
> once in her life and therefore for ever.
> . . . .

and ends with Humbert's translation of the last verse of Victor Hugo's 'Puisque j'ai mis ma lèvre':

> Then say to death, "Although your wing may brush
> the vase we brimmed, it will not overset.
> We cleanse with fire more than you clog with ash.
> Our love remembers more than you forget."[21]

After the characters have taken their leave, each in a quatrain, a final 'Apology to the Audience' from the Management explains that this is a unique performance since the audience will insist on

> . . . living, while we act, Harlequinade.

The company therefore withdraws,

> 'assured that, while there are two hearts to beat,
> this cast of two will stage our pantomime.'

It would be idle to criticize *Humoresque* for its departure from the traditional version of Harlequin. I think it is safe to accept that he saw it as a convenient peg on which to hang his poems, adapting it to suit his purpose. Pierrot was a rather pathetic character in French pantomime, a man in growth but a child in mind and manners; an apt model for the poet lover - naive, credulous, vulnerable and innocent under his appearance of maturity. Superficially, at least, Pierrot, rather than Harlequin, invites identification with Humbert: Harlequin is here a curiously ambivalent figure, as if Humbert could not make up his mind whether he was an enemy or an ally.

The chief interest of *Humoresque* lies in the fact that this is the first sustained treatment of two of the central themes of Humbert's poetry: on the one hand, the inevitable impermanence of love, and, on the other, the power of love to overcome death. Humbert's handling of the subject is characteristically ambiguous. The Song of Songs (the original of Humbert's 'High Song' - 'Das Hohe Lied') said: 'Fortis est ut mors dilectio' - 'love is as strong as death.' Humbert's fondness for sophisticated argument may have led him to maintain that love's triumph was not only over physical death but over love's own finitude: to have loved was an indefeasible fact. Without a doubt *Humoresque* drew extensively on Humbert's own experience - one has only to read the Alpine references - and there is nothing very surprising in that. One cannot but wonder, however, what Jessie made of it, for with hindsight it reads like the first of what Virginia Woolf shrewdly identified as Humbert's successive attempts at autobiography.

(iii)

April-June

In the middle of April Ann was to have the first of the operations which would eventually cure her disability. Mr. Kelsey Fry had brought in Mr. (later Sir) Harold Gillies, a leading plastic surgeon. Humbert had to go to Geneva for a week and arrived there on the eve of the operation. He spent several anxious days awaiting news from Jessie who was with Ann at the Duchess Nursing Home, Beaumont Street. Eventually the surgeon appeared satisfied that the operation had been a success. For all his regrets at leaving her to cope with this trial alone, Humbert had suggested that if Jessie agreed and the weather at Geneva improved, he might stay on for two or three days to get some sunshine further up the lake, in order to get rid of his persistent cough.

As always, there were tempestuous debates at the I.L.O., this time over the agreements reached at the London Conference the previous year, which the smaller nations, and Poland particularly, wished to reopen. The Italians joined in, claiming to have signed under a misapprehension and, wrote Humbert, 'generally behaving in a most Mussolinic way.' The French and German representatives, however, supported Humbert who was confident that he would accomplish what he had set out to do. But the Cabinet in London had been so tied up with the difficulties of the coal industry that they had not had time to send him instructions. Eventually he reported encouraging progress:

> All the five nations have asked me to act as their spokesman - a thing, as far as I know, that has never happened to any representative of La Grande Bretagne before! In particular the Germans are most friendly. Oudegeest - the secretary of the 2nd International and Vice-Chairman of the Governing Body (Workers' side) thanked me this morning on behalf of the workers for all that I had done for the International Labour Organization. He told me privately that any doubts that the workers had ever had about me were finally allayed.

In between these excitements he was busy writing 'Requiem', which he wanted to complete in time for publication in the autumn. He was also working on 'The Verdict' - a reference in one letter to 'Mrs. Jakes' suggests that it was an early version of *The Uncelestial City*. By the time the Governing Body adjourned, the weather, far from improving, had grown worse, and Humbert wrote that the one thing he wanted was to get back home to his family.

In the month between the end of this meeting and his next journey to Geneva, the General Strike occurred. The letters contain no reference to these events in which, in any case, he played a backroom role. But when the General Strike ended, the coal strike continued into the autumn, with increasing bitterness among both employers and miners.

In May a selection of Humbert's poems (chiefly *Kensington Gardens, The Unknown Goddess,* and *Lampoons*) appeared in *The Augustan Books of Modern Poetry, First Series,* one of fifty-six titles edited by Edward Thompson, and published by Ernest Benn between 1925 and 1926. The fascicule devoted to Humbert's poems went to four impressions between May 1926 and February 1931. Humbert edited the second series in 1927 - 1928.

In the General Preface, Edward Thompson explained the genesis of the Augustan Poets Series. It was originally to be called 'The Sixpenny Poets', the name by which Humbert referred to it in his letters to Jessie later in 1926. But by the time the publishers had realized the unfortunate connotations of that title the text was ready for the printers, and an 8-letter word had quickly to be found to fill the gap yet avoid infelicitous associations: they came up with 'Augustan', the title adopted for both collections.[22]

Humbert persuaded Jessie to agree to taking Ann abroad that summer to get a good spell of sunshine after the operation. He wanted to get rid of the Kensington High Street flat, which he judged to be too expensive and inconvenient, and he felt practically certain that by the autumn they would be in Geneva, which would be easy to reach if they were in northern Italy. His letters of May and June make numerous references to travel arrangements, medical checks for Ann, and arrangements for the storage of his books in a strong-room.

In the midst of preparations for the removal, Mrs. Harry Betterton, the wife of the Parliamentary Secretary to the Ministry of Labour, telephoned to tell Jessie that she had received cards for one of the first 'courts' (formal receptions at Buckingham Palace, at which people were presented to the sovereign) on 10 June and invited them to attend. Humbert had to decline, since the I.L.O. Conference was to be followed by a second, 'Seafaring Conference', beginning on 7 June, but thought that Jessie should be presented before he took up his Geneva appointment. Consola had very much wanted her to go too: 'I will be so proud,' she used to say, 'When Berto's wife bends the knee at court.' Jessie immediately began making a dress for the occasion.

On 31 May he wrote to tell her that he had finished "Paul Arthur" (i.e. *News of the Devil*) and sent it off to Benn's. Mgr. Nolens, 'the old Dutch papal Nuncio', was elected Chairman of the first Conference. One immediate consequence of this was a reduction in the number of I.L.O. dinners 'owing to the fact that Monseigneur is rather stingy, and is giving a lead of restraint!' Humbert welcomed the additional leisure for writing that this would give him. It may have been this Conference also which gave him the opening for one of his best-remembered shafts: winding up one particularly lengthy debate on a proposal which the prelate had firmly opposed, Humbert informed the assembly that 'Nolens volens we will get this measure through.'[23] The Conference was a tiring one for Humbert even though it passed without much incident. The Hours issue simmered on, and Humbert found himself making a speech on the subject which was all the more difficult in that the British government had still not reached a decision on the London Conference of the previous year. But on 4 June he wrote to Jessie: 'I have more or less got through all my jobs, and shall be able to report a complete success to Sir A[usten] Chamberlain, who is expected here on Sunday. I do hope that his arrival will have something for me!'

On Sunday 6 June the ceremonial opening of the new I.L.O. building took place, beginning

> with a Mass at 9 o'clock in the Cathedral followed by 3 hours of speeches in the Conference Hall, followed by a lunch to the German Minister of Labour, the French Min. of Lab., the Belgian M. of L., the President of the Swiss Republic, Michelis, Adatchi, Chatterjee, Barnes, Lord Burnham, Butler and myself, given by Thomas & Fontaine. Austen Chamberlain has been very naughty. The whole programme had been arranged so that he might make the first speech this morning. Ten minutes before it started he rang up (having arrived in Geneva an hour before), to say that he wasn't coming. And I had to stand up first before 600 people to make his apologies - a most painful ordeal!

The new building, a purpose-built edifice, rectangular, very plain, and said by its detractors to resemble a steam-engine, stood on land donated by the people of Switzerland. Humbert mentioned it briefly in *Portraits By Inference* (1934) ('a cinema-producer's guess at Sing-Sing'), when he was recalling the proposal to build the new League headquarters on the land of the Villa Lammermoor, for which the architects had designed a building larger than the land it was to stand on. The I.L.O. building was later enlarged, and finally exchanged for the 1970 modern design about one and a half miles away on a hillside near the World Health Organization.[24]

Jessie's presentation at Court duly took place on 10 June. The Bettertons had originally invited Jessie to dinner that day, but forgot and went elsewhere, so that Jessie called for them after dinner. She said that Mrs. Betterton, a very handsome woman, looked lovely in brocade. Mr. Betterton (later Lord Rushcliffe), looking very romantic in his court dress, asked Jessie: 'How do you like Muriel's fender?' (his disrespectful term for her flashing tiara). They arrived so late at the Palace that they were among the last of the presentations, and Jessie saw King George (V) glancing anxiously at the doorway of the gallery from which they emerged, as though to see if this was the end of the procession. The ladies wore short trains, so that two could curtsey at once, one to the King, one to the Queen. Humbert had sworn her to secrecy about the holiday, and Geneva, so that when Mrs. Betterton asked why she did not join him in Geneva, and where they were moving to, she had to dissemble. According to Jessie he wrote the sonnet 'Absence' for her on that day; it was later printed in *This Blind Rose*:[25]

> How should not absence from thy presence change me,
> since in thy presence all my future is,
> and in thy absence all that doth estrange me
> from that, and binds me to past miseries?
> I, like a shadow, when the lighted candle
> is snuffed, into a little pool of black
> shrink in a second, but, if you rekindle
> your flame, then on the instant I am back.
> O my bright candle, since it is your virtue
> and use to shine, and set your shadow moving,
> shine, well assured that naught in him can hurt you,
> and least his small and ghostly way of loving.
> Ghosts with God's word are laid, but mine with less,
> who only need for that a woman's "yes."

On 14 June he sent on to Jessie two flattering letters he had received from the Bettertons about her presentation. That same evening Lord and Lady Burnham gave a large dinner-party for the League and I.L.O. notables. Humbert was placed next to Mrs. Barton, the owner of the Villa Lammermoor, which stood in the great park that bore her name. 'She is a grand-daughter of Peel - & has been a great European figure (it seems) for a quarter of a century. She behaved all through dinner like a historical character reading her own memoirs. I was thoroughly cowed.' The calm elegance of the Villa and its gracious châtelaine were more flatteringly and generously described in Chapter X of *Portraits By Inference*, entitled 'Luncheon at the Villa Lammermoor', where 'None enters that heavy gate unless distinction, a mission, a reputation or pleasing youth command the benevolence of the owner.'[26]

(iv)

Italy

At the end of June, Jessie and Ann, together with Jessie's mother and sister, set off for Cannero, on Lake Maggiore, where Humbert later joined them. During the holiday, he told her that their financial situation was worrying him rather and that if the move to Geneva was delayed it might be a good idea to remain in Italy a little longer, since it was so cheap. It would be at least a year before he received anything from Consola's estate, and he did not expect it to be very much. (She left in fact nearly £6500, but what his share was has not been revealed.) Ann's operation had been expensive, and he wanted to be clear of debts when he started at Geneva. At the end of July he left to attend a conference in Paris on his way back to England, while they went to Bellagio on Lake Como, expecting him to join them later.

But after Paris, he returned to England for the whole of August. He wrote tender letters full of hope for a future which would recreate the climate of their early married life, and reported on the progress of 'Requiem'. On 6 August he wrote:

> With any luck I should have finished [it] in about a fortnight, and then my book for next autumn will be ready. If "The Publicist" is accepted for performance in the spring, & it looks as though it were going to be, I shall publish that as my spring book, though Benn's would rather have a straight book of verse. They have in any case asked me for a short story for their 1/- long short-story series. I have sent them "Mr. Fromage & George Gregory" and "The Great Undetective" to choose from. You remember one is about the don in Wadham Garden, & the other is about the little man at Balham, called upon to play the part of St. Peter. The only question is whether either of them is long enough.[27]

London in August was depressing, he said, especially after forty-eight hours of uninterrupted rain. The Sitwells, De la Mare, Gollancz, everyone but Civil Servants was out of town.

> I am thinking of learning American, because nobody in the streets understands English, and horn-spectacles don't suit the Americans as well as they suit you!

Mention of bills to be paid led him to complain:

> O what a d--d nuisance money is. Why the devil can't I just chuck all this, & come straight out to where all my thoughts are - Bellagio, & the one person in the world who really knows all about me - & loves me in spite of it!

He had written 'yards and yards of "Requiem"' but was slightly worried because a new book of verse by Edwin Muir called 'Chorus of the Newly Dead' looked 'rather like a clumsy anticipation of me. But it hasn't got my idea of all the persons in pairs.' He went on to list the pairs of 'Losers' and 'Winners', who were to be 'summed up in the final poem 'The Child'. In each group of two the first is a man and the second a woman. And each is intended to symbolize some tendency. I am only afraid lest the whole design should be a little heavy.'

The two books did indeed bear a superficial resemblance, but Muir's poem (written between 1923 and 1925), consisting of a number of 'types' whose lives either predestine them to alienation or provide a context in which solutions may be found, was at once more apocalyptic and less optimistic than Humbert's. Both works had this in common that the published version differed in some degree from the description given by their authors in letters written when the work was in progress. [28]

In a letter of 9 August Humbert quoted for Jessie's benefit the end of 'The Nun' (one of 'The Losers') which he thought was lovely:

> It is very quiet in the garden. Slowly
> the oleanders let their roses fold.
> The shadows reach my feet, and all the holy
> precincts of evening are suddenly cold.
> Sweet Christ! a nun
> lies down to sleep, and for the last time rejects the sun.
>
> The oleanders have terribly come to stand for Italy. I see them in the garden of the hotel, before I knew their names, & they seem to gather all the beautiful days into a whisper and a regret. "Rose bay, rose bay, where are your roses now!" But it's no good, is it, being sentimental, I have done what I had to do, & I don't like it any more, my dear, than you. But if it is right, I suppose it will bring its reward.[29]

He went on to say that he had only three 'Requiem' poems to finish. He wanted it out of the way in case he had to re-write "The Publicist". His 'Spring' poem, beginning: 'The sun-gold seas bank up and spill', had been printed in *The Saturday Review*.[30]

An interview reported in the *Bradford Argus* on what appears to be 6 August 1926 mentioned 'The Publicist' as a forthcoming production. On 16 August Jessie wrote to him in great distress about a press interview which he was reported to have given. From his reply it seems likely that she was upset at receiving no credit for her influence on his early poetry, and particularly on the *London Sonnets*. He was equally upset by her reaction which he put down to 'separation and geography.' But in his attempts to assure her that he did not take their present separation for granted, one can sense the desolation she increasingly felt, and her aching, mute feeling of isolation and loneliness.

On 27 August he wrote from the R.A.C. that he had just returned from a futile Conference with the Miners - 'Heaven knows when this thing will end.' He was working on 'Requiem' in the chess room:

> 'the poems were coming in spate, as they did when I wrote "Humoresque" at Folkestone. I wrote a poem for St Joan called "Voices", and then a poem for The Builder called "Words", and then suddenly without warning a quite astounding poem called "Rudolph Valentino reaches heaven". I had been very much impressed by the immense discrepancy between his obviously uneducated little mind and vulgar little soul & the celebrity of his life and death. And I thought of him arriving at the Gate, & Peter looking out, and wondering what on earth the funny little one-dimensional thing posing there could be. And then with a great rush the poem came. It has about 50 lines. The two best verses are:
>
> He was so trifling a thing
> he was so heart-rifling a thing
> that an angel was caught by the nebulous grace
> of his fabulous face.
>
> And seeing him so mean a thing
> so in-between a thing
> cried to St. Peter "O Peter be merciful
> to this mock-Parsifal."
>
> and it ends:
>
> Silver in mail and helm
> in an eternal film
> let him go flashing as if he played
> in a Crusade.

Make a new thing of him
an untrue Spring of him
and a shadow shall be heaven of shadows enticed for him
and a shadow be God, and a shadow be Christ for him.

I shall have it copied today, and send it to "The New Statesman". I think however that they may hesitate about printing it.'[31]

The paucity of letters between 9 August and 25 September - four in all - suggests that some were lost or concealed. Jessie and Ann stayed in Bellagio until the end of September at least, expecting him to join them there. The three of them would then go to Geneva, while her mother and sister would return to Scotland. In fact it marked for Jessie and Ann the beginning of a year of exile. On 25 September, replying to a reproachful letter from Jessie (she said once again that he did not answer her questions), Humbert went into some detail about his preparations for their forthcoming reunion in Venice. He had discovered that hotels on the French Riviera were cheaper than Italy, which suggests that they were considering a possible move to France, 'But we can talk about them, and all the other things when I come.'

When he duly joined them in Venice, it was decided that Jessie, her mother and sister, and Ann should all remain in Italy, in order to save money. They went first to Florence where they spent three unhappy months: they had brought no winter clothes with them, Jessie felt abandoned, her mother and sister grumbled.[32] Jessie also recalled in later years how she had had frequently to crush her desire to rush home, and how his letters helped her to forget the discomfort and concentrate on teaching Ann, going for walks in Florence and the surrounding countryside, and mending their old clothes.

On 25 September Humbert described meeting Siegfried Sassoon at the Holborn restaurant, where he dined with Monro and Aldington.

> I hadn't met Sassoon before. He is quite the most beautiful Jew I ever saw. He is fair and tall, and very shy, and with only a tiny glimpse of the Jew in his queer otherworld face. He hardly talked at all, and he is plainly still deeply under the influence of shell-shock. O that devilish war! Monro, for once, was not under the influence of drink, but of great worry. Unless he can raise £2500 in a month the Poetry Bookshop may have to close down. He is trying to form a limited company, but I fear that he won't get the money. I don't see how he can expect people to trust him with it.

(v)

News of the Devil

News of the Devil was published by Ernest Benn in October and made a more or less instant stir. Demand was such that a second impression was needed in October, a third in November and a fourth in December, as readers and reviewers recognized the quality of this remarkably sustained and at times very powerful satire in which seriousness and wit harmoniously blended. The title is taken from the opening poem entitled 'Fleet Street', a gem in the spirit of his earlier *Lampoons*:

> Here they publish,
> fresh and fresh,
> news of the devil
> and news of the flesh.
>
> And as for the world,
> they take the view
> that it simply consists
> of the other two.

His judgement would not have been different seventy years later.

The body of the poem, some twenty-eight pages of heroic couplets, relates the story of the redemption of Paul Arthur, a newspaper tycoon who, having grown rich and powerful by sedulously underestimating public taste, decides one day that he will control not only his readers' minds but also their souls: '. . . he would reorganize religion.' Observing the multiplicity of religions,

> each with a right of way
> to heaven, and all strong in the conviction
> that all the rest moved in the wrong direction,

he saw the solution: a universal syndicate which

> embraced all creeds from Jew to Wesleyan
> in one magnificent co-ordination
> of overlapping systems of salvation.
> You know the way the modern business man
> by intuition hits upon a plan,
> titanically scornful of the facts,
> and, without wasting time on thinking, acts.

What God needed, he saw, was efficiency: "Religion by Results", and the replacement of the private sector by one Church, a glorified Trade Union based on the principle of collective bargaining, while a programme of mass-suggestion through the Press would sell the idea to the public.

Discussions with God and the Devil (apparently during a heart-attack) about Arthur's plan of campaign allowed Humbert first to set against the cult of business the ideals of Arthur's brother, a poet; then to satirize the basic tenets of the popular Press, and the worship of war; and finally to assert the triumph of God's love. It must be said that Humbert's theology, here as elsewhere, is highly unorthodox, and relies on the persuasive power of a torrent of heart-warming images and sounds - faintly reminiscent of *The Hound of Heaven* - which suggest without actually embodying traditional Christian doctrine:

> . . . "Too late" will little irk or rue
> when the unhasting love of God breaks through
> the puny dams, the crumbling breakwaters
> of Time, and overwhelms the barriers
> that strain at Him, and tumble, and are gone,
> while the great tides of heaven thunder on,
> not drowning, but releasing, soul by soul,
> division in the undivided whole.
> Listen! the stuff that God is woven of
> is love of loving for the sake of love.
> . . . .
> your sins and you have here become a part
> of the immortal movement of the Heart,
> that does not judge, nor blame, nor yet forgive,
> but being needed by all things that live,
> needs all of them, . . .

The author of his obituary in *The Times Literary Supplement* chose four lines from *News of the Devil* to exemplify not only the best of his early verse but also to show how 'at his lyrical best he could evoke from words the ghostly sweetness of the violin, which he once described as "the voice of my own heart speaking":

> Nothing is here recaptured, but the thin
> perfume that reaches like a violin
> up to the fifth in frozen fern and frond,
> but the living green of music is beyond.'[33]

In *News of the Devil*, with its well-defined theme, a poetic vehicle he was at home in, and a certainty in his purpose, Humbert showed what a remarkable artist he could be.

On 17 November an invitation from the Old Boys Association of Bradford Grammar School to be guest of honour at their next dinner and to reply to the toast on behalf of literature reminded him of the cavalier treatment he received at the last dinner he had attended. He reported to Jessie that Benn wanted him to edit *The Sixpenny Poets*, and *The Daily News* had published an article of his.

> Then "The Saturday Review" rang up and asked me if I would write a poem on a horrible incident that happened stag-hunting at Minehead. The hind swam out a mile to sea, was pursued in motor-boats, & brought back by the hunt & given to the hounds to be killed! Isn't it unspeakably beastly! I don't know whether I can do the poem, but I'm going to have a d-d good try this evening. I think it's the most revolting thing I've ever heard of in England - I mean so far as animals are concerned. When you think of the fat rich leisured people living round Minehead going out to indulge in an orgy of murder, it makes you despair of humankind.[34]

He went on to list more requests for poems, and reviews, but added:

> Mind you I'm enjoying having all this work to do, & it does feel like the beginning of the breath of - well not fame (for that's too grand a word!) but certainly some sort of recognition, which hasn't come my way before.

His weight, he said, was now comfortably over ten stone and he feared he might become 'a little round man.' At a dinner of 'The Omar Khayyam Club' he sat next to "Dum-Dum" of Punch and Low the cartoonist - 'Ann's friend'. *The Saturday Review* wanted him to do a weekly causerie which he said he would think about. *Vogue* wanted reviews and a leader for their Christmas number; he was writing reviews and articles for the *Observer* too, but

> I would like to do a great deal of work that is well paid next year, and so emerge into the final sunlight of financial security. . . There are bad things - like separation, financial embarrassment & family anxieties - about us, but, Jessie, I do think that the thing we have waited for is actually trembling on the threshold.

On 28 November he was advising Jessie's mother on how to go about selling her property in Scotland: he expected property prices to rise as a result of a trade boom in the New Year now that the Coal Strike was settled. He talked of the Sixpennies he was editing, and the poets he had in mind for the February edition: three moderns (including Monro and Gerard Hopkins) and three 17th century mystics. There was a case for including Monro, he said: 'He's not a very good poet but he's done as much as anybody for poetry. He told me that last week Sir Henry Newbolt gave a reading at the Bookshop, and read a large slab of "N[ews] of D[evil]", which he described as one of the best poems of the last 50 years!' *The Spectator* printed a little poem from "The Uncelestial City" about Paddington and Waterloo.[35]

On 29 November he discussed with Gerald Barry the latter's suggestion that Humbert should write a weekly article for *The Saturday Review*, beginning with a series on Victorians reviewed as if by a contemporary, which he proposed calling 'Dead Letters'. The first would be a review of *In Memoriam* as if it had just come off the presses. There are only two letters for December, one on the 5th, saying he was up to his eyes with reviews and work on the Sixpennies, and trying to raise Jessie's spirits. The second, dated 23 December, lacks the first sheet or sheets. It reported that *London Sonnets* and *Shylock* were out of print, and that copies were being sold for £4 so he was asking Blackwells for 10% royalties.

For the first time in their marriage they spent Christmas apart. The effect on Jessie can only be imagined.

IV

1927

(i)

He wrote to wish Jessie a Happy New Year on 1 January. Arnold Bennett had invited him to dinner on 2 January, and A. A. B. for his birthday on 5 January. 'He is very pleased with me about his book, and the last time I saw him he spoke again about his Will. The Birthday Honours are very uninteresting - I'm not a knight yet. But you are, as you always have been, my lady!'

On 13 January he told Jessie that having agreed with Gollancz on one or two omissions from and additions to *Requiem*, it was now ready for publication. He wanted to publish *The Uncelestial City* after that, but Gollancz did not agree. The "Sixpennies" were causing him many problems: getting the right number of lines of the right kind to represent each poet involved him in long telephone calls and many letters, W. B. Yeats had still not submitted his selection, while Harold Monro threatened to withdraw his poems rather than have them cut.

On 16 January he went to have tea with George Moore, who lived in Ebury Street, at the opposite end to where Humbert had lived with Lascelles in 1910. The next day he described his excitement to Jessie:

> He has the whole house - a great double-room on each floor, and both rooms and the staircase walls filled with French pictures, and some English, including portraits of himself by Manet and Orpen.
>
> He is a very old man, older in his ways and more infirm in appearance than A.A.B., though he has clearly never had a stroke, and is probably no older. He has soft white hair, like fur, and the whole of his face is curiously on the slant to the left. He gives you the impression of having his head always cocked like a bird, though in fact he keeps it quite straight.
>
> He speaks slowly with a soft Irish drag in his words, but his mind is as lively and as vigorous as ever. He spoke first of the very great pleasure a review I had done on him in "The Observer" some months ago had given him. "It wasn't", he said, "that it was pleasant to me, but it was written. I hardly ever come on writing nowadays."

The letter went on to give Moore's account of how he came to write *The Brook Kerith* and *Abelard*, which Humbert greatly admired.[36]

> When he was showing me his pictures he showed me a little landscape of Mark Fisher. "Not a very good picture," he said,"but the man was born to paint you can see - as you were born to write." I was more pleased by that simple phrase than by all the other things that the critics have ever said of me. . . . "That's charming of you," I said," but if it hadn't been for my wife, I'd not be writing now." I told him that you were in Italy and he said, "You should go and live out of England for some years. Every writer should. You want the blood to flow in the opposite direction." I told him that I might be going to live in Geneva. "That won't do," he said, "Italy's what you need!" I left at 6.45 greatly exalted.

A little later he wrote to tell Jessie that while he was in Bradford for the Old Boys dinner he had gone with his sister Rita to Scholemoor to see his parents' grave.

> They have taken down the old tombstone and made the grass into a little paved garden with a crazy pavement, and mosses and flowers growing. The names are inscribed on the runnel. It is very charming, and very simple. And I think that she would have liked it. . . But it's odd, isn't it, that an Italian should sleep happily in a West Riding graveyard.

Still awaiting the call to Geneva, Jessie and Ann were glad to leave the cold of Florence for the sun and palm trees of San Remo. Later in the year they moved again, first to Monte Carlo and then to Nice. Humbert took advantage of a trip to Geneva to go to see them. They went on to Ospedaletti, a charming little place just a few miles west of San Remo, and were there when Humbert wrote on 18 February to tell Jessie that he had 'tinkered at the prologue for a play called "The Fanatics", in which Leon was showing an interest.[37] He thought he might incorporate an amended version of a poem he had written two years earlier, called 'The Voyagers', ending with 'a sort of song beginning: "If that be a sword, break it!"' The play seems not to have been published, if it was ever completed, but the poem appeared in *This Blind Rose.*

The next letter is dated 7 March. He was still working on 'The Fanatics', and discussing with Benn and others 'the whole programme', i.e. of his next publications. Blackwell had approached him about republishing *London Sonnets* and *Shylock Replies*, but in view of the proposal by Doran (a New York publisher) to bring out *Requiem*, *Kensington Gardens*, and *Lampoons*, in addition to Benn's intention of printing *The Uncelestial City* and one other book in 1927, he was disposed to let Blackwell wait. It seemed to him a formidable list and he was anxious not to overproduce.

At the end of March he managed a short visit to see Jessie for their wedding anniversary. They went to Milan for a week-end and saw 'Rigoletto' at La Scala. Ann said that Jessie came back singing 'La donna e mobile.' In a later letter Humbert referred to this 'little escape into fairyland . . . I loved every minute of it, & I bless the porter who decided that we were to have a car, & the concierge who got us seats for the Scala. It is an imperishable memory, isn't it?' On 7 April he sent Jessie the American edition of *News of the Devil*, which he said had an 'alarming' cover. He was making enquiries about a furnished flat or house for June, 'one which will take all of us at any rate at the outset.' - a hint that he looked forward to the departure of Jessie's mother and sister. He was going to write to Gillies to postpone Ann's operation on the advice of the Italian doctor.

The next set of "Sixpennies" were to be translations from Chinese, Persian, old Irish, Latin, French and the Greek Anthology. He found most of the Greek translations so impossible that he decided to rewrite a lot of them himself. This decision eventually led to his two books of translations from the Anthology, *Others Abide* (1927) and *Homage to Meleager* (1930). Benn's announced that *Requiem* would not now appear until 27 April: 'They had to re-set the whole book, because the first setting was a muddle.' The BBC had also asked him to do 'a series of things for them' which he said he might consider if they paid fifteen guineas a time. *The New Criterion*, a literary quarterly founded by T. S. Eliot, had sent him a score of books of verse to review. Eliot had also invited him to dine

> to discuss the future of the paper. It is being converted from a quarterly into a monthly, though I can't believe it will survive many months. . . I can't understand how a body so thin and white goes on living. My word if he were your husband you'd have cause to worry. I look positively robust and coarse beside him. He's had pneumonia twice, and my belief is that he has consumption. However, he's very bright and cheerful about "The Monthly Criterion" as it is now to be called.

Humbert's quip that, having reviewed A.A.B.'s book for *Country Life*, 'I expect him to give me £100 at lunch tomorrow', may not have been entirely jest, for he later wrote to Jessie:

> the old man . . . was, as I expected, hugely pleased with the review. I'm quite sure that whatever his intentions about his Will were, they have been confirmed and driven home. He was as excited as a child, and could talk of nothing else. He had a magnificent lunch in honour of the occasion, and observed (after two glasses of champagne, which he oughtn't to have drunk, & which he quarrelled with Browning [his manservant] about) that his old age had given him the son that his youth had denied!

In the same letter he announced his intention of doing his own translation of the Greek Anthology, which he would publish as a book the next year:

> It's asking to be done, & it suits me perfectly. Of course I can't keep absolutely to the Greek, but I can keep a d-d sight nearer to it than the bunglers who have tried before, and still produce poetry. . . I've got exactly the "Kensington Gardens" and "Humoresque" feeling. It's exciting but tiring.

He thanked heaven it was Budget Day, for it would be the first since his return on which there had not been at least one Committee to attend. 'Today is to be devoted to Winston's dirge. There won't I imagine be an increase in the income-tax, but there will be a number of new indirect taxes on tobacco, etc.' His forecast was remarkably accurate.[38]

Financial anxieties seem to have abated during these first months of 1927. His letters at this time are full of details about cheques he was sending her as they came in from magazines and publishers, and there is no mention of debts or particular financial worries on her part or on his; in fact, he wrote on 13 April that he did not want her to be uneasy for the sake of a pound or two. He looked forward to joining them soon in Monte Carlo and being shown the sights by her. He made jokes about things and people - of some samples of cloth for a 'light suit' he said that if he had chosen one and gone out in it 'I should have been instantly charged betting-tax!' He commented on the annual dinner of *The Saturday Review* which he had attended: 'There were the usual people there - Gerald Barry (the nice fat Editor), Ivor Brown - the dramatic critic -, Barley Webley, the long thin authority on Swinburne, Berham, the art critic, . . . and Edward Shanks, looking like a white slug. Barry is in trouble, because I think that the proprietor is beginning to tire of losing money. But on the whole "The S.R." has picked up a great deal since Baumann's day.'

On Good Friday, 15 April, he wrote from the R.A.C. where he was working on the translations:

> The fact is that the Greek Anthology is a fraud. For centuries all the silly old scholars have gone on saying it is great poetry, & the few poets who have ever read it have been awed into a slavish belief. In fact the great majority of it is the level of the memorial verses in a parish magazine. There are only about 4 poets in the whole lot (about 6,000). Its interest for the most part is purely historical. Meleager is the only poet of any importance, Simonides & Antipater of Sidon have some claims. But there is not a poem in the lot as good as Shelley's translation, & only about 3 as good as two of mine! I propose to announce this discovery to the world in my preface.

The BBC wanted a series of broadcasts from him: he was not keen, he told Jessie, but wanted as much money as he could get. A wrangle with Benn about money he was owed prompted him to threaten to employ an agent and to take his work to Heinemann: 'Really publishers are very slippery people.'[39] The next day he developed the theme further:

> Talking of "Vogue" I received the ominous letter to which one grows so accustomed in the newspaper world.

> It acknowledged my last review, & observed immediately that they were "reorganizing". That is normally the prelude to saying that one isn't wanted any longer! . . . The journalistic world is the most precarious I know. I have now written for about 10 papers, every one of which has changed proprietors, and Editors about 8 times! There have even been rumours about "The Observer", which I hope and believe are untrue. However, . . . as soon as one paper disappears another bobs up. So I've no doubt that if "Vogue" sends me packing, some successor will appear.

Jessie must have warned him about the awful fate of Sir James Masterton-Smith (who had a nervous breakdown through overwork after 16 months as Permanent Secretary in 1921), for he reassured her that he was in good health and having a lazy day or two over Easter.

Almost every letter for the rest of the month included specimens of his translations - mostly epigrams and epitaphs, sometimes demonstrating how he needed only two lines to say what previous translators had said in four. He went on to give his views on the art of the epigram:

> The esssence . . . is to avoid unnecessary words, &, of course, in this case to get as near to the letter and the spirit of the Greek original. The truth is that, except in about ten cases, only scholars, ignorant of verse, have tried their hand. Their idea of poetry is to use worn-out "poetical" words & phrases - repugnant both to Greek thought and English verse. I am approaching it as verse first and last, & I hope that the result will be satisfactory.[40]

On Easter Sunday he had tea with George Moore again, this time to discuss the French translation of *The Brook Kerith* which Humbert said 'is called "La Solitude du Kerith", and really is an amazing piece of work. I am reviewing it for next week's "Observer". G[eorge] M[oore] is trying to screw himself up to do a review of "Requiem". But I think that he'll fail at the post.' He had walked across the Park and [Kensington] Gardens to A.A.B's for lunch: 'The trees are just beginning, & everything looked as though it were waiting for you and Ann.' His tally of Greek translations now stood at twenty-seven. He was going to spend 'a melancholy lunch interval signing my name 275 times on the "de luxe" Requiem. They've arranged it properly this time. So that the ordinary edition is the First Edition. I haven't, of course, got copies yet. But you shall have the first. But I hope you will be pleased with the dedication, which I send with all my heart.'

He reported having no luck yet in the search for flats but expected to find something reasonable in Chelsea or Kensington: 'I don't want anything too far away from the middle of things for your sake.' The American press was giving *News of the Devil* a mixed reception: 'It has particularly annoyed a lady of the name of Babette Deutsch!'[41] He thought that the BBC talks he had been offered were probably as a stand-in for Desmond McCarthy who was going away for six months.

On 21 April he gave her the encouraging news that the *de luxe* edition of *Requiem* had been over-subscribed,

> which means that 275 copies at 10/6d have been sold. They only started selling the 6/- edition yesterday, & as they hadn't got either bound yet (& won't have for a week) it does seem rather a remarkable thing that people should buy copies like this in the dark. It does give me the feeling that things are rather moving in my direction.

The letter continued:

> The Hours Committee restarted its dreary sittings yesterday afternoon. All the Ministers are rather bored at having to be back in town after Easter. Sir P. Cunliffe-Lister arrived later as (he explained) he had just got away from lunch at Windsor. He asked me casually whether I'd known that he was staying with the King, when I arranged for the Cee at 3, & I said "yes, I had been told, but I'd forgotten whether he or the King told me"! He was duly irritated. I don't really mind him. We get on quite well, &, as he sees my name about more & more, he becomes less & less superior. He mentioned that "Molly" was anxious to meet you again![42]

When the Anthology was finished - he had done thirty-five out of the fifty or sixty envisaged - 'I must get back to "The Uncelestial City" which urgently needs attention. It is to be published in September.' (As will be seen, this proved not to be the case.) *Vogue* had written after its change of Editor to ask him to carry on, 'so that source of income won't be stopped for the moment.'

He reassured Jessie about his health, giving her his time-table as proof:

> I sleep at least 8 hours every night. I'm nearly always in bed by 11. I read for half an hour & then go off to sleep at once. The man brings tea at 8, I read the paper till 8.30: then I have my bath, and breakfast about 9. And then, as today, I write to you before going to the Office.

> So you see that even if I work hard between 10 a.m. & 11 p.m. I see to it that I rest between 11 p.m. and 10 a.m.! As to the cough, I will stop cigarettes for a fortnight as you ask.

Vogue now wanted not one, but two articles a month, to which he provisionally agreed, with some misgivings. The BBC, as he had guessed, wanted a fortnightly broadcast but for a five guinea fee which he thought derisory. At the BBC he met

> Fuller & Gorham (who had both been on the old "W.G.") and Sava, the caricaturist. Sava asked me whether I would give him a sitting . . . He is the first artist of any distinction that has asked. . . So that makes 4 portraits - poor old Shackleton,[43] the one for "The London Mercury", the one for "The Bookman", and now Sava's. . . Gollancz has asked me to dine with him at Pagani's on Monday night to celebrate (a) "Requiem" and (b) the first six Sixpennies. He will be [over]joy[ed] and surprised when he learns that I've written a new book in the last fortnight.

The Bermondsey Bookshop rang to ask him to stand in at the last moment for one of their Sunday evening lecturers. Despite being so busy he agreed: 'I do like the East-End audience. They're really interested, and even excited, & I think it's extraordinary that 2 or 300 working-class men and women should choose to spend their Sunday evening listening to verse.'

Leon M. Lion sent him 'a most amusing French play in verse, & has asked me whether I would like to think of making it into an English verse play for "The Ambassadors". . . It has the makings of a great success, but it would be a terrific job.' He was by now thinking of going to a hundred poems from The Anthology and making it his autumn book instead of "The Uncelestial City." Although the French play would bring in extra money, he seems in the end to have declined it.

On 25 April, reassuring Jessie that he was indeed planning to go out to her, he wrote: 'Sava's drawing of me is <u>brilliant</u>. He did two - one in detail, and the other in about 15 lines. The detailed one made me look very old, but otherwise (I thought) extremely like. The other one makes me look like a poet staring at the sun.' The BBC implored him to step into the breach and broadcast at 9.15 on Thursday. He agreed to do a fifteen minutes travel talk on Lac Leman, for which he could use some earlier pieces: 'I don't want to read verse again.'

He told Gollancz about his idea for *The Anthology* (now over a hundred translations); the publisher was most excited and wanted to publish it in July. Humbert thought there was a risk of overkill and preferred to release a few of the epitaphs in *The Spectator, The Saturday Review*, and elsewhere, saving the complete work for the next year. In addition to the sell-out of the *de luxe* edition of *Requiem*, Benn had sold five hundred of the ordinary edition.

Jessie must have become a little alarmed lest his writing pushed their Geneva hopes into the background, for he protested to her on 27 April that, on the contrary, Geneva was very much in his mind, since Thomas had written to say he wanted to discuss his whole position privately with Humbert as soon as he arrived in London the following week. Meanwhile, Gollancz was pressing for publication of *The Anthology* in July - what he called "the tradition of overwhelming output", while Humbert was terrified at the thought of five books in a year. And Heinemann's had rung up to ask him to go to see them with a view to being an "adviser" to the firm. 'Heaven knows what that means, but . . . if it means easy money, so much the better.'

T. S. Eliot wanted him to write a dialogue on "George Moore" for the May issue of *The New Criterion*, and Sackville-West (the poetess's cousin, not, as Humbert thought, her brother), who had temporarily succeeded Desmond McCarthy as literary editor of *The New Statesman*, wanted him to write for them. Humbert was at first reluctant but on 28 April told Jessie:

> I clinched with Sackville-West at the Holborn Restaurant. He is a queer shy young man. He wrote a novel last year, which was bitterly attacked by "The Daily Express" on the grounds of its immorality. Anything less immoral than this almost mortally shrinking creature I never saw. But it's possible that, like Aldous Huxley, he writes unpleasant stuff as a reaction against his own timidities. I don't know, because I haven't read it.

(ii)

Requiem

Humbert announced the arrival of *Requiem* in a letter dated 31 April (*sic*): 'much the most beautifully produced of my books.' He promised to send her a copy as soon as he received her Nice address, and said again that he hoped she would like the Dedication he had written. He expected a review of it in the next day's *Observer*.

On Sunday 1 May he sent her a copy of the *Observer* review:

> You will (I think) agree that it is the best I have ever had, & should start the book with a bounce. The review isn't signed, but I imagine that it is by Garvin. He wouldn't have signed it, because he is concentrating for six months on his book on Chamberlain, & has announced that he is doing no work in "The O", except his weekly article on the middle page.[44]

It seems unlikely that Humbert did not know or suspect that the author of the review was in fact Viola Garvin, J. L.'s daughter and Literary Editor of the paper. He expected reviews to come quite quickly, since *The Saturday Review* printed a note to say it proposed to review it at length, *The Spectator* put it in its library list, and Sackville-West told him that *The New Statesman* was doing an early review. 'The only misfortune is that Arnold Bennett is away, so that his powerful assistance won't be available.'

On 3 May he wrote that he found *Requiem* displayed in the Oxford and Cambridge Club, 'among the books at the top of the stairs where they exhibit the last arrivals', but was embarrassed at hearing it discussed by the diners at the next table. That same day he heard from Benn's that in addition to the limited edition, they had sold a thousand of the ordinary in three days. Victor Gollancz, admittedly tending to be over-sanguine, was speaking wildly of a best-seller. He turned out to be right. He pressed even harder for publishing *The Anthology* that year. He must have been very persuasive, for although Humbert said he would not change his mind, *Others Abide*, the title he gave to the translation, did come out in 1927.

That same afternoon Humbert went to the House of Lords and spent an hour briefing A. J. Balfour (now Earl Balfour) for a Debate.

> He really is extraordinary, [Humbert told Jessie the next day], 'His mind isn't a day older than when I met him in Munitions days. He said to me "Now it's my turn to stand on the mat!" He knew all about my writing. I've got to go down to the House of Lords again this afternoon to hear the Debate for which I was briefing B . . . The photos of the Sava pictures have arrived. . . if you look at them about 10 yards off you'll find they're not really too bad. But I'm afraid that they won't reproduce well in the Press.[45]

With his letter of 4 May he enclosed a tribute from Will Rothenstein which took his breath away. Rothenstein lived in Campden Hill now, not the Hampstead address which had been so inconveniently far from Humbert's modest Battersea dwelling in 1910.

> My dear Humberto, [he wrote], 'I am told that the Bradford trade is not what it was. But I say that Bradford manufactures are clearly at their highest. It is a particular pleasure to follow the steady crystallisation of your nebulae into a fixed star, the more so since for a time the world was grudging & ungenerous towards your gifts. But then I have always contended that we have to put gold under men's pillows in the night, while they sleep, lest we be arrested & cast into prison. Your new work, judging from the quotations in today's Observer, seems to me likely to move my bowels. I shall get it at once & be in your debt. Such debts, unlike others, are a lasting pleasure. Ever yours, Will Rothenstein.

'Aren't they a marvellous family!', wrote Humbert incredulously. 'When you remember what he could have done for us! And then he speaks of the world being grudging and ungenerous. Well - can you beat it!'

The success of *News of the Devil* may have had something to do with the advance sales of the new work, but one has the feeling in retrospect that word had somehow got about that a new star was about to enter the firmament. And there is no doubt that *Requiem* struck, and still strikes, the reader as a powerful and intense sequence, with little or none of the attitudinising which marred some of his earlier 'high style' poems.

The book retained the shape which Humbert had outlined in his letter to Jessie of the previous August, namely, Losers on the one hand - 'The Common Man', 'The Common Woman', 'The Soldier', 'The Harlot', 'The Huckster', 'The Nun', 'The Anarchist', 'The Respectable Woman'. And, on the other, Winners - 'The Lovers (He and She)', 'The Builder', 'The Teacher', 'The Saints (He and She)', 'The Uncommon Man, and the Uncommon Woman'. In a final 'Losers and Winners' poem, Humbert, not altogether unexpectedly, stood everything on its head, passionately advancing the proposition that only those who lose their lives and their world shall win them, while those who win

> . . . . never can
> do more than prove for the common woman and man
> . . . .
> that these are the losers of the world, and they have it,
> they are the lost archangels, and they rise,
> they have cheated the faith they had, and God forgave it,
> are blind and see in His forgiving eyes,
> and, having died,
> of life eternal are the bridegroom and the bride.

This impassioned, prophetic gloss on the Pauline doctrine that in what the world holds to be weakness and folly lie the strength and wisdom of God must have struck convincing and hopeful echoes in the jaded and disillusioned world of the twenties. The dedicatory poem announced something new and different - a poet unashamedly claiming to write as one seized of a vision which he had no choice but to tell:

> . . . . I sing
> not here, as once, of love and his first swallow
> that does not make, because it is, the spring.
> Nor was it written as other poems were
> because of human beauty and brief grace,
> . . . .
> . . . . but as the pool
> they called Bethesda, when the angel stirred it,
> was with some alien virtue wonderful,
> so was this written, as though I overheard it,
> whispered beyond the misted curtain . .
> . . . .
> I only know this poem is not mine. .

The emotion feels real and resounds in the reader, for example in 'The Huckster' - two poems about Judas. The first is a dramatic plea by 'the merchant', begging the priests to take back their thirty pieces of silver, while the second describes, in sonnet form, the Last Supper:

> There were thirteen that ate together, drinking
> strange wine, and biting on perilous bread.
> And one was speaking, and the rest were thinking
> more of his eyes than of the things he said.
> . . . .
> save one, who heard, but would not understand,
> afraid of blindness, if he dared to see.
> But even so there was a ray of light
> went out with him into the fatal night

'The cloistered nun', mentioned in Humbert's letter of August 9, 1926, is listed, paradoxically, among the Losers. Even so, in her Humbert pays tribute to

> . . . . man's unsatisfied
> desire for more than human holiness . . .

When 'The Respectable Woman', the last of The Losers, sings of her respectabilities, it is with the feeling that she may have missed the true singing:

They are singing, but I have not listened
in the open spaces in spring.
Their white feet in the dances have hastened,
but mine are not hastening.
. . . .
I have not heard nor seen them,
I have not danced nor sung,
and when love passed between them
he left my heart unwrung. . .

Among the Winners, 'The Uncommon Man' speculates on who the losers of the world may be:

We lose the world. And yet, in losing, see
by their lost sight, feel by their wasted touch,
and find the face of God bewilderingly,
because these others loved their dream too much,
because we love it
too little, and through them become the meaning of it.

We are the losers of the world, and we have it.
We are the lost archangels, and we rise. . .

There are interesting linking devices, with the 'Lucifer, Adam and Azrael' refrain most prominent. The religious themes are insistent, urgent, even anguished. In 'The Builder', for example,

There is one splendour of vision, another glory,
different and less, of the vision consummate
snatched from the void in steeple and clerestory
and the tall iron irresolutely great,
the builder's tale
of all the strivings of men that thus divinely fail.

(Lucifer, that fell from heaven, and Azrael -
space in triumphant darkness - you were lit
even with the burning of pinions as they fell,
. . . .
. . . . and all our pride
is that the desire of the heart is never satisfied.)

In the first of the three 'Teacher' poems, the teacher compares his work to that of the builder:

I also build, but not with steel nor stone

but with the shadowy bricks of innocence. . .
This is more than the upward anguish of the spire . . .

The final poem in 'The Teacher' section is the most moving of all, probably because it captures almost miraculously the feel of a class of small children and the fragility of their innocence:

They murmur, the children, like bees in summer
in a hot garden, like bees in a cup,
and, like light through branches, now gay, now dimmer,
thought touches a face that is lifted up.
My bees, with the pollen under your feet,
when the thought that we shared is no longer alive,
will aught that we dreamed of together be sweet,
will there be honey of ours in the hive? . . .

There are no remarkable metrical experiments, save for the insistent, repeated 'now' in the Coda: 'High Song':

The high song is over. Silent is the lute now.
They are crowned for ever and discrowned now. . .

which some critics (e.g. H. W. Garrod) thought weakened the force of the poem's burden: namely, that there was a thing to say, and it is said; winners and losers are only a theme now; no need for blame, no cause for praise; they were men and women; they have gone their way, as men and women must. The high song is over.

No book of verse since Masefield's *Everlasting Mercy* sold so abundantly - it was the best-seller in its first week - or was so much talked about. He was compared with Francis Thompson, even Shelley. H. W. Garrod, later that year, said in the lecture referred to earlier, ' . . . For it will not be contested, I think, that his *Requiem* has been the most successful poem of recent years. Rupert Brooke published nothing which had so notable a vogue. . . But forget Swinburne's *Poems and Ballads*, and for a vogue equal to that of *Requiem* you will perhaps be driven back to that morning of February 1812 when Byron "awoke and found himself famous".' Garrod went on to say that Humbert had enjoyed none of Byron's advantages - a nobleman when that still counted; wicked, when that was still romantic; a widely-travelled man, when that was still glamorous. 'Mr. Wolfe . . . has had to contend, not only with the temptations which his origins set him, but with the prejudices which they create. . . recognition came to Mr. Wolfe somewhat late; and I hope the more sweetly as from men who gave it grudgingly.'[46]

(iii)

After *Requiem*

In the week that *Requiem* appeared, Thomas and Butler came to London. Most of 4 May and a good deal of 5 May was spent in stormy meetings with the Ministry. The employers had complained bitterly of I.L.O. interference in English affairs, a charge to which an unfortunate circular from Thomas lent colour. Thomas countered with accusations of Britain's lack of interest in the I.L.O and even of hostility towards it. According to Humbert, Thomas said that no doubt their attitude would change when there was an English Director. Hot exchanges followed, all of this in the Minister's room at the House of Commons. When the Minister was needed in the House for a debate on The Trade Disputes Bill involving labour issues,[47] they took the argument to H. J. Wilson's room in Montagu House, where it went on until 8 p.m. Meanwhile, in the House of Lords, Balfour had pulled the rug from under everyone's feet by announcing firmly the Government's intention to ratify the Hours Convention. Had the contestants known this it would have saved a lot of unnecessary bitterness. As it was, Balfour's speech mollified everyone.

Eventually Humbert dined alone with Thomas at the Ritz, where, he said, Thomas poured out his heart, blaming Britain for not offering Drummond sufficient inducement to make way for Thomas, and consequently for Humbert too. However, he had had talks with the Foreign Office and expected eventually to take Drummond's place. Furthermore, by taking Butler with him, he would remove any obstacle to Humbert's appointment to the Directorship of the I.L.O. He had, of course, said much the same thing before, but Humbert felt that things might be moving his way.

Jessie had apparently advised him not to write a new book before he came to see her. He had, nevertheless, started one - *The Uncelestial City* but in a totally new form - 'a sort of picture of the soul, an H. G. Wells poem!' He already had the first two verses, which he sent to her:

"Creator of the spirit, self-created,
since all creation is embodiment
of what is bodiless by its own beauty weighted,
dull as that brightens, sinking in its ascent.

Be near us when we build the corruptible wall
of life's poor city in darkness, turn the brick
with the courses of dawn, and let your stars enthrall
Time's rages with their gold arithmetic."

'I shall probably alter it, but it gives you the new note.'

It is interesting and instructive to compare this first draft of these verses with the form they finally took, not as the first lines but as the 'Coda' of the book which emerged in 1930, which will be the concern of a later chapter:

> Creator of the spirit, self-created,
> since all creation is only thought ungodded
> by gradual matter, slowly separated
> from beauty that is for ever disembodied,
>
> be near us when we build our city, indulge
> the builders' plan with starshine, turn the brick
> with the courses of dawn, and let the sun divulge
> the secret of his gold arithmetic.

A letter of 8 May questioned the wisdom of Jessie's proposal to leave Nice for Cannes: 'Why not stay there for the rest of your time (not very long now) abroad?' The prospect of a month's holiday together on the Riviera after the I.L.O Conference (at the end of May) was tempting, but Ann's next operation ought not to be too long postponed. Perhaps somewhere neither too far nor too hot was indicated, when Ann had had a decent time to recover. *Requiem* was now in its third thousand, according to Gollancz, and he had started on the new "Uncelestial City" - 'After all this outburst I can't publish the little comic thing that I wrote more than two years ago.'

Jessie may have asked why they could not go straight to Geneva, for in another letter, postmarked 9 May but dated 16 April, he argued that they had practically paid off their debts, but there was still the overdraft and Ann's next operation, which he now suggested could take place at the beginning of July; they ought therefore not to spend money which they did not have.

From these considerations he rapidly moved on to flat-hunting and to the fortunes of *Requiem*. George Moore had liked it and was going to show it to Edmund Gosse. The latter, unfortunately, would not be able to review it in *The Sunday Times*, since that had already been done. He went on to draw interesting comparisons between George Moore and A.A.B. 'When (Moore) talks about books he never says a foolish thing, & he never does a wise one. . . A.A.B . . with all his selfishness and faults, is a very real human being, as much better than his writings as George Moore is worse.'. At the R.A.C. he had dined with Morrison, his old Oxford friend. Morrison said that he and Drewitt (their old philosophy tutor at Wadham) thought very ill of Humbert's verse. Morrison was still cataloguing the records of the City Companies, and working at palaeography. 'It looks as though he had at last settled down into a life's occupation.' It is difficult to recognise, in the post-war references to Morrison, the 'swell' whose company and approval Humbert had so diligently sought at Oxford.

Jessie's next letter to him brought the devastating news that, having received her copy of *Requiem*, she hated his Dedication. The dedication in question was not the poem of that title but the words on the opposite page, which said simply: 'For my visitor to a room on No. 10 staircase at Wadham College, and because of everything.' His first intention had been to say: '. . . because of days at Epping & Windsor, a motor-boat on the Kyles of E. Bute, & a red church in Morningside.' But then he thought that left out everything since the day in the Church, 'so I put instead "& because of everything."'

On a visit to him in his undergraduate days, Jessie had come alone to his room (which was against the College rules), but in all innocence, and was now afraid that her action would be viewed as either silly or wicked; alternatively, it might appear that the person addressed was someone other than herself. Humbert was clearly shattered by her reaction and said in effect that what he had thought of as a shared success was now of no interest to him at all. He had meant the dedication in all love, but since it had been such a disappointment to her he did not want to write about "R[equiem]" at all.

Jessie may have been more than usually tense because of her mother's health - a telegram on 12 May told Humbert that her mother had had an attack. While expressing concern and hope for her mother's speedy recovery, he also hoped that this would put the *Requiem* trouble out of her mind. He wrote that he was planning to join her in Nice on 19 or 20 May. It must be assumed that Jessie was sufficiently mollified, for the dedication was no more mentioned thereafter. Ann did not think much of Nice: 'very dull, I thought, and the sea full of sewage.'

After a short break in Nice, he went on to Geneva on 22 May where he was kept hard at work at the I.L.O. Conference, which was made no easier by tender national susceptibilities over representation (the Irish and the Canadians), language (the Spanish and the Germans), race (white and black South Africans). He expressed the rather forlorn hope 'that the Sabbath may induce peace and a better frame of mind.'

The mounting difficulties of the Conference - queries about the Italian delegate's credentials; the intolerable heat and congestion in Humbert's Mimimum Wages Committee room, inducing long speeches and short tempers; and, in addition to the perennial Hours debate, a new sub-committee on Russian and Armenian Refugees - all left Humbert longing for the day when he could join his family in the middle of June. Meanwhile, Drummond and Thomas still blew hot and cold and Humbert was beginning to think that neither had ever seriously meant business. Nor did he receive much encouragement from London. 'More and more,' he wrote on 7 June, 'I get the weary feeling that this organization, which started as the crystallized hope of the world, is degenerating into the crystallized boredom.' The Conference was characterized by naked national needs, carefully fostered antipathies, squalid jealousies, quarrels and intrigues; if this was happening so soon after the first impulse, 'what can the hope for ten years hence be?'

The next of his letters is dated 23 August, by which time Jessie and Ann were back in England. Ann's later recollection was:

> 'Finally in the summer of 1927, back to England. After a short stay in a hotel in Northumberland Avenue, we moved to a furnished house in Bournemouth (first in the centre, later further out near a golf-course). Humbert came at week-ends. 'Cursory Rhymes' was published while we were in Bournemouth. While we were in Italy Jessie became drawn to the Catholic church, which she later joined in 1937 or 38 I think.'[48]

By March 1928 *Requiem* was into its seventh impression: Humbert looked securely installed upon the heights of Parnassus. There remains the problem of accounting for the book's extraordinary success, given its time and its subject matter; what chords did it strike in the late nineteen-twenties which caused it to continue as a best-seller long after the *succès d'estime* had abated?

The explanation, I think, is to be found in the sense it roused in the reading public of a positive affirmation of hope. Beatrice Webb, in her Diary for 1928, adverted on two separate occasions to a malaise which for all her unbelief she deplored. On 2 May she noted as an intensely interesting though to the Webbs personally an unimportant phenomenon, namely the break-up of the Christian Church in Great Britain. If Dean Inge was anything to go by, no longer was belief in the supernatural or in any specifically Christian doctrine required of a candidate for ordination; only 'that he should have a sort of an idea that there is a Force that makes for righteousness at work in the Universe. . . The rotting away of this ancient structure [the Church of England], in sight of curious and contemptuous citizens, is ugly and distressing; Dean Inge acting as a cynical guide among the crumbling ruins adds a touch of ironic humour to the melancholy picture. . .'

And later, on 26 October, Aldous Huxley's *Point Counterpoint* prompted her observation that even those mild reflections of the consciousness of God, 'The Religion of Humanity' and its successor 'The coming of the Superman', had vanished from the public eye in her lifetime. The fashion was for the sub-human in art and literature and music; clever novelists such as Huxley, D. H. Lawrence, Norman Douglas, David Garnett, Compton Mackenzie, depicted men and women as morbid animals. She quoted a Cambridge undergraduate's words to his mother: 'Your generation lost faith in God. Our generation has lost faith in man.'[49]

Against this, *Requiem* advanced both a faith in God and a faith in man, couched in language which believed in the music of the word. In March 1928 Humbert outlined in a letter to Jessie the theme he planned to develop in a talk to the Whitefriars Club, a group of male journalists who met in the City at Johnson House. He identified his time as 'The Age of the Spirit that Denies - the Everlasting No.' What was urgently needed was 'the revival of the Spirit that Affirms - the Everlasting Yes.' He intended to expose the superficiality of pseudo-philosophies such as Spengler's (in *The Decline of the West*), whose 'favourite theory of a weary and worn-out civilisation is really only a superficial statement of postwar malaise, and the sooner it is killed and we get back to a belief in human endeavour the better for all of us.' He was also re-writing Das Hohe Lied, which illustrated that malaise.

It is worth noting the effect that *Requiem* had on two people in particular. Gustav Holst, according to his daughter, began reading Humbert's poetry in May 1927, 'It was *Requiem* that had first moved him so profoundly.' Correspondence followed and then a friendship: they shared so many likes and dislikes, hating anything slip-shod, passionately caring for accurate detail, loving solitary walks round London at any hour of the day or night. All of this resulted in *Twelve Humbert Wolfe Songs* which Holst composed in 1929.[50]

The other person, also a writer, was Vera Brittain, who related in *Testament of Experience* how the present of 'Humbert Wolfe's latest volume of poems', from her husband, George Catlin, in 1928 revived her project of writing a novel with war as the theme - what eventually became her autobiographical work, *Testament of Youth.*[51]

For the first time in over a year, the Wolfe family were now together, if not in the same place, at least in the same country; Humbert's literary success was an acknowledged fact. All that they still lacked, it seemed, was the call to Geneva.

Chapter Eight

1927-1930

'The echo of departing wings'

('Love and Friendship', *The Uncelestial City*, 1930)

I

1927

Others Abide and *Cursory Rhymes*

The summer of 1927 was in several respects a watershed: if it marked Humbert's 'arrival' as a poet, it also signalled, in their domestic life, a turning point which coincided with their frustrated Geneva hopes. Jessie and Ann, together with Mrs. Graham and Annie, returned to England during that summer and, after a short stay in a hotel in Northumberland Avenue, moved to a furnished house in Bournemouth. The pattern of their lives for the next two years was established, Humbert remaining in town for the working week and travelling to Bournemouth (and later to Tunbridge Wells) on Friday evening unless duties kept him in London until Saturday, as they increasingly seemed to do.

He continued to write regularly to Jessie, either from the Ministry or from the R.A.C. From something that Viola Garvin wrote in a personal appreciation of Humbert in 1944 or 1945, it could be inferred that during 1926/1927 he had a flat in London. Writing affectionately of the beginnings of Humbert's long and familiar association with *The Observer* when she was serving her apprenticeship as its Literary Editor, she recalled the

> evenings of poetry begun at the Café Royal or in Soho or in Charlotte Street when Wolfe and [Gerald] Gould and I were joined by James Stephens, Ronald Fraser, Francis Meynell, D. L. Kelleher, F. S. Flint, Eileen Power, Harold Monro . . . and his wife, Alida, Rose Macaulay, and many another. Then we used to adjourn to the flat, where Wolfe lived at that time, in Mecklenburgh Square, where we argued and quoted nearly till dawn.[1]

Although this account wants corroboration, it does suggest that, unless Viola Garvin's memory was at fault, Humbert had for a time a London base which he chose to conceal. The letters and family papers for 1927 and 1928 contain no reference to a London flat. He took a service flat in Artillery Mansions in 1929, with Jessie's full knowledge, as will be seen. Humbert began reviewing for *The Observer* in 1926, the year in which Garvin's daughter became the Literary Editor. According to her, Gerald Gould and Humbert were two of the four names picked by J. L. Garvin as possible reviewers of contemporary novels. The other two were Charles Morgan and P. C. Kennedy. Morgan soon moved on to become dramatic critic of *The Times*, and P. C. Kennedy was not to be found until it emerged that he was none other than Gould himself. For his first task, to review a batch of really bad and foolish novels, Humbert 'did an airy, wicked, naughty piece of writing which made us take him straight off fiction and reserve his charming mind and pen for books more in tune with them.'[2] When Humbert sent Jessie the glowing review of *Requiem* in *The Observer*, he must have known the identity of the reviewer.

Others Abide, Humbert's translations from The Greek Anthology, was published by Benn in September, the limited edition of four hundred signed copies selling at fifteen shillings. By the time the book came out Humbert's declared intention of informing the world of the superior poetical merits of his translations (*see* above, Chapter 7) had become the more modest aim of 'following the original as closely as he could. (Prefatory Note to the book) - perhaps he felt it otiose to add 'and still write poetry'. Whatever else lay behind the book's equivocal title, it was an unmistakable salute to his earlier poetic hero, Arnold, in turn acknowledging the supreme genius of Shakespeare. By the end of September the book had gone into a second impression, which for translations of such specialised, not to say limited, interest was in itself a measure of their perceived quality.

We cannot, of course, know how far its readership extended beyond those with a knowledge of Greek, although these alone would have far outnumbered any corresponding public of today. But since the myth of the opposition between literary and literal translation continues even now to flourish, it may safely be assumed that for critical readers fidelity to the text would have counted for more than poetic merit. Some said as much in their reviews, revealing their presuppositions as well as their inability to recognize that the measure of a translation is the success with which it faithfully conveys the original in a form which is natural to the target language, so that the reader has to be reminded that it was not originally written in English.

As with anthologies of jokes, the unremitting reading, in any language, of collected epigrams, epitaphs and dedications is subject to the law of diminishing returns. It will be enough here to compare a few of Humbert's versions with the earlier authorised translations of Paton and Mackail. In a letter to Jessie in April 1927 Humbert wrote (of an inscription on a grave by one friend to another):

The one that I adapted ran as follows:

> 'Though small the stone, dear friend, I raise to thee,
> Great was the love, whose memory I bless,
> I'll seek thee still: Death grant thee thought of me,
> Nor draught of Lethe bring forgetfulness.'

My version is:

> 'As small this stone, so great my love. And you
> despite all Lethe, friend, remember too!

Similarly, the earlier version of this love poem by Dionysius the Sophist read:

> You with the roses,
> What have you to sell?
> Say, may we buy your posies
> And you as well?
> For all the rose's grace
> is in your face.

Humbert's 'Rose-girl' simply said:

> Flower or girl, which do you sell none knows,
> since each, rose-girl, is equally a rose.

For all its qualities, however, *Others Abide* was unlikely to add significantly to Humbert's stature as a poet.

His health was a frequent topic in the letters of the last week in August and early September. He had to have teeth extracted, and suffered an attack of alopecia. For these and perhaps other unspecified ailments he was doing special exercises and receiving massage and high frequency heat and lamp treatment. He liked to tell the story of his visit to a specialist when he was suffering from a throat infection. After examining him thoroughly the specialist said, 'Your throat's all right, but I don't like the look of your nose.' 'Ah,' said Humbert to the embarrassment of the doctor,'That's your racial prejudice.'[3]

At the beginning of September Humbert mentioned that Gollancz 'had quarrelled with Benn's and is leaving them on May 1st. He has been in such a state that he has done nothing about the illustrations for "Cursory Rhymes"' - the first time the book had been mentioned in his correspondence. If nothing was done soon, 'they will just have to be issued unillustrated.' Fortunately that risk was averted: Albert Rutherston's charming illustrations were particularly successful, the originals of some of them fetching good prices at a sale in 1988.

Cursory Rhymes belongs with *Kensington Gardens* in the Wolfe canon. Although the opening 'Invocation - For my daughter Ann' addresses children in general, the poems, only a few of which had been previously published, convey the overwhelming conviction that they were inspired by and sometimes addressed to events in Ann's life, including her periodical operations and ill-health. These and her family's dealings with doctors no doubt account for the sardonic humour of the 'Poems Against Doctors' - whose avarice, ignorance, and curiosity are mercilessly pilloried:

> His greed is such that though you ache
> in every limb, be sure
> if there is nothing else to take,
> he'll take your temperature.

The miseries of a boarding-school upbringing have sometimes been held accountable for the peculiarly British obsession with children's books. But Humbert attended a day-school and had a generally happy childhood. A related theory holds that the claim of writers such as Barrie, Grahame and Milne to understand children rests on the fact that they themselves never grew up, and, like many of the adults for whom they wrote, constantly sought the emotional Eden of their earliest years.

This may be nearer the truth in Humbert's case, but the explanation is almost certainly much more complex than that, for although he enjoyed the company of young people, there is nothing to suggest that he had a special fondness for that of children, and his two books of verse which explicitly address children were arguably written at least as much with adults in mind, while the posthumously published *Kensington Gardens in Wartime*, which juxtaposed the gentle associations of the Gardens and a war which so callously denied them, emphasized most of all the loneliness of the poet who had walked there with his daughter twenty years before. If, as I suspect, the explanation for the special fascination which youth, as distinct from childhood, held for him is to be found in the same vision which he tried to express, admittedly with less than pellucid clarity, in 'The Locri Faun', then that poem is of pivotal importance for his poetical development.

In the case of *Cursory Rhymes* there seems to be no reason to search for more than fatherly affection and the sheer enjoyment of writing the sort of thing he was good at. The greater part of the sixty-six poems are grouped in three sequences: 'Praise of Famous Men' (very reminiscent of the 'Monuments' section in *Kensington Gardens*); 'The New Doll's House'; 'The Return of the Fairy'. In addition there are single poems or small groups of up to four poems on unconnected themes: 'Poems Against Doctors', 'Nurse', 'The Bluecoat Boy', 'The Zoo', 'The Sick Child of Kensington', and so on.

'Introduction I and II' superbly guy the 'poetry specially for children' school - perhaps a jab in the direction of de la Mare on an off-day? -

'Introduction - I'

They tell me, children,
    you have some
fugitive Elysi
    -um

where, while your baffled
    elders pass
through what to them is
    common grass

you walk in fields,
    where never fell
or snow or rain, through
    asphodel. . .

whereas, he bluntly assured them, when he was seven years old what he wanted most was to be himself,

and liked the daisy
    most, because
it went on being
    what it was. . .

and that being constantly the same was

. . . the circumstance
        that wrings
my heart in ordinary
        things.

'In Introduction II' he warned them not to look for adulation, 'or for an attitude/ of dim/ belief that you are/ seraphim.'

No! I've found
        that children, taking
them all round,

are not the least
        bit better than
their parents. . .

Some he has found quite impossible,

while others simply
are the plan
to which life draws
a gentleman.

. . . it takes all
sorts to be
a schoolroom, or a
nursery

but the best are

. . . children who
enchant the air
(like Ann) by
merely being there.

It was doubtless for these reasons that he chose for his Bluecoat Boy another unsentimental writer for children, Charles Lamb. The two Bluecoat Boy poems are additionally interesting in that they explicitly point to *The Uncelestial City*, on which, as we have seen, Humbert was already working. As the Angel in the Strand is speaking of

what they tell me would be witty
to name the Uncelestial City,

London is transformed - 'set working like a toy' - just as Spring was to transform it in the later work. Similarly, the half-affectionate, half-mocking verses on the statues in Westminster - Charles the First, Nelson, Edith Cavell, and the 'forgotten generals

who, preserved in
bronze or lead,
are no thicker
in the head'

- serve as a preliminary sketch for the broader and more sombre canvas of *The Uncelestial City*.

Occasionally a hint of archness, or of self-conscious cleverness, creeps in, for example in some of the 'Famous Men' poems, e.g. in, 'Lewis Carroll', Alice

on the other side of things
teaching that chess means
that, though pawns cannot be kings,
love will make them queens -

or 'Andrew Lang', whose

> books in brilliant rocket-spray
> burst about his head,
>
> and, as petal after petal
> climb the skies, and hang,
> "Love me," hear him cry, "a little
> since I loved you Lang."

which contrasts strangely with the charming whimsies of 'The New Doll's House', for example 'The Rather Immortal' visitors:

> Then once in every
> year for luck
> we'll send a tele-
> gram to Puck,
> and, ringing up the
> cowslip's bell,
> telephone to
> Ariel

and the gentle humour of 'The Return of the Fairy', where the poem about how the fairy made her new house is given the title of 'Unassisted Building Scheme'. Similarly, in 'The Garden',

> She had other strange habits,
> *e.g.* paraffin,
> which she used for her rabbits
> without and within.

In 'The Palace', with its allusion to Browning -

> And we'll take our rest at noontide
> at the inn of summer weather,
> whose ancient sign is the Time, and the Place,
> and the Loved One altogether -

he may perhaps be forgiven for mistaking, as Browning did, and Chatterton before him, the slughorn for a trumpet - a misreading of 'slogan', a battle-cry.

This genial, funny, touching collection ends with the evocation of his own childhood journey to Arnside, the 'Seaside' poem which, he later wrote in *Now A Stranger*, 'had lain hidden in a single dried seed. . . a single irrefragable word that held a whole summer holiday in three letters.' That word was 'fly', the lumbering, four-wheeled cab which conveyed the family and its mountain of luggage from Mount Royd to Manningham Station:[4]

> First, the luggage cart -
> eleven trunks, four cases, a bath, a perambulator
> and me on it for a start;
> but, not an ordinary cart, not an ordinary load,
> rumbling and grumbling down the steep side of Parkfield Road.
> No! a cart that has the tang of the sea about it, and the grip
> of the first strange mast against the skyline, of the first ship. . .

If there are occasional uncertainties of tone, almost as though he felt obliged to throw in a pinch of solemnity and his hand slipped, these are abundantly redeemed by an ease in the versification that suggests that he enjoyed the composing, perhaps recognising that his talent was being profitably challenged.

Although there is no mention of it in his letters, he had two other publications to his credit in 1927: the Introduction to *Poems by Edward Lear*, which he also edited, in the *Augustan Books of English Poetry* series; and the privately printed poem 'Veni Creator', already mentioned, which was reprinted in *The Uncelestial City.*

The expiry of the lease on the house in Bournemouth in October more or less coincided with further medical treatment for Ann, and Humbert suggested to Jessie that after a week together in London they might go abroad again if she could face it, or they could look for another place in Bournemouth, as well as a couple of rooms in London just for Jessie and himself. When the Governing Body of the I.L.O. met in Berlin in October, Ann was still being treated by Kelsey Fry and Jessie was staying at the Victoria Hotel in Northumberland Avenue.

From the Hotel Adlon, on the Unter den Linden, on 11 October he wrote that he was received by the Germans 'with more civility than I expected, & indeed up to the present have not had to complain of any anti-Semitic demonstrations. But they may be to come.' Next day he went on:

> The Germans are at any rate superficially changed. The officer class has disappeared from the streets. They speak quite openly and disparagingly of the Kaiser. But they have transferred their talent for submission to Hindenburg, whom they worship.

A few days later he described dining with the German Chancellor - Marx - and various other Ministers, in Bismarck's former house:

> I was shown the table at which Bethman-Hollweg signed the declaration of war. Yesterday [October 13] Fontaine, Thomas, d'Altéa, de Michelis & I had tea with Hindenburg! The old man is a marvel - 6ft 1 tall & straight as a larch - like a statue of himself rather than himself. He is simple - very much the Kitchener type - character, innocence, courage. I talked to him for about 20 minutes chiefly about modern German architecture, of which he knew nothing.

Early in September Humbert had voiced his fears, in a letter to Jessie, that H. W. Garrod, who had suffered a fractured skull in a street accident in Oxford, would be a long time recovering. By November, however, he was well enough to deliver the Poetry lecture on Humbert referred to earlier in Chapter 7, which was followed a week later by Humbert's own talk on 'The Craft of Verse.' While recognising that Humbert was 'a singularly accomplished craftsman' writing verse of 'melodious quality', Garrod criticised him chiefly for being satisfied with sales rather than with being as good a poet as he could be. There is something curiously unreal about this fastidious academic distaste for such vulgarities as money.

Arnold Bennett's *Journal* for Sunday, 4 December, recorded that he dined at the Savoy in the Pinafore Room, and that George Doran's party included 'the Colefaxes, Noel Coward, Joan Sutherland, Ethel Mannin, Humbert, Osbert Sitwell (sardonic), Rebecca West, Clemence Dane (highly ingenious). Fine dinner. I was too tired and gloomy to enjoy it much.'

After the Berlin visit, Humbert's next surviving letter, sent from Montagu House, undated but postmarked 19 December, said simply, 'Thank you so much, Jessie dear, for a lovely week', and was directed to a new address in Bournemouth, where Jessie was to stay until the following June. In connection with the possibility of some film work coming his way, he said that he might need to think of using an agent, and that Curtis Browne, the chief Literary Agent, had already asked to handle his affairs. He was still working at 'The Publicist': 'I think that perhaps I have struck something.' Gollancz had also acknowledged receipt of his novel: 'I'm more than half hoping that his reader will advise him against it - or perhaps only half. Because there were such hopes, and happiness, & never-to-be-forgotten days hidden between the covers, weren't there?' - almost certainly a reference to their Battersea days when he began writing *Utopia*. The novel was never published.[5]

On 22 December he wrote that Winston [Churchill] had asked to see him the next day, and that the Foreign Office had rung to ask him to be available to meet Sir Eric Drummond who was due in London on the 23rd or 24th. Jessie was not, he said, to expect the Secretary-Generalship as a Christmas present, 'but there may be some development.' Meanwhile he thanked God that they would be together that Christmas.

He was back in London on 28 December, writing to thank Jessie for 'the loveliest Christmas I remember. Don't bother about the bills!' On 30 December he brought her up to date with the progress of his talks with Locker-Lampson of the Foreign Office.[6] They were, as usual, inconclusive. The F.O. was worried about the German position and wanted to be sure that Humbert could get the I.L.O. post so that they could use that as a counter in bargaining. 'The Cabinet were determined to have one British post, and I seemed the most likely to get one or the other. . . I told him [Locker-Lampson] that I had talked to D[rummond], and that in fact the real questions were

(1) when was D. going?
& (2) who was Gt. Britain backing?
& (3) if me, for what was I being backed?'

He went on to tell Jessie that he had written to inform Churchill of what had happened, and all they could do now was wait and 'hope that 1928 will compensate for these last bitter years.'

II

1928

This Blind Rose and *Dialogues and Monologues*

At 11.45 p.m. on 1 January, after a very strenuous day with Albert Thomas, Humbert wrote to tell Jessie that Thomas had come to London to ask for the Secretary-Generalship of the League, in exchange for the Directorship of the I.L.O.

> That is the long and short of an interminable series of conversations, manoeuvres and counter-manoeuvres. Gt. Britain has not yet decided to accept. The chances are even. Winston is against, the F.O. for. There is to be a week for cons[ultatio]n. I am absolutely tired out! I have loathed missing you on New Year's Eve, but if we win you will forgive me - and if we don't, you will forgive me all the more.

In a detailed account of the conversations which he wrote the next day he summed it up as 'a plain political struggle with D[rummond], T[homas], and myself as pawns.' He was sure that Drummond would not go unless he got the Paris Embassy, which the Foreign Office would not give him unless they were sure that Humbert could succeed him at the

League. Churchill's chief concern was to keep the Secretary-Generalship for Great Britain; if Humbert got neither of the posts 'the Cabinet would know how to compensate me - a mysterious utterance!' - and, as it turned out, apparently meaningless too.

Jessie was to have brought Ann to London for dental treatment, but they both caught colds which kept them in Bournemouth and, as a precaution, Humbert in London. As part of his plan to get Jessie to spend a week in London with him, he suggested that 'Miss Piggott start lessons on Monday', perhaps the earliest of the few references to their arrangements for Ann's education. Apart from the special speech training which she needed, Ann had always been taught at home by Jessie, who had not wanted her to go to school lest she be teased for her poor speech. Ann, however, had conceived a great desire, which Jessie supported, to go to Oxford. Humbert at first ruled out the idea on the grounds that she had missed so much schooling, and there ensued a monumental three-day row until Jessie finally got her way. Perhaps the cost was an additional consideration, for in order even to attempt the first hurdle she would need more professional tuition than Jessie, for all her talent and skill, could supply. On the other hand, Humbert had saved a lot on school fees.

Ann was given the first of her governesses, the Miss Piggott mentioned in this letter. When later they moved to Tonbridge she had two teachers, one who taught her Latin and Greek, the other, headmistress of a local school, who taught her English. On their return to London and Battersea she had a further succession of private tutors to prepare her for the School Certificate examination. One was an old lady, 'not a very good teacher,' said Ann, who admitted that she herself was probably conceited and thought she knew more than she did. Another lady taught her French.

A slim volume, *The Silver Cat and Other Poems*, was published simultaneously by Benn in London and The Bowling Green Press in New York in this first month of 1928. The connection between the five poems is not immediately discernible, any more than is the reason for producing this slender offering, except the obvious one of profit for the publisher and perhaps for the poet. The title poem and two others were reprinted as part of *The Uncelestial City* (1930), and, to me at least, make more sense there than as poems standing on their own. 'Thus freedom comes, thus peace' is one of the best pieces of quasi-forensic oratory in *The Uncelestial City*, where it is the subject of and the defence against a charge of blasphemy tried before Mr. Justice Crayfish. The remaining two entries, 'The Immortal Hour' and 'Spring and Death', were reprinted in *Snow* (1931). They are the least convincing of the five, perhaps because, trying for high seriousness, they achieve only a rather strained portentousness. When one considers the sort of love poetry that some of his contemporaries were writing (e.g. Graves, or some of the early Auden), this collection strikes a rather endearingly old-fashioned note.

The fears for the survival of *The New Criterion*, which Humbert had expressed to Jessie earlier, proved to be well-founded, for Eliot's backer,

Lady Rothermere, withdrew her support at the end of the year. Eliot cast about for alternative financial support and enlisted Humbert's help in his efforts to interest Arnold Bennett in financing the magazine. According to Reginald Pound, Bennett's biographer, Bennett was no more impressed by Eliot's persistence than he was by the merits of his journal, although Bennett had written in much more encouraging terms to Eliot in 1927.

In Chapter XI of *Portraits By Inference*, entitled 'A Diary of Arnold Bennett', Humbert briefly referred to the visit they made to the sage of *The Evening Standard*:

> I read the following entry in Arnold's Diaries, which Mr.Newman Flower has edited with such discriminating fidelity: "T. S. Eliot and Humbert Wolfe came to see me about *The Criterion*. Their object was to get money. . ." It reminded me vividly of the scene - the back drawing room of No. 75 [Cadogan Square] with the beautifully bound manuscripts of his novels behind his head. Arnold with his dark tuft, rising like Shagpat's Identical, myself dark and conciliatory, and T. S. Eliot, pale, cold and speaking slowly with his soft persuasive voice like a white kid glove. And I dare say we did want money. Why not? as Arnold himself would have said. . .

Although Bennett later gave *The New Criterion* extracts of his Journal from 1910 onwards for publication, he noted in his Diary for Friday, 13 January, 1928:

> T.S.Eliot and Humbert Wolfe came for...tea to discuss with me the future of the New Criterion magazine. Their real object was to find out whether I would find capital. I showed little interest. The New Criterion is a dull production and always will be.

The journal was eventually saved by a fund set up at the instigation of Frank Morley.[7]

At the beginning of February the British and French governments were at loggerheads over the question of revising the Hours Convention, 'but the undercurrent has been the other thing all the time.' The 'other thing' - the succession at the League and the I.L.O. - festered on like an open sore for the rest of the year, as Humbert's letters show, with hope constantly renewed and just as constantly deferred.

On 15 February he went to give a lecture at Trinity Hall, Cambridge, and found an audience of about two-hundred and fifty in the Junior Common Room. 'They cheered and cheered, and rolled up with dozens of "Requiem" and "Others Abide" to sign.'

The gaps between the letters for 1928 suggest that a number have been lost or destroyed, and of those which have survived, many are little more than notes announcing his arrival or departure times and similar domestic items. Quite often matters such as the Hours issue are mentioned and occasionally some major political event enlivens his account. Thus, on 7 March, he wrote that 'the Foreign office are exceedingly fluttered about the Mussolini declaration re Austria', and foresaw that 'Mussolini will force Austria into a union with Germany. This has always been feared as one result of the Versailles smashing up of the Austrian Empire.'

The letter continued:

> The F.O. are also preoccupied with the Zinoviev debate. I know now who gave the letter to the "The Daily Mail". The man is an old and bitter enemy of mine from M[inistry] of M[unitions] days. I will tell you his name at the week-end. He's not a Civil Servant; and I don't think that he got the letter from official sources. Barber, whom I saw at the Club last night, is certain that the letter was a fake. He says that two sentences were taken from an article of his own in "The Morning Post", which consisted of a translation of a leading article in the Moscow "Pravda". The F.O., of course, honestly believed that the letter was genuine, but the debate may produce a certain liveliness.[8]

Another issue, not mentioned in any of the extant letters, but which also produced 'a certain liveliness', was that of the Bolivian Refugee Scheme, about which there is a susbstantial file in the I.L.O. archives in Geneva. For over two years Thomas and the I.L.O. had been monitoring a proposal to recruit a hundred refugee families from Russia, Yugoslavia and Lithuania for resettlement in Bolivia. The plan involved the Société Internationale des Migrations and the Bolivian Concession Company, and the first thirty families were due to travel in February. Thomas's firm stand against the Brazilian and Paraguayan authorities' procrastination in issuing transit visas for the Russian refugees was matched by Humbert's strenuous criticism of the scheme's intrinsic flaws, which he outlined in a Memo to Betterton in the first days of February. All recruitment for the scheme was immediately suspended, but the question of transferring responsibility for administering the fund from private hands to the body responsible for placing refugees, namely the I.L.O., remained to be settled.[9]

The forthcoming dinner at the Whitefriars Club on 15 March, at which Humbert was due to speak, and a dinner with his Minister, Steel-Maitland, at the House of Commons, to meet two German visitors about Ministry of Labour business, were, he wrote, 'the only two dinner appointments I have had in weeks!' The completion of a paper on "Modernist Verse" meant that he now had

> almost enough material for a book, i.e.
> The Craft of Verse (Bradford)
> Modernist Verse (Cambridge)
> The Civil Servant in Fiction (Institute of Administration)
> Satire (Bermondsey Bookshop)
> English Bards and French Reviewers (New Criterion)

Altogether they make nearly 50,000 words. With 10,000 more the book would be finished.

The additional words were found. With an essay on George Moore, a valedictory memorial to his Oxford friend, A. D. 'Drum' Keith, who died that year, and the susbstitution of 'The Difficulties of the Poet' for 'Satire', the book was not only finished but published in the autumn, under the title of *Dialogues and Monologues.*

The next collection of Sixpennies was occupying him in March. They were to be, he wrote, 'Edmund Spenser, Byron, D. G. Rossetti, Gordon Bottomley, Sacheverell Sitwell, and Translations from Dante by Laurence Binyon.' On 14 March he wrote the letter referred to in Chapter VII above, outlining his thoughts for the subject of his talk to the Whitefriars Club, to which he had already spoken the previous December. Two days later he described the dinner:

> . . . rather charming. It was actually in the garret of the house in which Dr. Johnson wrote the Dictionary. It is a long low room with sloping rafters. There was a single trestle table that ran the whole length of the room with about 35 men round it. It was lighted only with candles in sconces, & the food was plain old English with beer and port to drink. Most of the men were editors or big booksellers, or judges, & judging by their comments & speeches they liked me & what I said. It was over by 11 & I went on to the Savage Club for about 3/4 of an hour with Thomas Moult to console him about the attacks that have been made on his Barrie book.

On 20 March he announced that if Parliamentary business did not delay him he was to dine with Edward Shanks and J. C. Squire at the Rendez-vous 'to discuss my manifold iniquities in superseding them.' But on the next day he wrote: 'I had to go down to the House after all. So I didn't encounter the merited castigation at the hands of Squire & Shanks.' Instead he went back to his Club and wrote several reviews. 'Will Rothenstein crept in with his drawing-board this morning - & made a very good beginning. It's going to be, I think, a real portrait, the first that I have ever had. It will, I fear, be too expensive to buy.'[10]

The Bodley Head asked him to write an Introduction to an edition of Swinburne. 'I don't think that I dare take on still another job. However, I'll go round . . . to see them. I have a morbid terror of refusing work - & the possible pounds attached to it!' He then listed the articles to appear that week: one in *Country Life*, another in *The Saturday Review*; he had written 'the middle for 'The Spectator' last night, & I expect that "The Observer" will have the Henry James article. "Vogue" rang up & asked me to write an article overnight.' The wonder is, not that he could not oblige them, but that he found time and energy to write as much as he did, and that he was still short of money. The *Selected Poems by Swinburne*, with an Introduction by Humbert Wolfe duly appeared later that year.

They spent the week of their wedding anniversary together and he wrote on 3 April to tell Jessie that the money spent on it 'was one of the best investments of my life.' Although there is no indication of where they went, it seems to have involved taking a car. He had waited to write until after seeing the Foreign Office - presumably in the hope of good news about Geneva - 'but it was only Refugees.' This was almost certainly a reference to the Refugees debate going on within the I.L.O.

This Blind Rose, the first of his books to be published by Victor Gollancz, came out in the late Spring. The equivocal title (were 'blind rose' an adjective and a noun, or a noun and a verb?) was thought by some to be a typical piece of Wolfe mischief, but the poem of that name, the shortest in the book, is unambiguous. Indeed, this satirical, not to say cynical, epigram sits strangely both in the collection and as a title, if the latter is to be taken as indicating the theme of the collection:

> As this blind rose, no more than a whim of the dust,
> achieved her excellence without intent,
> so man, the casual sport of time and lust,
> plans wealth and war, and loves by accident.

The poems had been written, he wrote in a prefatory note, in the last five or six years, and, as we have seen, a few had been published in the different periodicals for which Humbert wrote. They were not arranged chronologically, but under various headings - Serenade; Ghosts; Flowers, Birds, Trees, Stars and the Moon; Verse and Music; Places, Question; Persons; Sonnets; Valediction; but even these groupings look fairly arbitrary, and some of the poems could have been differently placed.

The book contains some fine pieces, not least when he is most direct - the title poem, for example, or 'A Little Music' - 'Since it is evening,/ let us invent/ love's undiscovered/ continent. . . Since it is evening,/ and sailing weather,/ let us set out for/ the dream together./ Set for the landfall,/ where love and verse/ enfranchise for ever/ the travellers.' In a few he over-elaborates ('The Voyagers' and 'What am I afraid for?') or leans a little heavily on his models, in 'The Sirens', for example, with its echoes of Tennyson. The first of the 'Serenade' poems takes exactly the opposite view from 'Iliad' in *The Unknown Goddess*, namely 'that rhyme endures because of love,/ not love because of rhyme.'

The collection includes a number of poems mentioned earlier in his letters: those inspired by his discovery of Geneva and the Alps - 'A Hill Road by Zweilutschinen', 'Rue du Soleil Levant', 'Rue de Toutes Ames'; the Michael Collins poem, in which the 'old grey ghost of Parnell' half-enviously commiserates with Collins:

> "But you were killed at thirty-three, Michael,
> in battle; you died well.
>
> There was no breaking of an old heart for ye,
> nor pointing of the finger, and slow shame . . .
> Michael! It's me they've killed again, not you."

The 'Spring' poem, referred to earlier in his letter of August 1926 and printed in *The Saturday Review* (*see* Chapter 7 above), develops the images and language of sea-scapes in a profusion of richly evocative colours and sounds:

> The sun-gold seas bank up, and spill
> in leagues of ruffled daffodil,
> nor brine, it seems, but woodland scent
> aneles a lazy continent.
> . . . .
> spring sweeps the wood's cathedral nave
> with the green fury of a wave,
> . . . .
> till oak and elm and beech and ash
> in one viridian comber crash,
> while at their feet red vetches shine,
> sharp, and cold, and coralline.

His empathy with violins is seen once more in the poem of that name, where the alternation of verses of disyllabic with those of monosyllabic rhymes skilfully embodies the antithetical form of the poem:

> I have loved violins, and I have thought as I heard them
> that they were birds, crying at the other side of the wood,
> birds in the light beyond the dark wood, and none has snared them.
> I thought that they were birds crying, but I had not understood.
>
> They were a shadow, but not of song beyond the world;
> they were an echo, but not of invisible light.

They were love's first banners, tremblingly unfurled
by standard-bearers, marching alone in the night.

. . . .

For the fiddle soars up, and is lost in its own
silver cascade, that tumbles in rain,
out of the glory that it could not have known,
back to the dark earth that it spurned in vain.

. . . .

For they have become the voice of my own heart, speaking,
they have become that voice, and one voice dearer.
And they do not fall back to the earth, and there is no waking,
but they shine and rise like a star, and the star draws nearer.

'My Poems' seems to provide both an interesting piece of self-revelation and an insight into his creative activity:

As always when he has finished writing,
he who takes the pencil out of my hand
looks at me with bright, half-wondering malice,
and says, "Another poem by Humbert Wolfe.
Well, take your poem, and make the most of it!"
And at first, as I read the poem,
it is not my poem at all.
If it is a poem of mountains, it is as tall
and lovely as the mountains themselves.

. . . .

Or, if it is a poem of life, then like a meadow,
under trees in moonlight, life lies, all dreaming
and still, save for the little moving shadow
of wings between the meadow and the moon.
But presently, as I read,
the words lose their dew, the green
and fragrant thoughts are gradually cloaked
with the dust of the common road
that all feet tread.
And the poem is just a poem like any other
that I have written.

. . . .

But the true poem - the one that I have not written,
of which mine is the discarded husk,
is safe with him who wrote it,
and with the poets who, when this stranger smiled,
caught him by the wing, and, though they could not hold him,
found in their star-stained hands one golden feather,
which touched their page.

Having read it, one is left wondering whether it expresses the poet's painful awareness of the gap between the ideal which he perceived and what he actually achieved, or is simply another instance of Humbert hiding behind self-depreciation? Self-concealment is certainly the theme of 'Any Poet to Posterity', in which he asks to be remembered 'only/ as a voice once heard singing, as a cry/. . . Let those who write of me say, "None knew him!"

The final poem, 'Valedictory', bears no explicit dedication, but leaves a distinct impression that it was written principally with his mother, Consola, in mind:

> Bright hair, grow dim;
> close slender hands,
> for the long dream
> till the world ends
>
> No wind to ruffle,
> no pain to wring,
> now she may baffle
> everything.
>
> Grow dim, bright hair!
> Hands, close for ever!
> So she was fair;
> So let us leave her.

'The "Great Delusion" has not been dispelled - nor proved,' he wrote to Jessie on 12 April. 'But I've seen Austen's [Chamberlain, the Foreign Secretary] S[e]c[retar]y this morning, & he remained entirely cheerful. So I'm prepared to be so no less.' - a clear reference to their Geneva hopes. On 13 April he announced the arrival of an enormous parcel from the United States: four hundred and seventy title pages which he had to sign for the American edition of *The Craft of Verse*, described as an 'Oxford poetry essay.'

He said he had also received the Oxford Herrick for which he was to write the preface - in six weeks. This was the lovely four-volume edition published by the Cresset Press and delightfully illustrated by Albert Rutherston. He also had the Swinburne Preface and another article on the stocks: 'If Satan finds mischief for idle hands, mine won't be much use to him!'

The dearth of letters for the second half of April and the beginning of May is puzzling. He went to Geneva in the latter part of April, but there are no letters to mark the occasion, simply a reference to it in a letter from London to Jessie on 1 May. Albert Thomas wrote to him from France explaining that he had to vote in the French elections (*see* I.L.O.

archives). On 1 May Humbert described a great excitement both in the Press and in Whitehall in connection with his doings in Geneva, and that Sir Horace Wilson was full of worry about the excessive publicity that Humbert had acquired, but I have found no clear statement as to what the excitement was about. A week later he reported that the Minister had left a message with Betterton 'heartily congratulating me on the results of Geneva, adding that he didn't feel that he had made his view of my achievement clear when I saw him. It's a very long time since anyone threw me an official bouquet.'

Towards the end of May I.L.O. affairs took a dramatic turn, when Thomas upset the Second International (Workers) by an apparently violently pro-Fascist speech in Rome, and, it was thought, might be forced to resign. Humbert went to the meeting of the Governing Body on 29 May and spent two days in what he called 'a nightmare of comings and goings' as Thomas's enemies sought his removal. Humbert had to refuse their invitation to be nominated for the post, presumably because the policy of the Government was to support Thomas for the time being. Drummond wanted Humbert to save Thomas, and if he succeeded, as he thought he could and would, 'the French will be genuinely grateful. That at least is D's view.' Humbert's excited optimism in the rest of the letter suggests that he thought so too, although gratitude could not have been, in his own experience, a habit that governments had ever thought it wise to acquire or practise.

On 5 June he wrote that the atmosphere at Geneva made it hard to feel or to appear calm:

> I wish with all my heart for everybody's sake to become SG, but you can hardly imagine how huge a load it will be. . . not a day passes here - at any time of year - without a major or minor incident. Before the League was established nations nourished their suspicions of one another at long distances. Now they are all concentrated in one spot under a burning-glass. Personal amour-propre, the sensitiveness of the small (& unsuccessful) nations - the everlasting human desire to take the lead all bustle and crash. The Secretary General walks perpetually on red-hot plough-shares in an ordeal which lasts as long as his job. I don't mean by any of this that I wouldn't throw my cap over the moon when the word "Go!" or rather "Come!" is pronounced. But it does explain how I contrive to sound so little self-assured in my letters. . . But hearts up! We are nearer than ever before.

But two days later his disillusionment showed: 'I have increasingly felt that I am merely a pawn in an obscure and by no means attractive political game.' The process of saving Thomas's skin went on. The questions for consideration at a meeting of the League of Nations Council members in Austen Chamberlain's hotel room, said Humbert, were:

> (1) were the French prepared to support T through thick and thin and (2) were the Council prepared to indicate to the Governing Body that they would regard the disappearance of T without their consent as a serious matter.

In the absence of Briand and Stresemann, respectively the French and the German Foreign Ministers, the third question, who was to succeed Drummond, was shelved. Humbert reported that although the French agreed to support Thomas, the second point was difficult because of the delicate balance of autonomy and dependence of the I.L.O. vis-à-vis the League, which provided the I.L.O. grant but did not want conflict with the labour organizatons. A diplomatic compromise was eventually reached which looked likely to save Thomas.

Humbert went on to tell Jessie that he was to see Chamberlain later, and dine with him at Thoiry, where Briand and Stresemann had concluded their famous pact.

> I am going to tell them that as far as I am concerned the thing has gone on long enough. If by the end of next week they can't clinch the thing, I think that they had better find another candidate. I shall say that I gave up the certainty of the Directorship at their wish, & now I am kept hanging on month after month with nothing done . . . the strain is becoming intolerable. This will have the effect of finally forcing their hand.

In subsequent letters he reiterated his belief that the French were to blame for all the delay and deception; he had told Chamberlain bluntly that they were cheating.

On his return to London he told Jessie in a letter of 19 June the outcome of all the discussions in Geneva over Thomas's future. The governments' and employers' groups had voted by majorities in his favour. Humbert played an important part in persuading the workers' representatives that to dismiss Thomas was to play into the hands of Moscow. Eventually the Governing Body overwhelmingly declared its confidence in the Director. Immediately after the vote Humbert saw Drummond, 'and told him that I had brought it off, and that now it was his obligation of honour to see that I was not cheated.'

But the waiting continued throughout June and most of July. It had prevented his writing anything in Geneva but now he had managed to get into the Herrick Introduction which he completed towards the end of

July. The last letter for 1928 is dated 31 July. By then he still had nothing tangible to report about Geneva. They had been together to a Palace Garden Party, Jessie and Ann had moved to another hotel in Bournemouth, and now they were discussing holidays. He had thought of St. Jean de Luz or Monte Carlo for the sake of the sun, but Jessie clearly preferred Oban and the Caledonian Canal.

His poem, 'Troy', was published that year on its own as an Ariel poem, the twelfth in a series of seventeen in all, published by Faber and Gwyer, which included Belloc, W. H. Davies, de la Mare, Monro, Sassoon, Edith Sitwell, Belloc and Chesterton, and T. S. Eliot, whose *Journey of the Magi* was No. 8 on the list. All the poems were illustrated by recognised artists such as William Nicholson, Charles Ricketts, Eric Gill, John and Paul Nash, Albert Rutherston. Humbert's poem was illustrated by Charles Ricketts.[11] 'Troy' was later incorporated into *Out of Great Tribulation* (1939).

The next set of six Sixpennies, as he continued to call them, due to be published in the autumn, was to be the last for the time being, unless public interest revived, and Humbert had, not for the last time, to disappoint those who wrote to him with interesting suggestions for further collections, for example, of Fulke Greville, Dunbar and the early Scottish poets (an idea which had already occurred to Humbert), and Henry Vaughan. Replying to one such correspondent who, having failed to get his own translations from the Greek and Latin poets published, had applied to Humbert for inclusion in the Sixpennies, Humbert observed that few books of verse paid for their production costs, as the publishers well knew, and consequently they regarded books of poetry 'as a decoration to their list rather than as an asset.'[12]

In the autumn Gollancz published *Dialogues and Monologues*, the collection of seven essays, some originally written as articles, others delivered to a live audience, as the letter of March 1928 mentioned earlier clearly shows. If a common thread or theme can be identified - and Humbert took good care not to suggest any such thing - it might be described as a prose profession of his poetic faith.

The essay on George Moore ostensibly set out to paint a portrait which would correct the mistaken view that Moore was a facile writer concerned only with style, only half-serious (almost in the French sense of *sérieux* - the complimentary word reserved for solid professionalism). It is not beyond the bounds of possibility, however, that Humbert was obliquely defending himself, hinting that he too was a craftsman who had achieved his apparently effortless word-control by sheer grinding hard work. But modesty, of course, forbade him to say so overtly.

Four of the essays are in dialogue form, reviving a literary convention popular in Victorian times (for example, in Mallock's *New Republic*,[13]) but already virtually out of fashion in the nineteen-twenties. Whereas Mallock set his discussion in a country-house party, Humbert's disputations are placed variously in George Moore's house in Ebury Street (for an imaginary conversation with the Irish writer); on the *terrasse* of the Grand Hotel at Saint-Cergue; in an imaginary room in the Cour de Saint Pierre in Geneva; and on a bench on Hampstead Heath.

For much of its effectiveness *The New Republic* depended on the ease with which the protagonists could be identified behind their fictional doubles, for the persons were inseparable from the philosophical positions they held. Matthew Arnold, Benjamin Jowett, T. H. Huxley, Walter Pater, Ruskin and others are instantly recognisable in Mallock's brilliant parodies of their style. The identity of Humbert's disputants, on the other hand, was less important than the views they held, and so he presented their views fairly, even when he was disagreeing with them, but his concern throughout was to challenge their understanding of poetry, even by gentle mockery, rather than simply to expose them to ridicule as individuals.

In *The Craft of Verse* Humbert set out to define the nature of poetry, as the only way of satisfactorily showing that it was not the same as prose, a view hotly contested by some. As if to give his definition an appearance of objective validity, Humbert gets one of his opponents to formulate it, by means of the "What you are saying is . . .' device: 'verse is the expression with authority of what is significant in life by means of the fusion of thought and sound', adding that that is little more than to say that poetry is, in short, poetry. Humbert accepts that, but then proceeds to explore it further by applying it to some established contemporary reputations, beginning with Thomas Hardy, who, after two pages of examination, is judged to fail for want of music in his verse: 'In a word, Hardy does everything except sing, and if that is true, he is everything but a poet.' It has been said that for this supposed 'attack' on Hardy, Sassoon later punished Humbert's *Uncelestial City*.

The piece contains some fine ironic writing, including the barbs aimed at himself. The arguments in fact are a revealing commentary on attitudes to the Modernist movement, with Humbert insisting on 'detecting and branding the pseudo-innovators". For all his proximity to the poets and movements that he analyses, he shows himself to be a shrewd judge, and, though hindsight helps us to raise an eye-brow at some of his judgements, it is interesting to see that by the time he reaches the later essay on Modernism in Verse, the experience of 'Sailing to Byzantium' has clearly changed his view of Yeats.

In 'English Bards and French Reviewers', despite his admission that he has 'never discovered a satisfactory definition of poetry, nor yet any criterion which distinguishes satisfactorily between it and prose', he reopened the debate, his two French interlocutors providing him with the excuse for examining the two literatures in terms of 'le génie de la langue.' After comparing Bennett and Proust, Anatole France and George Moore, they engage with the Racine-Shakespeare debate. Humbert says that he has only recently come to recognise that real poetry is possible in French - and he cites his favourite examples: Hugo's 'mon âme a plus de feu que vous n'avez de cendre/ mon coeur a plus d'amour que vous n'avez d'oubli', and Hérédia's 'toute une mer immense où fuyaient des galères', as passing the test of 'inevitability'. 'These . . . lines have exactly what I seek in true poetry, verbal magic that passes far beyond the poet's mind and points beyond itself . . . At its highest moment verse trembles on the edge of thought. . .' But ultimately he believes that 'words in themselves have an almost absolute value', by which he means 'their own unsupported magic', and he quotes de la Mare's poem on winter in evidence. In his view the nature of the French language excludes that possibility, and for magic the French theorists have tried to substitute rules.

The next essay, 'The Difficulties of the Poet', needs to be taken in conjunction with the last of the dialogue essays, 'Modernism in Verse.' In both he tackles the problem of 'no certain guides and no definite goals' for the poet in that puzzled post-war period. After a rapid and comfortless survey of the post-war poets - Monro, Blunden, Sassoon, T. S. Eliot and Herbert Read, the Sitwells, Graves - he considers the case for satire in verse, citing his plea in the Preface to *Lampoons*, and a longish extract from *News of the Devil*, to illustrate his argument. But he finally sees that 'hate may blast but it cannot heal', and that if there is, as he believes, a place for the true satirist, it is for 'one who, knowing himself [to be] no better than his fellows, exposes his own weaknesses, and elevates that exposure into a universal demonstration.' This leads him to consider the case for abandoning obsolete traditional verse forms in favour of free verse. His wise and balanced conclusion is: 'Let the poet by all means invent a new form, but only if the new form is the inevitable expression of his own personality, and not because he is intellectually convinced that the old forms are wrong. . . The writer of free verse will only be justified if he can produce in the mind of the reader the sense of distant and lonely song.'

'Public Servants in Fiction' is in a much lighter vein. Starting from the highly tendentious premiss that Milton's sonnet 'On His Blindness' referred principally to spiritual blindness - 'that mental condition which leads a man, otherwise in possession of his four remaining senses, to adopt the Civil Service as a career' - Humbert developed the thesis that the life of the Public Servant is one in the high tragic vein. His coolly ironic stroll through the gallery of portraits of public servants in Dickens and Trollope is lit with such prophetic asides as: 'Trollope, in my view, is a writer of merit who is at the moment in danger of being damned by a sudden revival of interest in him.'

He shrewdly identified two Kiplings, the first with an infinite capacity for loving, the Kipling who wrote of the Public Servant abroad, especially in India; the second Kipling, with an equal capacity for hating, wrote of the Civil Servant at home. Humbert deliberately omitted the Diplomatic Service on the grounds that it serves no purpose at all. 'Even when ambassadors are admitted into serious literature the fact that they are engaged in the romantic avocation of preventing or propagating wars removes from them the stigma of being associated with Public Service.'

A propos the rash of novels occasioned by the War, he observed in a phrase which anticipated *Portraits By Inference* that 'the population was roughly divided into those who fought the enemy abroad and those who fought one another at home.' He concluded regretfully that Edward Shanks' *The Old Dispensables* was the only one that credibly described the Public Service as it really was.

The final essay, 'Drum' (the nickname of Alan Davidson Keith), was written soon after the death of this shadowy yet clearly central figure in Humbert's undergraduate life. By reason of its subject matter and its style, it belongs with *Portraits By Inference* and *The Upward Anguish.* It opens with him sitting in the Royal Automobile Club, reading his *Evening News* and 'trying to find an explanation of the revolt against life, which seems to me to be the dominant note of the day.' Everyone and every place of importance in his early life, with the exception of his family, passes through his reflections: Bradford, his teacher, Barton, with his message to Berto and to Albert Rutherston that 'Affirmation - that's the word - affirmation'; Oxford, Drewitt, metaphysics, politics, the Canning Club, Flecker - and finally 'Drum'. 'For everybody the secret of Oxford is different. For me it was "Drum". I cannot share it with anyone now.'

He wrote of 'Drum - large, gentle, and beloved, . . . unboyish wisdom in his eyes' affectionately, though briefly, both in prose and in verse, but, as so often, obliquely. Although Keith obviously meant a great deal to Humbert, and almost certainly more than he ever revealed in his writings, there is nothing to suggest they remained in contact after Oxford. At the end of it all we are left with another mystery, another mask.[14]

He dined at Arnold Bennett's on 2 November. The other guests were the Denison Rosses, Sir Arthur and Lady Sybil Colefax (the Solicitor General and his wife), Muriel Foster, and H. G. Wells. Bennett recorded that 'the uproariousness of the whole evening was terrific.'

At the end of the year, one single poem, entitled 'The moon and Mrs. Smith' was produced as a Poetry Bookshop Christmas card. From what Humbert's letters reveal - mostly indirectly - it probably formed part of the original version of 'The Verdict'. It was a curious, not to say macabre, subject for a Christmas card. Mrs. Smith was the universal name by which the charlady was known, although her real name was Jakes. In the scene described by the poem it is to be inferred that she has died of heart-failure. The poem was later incorporated into *The Uncelestial City*, in the final section: 'Retort By Mrs. Jakes - *morte* Smith:'

> Pausing in her cool affairs,
> through the basement window stares
> moon, and with cold witcheries
> makes a drypoint out of mess. . .
> Dishes in her silver pool

almost glimmer beautiful;
meat, torn papers, broken knife,
glitter with a secret life;
even the taps that splash and sprawl
become a lunar waterfall.
Last her pencils touch the chair
with a sly and dexterous air.
Face, clasped hands, and unshrugged shoulder
placid silver. Moon grows bolder,
inscribes her tranquil etching with,
"Life and death of Mrs. Smith.

III

1929

The Wall of Weeping and *Notes on English Verse Satire*

Early in 1929 Jessie and Ann moved yet again, this time to Tunbridge Wells. Why they moved, and why to Tunbridge Wells remains a mystery. It may be inferred from the earliest letter preserved from that year and dated 4 February that they had only just taken up the occupancy of a house or flat in Boyne Park, with as yet neither hot water nor a telephone, although these were soon installed. Jessie's sister and mother were still with them, but not in good health. Humbert was in London, waiting to see Drummond (who was held up by illness from travelling), and hoping to hear something definite. In this respect 1929 was no different from previous years: like W. S. Gilbert's policemen, Drummond kept saying that he was going, but he *didn't* go, not until 1933.

The first half of the year was marked by two serious crises, both of them relating to Humbert and each in its own way brought on by him. The first occurred in the second week of February when an anonymous letter attacking him arrived at his London flat. Later events suggest that this was almost certainly in Artillery Mansions, Victoria.

Who wrote the letter - Humbert took it for granted that the author was male - or what it said will probably never be known, but it arrived while Jessie was staying there. From Humbert's attempts to calm her fears and reassure her that there was no substance in the charges, the inference is that he was accused of some moral turpitude. Humbert tried to persuade her that the attack came from some malicious person who envied him his success; after all, he could not hope wholly to escape that sort of enmity. The letter was not blackmail, he said, nor could it, if challenged, be called more than a practical joke, but what made it particularly mean was that it gave acute pain to a most innocent person, presumably Jessie, although his words do not make it entirely clear.

He seems to have had his work cut out to convince Jessie, who told him that a bitter truth was better than a half-truth or a lie. One curious feature of his letters on this subject is that nowhere did he actually deny whatever he was accused of; he simply asked her to trust him, as the only way, however hard, of averting what might otherwise be a grave trouble. He had always known, he said, that if he had enemies they would attack him through her, just as Browning's enemies tried to strike at him through Mrs. Browning, Napoleon's through Josephine. And while he hoped that it would not happen again, he could not guarantee against a recurrence. Perhaps because his work involved so much industrial diplomacy, these parts of his letters read more like the reply of a professional conciliator than of a falsely accused husband. But he made a point of telling her that her pain distressed him if anything more than the accusations did, and that his feelings for her had not changed since he first met her, in proof of which he sent her a cheque to buy a brooch as a present from him.

There is no doubt that he had his detractors in the literary world. The young Auden attacked him in his 'Verse-letter to C. Day-Lewis' in March 1929:

> While Wolfe, the typists' poet, made us sick
> Whose thoughts are dapper and whose lines are slick.

One shorthand-typist of the time, who had joined the 'pool' at Montagu House in 1927, and was trying to read all the modern poets, has told me that Humbert was considered 'a highbrow', and that many of his poems exceeded her comprehension. She remembered her first sight of him as he entered Montagu House in front of her, his cloak and hat giving him a Bohemian appearance.[15]

Day-Lewis, a Wadham man (he went up in 1923) who admired Humbert's poems and was grateful for his help in his early days, described him as 'one of the wittiest men I have ever met, a figure of flamboyance and panache.' One poem which manifested Humbert's influence was 'Naked Woman with Kotyle', written on a dance theme and reflecting a Greek vase-painting:

> She moved to the slow
> Dance of supplication
> Her body's flow
> Was a moon in motion . . .

Auden, self-assured, dogmatic, intransigent, undoubtedly swayed budding writers like Day-Lewis and Stephen Spender who, if they would eventually have grown out of their admiring imitation of Humbert's poetry, would also have declared their independence rather more graciously. Sir Stephen readily admitted his own admiration as a schoolboy and an undergraduate. He had written an article in praise of Humbert - Betjeman's biographer called it 'fawning' - in *Cherwell* in November 1927, and later, in 1929, when he became Secretary of the University English Club and invited Humbert among other distinguished writers to speak, he sought his advice on how to earn a living as a poet. According to the rather unflattering account of their conversation in Spender's autobiography, Humbert talked mainly about the commercial success of his books, like 'one who buries his critics under his public', a clever remark no doubt, but foolish if it was Spender's reaction at the time, since pleasing the critics - if that were even possible - at the expense of his sales would profit him nothing; disingenuous if it was a later reflection, for none of those collectively known as the MacSpaunday is known to have published in order not to make money. In fairness it must be said that Spender was kinder about Humbert in his letter to me.[16] While one sees, therefore, that young, left-wing idealists full of notions of doing good for the workers in the Depression would almost be *required* to sneer at a successful, quasi-Establishment figure and a poet making grubby money out of his art, Auden's jibe reveals the snobbishness of many who considered themselves socially superior both to typists and to people like Humbert.

On 20 March Humbert was elected to The Athenaeum. Given the membership of this august club, his sponsors were likely to be men of some eminence. He was proposed by J. Alan Barlow, CBE (Assistant Secretary at the Ministry of Labour and later Under-Secretary at the Treasury after a short spell as Principal Private Secretary to the Prime Minister), and Sir A. Daniel Hall, KCB, FRS (sometime British Government Delegate to the I.L.O. Conference at Geneva).

Among the thirty-five signatories subscribing to his eligibility were F. S. Boas, Sir John Buchan (later 1st Baron Tweedsmuir, Governor-General of Canada, who died only a month after Humbert), Sir Edward K. Chambers, Sir Sydney Chapman, Sir Atul Chandra Chatterjee, the Hon. Gilbert Coleridge, J. L. Garvin (Editor of The Observer), Sir Henry Gooch, St John Welles Lucas, H. Cotton Minchin, Sir Richard Redmayne, KCB (fellow-author in the British Series of the Carnegie Foundation's Economic & Social History of the World War - he wrote on The British Coal Industry); Alban Dobson (son of the famous Henry Austen Dobson), G. Rostrevor Hamilton, Will Rothenstein and Albert Rutherston, Max Beerbohm, Douglas Jerrold (Director and former Chairman of Eyre and Spottiswoode), Sir Lynden Macassey, and Redcliffe N. Salaman. Although Humbert did not immediately give up his membership of the Royal Automobile Club, The Athenaeum was henceforward his principal club, whose writing paper he used as an alternative to Ministry of Labour paper.

The next letters begin in mid-March, from Geneva where the Governing Body of the I.L.O. was meeting. Jessie had asked him for proper letters, so he sent her 'a faithful and complete account of every minute of my time' - every detail of every meeting with every group of interested participants, all anxious to promote their own sectional interests. The success of the Hours Convention, for which he had worked for four years, was in jeopardy, partly because the French were intransigent, but even more because the Minister, Steel-Maitland, was no match for his opposite number, the Frenchman Loucheur - 'all that is clever and unscrupulous.'

> The conflict [Humbert wrote], was like that of a shark circling round a whale, with me trying to slip in between as a sword-fish. At meeting after meeting by mistranslating the Minister into what he ought to have said & not what he did say I saved crash after crash. I did in fact succeed in making France appear to be in the wrong although we have at the present not succeeded in getting revision. . . What is certain is that Steel-Maitland will be grateful to me all his life (he has said so again and again) for what I have done. And I know that he will throw himself with all his heart into doing what he can to help me in every way.

Another fond illusion!

It was most probably in the spring of 1929 that his translation of *Le Mur des Pleurs*, by the French Jewish writer Edmond Fleg, was published as *The Wall of Weeping*. The edition, simultaneously by Gollancz in London, and E. P. Dutton in New York, was limited to 750 copies. Edmond Fleg was born Edmond Flegenheimer in Geneva in 1874. After studies at the Ecole Normale Supérieure in France he won his *agrégation* in German and later served as a volunteer in the First World War. Drawing on Jewish literary and religious traditions, he celebrated the destinies of the Jewish people in a varied literary *oeuvre* which ranged from the theatre to poetry, novels, and essays.

I have not been able to discover how Humbert came to know Fleg or why he chose this particular work to translate, but it is easy to see how he would have been drawn to its theme: the Wandering Jew who is really the Messiah who will heal the ancient wounds not only of Israel but of the world; an affirmation of hope couched in evocative language, expressing a mystical, though imprecise, theology which appeared to embrace both Judaism and Christianity.

Since Fleg's original text is unlikely to be widely known or readily accessible even in France, Humbert's introductory 'Translator's Note', which attempts to justify the differences - principally of length and versification - between his version and the original, has a limited interest today, save in one respect: it firmly rejects Modernism and Free Verse. Discussing the impracticability of a Free Verse rendering he wrote:

> M. Fleg's habit of mind is, as I understand it, wholly opposed to that of the schools of Modernism. His is the spirit that affirms. It would be no less than a perversion to present it in terms of the spirit that denies.

I have found nothing to indicate what success, if any, the book enjoyed.

The second of the two crises in his domestic life occurred at the end of May. On the 30th, the day that the Conservatives were swept from office, he wrote to Jessie from Geneva of the distress and anxiety he felt about his 'muddle of finance,' but for which Jessie would have accompanied him this time. But the trouble is clearly much more serious than that. He speaks of his 'abominable irresponsibility' and echoes his woes of 1921:

> Once again money is the first thing of which I think in the morning & the last thing of which I think at night. But believe me I will never be a fool about money again - I have worried myself to distraction. I sit here thinking of nothing else - all the time. I can hardly believe that I have been such an idiot.

What folly he had committed was not immediately made clear. The Wall Street crash had not yet occurred, nor is there anything to suggest that the trouble arose from an unwise venture on the Stock Exchange. It is doubtful if he had much in the way of investments: money was too fleeting a visitor to put down any roots. For all that, one is left wondering how, on his salary and the extra income from his writings, even allowing for the burden of Jessie's family and Ann's operations, he managed to be on the brink of disaster, if not over the edge. But his incorrigible optimism immediately returns: 'But there - if only I can have sense now, & it's never too late, all should still be well - for all of us.'

Letters of early June discuss dispassionately the implications of the election results. Walter Citrine (later 1st Baron Citrine, P.C., K. B. E.), General Secretary of the T. U. C., and President of the International Federation of Trade Unions, was anxious that Humbert should be available for the Secretary Generalship, and promised to use his influence. He told Humbert frankly that Labour opinion was divided between those who mistrusted Humbert as the presumed architect of the Government's Hours policy, and the majority who regarded him as a a very able Civil Servant with a genuine interest in the League and in Social Reform. Citrine also said that the new Prime Minister, Ramsay MacDonald, was personally favourable.

But the process of transition from one government to another made life for its representative in Geneva exceedingly difficult. The flood of telegrams from London was so great that sometimes three contradictory ones would arrive at once, recalling him, cancelling the others, instructing him on the line to take on some issues, leaving him in the dark on others. Yet in spite of all the frenzied activity to make up lost time on an overloaded agenda, and the strain of the tensions between the different warring factions, as well as the weariness and discomfort of Geneva in June - he was there until the end of the month - he still managed to make some progress with *The Uncelestial City*.

On 22 June, in a lengthy answer to Jessie's complaint that she was 'a neglected wife', the mystery of the flat in London is cleared up. He had taken a flat in Artillery Mansions because he felt that 'for the purpose of writing I needed conditions a little different from those of every-day.' There is no suggestion that Jessie was unaware of this arrangement, which he said he had felt 'would bring us all happiness and give me the chance of writing freely.' He had counted on a short tenancy followed by a great improvement in their finances when the Secretary Generalship came through. The expense of the flat in addition to their other outgoings proved too much and, as it turned out, the Artillery Mansions scheme produced 'more pain and expense than all my other failures and follies.'

He clearly felt the need to defend himself from the suspicion of ulterior motives in all this, particularly in the light of the anonymous letters episode in the early part of the year (for it emerged that there had been more than one letter) which he said he had 'tried to explain.' The future, both in Whitehall and in Geneva, was uncertain and they could not hang anything on that peg. They had to find a way of straightening everything out, and not least their finances, and if this meant abandoning the flat and taking a house for the whole family, even with the additional expense of furnishing it, that was what they must consider.

Requiem, and *The Unknown Goddess*, it will be remembered, had made a deep impression on Gustav Holst, who began to write musical settings for some of the poems from the latter. 'And now, on Whitsunday, he glanced at 'The Dream City' . . . It might have been written for him to set to music.' Of the twelve songs, two were from *This Blind Rose* (1928), the remainder from *The Unknown Goddess*. 'The poems that appealed to him most were *The Thought* and *Betelgeuse*.' The songs were first sung that same year in Paris by Dorothy Silk at a private party given by Mrs. Louise Dyer, the founder of L'Oiseau-Lyre.[17]

The Minister of Labour in the new Government was Margaret Bondfield, who had been the Parliamentary Secretary in the earlier 1924 Labour administration. Beatrice Webb said that Humbert insolently boasted of the Minister's subservience to his influence and direction, but Mrs. Webb's dislike of Humbert may account for her readiness to involve him in the calumny that Miss Bondfield was the tool of her officials. On the contrary, she was by all accounts vigorous, decisive, courageous, and honest, with a strong sense of practicality. Her willingness to resist the Treasury would also have endeared her to Humbert.

He teased her, of course, as he did everyone, given half a chance; more often than not because he was constitutionally incapable of allowing a witticism to perish from disuse. When she summoned him to discuss the provision of facilities for women at employment exchanges, he allegedly replied, 'Certainly, Minister, at your convenience', but he can hardly have been the first, as he was certainly not the last, to give that joke an airing.

In 1929 Humbert left the General Department to become Director of Services and Establishments, with the rank of Principal Assistant Secretary (the equivalent of today's Under-Secretary), at a salary of £1200 rising to £1500, an upward move which defied the Treasury rule forbidding internal promotion at this senior level. The Establishments Officer combined the functions of a housekeeper and a personnel manager. For the next four years he would be responsible for representing the Ministry in most of its dealings with the Ministry of Works (on issues of accommodation), with the Stationery Office (on supply of materials and office machinery), and with the Treasury and staff associations (on questions of staffing, salaries, promotion, etc.).

He was now well placed to pursue even more vigorously his policy of encouraging talent and originality within the Ministry, particularly among the female staff. Dame Mary Smieton, not a fan of Humbert's, said that it was generally recognised in the office that he thought highly of Beryl Power and was instrumental in getting her transferred from her work as a Trade Board Inspector to the Administrative Class, where she appeared in 1930 with the rank of Principal to Miss Smieton's then Assistant Principal status. Humbert told Dame Mary that Miss Power 'had a mind like a knife.' 'In fact,' said Dame Mary, 'though she was indeed very able, she was less at home in that type of work. Her real métier was as a very forceful executive.'

Miss Power's transfer caused some resentment among the war veterans of the staff, whose promotion was very slow at that time. Moreover, although Humbert's action could be defended as a praiseworthy move against the rigidities of a caste- and sex-conscious system (less constrictive in the proletarian Ministry of Labour than in some others), the consequent imbroglio was said to have embittered the rest of her life. Less controversial was the helping hand he gave to Paul Goldberg, who had caught his eye as a very 'Bolshy' Secretary of the Staff Side of the Departmental Whitley Council. He wangled Paul into Oxford and then into an Assistant Principalship. Neither of these beneficiaries of his patronage rose higher than Assistant Secretary, probably because neither fitted gracefully into official moulds, but each represented a waste of talent in their previous role, and Humbert deserved credit for getting them out of it, whatever his motivation, at the cost of some unpopularity.[18]

In the autumn his *Notes on English Verse Satire*, No. 10 in the Hogarth Lectures on Literature series, was published by The Hogarth Press. This masterly survey of the field made few concessions to the reader. Its assumption of easy familiarity with a wide range of texts was no doubt characteristic both of the time and of the author: the educated man expected to know well, if not intimately, both Juvenal and Anatole France, and to be able to respond to asides on Charles Churchill and Robert Montgomery. It is certainly of a piece with much else of Humbert's writing - the certainty of opinion and judgement, the striving for (and often attaining) an epigrammatic quality in conclusions and reflections, the cheerful parading of his own prejudices, for example about the unsuitability of the novel, and of prose in general, as a vehicle for satire - a view which creates problems if one looks at Dickens, and indeed is contradicted by his words in the last chapter: 'Dickens, on the other hand, stands beside Rabelais as the one of the few great satirists whose work can actually be proved to have altered the abuses which it reviled.'

He is convincing on Samuel Butler, with whom his own satirical verse shows a great affinity, but seems to miss some of the point on Marvell as satirist. He makes a good case for the reinstatement of Dryden and Pope, who were only just recovering from their neglect in the 19th century, but offers an odd argument in distinguishing satire from verse - is he uncomfortably aware of the variability of his own work? It is significant perhaps that in the lengthy section on Pope he avoids mention of 'The Rape of the Lock' which would seriously weaken the main thrust of his arguments.

It is notoriously difficult to make sure judgements of one's own time, and it would be unfair to ask of Humbert a shrewd and well-informed survey of his contemporaries. The final chapter, 'The Victorians and Ourselves', nevertheless somewhat disappoints; it seems slightly lacklustre, even perfunctory, as though he had lost interest and was longing to write 'THE END' with a big sigh of relief. For instance, he misses almost all of the significance of Kipling, appearing to take him at the absurd valuation of rock-headed Imperialist, which contrasts sharply with the much more balanced view he demonstrated in *Lampoons*, in *Dialogues and Monologues*, and in other works. There is nothing on Hardy, or on Eliot (except to judge Prufrock, rightly in my view, as elegy/lament not satire), but he is interesting and penetrating on Chesterton and Belloc. It is hard to understand why such a lively, entertaining survey, prodigiously supported with quotation yet wearing its erudition lightly, should have received such a bad press.

IV

1930

(i)

The Uncelestial City

The family spent Christmas together at Tunbridge Wells, and then, early in 1930, they moved back to London: Jessie and Humbert to a two-room furnished flat in Artillery Mansions, a gloomy block in Victoria Street, while Mrs. Graham, Annie and Ann went to a flat in Battersea.

1930 was one of Humbert's most prolific years: in addition to his normal output of reviews and articles he had six books published. The first of these appeared in January, a further collection of his translations from the Greek Anthology, entitled *Homage to Meleager*, published in Britain by the Oxford University Press and in New York by The Fountain Press, in a special signed edition of 450 copies. This volume of love poems, epigrams, drinking songs, satires and dedications, unlike the earlier *Others Abide*, included the Greek text facing the translation.

The Cresset Press brought out in a limited edition his *Portrait of Heine*, a translation of some seventy lyrics, mostly from the *Lyric Intermezzo* and *The Homecoming*, which was re-issued by The Bodley Head in 1935, and reprinted in 1950. It became a commonplace in surveys of poetry of the twenties and thirties to remark on the affinity between Humbert and Heine, the Romanticism, the irony, the wit they had in common, and their shared delight in the feminine, double syllable rhyme. Like Humbert, Heine was a baptized Jew who was haunted by his Jewishness.

Despite his new departmental responsibilities, he continued to represent Britain at the I.L.O. throughout 1930. In a letter to Jessie from Geneva on 5 February he wondered if she was going to the performance of the songs (i.e. Holst's setting of twelve of his poems) at the Wigmore Hall that same evening, and 'who the songstress was to be.' It was in fact the same Dorothy Silk who had sung them in Paris the previous year. The composer's daughter later wrote:

> *Betelgeuse* was the song that made most impression at that first performance in 1930; the listeners held their breath as the remote quietness stretched into the farthest distance. There is a wealth of imagination in all the songs, with . . . their sensitive response to the rhythm of the words. . . Holst was so weary at the time that he scarcely heard a note. The other listeners held their

> breath, swayed by the magic of those gold leaves that
> never stirred on Betelgeuse.[19]

The I.L.O meetings (dealing with Coal and the finances of the I.L.O., as well as the ordinary business of the Governing Body) were long and tiring but he was still managing to work hard at completing *The Uncelestial City* and expected to deliver it to Gollancz by the middle of February.

The vexed issues of Coal, Textiles and Unemployment occupied further I.L.O meetings in Paris in April. On the 23rd he wrote that there were signs that the French were going back on their word over the Secretary Generalship. He found time to write an article about a new book on Thomas Hardy which *John o' London's* had sent him. He thought the book 'utterly useless - silly little scraps from [Hardy's] diary, a pathetic record of the last years of his life.' He foresaw an imminent revaluation of Hardy: 'I am surer every day that except for "The Dynasts" all his verse will disappear. His reputation will ultimately rest on "Return of the Native", "The Mayor of Casterbridge" & "Far from the Madding Crowd"'.

On 27 April, replying to Jessie's speculation about the next Poet Laureate, now that Robert Bridges had died, he discounted his own chance of being even considered, and thought Masefield would be appointed. Yeats, as an Irish Free State Senator, could hardly be offered or accept the post, while 'Kipling is impossible as a choice for the Labour Party . . . It wouldn't help me if I did get it. It would only mean deducting £100 from my M of L income to take the place of the Laureate's £100 per annum.' David Low's cartoon in the next day's *Evening Standard* pictured all the possible laureates, including Humbert, waiting to be interviewed by the Prime Minister. Masefield was in fact chosen and reigned until his death in 1967 (*see illustration*).

He repeatedly said how unhappy he was, not only at being away from Jessie, and in the frustrating atmosphere of the I.L.O. meetings, but because of their financial worries for which he was responsible. 'Life has been one unbearable rush,' he wrote on 29 April, '- with reporters, speeches, interviews, photographers, & cinemas.' The Minister had come over for one day's meeting, which had been filmed. They then lunched at the Elysée with the President of the Republic, Doumergue. On another day he lunched with Pierre Laval, then Minister of Labour, later head of the Vichy Government and executed in 1945 for collaborating with the occupying Germans.

May saw the appearance of *The Uncelestial City*, the book which he had begun writing years before, and completely re-shaped after *Requiem*. Despite the many references to the work in his letters, he never said, as far as I can ascertain, what originally inspired him to write it. It seems likely that it grew out of at least two, if not three, separate pieces. There was an unnamed 'comic' poem that he had begun work on early in the 1920s. There was also the poem which he called 'The Verdict', which probably centred either on the murder trial which later formed Book Four of *The Uncelestial City*, or, less probably, the blasphemy trial which occurs earlier in the book.

He had announced to Jessie in 1927 that the refashioned work was to be 'a sort of picture of the soul, an H. G. Wells poem' (*see* above, Chapter 7). The inherent difficulty of making it both of these was fortunately avoided by making it neither, but something rather more, a remarkably ambitious *tour de force*. It told the story of a judge who, at his death, and before being allowed into the Celestial City, was obliged to retrace the steps of his earthly life through the Uncelestial City. Not that it was in any sense a modern Pilgrim's Progress, despite the distant echo of Bunyan in the title. A more striking parallel might be drawn with Newman's *The Dream of Gerontius* (1865) and Eliot's *Gerontion* (1920), although there is clearly no direct debt to either of them. It is therefore worth examining how Humbert's treatment of the theme of death and judgement differed from that of his predecessors.

The Uncelestial City is not allusive in quite the same way as Eliot's poem is. It is not defiantly heroic, like *Gerontion*, nor quite as obviously self-dramatising, though there is a hint of 'I am myself alone', especially in the end section. A major difference from both Newman and Eliot is that, although Humbert's book is very much about sin and forgiveness, it is not about the experience of growing old and dying. Rather does it involve the protagonist in recognizing and accepting that he is what he is and has been, as is clear from a poem entitled ANAGNORISIS near the end of the book. Nor is there, as there is in 'The Dream', the consciousness of dying, with its attendant fears, or a journey towards purification. Doubtless Humbert felt that he was not the man to compete convincingly with Newman on that level. Nevertheless Mr Justice Crayfish's rediscovery of the parts and the sum of his past life does somehow echo Gerontius's

> For it drives back my thoughts upon their spring
> By a strange introversion, and perforce
> I now begin to feed upon myself,
> Because I have nought else to feed upon.[20]

Except for the prose 'Argument' at the start of each of the five Books which make up the work, the narrative is almost entirely indirect, by means of poems organized in dramatic form, whether as monologues or dialogues. The gatekeeper/fiddler provides a kind of Chorus, and some events are presented by poems which act as a comment upon them. The range of poetic styles, and forms, is enormous: from the lyrical to the satirical via the purely comic and demotic.

The work does more than use his own experience as the quarry from which the hewn stone will eventually be carved into a new shape; it is unmistakably autobiographical, albeit in a transmuted form, whether reflecting his own life and loves, or making reality out of discarded possibilities, as, for example, his toying with the law in 1908. And of course many favourite themes recur like old friends.

Book I traces the path of John Crayfish from his childhood in a barely disguised Bradford to Oxford and his choice of law as a career. His father's discussion with his conscience about whether the boy should go into the Blackford trade or choose Oxford and a professional career provides some satirical gems about the City:

In the City
they sell and buy,
and nobody ever
asks them why.

But since it contents them
to buy and sell,
God forgive them!
They might as well.

and

When I walk down
Threadneedle Street
I hear the multi-
tudinous feet
of those who crawl
and limp and caper
for the love of a handful
of crumpled paper.
Let them find it, or
let them lose it.
All of them die before
learning to use it.

The 'Blackford' poem, quoted in Chapter 1 above, is also here. The final comment on the City comes from the Fiddler:

If I had money, as I have none,
I'd buy the City, and sell it for fun
to a little black pig, who a long time since
started life as a fairy prince.
And while the others were all for trough,
he was over the hills and a long way off
catching the moon. . . . .
. . . .
And the deeper it plunges, the deeper they dig

this little pig, and that little pig.
"Grunt," says the first, and "Grunt," says his brother,
and each one gravely approves the other.

. . . .

But, it may be, Odysseus, that ancient wizard,
will catch my swine, and slit up his gizzard.
And the sty will blossom with olive and quince,
and the hog will be walking there straight as a prince.

At Oxford, John Crayfish and his college friend, Peter Arkwright, debate materialism in the Junior Common Room, Arkwright arguing that men, descended from apes, discredit their origin and yet have the audacity to claim a spiritual origin. Crayfish's answer is that the ape in man, by being the source of eternal conflict, is his passport to the angel. John takes the image of the pine-trees at Zweilutschinen, which 'in their green battalions clamber,/ like Hannibal's armies that Time has led astray', and combines it with an insistent reiteration of Juvenal's scornful apostrophe of the Carthaginian leader, in order to conjure up the desperate, impossible dream of humankind:

"I demens!" - still the Roman whisper scourges
the tree-enchanted Carthaginians,

. . . .

"I demens!" fight, and fail, and, afterwards,
with the shrill laughter of the ape within you,
mocking the tarnished shields and broken swords,
and in the teeth of certain death, continue!

. . . knowing as the pine-trees know
that somewhere in the urgent sap there is
an everlasting answer to the snow,
and a retort to the last precipice,

that, merely by climbing, the shadow is made less,
that we have some engagement with a star
only to be honoured with death's bitterness,. . .

Later, the two discuss the careers which are open to them, Arkwright maintaining a steadily cynical and Crayfish a consistently idealistic view. The first option, journalism, is the occasion for the best known of Humbert's squibs:

You cannot hope
to bribe or twist,
thank God! the
British journalist.

> But, seeing what
> the man will do
> unbribed, there's
> no occasion to.

Journalism is finally seen off with the help of Wordsworth, Davies, Blake, Yeats and Charles Wesley:

> The primrose on
> the river's brim
> was one-and-six a
> line to him.
>
> and though he grumbled,
> begged, and swore
> (believe me) it was
> nothing more.

and (on the lark):

> "Star and not song,
> sweet bird, thy stave is,"
> wrote Jobson, imi-
> tating Davies.
> . . . .
> Which written, Jobson
> went near by
> to lunch on lark and
> oyster pie.
>
> Which makes me wonder
> whether He,
> Jobson, who made the
> lark made thee.

Success in this career might lead to the House of Lords:

> and hide our heads among a crowd of peers,
> saying:
>
> > 'The House of Lords
> > are waiting for
> > the newspaper
> > proprietor.

Soap! Attention!
Listen! Beer!
"Glory to the
new-made peer."

Hark! the Heralds'
College sings,
as they fake his
quarterings.'

Politics and the Civil Service are speedily dismissed:

'Not for the world-shakers!'
Oh, think of Trollope and cathedral cloisters,
with quiet clergymen who thank their Maker
for planning Chablis when he thought of oysters.

In their discussion of teaching as a possible career Humbert pays unmistakable tribute to his own mentors, Barton and Battersby, with an uncommon depth of understanding and awareness:

And teaching is impossible unless,
like Heine's Northern fir under the false calm
of snow, a self-appointed loneliness
creates the desert and the waving palm.

There must be vicarious joy, and the sacrifice
of one's own summer for an unshared spring,
and to start the migrant swallows before the ice
back to their South, and never to stir a wing.

At best a kind of sainthood, and at worst
a drudgery, whose squalid hopes and fears
change what had seemed a martyrdom at first
into a gradual argument for Squeers. [21]

What about being purely decorative men-about-town?

Up and down Pall Mall and then
back to Piccadilly,
educated gentlemen,
exquisitely silly,
sit about, and lounge about,
talking, eating, drinking.
And the only thing they do without

There remains the law, which John, the romantic idealist, sees as essentially the defence of 'the hungry thief, the frightened cheat,/ and all the fools who ignorantly err.' Peter, the cynic, counters with a satirical swipe:

> 'Let me tell you, gentle sirs,
> advocates and barristers,
> that the firm you're working for
> is the old Solicitor,
> whose advice (you may recall)
> terminated in the Fall.'

John decides to choose the law; Peter says this is simply as a means of getting married, and not on merits. The Book ends with a farewell to Oxford and to youth: 'Agamemnon sleeps at last in Argos/. . . Oh, why do men love like heroes;/ and nightingales! why do you sing?'[22]

Without the help of the 'Argument' which introduces each book, Humbert's drift would in some instances be harder, if not impossible, to follow. With so much of the verse ringingly clear, one wonders, therefore, was Humbert wilful in obscuring some of the narrative working? Or was he attempting a kind of acknowledgement to the modern temper in epics (of which *The Waste Land* could be said to be the ultimate measure)?

Book II deals with Crayfish's first experience of love which in the space of ten years goes through all the stages from infatuation to inspired companionship, doubt, separation, agonizing regret and finally friendship in disillusion. He is also presumed to have made a marriage compatible with his career. It is in this section that The Silver Cat poem occurs. Another poem, entitled 'Two More Memories', under the disguise of a return to Oban, Kerrara and the Glencruitan Road of Humbert and Jessie's childhood, achingly conveys the gulf between memory and present reality:

> And in the midst my springs! was never water
> that had so cool a throat of lilied laughter,
> was never tide caught in the moon's long mesh
> under the wind so indomitably fresh.
> And after thirst so sharp, such hungerings,
> I found rank water and the yellow springs.

The rhyming couplets in 'Love and Friendship' admirably point the contrast between an exterior of graceful detachment and the underlying sadness of 'the echo of departing wings.'

Book III is devoted to incidents in the professional and family life of Mr. Crayfish. The condemnation of Kitty, the young prostitute whom he has to defend, seems to him unjust, although to say (as Humbert did here) that it was for being young and pretty is clearly a romantic simplification. But as Crayfish walks home the whole of spring seems besmirched and tarnished. Here the 'Spring in London' poems at first suggest the 'Bluecoat Boy' poems of *Cursory Rhymes*, but, as anger and self-disgust overcome Crayfish, the twin towers of Westminster Abbey are replaced by those of Wormwood Scrubs - 'the only abbey for such as Kitty/ in all the Uncelestial City!' - and there follows the poem which Humbert had based on Jessie's remark about London being built on lunatic asylums and prisons (*see* above, Chapter 6, 1923), which ended with the lines:

> a sullen distant drummer drubs,
> 'Youth and spring in Wormwood Scrubs.'

The prostitute (and those whom her case evokes) are given verses in the demotic style of some of the Battersea poems referred to in Chapter 5.

Ten years later, Crayfish, now a middle-aged father, discusses with Arkwright the shortcomings of modern youth, and particularly his daughter, Helen, who, though married, has become involved with a society spiritualist named Trodley. Arkwright points out that the young have become as two-dimensional as the cinema-world they inhabit, which gives rise to the poem beginning 'He was so slight a thing,' which Humbert had written on the death of Rudolph Valentino. There is also a clever poem about Piccadilly Circus:

> What is her message?
> Line by line
> the simple read
> who seek a sign:
>
> *Omnia ab uno disce!*
> Man shall his salva-
> tion win
> either by old Shetland
> whiskey
> or through Martin's
> London Gin.

The two old friends decide that after all they belong to a bygone age:

> Some day, when our work's done,
> if we go to Paddington
> and ask them to book us back
> half way through the almanac,
> the clerk will give us a ticket
> for Oxford, but just as they snick it,
> 'Stuff, stuff, stuff, stuff

and nonsense,' the engine will puff,
and shake with laughter and run
two old fools out of Paddington.

Two of Trodley's mediums have committed suicide, one while Trodley was with Helen. Crayfish agrees to represent Trodley. One of the suicides, Jones, died clutching a mysterious statue in his garden. The inference in this 'Garden God' poem (written in 1922, *see* Chapter 5 above) is that this was either Pan, or some evil deity. The second suicide, that of Sludge, is the subject of a longer poem arguing that if immortality means taking the burden of ourselves and our lives with us into eternity only to relive them all over again, then poor, helpless victims of circumstance like Sludge were better off dying young, - 'beauty and youth endure, and kindle a rose/death does not pluck.' If he takes his own life to avoid further pain, will God therefore deny him rest? Since Humbert uses the poem to have a go at the Church, whose clergy are too busy removing the awkward truths from religion, it is fair to remark that his argument is specious, resting as it does on an understanding of immortality which runs contrary to anything that could be called Christian belief, even of the blandest kind. The Fiddler's insistent song in this book, that everyone needs God's mercy which is greater than man's weakness, stands on more solid theological ground:

The saint, with the sinner,
let that one and this come,
for all that is human,
the *pax vobiscum*.

As so often with Humbert, as if he feared he may have been uncomfortably serious, he rounded this section off with a satirical couplet: the Coroner's inquest having judged Sludge's death to be suicide, and exonerated Mr. Trodley,

Jury returned the verdict, with a rider
suggesting that gas ovens should be wider.

The final section of Book III is concerned with a blasphemy case before the newly-appointed Mr. Justice Crayfish. A young poet, Stephen Jinks, is accused of having published blasphemous verse, of which a typical example is 'Reflections on the revival of Trade.' This gives Humbert an opportunity to vent his anger, pent up since the War, against the waste of lives, the profiteering, and the stupidity of ordinary people who allowed it to happen.

The alleged blasphemy attacks those who say that 'Peace and freedom will come again when we have made/ suitable arrangements about the revival of trade.' To them the poet says:

What you call peace
is a graveyard near a battlefield . . .
Write him this epitaph: 'He went
in order that investors might be sure of a safe fifteen per cent.'

The poem goes on to argue that freedom can be ensured by applying the Sermon on the Mount to business and industry, and demanding honesty from the Press.

And I shall say to these:
'You cannot traffick in peace,
and you cannot quote it as priced
in the Stock Exchange list. . .

Not thus comes peace,
nor freedom thus. But slowly
making more holy what is holy
from the guarded pool
of the spirit, swift, cold, and beautiful,
in mists diaphanous his rain
a god draws back again;
and, as the sun builds with clouds, of these
he builds his city of peace -
. . . .
and the music of meeting and the trumpet at the gate
sounding, "All ye who enter here, abandon hate."'

The prosecution quotes a number of satirical verses about the War, of which the most memorable is

Here in an English graveyard snore
the business men who won the war.
While by the foreign seas they crossed, it
happens, lie the men who lost it.

(The shallow critics who wrote that Humbert specialised in distracting attention from the War had clearly never seriously read any of his poetry.) In 'The Summing Up', faint and disturbing memories of his youth, and particularly of a memorable night at Zweilutschinen, haunt the judge, but he eventually sums up against the poet who is duly found guilty.

The whole of Book IV is devoted to the aftermath of a murder trial in which Mr. Justice Crayfish has passed a sentence of death. The affair is examined from the points of view of all the people affected, however remotely; finally, on the eve of execution, the judge is visited by the murderer's mother. Together they discuss the case but on completely different levels, until they both become aware of their own helplessness, and of the futility of life and death.

As in all the previous books, the Fiddler has the first word. This time he identifies himself explicitly with the rest of sinful humanity, while affirming mankind's capacity to defy failure and evil:

> It is easier to be angry than to pity,
> it is easier to condemn than to understand,
> easier to find the Uncelestial City
> than the dim counties of the Holy Land
> . . . .
> I too have judged men, being judged by these.
> And I too have loved far less than I have hated,
> . . . .
> Shall I not, therefore, now that the day is over,
> remember, if men sinned, that they have suffered,
> . . . . .
> Shall I not see that to live is to have relinquished
> beauty to the sequestration of the dark,
> and yet that the spirit of man, benighted, vanquished
> has folded wings, and shall use them as the lark
> . . . .
> . . . . not reaching where she has striven,
> but soaring ever beyond herself, ...

ANAGNORISIS tries to bridge the gulf between the judge and the condemned man's mother:

> Then let us show them as they really are
> each to the other, not as judge and char,
> but each the equal prey of circumstance.
> . . . .
> he by hopes dying, she by hopes born dead,
> equally spoiled, impoverished, misled;

But there is no common ground. The judge had done what he was required to do. Mrs. Jakes bitterly reminds him that

> it's easy to sit in a chair
> and be sorry for mankind. But Jakes sits there,
> and it's not mankind 'e's troubled for, not Jim,
> but the days to come you've took away from him.

Crayfish replies that he has listened to the bells that very night, with their promise of peace,

> But how shall we find peace? Not by denying
> the choices of life, nor standing still and crying,
> 'I dare not or I will not.' Each one takes
> his own burden of action, and his own mistakes
> walk with him like tall friends, and in the end,
> believe me, madam, man has no other friend.

Although judicial execution is at the centre of this fourth Book, I do not think that it is principally concerned to debate the issue of capital punishment, so much as that of individual responsibility and the extent to which any man is free. Despite the absence of any independent evidence on the subject, there is a strong hint that Humbert was himself opposed to the death penalty. But, perhaps because there are in Crayfish's story so many echoes of Humbert's life, I have always felt that on the question of responsibility the judge here represents Humbert's own view. If that be the case, this picture of heroic acceptance of the consequences of choice declining into numb stoicism puts the author's life and actions into a new and melancholy perspective.

The last of the five Books, entitled 'Retort by Mrs. Jakes, *morte* Smith' is about the death of the murderer's mother. 'The Moon and Mrs. Smith', referred to earlier, occurs at this point, as the poet for whom she works as a char returns home and, unaware that she is dead, writes the poem that is her epitaph. The whole work ends with the 'Coda' which Humbert had earlier published as 'Veni Creator': Creator of the spirit, self-created/ . . . be near us when we build our city/ . . . Be near us always, but most of all when dawn/ breaks, and we see thy City on the hill.

Perhaps because this, the first of his books that I read, made such a deep impression on me, while leaving me puzzled, uncertain as to whether the author was a Christian, a pagan, or even some sort of pantheist, I have always thought it the best book of verse he wrote. Never mind that in the end his reach may well have exceeded his grasp: the work commands respect by the enormous breadth of his canvas, the huge range of verse forms he essays, the variety of poetic voices - lyrical, satirical, elegiac - and the sheer power with which he drives the story on.

Against the felicities, the delicate but finely-honed thrusts of the satires, and the many fine narrative and elegiac pieces, must be set the tendency to playfulness which can trivialise the argument, as in some of the exchanges with Arkwright and parts of the Trodley affair. Elsewhere, in the Jakes episode, sentiment occasionally declines into sentimentality, as he endeavours to demonstrate (what is true) his great skill in handling a variety of poetic forms. *The Uncelestial City* shows that he *was* an original: it is difficult to think of anyone of his time remotely like him - but ultimately perhaps he was too clever for his own good.

Although the book was reprinted within the month, it was mauled by Arnold Bennett in *The Evening Standard* (15 May) and by Harold Nicolson in *The Sunday Express*, and later savagely parodied by Siegfried

Sassoon in *Poems By Pinchbeck Lyre*. Bennett's review, like many of his *Evening Standard* pieces, reads today as patronising, not to say pompous, and pontifical. Nicolson's was simply spiteful.[23]

That these adverse reviews hurt and angered Humbert is clear from a passage in *Portraits By Inference*. Yet despite the understandable bitterness and sadness that he felt, his generosity and lack of vindictiveness put his detractors to shame:

> I wrote a longish book of verse called *The Uncelestial City*, of which Arnold (Bennett) did not approve. He was at that time king-making and unmaking in the *Evening Standard*. He signed the deed for my deposition from the thronelet I had briefly occupied in an obscure corner of Rabesqurat's kingdom. Proudly, I suppose, I had assumed my circlet of asses' ears and apes' heads, and not very much did I at the moment like the wrench when Arnold pulled it off. He wrote to me before the review appeared an affectionate letter saying that he felt it his duty to review the book, adding "Magnus amicus Humbert, major veritas." The review, following on a friendly little notice by Mr. Harold Nicholson beginning, "This silly little book", naturally damaged the book and hurt the author.
>
> There are writers who tell you that they do not read their reviews, there are others who prefer bad notices to good. Such men are either liars or more than mortal. In this matter at least I am neither one nor the other. I wrote to Arnold, approving his literary integrity but indicating only too plainly that I wished he hadn't used it at my expense. We exchanged several letters of increasing complexity and dignity. We did not meet for several months. He was busy and I was, I imagine, sulking. Then suddenly I heard of his illness. Like the rest of the world, I took it to be a bad attack of influenza, but I began to be worried at its prolongation. Finally I plucked up courage and went round to see him. When I went in the butler asked me if I would mind washing my hands in antiseptic. I felt suddenly cold. Antiseptic, what, why? At the very far end of an interminable passage I heard a door open, and I heard, faint, illegible and terribly changed, a voice that I had known whisper "Who is it?" "It's I, Arnold," I cried, but the door closed. It never opened again for me.[24]

In 1930 Humbert began to write for a new weekly, *The Week-End Review*, founded by a group of writers who had seceded from *The Saturday Review*. Gerald Barry was the editor. [25]

The Governing Body met again in Geneva at the beginning of June. On 6 June Humbert wrote that he had discussions with Drummond and others: that Drummond was still stalling over his predicted departure. Miss Bondfield and the new Secretary of Mines, Emmanuel, later Lord, Shinwell were expected soon, and so he hoped for news on the future of the Ministry. When she arrived, Miss Bondfield went with Humbert to 'have it out' with Drummond. She was very blunt with the Secretary General and told him plainly that 'if the wishes of the Cabinet were consulted, he would go at once.' But Drummond fenced as usual and the Minister returned to London promising to represent her views strongly there.

Humbert was working on *Tennyson*, which was to be published by Faber later that year. His *Heine* was already with the Cresset Press. But he was feeling the after-effects of the failure of *The Uncelestial City*. He wrote on 12 June for Jessie's birthday, bemoaning the fact that they were still burdened with debt. A few days later he wrote that he could not make their plans for the autumn definite, because of their financial position: the Victoria flat was an expensive nuisance but what alternative was there?

The official record of the 14th I.L.O. Conference, held from 10 June to 28 June, listed the British representatives as Margaret Bondfield, PC, LL D, JP, MP, Minister of Labour; Emmanuel Shinwell, MP, Secretary for Mines; Adviser: Humbert Wolfe, CB, CBE, Principal Assistant Secretary Ministry of Labour and Substitute Governmental Delegate. The Report mentioned his speeches as Chairman of the Selection Committee, and quoted two contributions in typical vein. At the 11th session, 21 June a.m., under the Presidency of Mr. Chou (China), Humbert, after congratulating the Director on his Report, said:

> It is perhaps not improper that in the incense that curls up continuously round the Olympic dais upon which the Secretary-General and Director sits, a voice of tempered enthusiasm should occasionally be heard. . . I venture to say that if perhaps the Director could school himself not always to anticipate the friendly criticism which he is to receive, but to leave it to the critics, it might perhaps reduce the volume of the Report and augment its objectivity.

At the 19th sitting, 27 June am., in the debate on Hours of Work of Salaried Employees. Mr Hallsworth (Workers Adviser, British Empire) attacked the British Government and its delegates for

> looking down from their Olympian heights upon us lesser mortals struggling with the problems which faced the Committee.

Humbert replied:

> . . . But after Mr. Hallsworth's final note I thought that my natural modesty would impel me to disclaim any association with Olympian heights. I have never penetrated there, and for my part, and on this occasion so far as the British Goverment is concerned, we have never been lost on those lonely clouds. . .[26]

That summer Humbert, Jessie and Ann spent their summer holiday in Germany, on a tour devised by Jessie. They went first to Berlin, then on to Munich and Oberammergau, after which they had a walking tour of the Odenwald. Ann retained a memory of Humbert's energetic walking, while he maintained in a letter at the end of August that *they* walked him off his feet. It seems that there was also a memorable scene with an obtuse German railway porter who so infuriated Humbert that he literally danced with rage.

Jessie and Ann stayed on in Germany after Humbert came home. On 1 September he wrote from London to say what a heavenly holiday it had been, and regretted all his grumbling and bad temper, which he put down to extreme mental fatigue. 'It was a real joy to see you & Ann striding out like two athletic sisters, very young and fresh in your ridiculously attractive trousers.' He was negotiating something with Douglas Jerrold at Eyre and Spottiswoode; a later letter showed this to be *A Winter Miscellany*, which he had been asked to compile and edit. He had already made a good start on 'George Moore' and had arranged to go to see the writer who was on holiday in Dieppe.

On 6 September he was trying to discover the 'results of Ann's exam' - the School Certificate, without which she could not enter the sixth form at St. Paul's Girls School, Hammersmith. In the same month his *Tennyson* came out, No. 3 in the Faber series *The Poets On The Poets*. In three chapters of acute, sharply-observed analysis and commentary this fifty-page essay set out to counter the prevailing temper of criticism which had all but despatched Tennyson and Browning to poetic limbo. The choice of 'Maud' for his Tennyson rehabilitation is a fascinating one, almost perverse as a challenge, rather like defending Browning on the basis of 'Sordello'. This in some ways idiosyncratic reading of the Master - Humbert succumbing to the temptation to demonstrate half-a-dozen impossible things before breakfast - nevertheless makes a persuasive case.

The last chapter is of particular interest because it is a fresh statement of Humbert's conviction of the need for affirmation, here contrasted not with denial but with the agreement of yes-men. The decline which

Humbert identified in *The Idylls* was due to Tennyson's 'complete misapprehension of the true character of [Prince] Albert', who was, according to Humbert, 'a dangerous pedant whose rigidity of mind and temper might well have led to disaster.' Tennyson's readiness to accept at face-value the 'convenient popular fiction that the Prince Consort was a type of King Arthur' made his affirmation seem, to Humbert at least, less like an 'everlasting "yes"' and more like 'a dubious "aye" dictated by considerations of party policy. . . the angels of *The Idylls* had a little the air of figures erected to introduce the International Exhibition of 1862.' *Tennyson* was followed by *Early Poems*, Blackwell's reprint of his first two collections, *London Sonnets* and *Shylock Replies to Mr. Chesterton*.

At the beginning of November he was in Geneva once more. A Committee of Thirteen had been set up to deal with the question of the future of the League's staff. Humbert became involved in discussions with Drummond and Lord Cecil about conditions of service with the League. Only one question really interested him: 'Should the post of Secretary-General remain a temporary one?' The other two favoured a temporary appointment. When Humbert pressed for a definition, Cecil said "Not longer than seven years." (Drummond had been there for ten.) But nothing more definite emerged.

Towards the end of 1930, from Eyre and Spottiswoode, came *A Winter Miscellany*, an anthology of prose and poetry which he compiled, edited, and augmented with original poems of his own. The Preface is most revealing, firstly for its autobiographical content, especially the reminiscences of childhood in Bradford, informed by the 'representative truth of his personal mythology', as C. Day-Lewis's called his own autobiography. In addition, and for good measure, there are the jokes about the anthology's origins, the self-depreciation, the learning lightly stirred in, all done with great vivacity.

The anthology is organized in sections devoted to the countryman's winter, the traveller's, the soldier's winter, and so on. It is, without a doubt, a brilliant collection, exactly satisfying his declared intentions and full of good things: the expected, the half-remembered, the new. Humbert's own contributions to it were later reprinted in *Out of Great Tribulation* (1939).

(ii)

The Disclosure

The Uncelestial City, Humbert's first major piece of public self-revelation, was paralleled by an equally important but private self-disclosure. He suddenly and unexpectedly overwhelmed Jessie in a flood of confessions which, though she could hardly believe her ears, nevertheless explained a great deal that had puzzled her. In 1941 she described how in 1930 Humbert had sat on the floor of her bedroom, telling her almost with exaltation how for ten years he had invented excuses for excluding her from a large, and perhaps the most important, area of his life. He told her how he had decided in 1920 at the very last moment that he wanted to go to Sweden alone and had invented the story that no ladies were to be allowed to accompany the delegates to the Stockholm conference.

He explained that, as a writer, he had felt that he had a right to lead his own life - to travel, to meet people, and to keep all that side of his life to himself. He had refused on her behalf all invitations which came to them from any one in London whom he had met through his work in Geneva. He used to explain to them that because of Ann she never went into society.

For Jessie and Ann, however, life had become a state of permanent and excited tension, and Geneva the obsessive focus of all action. The repeated disappointment of not accompanying him, the farewells at Victoria, 'the gateway through which he vanished from me four or five times a year for almost ten years', the continuous postponements until 'next year' of the permanent position and life in Geneva, destroyed the continuity of their life in London by focussing their eyes on a life elsewhere which made London and England seem no more than a waiting room for Geneva.

Jessie's protracted exile in Italy and Monte Carlo, followed by her virtual rustication to the coast, seeing Humbert only at week-ends, when he was not absent in Geneva or elsewhere, had helped to create a gulf of whose increasing depth and width she gradually became aware. She accepted as genuine his protestations that he missed her, and wanted her with him. But she could see that he at least was able to make something of his absences: they were part of his work. In addition, he took his writing with him, he met people, made friends and led a social life from which she was increasingly excluded. In retrospect it seemed that he was creating for himself a zone of privacy, while feeding her scraps of information, partly through a need to lull her anxieties and partly through the irresistible urge he always had to reveal himself, even to show off, while preserving his own secret world, at once repelling and inviting questions, conducting his life in a blaze of concealment.

Why Humbert chose this moment to tell Jessie can only be conjectured. There is not a single reference to it in any of the letters, and Jessie's unpublished papers describe only the fact, without attempting to explain it. His transfer to a new Department in the Ministry probably heralded the end of his trips to Geneva. He could hardly continue to compartmentalize his London life and still keep her in ignorance. Other plausible but unverifiable reasons may have been that it was better to confess before Jessie found out from someone else - for example, from the anonymous letter-writer - or he may have volunteered the information in order to distract her attention from some other deception which he was anxious to conceal: 'un train peut en cacher un autre', as the French level-crossing signs remind us.

The admission can hardly have failed to affect their relationship, and although Jessie may appear to have been naïve, gullible, or simply anxious to believe the least possible ill of her husband, there is little doubt that she had a shrewd idea of the temptations to which he was exposed. After Humbert's death she recorded that, while they were still living in Artillery Mansions, they had stayed with his sister Rita at Burley-in-Wharfedale, and that Rita had let slip the apparently inconsequential remark that 'People are always asking me about Berto's love-affairs. Now he's become so famous. Like Byron and Shelley.' Jessie remembered feeling annoyed and wondering if Rita was simply being more 'in-lawish' than usual, or if there was indeed something to wonder about. And now, whatever Humbert might say in his letters, he obviously preferred his independence in London, and did not want the constant encumbrance of a family. In retrospect, 1927 can be seen to mark the turning point, the beginning of the disintegration of their marriage, the moment when things began to fall apart.

All of this goes a long way to explaining why Jessie was rarely named or directly mentioned in any of his published writings, although, of course, a number of his poems were written for or about her, and several of his books were dedicated to her under the classical pseudonym of Euterpe, Muse of Poetry. In *Portraits By Inference* (1934) he mentioned Jessie by name, but only briefly and *en passant*. To the best of my knowledge, *The Uncelestial City* was the last book he dedicated to her, and then only in the oblique inscription: 'To "My Visitor" who gave me "Requiem"', which concealed her identity from all but the knowledgeable, but could be construed as reminding her of the hurt he had felt at her rejection of the earlier dedication of *Requiem*.

There was undoubtedly a ruthless side to Humbert where Jessie was concerned. His treatment of her can only be described as cruel, and is explicable only by the same moral amnesia which he had identified in Lloyd George ten years earlier. In this respect Humbert bore witness to the truism that artistic merit has never been synonymous with moral rectitude. One is saddened to have to recognize this flaw in a character which showed so many other virtues, but no good purpose is served by denying what was obvious fact. Indeed, both *The Uncelestial City* and this latest domestic drama reveal the same truth that Sean Day-Lewis set out to portray in his biography of his father - 'not a picture of a hero or a villain but of a complicated and much-loved man of many contradictions.' One might also echo the same hope - ' . . . and that any new understanding will help towards more appreciation of his poetry, which was the point of his life.'[27]

Chapter Nine

1931-1936

'But how shall we find peace?'
(*The Uncelestial City*, 1930)

I

1931

In January Ann entered the sixth form at St. Paul's School, Hammersmith, to prepare for Oxford entrance, and Sir William Rothenstein completed his pastel portrait of Humbert which he presented to the sitter, inscribed with the words 'To Humbert from Will, January 1931.' In February Humbert was elected a Fellow of the Royal Society of Literature, but the paper on Arthur Hugh Clough which he had been invited to read to the Society was delayed by Whitehall commitments until May. It was eventually published in 1932, in the Society's *Eighteen Sixties* volume.[1]

In April 1931, when Jessie was once more busy nursing her mother, he was sent to Geneva in his capacity as head of Establishments at the Ministry of Labour to conduct an inspection of the League and of the I.L.O. Initially he expected to be there no more than four or five days, and planned to return as soon as he had completed his report. But the whole operation took much longer than he had bargained for, partly because of the size of the two organizations - each had a staff of four hundred - but mostly because the League's affairs were in such a mess. He wrote of mismanagement and a slackness of control that made the suspicion of corruption hard to dismiss, while 'in an atmosphere of mixed intrigue, fear, suspicion & ingratiating falsehood' finding the truth was no light task.

In Drummond's absence he was dealing chiefly with Avenol and Paulucci di Calboli, the two senior Deputies. 'All Geneva is humming with the news from Spain. The Spanish members of the Secretariat have quite simply gone up in flames' - a reference to the replacement of the Spanish Monarchy by a Republic. When Drummond returned to Geneva he was still as vague as ever about when he would give up his post, but equally clear that the jealousy between the French and the Germans made Humbert his only possible successor. In the middle of all that a telegram signed 'R. MacDonald' (Prime Minister) instructed Humbert to take over the I.L.O. Governing Body work instead of Somervell (a former Ministry of Labour official seconded to the League) and Lawson (the Parliamentary Secretary). By the time he came to submit his Report he said he had received a shocking insight into what his job would be if ever he became Secretary-General of the League. 'The I.L.O. seems like a dove-cote compared with this den of raging tigers.' Every single one of the senior staff had secretly dined him 'to explain exactly how they have been wronged & how by giving them everybody else's work everything could be put right.'

Although a senior position in Geneva seemed their best hope of solving their financial problems, 'I regard this world of Geneva seen now from below and within with genuine apprehension.' he wrote. But while the uncertainty dragged on for another year, if not two, subsequent correspondence in Ministry of Labour and I.L.O. files indicates that this was his last journey to Geneva as British representative at the I.L.O. The suggestion has been made that he had offended his masters by his conduct in Geneva; on one occasion he was said to have declared in a speech to the assembly that he was ashamed of the line his government was taking on a particular issue, and only a change of government had averted a massive rebuke. No evidence has survived to support this theory, and the overwhelming likelihood is that his change of department required him to hand over responsibility for I.L.O. matters to his successor.

On 15 May Duckworth published a collection of fourteen poems by Siegfried Sassoon, under the pseudonym of Pinchbeck Lyre, most if not all of which were parodies of Humbert. 'Coda', for example, mocked the 'Coda' of *Requiem*:

> *The Cat and Fiddle* is closed. Empty is the bar now.
> Nobody else will cork or uncork the bottles now. . .

and so on for a further fourteen lines. Similarly, the next poem, 'Requiem', with its recurrent 'Swing tripe, swing tosh!', lampooned the poem about Jakes's execution in *The Uncelestial City*, 'Swing dark, swing death!'

Sassoon may simply have thought it a good joke to produce this *jeu d'esprit*, as the Sassoon bibliography called it.[2] The collection's equivocal sub-title, "*It is the season of larks*", suggests something of the school-boy jokes that were common among many of the public-school bred literati of the time. According to Richard Church, however, Sassoon chose this as the most suitable form of chastisement for what he took to be Humbert's slighting reference to Hardy in a review. The offensive pseudonym behind which Sassoon hid lends credence to this view. But whether *Poems by Pinchbeck Lyre* began as a schoolboy jape, or arose out of a mistaken, or at least imperfect, interpretation of Humbert's admittedly dangerous mannerism, the effect of Sassoon's excoriating humour on Humbert's sales was said to be disastrous.

The time was against him too, for he was swimming against the stream of literary fashion, which has flowed more or less consistently in the opposite direction ever since, and certainly until the fifties or sixties. Rhetoric, sentiment, Heine-like ironic agony, have become taboo in poetry. Only the very brave or the very foolish have dared in the last sixty years to write a love lyric. Robert Graves, with whom in many ways Humbert had so much in common - writer of love poetry, wit, fantasist - was a notable exception. Humbert's readiness to display his emotions, in verse that occasionally verged on the perfervid, stands in sharp contrast to his younger rivals who for the most part wore their brains rather than their hearts on their sleeves. But first the war and then the influence on verse of the anti-establishment trend in the theatre worked against pre-war romantics. By the time the notion of a dominant fashion disappeared in the late sixties, with the rise of poets like Seamus Heaney, to whom Humbert would surely have warmed more than to the neo-Brutalists like Gunn and Hughes, it was too late: Humbert had been too long not merely dead but buried.

Snow, his next collection of poems was published by Victor Gollancz in June or July.[3] The first of the book's three sections is a sonnet sequence entitled 'Calendar', with a sonnet for each month of the year. The poems are without a doubt skilful, but perhaps a touch over-literary. One stands out from the rest - 'Bredon' - by reason of its directness and its echo of Heine. It takes the form of an exchange between (presumably) the poet and his lover:

. . . .
"Because a poet sang it, Bredon outstays
 the actual hills where, with my love, I'd lie,
and something in me is grieving all my days
 because Housman's girl went out alone to die.
. . . . We'll remember this
 perhaps hereafter when we think of June."

In the section headed 'Persons', there is a cluster of memorable tributes to his seventeenth century heroes: a sonnet on George Herbert, a tender adieu in 'Henry King - To His Saint', what might be called a serious pastiche in 'John Donne':

If that I love and love doth not suffice
I'll double self and love, and love thee twice,
and if that still fall short thou'lt find in me
of all known lovers such a company
 that thou shalt never know from morn to morn
 what old love's dead or what new love is born. . .

and a moving evocation of Marvell witnessing the execution of Charles I, which ends:

> . . .
> England was saved, the royal cause was dead,
> but Andrew Marvell heard, or seemed to hear,
> far trumpets in another Commonwealth.

'Consola' is a tender tribute to his mother:

> Aye! she was such
> as quiet possesses,
> gentle with fulfilment's
> gentlenesses.
>
> She went all slender,
> oft looking down,
> who wears death's splendour
> like an old gown.
>
> Heaven from the beginning
> was thrall to her -
> this bright unsinning
> Lucifer.

The penultimate poem is an Horatian 'Ode to Shakespeare', described as a version of 'Ode à Shakespeare' by Georges Lafourcade. My admiration for Humbert's technical virtuosity is tempered with regret that comparison with the original has proved impossible.

Finally, a direct, unadorned simplicity, free of jokes or show of self-abasement, in 'Envoi':

> Now go, my book, and take with thee
> the bright unwritten part of me.
> Tell them each poem bears the mark
> of the intact, majestic dark,
> that mercifully cloaks the eyes
> which saw, and lost, their Paradise.
> Tell them that he who overheard
> an incommunicable word,
> offers no other plea than this
> to the eternal silences.

In 1931 there occurred one of those spats for which the English literary world has always had a peculiar fondness. As A. Alvarez shrewdly observed, 'The English scene is peculiarly amenable to literary history; it is savage with gang warfare which, at a distance, can be dignified as disagreements between schools of verse.'[4] In essence it was another skirmish in the tribal warfare between progressive and conservative poetic camps which were respectively the opponents or the allies of *Georgian Poetry*. Hostilities in this instance were initiated by Roy Campbell, and originated in his feeling of alienation when he and his wife were enjoying the hospitality of Harold Nicolson and his wife Vita Sackville-West at Long Barn, in Kent, in 1927. Humbert's involvement in the subsequent *brouhaha* was in a sense peripheral and coincidental. Campbell, like Humbert, was writing regularly for *The New Statesman and Nation* and his affinity with the anti-Establishment views of Wyndham Lewis made him the obvious reviewer for Lewis's *Apes of God* in 1930. The editor's decision, however, not to print his review only served to inflame further Campbell's anger. His fierce rejection of the values of a fashionable literary coterie from which he felt himself to be excluded turned into an attack on coterie morals too when his wife fell in love with Victoria Sackville-West.

Until this moment, Campbell had had no scruples about his own love affairs and seemed to have accepted without protest the catholic sexual tastes of those at Long Barn. But when his own wife became involved, and contemplated leaving him, he was deeply shocked and hurt. He seems to have sought relief from and vengeance on this affront to his manhood in a long verse satire, *The Georgiad*, begun in 1929 initially as a straightforward attack on Bloomsbury immorality and Bloomsbury immoralists. This is not the place to discuss the central problem of *The Georgiad*, or the inherent contradictions in Campbell's own personality which the poem mythologises.[5] But it is clear that he was unable to resist the temptation to settle a number of other scores, and even to have sought new ones. Not content with savaging the sexual pyrotechnics of the Bloomsbury set and the grim and sterile sexual punditry of Marie Stopes, Havelock Ellis and Bertrand Russell, he widened his attack to pillory the mutual admiration the Georgians lavished upon one another's writing and, even more, their attempts to force the critical standards of their coterie upon others.

The voice of Androgyno, the hermaphroditic hero of *The Georgiad*, could in its Bloomsbury mode 'coo in satire gentle and polite/ to fill the soul of Humbert with delight:' or change to a growl and 'startle Humbert from his dreamy stare/ among the weeping willows of his hair,/ whereon, I only wish it for the best,/ he'd sometimes hang his harp up for a rest.' Humbert's appearance was further abused later: 'More like a weeping willow than a man,/ with trailing hair, as dreamy as a sheep,/ and a great bow (to make the typists weep).' Campbell accused Humbert both of the standard humility affected by the Bloomsbury group: 'until at last to Humbert's side I crawl/ and cower beside the humblest of them all', and at the same time of praising Campbell's attacks on other Georgians: 'And like poor Humbert (whom I still pursue/ in him addressing all your tribe and you) turn somersaults of such amazing daring/ as dislocate both dignity and bearing.' And much more of the same. The choice of *The Dunciad* as the model for this parodic effort emphasizes the parallel with Pope's London which the closed world of these metropolitan literary cliques so strongly resembled.

There is no evidence that Campbell had any grounds for personal animosity towards Humbert, other than his popularity as a poet. It seems to have been enough that he was successful: in Campbell's book that had to be his reward for writing the sort of poetry that Campbell disapproved of. It looks increasingly likely that it is to Campbell that Humbert owed the mistaken but oft-repeated label of Georgian, a classic case of guilt by association. He never was or even appeared to be a Georgian, as is clear from his earliest published poems, *London Sonnets*, and it may well be (as Rowland Smith suggests) that it was enough that he was a reviewer, like J. C. Squire, Arnold Bennett and Harold Nicolson, the other principal targets of Campbell's scorn.

Rowland Smith sees Humbert's satirical poem, *The Ranciad*, published in *The New Statesman* on June 27, 1931, as a riposte to Campbell. Since *The Georgiad* was not published until October of that year, this would make Humbert's poem something in the nature of a pre-emptive strike. That in itself is not implausible; it was widely known that Campbell was writing his satire, parts may have been 'leaked', and the two of them shared connections which could account for Humbert's foreknowledge. But although *The Ranciad* made some shrewd thrusts in the direction of the trend which Campbell represented, Humbert identified no one by name, nor would he have descended to the personal abuse to which he was himself subjected.

His satire consisted of a 78-line invocation to

> Divine Cacophone! ugliest of wenches
> at whose dread aspect all Parnassus blenches,
> ....
> .... Have I not also strayed
> by the Pierian spring, disgusting Maid,
> and spat into the waters, to ensure
> whatever else they are, they shan't be pure?
> Am I not willing with the rest to sneer
> at what in secret I respect and fear?
> Ready with sycophantic awe to flinch
> at anything that's written by the French,
> ....
> or like the comic juggler of the Halls
> toss in the air my vision's coloured balls,
> and, when they crash, anticipate with vigour
> the crowd by teaching them myself to snigger.

> Or call upon me in a reckless hurry
> to do the utmost violence to Murray [*probably a misprint for Murry*]
> and you shall find in me (I swear) the man to
> invent a new gorilla Esperanto,
> which, scorning English, with a jungle sound
> salts, as it causes, reason's hopeless wound.
> Nor will I stop at that. My Muse shall curb
> the native insolence of noun and verb,
> seeking that happiest of all conditions
> when verse is one long string of prepositions. . .

If this was indeed Humbert's counter-charge, as sharp as it was unusual, it would indicate how deeply he felt the attacks which were increasingly being made upon him after the first success of *Requiem*, as if the critics arrogated to themselves the role of Nemesis who would punish his presumption. The pettiness and spite displayed in the close hot-house atmosphere of these small and in part mutually exclusive literary groups of the twenties and thirties is also encountered where one would expect to find more measured and sober judgement. It is as if the historians of literature have been content in the main to repeat earlier plaudits and jibes, rather than take the trouble to read, or read carefully, the authors on whom they sit in judgement. Thus, C. H. Sisson, himself a Civil Servant who should have known better, dismissed Humbert as 'a journalist versifier.' Rowland Smith, in the Campbell study already mentioned, might on reflection have thought better of ascribing to Humbert's prominence as a Civil Servant 'a tinge of that middle-class amateurism' in his status as a writer which Campbell and Lewis so despised. 'Amateurism'? By what criteria could the latter be rated 'professionals'? And even if these distinctions could satisfactorily be established, on what grounds is the one to be held superior to the other?

Mr. Smith expresses surprise that Campbell should have attacked Robert Graves and Laura Riding; were they not after all just as critical of Humbert as Campbell was? Doubtless the enemy of my enemy must appear to be my friend, but shared dislike was clearly not enough. Moreover Mr. Smith endorses without question the Graves' antipathy towards Humbert, while his reading of a passage in *Dialogues and Monologues* about Humbert's English master at Bradford Grammar School - 'the knowing clubbiness of its tone . . . cliquish innuendo . . .' - argues a determination to put the worst possible construction on anything Humbert said: '*nec defuere qui in deterius referrent*', I can almost hear Humbert quoting.[6]

The last word is perhaps best left with one who shared Humbert's fastidious distaste for the publication of personal abuse. In a letter of 1952 C. Day-Lewis wrote:

> '. . . Personal satire, such as Campbell's, seems to me nowadays nearly always a parade or a bolstering-up of the writer's own ego, not a genuine detestation of what the satiree stands for. . .'

Like Humbert, he had had his share of abuse from Geoffrey Grigson:

> 'I dare say he felt he was being "sincere and honest" - people do, who believe they have a mission to clean up the literary or some other scene: but the *tone* of malice always betrays itself.'[7]

In all likelihood it was in August of that year that Humbert first met Pamela Frankau, the daughter of the author Gilbert Frankau and herself a novelist who had published her first novel, *Marriage of Harlequin*, in 1927 when still in her teens. She was now twenty-three years of age, Humbert forty-six. According to Pamela's cousin, the novelist Diana Raymond, the meeting probably took place at a party given by Viola Garvin.[8]

It was most probably about the same time that *Signpost to Poetry*, Humbert's Introduction to the Study of Verse, was published by Cassell. The three largely historical sections, which trace the origins and development of poetry, are clear, serious without being heavy, and display, as one might expect, the vast breadth of his reading and the catholicity of his sympathies. They are also refreshingly free of any suspicion of attitudinising, or coy self-depreciation.

But the last chapter, a mere ten pages, is in many ways the most interesting, chiefly because it is from start to finish a profession of faith in the survival of poetry, a ringing affirmation that, far from being dead, poetry was never more alive, or - and this is perhaps even more significant - more eagerly sought by the age. Furthermore, he contemplates without dismay or discouragement the rising generation and the movement away from traditional forms. Indeed, he goes further than his conclusion in *Dialogues and Monologues* or his observations on Fleg. He sees much that is good in Free Verse, and 'though much freakish rubbish is being written in that mode as in all other modes, it is a sign of health and not of decay in the body of poetry.' And he shrewdly observes that Eliot was not the revolutionary in form that he was taken to be; rather 'his innovation is an attempt to give the object of poetry a greater share in the poem than it has hitherto enjoyed.' He adds sagely that it takes a mind as richly stored and erudite as Eliot's to succeed, but that is no reason for not trying nor any grounds for despair. The book, in short, is a further example of the 'affirmation' which he believed to be so necessary in those otherwise depressed and depressing times.

For a good part of September Jessie was in Rye, while her mother was recovering her health in Battersea. The inference from Humbert's letters to her is that Jessie was recuperating from the strain of nursing her mother. He stayed at The Athenaeum during the week, joining Jessie in Rye for week-ends. The task of implementing the Treasury policy of cutting expenditure kept him working very long hours, as Civil Service staff were forcibly retired, or suffered swingeing reductions in salary and status. On September 16 he reported to her that

> we've saved in staff alone £100,000 a year - which means dozens and dozens of broken hearts and careers. My room has been a sort of shambles with the cattle trooping up to be pole-axed. It's a miserable and soul-racking job.

He hoped that by the end of the month the worst of the work would be over, and if there was an Election he saw the possibility of a breathing space: 'I need sleep & sleep & sleep!'

The General Election he had foreseen came at the end of October, a National Government was returned with MacDonald as Prime Minister, and Humbert got his break - in Monte Carlo. From 23 October to 17 November he stayed at the Hotel Mirabeau, doing nothing but eat and sleep, no writing, only sunbathing and playing the tables at the Casino - where he mostly lost. He thanked Jessie for giving him the holiday, presumably by forgoing her share in it - not for the last time, as will be seen, and perhaps not for the first either.

II

1932

In 1932 he published only one book, *ABC of the Theatre.* Produced by the Cresset Press in a black and silver cover, with illustrations by Edward Burra, it has more than a hint of Art Déco about it. Described in the Preface as 'this tenuous Rosciad', quite lacking in genuine malice, this slender, and essentially slight, volume of mild lampoons on the world of theatre folk nevertheless neatly picked off a number of targets in classical Humbertian fashion:

> G is Galsworthy. We could do after all
> with a little less worth and rather more gall.
>
> N is for Noel (Coward). His genius is not
> deep thinking but thinking a little a lot.
>
> R is Revue. And would it be vihil
> to say it is hocks et praeterea nihil?

- an echo in the strictest sense of 'vox et praeterea nihil', the description of Echo.

The Wadham College Library copy has a pencilled addition signed by him:

> R is for Reinhardt. He employed as a super-
> Virgin quite naturally Lady Duff-Cooper.

Only nine letters from this year have been preserved, either because the rest have been lost or because, having fewer occasions for writing to Jessie now that he was less frequently absent, those were all he wrote. Except for an inconsequential letter from Birmingham in June, they were all written between 11 and 18 November while Jessie was away in Bournemouth receiving sunlight treatment with their daughter, Ann.

The last reference to his mother-in-law in the letters had been in 1931. It is known that she died early in the 1930s, probably in 1931 or 1932. Jessie's only remaining immediate family, therefore, were her sister, Annie, and her uncle, Willie Graham, who lived in Edinburgh. The inference from the 1932 letters is that Annie was still in London and unwell. Humbert promised Jessie that he was 'attending to all your commissions' and had sent Annie books and newspapers, and telephoned every day for news of her progress. He meant to go round to see her but doubted that he would have time. In view of the antipathy that his female in-laws had for him, his unfailing care of and concern for them was remarkably generous, and cannot be discounted simply as a way of pacifying his wife.

He wrote that the crowds which disrupted Whitehall on Armistice Day reminded him of

> the mad plan I had [in 1918] of becoming a commercial cad. Your refusal to agree to it was not the least of the benefits that your unfailing love has conferred upon me.

He was very excited about a sort of play he had just started work on called *Reverie of Policeman*:

> It's very much more than a touching up of "The Publicist". It is in fact a wholly new thing. The stuff hasn't come like this since "Requiem".

A few days later he promised her:

> I'll remember not to make Policeman too earthly. Indeed the trouble at the moment is to bring him to earth at all.

He soon came to the view that it

> isn't actable. . . I shall call it a Revue in verse I think, but it has no commercial possibilities.

He eventually called it *A Ballet in Three Acts*, when it was published by Gollancz in 1933. His doubts about its theatrical future may well have been prophetic, but the play was actually produced by Evan John Simpson at The Mercury Theatre in 1936.[9] His letter of 14 November ends with his renewed apologies 'for all my bad tempers', and then almost casually, as one referring to an accepted if fairly new facet of Jessie's life, 'I hope that you're drawing?'

This new interest which was to open a door into a new life for her had begun, apparently quite accidentally, the previous year. She had done no drawing since her childhood but, as has been noted, she had intermittently written verse throughout their married life. One Sunday afternoon in 1931, sitting at the desk in the library of their flat in Artillery Mansions, she had begun writing a poem about a dream. Humbert had fallen asleep while reading in his big easy chair. As the light from the window behind threw the planes of his face into relief she had begun almost unconsciously to draw the shape of the shadows of his face on the sheet of paper before her. When Humbert awoke he had been impressed with the strange drawing which he said looked like a death-mask. The drawing lay about in the desk until he put it in a book to mark his place, and there it stayed until it fell out one day in 1932. Seeing it once more she became convinced that if a talent for drawing had lain dormant within her all those years she should make the effort to revitalize it.

She made other drawings of Humbert - 'strange large heads, which Helen Moggeridge (later Cooper) said were drawings.' This artist friend gave her some lessons in perspective and set her to draw from a cast of the head of Richard Hughes, whose mother had been the first outside person to see the original drawing she had done in 1931. A few days later she bought Jessie some paints, canvas and brushes and started her off on a flower-piece. When Jessie began her first independent painting, a head of Humbert in oils, she still had only a hazy notion of how to go about the task, and she did not always paint in the same room or the same light. The result, she said, 'was an uncanny likeness, with eyes that followed one all round the room.' But in trying to correct what Humbert's sister, Fanny, said was a fault in the jaw, she spoilt the whole 'and it vanished as if it had never been.'

In spite of indignant and destructive criticism from friends, relatives and artists, she persevered. Humbert to his credit enthusiastically encouraged her, and sat for her in the morning before he left for Whitehall - senior Civil Servants then began their day rather later than is the practice today. She now constantly carried a sketch-book with her, and drew him at every conceivable opportunity.

That summer, when they were on holiday in Trouville and he was writing *Now A Stranger*, she drew him in the courtyard of the hotel, on the beach, at the Casino, at cafés. When they got back to London, he took a room in Chelsea, where they went every week-end, and lived a simple life, while she drew and painted him. Helen Moggeridge had suggested that she train seriously at an art school, the Academy or the Slade. Towards the end of 1932 she went with Humbert to Oxford, where he was giving a lecture. When Albert Rutherston, then Ruskin Master of Drawing, saw her sketch-book he said, with surprise in his voice, "But you are *really* good, Jessie. Come and work with me at the Ruskin." In her circumstances, of course, that was unrealistic, and she was too old for the Academy, but he wrote to Schwabe at the Slade to introduce her, and she became a student there in 1933, working every week-end in her studio at her portraits of Humbert.

She later recorded that sometimes when he was sitting for her and would not keep still, he would say to her, laughing, "You'll have to paint me asleep, or dead." Nevertheless he was an eager sitter, which made her all the more disappointed when her efforts were unsuccessful. She said that it was not until the end of 1934, when she began the 'White Picture' in the library of 128 Mount Street (their home from 1934) that she achieved a genuine likeness of him, and that was followed by the portrait in the chair (*see illustration*) painted while he was translating *Cyrano de Bergerac* in 1935, and a portrait, never finished, of him in a blue pullover.[10]

In one of her letters Jessie had accused him of destroying invitations which he received (presumably those which included her), perhaps a reference, serious or simply jesting, to his admission of 1930. In reply he firmly denied even receiving, let alone destroying, any invitations, except for one from Oxford and another 'from the Sec'y of the Ladies Luncheon Club, saying that the lunch is at 12.30 at the Midland. That means a horribly early start.' The Club was, by inference, probably in a northern town. He had accepted to go to Oxford and proposed that they both stay at the Randolph 'where the dinner is.' This was most probably the occasion when Albert Rutherston saw her drawings.

In the last of this group of letters, on 18 November, he wrote: 'I'm <u>sure</u> that Ann oughtn't to try to swot Spenser just before the exam. Far better to have a couple of extra days real and artificial sunlight.' This was almost certainly a reference to the entrance examination for Oxford. There was a certain irony in the fact that the advice was addressed to Ann in Bournemouth, the scene of his earlier opposition to her Oxford ambitions (*see* Chapter 8 above). This letter also mentioned the dinner of the Omar Khayyam club the previous evening, at which he had arrived 'an hour late at 8.15 in time for the chicken and the ice! Speeches were made by Sadleir, Sir Thomas [later Lord] Horder, Low, Herbert Samuel and R. H. Mottram. I didn't speak because I was tired.'[11]

III

1933

Important self-disclosures, this time in print, make this a year of special significance. They came in the form of a lecture and two dramatic works, on the one hand; on the other, his first explicitly autobiographical venture - in so far as anything of his was altogether explicit - *Now A Stranger*, written during his holiday at Trouville the previous summer, and published in 1933 by Cassell. Little needs to be added to what has already been said in earlier chapters about this book. There are occasional pieces of over-writing, but these are more than compensated for by his skill in evoking people and places. He shows himself to be a shrewd self-observer, with some revealing asides; for example, when the infant Berto pretended to be able to read from Grimm's *Fairy Tales* but in fact recited the declension of 'mensa' - 'As only too often happened in his career, instead of being mulcted of the sixpence he was given another as a tribute to his memory.'

One noteworthy feature of *Now A Stranger* is the importance of other people in his story; as much as anything, they serve to give himself a sense of 'being', of identity. Even his use of the third person in autobiographical works acts in this way: he is a reflection of all that he meets and experiences, which he interprets in such a way as to give meaning to his own existence; and how sensitive he is to the resultant self-discovery, for example in the Murgatroyd incident related in Chapter I above. He cannot believe that he is so universally disliked, yet turns this mortifying revelation into a badge of distinction - or distinctiveness, which is ultimately much the same thing.

The revelations in the other three works are of a different order, and all the more significant because they are indirect. On 26 January he delivered the Arthur Skemp Memorial Lecture in the University of Bristol on 'Romantic and Unromantic Poetry.' In it he returned to the theme which had become a central one in his theoretical writing and lecturing, from *The Craft of Verse* in 1928 to *Signpost to Poetry* in 1931.[12]

He began by charting the violent transformation undergone by poetry in less than half a century, and concluded that many of those who had claimed to be anti-romantic revolutionaries were, despite themselves, 'witnesses to a faith that they professed to ignore.' He then examined what he judged to be the most lucid argument against romantic poetry, enunciated by Professor Irving Babbitt in *The New Laocoon*. The crux of Babbitt's case was, 'first that "a world of pure imaginative illusion" is inadmissible, and secondly that a great poet must effect a reconciliation between the wings of poetry and the spurs of prose.'

Invoking examples from Shakespeare to Browning, Humbert boldly argued that illusion is the one thing impossible for romantic poetry, which sees things as they are - for the poet. 'Illusion is to see the world as others see it, truth . . . is to see it as nobody saw it before and would never have seen it but for the artist's vision.' - a lonely vision and, as he elsewhere insisted, a distant lonely song.

Like Kant, Humbert remained convinced 'that in the long run beauty is the sense of order imposed upon the essentially disorderly by the operation of the Mind', and that is what justifies the artist's loneliness of vision - his 'solitude is always qualified by the presence of the object. . . The romantic and classic poets, in this argument, stand together.'

He then returned to the question of what accounted for the flight to Realism and concluded that 'what has happened in the world is that life has become one long time-saving device, and we do not know what to do with the time that we have saved.' The worship of this new mechanical, technological world required both obedience to the object and submission to the sub-conscious. A pasage from *The Waste Land*, beginning "The music crept by me upon the waters", makes the point for him, for the reader cannot automatically be assumed to share the chain of associations which this evokes for the author, and without those shared assumptions the reader has to make his own sense of the poem. Humbert's complaint is a reasonable one : 'All new art requires an athletic effort in those to whom it is presented. It must not, however, demand an impossible one.'

Wrong though he held the new theory to be, Humbert did not 'therefore pretend that all its exponents have failed to enrich our minds', and he saw evidence of exactly what was meant by romantic poetry in some of Eliot's verse, even though the beauty achieved was in defiance of the doctrine professed by its author. The romantic poet is grounded in the earthly, to which the cascade of his verse, no matter how high it reach, must in the end return, 'obedient to the long pull of that wise old enchanter - gravity.' And as a final illustration of that unchanging allegiance he read his poem in which the fountain was the image of verse:

> Keep out the birds! . . . .
> . . . . Their song is charged
> with music not by silence purged,
> nor beyond passion nor the taint
> of half-articulate complaint.
> . . . .
> Play on, bright fount! . . .
> rising again to gather up
> the starlight in your flawless cup,
> not image, nor similitude
> but a cool spring in a green wood,
> alone of all that mind has sought,
> the pattern of consummate thought.

I have dwelt at such length on this lecture, and quoted from the final poem, of deliberate purpose, for the poem was taken, as indeed in a sense was the lecture, from another work of his, published in 1933, *Reverie of Policeman*, which I have come to think is one of the key texts for the understanding of his poetry, his philosophy and his life.

Reverie of Policeman, which, as we have seen, he had begun writing in November 1932, was published by Victor Gollancz in this year. Superficially - although there is nothing superficial about it - *Reverie of Policeman* is a slightly surrealistic fantasy in verse about the triumph of love. A fairly stereotypical London bobby, benevolently patrolling his beat, sees the houses beginning to act strangely, their frontages rising like stage curtains to reveal not only the interiors but also the past and the future of the principal characters, namely The Gentleman in Evening Dress and The Satiric Poet, both in love with the Ballet Dancer. The Gentleman relives the destruction, through jealousy, of his love, the Poet wrestles with his pessimism about love, poetry and the world. Strange things happen: characters assume their shapes of earlier or later years, Policeman is transubstantiated into the Bust of Darwin and made to speak its lines. Sundry contemporary 'isms' and trends are introduced in order to be firmly refuted, and eventually all contradictions are resolved and Policeman sees his world restored to normality.

The reduction of the poem to such a relatively straightforward account admittedly involves a degree of simplification which would be more difficult were it not for the help supplied by Humbert's prefatory 'Argument', the same device which he had used in *The Uncelestial City* and for the same purpose. The question of the relationship between the 'Argument' and the poem - which was written first?, and is the 'Argument' really a trustworthy guide to the poem? - matters perhaps less than the light they combine to shed on Humbert's deepest convictions at the time. But first, *Reverie* deserves to be examined for the themes it deals with and for the place it occupies in his *oeuvre* as well as in his development.

A reader even slightly acquainted with Humbert's writings will be immediately struck by the echoes and borrowings from earlier works. It recalls not only *Humoresque* but even the earlier *Old Man of Königsberg*, of which Humbert was only part-author. The theme of the 'Coda' in *Requiem* is rehearsed again here: 'everything - pain and joy, failure and triumph, weakness and strength - counting each other out in the cancellation whose other name is quiet.' The houses bear a distinct resemblance to the Mount Royd villas of his childhood. The Dancer is the unchanged flame of love, against which death is powerless. But, of course, first love carries its own death-warrant: jealousy and despair end the cycle. The capacity of love to triumph over itself is conveyed by transcending the limitations of time and space. Policeman, Gentleman in Evening Dress and The Satiric Poet, therefore, appear to traverse past, present and future. They too in various ways recreate some elements of the Crayfish story.

As early as Act I we are in familiar territory:

> . . . . . . what did I ask
> of love, the clown, that holds the tragic mask
> before his face to puzzle fools?

and a little later:

> . . . . "Since you choose to doubt
> and blew yourself love's starry candle out, . . ."

The soliloquy put in the mouth of the Bust of Darwin to argue that purposeless continuance of the race is the only reality - love is an accident - recalls the debates in *The Uncelestial City*. Here Humbert is in his best ironic mode, cudgelling

> . . . mid-Victorian clichés
> about the Origin of Species,
> what oft were thought (he dimly guessed)
> before but ne'er so ill-expressed.

Borrowings and reminiscences of early poems abound, for example of 'Nous n'irons plus au bois':

> I'll walk no more in your wood. Cut are the laurels
> and a harsh wind with fallen timber quarrels.

News broadcasts on the radio introduce, for the first time in Humbert's poetry, Hitler and his attacks on the Jews, followed by references to the League of Nations and the I.L.O. A French bulletin reports a speech by the former Minister of Labour, Paul Boncour, whom Humbert had known in Geneva. Humbert's attempt at French verse was more successful in its rhyme than in its scansion - he seems to have baulked at the rigorous discipline of syllabic versification - and it may have been with relief that he took advantage of a burst of atmospherics to introduce a reworked version of *TheRanciad* in which Cacophone displayed the future of the world in all its synthetic violence (a clear allusion to Huxley's *Brave New World*, H. G. Wells, Spengler, and others).

He even used the radio in order to have a jab, a little unfairly, at Alfred Austin:

> The gods are speaking - in the words of fate
> uttered by a prophetic Laureate
> long since. Now listen, if you dare and can,

to the unchanging epitaph of man.
"Along the wire the electric message came.
he is no better he is much the same."[13]

A careful reading, particularly of the 'Argument', powerfully suggests that this was, at least in intention, a synthesis embodying in one composition the present state of his convictions about poetry, philosophy and love.

Policeman finds a fountain playing in the centre of a house, the fountain representing 'the cool movement of verse . . . independent of all action and all dismay.' In the play, the first part of the poem which he read at the end of his Skemp lecture occurs here. The Satiric Poet is at war with himself: 'bitterness unequally counterpoised with vision. He pursues the better though he sees the worse.' (No prizes for identifying *this* character!) In the silence which follows the collapse of the wireless set, the Poet is drawn back

> from the Hell where he had gone not to find but to lose Eurydice. And since his quest is the opposite of that of Orpheus, the result is also the opposite. Cacophone changes imperceptibly into Euterpe - the other half of the nature of verse, which, like the first, is the projection of the poet's mind. . . He is forced to face his own past and his own heart.

The final lines of the 'Argument' resound not only with echoes of themes adumbrated in *The Uncelestial City*, but even more with the conclusion of the *Romantic and Unromantic Poetry* lecture:

> Each man has dominion over his own dream, if he will dream it true. The poet, like all men and all lovers, is the creator of his own world. . . Thus adjured [the Poet] settles down to write the prologue of the play as it should, and therefore must have been. He completes his seven sonnets, and as he reaches the beginning of the play the miracle occurs. All the shadow-play of the past is destroyed and Eurydice returns. The poet is left with the whole play to re-write and in the silence, where there is nothing left but his creative soul, the fountain-thought returns and rocks life in the brilliant crystal of its arms.

(At this point in the play the final lines of the Fountain poem are heard.)

> All is over. There is no play and Policeman is in the street again where he began. Since the play has been torn up nothing has happened, and he continues upon

> his beat having by mere continuity established the law
> and order of love upon their unshakeable foundation.

At this level, therefore, *Reverie of Policeman* appears to me to be a text of crucial importance in the assessment of Humbert's development as a poet, not so much for reasons of poetic skill or inspiration as for the recapitulation which it provides of virtually all of his work to date. But equally, if not more importantly, it goes a long way towards accounting for Humbert's attempts to cope with developments in his private life.

In this play/ballet, Humbert quite obviously played both character and author: The Satiric Poet is meant to represent at least an aspect of himself, and so may The Gentleman in Evening Dress have been too. A detail which puzzled me for a long time was why he chose to omit both definite and indefinite articles in all references to 'Policeman'. The conclusion I reached, that the unaccompanied noun was intended to be taken as a proper name, is supported by the first sentence of 'Argument': 'Policeman is chosen as the chorus and commentary of the ballet because there is essential humanity in the simplicity of law and order at the bottom of the ladder.' He might have added that Policeman is another name for our old friend the Constable from *Humoresque*, himself a throwback to the Constable of the pantomime harlequinade.

But more than that, *Reverie* could be said to be for the two male characters (who increasingly look like two sides of one person) a voyage of self-discovery, in which Policeman exercises the function of what our age would call the non-judgmental, non-intrusive, non-directive therapist or counsellor. The object and term of the journey is to learn to accept oneself and find wholeness once more: what an older tradition would have sought through sacramental absolution. The difference is that the latter was conditional on repentance and *metanoia* - 'conversio morum' - a total reversal of the direction of one's life, which the former conveniently by-passes, sometimes achieving its desired objective by a simple process of rationalisation. At a deeper level, therefore, of which Humbert may perhaps not have been entirely conscious, *Reverie of Policeman* may plausibly be explained as a commentary on and a rationalisation of his own tangled life at this time. The suggestion of day-dream, or musing by free association, inherent in the title-word, *Reverie*, tends to support the notion that this is a piece ultimately of self-justification, explaining past errors and confusions and allowing a new start - the poet writes a new play.

Humbert had claimed, when he first told Jessie in 1932 about his idea for *Reverie*, that it would be quite different from *The Publicist*, an earlier dramatic attempt (*see* above, Chapter 7, section (iv) and footnote 27), never published, let alone performed, as far as one can tell. The fact is, however, that *Reverie* owed more to *The Publicist* than he was prepared to admit.

The undated typescript of that name in Wadham College library describes it as 'A Play in Two Acts and One Interlude.' It was written in rhyming couplets and described the final stages in the life of the Publicist of the title, who had abandoned his youthful aspirations to poetry in favour of business and was periodically haunted by the Muse, Euterpe, who also stood for truth. The play was about his recognition of his betrayal of Euterpe and of his true self, which could be expiated only by his death.

The Publicist was shot through with echoes of *Humoresque*, Paul Arthur and *News of the Devil*, Mr. Justice Crayfish and *The Uncelestial City*. Some elements in it were cannibalised to make parts of *Reverie of Policeman*. Of particular interest is the transformation, in Act Two, of all the players into characters in a Harlequinade, with the Publicist playing Harlequin. It confirms the impression one has that what could be called the dramatic works - *Humoresque, News of the Devil, The Uncelestial City, Reverie of Policeman* - are all variations on the same theme; in a sense Humbert thus far had been forever writing the same play. But not entirely, for *Reverie of Policeman* marked to some extent a return to an earlier, fantastic stage in his writing. *The Uncelestial City* was realistic in a way that none of the others was, not even *News of the Devil*, with whose protagonist *The Publicist* had so much in common. Henceforward his dramatic or quasi-dramatic writings would be firmly fixed in the fantastic mode: *The Silent Knight* (which was his by adoption, though not in origin) and *X at Oberammergau*. And perhaps that is why to some extent they fail of credibility, where *The Uncelestial City*, by reason of its greater realism, does not.

Humbert's *George Moore*, first published in 1931 by Harold Shaylor, Gower Street, in a collector's edition, handsomely bound and boxed, and signed by the author, had been published in New York in 1932, and was now reissued in London, in the Modern Writers And Playwrights series of which Thomas Moult was the General Editor. In the Preface to this revised edition Humbert explained that Moult had asked him in 1930 to write the book. On Moore's death earlier in 1933 Humbert persuaded Thornton Butterworth, who had acquired the book from Shaylor's executors, to republish it. The dust-jacket described Humbert as 'himself a writer and poet of the first rank [who] deals with George Moore's works faithfully and in a spirit of sympathetic criticism.'

It is easy to see, from the Preface, why Moore might have been embarrassed by the monograph - he probably had a shrewd idea of what posterity would make of his work, and Humbert, so close to him, could not but be a fervent hagiographer, though an extraordinarily skilful and winning one. Humbert is his characteristic infuriating and captivating self - the ponderous and rather arch dialogue with the publisher contrasting sharply with such felicitous gems as 'clothed like uneasy propositions in Euclid', 'Austin Dobson in a moment of aberration'. One wonders what Moult made of the text when he got it. Perhaps he wondered himself what the readership would make of it, but decided its felicities were worth the risk. For all Humbert's high opinion of Moore's enduring qualities as a writer, it is doubtful whether today even the well-read could summon up many titles beyond *Esther Waters* and *The Brook Kerith*, let alone lay claim to a strong reading acquaintance.

A fourth publication that year was his Introduction to *The Life of Percy Bysshe Shelley as comprised in The Life of Shelley by Thomas Jefferson Hogg, The recollections of Shelley and Byron by Edward John Trelawney, Memoirs of Shelley by Thomas Love Peacock*. With such a title, it comes as no surprise that the work required two volumes.

It was probably in the latter part of this year that Humbert became head of the Employment and Training Department, where he remained until 1938. Senior and respected civil servants who were juniors at the time have paid just and generous tribute to the importance he attached to training, particularly of the administrative class of civil servants in the Ministry - that is, the grade of those who formed and influenced policy - and to the imaginative and energetic steps he took to ensure that it occurred.

The grade at which the administrative class entered the service in 1929, when he took over Establishments, was that of Assistant Principal, essentially a training grade, in which people did not expect to remain long. The administrative class was quite small, and within the Ministry of Labour (less hidebound than most in its recruitment and promotion policies) promotion was fairly rapid. Not all entrants came directly from university. Some, like Beryl Power and Paul Goldberg, were promoted from the executive class. Humbert was keen that people should enter the administrative class relatively young, and certainly before the age of fifty.

Sixty years later, one former Assistant Principal remembered the Ministry of Labour as a popular choice among candidates and difficult of entry. He bore out Richard Church's testimony that it attracted more people from unusual backgrounds than most other Whitehall departments. Most of all he vividly recalled Humbert's insistence that the administrative class should gain experience in the field, especially in the provinces. A new Assistant Principal would be sent out for six months to observe what went on in a region. He would do no one's work, simply watch and learn. He would stand behind the counter in a labour exchange and talk to the clerks about the problems they encountered, visit factories, sit in on industrial disputes and arbitration, and talk to regional managers. Humbert's staff were never left in any doubt that for him the quality of the service both at the highest level in Whitehall and at every employment exchange in the country was paramount. This particular junior recorded that in six months he had visited over a hundred factories in the Midlands and Tyneside, seen most if not all of the labour exchanges between Birmingham and Newcastle, and learnt more about practical government than ever he would have in an office in Whitehall.

He noted also the evidence of Humbert's popularity with the women staff. 'On the bureau of every chief woman officer in the exchanges there was a photograph of Humbert' - doubtless a slight exaggeration, for he had his critics even among the women. But tributes abound to Humbert's pioneering work in training, which made the Ministry the envy of other parts of the Civil Service and the model which they increasingly imitated.[14]

By the end of 1933, the scale of unemployment in certain areas and the special problems which it brought in its train led to the introduction of a regional policy, which initially set out to deal with the problems of four 'special areas': Durham, West Cumberland, South Wales, and south-west Scotland. To Humbert's responsibilities for the training of Ministry staff - essential in a department with so many out-stations - was now added that of overseeing the training institutions, particularly the Government Training Centres and the Instructional Centres. The training or re-training of skilled workers from one industry in the skills of another was the logical concomitant of geographical mobility: the transference of the unemployed from depressed regions would meet neither the economic needs of industry nor the social needs of the unemployed unless the latter were equipped with the skills required by the industries of the regions to which they were transferred.

Inevitably, the Ministry of Labour's premises and staff, other than at the Whitehall headquarters, were organized on a regional basis, under Regional Controllers whom Humbert called up to London once a month to keep him and one another constantly informed. Members of the Headquarters staff might be sent out to be Regional Controllers - they were paid about the same as Assistant Secretaries. One of his favourite sayings was: 'Regional Controllers are the eyes and ears of the department.' He listened to them and looked to them for fresh thinking. More often than not, matters in the regions needed prompt action. For this the staff of labour exchanges relied on Headquarters' Instructions, a manual of practice which Humbert was largely responsible for elaborating.

Other ministries such as Customs, Inland Revenue, Health, and the Home Office had out-stations and regional offices but nothing resembling the organisation and communication within the Ministry of Labour. Consequently, if Ministers wanted someone for a new and awkward job they tended to draft someone from the Ministry of Labour, whose training practices were eventually adopted by the other ministries.[15]

The only two of Humbert's letters from 1933 to have survived refer to his new responsibilities in this area. Emergency meetings of Training Centre Managers, and inspections of training centres took him on a long journey from London to Bristol, York and Edinburgh. On 6 October, just before setting off from London, he wrote to Jessie, who was in Oxford seeing Ann installed at Somerville for her first term as an undergraduate:

> I do realize how in some ways bitter a moment this is - and yet how great a moment of triumph. It is the culmination of years of devoted and unexampled work brilliantly rewarded. But when you see Ann actually taking to the water for which you have prepared her it is naturally a sharp pang. You say that you are returning to an empty world. I'll do my best to disprove that. . . Here is one great object achieved. Now for the next.

From York he wrote on 9 October: 'I had hoped as you know that you could come too' - and so visit relatives in Edinburgh - 'but I simply haven't the money this week.' He now had the additional burden of Ann's Oxford fees, but the hand-to-mouth economics which this bald statement reveals suggests that their financial situation was more parlous than ever. He added, however, that he would have to go up again about a month later for the Scottish Advisory Council: 'We can then go up together and give Uncle Willie warning in advance.' He briskly disposed of Jessie's anxieties about Ann - he seems to have had few himself: 'I'm glad that Ann has settled in. It must be a horrible wrench to leave her there. But I've no doubt that she'll be all right.'

IV

1934

The year began inauspiciously. Early in February Ann was ill - the letters do not refer to any operation - in a nursing home in Oxford, where Jessie had gone to be with her, but she appears to have recovered sufficiently by 20 February for Jessie to return to Artillery Mansions. A more serious threat came from the bank, which had returned Humbert's cheques unpaid, and threatened to cut off his credit. Humbert assured Jessie that it was all a mistake, arising from a mix-up over cheque books; cheques from publishers were coming in, and that if he could 'land the Insect Book (to be called "Subject to Beelzebub") on the Cresset Press we can breathe again.' This last sounds like *Stings and Wings*, published by Ivor Nicholson and Watson the following year - the poem dividing the two halves of the book was called 'To Beelzebub' and drew a parallel between the fallen archangel and the inhabitants of the winged insect world, which

> . . . . like you, remember,
> between the worm-casts and the venomed stings,
> when the sword falls, the agony of wings.

The letters optimistically go on to discuss plans for a dinner party for ten people ('that means about £8,') as well as the possibility of a week at the sea-side. He thought that Jessie's offer to raise £100 - one does not know how - would not be necessary, and he might persuade Leon [Lion] to buy one of his portraits. He sounded cautiously optimistic about his forthcoming interview with the bank manager.

But on 15 February he reported 'a pretty grim hour at the Bank yesterday.' The threat of having his securities, 'i.e. my Life Insurance Policy', called in was narrowly averted, and he eventually left, 'sufficiently encouraged about the state of my credit to wire you at lunch today to pay the first week at the Home', that is, the Oxford Nursing Home where Ann and Jessie had stayed. By 17 February he was reassuring her that 'we needn't look forward to a life of penury and pinching. After all, we have £1400 [presumably his salary] to spend in ten months which isn't too hopeless. And that even if nothing else comes our way either through your efforts or mine.'

And on the following day he returned to the theme. He referred to two bitter disappointments - 'the play and Geneva', the latter irretrievable. Albert Thomas had died suddenly in 1932, and been replaced by his deputy, Harold Butler. Sir Eric Drummond, who eventually obtained the Rome embassy in 1933, had been succeeded at the League of Nations by his deputy, the Frenchman, Avenol. But Humbert was hopeful that the play, entitled "Salvation Somehow", would still revive.[16] He was putting the finishing touches to 'the Methuen book' (presumably *Portraits By Inference*, published later that year) and did not doubt that 'with strict care we shall be able to get through, afford a holiday and even have a surplus on which to contemplate removal.'

These concerns were set against a background of debates on the Unemployment Bill then before Parliament, which he had to attend in order to brief his Minister, meetings of Divisional Controllers, meetings connected with Industrial Transference, for example with the Scottish Still Manufacturers 'who want to remove their works and their workpeople at the Government expense to Northamptonshire', and a dinner with the Association of Education Committees to discuss Juvenile Employment. The following week he would have to spend two days inspecting Training Centres in the London area, and two more the week after that at the centres in Norfolk and Warwickshire. 'This is because the Bill is making new provisions for Training and we must have certain additional information for the report stage.' And on top of all that he had a bad attack of tooth-ache which required the attentions of the dentist.

On 27 March he wrote from Newcastle-on-Tyne to describe the two exhausting but interesting days he had spent inspecting three training camps in Scotland, and two in the Newcastle area. The next day he was to return to the Scottish Borders to see two more camps before returning to London.

The biography of Sylvia Townsend Warner quotes his review of *Whether a Dove or Seagull* in *The Observer* of 8 April. The book was a collection of poems by Warner and her lover, Valentine Ackland, fifty-four by one, fifty-five by the other, but none of them individually attributed. Warner's biographer implies that Humbert, a keen admirer of Sylvia's poetry, was one of the 'few reviewers who got past the novelty of the presentation to discuss the poems themselves.' Most of the reviews concentrated on trying to identify the authorship of the various poems and to compare their quality. He was also unusual if not unique in guessing that Valentine was a woman, and in finding in the book 'a growing together - accidental perhaps in fact but not in essence - which gives a strange unity to the whole.' [17]

He may, of course, have known who Valentine Ackland was, even of the relationship between them - he knew more than one such couple (e.g. Radclyffe Hall, whom he had met in 1933, and Una Troubridge, and later Souline), just as he almost certainly knew some male homosexuals - or he may simply have had the sort of sensitivity, flair or 'nose' to sense the relationship without any previous knowledge.

He can hardly have finished writing the review when he fell ill with an ear infection. When the threat of a mastoid operation loomed, he called in Lord Horder, the society physician whom he had got to know through their mutual membership of the Omar Khayyam dining club. Horder immediately took complete charge of his case, giving the physician and surgeon strict instructions to do nothing without consulting him. The mastoid operation which Humbert feared (Jessie said that he had undergone one such as a child) was avoided: the trouble was an abscess in his middle ear, which was cleared up by a prick from the outer ear and fomentation. But it left him in a state of mental disturbance which Jessie attributed to his anxieties about money.

Easter Sunday fell on 1 April, a bitter irony, for with this illness, Jessie later said, all the troubles of their lives seemed to have reached a culminating point. The cheques which could not be honoured, the suspension of credit, her own allowance not paid since January, the discovery that the cheques which she had signed were drawn on her own small savings, the rent on their flat unpaid for so long that it was a wonder they had not been evicted, Ann's fees still to be paid - the catalogue of disaster seemed unending.[18] In desperation she telephoned their old saviour, Owen Smith, not knowing that the earlier debt had never been repaid. He rallied to their aid, and guaranteed a loan for them which not only paid their debts but allowed Humbert to go for a holiday when he was fit to travel and also enabled them to move to a flat in Mount Street later that year.

Humbert delivered the Oxford Zaharoff Lecture for 1934 on 'Ronsard and French Romantic Poetry' (it was published by Oxford in 1935). The publication of his translation of Ronsard, *Sonnets Pour Hélène* (Eyre and Spottiswoode), in the same year indicates that the two events were connected. In a lively and informative Preface, with familiar echoes of his views on the state of English taste in poetry, he made a good and persuasive case for Ronsard, not so much modifying his earlier doubts on the possibility of poetry at all in a language such as French, as underlining the deadly influence of Malherbe.[19]

Whether Humbert was always right in his intention to stick tightly to the original text (which he also claimed in his translation of Heine, but did not strongly follow) was and will be debated. Some odd phrases creep in here and there- 'tipple at your eyes', 'trunkèd elephant' (is there another kind?). But it was a remarkable achievement and for many whose command of French would not claim to be of the surest, the discovery of Ronsard which Humbert made possible for them must have been a rich and rewarding experience. It is impossible to do justice to the one hundred and forty-one translations in this volume - the one hundred and forty-second Sonnet is an untranslateable anagram on the name of Hélène de Surgères. Let part of one, perhaps the most famous, suffice to exemplify the empathy bridging the centuries between one poet and the other, his translator:

> Quand vous serez bien vieille, au soir, à la chandelle,
> Assise aupres du feu, devidant et filant,
>
> . . . .
>
> Vous serez au fouyer une vieille accroupie,
> Regrettant mon amour et vostre fier desdain.
> Vivez, si m'en croyez, n'attendez à demain;
> Cueillez dés aujourd'huy les roses de la vie.
>
> When you are old, at evening candle-lit
>   beside the fire bending to your wool,
>
> . . . .
>
> but you, a crone, will crouch beside the hearth
>   mourning my love and all your proud disdain.
> And since what comes tomorrow who can say?
> Live, pluck the roses of the world today.

At the end of April, when Humbert was sufficiently recovered to travel, he and Jessie went to Brighton and stayed a month at the Metropole. At the end of May or early in June, he went back to the office for a day, took more sick-leave and went to Eastbourne for a second month's convalescence. He did little but laze and read, but found himself extremely reluctant to begin writing, or even the reviewing which he had undertaken to do. During the week Jessie continued her studies at the Slade, did the housekeeping, and tried to restore what order she could to their affairs. She joined him for week-ends, and apparently did some painting while she was there: one of his letters mentions 'four first-rate water-colours.' Then, as the real holiday season approached and he returned to London, they received the timely offer of a cottage in Cornwall.

But Humbert suddenly decided that he simply had to go to France. 'I must hear French spoken,' he said, and suggested a villa in the south of France. Jessie gently pointed out that it was only by the greatest good fortune that he had had ten weeks at the coast. A cottage in Cornwall would give him another month or more of rest and recuperation. But Humbert was adamant that it had to be France.

Jessie therefore went to ask Lord Horder if Humbert's health really required a French holiday. He seemed to think that Humbert should be judge of that, and suggested that Humbert should go alone. Jessie was understandably concerned. She was tired, Ann had been ill and was not yet really fit, there was the removal planned for September or October, and even a holiday in France for Humbert alone would seriously strain their finances. But Horder simply said that Humbert was his patient, they were not. Jessie said that if he really thought it was necessary for Humbert, it would somehow be managed.[20]

Humbert was surprised when she suggested that he go alone, but produced a cheque for £60 or £70 from the *English Review* and said that that would doubtless help. It ought really to have gone straight into their bank but Jessie generously let him have his holiday, in the hope that he would come back restored, and contented in mind, which would be to the benefit of them all.

And so at the beginning of August he went off to the Auberge de la Colombe d'Or, at St. Paul, about four miles from Vence in the Alpes Maritimes, which had been recommended by his friend Cotton Minchin. An undated page headed 'Directions for Correspondence', found among the letters for 1934, instructed Jessie to tell E. V. Rieu, at Methuen's, that his illness was much worse and more prolonged than expected, that he was rapidly convalescing, had written one hundred and forty pages and expected to finish one hundred and eighty by the end of the week, of which a hundred and twenty-five would be delivered in a fortnight [presumably the typescript]. Alternative titles were suggested - 'The White Trousers of Mr. A. B.' or 'Ghosts at No. 6', both of which were eventually used as chapter headings in the book which appeared later that year as *Portraits By Inference*.

The remaining letters for 1934 were all written during this convalescence, between 6 August and 2 October. At first he spent his time at St. Paul much as he had done at Eastbourne, rising late, taking gentle walks, eating and retiring early, and writing nothing more taxing than these letters. As the heat increased he began to have doubts about the suitability of the small hotel with its 'unpleasantly noticeable sanitation', and thought he would investigate the possibilities of something bigger on the coast or up in the mountains. He also felt the onset of an urge to write, perhaps a play, in addition to 'the B.B.C. prologue'. This last was a reference to his contribution to a series of radio programmes called *The Pilgrim's Way*, in which a combination of music and verse would 'illustrate the progress of man - the pilgrim of the world - through the varying moods, which are the milestones on the path from the cradle to the grave.' The original conception, he said, came from Mr. Iremonger, the Director of Religious Broadcasting of the B.B.C. The programmes were broadcast over a period of two years, first at monthly, later at bi-monthly intervals.[21]

It seemed that as his vitality returned he became bored with the hotel at St. Paul, and with the chattering second-rate painters who flocked there. He wrote on 21 August that he proposed to go up to Briançon in the mountains on the Italian frontier. On 25 August he announced that he was now installed in the Grand Hotel there (alt. 1326m), which was better in every way than the 'Colombe d'Or' at St. Paul, which now apparently had suffered not only from a blight of painters but also a 'colony of imbecile American dancers - like things out of Sinclair Lewis', and nightly invasions of the terrace of the hotel by the great and the grand who came to dine there. Among these, he revealed on 31 August, had been Winston Churchill who had come up one night with Castlerose. 'I hid on the lower terrace because I still felt too bothered to cope with him.'[22] And finally the Minchins, who had recommended the hotel and took him out in their car, 'were the last word in benevolent boredom.' One of the merits of Briançon was the absence of English people.

Since arriving in Briançon he had begun walking once more, but only along broad paths through pine-woods or over mountain roads, avoiding all climbing, and he proposed 'to begin at once a little travel-book, like "Portraits by Inference"'. Jessie must have been greatly reassured to read that he had 'begun to think of a new book, poems, and a proper life of work with a proper house.' She had been negotiating for one in Clarges Street, although that eventually fell through, but she eventually found another Mayfair flat, 128 Mount Street, into which they moved later that year.

He commented in one letter on the curious contradiction of Briançon, which was both garrison town and centre for the cure of consumptives: 'here all the skill of all the doctors is used to restore life and half a mile below are the huge barracks designed to ensure death!' His letters begin once more to give Jessie the first sight of the poems he was beginning to write. One staggering surprise he had on an otherwise dull day-trip by bus to Grenoble over the Col de Lauteret - the weather cheated his hope of seeing the massif of Mont Blanc a hundred and twenty miles away - was the sight of the village of Rioupéroux. 'I couldn't see the mountains but I could hear the roaring Romanche river . . . and could with aching clarity remember the day at Oxford when Flecker read me the poem:

> High and solemn mountains
> Guard Rioupéroux
> Small untidy village

Where the river drives a mill!'

As soon as he reached Grenoble he wrote the poem which began

It was raining, Flecker, in dark Rioupéroux.
All Grésivaudan's vale was hidden with cloud.
But, as I passed beside the river, you
stood at my shoulder, as though the mist allowed
your gentle ghost to walk...

He admitted that he was not happy with the ending:

.... But in Rioupéroux
youth walks with love for ever because of you.

and changed it to:

who looks for love and youth finds only you.

He said that he had spent the night in Grenoble and gone back next day to find Rioupéroux in brilliant sunshine, and therefore he intended to write a second sonnet. In the nine six-line stanzas which this eventually became, he conjured up their undergraduate conversation in a swirling, tumbling, deceptively loose yet fundamentally regular rhythm that captured the inexorable rush of the waters of the Romanche. Both poems were eventually published in *Out of Great Tribulation* in 1939.

From time to time he suggested to Ann the names of writers whom she might approach as possible speakers for the English Club at Oxford of which she had become secretary: Drinkwater, P. G. Wodehouse, St. John Irvine and G. B. Stern. Some he approached himself on her behalf. One letter mentions a reply from T. S. Eliot 'which shows that he means business.' He suggested C. Day-Lewis - 'one of the fashionable group of new poets' - , Randolph Churchill, Daphne du Maurier, and Lilian Bayliss, and offered to write to them too.

He had had the idea for some time, probably ever since their holiday in Germany in 1930, of a long poem called 'X at Oberammergau.' He returned to it now: 'You remember that I projected the idea of Christ Himself coming to play the part and being crucified? I've about 100 lines, beginning with Mt. Kofel waiting for the return of Wotan and am now going on to the talks about the play in the village.' He enclosed the second of two poems about Kofel, entitled 'Germany and France', in which the mountains speak to each other:

Prorel said to La Meije,
'If they murder, what is men's wage?'

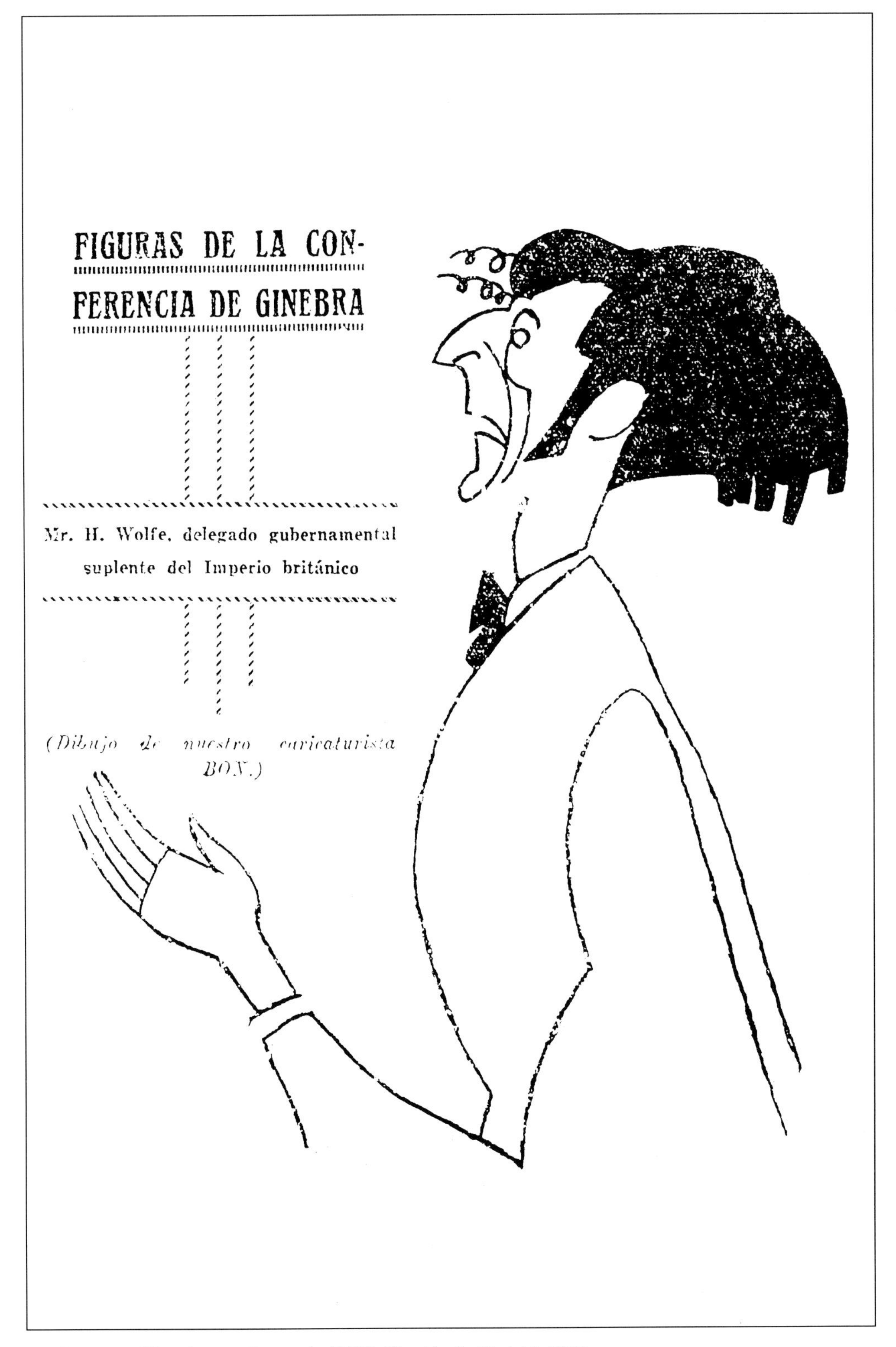

FIGURAS DE LA CON-
FERENCIA DE GINEBRA
Mr. H. Wolfe, delegado gubernamental
suplente del Imperio británico
(Dibujo de nuestro caricaturista
BON.)

13. Cartoon of Humbert at Geneva by BON, Heraldo de Madrid, 1925

Lazar
1927
Humbert Wolfe
Premier Secrétaire adjoint au
Ministère du Travail Empire Britannique

14. Sketch of Humbert at ILO Geneva, by Oscar Lazar, 1927

15. Humbert and Jessie on holiday at Trouville in 1932

16. Portrait of Pamela Frankau c.1940

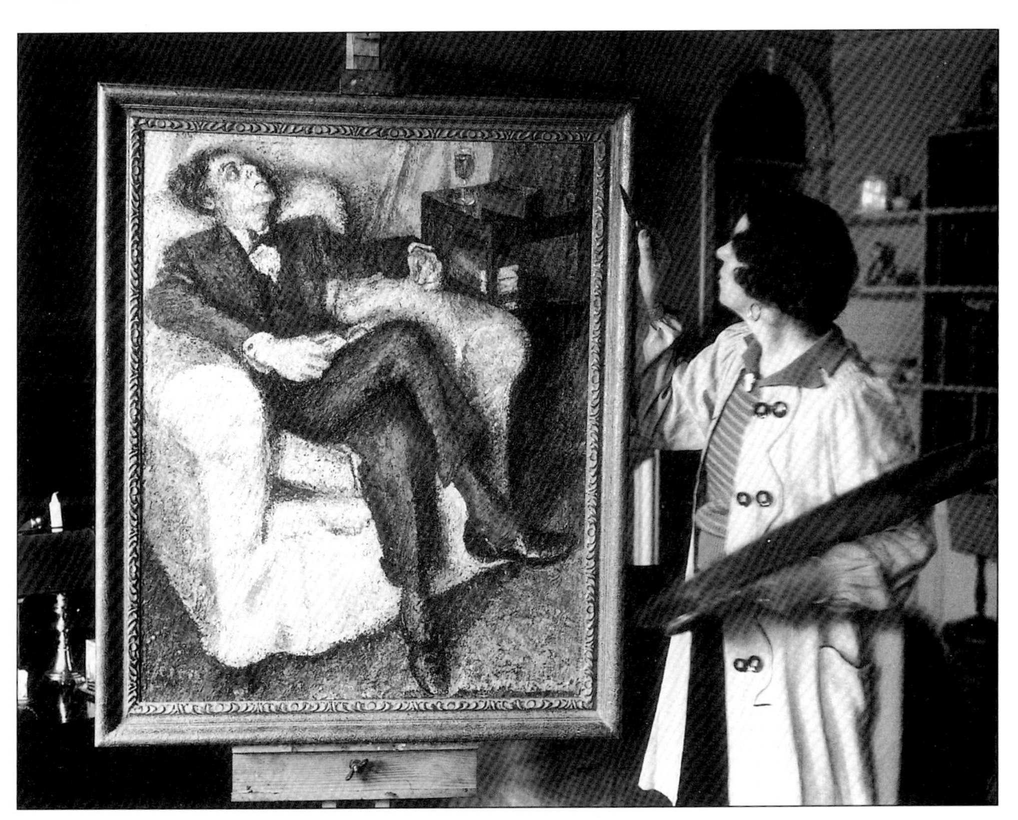

17. Jessie and her portrait of Humbert asleep, in their Mount Street flat, 1935

18. Candidates for the Poet Laureateship: Evening Standard cartoon by Low, 1931

La Meije said to Prorel,
'Their self-created Hell.'
Croix de Toulouse said to Mélezin,
'But to conquer is to be man.'
Mélezin said to Croix de Toulouse,
'Men have only what they refuse.'
Kofel said to the mountains of France,
'Glory rewards romance.'
The mountains of France said to Kofel,
'Offal to offal.'

The poem, unaltered, formed the third part of the PROEM of *X at Oberammergau*, published the following year. His writings from this time onwards, and indeed from 1933 or earlier, unmistakably identify the threat which Nazism posed not only to the Jews and to peace, but to all of the values of the Christian West.

On 22 September he raised the question of his return to England. He really wanted to stay longer at Briançon, not least because *X at Oberammergau* was coming on well - 'it is a mixture of the manner of "Requiem" and "News of the Devil." On the other hand I don't think that the Office would much like another week and I shall run out of money in a week's time.'

According to a former member of the Ministry staff, then in the Establishments Department, Humbert had been informed that when his six months sick leave was up (on 27 September) he would automatically go on to half-pay. 'He was back immediately!'[23] Be that as it may, he stayed another week (his thanks to Jessie, expressed in the next letter, suggest that she found the extra money for him), going up to view the glacier of La Meije at Le Lautaret on 1 October. On 2 October he announced that he would be back in London on 7 October. He had written over a thousand lines of the new poem and thought he might complete it before he left. 'I believe in my heart it is the best thing that I have done.' He said that he had never been so well for years and 'I think you will agree that the holiday has worked wonders.'

When he got back to London they moved into 128 Mount Street, which Jessie always remembered with great affection as a charming and comfortable flat in which she felt happy and safe. It had a pretty little staircase and a good north light for Jessie's painting, and from the small dining room that overlooked Farm Street, a view across the rooftops to the Houses of Parliament, Westminster Cathedral and, in the distance, the Surrey hills.

But the heart of the house was the library. It had always been the principal room in their house, ever since the first small room in Battersea. It had moved with them, accumulating books and shelves on the way, and had grown until the collection now surrounded completely the two front rooms, which were separated by a sliding door, the stubs of dividing wall into which it disappeared making deep bays lined on both sides with books. The smaller half of the room, which Jessie used as a studio, had the additional charm of a corner of sloping ceiling, formed by part of the steep gable which contained the whole of their maisonette.

Jessie found great pleasure in painting Humbert in the midst of his books -

> Rows and rows and rows of books
> Gave me many coloured looks -

from Victorian sub-fusc to sprightly modern; from the white-backed set of Eden Philpotts, the emerald green of Virginia Woolf, the sombre Pater and the dark crimson of Jane Austen, to the rainbow of Firbank, the woodland green of Trollope and the discreet dark blue of the Lady Murasaki. Special editions were in a glass case - the George Moores, the volumes of the Golden Cockerel and Nonesuch presses, glittering boxed limited editions and the dark, gold-tooled leather of the Aldine Poets from A.A.B's library.

He never stopped arranging them, she said. He would suddenly put down whatever he was reading, get up from his chair, walk over to the shelves and without hesitation remove a book from one shelf to another. Sometimes he would spend a whole evening in this way. If Jessie had taken a book from the shelves to read, and gone out of the room, leaving it lying ready to take up again, on her return it would be back in its place on the shelf. The illustration showing Jessie with her portrait of Humbert gives just a hint of the elegant charm of the room.

Portraits By Inference duly came out in the autumn, published by Methuen. At first sight it appeared to be simply a series of reflections on people and events whose significance, it was implied, might well extend beyond their connection with him. Arranged more or less in chronological order, these sketches covered the period beginning with the Canning Club at Oxford in 1906 or 1907, and ending in the early 1930s. In between, the reader met Flecker at Oxford, the New English Art Club in the London of 1908, Sir Alfred Bateman and Paris in 1910, Sir Henry Irving, the Salamans and their guests in Porlock, Balfour and the ghosts of No. 6, Whitehall Gardens, Mrs. Barton and her guests at the Villa Lammermoor, Arnold Bennett, George Moore, and finally Albert Thomas and Arthur Fontaine at the Stockholm Conference of the I.L.O.

In the absence of any clear evidence from Humbert himself, it is interesting to speculate on his motives for writing this book. Was it an exercise in nostalgia, an oblique piece of autobiography, or an attempt to compensate for his sense of never quite having made it to the ranks of the great and the good? While emulating the 19th century gossips, he remains quintessentially Humbertian in acting the part of the humble (but sardonic) participant-observer. In some lights he bears an uncanny resemblance to Prufrock: 'I am not Hamlet nor was meant to be; /Am an attendant lord . . .' The humility is not entirely convincing, for the spotlight is unerringly trained upon the wings as much as on the centre of the stage

The collection is vastly entertaining. His cricket-lore is a trifle shaky: Spooner was not a demon bowler, but a classical batsman - he probably meant Spofforth. But every chapter is a densely packed canvas, reminiscent of the pictures one used to see in periodicals like *The Illustrated London News*, where every conceivable participant and even those with merely walking-on parts were cunningly included in what appeared to be the recreation of a real historical event. It was thanks to this device that some, at any rate, of Humbert's heroes and villains received a measure of their deserts, although the villains on the whole got off very lightly.

When his emotions are fully engaged he writes with great precision and economy, for example on the Irving performance at Bradford, and the bathetic fall is just right. He is tantalisingly oblique on Balfour, but at least leaves one with a wish for more on the subject, indeed on the whole topic of the conduct of the 1914 - 1918 war. Is this the incorrigible Humbert, constitutionally unable to commit himself to a major theme, or the Civil Servant seized with professional discretion? With so much already said, this sudden access of reticence is baffling.

As part of the three-tier system of unemployment relief with which the Government aimed to replace the Poor Law, the Unemployment Assistance Board, originally planned for 1933, was set up in June 1934, with Betterton, now Lord Rushcliffe, as its part-time chairman at a salary equal to that of the Prime Minister. Humbert's fellow Assistant Secretary, Wilfrid Eady, who had been Secretary of the Industrial Transference Board in 1928 and subsequently in charge of Transitional Payments, became Secretary of the U.A.B., providing the perfect opening for a vintage Humbert witticism. The U.A.B., he said, was created '"to provide for the poor and Eady," neatly capped and very much *ad hominem* by T. W. Phillips with "also to keep the Wolfe from the door."'[24]

V

1935

In his Introduction to the *Life of Shelley* (1933, J. M. Dent), Humbert stressed the need to paint a truthful portrait of the hero, without erasing the lines on the forehead:

> 'A good biographer and a true man of letters will not deliver himself to indiscriminate adulation . . . It is the biographer's duty never to lose the man in his deeds,

> and never to gloss over actions which, though discreditable, are still wrinkles that gave the brow its character.'

It is important to bear his admonition in mind when considering the juicy though minor scandal which set the London literary scene buzzing with excitement early in 1935. Despite adverse reviewers and critics Humbert had continued to enjoy considerable public esteem. He was invited to be the first President of the Society of Civil Service Authors which was founded in 1935. At the beginning of February the organisers of the Bath Festival of Contemporary Arts asked for one of his manuscripts for their exhibition; he sent them *Portraits By Inference.*[25]

But all through that winter a time-bomb had been ticking away and now it exploded. In that same month of February there appeared in *Nash's Pall Mall Magazine* a long short story, more like a short novel, of some 20,000 words by Rebecca West, entitled *The Addict.* Sub-titled 'Portrait of a man - his loves, his labours and his lies . . .', it depicted a bank employee poet, addicted to women, who deceives not only his good, simple wife but all of his girl-friends too, and concocts for the purpose the fiction of a spendthrift, jealous and violent wife who will not divorce him. He eventually meets his nemesis, to the evident satisfaction of the author.

Pamela Frankau, whom Humbert had met in 1931, had fallen in love with him and he with her. In 1932 he gave her a signed copy of a photograph of Will Rothenstein's portrait of him, inscribed "After a year, Pam from Humbert, 31 August '32." For several years Pamela had been very much the protégée - part awed disciple, part young friend - of Rebecca West, and a useful companion for Rebecca's son, Anthony. They spent holidays together in the south of France - Victoria Glendinning's Life of Rebecca has photographs of them on the rocks at Agay - but when Rebecca discovered Pamela's deep attachment to this man old enough to be her father, married, about whom all manner of stories circulated in the literary world, her deep disapproval was compounded with hurt pride and jealousy.

Her habit in such situations was to relieve her seething emotions in long, furious letters. This time she seems to have sought release by means of a short story. It was without any doubt an attack on Humbert (the 'Addict' of the title) as a punishment for having 'stolen' Pamela. I do not know if Rebecca West was in love with Pamela but there was certainly, as Diana Raymond (Pamela's cousin and biographer) said, 'an emotion compounded of jealousy and the outraged pride of the master who sees his star pupil evade his sphere of influence, and take a massively wrong turning.' It was also intended to punish Pamela for her betrayal. But the portrayal of Pamela as a silly masochistic child was not the real point of the story. Rebecca's chief target was Humbert, who was easily identifiable as the bank employee (a Civil Servant in the first draft) and poet, Claude Cambray. Rebecca thought that she was safe from a libel action - he was too vulnerable to scandal as a senior Civil Servant - but none of his friends and colleagues could fail to recognise him in the portrait.

Although she had shown the story to others, Rebecca waited until just before publication before telling Pamela, who was in any case bound to find out within a few days. To Pamela she maintained that the story was meant to be funny, and that Humbert would see it as such. Romancing, the main theme of the story, was part of his stock-in-trade. She quoted the example of one of the addict's favourite fabrications: how his absent-mindedness had led to the tragic death of one of his children, whereas in fact his family were all alive and in the best of health. When Pamela told her of the death of Humbert's two babies, one of his cruellest memories, Rebecca was devastated. She swore she never knew, but it was too late to change the story now, a matter of days before publication. She asked Pamela to show Humbert the piece, but Pamela said that would not be necessary: his 'friends' could be relied upon to perform that service. And, as Diana Raymond told me, 'It certainly gave rise to a small literary explosion', with all the accompanying *schadenfreude* in which the occupants of that enclosed world so eagerly revelled.

Humbert had no shortage of female admirers: Viola Garvin certainly was very fond of him - Pamela later teased him about her - and she was widely believed to be in love with him, though how far her feelings were reciprocated is impossible to say. He seemed to have been close to Dame Rachel Crowdy, the Chief of Social Questions at the League of Nations, but I have found no evidence of more than that save for hearsay reports. He was given to sending poems to ladies, but as often as not it was simply his way of saying 'thank you' for their kindness to him (Lady Maufe bequeathed to Wadham College several little poems written to thank her for dinner), or to make amends for some gaffe (e.g. erasing G. B. Stern's memo pad).

Part of the trouble was his undoubted appetite for admiration, even adulation. Some of these admiring friends, the Maughams, for instance, were much of an age with Pamela, and since she was young, he wanted to like and be liked by those of her age group. Robin Maugham's sometime fiancée, Gill Dearmer, said that at fifty years of age Humbert appeared to her and her friends as an old man, as he did to Pamela's friend, the actress Margaretta Scott. They rather wondered at his zest for the physical games they played at Tye House, the Maughams' country house near Heathfield, and recalled his near collapse from exhaustion on one such occasion. He was very attached to Robin's sister, Kate Mary Bruce. She was equally very fond of him and according to Diana Raymond, 'was always looked on as the only real rival to Pam in Humbert's wide affections.'

But his relationship with Pamela was different. Furthermore, it involved serious and cruel deception of Jessie. It may well be that by the time he realized how deeply involved he was it was too late to extricate himself without jeopardizing his relationship with both Jessie and Pamela.

Like many men, he wanted to have his cake and eat it, and provided that he could keep Jessie in ignorance, if not of Pamela's existence, at least of her place in his affections, he might just avoid any serious unpleasantness. I do not know what Pamela hoped for at this stage in their relationship but he, at any rate, did not at that time, if indeed he ever did, actively seek to abandon Jessie and his domestic responsibilities in order to set up house with Pamela. But by 1935 their liaison was sufficiently widely known for Rebecca's story to be sure of an appreciative readership.

The characters in *The Addict* were, as they were intended to be, easily recognisable. 'Claude Cambray', the 'addict', was of course Humbert. 'Agatha Marley' was clearly Pamela: when the latter went to see Rebecca in a Nursing Home after the story burst, she announced herself as Agatha Marley. 'Valerie' was Viola Garvin (who suffered from the aftermath of polio), and 'Sylvia Spain' was Kate Mary Bruce, wife of Bobby Bruce who appeared as Sylvia's husband, Cecil Spain.

The portrayal of Humbert's appearance and character was clever, though savage, and Claude Cambray's excuses for not including his wife in his social life, as well as for not abandoning her, matched a lot of what is known through, for example, Jessie's unpublished papers. The same is true for the details of his delicate digestion and occasional ill-health. The story was also in some respects prophetic - e.g. Cecil Spain's suggestions about a separation; at the least it anticipated events in a remarkable way.

Pamela said later, 'She (Rebecca) represented Humbert as dirty, unpopular, stingy, greedy, and wholly without talent: a liar, a sponger, a *noceur* somewhat handicapped by impotence, a painstaking deceiver of his good simple wife and all his girl friends . . . one of whom was me.' The suggestion of impotence is both curious and revealing. Diana Raymond observed that Claude's affairs 'somewhat improbably stop short of consummation' but the suggestion has been made elsewhere that Humbert was less of a 'stud' than has been thought - that, with the exception of Pamela, his 'affairs' were more in the nature of romantic attachments. Others, however, are quite sure that they were - and were widely known to be - full-blown liaisons. In the end, however, Humbert's observations on Shelley apply here. Whether, like Shelley, he was 'hopelesssly irregular in matters of sex, or habitually maligned by interested (and sometimes disinterested) gossips and scribblers . . . is of importance only to the prurient.'

Diana Raymond found Rebecca's story 'unsatisfactory as a whole; Rebecca's prejudices were working overtime, and this always detracts from any literary work. And I had the feeling that it was meant to be funnier than it was - or perhaps the virulence of Rebecca's feelings about Humbert prevented the jokes - or the satires - from making their mark.' She concluded: 'I don't think Rebecca knew Humbert well: certainly she didn't know . . . about the death of his two babies.'

Although *The Addict* was undeniably repetitive and overlong, its author did not seem able to sustain the savagery of the initial onslaught on

Claude/Humbert's character. Gradually, as the story unfolds, the compulsion of the artist to write as good a story as she could somehow softens the attack, or makes her forget her initial purpose, and although Claude/Humbert is finally shown to be a weak, pathetic, rather ridiculous figure, he is entirely credible and the bathetic ending is artistically perfect. The reader recognises a type and says, 'Yes, I have known characters like that, people who seem to spend their lives setting traps for themselves and expend all their energies trying to avoid falling into them.'

When Humbert heard about the story from Pamela, he sat, she said, like a stunned child. No doubt he was wounded as much by the wide circulation the story immediately received as by its inherent hurtfulness. But he appeared to get over the episode fairly quickly, more (Pamela thought) from absent-mindedness than from Christian charity. He said himself that his faculty for forgetting everything but that which was immediately in front of him had begun to develop by the time he was nine years of age (*see* earlier, Chapter 1). He may also have judged that his best defence was an olympian disregard for the insult: if it was seen to be unworthy of powder and shot it might appear to have fallen wide of the mark.

It was ten years before Pamela forgave Rebecca, and in between wrote a novel in which her erstwhile mentor was maliciously portrayed. Humbert commendably persuaded her to tone down the more savage bits. Later still Rebecca's son, Anthony, also wrote a cruel satire on his mother. Neither of these books had any lasting success, nor does *The Addict* appear in any collection of Rebecca's works. Diana Raymond wisely said of them all: 'Hatred, it seems, does something to poison the root of a work; in the end it withers.' Ultimately, as Pamela observed, the only one to come out well from it was Humbert.[26] But perhaps the most curious feature of the whole affair is that news of the story seems never to have reached Jessie who remained totally unaware of the furore surrounding her husband.

Kate Mary Bruce and her husband lived at 79 Cadogan Square, where they entertained many literary people. His friendship with them brought Humbert in contact with her sisters, Diana (Marr-Johnson) and Honor (Earl), her brother Robin, and their mother, who lived close by at 73 Cadogan Square. Their father was Lord Maugham, Lord Chancellor until his resignation in 1939 or 1940. Somerset Maugham was their uncle; he and their father were at odds. Lady Maugham was very fond of Humbert - her letters to Robin showed that she liked Humbert's company - but no evidence has survived to suggest that he had any dealings, friendly or otherwise, with Lord Maugham. A contemporary witness said that 'Aunt Nelly' (Lady Maugham) would invite Humbert to her parties but not Pamela, because of the peculiar conventions of the time. A man, if invited to a dance, could take a girl, but a girl could not take a man.

Robin Maugham met Humbert and Pamela about the time that he went up to Trinity Hall, Cambridge in 1934. In his autobiography he wrote affectionately of them both, of Humbert's visits to Tye House, his skill with crosswords and his wit. When war threatened in 1938 he discussed with Humbert the possibility of some sort of national service work. In 1939 Robin and Pamela were members of the editorial board of a magazine called *Spark* which never appeared because of the outbreak of war.[27] He signed his letters 'Kardomah' and they remained on affectionate terms until her death.

It was probably at the beginning of 1935 that Gill Dearmer met Pamela and Humbert at a party, possibly given by G. B. Stern in her rooms in Albany. She was just seventeen in January and had not long known Robin Maugham, to whom she became half-engaged for a time. She was the daughter of Percy Dearmer, Canon of Westminster Abbey, best remembered for his hymns and for his advanced theological views - the David Jenkins of his day, she later said. Humbert used to make her cross by introducing her as 'the daughter of a Canon of Westminster who doesn't believe in God', and by making fun of her godmother, who was much in favour of the ordination of women. She said that her father wrecked his career by supporting her stand.

Humbert seemed to her at the time 'terribly old', with his grizzled hair and his head which in some ways resembled her father's, but she remembered above all his 'immense kindness to us young ones - he was interested in what we were up to.' 'When Robin went to Mexico after Somerset had seduced him, Humbert tried to reassure me, saying that "he's being very naughty just now but I'm sure he'll come back."' She was depressed by this but thought later that Humbert was gently warning her what to expect and thus letting her down lightly. She was heart and soul in love with Robin for three years and in her unhappiness at his desertion Humbert and Pamela were a great comfort.

One day she was telling Humbert that at a dinner-party at the Maughams she had met Harold Nicolson. Humbert's comment - 'I wish he had been eaten by an elephant' - surprised her. She assumed that he was referring to Nicolson's anti-semitism, but there may have been also some residual bitterness at Nicolson's dismissive review of *The Uncelestial City*. For all their fondness for Humbert, the Maugham family, too, were unthinkingly anti-semitic in their speech. No doubt Humbert had all this in mind when he wrote in *Now A Stranger* about the latent anti-semitism in Britain.[28]

On 29 March Humbert and Jessie celebrated twenty-five years of marriage. Jessie later recalled the toast he had given: 'These have been good years. Here's to the next twenty-five.' On 30 May Pamela was introduced for the first time to their home. Jessie remembered her first sight of this 'sleek-haired, black-eyed young woman with a husky voice' whom Humbert had invited to make up the numbers for a little dinner party. Pamela was a strikingly good-looking young woman. Gill Dearmer reported that 'You could see why people found her attractive - a sort of

Nefertiti type.' Rebecca West described Pamela as 'resembling Disney's Bambi.' It was not long before Pamela was sitting to Jessie for her portrait.

The long poem *X at Oberammergau*, begun the previous September in Briançon, was published in the spring or early summer by Methuen, and dedicated to 'Tommy, Lord Horder.' It ingeniously used the Passion Play to wage a fierce but controlled attack on Nazism, an onslaught so outspoken for its time that Methuen's prudent disclaimer that the poem was in any way 'a criticism of a political system or of any person connected with that system' will hardly have convinced a single reader.

Much more, however, than a simple Philippic, the poem works out the age-old conflict between Christianity and Paganism in a veritable re-enactment of the Passion. The actor who should have played Christ falls ill and a stranger - X, the unknown quantity - found wandering in the snow takes his place. The Nazi State Commissioner, aptly named 'Kanalgeruch' (sewer- or gutter-stench), scents a Jew in the substitute actor who, however, produces a remarkable effect on many in the little Bavarian community. Mary the Mother, Mary Magdalen and the disciple John accept the challenge of the stranger, others do not. The players gradually become merged in the parts they play; a mesh of conspiracy is rapidly woven about X; his fellow-actors, led by Judas, enter into the plot against him, and the drama moves inexorably to its inevitable conclusion, in Humbert's poem skilfully inferred rather than directly portrayed.

Most of the reviewers found the poem deeply impressive, both for its theme and for Humbert's treatment of it. They saw that it was not just another bitter satire, although there was satire in it, for example in the portrait of Herr Hans Kanalgeruch:

> Gangster by choice, storm-trooper, and then putscher,
> his civic occupation as pork-butcher,
> made it seem more than probable that he might
> have been designed as Nature's Anti-Semite
> by God and by His first pan-German Bishop
> to visit Oberammergau and dish up
> a Passion-Play purged of the ugly libel
> that the Jews had some connection with the Bible.

There is nobility, pathos, great lyrical beauty - some of the lyrical parts were judged to be the best of their kind that he had done:

> This is another love that has no need
>   to give or take, to slumber or to waken.
> It has not motion yet in its intimate speed
>   the source of life itself is overtaken,
>   and it is lavish
> with all the leisurely passion time cannot ravish.

The dramatic and narrative parts were equally effective and vivid: the scene between the village women and the village idiot a model of fine, indirect and concentrated writing. The dialogue in couplets was handled with great ease and freedom, as for example in the discussion between the Procurator, Peter, Judas and Kanalgeruch in the House of Pontius Pilate. The audience of tourists of different nationalities have a little too much of stereotypical caricatures - film-Americans, pseudo-intellectual Frenchmen, simplistic Germans, slightly snooty English - for their final reaction to X ('He gets me where I live . . . Almost mine eyelids burn') to be entirely convincing. If it was accurate 1930-speak, all one can say is that nothing dates so quickly as the contemporary. Otherwise it looks very much like Humbert simply showing off.

The ending, expressing the triumph of the Resurrection, re-echoes the 'Go down to death' with which the second part of the poem ended:

> He has gone down to death by a steep longer
> than any after him shall face. 'Tis pathless,
>
> . . . .
>
> and while the dead with pitiful hands implore him,
> and the devil mocks, 'Behold the crucified!'
> immutable
> by his mere presence he makes a heaven of hell.
> He has gone down to death. Cease, women, your sorrow.
> There is nothing for you to lament and naught to cry on.
> He has taken death under his arm like an arrow
> whose barb is broken. Lift up your gates, O Zion. . . .

One interesting response to the poem was that of Gilbert Murray, Regius Professor of Greek at Oxford and an agnostic, but not unsympathetic to religious experiences outside his personal belief. Writing to Humbert in May about a quite different matter, he went out of his way to list all the things he had enjoyed both in the technical accomplishment of the verse and the emotive power of the story.[29]

Of all Humbert's religious poems this was the most concentrated in its subject: the spiritual conflict between good and evil, hatred and love, and the power of the person of Jesus to reach out and touch the human heart in a way that no religion of blood and race could ever hope to do. But by thus limiting his field - and that is not meant as a criticism - he also reveals, it seems to me, the limitations of his own religious position. The lovely tailpiece refutes the agnostic theology of the PROEM to Part II, but is still hesitant of accepting the full implications of the Redemption. Perhaps this is what H. W. Garrod had in mind when he suggested in 1927 that when Humbert finally found his subject-matter and himself, 'I should not be surprised if the two things proved one and the same; nor, yet again, if Mr. Wolfe one day merged both in the Catholic Church.'

Well, as we know, he did not take that step, but had he lived he might have done, as Jessie, Ann and eventually Pamela Frankau all did.

Humbert's increasing identification with the persecuted Jews in Germany was noted by J. B. Priestley, as has been mentioned already (*see* Chapter I). Satire was the only way of fighting back that he knew; perhaps, in view of his official position, the only way available to him. At some time in the mid-thirties he produced a pastiche of *Der Struwelpeter*, in which the Nazis in general, and their chief representatives in particular, along with their favourite dogmas, were pilloried in verse and cartoon. The book was called the *Truffle Eater*, and its author disguised under the *nom de guerre* of Oistros (Greek for a gadfly). It does not figure in the list of his published works and it may be that he preferred not to broadcast his authorship, but his daughter, who gave me my copy of it, was in no doubt as to its origin.

A work more closely related to *ABC of the Theatre* and *Lampoons* was *Stings & Wings* (1935), illustrated by A. Savory, and published by Ivor Nicholson and Watson. It was a collection of amusing, cautionary and at times semi-philosophising verses inspired by different varieties of insect. The Stings outnumbered the Wings by nearly three to one, and on the whole were rather more successful verses, gloriously playful, but very skilfully varied. There were generous helpings of satire -

> Ladybird, ladybird, fly away home!
> Athens is burning, the Goth is in Rome,
> Russia's gone Bolshevik, Germany's Nazi,
> de Valera in Ireland has mesmerized Patsy.
> The world is all jaundiced in layers of chrome.
> Ladybird, ladybird, for God's sake fly home!

'Wasps', with its superb image of 'you jerseyed champion of spite', combines irony, blunt sarcasm, and verbal legerdemain -

> If I could rhyme your name with asps
> it would be more appropriate, wasps,
> or if I could, when something rarsps,
> invoke your tribe, how useful, warsps,
> or, when the dentist plies his forcps,
> how natural to think of worsps.
> Instead of which, in general osps
> I lie, and curse the sound of wasps. . .

He is by turns fancifully allusive in 'A Runnable Stag-Beetle', Punch-archetypal in

> 'The Gnat'

When the ark
 reached Mount Ararat,
why didn't Noah swat
 the gnat?

Or if he was too drunk
 to strafe it,
couldn't he hand the job
 to Japhet? . . .

and wryly self-regarding in

'The Greenfly'

Don't call the creature parasitic,
 nor mutter, "Off! Obscene fly."
Good work attracts the insect-critic,
 as roses do the greenfly.

The specimens in the 'Wings' section sit a little oddly after the earlier ones, perhaps through too much striving after effect, demonstrating poetic virtuosity, thumbing his nose to the critics. 'The Death-Watch Beetle' is interesting for its resemblance, in style, tone and versification, to 'Journey's End' - 'What will they give me when journey's done?' - in *The Unknown Goddess*:

"What manner of time does your watch keep
strange timekeeper?" "The time of sleep."

"I see no movement in the hands."
"And yet the sleeper understands."

"The sleeper understands! But how?"
"You cannot understand it now."

"And shall I never?" "In the end
you'll ask no other time-piece, friend."

One other book came out in 1935, *The Fourth of August*, published by Eyre and Spottiswoode. This was a curious narrative, told in a sequence of seventeen sonnets, of a woman, her poet husband, and an old university friend of his who arrives unexpectedly at their house on the fourth of August. The visitor and the woman fall in love - or realise that they have always been in love, it is not entirely clear which; they all have a meal, talk a lot about Oxford days and people, and of the threat of war, and then the visitor departs into the night and war. I have not found a single reference to it in Humbert's letters or in Jessie's unpublished papers, and it seems to have made few ripples in the critical press. It reads like a private reverie on times past, with the First World War to end the idyll. The whole thing is rather baffling, but neither the subject matter nor the poetical inspiration is of sufficient inherent interest to make solving the puzzle an urgent priority.

Some time in 1935 Humbert was approached by Alexander Korda about making a translation of Edmond Rostand's play, *Cyrano de Bergerac*, for a film which he planned to make with Charles Laughton in the title rôle. The translation was completed in three weeks, after which he and Laughton were sent away to improve on his version, thought by Korda and his literary advisor, Lajos Birò, to be just a little too faithful to the French original. The Introduction to the text which Humbert published in 1937 retails the saga of his dealings with Korda and Birò, and the memorable and altogether more enjoyable though equally taxing experience of working with Laughton. Neither this nor the account given in Simon Callow's life of Laughton enables any precise dating of events to be made, but from references in Humbert's letters it is clear that the business dragged on for a long time, throughout the autumn and into the next year.[30]

One day in the summer of 1935, while Ann was on holiday in Lausanne, and Jessie was painting Humbert as he sat busily translating *Cyrano*, he said it was time to be thinking of holidays. He said he was thinking of Briançon again, but there was only enough money for one of them to go, and as he was anxious to finish the travel book he had started the previous year in Briançon (*P.L.M.*), they should look on his holiday as an investment for them all. Jessie was unwell herself and very tired, but, swallowing her disappointment, she gave in.

From the Paris-Lyon-Palais Hotel in Paris, on his way to Briançon, he wrote on 8 September to tell her that he hated leaving her in pain but that 'another sequestration was vital to my mental and physical health.' All the letters from Briançon, where he stayed until some time in October, made the same point in one form or another, adding on occasion a hint of moral blackmail - 'I've to pay the bills so my good health is paramount.' Jessie, who had to manage everything, including repayments and insurance premiums, out of the monthly allowance that he paid her, and whose health remained poor throughout his absence, could have advanced the same argument, but to what purpose?

During his holiday he worked at "P.L.M.", initials which for French travellers signify the Paris-Lyon-Méditerranée train, but which, characteristically, he re-interpreted as 'Peoples, Landfalls, Mountains.' It was published in 1936 by Cassell. He was also writing parts of the BBC series, *The Pilgrim's Way*, as and when the schedule required them. Problems with his *Cyrano* translation interfered with these other commitments. Press-reports of an interview given by Laughton seem to have suggested that the actor was not happy with progress so far.

Humbert had gained a quite different impression from his sessions with Laughton in London, and he had subsequently written offering to make any alterations that Laughton thought necessary, but had received no answer.

On 27 September he wrote to Jessie that Sir Thomas Phillips, Permanent Secretary at the Ministry, was happy enough to let him have as long a rest as possible. His last letter from Briançon, on 3 October, said that he expected to finish "P.L.M." by 6 or 7 October. This is also the last surviving letter to Jessie from 1935, no doubt because he returned to London soon after. A letter to Robin Maugham sent from London at the end of October refers to continuing problems with "Cyrano."

Throughout the autumn, Jessie, still sublimely ignorant of the affair, continued to work on Pamela's portrait which, when almost completed, was displayed at a fancy-dress party at Mount Street on the occasion of the Slade dance. P. H. St. John Wilson, then a Principal under Humbert in the Training Department, recalled being invited to Mount Street about this time, on the occasion of the Three Arts Ball. His description of the party so closely matches Jessie's recollection that they both must almost certainly have been describing the same event.

He wrote: 'Humbert had conceded to the occasion to the extent of donning a magnificent turban. When I commented on the splendour of his appearance he said, with a characteristic sweep of the hand over the top of his head, "Well, I suppose I am an oriental of a sort."' Jessie described Humbert as looking that night in his evening dress and turban "like George Arliss in 'The Green Goddess'."

St. John Wilson's account continued:

> It appeared that the gramophone had ceased to operate, and as a gramophile I volunteered to fix it. At this point there was momentary alarm as the lift or something had caught fire, but this was soon under control, and I bent to my task. Wolfe watched my ultimately successful efforts with admiration. "Faced with a situation such as this," he observed, "I have to content myself with giving the instrument a sharp blow."

Jessie went as a moujik, her sister as a harlequin and Ann as a Jane Austen lady. A friend of Ann's had come in a Pilgrim Father's costume, Edward Keeling, MP, wore the bright red uniform of a bell-boy. Michel Salaman came as himself, and Anthony West, brought by Pamela, was in a vaguely Napoleonic uniform. Pamela was dressed as the young Byron, which corresponds closely enough to St. John Wilson's description:

> Acting on my settled principles at that unattached moment of my life, I approached the most attractive

> female visible, a boyish piquant figure in a sort of Sidney Carton Regency get-up, with one of those curly-brimmed hats that narrow off at the top. It turned out to be Pamela Frankau.
>
> Possibly because I could claim with truth that I had enjoyed reading (at School) her father's Byronic poem 'One of Us' and avoided comment on her father's novels, of which she was fiercely defensive, I was favoured to the extent that she accepted my tentative offer to drive her back to Chelsea, where we both lived at that time. As the night wore on and the party began to break up, I became dimly aware that something was not quite right, as apart from the Wolfes (Humbert squatting cross-legged on the hearth looking more oriental than ever and discoursing happily), only Pamela and I were left. By this time my sense of having strayed into uncharted waters had become a conviction, but it was by now too late to make an unobtrusive getaway, and I had to wait until at last Pamela signified her readiness to depart. I deposited her in Pont Street without further incident, and never saw her again . . . To this day I have no idea whether I was playing unwilling gooseberry or a useful part in a screening operation. Certainly, if Wolfe entertained the suspicion that I was attempting to pinch his current girl friend (a relationship of which I learned when the information was of no use to me) he did not allow it to cloud our official relationship.[31]

The same colleague, in his capacity as the Ministry's Press and Public Relations Officer, attended Humbert, with his Private Secretary and a forbidding looking Assistant Accountant General, to be examined by a House of Commons Committee on the subject of Public Relations. During their long wait in an ante-room Humbert beguiled his audience with recollections of George Moore, complete with a convincing Irish accent. By the time they were admitted to the Committee Humbert was too exhausted to do justice to his brief (which he was suspected of not having read). Fortunately the Committee was running short of time and the Chairman was a fellow-Jew well known to Humbert (probably Isidore Salmon), and after some brilliant cross-talk between the two protagonists on unrelated subjects the party escaped.

VI

1936

In each of the previous two years February had been a cruel month for Jessie. February 1936 proved to be the cruellest of all.

At the beginning of the month her uncle, Willie Graham, had fallen ill and she had hastened to his bedside in Edinburgh, where she stayed three weeks. Only five letters from Humbert have survived, written between 10 February and 14 February. He reassured her that the house (Mount Street) was 'running like clockwork', although her cat, Ginger, 'mows' disconsolately outside her door. He posted books to her - *The Fourth of August*, which his letter implies had recently come out, along with *P.L.M.*, the composite account of his two holidays in Briançon.

The first word that *P.L.M.* prompts in the reader is 'whimsical' - there is a hint of relaxed inconsequentiality about this succession of descriptions and anecdotes, with no sign of the satirical Humbert, or rare, softened glimpses only. Some hilarious episodes, such as the bus-journey from Cagnes, make up for over-extended jokes like the tale of the missing trunk. Descriptions and atmosphere are rendered with artful ease, though the portraits of People vary greatly in quality. In some, like that of M. Roux, Humbert perfectly balances caricature, exaggeration and solemnity; in others, the artifice shows. All in all it is a pleasurable experience, but of Humbert cruising only at half-speed. Any criticism of what looks like slipshod proof-reading is forestalled by his preliminary disclaimer that 'No responsibility is taken either for the French accents or grammar in this book. That, after all, is the affair of the French Academy.' A book was no sooner finished than he seeemed to lose interest in it, his mind already at work on the next one.

The *Cyrano de Bergerac* saga was still in full swing during Jessie's absence in Scotland. He reported on 12 February that Laughton had telephoned and they were to meet that same evening. 'There is a crisis on between him and Korda. One or two of the papers have referred to it and suggested that the whole thing is to be abandoned. This is not so, but there are weeks of work ahead before the actual photography begins. I am not dispirited but extracting the money is a matter of extreme labour.' Earlier he had written that 'Korda and Birò were . . . lavish in promises.' He was hoping that his bank manager would believe him, which indicates that his difficulties there were not yet resolved, and also explains the very courteous letter from the Secretary of the Royal Society of Literature reminding him that he had paid no subscription since 1931; they had been very forbearing because of his illness in 1934, but that he now owed

£8.8s plus the current year's subcription. The R.S.L. archive provides no information as to any action that he or the Society subsequently took.

But on 13 February he wrote that 'the position about "Cyrano" becomes daily more intricate. . . I have received categorical assurances that it is only postponed; that Laughton will act personally; and that no word shall be used that I haven't written.' Meanwhile, Hutchinson had accepted his translation for publication and would discuss terms the next day.

On 14 February he gave Laughton lunch at the Athenaeum. 'You can imagine the suppressed gaping of all the old men at his appearance. Sir W. Rothenstein insisted on coming to speak to him for about ten minutes and tried to sell him a picture!' Assurances from Laughton and a satisfactory talk with Hutchinson meant that he would shortly be sending her the means of paying the rent and the electricity bill. He had occasional attacks of rheumatism, though less frequently than before, and had a crushing work load at the Ministry, 'with the Agricultural Insurance Bill in being, and the Unemployment Regulations in sight.' He added that 'the negotiations for the Deputyship continue briskly.' If this was, as it appears to have been, a reference to the post of Deputy-Secretary at the Ministry, it is all the more mysterious since the current holder of the post, Sir J. F. G. Price, had been promoted to it only the previous year, and stayed there until 1938.

Willie Graham did not recover from his illness; his funeral and the immediate sequel kept Jessie in Edinburgh until the third week in February. Humbert had travelled up for the funeral and the few days after their return had been very busy. On the morning of 21 February, tired, unwell, and still worried about their finances, she stood in her little studio at Mount Street, wanting to put the finishing touches to Pamela's portrait but feeling she should first attend to the preparations for a supper-party which Humbert felt he had to give for two departing colleagues a few days later.

According to the record which Jessie later made of events, her musings were interrupted by a telephone call, followed by a visit, from which she learned for the first time of Humbert's affair with Pamela, and of their holiday together in Briançon in 1934. A few of the details in Jessie's version of events are inconsistent with what can be independently verified. Nevertheless, her account is substantially accurate. Pamela admitted to having been Humbert's mistress for four years and to having been with him in Briançon not once but twice, in 1934 and 1935. After that Humbert could hardly protest his innocence, but all he said, according to Jessie, was that he had to live his own life, as he pleased. Jessie decided to go home with her sister for the night and to go to Oxford the next day to see Ann.

In her account Jessie wrote that, reflecting that night on the cataclysmic events of the day, she saw, illuminated with all the fearful clarity of a lightning flash, the explanation for all that had for so long made no sense, all the mysterious events and crises of the past few years; the sudden entry of Pamela into their lives; Humbert's frequent late nights, attributed for some time to *Cyrano*, more recently to late sittings in the House, or meetings at the Air Ministry. The desire to avenge herself of all this deceit was strong, but she quickly rejected the temptation to sue for divorce; the ignominy of it might punish Pamela and any other women with whom he may have misbehaved, but it would utterly destroy Humbert and make things even harder than they already were for Ann. The only solution was to persuade Humbert to be and to remain sensible, to see that between the despised narrow existence of the bank-clerk and these romantic extravagances there had to be a middle way.

Returning to Mount Street the next morning to pick up some clothes, she found a letter which Humbert had left which showed, she said later, that he had not yet fully realized what had happened. He spoke of "blackmailers" and went on to say: 'The question is whether you will immediately disorganize the structure you have patiently built, or whether you will take a little time for reflection.' She saw no sign that he felt in any way connected with, still less responsible for, the upheaval. It was as if a meteor had descended from outer space, and he expected her, as usual, to clear up the débris. He said he would be staying at The Athenaeum, where she could find him at any hour of the night, and that he would return home whenever she asked him to do so. But before she could bring herself to see him and talk things over, she became seriously ill and had to go into a nursing home until June, by which time her chance of talking things over with him had gone.[32]

Chapter Ten

1936-1940

'A distant, lonely song'
(Dialogues and Monologues)

I

1936

Jessie wrote after Humbert's death that on the morrow of these revelations she was quite certain that he did not want a divorce, although she had no doubt that Pamela wanted to marry him. Pamela, however, for all her determined independence, seems at this stage to have subordinated everything to her love for Humbert, settling for whatever part of himself and his life that he was prepared to give her. But as time went on and the separation between Humbert and Jessie became an established fact, Pamela saw the possibility of a permanent relationship with him, and all the more so as she became the principal focus of his affections.

But in February 1936 Jessie could only think of the others before Pamela who had tried to 'collect' her husband. It seems clear that she laid the blame more on them, for wanting to catch him, than on Humbert for being willing to be caught. There were, she wrote, as many sides to Humbert as there were to a Harlequin's dress, and each of these women, no doubt, matched one of these Harlequin colours. But the conflict was between herself and Humbert. Jessie was determined not to give up husband, daughter or home, without a fight. She believed that he no more wanted their marriage to end than she did, but he did not want to agree to any limitation on his actions. And therein lay their conflict. Had she not been ill there was a chance, albeit a faint one, that they might somehow patch things up. But by the time she emerged from her illness the damage was beyond repair, and for the next four years she was to remain in a curious state of suspension, neither ex-wife nor entirely wife. Letters were exchanged between them but according to Jessie his became increasingly the adroit evasions of a Civil Servant determined not to answer awkward questions.

In May Humbert's *Reverie of Policeman* was staged by Evan John Simpson at The Mercury Theatre in Notting Hill Gate, later the home of the Ballet Rambert. How long a run it had has not been possible to discover, but it can hardly have lasted beyond the first week in June. The producer, Simpson, however, wrote a letter of commiseration and encouragement to Humbert on June 10, saying that it was hard luck, but *Reverie* had lasted longer than many he had known, and might well have lasted longer but for the shallowness and laziness of theatre-going Londoners who wanted only what they were used to. He hoped that Humbert would not give up playwrighting, and considered it a privilege to have been the producer of something as inspiring and entertaining as *Reverie.*[1]

The series of BBC programmes, *The Pilgrim's Way*, already mentioned, also appeared, under the imprint of Ivor Nicholson and Watson. Humbert's Preface to *The Pilgrim's Way*, which ostensibly set out to explain the underlying conception, is another manifestation of his self-depreciation, professing ignorance of both prose *and* verse. His initial idea had been 'to illustrate the progress from youth's hope and certainty through the doubts of adolescence, by way of the consummations of love, past the growing anguish and despair of later years to final peace when, at the end, all trouble is laid aside.' The sequence has a familiar ring. But the prospect of a succession of increasingly gloomy broadcasts lacked any appeal other than that of logic and the planners were obliged to 'temper our Wolfe to the shorn lamb.' The broadcasts were to project successive moods by a combination of verse and music. Humbert was asked to select the verse and write a Prologue for each broadcast, a task which he accomplished for sixteen of the seventeen broadcasts, the exception being accounted for by his ear infection (here described as a mastoid operation) in 1934.

The series was a very ambitious project: it is small wonder that the Reithian BBC pursed its collective lips from time to time. The anthology seems in large part predictable - a sort of superior school collection. Those whose memory extends that far back may recall another such, by S. P. B. Mais. The absence of all but a small sample of contemporary verse, and that not exactly representative of its authors' work (Owen, Spender, Sassoon), is not altogether surprising. But the choice of music (with the identification of the records, all H.M.V. or Columbia recordings) and the names of the readers (Felix Aylmer, Robert Harris, Robert Speaight among them), which are supplied at the head of each section, will have a special interest for historians and for survivors from those days.

Humbert's association with the BBC, as an occasional broadcaster and a rather more frequent contributor of articles to the *Radio Times*, began, as we have seen, in 1925 with his reading of selections from his poems on 10 September (*see* above, Chapter 7, II (iii)). In 1927 he gave a talk on "The Lake of Geneva". His first article appears to have been written in 1928 at the request of Val Gielgud, then assistant to the Acting Editor of *The Radio Times*, Eric Maschwitz. Gielgud wanted a thousand-word piece on the possibility of picking up from the ether the waves of conversations from past ages and past figures of history - a plausible but now discredited pseudo-scientific fancy reminiscent of Addison's tale of the frozen words which became audible once more when thawed. It is easy to imagine the appeal of such a subject to Humbert's fantasising gifts.[2]

Gielgud and Maschwitz had negotiated the publication of further pieces by him in 1928 and 1929, but, although there were subsequent broadcasts of his poems, there is a gap in the correspondence with the *Radio Times* until 1936 when Maurice Gorham was editor. Gorham was anxious that Humbert should be one of the first contributors to a new version of a section of the *Radio Times* called "The World We Live In", in which different writers would offer a point of view on the problems raised by broadcasting and its influence on modern life.

Humbert occasionally and wittily reminded Gorham about unpaid fees, once writing: 'A certain silence has brooded over your finance department. Could you persuade them to break into song?' But from 1937 Gorham increasingly found reasons for rejecting his contributions (poetry was no longer an affordable luxury, etc.), and it begins to look as if his poems and articles no longer fitted in with editorial policy.

Between 1936 and 1940, however, there were many exchanges of letters with Val Gielgud (now Director of Features and Drama) interspersed with internal memoranda, on proposals to broadcast Humbert's version of *Cyrano de Bergerac*, as well as *Reverie of Policeman* and his unpublished play *Salvation Somehow*. His adaptation of *Cyrano* was eventually broadcast in 1938, with Ralph Richardson in the part of Cyrano. A fee of fifty guineas was authorized for a repeat broadcast in 1939, and correspondence continued about a further production of *Cyrano* with a cast which might (doubtfully) include John Gielgud in the title role. In December 1939 Humbert proposed a reduced version lasting only an hour, to be called "Panache", for broadcasting in the New Year, 'if only as something of a gesture to France.' He mentioned 'Pamela's show' (her pantomime) with which he hoped that she would score a huge success. On the day Humbert died, Val Gielgud replied to his suggestions for casting: Margaretta Scott was said to be passionately anxious to play Roxane, and Diana Wynyard was another possible. But the project, like the correspondence, seems to have ended with Humbert's death. Extracts from his translation of *Cyrano* were included in a music programme in 1953, and twice in the 1950s the BBC considered broadcasting *The Silent Knight* but decided that despite its merits the play was likely to have only a limited appeal. From time to time poetry programmes have included readings of his poems, and one devoted entirely to his verse, called "The Poet In Whitehall", was broadcast on Radio 3 in 1981.[3]

Humbert's friend and quasi-patron, A. A. Baumann, died on 20 June, 1936, which probably explains why *Personalities*, the volume of selected writings which appeared in 1936, was edited by Humbert: Baumann was by then too ill to supervise the edition himself. Another, slightly more public, task which Humbert was asked to undertake about this time was that of sitting as one of the judges chosen to select the lady whose recorded voice would be used for the Post Office Telephones' 'speaking clock', whose more popular title (almost certainly a press invention) was 'The Girl With The Golden Voice'.

In June Ann took her finals at Oxford and came down to find a largely unsympathetic world. She still needed further surgery to repair her disabilities and she had difficulty finding work. She had hoped for an opening in journalism, which everyone at Oxford had assumed would be easy in view of Humbert's connection with *The Observer*, but it proved not to be so. She continued to live with Jessie at 128 Mount Street. Humbert had taken a flat at 75 Eccleston Square.

He had not yet secured the promotion he hoped for and the form his efforts in this direction took, sharpened possibly by financial stress, may have hindered rather than helped. As a junior colleague later remarked, inability to restrain the wise-crack rising to one's lips is not the best way of ingratiating oneself with the Important. A typical example was Humbert's noisy arrival in the Official Gallery of the House of Commons one evening about this time. Ministry officials often attended Debates in which their Minister was speaking, in order later to 'assist' the official reporters to get their master's speech recorded for posterity.

> Humbert suddenly made an impressive appearance, slapping down the hinged desks of the other occupants of that cramped space as he came until he reached me in the seat nearest to the Speaker's chair. Having by then, so to speak, secured the undivided attention of the House, he sank down beside me and enounced clearly: "You know, St. John. I *do* wish I was still living with my wife; she's got such a nice flat in Mount Street," and followed this up with an equally audible account of the alleged intrigues which stood in the way of his promotion, mentioning the names of several prominent statesmen then sitting within easy earshot on the Front Bench.[4]

Humbert's readiness to challenge Treasury policy, his unpopular commitment to the I.L.O., and, above all, his outside interests, which may have suggested contumacious priorities, made him suspect in some civil service quarters, and may have accounted, in part at least, for his being passed over for promotion. Direct documentary evidence for this, of course, is not to be found, but Humbert's dictum may legitimately be invoked: 'Believe me! a good guess is worth a ton of official records.'[5]

Humbert's club, The Athenaeum, had decided that it should make some provision for ladies. In March 1936 premises were acquired at No. 6 Carlton House Mews. Building began in May, and after the annual closure of the club for the month of August, the 'Ladies Side' was opened in September. Humbert invited Pamela and Gill Dearmer to the opening, but once there he disappeared - to be 'with his chums' - to Pamela's considerable annoyance. She and Gill took their revenge by composing embarrassing and increasingly scurrilous telegrams which they sent to him and which were carried in by the butler at regular intervals throughout the evening. The worst ones that Gill could recall were:

> Come and stay and bring your organ.
> Love and kisses, Hilda Morgan.

(almost certainly a fairly well-known novelist of the time, Hilda Vaughan, married to the author Charles Morgan), and

> Wishing I had met you sooner
> Than old Radclyffe. Love from Una.

- an allusion to Radclyffe Hall and her partner, Lady Una Troubridge. The telegrams would not have cost them more than sixpence a time and they succeeded in making Humbert very cross.[6]

Princess Bibesco, another of Humbert's admirers, is said to have made him a present of an orange tree about this time. Whether or not she intended it for The Athenaeum garden, that is where it found a home, although the likelihood is that it was a mock-orange, and no record of the bequest has survived.

Employment was precarious in the theatrical world for young women like Gill Dearmer: she was paid only thirty shillings a week by the Open Air Theatre or Covent Garden or wherever she was working, "and they [Humbert and Pamela] would play vingt-et-un. He began by explaining the rules and when I said 'I see: it's nines instead of 21', Humbert said 'Ha, now we'll start.'" Pamela was fond of gambling and wrote one of her novels about a gambler.

In the autumn of the year H. G. Wells retired from the International Chairmanship of the P.E.N. Club, and was succeeded by Jules Romains. Humbert took Wells's place as British member of the Executive. P.E.N.. (standing for Poets, Playwrights, Essayists, Editors and Novelists) was an organisation started in England many years before under the Chairmanship of John Galsworthy, in order to foster interchange of literature, and now had branches in practically every country of the world except Germany and Russia. Increasingly in the inter-war years it concerned itself with supporting writers who for political or other reasons suffered hardship in various parts of the world.

Humbert's position in Whitehall was undoubtedly for P.E.N. a useful means of access to information and influence. Equally valuable, according to Storm Jameson, was his command of French, particularly when, under Romains' presidency, discussions had to be conducted in French. Add to these his political astuteness and the combination became priceless, as for example when H. G. Wells convinced himself that a P.E.N. Congress in Rome would be the ideal oppportunity to face down the fascists with

P.E.N.'s freedom of speech and democratic principles. Humbert knew from experience that it was more likely to flatter fascist vanity. When he learned that the French were equally opposed to the idea he suggested translating the whole scheme on to the plane of general principles, in which rarefied atmosphere it died.

II

1937

The money question had by now become acute. Jessie had written to ask Humbert to use his influence to get work in journalism for Ann but he had been unhelpful. He would not meet Jessie either to discuss Ann's present difficulties or to arrange about her future. On the morning of Humbert's birthday, 5 January, Ann went to see him at Montagu House. She remembered his saying that he still dreamt every night about Jessie. He declined the invitation to return to Mount Street for lunch, pleading a lunch engagement with Jules Romains, who was in London for a meeting of the P.E.N. Club Executive. She was not to know that she would never see him again.

But his letter to Jessie of 10 January (the only one that has survived from this period, and the last in the whole collection) sounded a rather more encouraging note. As proof that he did not intend the olive branch to wither, he said that he would be taking out a further insurance policy for Ann, which would provide her with £100 a year for twenty years on his death, or a lump sum of £1500. This was in addition to the old policy which with dividends was now worth £2700. He thought there was nothing to fear from the statutory medical examination, since Lord Horder was more than satisfied with his health. He had also written to two or three papers to try to get some paid reviewing work for Ann, and hoped that this might prove fruitful. And he had taken over and reduced one of the larger debts.

At the January meeting of the P.E.N. Executive, Humbert's I.L.O. experience was invoked in order to discover what provision if any was made in individual countries for assistance to unemployed and aged writers. The I.L.O., however, in its reply disclaimed competence in this area since, unlike journalists, authors did not normally have contracts of employment. The International Institute of Intellectual Cooperation (part of the League of Nations) had been authorized to collect information but had done nothing yet since it was more concerned about the unemployment of young graduates.[7]

The *Cyrano de Bergerac* film project had finally fizzled out. Lajos Birò made a provisional camera script which he and Humbert worked on; a director of photography was appointed, Laughton's phenomenal energy and enthusiasm continued unabated, but Korda finally lost interest, most probably, as Humbert suggested in his Preface to the translation, because he became convinced (or was persuaded by Lajos Birò) that a period film in verse would simply not make money. He moved on to other schemes and Humbert was left in the dark, not knowing what was happening. His reference in the letters of February 1936 to an agreement with Hutchinson suggests that he had taken some steps to salvage what he could, but, according to Jessie, at the end of 1937 he was still expecting several thousands from London Films for his translation.[8]

At all events, his translation of *Cyrano* was published in 1937. His Preface not only describes the hopes, fears and ultimate disappointment of the venture, it also graphically conveys Korda's unique style of doing business and paints a vivid picture of his and Laughton's collaboration and the discussions of the problems of translation to which this gave rise. Simon Callow, in common with many writers, thinks that these problems remained unresolved until Anthony Burgess's 'miraculous version' for the Royal Shakespeare Company in 1984. His verdict on Humbert's version ('and very decent it is, too') is perhaps unintentionally condescending.[9]

Clough Williams-Ellis, the unorthodox and charismatic architect, had sold his house to the Laughtons, and through them got to know Humbert and, he wrote in his autobiography, 'thereafter saw as much as I could of him.' He quoted with approval one of Humbert's 'delighful "epitaphs in advance" on the Gloomy Dean' - Dean Inge - from *Lampoons*:

> Hark! the herald angels sing
> timidly, because Dean Inge
> has arrived, and seems to be
> *bored* with immortality.

The architect, wrongly surmising that Humbert was himself a refugee from an earlier purge, went on to recall Humbert's efforts on behalf of refugees from Hitler's Germany ' - and help them he did most devotedly, incidentally landing me . . . with a couple of Austrian architects for whom I had to find face-saving work of some sort in my war-shadowed and overstaffed office.'[10]

Humbert found time to lecture at the Cambridge Summer School with Edith Sitwell and Middleton Murry. Ethel Mannin reported a delightful story of how Humbert once visited the Sitwells at their paternal home in the country (Renishaw, presumably], and how when he got there dinner was over and there was nothing to eat, 'but they said, "Oh, well, never mind," and showed him to his room, and Edith came in and said should she read him one of her poems, and he said, "If you must," so she did.'[11]

His next book, *Don J. Ewan* (1937, London, Arthur Barker), was a satirical review of world history in six Cantos (plus a Prologue and an Epilogue), varying in length from eighteen to forty-one eight-line stanzas. He set himself the task of making 'my diagnosis/of the mistakes, called by their makers history,/ through the life-story of that most unlucky/ gentleman, Don J. Ewan of Kentucky', a journalist, though for once a not unsympathetic figure. It is no surprise to see some favourite targets pinked, even bludgeoned: the American Press - one wonders what he would have done with today's tabloids - , Hollywood, the Old World. The talent for the memorable phrase remained undimmed - 'the lounge, a morgue for chairs' [Canto I, vi]. It was a bold challenge, taking on Byron in his own stanza form, but he quite often succeeded in getting an authentic ring. It is tempting to think, for example, that Byron would have liked the telegraphed bathos of Canto III, xxiii:

> What did we speak of - girls, for whose bright tresses
> the ships had sailed, and men, whose locks bronze-curled
> were what the sculptor dreamed of lovelinesses
> when Troy in terror watched the sails unfurled?
> You can't imagine? You may have three guesses.
> You give it up? Of nothing in the world
> but slimming, and the influence of calories,
> with some reflections on the falls of salaries.

The 'German' Canto IV disappoints slightly, perhaps for being insufficiently focused. But the touch returns in Canto V, where he compares Themistocles before Salamis with Marshal Foch, and the Spartans with Haig; and the 'heroes' of the French Revolution who

> fed the guillotine a fritto misto
> of king and queen well flavoured with aristo. (V, x)

And finally London, in Canto VI. The whole is a brilliant, entertaining piece, which tries hard to see all that is wrong with the world, and still cannot stop optimism from breaking out. Fifty or more years later, however, one wonders how many of the allusions, classical or relatively modern, the late twentieth century reader would pick up.

The Silent Knight, 'A Romantic Comedy in Three Acts, by Humbert Wolfe, from the Hungarian of Eugene Heltai' (1937, London, Heinemann) was first performed on 16 November, 1937 at The St. James's Theatre. The cast for that first performance was a litany of names to conjure with: Diana Wynyard, Anthony Quayle, Ralph Richardson, Laidman Browne, Margaretta Scott, Douglas Jefferies, and others. The play, which ran for about six weeks, was produced by Gilbert Miller, who went on to produce some of the West End's greatest successes.

The play, set in 1476, tells the story of Peter Agardi, a brave young Hungarian knight who bargains with the lovely widow, Zilia, that for a kiss he will do anything she demands. She commands silence for three years so that he shall not boast of his conquest. The Emperor orders her to cure Peter of his silence or die. She fails but when at the moment of execution she declares her love for the Knight, the headsman is revealed as Peter and all ends happily. The play is not exactly a lost treasure, but it is pleasant enough and the couplets work quite well. Contemporary witnesses say that it rather suffered from the proximity of three J. B. Priestley plays concurrently running in West End theatres, *Time and the Conways, I Have Been Here Before*, and *Music at Night*. Twice in the 1950s the BBC considered broadcasting the play but decided that despite its merits it was likely to have only a limited appeal.

One of his sisters told a story that Humbert, who knew Priestley well enough, met him one day in a restaurant or a club and exclaimed delightedly, 'I've just heard that some journalist has described me as the handsomest poet in London. Can you believe that?' 'Aye,' said Priestley, 'I've seen the others!'

All this prodigious literary activity was naturally viewed by his colleagues and superiors in Whitehall, but not by Humbert himself, as strictly peripheral to his work in the Ministry, which was acquiring increasing status as an economic, as distinct from a merely social, department. As the Ministry's representative on the newly created Inter-departmental Committee on Public Capital Expenditure, Humbert more and more often chaired its meetings in the absence of the Treasury official, and, capitalising on the opportunities which this afforded, used his authority to challenge the Treasury's endemic gloomy assumptions (e.g. that increased public works during a depression inevitably invited loss of confidence) as well as to close some of the loopholes by which the Treasury habitually evaded its obligations.

But his major achievement was to rewrite the Committee's conclusions, thus ensuring that they gave positive rather than negative signals. For example, he emphasised that the 'formidable practical difficulties' foreseen by the Treasury were not a reason for doing nothing. Similarly, postponement of capital works in a boom economy was not just 'common sense', as the Treasury said, but had the dual purpose of reducing inflationary pressure and of keeping some public work in store for any future depression where they would be of real value. And thirdly, he secured the inclusion of a commitment to implementation and constant monitoring of such programmes.[12]

Interesting though all this is to the student of social and economic history, its significance for me lies in what it reveals of the man, namely that he identified the needs of his time as basically the same in all spheres, and so his response both as Civil Servant and as Poet was identical, and positive. It revived the theme of his address to the Whitefriars Club in 1928 (*see* Chapter 7 above) and recalls the words of his teacher, Barton, quoted in 'Drum', in *Dialogues and Monologues* (1929): 'Affirmation - that's the word - affirmation.'

One day early in December, Jessie went to Whitehall in person to see Humbert. She waited in a taxi outside Montagu House until he eventually emerged in his black squash hat and fawn overcoat, with his rapid, buoyant stride. She went over and asked him to come and speak to her. He was not at all pleased at first, but got into the taxi and said he was lunching at The Savoy; would she drive there with him? During the journey his manner gradually softened and he thanked her for having had the courage to come, but said he was leaving for Scotland that night; she therefore agreed to meet him to talk things over when he returned.

There was little time for discussion before they reached The Savoy. He disapproved of a further operation for Ann on the grounds of 'the risk', a strange reason in Jessie's view, since she had written to explain that Ann needed further surgery to improve her appearance and speech. But he waved away Jessie's anxieties about money. He was soon to be promoted, London Films were going to pay him thousands for *Cyrano*, and other dramatic ventures would bring in further large sums. In the courtyard of The Savoy he got out, then got back into the taxi, took her in his arms and kissed her, saying that he would write when he got back from Scotland, and they would meet and talk it all out. She went home feeling that it was going to be all right in the end. It was the last time she saw him alive.[13]

III

1938

The Amulree Committee which was set up in 1938 to consider the issue of paid holidays may have been the occasion for some teasing that Humbert endured from Pam and Gill. Lord Amulree, formerly William Warrender Mackenzie, P.C., K.C., was a lawyer who had acted as Arbitrator and Conciliator in industrial differences on behalf of the Board of Trade and the Ministry of Labour from as far back as World War I. He had also been briefly Secretary of State for Air and President of the Air Council (1930 - 1931).

Gill recalled that 'Pamela was always needling Humbert about the grand people he was off with, who weren't at all literary.' On one such occasion, when Humbert was showing off about his connection with Lord Amulree, Pam began to compose a verse, in the style of Lewis Carroll, in which they all eventually joined, Pam, Gill, and Humbert too. The poem was called 'The Great Lord Amulree', and began:

> Beware the great Lord Amulree,
> a colonel in the camelry,
> whose dromedary slides and skids
> at evening on the pyramids.

Humbert's verse ran:

> Who built latrines, Herren und Damen,
> Upon the tomb of Tutunkhamen,
> With a private entrance for his sweetie
> Who looked, he said, like Nefertiti,
> And put her to a nightly use
> Beneath the folds of his burnous.

The verses became more and more indelicate as they wrote it, said Gill, but these were all she could remember fifty years later.

On the retirement of Sir James F. G. Price early that year, Humbert finally got his promotion to Deputy Secretary in the Ministry of Labour. His continued advancement within the same Ministry, in contravention if not in defiance of a Treasury ruling, clearly signified that he was too valuable an asset for the Ministry to risk losing him to another department. Perhaps the threat of war, and the necessary preparations for that eventuality, required his unique experience, gained in the Ministry of Munitions twenty years earlier and in the intervening period. Some of his contemporaries have suggested that the prospect of war had galvanised his energies once more after a period when he seemed to be bored with Civil Service work.

Be that as it may, the published Evidence submitted to the Royal Commission on the Distribution of the Industrial Population, known as the Barlow Commission, before which he appeared on 2 and 3 February, 1938, described him as 'Principal Assistant Secretary and Deputy Secretary Designate, Ministry of Labour'. His evidence testified, directly and indirectly, to the Ministry's increasing status and its confidence in its ability to fend off attack from whatever quarter, Treasury, Board of Trade or industry. The introduction of new industries in the Special Areas (*see* above, Chapter 9) was a good example, and Humbert was not afraid to challenge the accepted doctrine of the infallibility of market decisions, declaring to the Royal Commission that 'The economic interest of a given manufacturer is not necessarily a national interest.' Indeed, by virtue of its influence as a leading social services department and as a serious factor in determining economic policy, the Ministry was beginning to be seen as an essential training ground for ambitious politicians of all ages, as the list of its post-war Ministerial alumni bears witness.[14]

Writing on 7 February to thank Harold Butler at the I.L.O., who had sent congratulations on his promotion, Humbert said: 'It is a dreadfully long time since I worked with you in Geneva. I do not think it likely that the change of post will bring me into ILO work again,' adding that he would nevertheless enjoy meeting old friends.[15] Jessie's recollection that the announcement of his promotion coincided with their twenty-eighth wedding anniversary (that is, on or near 29 March) indicates simply that his promotion was announced on one date but took effect on another.

Shortly before the date of their anniversary Jessie sent Humbert a note enclosing the card she had had printed for a party on 29 March, and suggesting that he should come back then and let bygones be bygones. She delivered the note herself to his flat at 75 Eccleston Square. On the day that she took it Humbert was himself giving a large party. Presumably she did not see him but her note proposed absolute freedom for him; they would meet only in public or for Ann's sake. He turned down her offer and refused to countenance the expense of a party even for Ann, and instructed his lawyer to write and tell her so.

The Spring of 1938 saw the publication by Cassell of the sequel to *Now A Stranger* (for such in its own fashion it was), entitled *The Upward Anguish*, a somewhat disconnected series of sketches in which he described his Oxford days. The 'anguish', as has been pointed out earlier (*see* above, Chapter 3), was in the main a social anguish for the young Umberto Wolff from Bradford, 'race-conscious, class-conscious, precocious, imaginative, very thin-skinned, rather impudent, and quite indestructible', as one reviewer put it.

The Edwardian Oxford which he portrayed appeared to many in 1938 as much a bygone age as it does to us. And yet, by not too persistently monopolising the foreground, he managed to transform episodes like 'First Term' into a universal experience, Everyman's rite of passage. There is, in addition, more than a suggestion of cinema technique, less an obvious borrowing than something absorbed during years of assiduous film-going. Comparison with *Now a Stranger* is unavoidable. The style is as distinctively measured, but a more noticeably mannered tone alternates with those exact, ironic passages that distinguished much of the earlier book (*see*, for example the Scholarship Exam chapter); the humour, however, is engagingly offered in good measure. 'Albert in Oxford', by comparison, seems to skate on the surface of things and events, without tracing a significant pattern. Fans of Jerome K. Jerome would love his use of the 'Three Men' section on putting up a tent - the humour in this chapter is Humbert at his most unaffected. By contrast, so often in the 'philosophical' dialogues he casts himself as the unserious mocker, invariably 'rebuked severely' by his companions. One is not sure what to make of this: is it a man wanting to be taken as a serious poet and scholar, yet volunteering for the post of court jester? Or simply another example of Humbert in self-depreciating mode? Another insistent theme is 'cleverness', its nature and (for Humbert) its two-edged character. This is perhaps the most illuminating theme in his reflections on aspirations and achievements.

Believing that his absence was only a temporary interruption in their life, Jessie stayed on in Mount Street. Payment of her allowance was becoming more and more irregular, while payment of interest on the loan, life insurances and ordinary expenses were all too regularly required. Her lawyer did all he could to get Humbert to make regular payments, but although his income was not negligible, it would not run to the upkeep of two establishments, foreign travel, entertaining his friends at his favourite hotels and restaurants, The Berkeley, The Ivy, The Savoy, and the like, and also repay the loan. She formed the opinion that he was taking advantage of her patience to avoid any attempt at making savings or at actively helping Ann, and therefore, although divorce was the last thing she wanted, she began to threaten legal action.

Humbert did not want a divorce either, probably because it would cost him more than if he left things as they were. If anything remained of his inheritance from his father's will, he stood to lose it under the terms of the agreement he had signed at the time of his marriage, which stipulated that in the event of a separation through any fault of his that he admitted in writing or was found by a Court of Law, the money from his inheritance and the income therefrom were to become Jessie's absolutely. The irony was that he had said at the time that although this proviso was 'wildly unnecessary' it ought to be included as a protection for Jessie. At all events he replied that if she made any move to divorce him he would resign from the Civil Service, thus leaving her and Ann penniless. As she wrote herself after his death, such a threat sounded more like Consola than Humbert, no matter how angry he might be. But he probably counted on her not to start an expensive action, even one likely to succeed, when the financial situation was difficult enough already.

But Jessie claimed that he left her no alternative unless he undertook to safeguard Ann and herself, and formally to acknowledge and take over the loan which she had raised in order to save him in 1934. In exchange for his agreement to this, she consented, much against her inclination, to sign a Private Deed of Separation in August 1938. She hoped, however, that it would not be long before they could tear it up, and in that frame of mind left London to go with Ann to Scotland, Oban and Ganovan Bay, where she and Humbert had first met.

At the news of the Munich crisis in September Jessie returned to London where she received a message from Humbert through his lawyer that she and Ann should go to live in Dorset. This solicitude for their safety touched her but she replied that they were determined to stay and take up A.R.P. (Air Raid Precautions) work. But first Ann went into hospital for what they hoped would be almost the last of her operations.

It was about this time, said Gill Warr, that Humbert got all the young in their group to sign up for all manner of voluntary service - distributing gas masks, the army etc. - 'we all joined up to send the numbers up and give Humbert something to rattle at the Germans'. She remembered taking something to do with recruiting to his office and when she put down her typewriter it went on making dreadful ticking noises and the police all thought it was a bomb. When in the autumn of 1938, after Munich, she went to Grenoble (the crisis had delayed her), he went out of his way to give her introductions to friends in France, including the director of the Art Gallery in Grenoble who showed and explained to her his collection of Matisse paintings, and to Jacques Chevalier, the philosopher, then Doyen at the Faculté.

During the Munich crisis the Permanent Secretary to the Treasury, as head of the Civil Service, issued an order requiring Civil Servants above a certain rank - Humbert's certainly came within its scope - to inform their departmental office of their whereabouts each night, in case of emergency. John Walley, then in Establishments, told off one of his staff, C. H. Sisson, an Assistant Principal at the time, to produce a list of the senior staff addresses. All but two were accounted for: Harold Emmerson, who was away on a walking holiday, and Humbert, who had flatly refused to divulge his address. Sisson was sent back with the message that the order emanated from the Cabinet Office and that Humbert was to comply. The messenger finally returned with the names and addresses of six ladies, the last of them Jessie's.[16]

The question which inevitably poses itself is this: from the time when he first began to be regularly and frequently absent, in Geneva and elsewhere, until the formal separation in 1938, were his protestations of love for Jessie a fiction or not?

As I have already suggested, the evidence of affairs with others besides Pamela is slender, in that it is now largely second-hand. Some witnesses are more credible than others, of course. One of them, Diana Raymond, who was in close contact with her cousin Pamela from 1934 onwards, is in no doubt that Pamela would have married Humbert as soon as he was free, and that her sometimes painful jealousy of his other women friends indicated that these were more than insubstantial romantic attachments.

Jessie herself, in her unpublished papers, said, and seems to have believed, or persuaded herself, that all these affairs, including the latest with Pamela, were annoying but fundamentally unserious and transitory 'Byronic adventures', and that as soon as he tired of Pamela or she of him he would return home. It was as if she were saying: 'He was a man, he was attractive to women, and susceptible to their flattery; no further explanation is needed.' Ann shared her mother's view of the other 'affairs' but thought that Pamela was the only serious rival to Jessie in Humbert's affections. But Jessie's papers also suggest, to me at any rate, that Jessie was divided between wanting to minimise the seriousness of these escapades, and seeing them as a real threat to the stability of their family.

His relationship with Pamela was different from the others, however, in that he actually did something about her: he left Jessie for her. But would he have done so if the cat had stayed in the bag in February 1936? Did the disclosure of their affair bring matters to a point where he *had* to do something? One can only speculate: there is no way of telling for certain. I prefer to leave the mystery as they left it.

The earlier question - were his protestations of love for Jessie a fiction or did he still love her? - is another matter, and one that cannot be ducked. On his own admission (unless Jessie made it up, which seems unlikely), Humbert deceived Jessie over the question of her accompanying him abroad, perhaps even of their ever living in Geneva. If he was lying about these matters, was he to be believed when he wrote that he loved her? I think, on balance, that he was.

There is no reason to doubt that Humbert meant what he undertook when he married Jessie - one can imagine him rolling his tongue round the sonorous phrases of the marriage service -'forsaking all other cleave to his wife; they shall be two in one flesh' - just as he did those of his baptism in 1908. And there is nothing to suggest that for the first ten years of their marriage there was any disharmony between them, despite the tragic loss of two babies, the anxiety about Ann's condition, the trauma of war and the ordinary worries of day to day life.

But then he began to be known in literary circles, which rapidly became his social circles too. The most plausible explanation is that he wanted the best of both worlds - not necessarily to the point of the adulterously illicit (except perhaps with Pamela), but almost certainly in the sense of relishing the excitement of being sought after by pretty and well-connected women. He genuinely enjoyed the stimulus (some of it intellectual and artistic) which they provided, while retaining the solid basis of his home and his marriage which met some of his needs even if it lacked the sparkle of these other relationships. Sparkle after all is a quality associated more with surfaces than with depths.

Whatever it was that kept him from leaving Jessie, it did not extend to involving her in every aspect of his life, nor was it enough to exclude additional emotional involvements. The answer to this enigma may well lie in the years between 1920 and 1926, and perhaps less in the events of this period than in his growing realization that he wanted a life outside the narrow confines of home and Whitehall. His letters show that right up to the 1930s he still talked to Jessie about what he was writing, though progressively less about her part in inspiring any of it. Even in 1930 (though not after that) they were full of publication figures, and projects for new books, and the money all these activities would generate. But no longer did he say, as he said in 1920, that he wrote less well when away from her, and only occasionally did he send her poems as he wrote them, for her inspection or approval. He admitted (in 1930) that he wrote affectionate-sounding letters mostly to keep her quiet.

Her reaction to the Dedication of *Requiem* seems to have been as hurtful to him as it was totally unexpected. My impression is that he was in fact more hurt by her reaction than she was by the Dedication. I suspect that the whole affair was the occasion rather than the deep cause of her outburst, which increasingly looks like a collapse under the last straw at a time when she felt neglected and unhappy, kept on the brink of Geneva yet at arm's length. Humbert, on the other hand, seems to have felt that if she so misunderstood him, he could henceforward share his inner life less and less with her.

It is a truism that a man can be simultaneously an inveterate deceiver and an idealist; fiercely jealous of his freedom yet emotionally dependent;

at once likeable and blameworthy. The evidence is there that Humbert's character was such an amalgam. But why he clung to his marriage until it could no longer be saved can only be explained, I think, because one part of him wanted to be a loving husband and father, folded in a warm domesticity which replicated the safety and security of Mount Royd, but free of Consola's imperious rule, while another part of him was the compulsive prospector, the dedicated explorer of greener fields.

IV

1939

Although it was now virtually three years since Humbert had left Jessie, contemporary references suggest that his and Pamela's relationship was not crystal clear to everyone. Vera Brittain noted on 7 March that she had gone to Humbert's flat (in Euston Square, she said - undoubtedly a misreading of Eccleston) with Pamela, Compton Mackenzie and others. 'Pamela was doing the honours but I couldn't make out whether she lived there with him or only visited. He [Humbert] showed me a photograph of Viola Garvin and told me her lameness resulted from the removal of her knee-cap muscles as a child. He showed us all his review books with autographed letters in them.'[17]

Outraged press and public opinion after Munich had led to huge spontaneous offers of service by the civilian population; over half a million people (including Jessie and Ann) enrolled in the A.R.P. during the crisis weeks. Men and women in the professional and scientific world offered their services in such numbers that a Central Register was created as a separate branch within the headquarters organisation of the Ministry of Labour to record the names and qualifications of the applicants. Kenneth Clark and Humbert were asked to draw up a list of writers, artists and archaeologists whose services could be similarly employed.

As far back as 1922 the Committee of Imperial Defence had advised that plans should be drawn up to deal with the unlikely eventuality of another war. Two Sub-Committees were set up, one, under the chairmanship of Sir W. Graham Greene, to address the question of the Control of Manpower, the other to consider supply problems. By October 1938 it was the view of the Manpower Committee that, in order to make the best use of all the offers of help, the Ministry of Labour should produce and distribute as widely as possible a Handbook on National Service which would 'explain what types of people were wanted for particular services and set out . . . the principles on which the Schedule of Reserved Occupations was compiled.' In January 1939 the Handbook was launched by a Prime Ministerial broadcast and a rally in the Albert Hall, and distributed to every household in the country.[18]

The Handbook was written by various Departments; Humbert edited it and ensured that it was accurate. In an after-dinner speech he said that he was the only living author whose first edition had run to twenty-million copies. Some civil service colleagues resented his taking the credit in this way, but he could no doubt have invoked the dictum: *qui facit per alium, facit per se.*

Humbert's central involvement in the manpower issue brought him into a new association with the BBC which was collaborating with the Ministry in the preparations for war. A recruiting drive by radio was planned for the month of June, with Churchill and Eden as possible broadcast speakers. But in informal discussions between representatives of the Ministry, the BBC and the Lord Privy Seal's Office, this last idea was turned down by the government.[19]

By the end of September 1939, however, concern about the slow rate at which the build-up of the Forces was proceeding led to the creation of an inter-departmental committee under Humbert's chairmanship to make a statistical investigation of the proposed munitions programme 'with a view to determining more exactly the labour demands on various categories that will arise and to defining the resultant problems that will have to be surmounted.' It was to submit its report in January 1940.

H. M. D. Parker's account of all the manpower problems before and at the beginning of the war, and how they were dealt with, reads like an eerie paraphrase of *Labour Supply and Regulation.* The problems were the same; the slowness, if not the unwillingness, to face them was the same; the solutions accepted, reluctantly or otherwise, were often the same. There is, however, an apparent contradiction between the comfortable belief in the unlikelihood of conflict and the plans set up as early as 1922 for the war-time organisation of the manpower and resources of the country. It may be that, as Parker suggests, the former attitude was that of the Government, the latter that of the Committee of Imperial Defence (whose scheme for national mobilisation in the event of war was itself more an academic exercise than a serious expectation). But in view of all the experience gained during World War I, not least by Humbert at Munitions, and so much of it recorded in his *Labour Supply and Regulation* (Oxford, 1923), Parker's dismissal of the Ministry's capability of assessing manpower requirements is surprising. All the discussion of 'Dilution' and related issues in Humbert's book suggests that they knew a great deal about skilled and unskilled work, as well as about the unions' habitual protection of skilled labour.[20]

The jacket of Humbert's next book of verse, *Out of Great Tribulation* (1939, London, Victor Gollancz) announced it as 'New Poems', but, as the prefatory note and the 'Dedication' poem indicated, this was a retrospective collection, a baring of the throat to the critics (how that self-depreciatory note persists!):

. . . this rusty fern, these browned
leaves for my laurel.

Let my lovers and haters
tear them apart
. . . .

They are theirs. I leave them
for ever now.

Beyond doubt, the collection contains some memorable poems, chiefly when Humbert is not striving for lush effects -

You must not ask
that in my middle years
I'll pluck the stars
for jewels at your ears.

You must not think
that I will rob the West
to hang the sun's disaster
at your breast.
. . . .

I do but bring
these cold, these dim, these pale
cadences of the
tired nightingale.

And when you hear
. . . .
say in your heart,
"You might have sung,
Hélène, Ronsard,
had you, like her, been young."

In 'Another Way' the power of the impossible dream transforms a drab working class suburb into a wonderland:

There is another way past the brickyard
past the board school playground and the petrol pumps.

. . . .
Nor let those clouds pretend that they are mountains.
The wild moraine, the glacier, the peak
are, as you see, an accident of vision,

. . . .
And that's not music that surpasses Mozart
with a more magical flute than aught he played with.

. . . .
And you're not young, as you suppose and wearing
strange silks, nor with a lady at your side
that would have been a princess in Palmyra,
walking beside her lover as a bride. . .

Other poems more explicitly recall his Yorkshire childhood, 'Bradford', for instance:

There is an old loom, and old warp and woof,
older than the knitting fingers of the roaring machine,
. . .
it wove with the trees from shoulder to sturdy shoulder
of the great moors and made its pattern of this.

There is the second loom. This was of man's making,
his stubborn answer to the beauty he cannot control,
. . .
These are the Bradford men. They are not smooth nor gracious;
they have no tricks of manner nor ways to flatter; . .
But the heart within them as their own moors is spacious . . .

Similarly 'The School': There was a boy. . . . .

. . . .
He stands between his childhood and his age,
between this shadow and that further shade,
but, like all men, he has for heritage
the truth and beauty other men have made. . . .

and 'Hollings Hill':

Last year (a hundred years ago?)
I walked up Hollings Hill.
. . . .
into a quiet place
where all that cracked or flawed or broke
resumed its ancient grace. . . .

The poems which he wrote for *A Winter Miscellany* are gathered here. The two sonnets which make up 'Countryman's Winter' are remarkable for the understated way they convey the matter-of-factness of the season to the farm-labourers,

but to a boy, who wearily has trod
    streets, where dull houses stretch in endless row,
strange as the music of the woodland god
. . . .
but I who read their movements like a tale
    by Thomas Hardy in charmed silence waited.
Then with a happy sigh, but head bent down,
trudged back through moonlit snow to Bradford town.

Other experiences which marked him indelibly years earlier can be identified in 'Sport at Minehead' (*see* earlier Chapter 7, III (v) 1926) which combines echoes of 'Drake is in his hammock' with 'A runnable stag':

The hunt is up at Porlock and the hounds are well away.
(Satan, are you sleeping there below?)
. . . .

And the world is like a blessing, with the hunt at Minehead guessing
it's a perfect day for slaughter, and by God! they ought to know.

and another anti-hunt poem, 'Hares':

I think that men who would hunt hares
would hunt anything.

Satire is generally less in evidence here, but 'Turn again Dick Whittington (*Theme with variations: A Contribution to Modern Technology*)' deftly sends up Eliot's knowing allusions -

. . .
Valiantly the spectres gibber,
poor rats behind the arras -
Polonii clenching the stuff in
dead men's teeth - but they only embarrass
the dignity of Styx - the oldest man ribber
that keeps on rollin' for ever and says nuffin'.
Because there is nuffin' to say?
Or because there is too much to impart . . .
and the news of the day
is the blood of the journalist.
As the blood of Viscount Rothermere
is the seed of the Press. . .

The poem ends with a *Note* - 'For the better comprehension of this poem readers are recommended to begin by mastering all the volumes in the

British Museum. A knowledge of Middle Aramaic, though not indispensable, will be helpful.'

The poems are grouped in sections variously headed, e.g. 'Places', 'Conversations', 'Hail and Farewell', 'Questions and No Answers' - which not surprisingly includes 'Victoria - The Lost leave-Trains':

> . . . .
> They go, as they used to go, terribly
> dragging the heart with the red
> light, that dimmed eyes could barely see,
> and with the murmur of last words said. . .

and 'Valedictory' poems to a variety of departed heroes, from Aristide Briand and George V to 'Drum', Gerald Gould and G. K. Chesterton.

Holidays that summer were out of the question. Even a week-end in Boulogne in August with Pamela, Margaretta Scott and others was cut short when Humbert was suddenly recalled by Whitehall and they all had to come home. Margaretta Scott recalls that they saw James Agate on the ferry.

Humbert continued to receive enquiries and requests from writers who wanted to be put on his list for civilian or military service. John Betjeman wrote to Kenneth Clark about a list of writers to add to the one that Clark and Humbert had drawn up for employment during the forthcoming war. He also sought Humbert's help in getting his name removed from the Schedule of Reserved Occupations, and after Humbert's death wrote to Jessie to record his appreciation of Humbert's efforts on his behalf. Storm Jameson recorded in her autobiography that earning a living as a novelist at that time seemed not only unlikely but also slightly indecent, and that Humbert promised to find other work for her when she had finished her current novel. John Pudney was another writer who asked to be put on the Register. Some, like Evelyn Waugh, stated the kind of work they fancied or felt equipped to do.[21]

On 6 December Pamela Frankau's pantomime, *Who's Taking Liberty?*, opened at The Whitehall Theatre. It ran until some time in January 1940. Humbert's poem in honour of the men killed aboard HMS Exeter in what came to be known as the Battle of the River Plate was written towards the end of December. According to Pamela Frankau, he claimed to have written it on his knee during a meeting of the Manpower Commission while the messenger from the newspaper office where it was overdue waited impatiently outside the door. It was by no means unusual for him to compose in this way: 'He could, would and had to, write at all times and in all places. I have seen him at work in a crowded railway carriage, in a room full of people talking, at a table in a restaurant.' The popularity of the HMS Exeter poem surprised him. But he was frequently just as surprised by what he had written or said. Pamela Frankau remarked on the 'headlong quality' of his wit: 'Often he was half-way through an epigram before he saw it coming.' And just as at Oxford someone had said that his eyes often looked astonished at what his mouth had just said, so even now he could also look surprised at what his pencil had just written - even if he then decided that it was utterly meaningless and crumpled up the finished product into a ball.[22]

V

1940

The apparently ceaseless flow of poems - Finland, the University of Jerusalem, HMS Exeter, and more - was of course no indication of any relaxation of the pressures within the Ministry. The Wolfe Committee report was due, and was duly submitted, in January. Colleagues in Whitehall all testified to the energy with which he threw himself into the work of equipping the nation for the struggle ahead. And, as was only to be expected, sooner or later he would pay the price.

Twenty years later, Pamela Frankau wrote:

> We might have guessed, in the early months of war, that he would not see the end. He burned himself out. Those of us who haunted his rooms at that time will long remember how much we took from him, in counsel, in practical help, in the reassurance that infected us with his own faith. He seemed to grow younger then. He was on top of his work, at peace in his private life, entrenched among his friends. Humbert's war was a crusade and he had chafed at its postponement since the month of Munich. Now he leaped at it.
>
> "*I demens*! fight and fail."
>
> It was his body that failed. Throughout his life his powers of recuperation had seemed limitless. He was the only person who knew when they were exhausted; he saw death coming. I quote him verbatim, as he spoke three days before he died. "Yes, I know I should see a doctor. But he would only tell me that I must lay off work for three months. And that, at this moment in history, I could not bear. I would rather die than that." He said it solemnly, not sadly, and added a little while afterwards, "The thing that I love most is England."[23]

On the eve of his birthday he had complained of feeling some discomfort, but thought it would pass. He got up in the night, had a drink of water, walked about a little, and returned to bed. In the morning of 5 January, his fifty-fifth birthday, the housekeeper who brought him his morning tea found him collapsed. Lord Horder and Dr. Lankester were called but it was too late. He was declared dead, of advanced arterio-sclerosis brought on by a combination of overwork, high blood-pressure, and no doubt excessive smoking and too little rest.

Jessie received the news of his death from Ann who telephoned from her office in the Ministry of Information. They made their way to Eccleston Square but did not meet Pamela, who slipped away quietly. Jessie was left to deal with Humbert's lawyers, doctors and executors, all of whom were unfriendly and only grudgingly allowed her some say in the funeral arrangements. She recorded later that about this time she had been dreaming so often of being married all over again to Humbert - curiously echoing her earlier dream, shortly before Consola's death, in which her mother-in-law had announced to her astonished family that she was going to be married again: 'I am going to join my lover.'

His death was announced on the radio, and tributes immediately appeared in the press. His Minister, Ernest Brown, and former colleagues such as Beveridge, understandably emphasized his distinguished work as as a Civil Servant. Robert Lynd, in *The News Chronicle*, typified the majority who tried to do justice to the variety of his talents and differed only in the detail they selected in order to illustrate a common theme: his extraordinary ability to combine so many activities into one short life. Others, more or less privately (for example, Virginia Woolf in her diary), honoured the virtue of consistency by being as unkind to him in death as they had been during his life.

Jessie got her way to some extent over the funeral arrangements. Humbert was buried quietly in Kensal Green, with a hawthorn in place of a stone to mark his grave in accordance with his wishes. A Memorial Service, conducted by the Dean of Lichfield, his former collaborator at the BBC, the Very Reverend F. A. Iremonger, was held on January 11 at St. Martin-in-the-Fields.

The Times of 12 January printed the names of over two hundred of the people present at the service. In addition to the family, there were represented the many fields in which Humbert had made such a profound and significant impression: ministers and politicians, the Civil Service and the Forces, Industry (both Employers and Unions), the I.L.O.; the arts, publishers and the Press (Sir John Squire, the Poetry Society, Richard Church, James Agate, Ivor Brown, Victor Gollancz, Edward Hulton, Viola Garvin, the Rutherstons, Sir William Rothenstein, the Maufes, and many more). And finally, if they can be separated from the others, friends: the three Maugham sisters, Beryl and Eileen Power, Dame Rachel Crowdy, and many more.

Although Pamela wrote in 1949: 'We packed St. Martin-in-the-Field for his memorial service', she was not listed among the attendance, and her absence can be readily understood; but her mother was there. Another absentee was E. C. P. Lascelles, who contrived to miss this, as he had missed most of the other important events of Humbert's earthly career. Lady Maugham was reported to have said, with characteristic acidity, 'Kate Mary was there, up among the widows.'

The I.L.O. sent its condolences; at the 89th Session of the Governing Body, on Saturday 3 February, the Chairman paid tribute to Humbert's distinguished contribution to the I.L.O. as representative of the British Government, and the Governing Body honoured his memory with a minute's silence.

Only the day before he died he had told his publisher, Heinemann, that his latest book of verse, *Kensington Gardens in War-Time*, was complete but for half-a-dozen poems and the choice of titles. It was published, without re-arrangement or amendment, in February or March. The flora, fauna, monuments and visitors of the earlier *Kensington Gardens* recur, as one might expect, but viewed with an older, more rueful if no less ironic gaze, and, significantly, without the joyful promise of Spring. The peaceful, idyllic associations of the Gardens contrasted with the harsh circumstances of war provided the perfect setting for some of his best and most characteristic work; the irony all the better for compression, the pathos delicately restrained, his wit neatly polished. A good example is 'The Anti-Social Reformer':

> In peace I hardly
> give a damn
> if there are babies
> in a pram.
>
> How strange that
> when it comes to war
> I want about
> a million more.

For Humbert - perhaps for most people - the Gardens were essentially a place for children. Two of the poems, both untitled, make particularly poignant references to his own special loss:

> A man who thirty years ago
> walked in the Gardens and overheard
> . . . .
> returns alone to sit and ponder
> under black trees and tries to guess
> where was it - here or there or yonder -
> the unrecaptured loveliness . . .?

O no! you fool, it was her power -
your lost but unforgotten child.

And

. . . .
It is no good hoping
she will step out from behind a tree.
She is the one thing between earth and heaven
I shall not see.

He is reminded, too (as who of his age could fail to be), of the earlier war:

All along the Broad Walk
listen how the soldiers talk,
ghost to ghost and shade to shade.
"This was where (I think) we played.
This was where we meant to bring
a girl to match the green of spring;
this was where we said good-bye
to all of that. I can't think why."

Epilogue

'The high song is over'

Photographs of Humbert in the nineteen-thirties bear out the dominant memory that people retained of him: the strong, bony, almost haggard face, with the fine eyes of a great comic performer, the pupils curiously ringed, his appearance made more striking by his individual style of dress, his unmistakable bow tie and malacca cane. The studied body language and carefully inflected voice added the finishing touches to this portrayal of an actor who had mastered his part to the last detail. The result, a masterpiece of self-creation, a succession of impersonations. He deflected unwelcome curiosity by pretending to be who he really was; the superficial observer saw the impersonation but not the reality.

Critics habitually said that he could not decide which he wanted to be, a writer or a civil servant. In fact there is little to support the view that, had he devoted all his energies to being only one of them, he would have been more successful. He might indeed have lived longer, but it is doubtful whether he would have been happier. What enabled him to do both without subordinating one to the other were, on the one hand his undoubted powers of intense concentration, and on the other a superabundance of nervous and intellectual energy whose ultimate source, so Storm Jameson surmised, lay in an impulse to frustration and self-punishment. The underlying melancholy of his poetry echoed the conflict between dream and reality which haunted him from his earliest days. He wrote in his letters as if his multifarious activities were all in pursuit of security. But for all his shrewdness he was manifestly not a prudent man. It was as if he accepted or arranged for himself stumbling-blocks in the way of doing what he most wanted to do.

I have often wondered where he got the profound insight which his poems on teaching revealed: 'like light through branches . . . thought touches a face that is lifted up'; 'the sacrifice of one's own summer for an unshared spring . . at best a kind of sainthood, and at worst a drudgery...' I think the explanation is simply that, from an early age, he felt somehow responsible for relieving the miseries of human kind. That was what made him both the unusual poet and the unusual civil servant that he was, highly competent but never a bureaucrat. It was revealed in his telling comment that the most efficient bureaucratic solution presupposed a state that was either above or below the nature of man. He never lost sight of the truth that he lived, worked and wrote for and in a world of frail, fallible and foolish human beings.

His humanity went to extraordinary lengths of kindness, while his position both as a civil servant and as a successful man of letters enabled him at the same time to play the patron, the actor-manager and sometimes the devil. He enjoyed pricking the bubbles of pretentiousness, and the self-important got short shrift. But for all his malicious wit, he was considerate to a fault, and in his judgements on other writers he was if anything too kind. This 'damned show-off', as J. B. Priestley called him, had no great opinion of himself; the complex, vain and worldly exterior hid a vulnerable, simple, and humble man; the ironical observer of human folly, an incorrigible optimist; the sceptic who doubted the value of all human effort, including his own, was a man who delighted in life.

What the full reality was which lay beneath all the impersonations and performances is impossible to say. Certainly no saint, nor even a man fully reconciled to himself. Equally certainly, more than simply a puppet-master or the author of his own dramatic performances.

This study set out to bring to life this fascinating character, to try to account for my almost life-long interest in him, and to repair, if possible, the neglect and misunderstanding from which his reputation as a poet has suffered for fifty or more years. In the end, I cannot claim to have achieved these aims, only to have tried my best. Humbert Wolfe began for me as an enigma and, at the end, he remains one. The space in between has been, for me at least, one of immense enrichment. I am sure that he is still safe behind his mask, as much a mystery as ever.

The last word in this portrait lies, fittingly, with Humbert, and, equally fittingly, with the final poem from *Out of Great Tribulation*, the last of the books he published in his lifetime:

'Epitaph'

Now it is time to sleep
I only ask
to be allowed to keep
unpierced the mask.
behind whose close
and changing covers
I hid myself from foes
and lovers.

Appendices

AI
Departmental Organisations on 1 June, 1915

I. Munitions Supply Organisation under the War Office

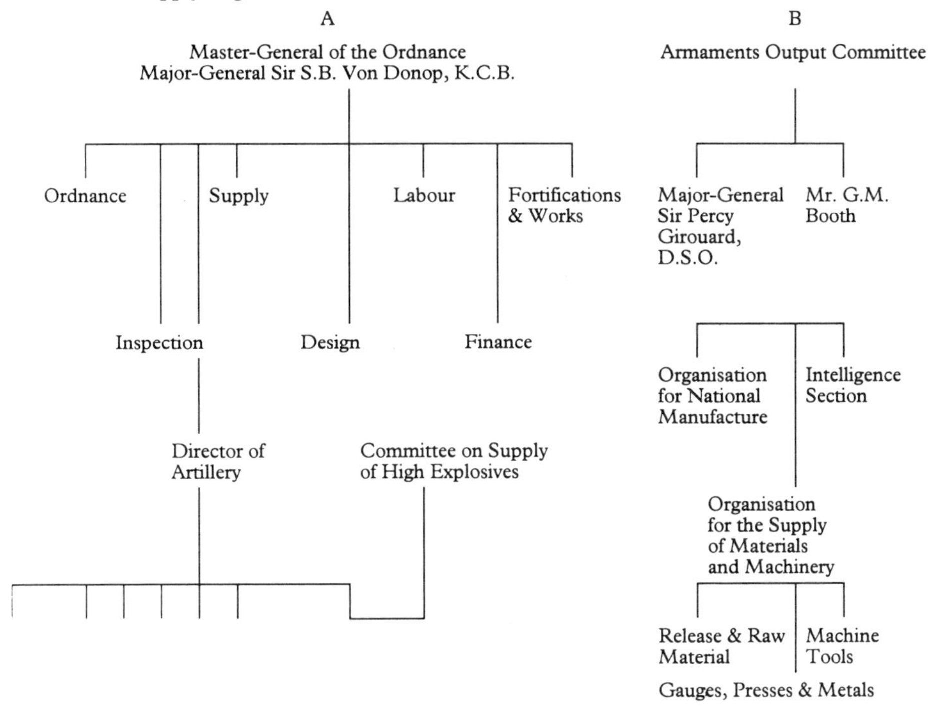

II. Organisation at 6, Whitehall Gardens

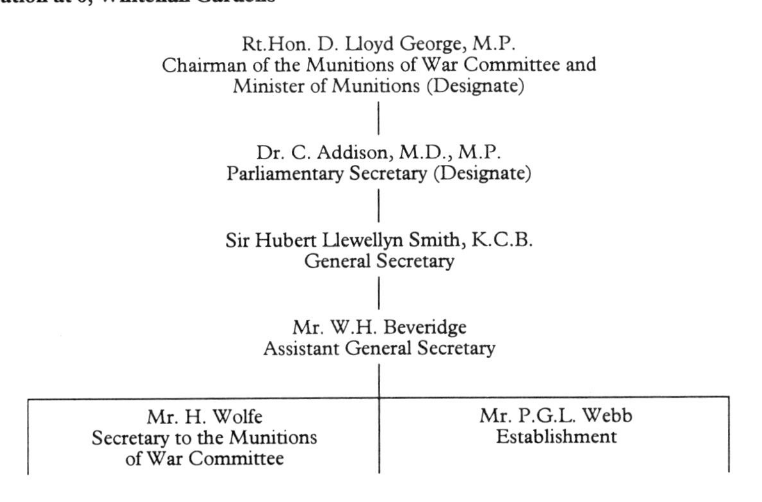

AII
Departmental Organisation on 1 July, 1915

Minister of Munitions
Rt. Hon. D. Lloyd George, M.P.

General Secretary

Parliamentary Secretary

Parliamentary Military Secretary

Sir H.Ll. Smith, K.C.B.

Dr C. Addison, M.P.

Maj.-Gen. Ivor Phipps, D.S.O., M.P.

Secretariat & Labour
Mr W.H. Beveridge
Assistant General Secretary

Munitions Supply
Maj.-Gen. Sir P. Girouard
Director-General

Explosives Supply
Rt.Hon.Lord Moulton, K.C.B., F.R.S.
Director General

Engineer Munitions
Brig. L.C. Jackson
Director-General

AIII
Organisation on July, 1916

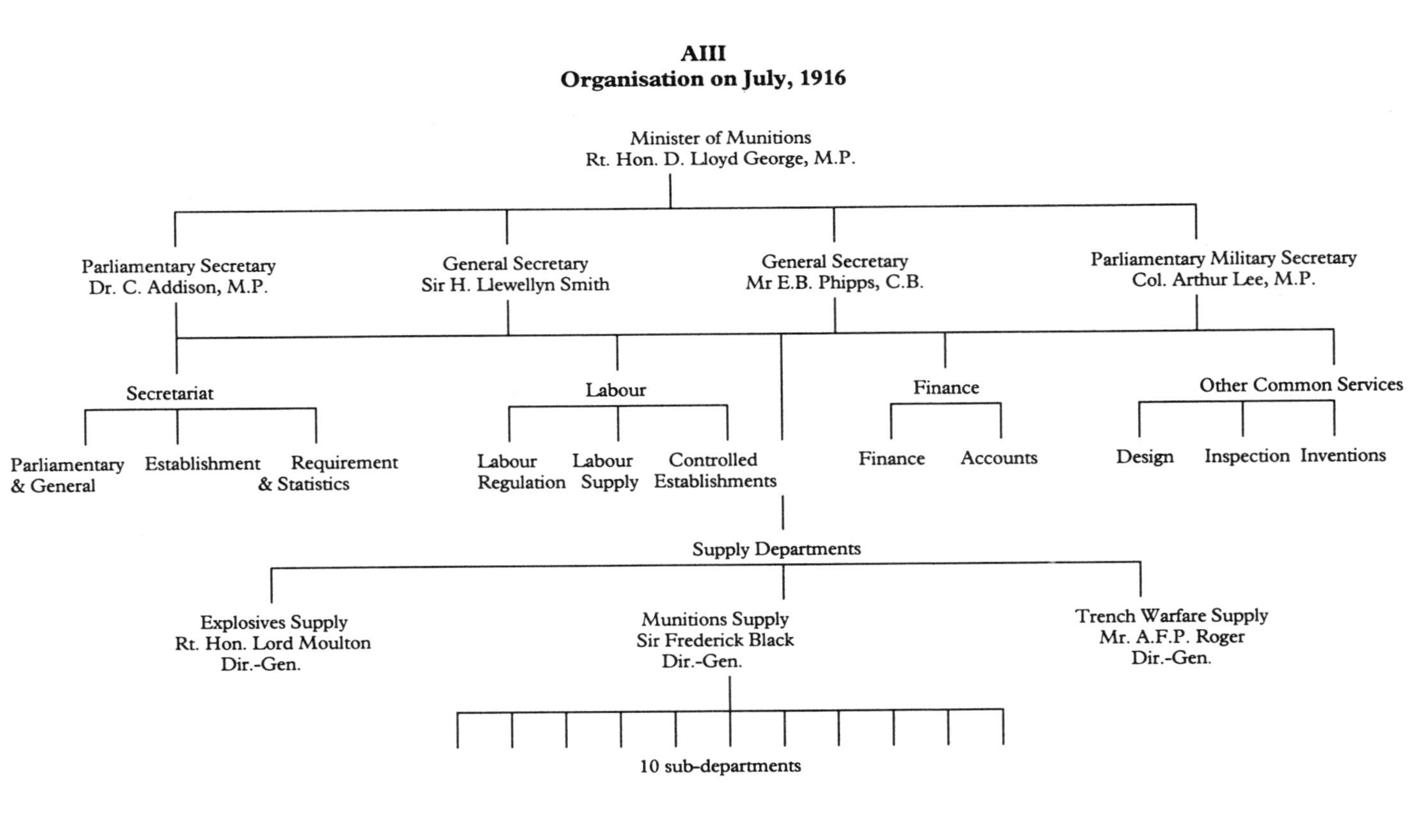

Minister of Munitions
Rt. Hon. D. Lloyd George, M.P.
Parliamentary Secretary
Dr. C. Addison, M.P.
General Secretary
Sir H. Llewellyn Smith
General Secretary
Mr E.B. Phipps, C.B.
Parliamentary Military Secretary
Col. Arthur Lee, M.P.
Secretariat
Parliamentary & General
Establishment
Requirement & Statistics
Labour
Labour Regulation
Labour Supply
Controlled Establishments
Finance
Finance
Accounts
Other Common Services
Design
Inspection
Inventions
Supply Departments
Explosives Supply
Rt. Hon. Lord Moulton
Dir.-Gen.
Munitions Supply
Sir Frederick Black
Dir.-Gen.
Trench Warfare Supply
Mr. A.F.P. Roger
Dir.-Gen.
10 sub-departments
Imperial Munitions Board
Tank Supply Committee
American Organisation

AIV
Departmental Organisation on 1 July, 1917

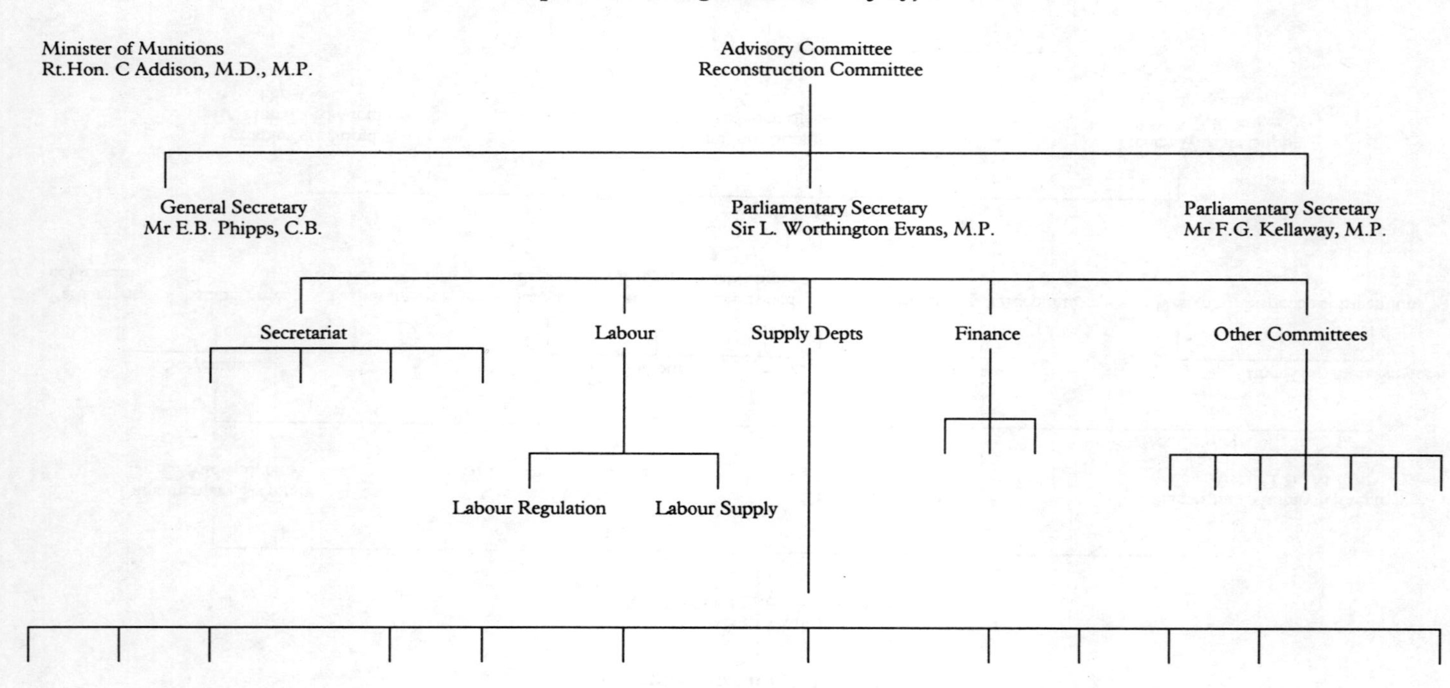

AV
Departmental Organisation on 1 July, 1918

Minister of Munitions
and President of The Munitions Council
Rt.Hon. W.S. Churchill, M.P.

Parliamentary and Financial Secretary:	Sir L. Worthington Evans, Bt., M.P. Vice-President: Munitions Council
Parliamentary Secretary:	Mr. F.G. Kellaway, M.P. Vice-President: Munitions Council
Secretary:	Sir W. Graham Greene, K.C.B.
Assistant Secretary:	Mr. J.E. Masterton Smith, C.B.

The Munitions Council

Group (Department)		Council Member
SEC.	(Secretariat)	Sir W. Graham Greene
D	(Design)	Maj.-Gen. The Hon. Sir F.E. Bingham, K.C.M.G., C.B.
S	(Steel & Iron)	Sir John Hunter, K.B.E.
M	(Materials, etc)	Sir Ernest Moir, Bt.
X	(Explosives)	Sir Keith Price
O	(Ordnance)	Sir James Stevenson, Bt.
W	(Warfare)	Brig.-Gen. Rt. Hon. J.E.B. Seely, C.B., D.S.O., M.P.
A	(Air)	Sir Arthur Duckham, K.C.B.
L	(Labour)	Sir Stephenson Kent, K.C.B.

(Additional Council members representing Ministry of Munitions in Paris, War Office, etc.)

BI

Ministry of Labour Administration and Personnel: Ministers

Minister		Parliamentary Secretary
1916	(Dec) John Hodge	W. C. Bridgeman
1917	(Aug) G. H. Roberts	
1919	(Jan) Sir R. Horne	G. J. Wardle
1920	(Mar)T. J. Macnamara	Sir C. A. M. Barlow
1922	(Oct) Sir C. A. M. Barlow	A. Boyd-Carpenter
1923	(Mar)	H. B. Betterton
1924	(Jan) T. Shaw	Margaret Bondfield
	(Nov) Sir A. Steel-Maitland	H. B. Betterton
1929	(June) Margaret Bondfield	J. Lawson
1931	(Aug) Sir H. B. Betterton	M. Gray
	(Nov)	R. Hudson
1934	(June) O. Stanley	
1935	(June) E. Brown	A. Muirhead
1937	(May)	R. A. Butler
1938	(Feb)	A. Lennox-Boyd

BII

Ministry of Labour Administration and Personnel: Officials

	Permanent Secretary	Deputy Secretary	Principal Assistant Secretary
1916	Sir D. J.Shackleton, KCB		
1917			H. B. Butler
1919		E. C. Cunningham	F. G. Bowers T. W. Phillips A. W. Watson H. J. Wilson
1920	Sir J. Masterton-Smith and Sir D. J. Shackleton		H. Wolfe
1921	H. J. Wilson		
1924	Sir H. J. Wilson		T. W. Phillips J. N. Barlow
1929			J.F.G.Price C. W. G. Eady F. W. Leggett
1930	Sir F. Floud		
1933			J. A. Dale
1934			
1935	Sir T. W. Phillips	Sir J. F. G. Price	J. S. Nicholson
1938		H. Wolfe	J. M. Glen C. B. Hawkins G. H. Ince

Works by Humbert Wolfe

I

Poetry, Verse Plays and Verse Translations

London Sonnets. Oxford 1920.

Shylock Reasons with Mr. Chesterton, and Other Poems. Oxford 1921.

Kensington Gardens. London 1924, New York 1927.

Lampoons. London 1925.

The Unknown Goddess. London 1925, New York 1925 (with 2 new poems), London 1927.

Humoresque. London 1926.

News of the Devil. London 1926, New York 1926.

[Thirty-four poems] *Augustan Books of Modern Poetry*, First Series. London 1926. Selection.

Cursory Rhymes. London 1926, Garden City NY 1928.

Others Abide. London 1928. Verse translations from the Greek Anthology.

Requiem. London 1927, New York 1927.

Veni Creator! privately printed 1927. Reprinted in *The Uncelestial City*, 1930, below.

This Blind Rose. London 1928, Garden City NY 1929.

The Moon and Mrs. Smith. London 1928. Christmas card, containing a poem reprinted in *The Uncelestial City*, 1930, below.

The Silver Cat and Other Poems. New York, London 1928.

Troy (Ariel Poem) London 1928.

The Wall of Weeping, by Edmond Fleg. Translated from the French by Wolfe. Limited edition of 750 copies. London 1929, New York 1929.

Early Poems. Oxford 1930, New York 1931. Contains *London Sonnets* and *Shylock Reasons with Mr. Chesterton*. With a preface by Wolfe.

Homage to Meleager. New York 1930 (464 signed copies). Verse translations from the Greek.

Portrait of Heine. London 1930, 1935 (as Selected lyrics of Heine), reprinted 1950.

The Uncelestial City. London 1930, New York 1930.

Snow. London 1931.

ABC of the Theatre. London 1932.

Reverie of Policeman: a ballet in three acts. London 1933.

Sonnets pour Hélène, by Pierre de Ronsard, with English renderings by Wolfe. London 1934, New York 1934.

The Fourth of August: a sonnet sequence. London 1935.

Stings and Wings. London 1935.

X at Oberammergau: a poem. London 1935.

Cyrano de Bergerac: a translation of Rostand's play. London 1937.

Don J. Ewan. London 1937.

The Silent Knight: a romantic comedy in three acts from the Hungarian of Eugene Heltai. London 1937.

Out of Great Tribulation. London 1939.

Kensington Gardens in War-time. (posthumously) London 1940. See also *A Winter Miscellany*. London 1930, below.

II

Other Works

Circular Saws. London 1923. Short stories.

Labour Supply and Regulation. Oxford 1923 (Economic and social history of the World War: British series).

Edward Lear. Edited selection with introduction by Wolfe (Augustan Books of English Poetry) London 1927.

The Craft of Verse: Oxford poetry essay. New York 1928.

Dialogues and Monologues. London 1928, New York 1929. Essays on literary topics.

The Poetical Works of Robert Herrick. 4 vols. London 1928. With a preface by Wolfe.

Selected Poems by Swinburne. Introduction by Wolfe. London 1928.

Notes on English Verse Satire. London 1929, New York 1929.

Tennyson. London 1930.

A Winter Miscellany [in prose and verse], edited and compiled by Wolfe, and including original poems by the editor. London 1930, New York 1930.

George Moore. London 1931, New York 1932, London 1933 (revised edition).

Signpost to Poetry: an introduction to the study of verse. London 1931.

The Life of Percy Bysshe Shelley as comprised in The life of Shelley by Thomas Jefferson Hogg, The recollections of Shelley and Byron by Edward John Trelawny, Memoirs of Shelley by Thomas Love Peacock. Introduction by Wolfe. 2 vols. London 1933.

Now a Stranger. London 1933. Autobiography.

Romantic and Unromantic Poetry. Bristol 1933 (Arthur Skemp memorial lecture).

Portraits By Inference. London 1934. Reminiscences and sketches of contemporaries.

Ronsard and French Romantic Poetry: the Zaharoff lecture for 1934. Oxford 1935.

P.L.M.: Peoples, Landfalls, Mountains. London 1936. Travel in France.

Personalities: a selection from the writings of A. A. Baumann. Edited by Wolfe. London 1936, New York 1936.

The Pilgrim's Way. London 1936. An anthology, chiefly of poetry, selected by Wolfe.

The Upward Anguish. London 1938. Autobiography. Contains *The Old Man of Königsberg, or, Kant and re-Kant: a Greats Week Pantomime*, in verse written in part by Wolfe and published separately.

Truffle Eater. London (no date, probably between 1933 and 1936). Published under the pseudonym of 'Oistros'.

Twelve Humbert Wolfe Songs: music by Gustav Holst. Introduced by Imogen Holst. London 1970.

Wolfe also edited the second set of Augustan Books of English Poetry. London 1926.

Writings on Wolfe

Apart from mentions and incidental comments in the writings of contemporaries and in books about twentieth century writers, the following is as complete a list as I have been able to make of articles written specifically about Wolfe during his lifetime and since his death.

Gorman, H. — Humbert Wolfe. *Bookman* (New York) 65. 1927

Garrod, H. W. — Mr. Humbert Wolfe. In his *The profession of Poetry*. London 1929

Arns, K. — Humbert Wolfe. *Zeitschrift für französischen und englischen Unterricht 30*. 1931.

Gilbert, T.R. — Humbert Wolfe. *London Quarterly & Holborn Revue, 165*. 1940.

Shillito, E. — A satirist of these days. *Christian Century 7*. February 1940.

Wells, H. W. — Humbert Wolfe: a modern English Heine. *Sewanee Revue 49*. 1941.

Bentwich, N. — Humbert Wolfe, poet and civil servant. *Menorah Journal 31*. 1943. Includes 3 poems.

Bushnell, A. — Humbert Wolfe. *Poetry Review 34*. 1943.

Garvin, V. G. — Two Observer reviewers: Gerald Gould and Humbert Wolfe. *English 5*. 1944.

Notes and References

N.B. References to the writings of Humbert Wolfe are by title only.

Preface

1. *Weekend Telegraph*, 7 January 1989.

Prologue

1. It has not proved possible to trace the newspaper in which the poem appeared.
2. *Whitaker's Almanac* 1940.
3. *Reverie of Policeman* (London, 1933), pp. 33, 79 & 95, where in each instance it is 'love's starry candle'.
4. *Humoresque* (London, 1926), p. 68.
5. *Now A Stranger* (London, 1933), pp. 84 - 90. A less romantic view of pantomime is to be found in the preface to *A Winter Miscellany*, pp. 25-27, written three years before *Now A Stranger*, in 1930. Musing on 'The Winter of the Reveller', he wrote:

   > 'It's true, of course, that we have lost the taste for gargantuan enjoyment. . . The pantomime was not the theatre at all. It was only the national unbuttoning of the waistcoat after a meal of incomparable indigestibility. It was everybody's post-prandial nap.'

6. The French word for the black velvet mask worn at a masked ball was 'loup' - wolf, an interesting but doubtless fortuitous association.

Chapter One

I

1. Staats Archiv, Schwerin.
2. Emido de Felice, *Dizionario dei Cognomi Italiani*. Among the more notable bearers of the name in recent times were David, a famous rabbi who died in Asti in 1892, Humbert's cousin, Umberto Terracini, the lawyer, journalist and communist senator who, with Togliatti, was a founder member of the Italian Communist Party,

and Dr. Lore Terracini of the University of Turin. *see Panorama Biografica degli Italiani d'Oggi*, a cura di Gennaro Vaccaro, Vol.II I-Z (Firenze 1956).

3. Background supplied by Dr. Lore Terracini.
4. Archivio Storico, Commune di Genova, 1871 Census.
5. The letter which records his appointment to a partnership describes him as a long-serving employee. cf Brandt MS, Hallward Library, University of Nottingham.
6. quoted in *Now A Stranger,* p 56.
7. I am indebted to Alan Longbottom (Bradford Jewish Register) for a reference to 'nuestros commandit.', suggesting that Simon, Israel & Co. were sleeping partners in a firm in S. America; another reference mentions Puerto Suarez, 1906 (Brasil?) and Stofen & Schmack Müller (formerly Voss & Stofen) with whom Simon. Israel & Co. are thought to have had connections.
8. *see* G. Firth: *Bradford and the Industrial Revolution* (Halifax, 1990), and D. James, *Bradford* (Halifax, 1990). Titus Salt built Saltaire, the largest of the model villages developed by Victorian industrialists, as much, it seems, from fear of political dissent as from paternal or commercial motives: Bradford had seen a near-revolution in 1840, it was the birthplace of the Independent Labour party in 1893 and gave support to the political activists who had fled to England from Germany after 1848: cf Rosemary Ashton's '*Little Germany - German Refugees in Victorian Britain*' (OUP 1986).
9. David James, *op. cit.* p 32.
10. Burgess Roll, Bradford Central Library.
11. J. B. Priestley, *An English Journey*, 1934, pp. 160 - 161.
12. *Now A Stranger*, pp. 116, 125 - 126.
13. *ibid.* pp. 119-120 and Jewish archives in Bradford Central Library. The brochure published to mark the centenary of the Synagogue records, among the rabbi's efforts to supplement his income, his advertised rates for marriages, Bar-Mitzvahs and 'Cut-price circumcisions'.
14. *Now A Stranger,* p. 123. Humbert's fellow-Bradfordian, J. B. Priestley, in his *English Journey* (1934) draws a very similar picture, and recommends *Now A Stranger* for "a glimpse of what life was like in that colony for at least one small boy". (*English Journey* p.160) Over fifty years later Michael Wharton in his autobiography, *The Missing Will,* describes a remarkably similar childhood in Bradford at the time of the First World War.

II

15. *Now A Stranger*, p. 3.

16. *Aeneid,* Bk. vi, *see* translation in *Early Poems* (1930), 'Orpheus', p. 105.
17. *Now A Stranger,* pp. 37-38. It was recognisably the same a century later - *see* illustration.
18. *Cursory Rhymes,* 1927, p. 117, illustrated by Albert Rutherston, one of Humbert's lifelong friends, whose personality and appearance are vividly described in *Now A Stranger.*
19. In addition to Humbert's nine pages of vivid recollections of the two doctor brothers, Hermann and Adolf Bronner, in *Now A Stranger, see* Rosemary Ashton *Little Germany,* pp. 172 -173, 247 & pp. 280 n105, for an account of their medical and cultural contribution to Bradford.
20. *Now A Stranger, passim.*
21. On the occasion of questions raised in Parliament about Humbert's German origins.
22. *Now A Stranger,* p. 196. This recollection appears inconsistent with what is known of her deafness - *see* n.24 below.
23. Unpublished papers of Jessie Wolfe.
24. Jessie, in an unpublished paper, recalled an incident on the shores of Lake Como, when Consola retailed to her companions the conversation of some German tourists who were certainly too far away to be overheard.
25. *Now A Stranger,* pp. 180 -181. Information provided by Alan Longbottom (Bradford Jewish Register) says 1887; *Now A Stranger* says 'in the boy's sixth year', which would be 1891. Both sisters settled in Bradford. Sylvia subsequently became a teacher of Italian, connected with the University of Leeds, Rosetta a dressmaker. Neither appears to have married.
26. *Now A Stranger,* p. 184.
27. *ibid.*p. 184.
28. *ibid.*p. 182.
29. *ibid., passim.*
30. The 'M's were almost certainly the Mahlers, *q.v.*
31. *Now A Stranger,* pp. 187-195.

III

32. *ibid.* p. 9.
33. *ibid.* p. 5.
34. *ibid.* pp. 14-15. A resort north of Morecambe, apparently a favourite with Humbert - he returned there before going up to Oxford; see *The Upward Anguish.* This passage suggests evidence of conflation, for if Oswald was twelve, Humbert could not have been seven years old - there were barely two years between the boys.

35. *ibid.* pp 15-19.
36. *ibid.* pp. 20-22.
37. *ibid.* Chapter 4. This outing was to play a special part in the genesis of Humbert's poetic vocation; *see* Chapter 2 later.
38. *ibid.* pp. 114-115.
39. *ibid.* pp 130-131.
40. *see* above n11. I have been unable to identify the later Priestley work in which I first read this some years ago.
41. Victoria Glendinning: *Edith Sitwell*, 1981, p. 9.
42. attributed to the 'M's in *Now A Stranger*, p. 41.
43. e.g. in the episode of 'chumping', i.e. stealing wood for the Guy Fawkes bonfire. Berto, engaged in this mischief, got himself appointed guardian of the woodstore by the victim, Mrs. Bronner, and was duly rewarded with extra wood for his stewardship, *ibid.* Chapter 2.
44. *ibid.* p. 137.
45. *ibid. passim.*
46. *ibid.* pp. 71-74. The poem 'Seaside' is in *Cursory Rhymes*, 1927, pp.123 - 124.
47. *ibid.* pp. 77-78.
48. *ibid.* pp. 80-81. Whether this was the original German '*Der Struwelpeter*' or the English translation is not known, but the book marked him deeply and he was to draw on it in the thirties for his attack on Nazism called '*The Truffle-Eater*' - *see* later Chapter 9, 1935.
49. Article by Humbert in *The Yorkshire Observer*, 20 April, 1939.
50. *Now A Stranger*, pp. 90-92.
51 *ibid.* pp. 133-136.
52. *ibid.* pp. 140-154.
53. *ibid.* pp 154-161. It is hard not to entertain a suspicion that this account was intended to justify as much as to explain the adult Humbert, for whom being different became increasingly important. The events in this story hardly seem to justify the attack on Mr Rendell's character. Moreover, it is as if Humbert became so engrossed in making his story as amusing as possible that he forgot his original intention of showing up the master in a bad light and ended up with a quite engaging portrayal of him. Other examples of a similar kind (e.g. in *The Upward Anguish*) confirm the impression that although Humbert rarely resisted the temptation to be witty at other people's expense, he meant no malice by it and rarely harboured any grudges himself. Perhaps he felt in some way grateful to his victims for affording him such splendid opportunities.
54. *ibid.* pp. 32-35.
55. *ibid.* pp.161-163.

56. It is in this connection that Archie Hamilton emerges as a faithful, steady, stubbornly courageous and honest friend - *see Now A Stranger*, pp. 165-168. Archie was the son of a doctor and lived near the Wolffs, on Manningham Lane. Archie later became a doctor, married Humbert's youngest sister, Sylvia, and died a few months before Humbert.
57. Information supplied to Ann Wolfe by Sir Geoffrey Burton.
58. *Now A Stranger*, p. 171.
59. *ibid.* pp. 119-129.
60. *The Upward Anguish,* p. 2 and p. 4.
61. Reported by his sisters and Jessie (unpublished papers).
62. *Now A Stranger*, pp. 172-173.
63. *ibid.* pp. 200-202.

Chapter Two

1. The likeliest explanation for what look like three attempts at the Higher Certificate is that the first of these was the old School Certificate, and the second a practice shot at the Higher Certificate, before the final, serious, examination in 1903.
2. *Now A Stranger* p. 171.
3. The description of the old school in *Now A Stranger*, p. 132, is borne out by Sir William Rothenstein in *Men and Memories*, Vol. I 1872 - 1900.
4. *Now A Stranger* p. 135.
5. Information supplied to Ann Wolfe by Sir G. Burton.
6. *Now A Stranger*, pp. 99 - 100.
7. *ibid.* pp. 199 - 200. After Martin Wolff's death, "in my tenth year" according to *A Winter Miscellany*, p. 12, they left Mount Royd to live at No. 4 Oak Mount, a road just behind Mount Royd. They were certainly living at that address in 1902.
8. The Preface to *Early Poems*, p. ix (Blackwell 1930), shows that he had considered rewriting those of his early poems 'in which the 'prentice hand has most obviously failed' but having experimented in revising one poem 'I found that I was ploughing the sands.' But the poems may have undergone revision before being published in the original *London Sonnets*.
9. *The Yorkshire Observer*, 28 January 1927.
10. *The London Mercury*, 26 May 1936.
11. Newspaper interview in *The Yorkshire Observer*, 20 April 1939.
12. *The Oxford Magazine*, Eights Week Number, 1904. In 1960 Sir Geoffrey Burton, who had become Chairman of Governors of Bradford Grammar School, wondered if Humbert could have improved upon the following rendering offered by a recent Classical VIth at Bradford:

"In tumulum large Lethaeum funde papaver,
quo gravius mortis premat alta quies.
Et capiti lauro textam super adde coronam,
laurea cui vivo nulla corona data est."
(Information supplied by Ann Wolfe.)

13. *The Upward Anguish*, p. 43.
14. *ibid.* pp. 38 - 45. Humbert said that they took the train to Kent Bridge but this was almost certainly Kents Bank, on the western side of Grange, from where they could strike northwards towards the lake. Sir Geoffrey Burton confessed in later life that he could not recollect uttering all the words attributed to him or vouch for many of the discourses recorded, but he retained vivid memories of other events of their holiday.
15. *ibid.* p. 43.
16. Sir William Rothenstein, *op. cit.* p. 25.
17. *The Upward Anguish*, pp. 43 - 44.
18. *ibid.* p. 46.
19. *ibid.* pp. 45 - 46.
20. Bradford Grammar School collection: *Poems*; *see* later Chapter 3 (iv).
21. Jessie Wolfe, unpublished papers.
22. Jacquetta Hawkes: *Mortimer Wheeler: Adventurer in Archaeology*, p. 31; *see* also pp. 16 -17. Wheeler's father had become editor of *The Bradford*, later *The Yorkshire Observer* in 1890.
23. *The Upward Anguish*, pp. 4 and 16.
24. *The Uncelestial City*, p. 17.
25. *The Upward Anguish*, p. 17.

Chapter Three

I

1. cf J. McMurtry, *English Language, English Literature: The Creation of an Academic Discipline*, London, 1985, pp. 160-163; also S. J. Curtis, *History of Education in Great Britain*, 7th ed. 1967, pp. 135-136, & p. 458, and Sir Charles Mallett, *History of the University of Oxford*, 1927 Methuen.
2. For the scholarship examination and Oxford, *see* chiefly *The Upward Anguish* (Cassell, 1938); 'Humbert Wolfe at Oxford' in *The Yorkshire Post* 8 June, 1938; 'Masters and Boys' by Humbert Wolfe in *The Yorkshire Observer*, 20 April,1939.
3. *The Upward Anguish*, p. 1.

II

4. *ibid.* pp. 53 - 54. On Keith, *see* later, Chapter 8, n14. Allen gained a First in Theology in 1908 and later became Assistant Bishop of Oxford. Measham entered the GPO and rose to become Regional Director of the Scottish Region; he kept a photograph which corroborated Humbert's self-portrait. Evelyn-White died tragically in 1924; 'pale as papyrus' clearly refers both to his poor health and to his interest in Papyri, on which he became a considerable authority.
5. Information supplied by Ann Wolfe.
6. For example Chapter 7, conversations with Flecker and others on philosophy, which capture with perceptive accuracy the callowly clever dialogue which must have been more fun to take part in than it is to read.
7. *Requiem*, published in 1927, was the book which effectively established Humbert's reputation as a poet.
8. Obituary article in *News Chronicle*, 6 January 1940.
9. *The Upward Anguish*, p. 58.
10. *The Upward Anguish*, pp. 57-61. Keith was already dead when the book was published in 1938. The dedicatory poem was re-printed in 1939 in *Out of Great Tribulation*; *see* also later, Chapter VIII (ii) 1928, and *Dialogues and Monologues.*
11. *The Oxford Magazine,* March 1904.
12. *The Upward Anguish*, pp. 159 - 162.
13. On Morrison's refusal to sit Ancient History in Greats, and subsequent move to Cambridge, *see The Upward Anguish*, p. 153; also present work, Chapter 4. Likewise for Flecker's move to Cambridge, and Humbert's encounter with Rupert Brooke.
14. *The Upward Anguish*, p. 93.

III

15. Information supplied to Ann Wolfe by Ward, Burton & Measham.
16. *The Upward Anguish*, pp. 76-77.
17. *see The Oxford Magazine* 1907 Feb 20: 'Mr. R.A. Knox wanted Germany to try Socialism as an *experimentum* in her *corpus vile.* Mr. Knox was very crisp.' It is tempting to see in the phrase the origin of Evelyn Waugh's *Vile Bodies.* The origins of the phrase are obscure; it sounds classical but made its way into English only in the 19th century [Bliss, *Dictionary of Foreign Words and Phrases* 1966] and was variously invoked to justify vivisection and the trials of poisons, as well as being a recommendation to try out a probably unsuccessful experiment on something of little value: 'First try the gilt before the gold.' *The Stanford Dictionary of*

Anglicised Words and Phrases (1964 edition) cites De Quincey's *Confessions of an English Opium Eater* (1822) where the phrase is quoted but as one familiar to the reader, not as a coining of De Quincey's. The likelihood is that the joke was in university currency well before the arrival of either Knox or Wolff, and was trotted out regularly, with as many putative parents as there were generations of undergraduates.

18. This was the debate which he cites as the occasion of his first year failure: 'the Isis said afterwards "U. Wolff (Wadham) made a dull and unconvincing speech."' The reader is left with a suspicion that it suited Humbert's autobiographical purpose to recall the more damning of the two reviews. (*The Upward Anguish*, Chapter 8.)
19. On his glazing of the eyes - often when he was pondering a reply: virtually everyone I have spoken to or read noted this curious lizard-like phenomenon.
20. *see The Upward Anguish*, p. 95, for his ambitions, and pp. 166-7 for 'the Scholar's climbing instincts'.
21. *see History of The Oxford Canning Club, 1861-1911*, edited by Harold Steinhart. Reports of debates suggest that Humbert's Catholic leanings may have owed something to The Canning's Anglo-Catholic view of Church and State.
22. R. A. Knox subsequently became chaplain to the Roman Catholic undergraduates at Oxford, and a well-known writer and preacher. He was created a Domestic Prelate by Pope Pius XII. His best-known writings are probably his English translation of the Vulgate Bible (Burns Oates and Washbourne, 1945 and 1949) and *Enthusiasm*, his study of some XVII and XVIII century religious movements (Oxford, 1950). For Humbert's recollections of his political frequentations at Oxford, *see The Upward Anguish*, pp. 177 - 180.

IV

23. This is at variance with the evidence of the Bradford Grammar School archive which contains a poem dated September 1906 but nothing for October.
24. R. J. R. Measham, paper in Wadham archives.
25. 'The Old Man of Könisgsberg': appendix to *The Upward Anguish*. Ferdinand Canning Scott Schiller, 1864-1937, Fellow of Corpus Christi College, later Professor of Philosophy in the University of S. California, claimed to have discovered his generalized Pragmatism, which he called 'humanism', before he met William James (*see* Concise Encyclopedia of Western Philosophy and Philosophers, ed. J. O. Urmson, 2nd edition, London, 1975).

26. *see Bradfordian* for July 1907: "Wolff consoles himself for his defeat in Schools by publishing libels on his examiners. Mr. Schiller, of Corpus, has been heard to say that the author of 'fiat experimentum in corpore vili' shall repent of his Wadham levity." This is most probably a reference to *The Old Man of Königsberg*. Why *The Bradfordian*'s correspondent should have made the mistake about Berto's 'defeat in Schools' is a mystery.
27. *Portraits By Inference*, pp. 9 - 10.
28. Humbert wrote about the state of poetry in Oxford in two separate accounts of his meetings with Flecker, first in 1934 in *Portraits By Inference*, pp. 9 -22, then again in 1938 in *The Upward Anguish*, chapter 7 - 'Poets and Metaphysicians in Oxford' - *passim*. While both books agree about the state of poetry, their accounts of the meetings with Flecker differ on several points.
29. *The Upward Anguish*, p. 150.
30. Jessie Wolfe: unpublished papers. There is little doubt, however, that she was more than fifteen when Berto wrote to her from Oxford. A longer version of the poem occurs in a letter from Humbert to Jessie in 1910 - *see* later in Chapter 4.
31. *see* later Chapter VIII. G. Sampson, in his *Concise Cambridge History of English Literature*, p. 1020, said of Humbert: 'something of an echo poet: he frequently reminds the reader of someone else, perhaps Heine most of all?'
32. Books I - IV were published in 1890, with reprints in 1891 and 1894.
33. *see* later Chapter 9.

V

34. *The Upward Anguish*, p. 205.
35. 'Oxford', in *The Unknown Goddess*, 1925.

Chapter Four

I

1. Jessie Wolfe: unpublished papers
2. 'In this case, Mr Wolfe's birth certificate was sent to him on loan on 16 March 1909 in connection with a legacy and not returned.' - letter from Civil Service Commission, 1985.
3. *The Uncelestial City*, p. 67, mentions Glencruitan Road, where the Wolffs stayed when holidaying in Oban.
4. *A Winter Miscellany* Eyre & Spottiswoode, 1930, p. 23.

5. Jessie Wolfe: unpublished papers. Jessie's own views on the matter were apparently not sought.
6. Although his wife's papers suggest that he was baptized and confirmed in St. Paul's Cathedral, no trace of either ceremony is to be found in the Cathedral records. Searches in the Westminster Archives and the Greater London Record Office of the baptismal registers of all churches dedicated to St. Paul in the central London area have proved equally barren. It seems likely that Jessie was mistaken about the name of the church.
7. *The Upward Anguish*, pp. 65 - 67.
8. *The Upward Anguish*, pp. 147 - 150.
9. Jessie Wolfe: unpublished papers; *see* also *The Uncelestial City*, p. 231, 'The Broken Bread.'
10. Jessie Wolfe: unpublished papers.
11. *Haddingtonshire Courier*, 6 February 1880 (especially for Balfour's references to 1872 Education Act); and Mr. A. B. Ellis, Rector of the Academy, 1991, to whom I am indebted for the earlier history of the school.
12. Mr. A. B. Ellis, letter to the author, 1991.
13. Ann Wolfe: letter to the author, 1991
14. *ibid.*
15. Ann Wolfe: conversation and letter, 1993.
16. The Pimlico house was probably 99 St. George's Square, where Berto lived in May 1908
17. For the New English Art Club, and for Michel Salaman, in addition to *Portraits By Inference*, *see* Susan Chitty: *Gwen John 1876 - 1939*, p. 38; and Sir William Rothenstein's *Men and Memories*, Vol.1, pp. 356 - 357, and Vol. 2, p. 10 and p. 32. Jessie thought that Humbert met Salaman at Oxford.

II

18. Jessie Wolfe: unpublished papers.
19. Oswald had embarked on a business career on leaving school in 1896 and before long was sent to gain experience in Germany.
20. Jessie Wolfe: unpublished papers.
21. *ibid.*
22. *ibid.* In 1909/1910 a 'working class' income (i.e. artisan, not labourer) was probably £110 p.a. at best.
23. *ibid.*
24. The typescript collection of poems in the Bradford Grammar School archives bears, in addition to his name, the address '17 Hallam Street'.
25. Jessie Wolfe: unpublished papers.

26. The typescript copy of 'The Great Adventure' appears to be corrupt, but repeats the apparent lack of concord between 'soul' and 'embrace . . . founder' in the last two lines, which Berto probably justified as a subjunctive so as to make the last line scan. The title and contents of his first published collection of poems, '*London Sonnets*' (1920), justify the inference that the idea for the book originated in the suburban sonnet competition of 1909.
27. *London Sonnets*, p. 38. The intervening time has allowed for a generalised rather than a particular response (originally no doubt dashed off in a hurry), and the result is a better poem. But it is interesting to note what he retains of the original, and the switch from 'lips' to 'tips', a touch of English rather than Continental gallantry! But the final exclamation mark of the original is more logical than the question mark of the later, published poem. Many of the poems in the 1930 re-edition show signs of slip-shod proof-reading. In a letter to Jessie (August 18, 1926) Humbert confirmed that this sonnet was by way of an answer to to Jessie's, and the other two on 'Love' were a continuation. He added: 'The "London Sonnets" proper were all written at Battersea.'
28. Jessie Wolfe: unpublished papers.
29. *see Now A Stranger* and present work, Chapter I.
30. Jessie Wolfe: unpublished papers.
31. Lascelles, Major Edward Charles Ponsonby, 1884 - 1956; son of Lt. Col. H. A. Lascelles; served in the Boer War, joined the Board of Trade, was called to the Bar 1911, married (1911) Leila, daughter of Sir Vincent Kennett-Barrington. The combination of military distinction, upper class background, and shared Civil Service and legal ambitions would explain Berto's desire to cultivate his acquaintance. For details of his subsequent career, publications etc., *see Who Was Who*, vol. 5, p. 638.
32. For the engagement party and the house-hunting, *see* Jessie Wolfe: unpublished papers

III

33. Ann Wolfe is also sure that the wedding was in Edinburgh but does not know in which church. Humbert's letter of May 11, 1927 to Jessie mentions 'the red church in Morningside' - a clear reference to their wedding.
34. Preserved in the typescript poems (Ruth Atkinson): p. 57 in *Verses*, and also in *Poems*, dedicated to Consola, December 24 1904. It is also in the typescript collection of *47 Poems*' and dated 22 Sept 1904, in the Bradford Grammar School Archive.
35. Jessie Wolfe: unpublished papers.

36. He had a fondness for this Shakespearian phrase; it occurs in his letters and in *Now A Stranger*, to describe Bradford Grammar School (*see* above, Chapter I).
37. Jessie Wolfe: unpublished papers.
38. *ibid.*

IV

39. Humbert was to work with the man in question, H. B. Butler, years later at the International Labour Office in Geneva.
40. Jessie Wolfe: unpublished papers.
41. Jessie Wolfe: unpublished papers. The present appearance of the house, now a holiday guest-house (1987), bears out many of the details of Jessie's description: the thatched roof, the veranda surrounding the house, the black-and-white paved hall, etc. The chapter in *Portraits By Inference* entitled 'Gerard Chowne's Carpet', pp. 23 - 31, describes a visit to the Salamans' house at Porlock for Christmas in 1911 or 1912. This graphic and probably ornamented account is identical in a number of details with Jessie's description of their first visit in the summer of 1910. It also contains one of the rare references to Jessie to be found in Humbert's prose writings. Michel Salaman also encouraged Jessie in her painting in the 1930s. The Salamans' daughter, Merula, married the actor Alec (later Sir Alec) Guinness.
42. Frank Sidgwick, a partner in the publishing house of Sidgwick & Jackson from its foundation in 1909, and the author of some light verse, was the son of Arthur Sidgwick (Fellow of Corpus Christi College, Oxford), and the nephew of Henry Sidgwick (Knightbridge Professor of Moral Philosophy, Cambridge, founder of Newnham College, and a member of the group known as 'The Apostles'). Frank Sidgwick published Rupert Brooke's first volume of poetry, *Poems*, in December 1911. His brother Arthur, a fellow of University College, Oxford, who died of wounds in September 1917, was the author of several books, including a collection of poems entitled *'Jones' Wedding'*, which is mentioned in the chapter of the same name in *Portraits By Inference*.
43. The difficulties Humbert later encountered when he applied to the trustees for assistance to pay for Ann's operations may have arisen from Mr Mahler's reluctance to make any exception, particularly since he and Berto did not get on well. But this is conjecture.
44. Jessie Wolfe: unpublished papers.
45. *London Sonnets*, 1920 and *Early Poems*, 1930, p. 38.
46. *Early Poems*, 1930, Preface pp. xi-xii and p. 99.

Chapter Five

I

1. J. A. M. Caldwell, 'The Genesis of the Ministry of Labour', in *Public Administration* XXXVII (1959), p. 367.
2. Roger Davidson, 'Llewellyn Smith and the Labour Department', in *Studies in the Growth of Nineteenth-Century Government*, ed. Gillian Sutherland (London, 1972) p.237.
3. *Ibid.* p. 239.
4. *Ibid.* p. 245.
5. *Ibid.* p. 246.
6. W. H. Beveridge, *Power and Influence*, 1953, pp. 72 - 73.
7. *see* Martin Gilbert, *Winston Churchill: A Life*, 1992, p. 196.
8. *Ibid.* p. 197, and W. H. Beveridge, *op. cit.* pp. 71 - 78.
9. W. H. Beveridge, *op. cit.*, p. 78. Beveridge's footnote about Humbert's origins is inaccurate (*see* above, Chapter I).
10. *Ibid.* p. 91 .
11. Humbert Wolfe, *A Winter Miscellany*, (1930), p. 24. Also *Portraits By Inference*, pp. 71 - 72; this and the account of events on August 3, 1914, (pp. 89 - 90) are the only two places in the book where he mentions Jessie.
12. W. H. Beveridge, *op. cit.*, p. 119.
13. Humbert Wolfe, C.B.E., *Labour Supply And Regulation*, (Economic And Social History Of The World War, British Series, Carnegie Endowment for International Peace, Oxford, 1923), pp. 2 - 3.
14. *Ibid.* p. 13.
15. *Ibid.* p. 15.
16. *Ibid.* pp. 16 - 17.
17. *Ibid.* Editor's Preface, p. v.
18. *Ibid.* pp. 3 - 5.
19. *Ibid.* p. 6.
20. *Ibid.* p. 17.
21. Humbert Wolfe, *Portraits By Inference*, pp. 97 - 98.
22. Humbert Wolfe, *Labour Supply and Regulation*, p. 63.
23. *Lloyd George - A Diary*, ed. A. J. P. Taylor (1971), p. 49, and Wolfe, *Labour Supply and Regulation*, pp. 60 sqq. There may be no *real* discrepancy between Frances Stevenson's account and Humbert's, since his relates to April and early- rather than mid-May, though he *does* suggest that Booth and Girouard were agreed on the former's national factories scheme and on the need to spread contracts. But if either she or Lloyd George distorted the facts, that may have a bearing on Humbert's reported fall from favour in June.
24. Blanche Dugdale, *Arthur James Balfour*, vol. II.
25. Humbert Wolfe, *op. cit.* p. 64.

II

26. Lord Beveridge *Power and Influence*, p. 124. and *The Survey of London* Vol. XIII, The parish of St. Margaret Westminster (Part II), Chapter 13, LXX - No. 6 Whitehall Gardens, pp. 193 - 195.
27. *see History of the Ministry of Munitions* (HMSO), Vol. II, Part I, Chapter 2, p. 19, and Appendix I.
28. H. Wolfe, *Portraits by Inference*, p. 120.
29. H. Wolfe, *op. cit.*, Chapters 8 and 9.
30. R. Church, *The Voyage Home* (1964), p. 81. Rodney Lowe, in *Adjusting To Democracy* (Oxford, 1986), p. 23, cites this in confirmation of John Maynard Keynes' summing up of Lloyd George; *see* also Beveridge, *op. cit.* p. 140, for Lord Beveridge's complaint about the way Lloyd George recanted in December 1916 the compulsion (industrial conscription) which he had defended in June and November 1915. Dr. Lowe remarks on the similarity in the temperaments of Lloyd George and Humbert Wolfe. Jessie Wolfe's papers support this view, but she may have been somewhat biased.
31. *see* R. Lowe, *op. cit.*, also Lord Beveridge, *op. cit.* p. 129.
32. Humbert Wolfe, *Labour Supply and Regulation*, p. 99.
33. David Lloyd George, *War Memoirs*, Vol I.
34. Beveridge, *op. cit.* p. 126, and Appendix A, Section 5, p. 374. Also, Sir Llewellyn Woodward, *Great Britain and the War of 1914 - 1918* (Methuen, London, 1967), p. 467n.
35. David Lloyd George, *op. cit.* Vol. I, p. 220; Lord Beveridge, *op cit.*, and B. B. Gilbert, *David Lloyd George - a Political Life*, (1992), pp. 200 - 201.
36. *War Memoirs of David Lloyd George*, New Edition, Vol. I, p. 147 (Odhams, 1938).
37. Wolfe, *Portraits By Inference*, p. 116.
38. Wolfe, *ibid.* pp. 120 - 121.
39. *History of the Ministry of Munitions*, Vol. II, Part I, Appendix VII, pp. 257 - 259; *see* the same for details of the 100-odd buildings occupied by the Ministry by the end of the War. The subsequent restoration of Armaments Building to Agriculture and Fisheries fittingly completed the ploughshares-swords-ploughshares cycle; *see* also Beveridge, *op. cit.* p. 125.
40. *History of the Ministry of Munitions*, Vol. II, Part I, Chapter V, pp. 110 and 115, and Appendix II.
41. Wolfe, *Labour Supply and Regulation*, pp. 66 - 67.
42 Wolfe, *Portraits By Inference*, pp. 109 sqq.
43. *History of the Ministry of Munitions*, Vol.II, Part I, Chapter V, p. 109, and Appendix III.
44. Wolfe, *Portraits By Inference*, pp. 99 - 102.
45. *History of the Ministry of Munitions*, Vol.II, Part I, Appendix IV.

46. Correspondence with Sir John Walley. There is no evidence of a change by Deed Poll; Humbert seems to have announced simply that henceforward he wanted to be known as Humbert Wolfe.
47. *History of the Ministry of Munitions*, Vol. II, Part I, Chapter VI, Section (iv), p. 174.
48. *History of the Ministry of Munitions,* Vol. II, Part I, Appendix V, and Supplements, p. 275; for Churchill's early tussles with colleagues and strikers, *see* Gilbert, *op. cit.* pp. 376 sqq.
49. *see* Rodney Lowe, 'The Ministry of Labour 1916 - 19: a Still, Small Voice?', in *War and the State*, ed. K. Burk (1982, London), pp. 111 - 119; also R. Lowe, *Adjusting to Democracy* (Oxford, 1986), p. 53.
50. PRO: LAB 2/254/ML12475/2, and C. J. Wrigley, in *David Lloyd George and the British Labour Movement* (Harvester Press, New York, 1976), pp. 200 - 202.
51. Information supplied to Ann Wolfe. For the soldiers' revolt, see Sir Harold Butler, *Confident Morning* (Faber 1949), pp. 140 - 141.
52. For all of this disagreement *see* PRO: MUN 5 / 323 / 160 Part IV (1918)); MUN 5 / 328 / 160 R2 (1918); MUN 5 / 323 / 160 Part II (1918).

III

53. *Portraits by Inference*, 1934, pp. 90 - 91.
54. *Ibid.* pp. 131 - 132.
55. Norman Douglas, *Alone*, Introduction, which, when published separately, was entitled *The Tribulations of a Patriot* (1921).
56. *Portraits by Inference*, p. 160.
57. *see* Richard Aldington, '*Pinorman*' (1954); Norman Douglas, *op. cit*; Mark Holloway, '*Norman Douglas*' (1976), pp. 229-232.
58. Conversation with Ann Wolfe.
59. Binyon's "For the Fallen", however, was written in September 1914, *before* the fallen actually fell. For the subtle distinction between poetry of protest and poetry of bereavement in the First World War, *see* Geoff Dyer, *The Missing of the Somme* (London Hamish Hamilton, 1994).
60. These lines appear to have been inspired by Emerson's 'Give All to Love'. In the last chapter of *Portraits By Inference*, p. 193, writing of an International Labour Office gathering in Stockholm in 1921, Humbert unwittingly attributed to Emerson the ending of 'The Gods of The Copy-Book Headings':

    'heartily know
    when the half-gods go
    the gods, the gods return.'

Emerson actually wrote: 'the gods, the gods arrive.' - another example of Humbert's sometimes careless proof-reading.

61. Sir John Squire, Introduction to the *Last Poems* of John Freeman (London, 1930). For Humbert's later judgement on Imagists, Georgians, and others, *see Dialogues and Monologues* (1928), especially the section on 'Modernism in Verse', pp. 197 - 253.

Chapter Six

I

1. *See* Appendix B; also PRO:LAB 2/ 1718/CEB 186, and R. Lowe, *Adjusting To Democracy* (OUP 1986), Appendix I, p. 251.
2. R. Lowe, *op. cit.*, p. 52.
3. Peter Jenkins, *The Battle of Downing Street* (1970), p. 5, quoted in Lowe, p. 52.
4. Richard Church, *Voyage Home* (Heinemann 1964), pp. 26 -27.
5. H. B. Butler, *Confident Morning*, 1946, p. 117. Lowe, *op. cit.* p. 53, is slightly misleading since the figures he quotes relate to 1932. *See* also Church, *op. cit.*, for the account of his transfer thither from Custom House in the autumn of 1920.
6. Humbert Wolfe, *Labour Supply and Regulation* (OUP 1923), p. 298.
7. H. B. Butler, *op. cit.*, p. 131.
8. Sir Godfrey Ince, *The Ministry of Labour and National Service* (George Allen and Unwin, London,1960), p. 33.
9. *see* R. Lowe, *op. cit.*, p. 68. Trade Boards are extensively dealt with in Lowe's account of the Ministry of Labour between the wars.
10. R. Lowe, *op. cit.*, p. 41.
11. R. Church, *op. cit.* p. 29.
12. *ibid.* pp. 30 - 31.
13. Alan Watts in *Tempo*, the house magazine of the now defunct Department of Employment, September 1972.
14. R. Church, *op. cit.*, p. 82.
15. H. W. Garrod, *The Profession of Poetry & Other Lectures* (Oxford 1929), p. 196.
16. R. Church, *op. cit.*, p. 107.
17. John Rowland Fothergill, 1876 - 1957, described by Susan Chitty in *Gwen John* (Hodder & Stoughton, 1981), p. 55, as 'painter, dandy and amateur inn-keeper', opened The Carfax Gallery, in Ryder Street, off St. James's, c. 1902. Augustus John had an exhibtion there in 1903. In 1907 Fothergill published privately his book *The Slade: 1993 - 1907*.
18. Oswald later went to Spain, remarried, made a fortune, was British consul during the Second World War, and died in Madrid in 1956.

19. Humbert Wolfe, *Portraits By Inference* (1934), pp. 40 - 41.
20. *see* earlier, Chapter 5.

II

21. PRO:LAB 2/1822/CEB 461/2/1922 - also quoted by Lowe, *op. cit.*, p. 78.
22. R. Lowe, *op. cit.*, p. 101.
23. PRO: LAB 2/831/TBD100/A43.
24. *see* R. Lowe, *op. cit.*, Ch. 4, *passim.*
25. PRO: LAB 2/831/TBD100/A43.
26. R. Church, *op. cit.* p. 82.
27. R. Church, *op. cit.* pp. 82 - 83.
28. *see* R. Lowe, *op. cit.* pp. 104 - 5, for the significance of the Memorandum setting out possible amendments to the Trade Board Act, supplied to Lord Cave.
29. PRO: LAB 2/935 TB252. 1925.
30. *Ibid.*
31. *see* Church and Lowe; also information supplied privately by Sir John Walley, and by Mrs. Goodwin, a Ministry of Labour typist in the 1920s and 1930s.
32. PRO:LAB2/1029/11 (TB 357 1924).
33. PRO:LAB2/14/TB147 1924.

III

34. George Barnes, Labour Minister of Pensions in the 1917 coalition; a member of the War Cabinet and Minister Plenipotentiary at the Paris Peace Conference: 'solid, shrewd and sensible' (Butler). He wrote a book about the origins of the I.L.O. in 1926, to coincide with new I.L.O. building in Geneva.

    Sir Malcolm Delevingne, Butler's former chief at the Home Office, wrote *The Origins of the International Labour Organisation*; spiritedly and successfully resisted the Ministry of Labour's attempts to annex the inspection of factories in 1918, *see* Butler, *Confident Morning*, p. 158.

    Harold B. Butler, *see* Chapter V earlier; he succeeded Albert Thomas as Director-General in 1932. He later became a fellow of All Souls, and the first Warden of Nuffield College.

    Edward Phelan, an Irishman, graduated in science at Liverpool and went into the Civil Service. He arrived at the I.L.O. via the

Foreign Intelligence Section of the Ministry of Labour, which, as its youthful head, 'he had brought to a fine point of efficiency.' (Butler, *Confident Morning*, p. 157.) Phelan 'minded' the I.L.O. during the Second World War, and was Director-General 1941 - 48. Author of *Yes and Albert Thomas* (Cresset Press, London, 1949).

35. *see*, in particular, PRO:CAB. 27/272 and CAB. 24/172/CP 198(25); also Rodney Lowe, *op. cit.*, p. 96, and Stewart, *Britain and the I.L.O.* (HMSO 1969). Fifty years later, Parliament had still not ratified the Hours Convention, *see* Hansard 1969, vol. 784. col. 955 - 6. Albert Thomas: son of a baker, rose to be a university professor and a leading socialist député; Minister of Munitions during First World War. The I.L.O. 50th anniversary book (p. 86) called him 'more than the first Director of the Office; he was its natural leader and, to a great extent, its creator.' Both Phelan and Butler have described how he shaped the Office so that it should fulfil the function he intended for it, i.e. not merely to be a clearing house for information between its constituent members but also and even more to change national laws and practices. This was probably at the root of the hostility shown towards the I.L.O. by some Ministers and Civil Servants in Britain. Violet Markham voiced the universal view that he was 'the outstanding and dominating figure of the whole proceedings.' (*Return Passage*, p. 167.) But Sophy Sanger thought he was above all a shrewd politician. (A. M. Allen: *Sophy Sanger: A Pioneer in Internationalism*, (Glasgow, 1958), p. 132 and 153 - 4.)

    Arthur Fontaine, the President of the I.L.O., 'was not only the permanent head of the French Ministry of Labour and therefore the official key to the French position [at the Labour Commission of the Peace Conference], but a man of unusual talent and culture in his own right. . . . A close friend of André Gide, Paul Valéry and Carrière, he was at the centre of the literary and artistic life of Paris. . . . With a rational rather than an emotional approach to social problems, he was a perfect product of the French liberal tradition. At bottom he had little sympathy with the messianic fervour of Albert Thomas. But as a man of high character and ideals he was a convinced adherent of the new international faith.' (H. B. Butler, *Confident Morning*, p. 168.)

36. *see* E. Phelan, *Yes and Albert Thomas*, pp. 80 & 117; and Humbert Wolfe, *Portraits By Inference* (1934), Ch. X and Ch. XIII; also A. M. Allen's *Sophy Sanger: A Pioneer in Internationalism*, (Glasgow, 1958), p. 174.

37. The two letters are in the Archives of I.L.O., Geneva, Cabinet File 1932 - 38 RL 25/1/1/1.

38. The title of Phelan's book about the work of Albert Thomas in the I.L.O., *Yes and Albert Thomas,* was taken from Humbert's description of the toast at the end of the Stockholm banquet, in *Portraits By Inference* (Methuen 1934), pp. 193 - 194.
39. Private letter from Ann Wolfe to the author; *see* 'Unassisted Building Scheme' in *Cursory Rhymes* (1927) for a reference to 'the bus that stops opposite Barker's', and the drawing by Albert Rutherston on p. 101, of the girl dancing in the garden and a view of the church in the background.
40. A reference to Flecker's 'The Old Ships': 'And yet so beautiful I watched in vain/To see the mast burst open with a rose,/And the whole deck put on its leaves again.'
41. A modified version of this poem appeared, with another, 'Rue du Soleil Levant', in *This Blind Rose* (1928). The street, along with others, also provides the setting for No. XII in *Circular Saws,* 'Ars Longa, Vita Brevis.'

IV

42. *see* R. Lowe, *op. cit.*, passim.
43. Violet Markham, *Return Passage* (1953), p. 167.
44. e.g. I.L.O. Archives, Geneva, D312/25 1922, correspondence between Humbert and H. B. Betterton concerning inaccuracies in the I.L.O. Official Bulletin, vol. 5, No. 9 (1 March 1922).
45. These experiences are reflected, with varying degrees of directness, in a wide range of his writings, starting with No. XII of *Circular Saws* (1923), 'Ars Longa, Vita Brevis', which is set in the old town of Geneva; 'Monnetier Mairie', in *The Unknown Goddess* (1925); in *Humoresque* (1926), pp. 53 - 55: 'Jura', 'Mountain Flowers', and 'Alpine Chaces'; in *This Blind Rose* (1928), 'Mountain Flowers', 'A Hill-Road By Zweilutschinen', 'Rocher de Naye', 'The Alpine Cross', 'Youth'; in *The Uncelestial City, passim,* but notably in the J.C.R. debate, pp. 34 - 35, and on pp 61, 68, 151, and 201; and finally in *Out of Great Tribulation,* 'The Calm Mountain-Valleys'.
46. Humbert Wolfe, 'My Desk', in *The Unknown Goddess* (1925), inspired or occasioned by Jessie's failure to tidy/dust it.
47. Probably Edward William Dirom Cuming, 1862 - 1941, writer and editor, principally of books about sport, especially hunting; edited several Surtees books.
48. In 1900, Pavlova and Fokine in St. Petersburg; 1910, Fokine's Carnaval; also another in Berlin 1922. Picasso, who returned constantly to the theme throughout his career, painted a huge number of 'Arlequins' during his 'blue' and 'rose' periods, his curtain for the Russian ballet *Parade* being arguably his finest production in this area (*see* Sacheverell Sitwell's Preface to Cyril

Beaumont's *The History of Harlequin* (London, 1926), and Thelma Niklaus, *Harlequin* (New York, 1956), Ch. 7; also for Agatha Christie and D. L. Sayers). By a curious coincidence, Pamela Frankau's first novel, published in 1927, was entitled 'Marriage of Harlequin'.

49. *see Evelyn Waugh and his world*, edited by David Pryce-Jones, Weidenfeld & Nicolson, 1973, p. 68.
50. One of the family who owned Lyons; knighted c. 1933, see *Who Was Who*, vol. 4.
51. *see* M. Gilbert, *Churchill: A Life*, (Minerva, 1992) p. 452.
52. Léon Jouhaux, General Secretary of the French Workers' Federation, stood out: 'massive . . ., impenetrable, suspicious, determined, . . . a man of considerable political sagacity in the outward trappings of a demagogue . . . Though at times he used socialist jargon, I doubt if he was much of a socialist at heart.' (Butler, *op. cit.*); his chief concern was to preserve the independence of the French trade union movement. Jan Oudegeest, the Dutch workers' representative and Secretary-General of the I. F. T. U.

    Mgr. Nolens, a well-known Dutch prelate, was the permanent head of the Dutch delegation, and was elected President of one of the I.L.O. sessions. Although not himself a Minister he exerted great influence in the Catholic party which held the balance of power in Holland, and 'was reputed to have made and unmade Cabinets.' (Phelan, *op. cit.*, p. 97.) He provided Humbert with the excuse for one of his best recorded witticisms (*see* later).

    Ernest Mahaim, one of the Belgian delegates, Secretary of the Belgian Section of I.A.L.L. Baron Mayor des Planches, the President of the Genoa session of the I.L.O Conference in 1920, was 'an ancient Italian diplomat with the courtly manner and flowery phrases of a bygone age.' (Butler, *op. cit.* p. 169.) Eduard Benes was Minister of Foreign Affairs of the Czechoslovak Republic and often seen at Geneva. Sir James Lithgow represented the British employers.
53. quoted in Gilbert, *op. cit.* p. 456. For Churchill's acknowledgement, *see* Gilbert: *Winston S. Churchill*, vol. IV, Companion Part 3, p. 2126.

V

54. Violet Markham *op. cit.* pp. 166 - 168, for observations on Geneva, I.L.O. and the White Lead issue, also on Betterton, Albert Thomas, and Humbert Wolfe.

55. Thomas Gavan-Duffy, 1867 - 1932, for 23 years General Secretary Cumberland Iron Ore Miners, Labour M.P. for Whitehaven, 1922 - 1924; Lt. Col. G. R. Lane-Fox, M.P., Parliamentary Secretary, Department of Mines, Board of Trade - see *Hansard*, 1923, vol. 166, col. 782 -87.
56. The whole poem, of which these lines, slightly modified, form the end, appeared later as 'Wormwood Scrubs' in *The Uncelestial City*, pp. 98 - 99.
57. I have found no evidence that these were ever published.

Chapter Seven

I

1. H. W. Garrod, *The Profession of Poetry & Other Lectures*, (Oxford 1929), pp. 198 - 199.
2. quoted in Lowe, *op. cit.* p.97; see also Phelan, *Yes And Albert Thomas*, (New York 1949), p. 250.
3. *see* Violet Markham, *Return Passage*, (1953), pp. 166 - 169; also Salvador de Madariaga, *Morning without Noon*, Saxon House 1974.
4. Private communication from Sir Harold Emmerson. Bondfield, Rt. Hon. Margaret, 1873 - 1953; eminent trade-unionist, public servant and politician. Chairman of T.U.C. General Council 1923; Labour M.P. 1923 - 24, and 1926 - 31; Parliamentary Secretary Ministry of Labour 1923 - 24, Minister of Labour and first woman Cabinet Minister 1929 - 31; worked with League of Nations and I.L.O. throughout the 1920s.
5. *Diary of Beatrice Webb*, edited by Norman and Jeanne MacKenzie, (Virago 1985), Vol. 4 (1924 - 43), p. 247, 28 July 1931; Richard Church's graphic account of the event is suspect if only because in 1924 Margaret Bondfield was not a Cabinet Minister and Humbert was not yet a member of the Athenaeum: both of these elevations came in 1929. Church also implies (*op. cit.* p. 84.) that two Liberal MPs in particular harassed her in the House; one of them, Sir Geoffrey Mander, became a Member of Parliament only in 1929.
6. Private communication from Sir Harold Emmerson. The identification with Bowers is assumed in Lowe, *op. cit.* p. 68.
7. Bernardo Attolico, 1880 - 1942: *see Enciclopedia Italiana, Appendice II 1938 - 1948,* and *Dizionario Biografico Degli Italiani*, vol. IV, pp. 556 - 559. Attolico was Senior Vice Secretary-General of the League of Nations, 1922 - 1926; he then held a succession of embassies until his death in 1942. Salvador de Madariaga, *op. cit.*, in a graphic description on p. 20, called him 'an honest liberal' who was sacked from his Geneva post in order to make room for

Mussolini's 'own personal assistant, Paulucci di Calboli Barone', who is also mentioned in Humbert's letters from Geneva.

8. Giacomo Mateotti, 1884 - 1924. Markham, *op. cit.*, pp. 166 - 169.
9. Rusoni is probably a misprint for Edmondo Rossoni, *see Enciclopedia Italiana, Appendice I*, p. 984. His Excellency Signor De Michelis was Chairman of the Governing Body at the time of the Washington Conference, and a frequent member of later sessions. Francisk Sokal, the Director of the Polish Ministry of Labour, was another regular participant.

II

10. ILO Archives, Geneva: RL 25/1/1/1 Relations with Ministry of Labour London (HW) 4 March 1925.
11. Curzon, after several years as Foreign Secretary, had accepted the post of Lord Privy Seal in Baldwin's government. In 1925 Balfour became Lord President of the Council.
12. *H. W. Garrod, op. cit.* p. 199. *Pace* Bevis Hillier (*Young Betjeman*, 1989 Cardinal, pp. 337 - 8), the Iliad poem was certainly touched off by *Iliad*, Bk. VI, ll. 355 - 358, in which Helen confesses her mad infatuation ("atè" in Greek), to which 'mad heart' is a direct reference. For a detailed study of Owen's half-rhymes, *see* in particular Dennis Welland: *Wilfrid Owen: A Critical Study*, Chatto & Windus, (London 1978), pp. 104 - 124. It is interesting to note that in 1920 *The Times Literary Supplement* came near to atrributing Owen's "imperfect rhymes" to bad craftsmanship.
13. *See* Imogen Holst's biography of her father, O.U.P. (London 1988), p. 139. Betelgeuse, nearly 600 million light years from the sun, was the first star whose apparent diameter was measured, in 1920, by Michelson's stellar interferometer. *See* Chapter 9 in this present work for Holst's subsequent association with Humbert.
14. Norman Douglas, *South Wind* (London, Martin Secker [1917] 1934 impression), pp. 343 and 369.
15. Quoted in *The Upward Anguish*, p. 85.

III

16. Jessie Wolfe: unpublished papers.
17. *Ibid.*
18. Storm Jameson, Autobiography: *Journey from the North*, vol. 2. (1970). p. 28.
19. David Low, *Autobiography*, (1956), pp. 141 - 142, and personal communication from Maire Gaster, daughter of Robert and Sylvia Lynd.

20. H. W. Garrod, *loc. cit.* p. 207, wrote: 'Mr. Wolfe knows that the decasyllabic line is scanned, not by syllables, but by breaths', and that by that measurement 'I should not be surprised if he were not found an exact metrist.'
21. Votre aile en le heurtant ne fera rien répandre
    Du vase où je m'abreuve et que j'ai bien rempli.
    Mon âme a plus de feu que vous n'avez de cendre!
    Mon coeur a plus d'amour que vous n'avez d'oubli!
22. The 1943 reprint of the Rupert Brooke volume in *Augustan Poets* contains the General Preface in which may be found a fuller account of the venture.
23. Quoted by G. A. Johnston in *The International Labour Organization*, p. 30, Europa Publications, (London 1970).
24. For all this, *see* Butler, *Confident Morning*, Phelan, *op. cit.*, Stewart, *Britain and the I.L.O.*, (HMSO 1969), and of course *Portraits By Inference*, chapter X.
25. This account is based on Jessie Wolfe's unpublished papers.
26. But the point of the chapter is really to give him the opportunity to describe his meeting with Aristide Briand, whose presence in Geneva is referred to in a letter of June 17, but not the lunch described in *Portraits*.
27. I have not succeeded in finding these stories anywhere in England, although a copy of "The Publicist" is lodged in Wadham College Library.
28. For a more detailed account of this poem, see *Edwin Muir: Man and Poet*, by P. H. Butter, Oliver & Boyd, (London & Edinburgh 1966).
29. *see This Blind Rose*, p. 40, for 'Oleanders'.
30. *This Blind Rose*, p. 47.
31. It eventually appeared, not in *Requiem*, but in *The Uncelestial City*, pp. 105 - 107, slightly amended, no longer explicitly referring to Valentino but describing any Hollywood film star and his female counterpart.
32. private communication from Ann Wolfe.
33. *The Times Literary Supplement*, 13 January, 1940. p. 22.
34. *See* 'Sport at Minehead' in *Out of Great Tribulation* (1939) p. 110.
35. I cannot find it in the published work, and can only conclude that it was dropped or fundamentally altered when Humbert revised the whole idea for the book in 1927 - 1928.

IV

36. This account was reproduced in *Dialogues and Monologues* (1928) and in *George Moore* (1930, revised 1933).
37. Leon M. Lion, 1879 - 1947, actor, playwright, producer.

38. cp M. Gilbert, *Churchill: A Life*, Minerva, (London 1992), p. 481.
39. Victor (Sir) Gollancz, 1893 - 1967 was managing director of Benn Ltd from 1920 to 1928. Then he set up on his own. The Chairman of the firm was Sir Ernest Benn (1875 - 1954). Arnold Bennett said that Benn's 'always wanted something for half-nothing.'
40. One has only to look at the English verse of good classicists such as R. A. Knox (who won prizes for his Greek verse) to see how right Humbert was. Knox's translation of the hymn 'Ave maris stella', for example, reads in parts like a weather forecast: 'Clouded prospects brighten'!
41. Babette Deutsch, 1895 - 1982, American poet, critic, novelist, translator; *see* Jean Gould, *American Women Poets*, (1980), and *The Feminist Companion to Literature in English*, (Batsford 1990).
42. Sir Philip Cunliffe-Lister, 1st Viscount (later 1st Earl) Swinton, 1884 - 1972. His family name was Lloyd-Greame; he changed it to Cunliffe-Lister in 1924. He was President of the Board of Trade 1924 - 29.
43. Possibly the artist William Shackleton, 1872 - 1933, another alumnus of Bradford Grammar School.
44. J. L. Garvin, Editor of *The Observer* from 1908 to 1942.
45. Anastas Botzarich Sava, 1896-1934, son of the court painter to King Peter of Serbia. A remarkable linguist, he abandoned the diplomatic career planned for him in order to become a sculptor, painter and caricaturist (*see* Fine Arts Society Catalogue no. 708, 1926, and Who's Who in Art, 1935). Sadly the drawings of Humbert have proved untraceable.
46. H. W.Garrod, *op. cit.* pp. 195 - 196.
47. The Act, said Lowe, *op. cit.* p. 105, gave vent to anti-union bias in the aftermath of the General Strike, although the significance of the Act's industrial clauses proved eventually to be more symbolic than real.
48. Personal communication from Ann Wolfe.
49. Beatrice Webb, *op. cit.* pp. 143, & 152 - 153
50. *See* Imogen Holst, Introduction to *Twelve Humbert Wolfe Songs by Gustav Holst*, Stainer & Bell, (London 1969); and *Gustav Holst - A Biography*, by Imogen Holst, O.U.P., (1938), 2nd edition, 1969.
51. Vera Brittain, *Testament of Experience*, (Virago 1979), p. 76.

Chapter Eight

I

1. *See* 'Two *Observer* Reviewers: Gerald Gould and Humbert Wolfe', by Viola Gerard Garvin, in *English: vol. 5. 1944-5, No. 25*, pp. 4 - 7.
2. Viola Garvin, *ibid.*

3. Robert Lynd's obituary of Humbert Wolfe in *News Chronicle*, 6 January, 1940.
4. *Now A Stranger*, pp. 72 - 73. If *Circular Saws*, *Kensington Gardens* and *Cursory Rhymes* bring to mind Lewis Carroll, Kipling, Barrie and Graham, it is by way of what George Sampson called the 'coloration' which Humbert took on from his omnivorous reading, in English, Latin, Greek, French or German.
5. Kunitz and Haycraft's *Twentieth Century Authors - Biographical Dictionary*, The H. W. Wilson Co., (New York, 1942), pp. 1540 - 1541, mentions 'a novel called "The Count of Saldeyne," consistently refused until 1915 by all publishers, and then put away.' But it includes the novel in 'Principal Works', as if it were published in 1915.
6. Locker-Lampson, Rt. Hon. Godfrey, P.C. 1975 - 1946, Under-Secretary of State for Foreign Affairs 1925 - 1928; member of the British Delegation to the League of Nations 1928.

II

7. *See The Journals of Arnold Bennett, III, 1921 - 1928*, edited by Newman Flower, (Cassell, 1933); *Letters of Arnold Bennett*, ed. James Hepburn, (Oxford, 1966), Vol. I, p. 368, vol. III, p. 286; Humbert Wolfe, *Portraits By Inference*, Ch. XI, p. 153 sqq.; *Arnold Bennett*, Reginald Pound, (Heinemann, 1952), p. 40, and p. 326; *T. S. Eliot*', by Peter Ackroyd, (Hamish Hamilton, 1984); *Arnold Bennett The Evening Standard Years*, ed. Andrew Mylett, (Chatto & Windus, 1974). In all of these accounts there is hardly any mention of Humbert. Extracts from Bennett's Journal appeared in *The New Criterion* in December 1927, January and February 1928.
8. The Zinoviev Letter (1924) purported to be revolutionary instructions from the President of the Communist International in Moscow to the Central Committee of the Communist Party in Britain; *see* Beatrice Webb, *Diary vol IV 1924 - 1943*, ed. Norman & Jeanne MacKenzie, Virago 1985, Introduction, pp. 5 - 6, on the 'Red Scare' which finally brought the government down. The Zinoviev letter incident occurred during the election campaign: a forgery by a White Russian émigré, improved upon by a British agent, Sidney Reilly, and passed off on the Conservatives and the F.O., though many saw or suspected it was a forgery; *ibid.* pp. 42 and 44, for MacDonald's mishandling of the affair.
9. I.L.O. Archives, Geneva: Cabinet File 1932 - 38 Dossier No XL File No. 5/2/1'Refugees: General Correspondence'; XL 25/1/1/1 9 Feb 28; and parts of XR 25/1/16 (Relations with Ministry of Labour.)

10. This may have been the pastel portrait completed in 1931, now in the possession of his daughter and reproduced here with her kind permission.
11. Charles de Sousy Ricketts RA (1928), 1866 - 1931; he specialised in wood engravings and lithographs: *see Dictionary of British Book Illustrators of the Twentieth Century*, by Brigid Peppin & Lucy Micklethwait, John Murray, London 1983, and *Dictionary of British Book Illustrators & Caricaturists*, (Simon House, 1978).
12. Correspondence with W. Fraser Mitchell, 1928, Department of English, Armstrong College, Newcastle-on-Tyne (by kind permission of the Special Collections section, University of Edinburgh Library). Henry Vaughan was the suggestion of Mr. John Walley in 1929, a few months before he joined the staff at Montagu House as an Assistant Principal; he eventually became Deputy Secretary at the Ministry of Social Security and National Insurance and was knighted in 1965.
13. First published in 1877, re-issued, with an introduction by John Lucas, by the Victorian Library, (Leicester University Press, 1975).
14. A. D. Keith died on February 22, 1928, in a North Wales nursing home at the age of 42. On graduating in 1907 he entered the Indian Education Service and went to teach Literature in Government College, Rangoon. He married Enid Gilliat in 1909 who bore him two sons. He left teaching to become a barrister and entered the Burmese Bar, where he practised until 1927. There is a brief obituary in vol. VI of *The Wadham Gazette*. Other volumes of *The Wadham Gazette* contain references to his university years and later career, but some of the index entries are unreliable.

III

15. Personal communication from Mrs. Jessie Goodwin.
16. C. Day-Lewis, *The Buried Day*, London, (Chatto & Windus, 1960/1966), p. 177; Stephen Spender, *World Within World*, (Hamish Hamilton, 1951), pp. 98 - 99. The late Sir Stephen Spender told me in 1982 that his article, entitled 'Thou art free', appeared in *The Isis*. When he wrote slightingly of Humbert in the 1930s he received a reproachful letter reminding him of his earlier words of praise. Spender said that Humbert received him kindly when he sought his help in obtaining war work in 1939, although nothing came of this. He told me that he still knew by heart and admired two of Humbert's epigrams about George Moore and Kipling. Sean F. Day-Lewis, in *C. Day-Lewis: An English Literary Life*, (Weidenfeld & Nicolson, London 1980), pp. 37 - 38, tells the story that when his father announced the title of his recitation: 'Naked Woman with Kotyle', to the Jawbone Club, Tom

Hopkinson, later Editor of *Picture Post* and other journals, drily remarked, 'Lucky chap, old Kotyle.'

17. *See* her Introduction to *Twelve Humbert Wolfe Songs by Gustav Holst*, (Stainer & Bell, 1970).
18. Personal communications from Dame Mary Smieton and Mr. P. H. St. J. Wilson. For a fuller account of the organisation of the Ministry and the Civil Service, see Sir Godfrey Ince: *The Ministry of Labour and National Service*, (London & New York, 1960), pp. 184 - 185; T. A. Critchley, *The Civil Service Today*, (Gollancz, London, 1951), pp. 35 - 36, and 109; Frank Dunnill, *The Civil Service: Some Human Aspects*, (George Allen & Unwin, London, 1956), pp. 23 - 30, 73 - 94, 225 - 6; G. K. Fry, *Statesmen in Disguise*, (Macmillan, London, 1969), pp. 50 - 51.

IV

19. Imogen Holst, Introduction to *Twelve Humbert Wolfe Songs by Gustav Holst*, (Stainer & Bell, 1970), p. 3. Miss Holst mentions on p. 4 'a recent recording' made by Peter Pears and Benjamin Britten at the Maltings, Snape (Argo ZRG 512); *see* also *Gustav Holst - A Biography*, by Imogen Holst, (O.U.P., (1938), 2nd edition, 1969), p. 141.
20. John Henry Newman, *Dream of Gerontius*, (1865). On Eliot's *Gerontion*, see *Poetry of the 1920s*, ed. Sydney Bolt, (Longmans, 1967), pp. 7 - 14; also David Daitches, *The Present Age*, (1958), Chapter 2, pp. 22 - 29.
21. A graduate student-teacher to whom I quoted these lines asked: 'Please, what's a Squeer?' The poem, together with the one quoted from *Requiem* earlier, ranks in my view as the most profound poetic expression of the reality of teaching.
22. Originally written for *The Wadham Gazette*, vol. VI, p. 339: 'In Memoriam A. D. Keith', *see above* n.14.
23. *Arnold Bennett: The Evening Standard Years: Books and Persons 1926 - 31*, ed. Andrew Mylett, (Chatto & Windus, 1974), pp. 375 - 376. In 1927 Bennett had written: '[Humbert Wolfe] is rounding Byron Corner.' (*ibid.* p. 22.)
24. Humbert Wolfe, *Portraits By Inference*, (Methuen, 1934), pp. 162 - 163. Bennett died in 1931.
25. *See* Vera Brittain's *Testament of Experience*, (Virago, 1979), p. 65. She was invited to review for the new weekly.
26. I.L.O. Conference Reports.
27. Sean Day-Lewis, *op. cit.* Preface, p. xi.

Chapter Nine

I

1. Royal Society of Literature, *The Eighteen Sixties*, (C. U. P. 1932). See also Wolfe correspondence (mostly concerned with arrears of subscription) in the Society's Library.
2. Geoffrey Keynes, *A Bibliography of Siegfried Sassoon*, (London, 1962), pp. 85 - 86.
3. The proof copy presented to Wadham College Library is signed June 19/31. The first edition copy in my possession belonged to Humbert's friend Ivor Brown, a former Civil Servant, dramatic critic of *The Saturday Review* from 1923 to 1930, and of *The Observer* from 1929 to 1954, becoming editor from 1942 to 1948. He also wrote novels, books on politics, and essays.
4. A. Alvarez, Introduction to *The New Poetry*, (Penguin 1962), p. 18.
5. For a more complete account of *The Georgiad see* Peter Alexander's *Roy Campbell - A Critical Biography*, (O.U.P. 1982), especially pp. 93 - 99, and Rowland Smith's *Lyric and Polemic - The Literary Personality of Roy Campbell*, (McGill - Queen's University Press, 1972), Chapter 3.
6. Tacitus, *Annals*,13.14
7. C. Day-Lewis, letter to Peter Russell, editor of *Nine*, a literary quarterly, 23 December 1952, quoted in Sean Day-Lewis's *C. Day-Lewis: An English Literary Life*, (London, 1980), pp. 207-8.
8. Pamela Frankau (1908 - 1967), daughter of Captain Gilbert Frankau (1884 - 1952) whose mother, Julia, wrote under the name of Frank Danby. His father was a cigar importer. Gilbert went to Eton, entered the family business, then the Army in World War I, and later the RAF. He wrote novels and poetry, was thrice married. One of his wives, née Dorothea Drummond-Black, was Pamela's mother. His brother, Ronald Frankau, became a well-known music hall comedian. Pamela's book, *Pen To Paper*, movingly describes her strained relationship and eventual reconciliation with her father.

II

9. *See* letter from Evan John Simpson, dated 10 June 1936, No. 106, 'John E. Simpson', in Manuscripts Collection, University of Nottingham Library. For a fuller treatment of *The Publicist*, *see* the next section, 1933, in connection with *Reverie of Policeman*.
10. Jessie Wolfe, unpublished papers. She painted both in oils and water-colour, and her forte seems to have been portraiture. Her painting career was intensive, but brief. She held her first

exhibition in 1938 at the New English Art Club, but painted little after the summer of 1940. In May 1958, two years after her death, a memorial exhibition of her portraits and flower paintings was held in Foyles Art Gallery.

11. Michael Sadleir (1855 - 1952), author of *Fanny by Gaslight*; Sir Thomas [later Lord] Horder, society physician (*see* n20 below); David Low, the cartoonist; Sir Herbert Samuel, later 1st Viscount Samuel, P.C., G.C.B., G.B.E., High Commissioner for Palestine 1920 - 1925, Leader of the Liberal Party in the Commons 1931 - 1935, and in the Lords 1941 - 1955; Ralph Hale Mottram (1883 - 1971), author and Fellow of the Royal Society of Literature.

III

12. The lecture was published in the same year by The University of Bristol.
13. The authorship of the famous couplet, slightly misquoted here, is now disputed, I understand.
14. Interview and correspondence with Sir John Walley, P. J. St.J. Wilson, CB, CBE, Sir Harold Emmerson and others.
15. Interview with Sir John Walley, 1989. Rodney Lowe has pointed out in *Adjusting to Democracy* (Oxford 1986) the increasing recognition from the 1930s onwards that the Ministry was also the essential training ground for ambitious young politicians. After the Second World War, among the young and not-so-young hopefuls who trooped through its portals may be listed R.A.B. Butler, Bevan, Robens, Macleod, Heath, Castle, Shirley Williams, Whitelaw, Foot, Prior and Tebbitt. Its demise (in its final lineaments as the Department of Employment) in 1995 marks the end of its contribution to political advancement.

IV

16. There is no trace of any play with that title in his published works, or in any papers preserved in this country, nor does it sound remotely like the two plays by him that were produced.
17. *Sylvia Townsend Warner*, by Claire Harman, (Minerva 1989), pp. 132 - 133. Humbert used his good offices in 1938 to obtain a visa for Souline, the lover of Radclyffe Hall, whose book, *The Well of Loneliness* (1928), had been suppressed after a court had found it to be obscene. Vera Brittain defended the book at the time and in her last book, *Radclyffe Hall: A Case of Obscenity?* (1968). *See* also Michael Baker's biography of Radclyffe Hall: *Our Three Selves* (Hamish Hamilton, 1985), pp. 320 and 324.

18. A week before their wedding, Humbert had formally committed himself to making an annual allowance to Jessie; *see* letter to J.C. Graham, 21 March 1910.
19. Boileau had written approvingly: 'Enfin Malherbe vint', to which de Banville added the damning rider: '. . . et la poésie, en le voyant arriver, s'en alla!'.
20. Thomas Jeeves Horder (1871 - 1955), 1st Baron of Ashford (1933), besides being Extra Physician to various members of the Royal family (including Edward VIII, George VI and Queen Elixabeth II), was also adviser and consulting physician to many governmental and national bodies connected with labour, health, insurance and pensions. Humbert consulted him periodically.
21. *The Pilgrim's Way*, (Ivor Nicholson and Watson, 1936), Foreword, p. (v). The Very Rev. Frederic Athelwold Iremonger (1878 - 1952), who became Dean of Lichfield in 1939, was BBC Director of Religion from 1933 to 1939. After Oxford he had worked in various East End parishes, edited *The Guardian*, a liberal Church of England newspaper, from 1923 to 1927, and was Chaplain to the King (a fairly honorific title) from 1927 to 1939. He officiated at Humbert's Memorial Service in St. Martin-in-the-Fields in 1940.
22. Apparently corroborated in Martin Gilbert's *Churchill: A Life*, p. 532, although not surprisingly Humbert is not mentioned.
23. Sir John Walley, private communication.
24. Quotations supplied in a private communication from P. H. St.J. Wilson.

V

25. *see* Humbert Wolfe Correspondence with R. W. M. Wright in Bath Reference Library.
26. Pamela Frankau told the story in the American edition of *Pen to Paper* but identified the characters only by letters - A, B, C, etc. I am profoundly indebted to Diana Raymond for her enormous help with all of this story, for the opportunity of reading *The Addict*, and for allowing me to quote from her biography of Pamela Frankau, as well as from her letters to me. Thanks to her I was also able to interview Diana Marr-Johnson and Mrs. Gillian Warr (formerly Gill Dearmer) who supplied further details about the Maugham family, Humbert and Pamela. For photographs of Pamela, Anthony and Rebecca, *see* Victoria Glendinning's *Rebecca West*, Weidenfeld and Nicolson, (1987).
27. cf Robin Maugham's autobiography *Escape from the Shadows*, (1972), pp. 109 - 110 and Appendix II, p. 253.
28. Interview with Mrs. Michael Warr (née Gillian Dearmer).
29. Gilbert Murray Letters, vol. 71, Bodleian Library, Oxford.

30. *See* Introduction to Humbert's translation of *Cyrano de Bergerac*, (1937), Hutchinson; and Simon Callow, *Charles Laughton: A Difficult Actor*, (Methuen, 1987), pp. 94 - 95, 100 - 103.
31. P. H. St.J. Wilson, private communication.

VI

32. This letter appears not to have been preserved.

Chapter Ten

I

1. *See* Correspondence with E. J. Simpson, Hallward Library, University of Nottingham, Access 158.
2. Addison, *The Tatler*, No. 254, November 23, 1710, attributed the story of the Frozen Words to Sir John Mandeville's Journal; earlier, both Plutarch and Rabelais credited the Greek Antiphanes with being the author; the tale occurs also in Castiglione's *Courtier*, in the works of Calcagninus, Peter Heylin, and in Ned Ward's *London Spy*. *See* Richmond P. Bond, *The Tatler: The Making of a Literary Journal*, (Harvard University Press, 1971).
3. I am indebted to the BBC Written Archives Centre for access to the Wolfe Correspondence.
4. P. H. St.J. Wilson, private communication.
5. H. Wolfe, *Portraits By Inference*, p. 147.
6. I am indebted to the Librarian of the Athenaeum for the historical background. The Ladies Annexe in Carlton House Mews was closed for the war and pulled down in 1961. The present Ladies Annexe in the converted billiard room of the main club dates from about 1962.

II

7. *See* I.L.O. Archives, Geneva, for Correspondence between Humbert Wolfe and Harold Butler, 1937.
8. Jessie Wolfe, private papers.
9. Simon Callow, *op. cit.* pp. 100 - 101.
10. Clough Williams-Ellis, *Architect Errant*, Constable, London (1971), pp. 155 - 156.
11. Ethel Mannin, *Confessions and Impressions*, Jarrold, London (1930), p. 204.
12. R. Lowe, *Adjusting to Democracy* (Oxford, 1986), pp. 221 - 222.

13. Jessie Wolfe, unpublished papers.

III

14. Royal Commission on the Geographical Distribution of the Industrial Population, *Evidence*, 10th and 11th Days, qq. 2601 and 2651. The Commission sat from July 8 1937 to August 1939, but the war delayed publication of the report until January 1940. *See* also Lowe, *op. cit.* pp. 228 -233, 239 and 239n.
15. I.L.O. Archives, Geneva. Cabinet File 1932 - 38 XR 25/1/16, 'Relations with Ministry of Labour'.
16. Information supplied by Sir John Walley.
17. Vera Brittain, *Chronicle of Friendship: A Diary of the Thirties*, ed. Alan Bishop, (London, Gollancz, 1986) p. 343.

IV

18. H. M. D. Parker, *History of the Second World War: Manpower* (London, 1957, HMSO and Longmans, Green and Co.), p. 51.
19. *See* Asa Briggs, *The History of Broadcasting in the United Kingdom*, (OUP, 1965) II, pp. 657 - 8.
20. H. M. D. Parker, *op. cit.*. Subsequent proposals based on Beveridge's further survey in the autumn of 1940 reflect the thinking, if not the identical arithmetic, of the Ministry of Munitions during the First World War, where Beveridge was responsible for Labour Supply until he moved to the Ministry of Food at the end of 1916. *See* C. Wrigley, *History of British Industrial Relations*, Vol. 3, *1939 - 79*, ed. C. Wrigley, (Edward Elgar, 1996), pp. 12 -43.
21. *John Betjeman Letters*, Vol I, ed. Candida Lycett-Green, Methuen, (1994), letter of 20 September 1939; Bevis Hillier, *op. cit.*, p. 338; Humbert Wolfe Letters, University of Nottingham Hallward Library, Access 158, Nos. 91 and 120; Storm Jameson, *Autobiography*, vol. 2. *Journey from the North,* (1970), p. 30.
22. Pamela Frankau, *Humbert Wolfe*, typescript of a newspaper article (possibly *The Marylebone Mercury*, 1949).

V

23. *ibid.*

INDEX

Humbert Wolfe and Jessie Wolfe are referred to as HW and JW; Pamela Frankau as PF. References to illustrations are in italic numerals.

Ackland, Valentine, 330
Acts and Bills, Parliamentary
  Agricultural Insurance, 351
  Labour Exchanges (1908), 113-4
  Munitions of War (1915), 119-20, 125-6, 150
  Munitions (1917), 133
  Piers and Harbours, 163
  Port of London, 111
  Superannuation (1859), 112
  Trade Board Amendment (1918), 151
  Trade Disputes, 250
  Unemployment (1934), 329
  Unemployment Insurance (1911), 114
Adams, Professor W.G., 135
Addict, The, 338-41, (*see also* West, Rebecca)
Addison, Dr. Christopher, MP, 123, 131, and Appendices AI-AIV
Addision, Joseph, 354-5 & n2
Agate, James, 373, 375
Agnew, William Lockett, 123
Aitken, (Sir) Max (later Lord Beaverbrook), 130
Aladdin at Theatre Royal, Bradford, 1-3
Albert, Prince, HW's judgement of, 303
Aldington, Richard, 138, 173, 232
Allen, G.B. (later Assistant Bishop of Oxford), 50 & n4
Alvarez, A.A., 310-1 & n4
Amery, L.S., 61
Amulree, Lord, 362-3
Ariel Poems, The, 275
Aristotle, 117, 144
Arnold, Matthew, 42, 81, 144, 256
Artillery Mansions, the Wolfes' address 1929-1934, 256, 279, 284
Asquith, Cyril, 127
Asquith, Herbert Henry, lst Earl of Oxford and Asquith, 113, 122, 131, 189
Athenaeum Club, The, 214, 281, 356-7 & n6
Atkinson, Rita, *see* Wolff
Atkinson, Ruth, HW's niece, 64
Attolico, Bernardo, 196 & n7, 197, 202, 216, 218
Auden, W.H., 265, 280-1
Augustan Books of Modern Poetry, 226 & n22, 235, 236, 238, 243, 268, 275
Austin, Alfred, 322-3
Avenol, Joseph Louis Anne, 307, 329
Aylmer, Felix, 354
BBC, HW's dealings with, 205, 213, 239, 242, 243, 332-3, 354-5, 369
Balfour, Arthur James (later Earl of): and foreign languages, 166
  munitions crisis (1915), 120
  HW's admiration for, 130-1
  HW briefs him for Hours Convention Debate, 245, 250
  at opening of Knox Academy, 82
  possible sucessor to Curzon as Foreign Secretary, 203 & n11
Balfour, Harry: on HW as fellow-lodger, 85
  speech at HW's wedding, 98
  lunches with HW, 103
  on HW as conciliator, 134-5
Banville, Théodore de, 331n19
Barber, W.E., 32
Barfield, Miss, 155
Barfield, Owen, 155
Barlow Commission, HW's evidence to, 363 & n14
Barlow, J.A.N., 214, 281 & Appendix BII
Barlow, Sir Montague, *see* Montague-Barlow
Barnes, George, MP, 165 & n34, 227
Barrie, Sir James, 258
Barry, Gerald: with HW at annual dinner of *The Saturday Review,* 240
  becomes editor of *The Weekly Review,* 301
Barton, J.E. writer and teacher: at Bradford Grammar School, 32, 33, 34
  encourages HW to write poetry, 40, 42, 43
  his 'charmed circle', 44
  victim of HW's practical joke, 33
  when Head Master of Crypt School, entertains HW and friends, 51
  views on Raleigh and Arnold, 55
  need for 'affirmation', 290 *see also* 254
  HW's tribute to Barton and Battersby (*q.v.*) in poems on teaching, 293
Barton, Mrs., 228
Bateman, Sir Alfred, 102, 104, 213, 336
Battersby Caryl, 8, 32, 174-5, 293
Baumann, A.A., HW's dealings with, 158-9, 236, 239, 241, 251
  death of, 355
Bayliss, Lilian, 334
Beacon, The, 205
Beerbohm, Max, 100
Belloc, Hilaire, 215, 286
Benn, Ernest, publisher, (*see also* Victor Gollancz): Arnold Bennett on, 240n39
  asks HW to edit 'Sixpennies', 235

dealings with HW over *Kensington Gardens,* 174
Humoresque, 220
Augustan Books of Modern Poetry, 226, 235-6, 243
News of the Devil, 227, 233,
Requiem, and other projects, 229, 243-4 245
The Anthology (Others Abide), 243, 256,
The Silver Cat, 265
HW's wrangles over money, 240
Bennett, Arnold: adverse review of *The Uncelestial City,* 299-300
attacked in Roy Cambell's *The Georgiad,* 312
Benn Bros, comment on, 240n39
deaf to HW's and Eliot's pleas on behalf of *The New Criterion,* 266
dinners with HW, 263, 278
not available to review *Requiem,* 245
Bermondsey Bookshop, The, 218, 243
Bethman-Hollweg, Theobald von, 263
Betjeman, (Sir) John, 57, 373
Betterton (Sir) Henry B. (later Lord Rushcliffe): attends ILO as Parliamentary Secretary, 184, 185, 198, 202 & Appendix BI
attends JW's presentation at Court, 228
chairs Unemployment Assistance Board, 337
memo from HW on refugees, 267
conveys Minister's congratulations to HW, 273
Betterton, Mrs, 184
invites Jessie Wolfe to Court, 226, 228,
letters to Jessie, 228
Beveridge, (Sir) William (later Lord): Director of Labour Exchanges, 111-4
recruits HW to Labour Exchanges Department, 113
HW and outbreak of war, 116
Munitions of War Committee, 122
Munitions Ministry, Assistant General Secretary, 123, 124, 128, 129, and Appendices AI, AII & AIII
on HW's value in drafting legislation, 125
businessmen in Ministry of Munitions, 126
on destruction of Wienerwald, 142-3
Bevin, Ernest, 186
Birò, Lajos, dealings with HW, 347, 350, 358-9
Bissett, A.M., 54
Blackwell, Basil, 139, 236, 238
Blackwood, Basil, 113
Blake, William, 292
Blanco-White, Mrs. Amber, 133, 155
Bloomsbury, 311
Blunden, Edmund, 277
Boas, F.S., 281
Boileau-Despréaux, Nicolas, 331n19
Bolivian Refugees Scheme, HW's views on, 267
Boncour, Paul, 322
Bondfield, Margaret, PC, MP:
adviser to ILO delegation, 184 & *12*
attends ILO as Minister, 284, 301 and Appendix BI
character, 284
relations with HW, 195-6 and nn4, 5, 284-5
tackles Drummond with HW, 301
Booth, G.M., 121-2, 126 & Appendix AI
Bowers, F.G., 196 & Appendix BII
Bowley, A.L., 117
Boyd-Carpenter, Maj. A., MP, 183, & Appendix BI
Bradford: industrial and social history, 7-10,
'Little Germany', 8, *see also* Jews in Bradford
in HW's writings, *see under* HW
Bradford Argus, The, 210, 231
Bradford Grammar School, 23-8 *passim,* 31-45 *passim*
HW archive, 64
Bradford Grammar School Old Boys Association, 235
Bradfordian, The, 32, 33, 34, 40, 55, 144
Briand, Aristide, 274
HW's poem on 373
HW's meeting with, 228n26
Bridges, Robert, 288
Brittain, Vera: effect of *Requiem* on, 254
visits HW and PF, 368
Britten, Benjamin, 288n19
Bronner brothers, 14 & n19
Bronner, Mrs., 23n43
Brooke, Rupert, 86, 142, 147
Brown, Ivor, 240, 309n3, 375
Browne, Laidman, 360
Browning, Robert, 42, 261, 280, 302
Browning, Elizabeth, 280
Bruce, Bobby, 340, 341
Bruce, Kate Mary (née Maugham), 340, 341
Buchan, Sir John (later Lord Tweedsmuir), 281-94
Buccleuch, Duke of, 149
(see also Montagu House)
builders, speculative, *see* Yates
Burgess, Anthony, 359
Burn, William, 149
Burnham, Lord, 179, 181, 227, 228
Burns, Robert, 102
Burra, Edward, 315
Burton, (Sir) Geoffrey Pownall, 27, 33, 41, 42, 48, 49, 51, 57, 74

Butler, (Sir) Harold B.: at Ministry of Labour: Assistant Secretary, 133 and Appendix BII
battles with other Ministries, and with HW, 133-4
description of Montagu House, 149-50
role in amending Trade Boards Act, 151
role in creation of ILO, 151, 165 and n34
at ILO: Deputy Director, 151, 165
'interpreter' for Margaret Bondfield at ILO, 195
congratulates HW on promotion, 363
at Travellers Club with HW, 177
the Butlers' house in Geneva, 199
at opening of new ILO building, 227
with HW to see Drummond, 211
in London with Thomas, 250
on translations at ILO, 180-1
ILO Director after Thomas' death, 329
Butler, Mrs., 172
Byron, Lord, 249, 360

Caldwell, J.A.M., 111
Callow, Simon, 347, 359
Campbell, Roy: attacks HW in *The Georgiad,* 311-4
Castlerose, Valentine Edward Charles, Viscount, 333
Cave, Lord, 162,
see also Cave Committee, *under* Royal Commissions
Cecil of Chelwood, Viscount, 303
Chambers, Sir Edward K., 281
Chamberlain, Sir Austen, 227, 272, 274
'Chanak Affair', 179 & n51
Chapbook, see Monro, H.E.
Chapman, Sir Sydney, 281
Chatterjee, Sir Atul Chandra, 227, 281
Chatterton, Thomas, 261
Cheatle, R.H.M., 61
Chesterton, G.K., 215, 286, 373
Chevalier, Jacques, 366
Church, Richard, 125, 149, 152-4, 155, 161-2, 164, 308, 375
Churchill, Charles, 286
Churchill, Randolph, 334
Churchill, (Sir) Winston S.: appendicitis, 180, 183
Budget Day, 240
December 1939, 1
reorganizes Ministry of Munitions, 132 *and* Appendix AV;
social reform, 112-3
dealings with HW: HW avoids at St Paul de Vence, 333
election defeat, HW commiserates, 183
memo to prove HW not a German, 132
opposed to Thomas' proposals, 264
sends for HW, 263
suggested for recruitment broadcasts, 369
Chrystal, George, 85, 102
Citrine, Walter, 1st Baron, 283
Civet Cat, The (public house sign), 167
Civil Service, *see also under* Ministries:
administrative grade, entry to, 326
Commissioners, 78
Examination, 73-4, 77
uncertain access to politics, 77
HW's enters, 77-8
Head of, *see under* Treasury
Post-war reorganisation of, 151, 160
Clark, Kenneth (later Lord), 368, 373
Clay, Sir Henry, 32, 133
Clough, Arthur Hugh, 81, 307
Cole, G.D.H., 117
Colefax, Sir Arthur & Lady, 263, 278
Coleridge, Hon. Gilbert, 281
Collins, Michael, 175, 270
Commissions, Royal
Pilotage, (Bateman), 102, 103-4
Distribution of the Industrial Population (Barlow), 363
Working & Effects of Trade Boards (Cave), 162-3, 170
Committees (under chairman)
Amulree (Holidays with Pay), 362
Cabinet Committees
Economies (Worthington-Evans), 177
Unemployment (L.J.), 177
Geddes (National Expenditure), 151, 170, 189
Graham Greene (Imperial Defence: Control of Manpower), 368
Hours, 242
Lloyd George (Munitions of War, 1915), 122, 123, 124
Phillips (Public Capital Expenditure), 361
Salmon (House of Commons on Public Relations), 349
War Office: Armament Output, 126
Wolfe (Munitions Programme 1939), 369, 374
Conservative Party, HW joins at Oxford, 60-1
Cornford, Capt. F.M., 135
Coward, Noel, 263, 315
Coxhead, Mr., 108
Crowdy, Dame Rachel: friendship with HW, 339
attends HW's Memorial Service, 375
Cuming, E.W.D., 174 and n47
Cunliffe-Lister, Sir P., 242 & n42
Curtis Browne, 263
Curzon of Kedleston, Marquess, 123-4, 203 & n11

Daily Chronicle, The, 215

Daily News, The, 235
Dane, Clemence, 263
Davidson, R., 112
Davies, W.H., 143, 205, 292
Day-Lewis, Cecil: Auden's *Verse-letter to C.Day-Lewis,* 280
autobiography, 303
HW suggests him as speaker, 334
'Macspaunday', 281
personal abuse, views on, 313-4
youthful admiration for HW, 280, 281n16
Day-Lewis, Sean, 281n16, 305
Dean, Sir James, 208
Dearmer, Very Rev. Canon Percy, 342
Dearmer, Gillian, *see* Warr
Decachord, 205
De La Mare, Walter, 203, 215, 229, 258, 277
Delevingne, Sir Malcolm, 165 & n34, 184
Delius, Frederick, 9
De Michelis, His Excellency Signor Giuseppe, 198 and n9, 216, 227, 263
Dennison Ross, 278
Deutsch, Babette, 242 and n41
Dickens, Charles, 99, 277, 286
Dobson, Alban, 281
Dobson, Henry Austen, 281, 325
Donne, John, 45, 309
Doran, George H., 238, 263
Douglas, Norman: attacks HW, 137-9,
HW's reply, 209-10,
Beatrice Webb on, 253
Doumergue, Gaston, 288
Drewitt, J.A.J.: compared with Barton *(q.v.),* 57-8
hero of *The Old Man of Königsberg,* 62
philosophy tutor at Oxford, 51
wedding present to HW, 101
Drinkwater, John, 334 & *18*
Drummond, Sir Eric, (Earl of Perth),
Secretary-General, League of Nations:
ambitions, 197
HW as possible successor, 197
discussion with HW, 202
stalling tactics over his departure, 211, 217, 250, 252, 279, 301, 303, 307
suspicion of being a political pawn, 264
wants HW to ensure Thomas' survival, 273, 274
becomes Ambassador in Rome, 329
Dryden, John, 286
Duffy, Thomas Gavan, *see* Gavan-Duffy
Dugdale, (Mrs. Edgar) Blanche, 122
Du Maurier, Daphne, 334
Dunbar, William, 82
Duncan, Sir Andrew, 179
Dyer, Mrs. Louise, recital of HW songs, 284

Eady, Sir Wilfrid, 337, and Appendix BII
Earl, Honor, Mrs. (née Maugham), 341, 375

Eccleston Square, No. 75, HW's address from 1938, 364, 368, 375
Eden, (Sir) Anthony (later Earl of Avon), 369
Edward VII, King, funeral procession of, 100-1
Eliot, T.S.: at Poetry Bookshop, 173
Crayfish, possible inspiration for, 188-9
dealings with HW over *The New Criterion,* 239, 244, 265-6
Gerontion and *The Uncelestial City,* 289
HW's assessment of Eliot in *Signpost to Poetry,* 314
HW's judgement on Prufrock in *English Verse Satire,* 286
HW's pastiche in 'Turn again Dick Whittington', 372-3
Eliot replies to Ann Wolfe, 334
Ellis, Havelock, 311
Emmerson, Sir Harold, 366
Employment Exchanges, 112-5
English Studies at Oxford, *see under* Oxford
Epitaux, M., 201
Evelyn-White, H.G., 50 and n4

'Fascismo', *see under* ILO: Italian delegates
Flecker, John (James) Elroy: meets HW and hears his poems, 63
HW's admiration for, 86
HW's epitaph poem, 142
HW's garbled quotation, 167 and n40
HW mentions Flecker in *Dialogues and Monologues,* 278
HW's poems on Rioupéroux, 333-4
Fleg, Edmond, 282-3
Flint, F.S., 154, 255
Fontaine, Arthur, 165 and n35, 166, 179, 196, 227, 263
Fontaine, Mme., 172
Fothergill, John, 157-8 & n17, 176
Fox, Victor, 55-6, 103-4, 141
France, Anatole, 276
Frankau, Gilbert, 314 & n8, 349
Frankau, Pamela: *16,* affair with HW placarded in *The Addict (q.v.),* 338-41
attends Wolfes' fancy dress party, 348-9
meets HW, 314 & n8
pantomime, *Who's Taking Liberty?,* 1, 373
relationship with HW, 338-42, 353, 368,
Roman Catholicism, conversion to, 345
rude telegrams to HW, 356-7
visits Boulogne with HW, 373
writing on HW: description of HW's voice, 152

HW's manner of composing, 373
obituary of HW, 374-4
his wit, 'headlong quality' of, 373
Fraser, Ronald, 255
Fry, Sir William Kelsey, Ann Wolfe's dental surgeon, 218, 225, 262

Galsworthy, John, 357
Garnett, David, 253
Garrod, H.W., Fellow of Merton, Oxford Professor of Poetry: at Ministry of Munitions, 130, 137
Oxford Poetry lecture on HW (1927): tribute to HW's success, 154, 249
HW's 'whimsical punctuation', 191
HW's 'false rhymes', 205
Humoresque, 221, 222-3
criticizes 'Coda' in *Requiem,* 249
injured in street accident, gives Poetry lecture, 263
predicts HW's conversion to Catholicism, 344
Garvin, J.L.,245, 256
Garvin, Viola: affection for HW, 255, 339
association with HW recalled, 255-6
attends HW's Memorial Service, 375
eulogizes *Requiem* in *The Observer,* 245
introduces HW to Pamela Frankau, 314
lameness explained to Vera Brittain, 368
portrayed as 'Valerie' in *The Addict (q.v.),* 340
Gavan-Duffy, Thomas, 186, & n55
Geddes, Gen. Sir Auckland, 130
'Geddes Axe', *see* Geddes Committee, *under* Committees
Geddes, Sir Eric, 128, 153, 179
Geddes, Irvine, 179
George V, King, 228, 373
Georgiad, The, see under Campbell, Roy
Georgian Poets, 143-4, 173, 311-2
Gielgud, (Sir) John, 355
Gielgud, Val, BBC dealings with HW, 354-5
Gilbert, W.S., 279
Gilliatt, A.E., 54, 61, 73, 74
Gillies, Sir Harold, 225, 238
Girouard, Sir Percy, 122, 124, 126-7, 129, Appendices AI & AII
Gladstone, W.E., 123
Godart, Justin, 199, 211
Goldberg, Paul, 285, 326
Gollancz, Victor: acknowleges receipt of HW's novel, 263
attend HW's Memorial Service, 375
celebrates success of *Requiem* and *The Sixpennies* with HW at Pagani's, 243,
talks of 'a best seller', 245
discussions with HW about *Requiem* and *The Uncelestial City,* 236
first meeting (probably) with HW, 174
leaves Ernest Benn, 252n39, 257
publishes HW's *This Blind Rose,* 269
wants to publish *The Anthology,* 244
Gooch, Sir Henry, 281
Gorham, Maurice, 355
Gosling, Harry, CH, MP, 186
Gosse, Sir Edmund, 251
Goudge, Elizabeth, vii
Gould, Gerald, 255-6
Graham family: *7*
origins 82,
relations with HW, 169, 190
Graham, Annie (JW's sister): *7,*
visits the Wolfes in Battersea, 101, 103
living with Wolfes in Kensington, 217
in Italy, 229, 232
in Bournemouth, 255
with Mrs. Graham in Battersea flat, 287
ill in London, 316
Graham, Mrs Euphemia, née Alexander, JW's mother: *7,*
marries Joseph Chalmers Graham, 82
at JW's wedding, 97
visits Wolfes in Battersea, 100, 109
financial problems, 190
lives with Wolfes in Kensington, 217
suffers stroke, 216
with JW in Italy, 229, 232
advice from HW on property sale, 235
ill in Nice, 252
with JW in Bournemouth, 255
moves to Battersea, 287
death, 316
Graham, Gilbert ('Gub') Malise, JW's brother: *7,*
helped by HW and JW, 169, 190
relations with HW and Ann, 190
Graham, Jessie Chalmers, *see* Wolfe
Graham, Joseph Chalmers, JW's father: *7*
HW asks permission to marry daughter, 79, 80
biography of JCG, 82-3
relations with HW, 85
consents to daughter's marriage, 86
HW and JW holiday with Grahams, 107
HW's marriage settlement, 109, 365
death, 169, 185
Graham, William ('Willie'), JW's uncle, 316, 350, 351
Grahame, Kenneth, 258
Graves, Robert, 207, 265, 309, 313
Gray, Thomas, 223
Greene, Sir W. Graham, 387, Appendix AV
Greenwood, Arthur, MP, 133-4
Grenfell, Julian, 60

Grigson, Geoffrey, 314
Guedalla, Philip, 187
Guinness, (Sir) Alec and Lady, 107n41
Gunn, Thom, 309

Hall, Sir A. Daniel, 281
Hall, Radclyffe, 330, 357
Hallsworth, Joseph, 301-2
Hamilton, Archibald, HW's brother-in-law, 27n56, 49, 102, 216
Hamilton, Sylvia, *see* Wolff
Hamilton, G. Rostrevor, 281
Hardy, Thomas, 40, 99, 286, 288, *see also* Sassoon, S.
Harrris, Robert, 354
Hazlehurst, Cameron, 117
Health, Ministry of *see under* Ministries
Heaney, Seamus, 309
Heine, Heinrich: HW's imitation of, 67
  affinity with and translation of, 287
Heinemann, publishers, HW's dealings with, 240, 244
Heltai, Eugene, 360
Heron, Cyril, 105, 109, 178
Heron, Fanny, *see* Heron, Cyril *and under* Wolff
Herrick, Robert, 272, 274
Hilton, John (later Professor), 161
Hindenburg, Field-Marshal Paul von, 262-3
History of the Ministry of Munitions, see under Ministry of Munitions *and* HW
HMS Exeter, 1 & n1, 373
Hodge, John, MP, Appendix BI
Hollway, Mark, 138
Holst, Gustav, 209, 254, 284, 287
Holst, Imogen, 287-8 & n19
Hopkins, Gerard Manley, 236
Hopkinson, Tom, 281n16
Horder, Thomas Jeeves (later Lord), HW's friendship with, 318 & n11, 330, 332 & n20, 375
Horne, Sir Robert, MP, 153, 177, Appendix BI
hours, 168
  see also Washington Hours Convention
Housman, A.E., 203, 215
Hughes Ted, 309
Hugo, Victor, 224
Hulton, Edward, 375
Huxley, Aldous, 143, 253

I.L.O.: chiefly Ch. 6-8, *passim*
  creation of, 151, 165
  delegation dinners, 182
  disorderly debates, 198
  financial problems, 184-5, 195, 204
  influence of Albert Thomas, 195
  hours convention, 165, 168, 171, 180
  HW sent to inspect, 307-8
  Italian delegates, 198, 225, 252
  Mateotti murder, 198
  new building, 185, 201
  opening of, 227
  personalities, 165n34, n35, 179n52
  relationship to League of Nations, 274
  represented at HW's Memorial Service, 375
  struggle for national interests, 170-1, 195, 252, 273
  tribute to HW, 376
  white lead debate, 168, 184
Imagist Poets, The, 143, 154
Inge, Dean, 253, 359
Iremonger, Rev. F.A., 333 & n21, 375
Irvine, St. J., 334

James, Henry, 269
Jameson, Storm: judgement on Consola and HW, 219
  asks HW for war work, 373
  on HW and P.E.N., 357
  judgement on HW, 379
Jefferies, Douglas, 360
Jenkinson, A.J., 135
Jerrold, Douglas, 281, 302
Jews in Bradford, 8-10, 14-17, 28, 43, 93-4
Joad, C.E.M., 149, 164
John, Augustus, 86
John, Gwen, 86
Jouhaux, Léon, 179 & n52, 196
Juvenal, 215, 291

Keats, John, 42
Keeling, Edward, MP, 348
Keeling, Rev. Dr. W.H., 32, 52
Keith, A.D.: 'Drum', friendship with HW at Oxford, 50, 51, 53, 55, 61, 73, 74
  death of, 268
  HW's essay on, 278 & n14
Kellaway, F.G., MP, 130 & Appendices AIV & AV
Kelleher, D.L., 255
Kennett-Barrington, Leila, 100, 110
  see also Lascelles, E.
Kensington High Street, No. 72, HW and Jessie living at, 167, 190
Kent, Sir Stephenson, 131, 157 & Appendix AV
Kershaw, Sir Louis, 184
Keynes, J.M., 215
Kipling, Rudyard, 142, 206, 277, 286, 288 and *18*
Kitchener, Field-Marshal Lord, 120, 124, death of, 131
Knox Academy, 82-3
Knox, John, 86
Knox, (Mgr) R.A., *Enthusiasm,* vii, ix

'experimentum' joke, 58 & n17
with HW in the Canning Club, 60-1
subsequent career, 61n22
as translator, 241n40
Korda, Alexander, dealings with HW, 347, 350, 359

Labour Exchanges, *see under* Employment Exchanges
Labour, Ministry of, *see under* Ministries
labour problem in 1914, 117-20, 121
see also under Humbert Wolfe
Lafourcade, Georges, 310
Lamb, Charles, 260
Lane-Fox, Lt.Col. G.R., MP, 186 & n55
Lankester, Dr., 375
Lang, Andrew, 261
Lascelles, Hon. E.C.P., friendship with HW, 96 & n31, 98, 108, 110, 133, 213, 376
Laughton, Charles, 347, 350-1, 358-9
Laval, Pierre, 288
Lawrence, D.H., 220, 253
Lawrence (Arabella) Susan, MP, 196
Lawson, J., MP, 308 and Appendix BI
Lecoq de Boisbaudran, 42
Lewis, (Percy) Wyndham, 311
Lion, Leon, 238 & n37, 243, 329
Lithgow, Sir James, 180, 183
Llwellyn-Smith, Sir Hubert, 104, 112, 113, 122, 123, & Appendices A1-AIV
Lloyd, G.I.H., 135-6
Lloyd George, David: social security, 112
World War I, 120, 122, 123, 124-9 131, 136 & Appendices AI-AIII
HW's relations with and opinion of, 124-5 & n30
HW's resemblance to, 305
Lloyd George on HW, 126
and ILO, 165
linguistic skills, 166
Lloyd-Green, Philip, 85, 102
Locker-Lampson, Godfrey, MP, 264 & n6
Lohr, Marie, 98
Longbottom, Alan, (Bradford Jewish Register) 9n7, 16n25
Loucheur, L., 282
Low, (Sir) David, friendship with Wolfes, 220, 235, 318
Evening Standard cartoon, 288 and *18*
Lucas, St. J. Welles, 281
Lynch, Bohun, 213, 215
Lynd, Robert & Sylvia, friendship with HW, 52, 220

Macassey, Sir Lynden, 281
Macaulay, Rose, 115, 255
MacDonald, James Ramsay, 283, 307, 315 and *18*
Mackail, J.W., 256
Mackenzie, Compton, 253, 368
Macmullan, C.W.K., *see under* Munro, C.K.
Macnamara, T.J., MP, 160-2 & Appendix BI
Mahaim, Ernest, 179n52, 181
Mahler, Hermann & Laure: relations with Wolffs, 17 & n30, 29
dealings with Wolfes, 93, 109n43, 216
Mahler, Sichel & Co., 78
Malherbe, François de, 331 & n19
Mallock, W.H. and *The New Republic*, 275-6
Mannin, Ethel, 263, 359
Markham, Violet, 171, 184, 195, 198
Marr-Johnson, Diana (née Maugham), 341
Marrs, R., 54, 56, 61, 62, 73
Marsh, Sir Edward, 144, 173
Marvell, Andrew, 286, 310
Mary, Queen, 239
Masaryk, Thomas Garrigue, 200
Maschwitz, Eric, 354-5
Masefield, John, 203-4, 215, 249, 288 and *18*
Masterton-Smith, Sir James, 132, 157, 161, 241, Appendices AV & BII
Matteotti, Giacomo, 198
Mathew, Rev. Mr., 97-8
Maugham, Lord & Lady, 341, 376
Maugham, Diana, (*see* Marr-Johnson)
Maugham, Honor, (*see* Mrs. Earl)
Maugham, Kate Mary (Mrs. Bobby Bruce), 339, 340, 341, 375
Maugham, Robin, 339, 341, 342, 348
Maugham, Somerset, 104, 341
Maurois, André, 222
McCarthy, Desmond, 242, 244
Measham, R.J.R., 50 & n4, 56, 61, 62, 73-4
Meredith, George, 104
Meynell, Francis, 255
Miller, Gilbert, 360
Milne, A.A., 258
Milton, John, 37, 42
Minchin, H. Cotton, 281, 333
Ministries
Admiralty, 117
Board of Trade: especially Chapter 4 & Chapter 5 *passim*
HW enters, 78
function of, 111
Labour Department, 112
Labour Exchanges Department, 111, 112-3,
permanent officials, quality of, 112-3
preparations for war, 116
low status of President, 112
Customs, 327
Health, 327
Home Office, 117, 327

Inland Revenue, 327
Labour: creation and early difficulties, 131, 133-4
low status, 151
democratic and egalitarian ethos, 154, 326
economic and social function, 361, 363
HW transferred to, 131, 149
model for other Ministries, 327
Montagu House, 149-50 & *10, 11*
post-war objectives, 150-1
role of Ministry in creating and maintaining ILO, 151, 165, & Chapters 6 - 8 *passim*
Trade Boards, 151, 160-4
Munitions, Ministry of: account of, Chapter 5 *passim,* especially 123-36 & *8, 9*
businessmen, 126-7
created, 122-3
expansion, 128-9, 132
HW transfers to, 123
History of, and HW's criticisms, 135-6
Lloyd George and the Ministry, 123-9
notable figures, 124, 129-30
premises, 123, 124, 129-9
successive reorganisations, 128, 129, 131,
132, and Appendices A1-AV
Treasury: assumes control of Civil Service, 160
HW's resistance to, *see under* Humbert Wolfe; Permanent Secretary becomes Head of Civil Service, 160
Monro, Alida, 255
Monro, Harold: 173, 174, 189, 232, 236, , 255
The Poetry Bookshop, 173
The Chapbook, HW's poems in, 173, 174
Montagu, Edwin, MP, 124, 130, 131
Montagu House, 149-50 & *10, 11*
Montague-Barlow, Sir Clement Anderson, MP: *see also* Barlow Commission
appointed Minister of Labour, 183 and Appendix BI
career and character, 167
HW substitute for, 171, 179
walks with HW to Zweilutschinen, 172
Mongomery, Robert, 286
Moore, George: HW's visits to, 237, 241
compares with A.A.B., 251
essay on, 268, 275
book on, 302, 325-6
Morgan, Charles, 256
Morgan, Hilda, (Vaughan), 357
Morrison, J.H., 55, 86, 90, 157, 251-2
Mossman, K., 34
Mottram, R.H., 318 & n11
Moult, Thomas, 268, 325
Moulton, Lord, 124, 127, 129-30, and Appendiices AII & AIII
Mount Royd, Bradford, 13-14 & *1, 2*
Mount Street, No. 128, the Wolfes' address from 1934, 333, 335-6
Muir, Edwin, 230
munitions shortage (1914-15), 120-2
Munitions, Ministry of, *see under* Ministries
Munro, C.K. (Macmullan), 154
Munro, Sir Thomas, 130, 133, 134
Murray, Gilbert, 344
Murry, Middleton, 359
Mussolini, Benito, 267

New English Art Club, The, 85-6, 336
Newbolt, Sir Henry, 236
New Criterion, The, 239, 244, 265-6
Newman, John Henry, Cardinal, 289
Newton, Mr. 'X', 23, 24
Nicolson, Hon. Sir Harold: attacks *The Uncelestial City,* 300
is attacked by Roy Campbell, 311-2
Nijinsky, Vaslav, 115
Nolens, Mgr., 179 and n52, 198, 227

Observer, The, 244-5, 255, 256, 269
Omar Khayyam Club, The, 318, 330
Onions, Oliver, 32
Oudegeest, Jan, 179 & n52, 196, 202, 225
Outlook, 175, 205
Owen, Wilfrid, 205-6, 354
Oxford: English Studies at, 47-8, 63
place in HW's life, *see under* HW; poetry at 63
Oxford Magazine, The, HW's poems in, 38-9, 40, 54, 58, 63, 74

P.E.N. Club, The, 357-8
Parker, H.M.D., 369
Paton, W.R., 256
Paulucci di Calboli, 196n7, 307
Pears, Peter, 288n19
Pelham, Hon. Thomas Henry William, 111
Phelan, Edward Joseph, 165 & n34
Phillips, Sir Thomas W., 113, 213, 337, 348, & Appendix BII
Piggott, Miss, 265
Poetry Bookshop, The, *see* Monro, H.E.
Polaire, Emilie-Marie Bouchard, 99
Pope, Alexander, 42, 215, 286, 312
Poulton, Councillor Edward Lawrence, 180, 183
Powell, J. Enoch, vii
Power, Beryl: HW's patronage of, 155, 162, 285, 326

attends HW's Memorial Service, 375
Power, Eileen, 155, 255, 375
Price, Sir James, F.G., 351, 363, & Appendix BII
Priestley, J.B.: on HW's Jewishness, 9, 10n14, 21, 345
on HW's voice, 152
competition between their plays, 361
HW a 'show-off', 380
Primrose, Neil, 130
Proust, Marcel, 276
Pudney, J.S., 373
Punch, 205

Quayle, Anthony, 360
Queen, The, 205

Rabelais, François, 215, 286
Racine, Jean, 276
Raymond, Diana, 338, 339, 340, 366
Read, Herbert, 277
Redmayne, Sir Richard, 281
Rendell, Mr. (Bradford Grammar School), 25-7,
Rey, C.F., 113, 129
Richards, H.P., Dean of Wadham, 50
Richardson, Ralph, 355, 360
Ricketts, Charles, 275 & n11
Riding, Laura, 313
Rieu, E.V., 332
Romains, Jules, 206, 357
Roper, Garnham, 101
Rossoni, Edmondo,198
Rothenstein, (Sir) William, R.A.: at HW's Memorial Service, 375
connections with Wolff family, 32, 35
dealings with HW, 55, 85, 102
letter to HW on success of *Requiem,* 245-6
New English Art Club, 85
portrait of HW, *frontispiece,* 268-9 & n10, 307, 338
tries to sell Charles Laughton a picture, 351
Rothermere, Lady, 266
Royde-Smith, Naomi, 115
Russell, Bertrand, 311
Rutherston, Albert: attacked by Norman Douglas, 138
encourages Jessie's painting, 318
friendship with HW, 32, 55, 56, 62, 85, 92, 93, 94, 278, 375
illustrations for HW's books, 14n18 and *1,* 173, 174, 187, 257, 272
New English Art Club, 85

Sackville-West, Edward, 244
Sackville-West, Vita, attacked in *The Georgiad,* 311
Sadleir, Michael, 318 & n11
Salaman, Chattie, 86, 105, 106, 189
Salaman, Merula, (Mrs., later Lady, Alec Guinness), 107n41
Salaman, Michel: befriends HW, 86; invites Wolfes, 105, 106-7, 189
Salaman, Redcliffe N., 281
Salmon, Isidore, 178, 349
Salt, Titus, 9 & n8
Saltaire, 9n8
Sampson, George, judgement on HW, 67n31, 143-4
Samuel, Herbert, Viscount, 318 & n11
Sassoon, Siegfried: 155, 354
HW meets, 232
attack on HW, 276, 299-300, 308
Saturday Review, The, 158, 159, 230, 235, 240 244, 245, 269, 301
Sava, Anastas Botzavich, 243, 245 & n45
Savory, A., 345
Schiller, F.C.S., 'The Pragmatist': HW's joke, 58, 62 and nn25 & 26
Scott, Margaretta, 339, 355, 360, 373
Shackleton, Sir David, 161, 162, 163, 170, 180, 183, Appendix BII
Shackleton, W., 243 & n43
Shanks, Edward, 174, 240, 268 (*see* Squire, J.C.), 278
Shaw, Tom, MP, 195 and Appendix BI
Shaw-Taylor, Patrick, 60
Shelley, Percy Bysshe, 47, 240, 249, 305, 326
Shinwell, Emmanuel, MP (later Lord), 301
Shotwell, J.T, 181
Sidgwick, Arthur, and Frank, 108 & n42, 147, 159
Silk, Dorothy, 284, 287-8
Simon, Israel & Co., 6, 8 & 9n7
Simon, John, Lord, 52, 123, 211
Simpson, Evan John, 317 & n9, 353-4
Sisson, C.H., 313, 366
Sitwells, The, 229, 277
Sitwell, Edith: 21; 200, 275, and *18*
HW lectures with, 359
Sitwell, Osbert, 174, 189, 263
Sitwell, Sacheverell, 174, 175, 189, 268
Sixpennies, see *Augustan Books of Modern Poetry*
Skemp, Arthur (Memorial Lecture), HW delivers, 319-20
Smieton, Dame Mary, 285
Smith, F.E. (Lord Birkenhead), 52, 77, 211
Smith, Owen: at Ministry of Munitions, 129
loans to Wolfes, 169, 177, 330
Sokal, Francisk, 199 & n9, 200
Somervell, R.C., 307-8
Souline, Evguenia, 330n17
Speaight, Robert, 354
Spectator, The, 174, 205, 214, 236, 244, 245,

269
Spender, Sir Stephen, 280-1 & n16, 354
Spengler, Oswald, 254, 322
Squire, Sir John C., 144, 174, 268, 312, 375
Stealing from the rich, *see* Lecoq de Boisbaudran
Steel-Maitland, Sir Arthur, MP, 202, 267, 282, and Appendix BI
Stephens, James, 255
Stern, G.B., 152, 334, 339, 342
Stevenson, Frances (Lady Lloyd George), 122, 126
Strauss, Rabbi Dr., 10 & n13, 28, 43
Stresemann, Gustav, 274
Stopes, Dr. Marie, 311
Sunday Express, The, H. Nicholson's review in, 299
Sutherland, Joan, 263
Swift, Jonathan, 215
Swinburne, A.C., 139, 249, 269, 272

Tallents, Sir Stephen, 113
Temperley, Mrs. H.W.V., 135
Tennyson, Alfred, Lord, 35, 36, 42, 72, 81, 99, 302-3
Terracini family, xv (Genealogy), 5 & n2, 6 & n3
Terracini, Consola, *see* Wolff
Terracini, Rosetta, 16 & n25, 93, 100-1
Terracini, Sylvia, 16 & n25, 93
Thomas, Albert *(see also under* Humbert Wolfe): appointed Director of ILO, 165
biographical summary, 165n35
Bolivian Refugee Scheme, 267
death of, 329
firm director of ILO, 165, 195
first exchanges with HW, 166
HW saves Thomas' skin, 273-4
London visit & discussions with HW, 244, 250, 264
manoeuvrings within ILO, 197, 201, 211, 217, 252
opening of new ILO building, 227
political ambitions in France, 196, 199, 201
tea with Hindenburg, 263
threatens resignation over budget, 185, 204
prolixity criticized by HW, 301
HW's tribute in *Portraits By Inference,* 166
Thomas, Mme., 172
Thompson, Edward, 226
Thompson, Francis, 207, 249
Toynbee Hall, 112
Trade Boards, *see under* Ministry of Labour
Treasury: 160-1, 195, 315, 361
challenged by HW, 155, 160-1, 361, 363, 366
Trollope, Anthony, 277
Troubridge, Lady Una, 330, 357

Valentino, Rudolph, 231-2, 295
Vaughan, Henry, 205, 275
Vaughan, Hilda (Mrs. Charles Morgan), 357
Verlaine, Paul, 63, 206
Virgil, 13n16

Wadham College, Oxford, 48-79 *passim,* 211, 339
Walley, Sir John, 275n12, 366
Ware, Sir Fabian, 32
Warner, Sylvia Townsend, 330 & n17
Warr, Mrs. Gillian (née Dearmer), friendship with, recollections of HW & PF, 339, 342, 356-7, 362-3, 365-6
Washington Conference, 165
Washington Hours Convention, 165, 168
Waugh, Alec, 174
Waugh, Arthur, 174, 187
Waugh, Evelyn, 57, 174, 176, 373
Webb, Beatrice, 112, 195-6, 253, 284
Webb, Sidney, 112, 113
Webb-Peploe, Prebendary, 147
Webley, Barley, 240
Weekly Westminster Gazette, The, HW submits poems, 90, 139, 175, 187, 205
Wells, H.G., 99, 250, 278, 289, 322, 357-8
Wells, 'Juffy', (Fellow, later Warden of Wadham), 49, 63, 99, 215
Wesley, Charles, 292
West, Anthony, 338, 341, 348
West, Rebecca, 263, attacks HW & PF in *The Addict,* 338-41, 343
Wharton, Michael ('Peter Simple'), 10n14
Wheeler, (Sir) Mortimer, 44
Whitefriars Club, The, 254, 267-8
Whitehall Theatre, The, 1, 373
Whitley Councils, 133-4
Williams-Ellis, Clough, 359
Wilson, (Sir) Horace J., 161, 163, 164, 213, 250, 273, Appendix BII
Wilson, P.H. St.J., 348-9, 356
Wodehouse, P.G., 334
Wolfe, Ann (HW's daughter): *7,* birth, 115
successive operations, 115, 169, 218, 225, 226, 251, 356, 362
inspires *Circular Saws,* 175-6
education, 265, 302, 307, 318
studies at Oxford, 328, 334, 356
difficulty in finding employment, 356, 358
receives news of HW's death, 375
Wolfe, Humbert
ambition: 44-5, 47, 52-3, 55, 56, 59-60, 73, 77-8, 93, 113, 155, 185, 196, 197, and Chapters 7 & 8 *passim*

ancestry: xv (Genealogy), 5-7
appearance:
as a child, 21, 27-8, *3, 4*
adolescent, *5*
undergraduate, 50, *5*
wedding portrait, *6*
in 1920s, 152-3, *12, 13, 14*
in 1930s, 379, *15, 17, 18*
articles and reviews, 115-6, 158, 159, 175, 235, 236, 239-40, 240-1, 243, 244, 256, 268-9, 287, 288, 301, 311, 330, 331, 354-5
autobiography, successive attempts at:
Chapter 1 *passim,* 225, 289-90, 319, 324-5, 336-7, 364
baptism & confirmation: 80-2, 108
birth: 7
at Board of Trade: 78, 111-4
Bradford Grammar School: 24-8, Chapter 2
broadcasting: *see* BBC
Cave Commission: 162
C.B.: 211-2, 213
C.B.E.: 132
childhood: Chapter 1
cinema: love of, 147, 202
influence of, 364
civil service, enters, 78
conciliator and negotiator: skill as: 134-5, and at Geneva, 182, 185, 196, 198, 225, 273, 282; in PEN, 357-8; in 1930s, 361
Consola, relations with: 15, 22, 87-9, 94-6, 98, 105-6, 114, 147, 158, 190, 204-5, 216, 219-20
courtship: 65, 79-80, 82, 85, 86-96 *passim*
daughter, relations with: 115, 159, 169, 175-6, 191, 192, 208, 258, 260, 265, 302, 328, 334, 358, 362, 364, 365, 376-7
death and funeral: 375-6
education: 22, 23-8, Chapter 2
encourages talent and women in Ministry of Labour: 155, 285, 326
financial problems: 87, 99, 109, 157, 158, 159, 169-70, 177, 226, 229-30, 232, 235, 251, 269, 283, 284, 288, 301, 308, 328, 329, 330, 332, 347, 350, 358, 362, 364-5
Frankau, Pamela, relationship with: *see* Frankau, Pamela
Garvin, Viola, relations with: 255-6, 339
Geneva: *see* ILO (main index key-word, and below)
Harlequin: viii, 2, 3, 141, 175, 221, 222, 224, 325
health problems: 22, 90, 94, 137, 225, 257, 330, 331-2, 335, 340, 347, 374-5
HMS Exeter, HW's poem on: 1 & n1, 373, 374
ILO: *12, see also* ILO
HW appointment to, 166
last attendance at, 307-8
ILO tribute, 376
Jessie: *see also* Jessie Wolfe
childhood meeting with, 44
courtship and engagement, 65, 79-80, 82, 85, 86-96 *passim*
marriage and early married life, 96-110
letters to, 90, 91-2, 156, and Chapters 6-10 *passim*
poems to, 64-5, 91-2, 139, 146, 228
reveals deception of, 303-4
separation from, 352-3, 364-5
Jewishness: 9-10, 20-1, 22, 24, 28, 43 ,53, 80-1, 138, 345, 364
journalists & newspapers, satires on: 121, 187-8, 233-4, 291-3
Korda, Alexander, dealings with: 347, 350, 358-9
Laughton, Charles, dealings with: 347, 350, 351, 358-9
library, importance of *and* description: 100, 335-6
Lloyd George: *see also* Lloyd George
relations with, 124-5
joins his staff, 123
judgement on, 125 & n30
moral resemblance to, 305
marriage: 96-8
Ministry of Labour: joins, 131, 149
significant contribution to, 154-5, 326-8, 361, 363, 368-9
Ministry of Munitions: *see also under* Ministries
appointment to, 123
account of, 123-136
history of, 135-6
name change: 132
Churchill's intervention on, 132
naturalisation: 15
Nazism, attacks on: 335, 343-5
Oxford, significance of: 44-5, 47,74-5
Paris, visit with Jessie: 104-5
pantomine, first visit to: 1-3
writings on, 2-3, & n5
P.E.N.: 357-8
poems: first attempts, 34-43, 62, 63-73
see also Works, genesis and publications *below*
promotions: 113-4, 149, 363, & Appendix BII
pusillanimity as a child: 19-20
Radio Times, writing in: 354-5

religion, *see also* Wolff, Consola *and* Jews in Bradford
in childhood and at school, 10, 28, 43
Anglo-Catholic leanings at Oxford, 60n21
conversion, 80-2
religious faith, 145
siblings, relations with: Chapter 1 *passim*, 101, 109, 158, 178, 204-5
Society of Civil Service Authors, first President of: 338
speed of work: 113, 125, 175, 189, 373
Switzerland, poems inspired by: 172-3 & n45
Trade Boards: *see* Ministry of Labour
training, innovations in and importance of: 326-7
Treasury, relations with: 155, 160-1, 361, 363
Wadham College: first visit to, 48-9
enters as Scholar, 50
life at, 50-73
leaves, 74
returns to, 211
walking: love of, 8, 34, 41, 254
in Switzerland, 168, 172, 199-200
walking holiday in Germany, 302
at Briançon, 333
West, Rebecca, attacks him in *The Addict:* 338-42
wit:153-4, 161-2, 181, 195-6, 337, 362-3
at expense of others: 27n53, 29, 189, 195-6, 215
Works, genesis and publication:
ABC of the Theatre, 315-6
Augustan Books of English Poetry First Series, 226
Augustan Books of English Poetry Second Series, 235, 236, 243, 268, 275
Circular Saws, 175-6, 187
Craft of Verse, The, 268, 272, 276
Cursory Rhymes, 257-8
Cyrano de Bergerac, 347, 359
Dialogues and Monologues, 268, 275
Don J. Ewan, 359
Early Poems, 103, 139, 303
Edward Lear, 262
Fourth of August, The, 346
Herrick, Robert, Poetical Works of, 272, 274-5
Homage to Meleager, 238-9, 287
Humoresque, 220
Kensington Gardens, 173,191
Kensington Gardens in Wartime, 376
Labour Supply & Regulation, 136, 185
Lampoons, 203, 213, 214
London Sonnets, 92, 103, 139
Moon and Mrs. Smith, The, 278-9
George Moore, 302, 325
News of the Devil, 189, 214, 227, 233
Notes on English Verse Satire, 285
Now a Stranger, 318, 319
Others Abide, 239-40, 241, 243-4, 256
Out of Great Tribulation, 275, 303, 334, 369
P.L.M., 333, 347, 350
Personalities, 355
Pilgrim's Way, The, 333, 347, 354
Portraits by Inference, 332, 336
Portrait of Heine, 287
Publicist, The, 229, 231, 263, 325
Ranciad, The, 312
Requiem, 226, 229, 230, 244
Reverie of Policeman, 316, 321
Romantic and Unromantic Poetry, 319
Ronsard & French Romantic Poetry, 330
Percy Bysshe Shelley, The Life of, 326
Shylock reasons with Mr Chesterton, 139
Signpost to Poetry, 314
Silent Knight, The, 360
Silver Cat, The, 265
Snow, 309
Sonnets pour Hélène, 330
Stings and Wings, 328, 345
Swinburne, Selected Poems by, 269, 272
Tennyson, 301, 302
This Blind Rose, 157-8, 269
Troy, 275
Truffle-Eater, The, 345
Uncelestial City, The, 172, 186n56, 188, 189, 226, 242, 250-1, 260, 265, 288
Unknown Goddess, The, 205
Upward Anguish, The, 364
Veni Creator!, 250, 262
Wall of Weeping, The, 282
Winter Miscellany, A, 302, 303
X at Oberammergau, 334, 343
young people, encouragement of, interest in: 258, 342, 374
Yorkshire: 7-8, Chapters 1 & 2 *passim*, 370-2
Zaharoff Lecture: 330-1

Wolfe, Jessie Chalmers (Graham): *6, 7, 15, 17,*
Bradford Jews, her first experience of, 93
character, 85
Consola, her description of, 89-90
courtship and marriage, 79, 86-98
death of first-born, 110
death of third child, 147
dreams and superstitions, 115, 218-9, 375
early life, 83-5
educates daughter at home, 265

exile in Italy, 229-53 *passim*
first sight of HW, 44
painting, discovery of her talent for, 317-8
portraits of HW, 317-8
portrait of Pamela Frankau, 343, 351
separation from HW, 351-2, 365
Wolff family origins, xv (Genealogy), 5
Wolff, Consola *(see also* Terracini): *3, 5*
birth, 5, 6
marriage to Martin Wolff, 7
character and appearance, 15-18, 20
deafness, 15n22, 16, n24, 89-90
dreams and superstitions, 97
religious indifference, 10, 28
idiosyncratic English, 87, 88, 89, 95-6, 114, 204-5
illness and death, 216-7, 218-9
attitude to Humbert's marriage, 87-8, 94
to his new home, 92-6, 98, 105-6, 147
relations with and influence on Humbert, 15-16, 22-3, 29, 35-6, 77, 90, 114, 204-5, 216, 219-20
Wolff, Fanny (Mrs. Cyril Heron, HW's elder sister): 7, 23, 29, 87, 95, 105, 178, *3,4*
Wolff, Martin: *3*
birth, 5
marriage to Consola Terracini 7
move to Bradford 7-10, 14-15, 16-17
illness and death, 30
Wolff, Oswald (HW's elder brother): *3, 4, 7,* 17, 19-20, 22, 23, 24, 28, 30, 83, 87 & n19, 99, 109, 158, 178, 204-5
Wolff, Rita (Mrs. Edgar Atkinson, younger sister of HW): *3,* 14, 22, 23, 29-30, 94, 97, 101, 102, 217, 219, 305
Wolff, Sylvia (Mrs. Archie Hamilton, younger sister of HW): *3,* 14, 22, 23, 29-30, 87, 94, 97
Wolmer, Viscount, 59, 60, 73
Woods, Gabriel, 55, 59, 63, 73
Woods, Maurice, 55, 60, 73
Woolf, Virginia, 225, 375
Wordsworth, William, 68, 69, 70, 72, 292
Works/Shop Committees, 133-4
Wright-Henderson, Rev. Mr. (Warden of Wadham), 81
Wynyard, Diana, 355, 360

Yates, H.C. St.J., 54
Yeats, W.B., 215, 236, 276, 288, 292
Yorkshire Observer, The, 37, 40
Young, G.M., 60, 61
Young, (Sir) E. Hilton, 177

Zaharoff lecture, 330-31
Zinoviev letter, 267 & n8